Caffeine, Coffee, and Health

MONOGRAPHS OF
THE MARIO NEGRI INSTITUTE FOR
PHARMACOLOGICAL RESEARCH, MILAN

Series Editor: Silvio Garattini

---

*Out of print.

MONOGRAPHS OF
THE MARIO NEGRI INSTITUTE FOR
PHARMACOLOGICAL RESEARCH, MILAN

Caffeine, Coffee, and Health

Editor

Silvio Garattini, M.D.

*Mario Negri Institute for Pharmacological Research
Milan, Italy*

Raven Press New York

Raven Press, Ltd., 1185 Avenue of the Americas, New York, New York 10036

Made in the United States of America

Library of Congress Cataloging-in-Publication Data

Caffeine, coffee, and health / editor, Silvio Garattini.
     p.   cm.—(Monographs of the Mario Negri Institute for
Pharmacological Research, Milan)
   Includes bibliographical references and index.
   ISBN 0-88167-961-5
   1. Caffeine—Toxicology. 2. Caffeine—Health aspects. 3. Coffee—
Health aspects. I. Garattini, Silvio. II. Series.
   [DNLM: 1. Caffeine—adverse effects. 2. Caffeine—pharmacology.
3. Coffee—adverse effects. 4. Coffee—metabolism. QV 107 C12852]
RA1242.C14C34 1992
615′.785—dc20
DNLM/DLC
for Library of Congress   92-49681
                                                  CIP

9 8 7 6 5 4 3 2 1

Contents

Contributing Authors

Maurice J. Arnaud, Ph.D.   *Nestec Ltd., Nestlé Research Centre, Vers-chez-les-Blanc, CH-1000 Lausanne 26, Switzerland*

Karl Bättig, M.D.   *Behavioral Biology Laboratory, Swiss Federal Institute of Technology, Turnerstrasse 1, CH-8092 Zürich, Switzerland*

John William Daly, Ph.D.   *Laboratory of Bioorganic Chemistry, National Institute of Diabetes, Digestive, and Kidney Diseases, National Institutes of Health, Building 8, Room 1A15, Bethesda, Maryland 20892*

Amleto D'Amicis, Ph.D.   *Human Nutrition Unit, National Institute of Nutrition, Via Ardeatina 546, 00178 Rome, Italy*

Makito Emura, Dr.rer.nat.   *Institute of Experimental Pathology, Hannover Medical School, Konstanty-Gutschow-Str. 8, DW-3000 Hannover 61, Germany*

Silvia Franceschi, M.D.   *Epidemiology Unit, Aviano Cancer Center, Via Pedemontana Occ., 33081 Aviano (PN), Italy*

Silvio Garattini, M.D.   *Mario Negri Institute for Pharmacological Research, Via Eritrea 62, 20157 Milan, Italy*

Siegfried Heyden, M.D., Ph.D.   *Department of Community and Family Medicine, Box 2914, Duke University Medical Center, Durham, North Carolina 27710*

Carlo La Vecchia, M.D.   *Department of Epidemiology, Mario Negri Institute for Pharmacological Research, Via Eritrea 62, 20157 Milan, Italy*

Alan Leviton, M.D.   *Department of Neurology, Children's Hospital/ Harvard Medical School, 300 Longwood Avenue, Boston, Massachusetts 02115*

Ulrich Mohr, M.D.   *Institute of Experimental Pathology, Hannover Medical School, Konstanty-Gutschow-Str. 8, DW-3000 Hannover 61, Germany*

Rogelio Mosqueda-Garcia, M.D., Ph.D.   *Departments of Medicine and Pharmacology, Vanderbilt University Medical Center, Room CC-2218 MCN, Nashville, Tennessee 37232*

Delphine Purves, B.Sc., Ph.D. *Division of Pharmacology and Toxicology, United Medical and Dental Schools of Guy's and St. Thomas's Hospitals, Guy's Hospital Campus, University of London, London SE1 9RT, United Kingdom*

Margrit Riebe-Imre, Dr.rer.nat. *Institute of Experimental Pathology, Hannover Medical School, Konstanty-Gutschow-Str. 8, DW-3000 Hannover 61, Germany*

David Robertson, M.D. *Departments of Medicine, Pharmacology, and Neurology, Vanderbilt University Medical Center, 1161 21st Avenue South, Nashville, Tennessee 37232*

Rose Marie Robertson, M.D. *Department of Medicine, Vanderbilt University Medical Center, Room CC-2218 MCN, Nashville, Tennessee 37232*

Jan Snel, Ph.D. *Faculty of Psychology, University of Amsterdam, Roetersstraat 15, 1018 WB Amsterdam, The Netherlands*

Frank M. Sullivan, B.Sc. *Division of Pharmacology and Toxicology, United Medical and Dental Schools of Guy's and St. Thomas's Hospitals, Guy's Hospital Campus, University of London, London SE1 9RT, United Kingdom*

Dag S. Thelle, M.D. *Department of Epidemiology, Nordic School of Public Health, Box 12133, S-402 42 Göteborg, Sweden*

Odin van der Stelt, M.Sc. *Faculty of Psychology, University of Amsterdam, Roetersstraat 15, 1018 WB Amsterdam, The Netherlands*

Rinantonio Viani, Ph.D. *Nestec Ltd., Avenue Nestlé 55, 1800 Vevey, Switzerland*

Hans Welzl, Ph.D. *Behavioral Biology Laboratory, Swiss Federal Institute of Technology, Turnerstrasse 1, CH-8092 Zürich, Switzerland*

Preface

Coffee is one of the beverages consumed most widely throughout the world—in developed and developing countries. Therefore, it is logical and understandable that its effects should arouse interest and controversy, especially in regard to health. To complicate the matter, coffee is not a homogeneous drink, as it may vary depending on the type of beans used and how the brew is prepared.

The use of coffee has long been accompanied by debate about its beneficial effects and possible risks. Innumerable studies have been conducted—experimental, clinical, and epidemiological—and a great amount of data has been accumulated. It appeared interesting to assess the situation, to summarize current knowledge, and to establish in what areas more research is needed. To reach this goal we identified some of the world's specialists in this field, asked each one to write a chapter on his/her specific area, circulated these chapters among the specialists, and held a workshop to discuss and agree on the final form of the contributions. The result is this book, a rich collection of detailed information on the relationships between coffee and various body functions, such as the central nervous and cardiovascular systems; its effects on reproduction; and its relationship to certain pathological conditions, including cancer.

The findings appear to be reassuring, but one must keep in mind that moderation is as important in coffee consumption as in anything we eat and drink.

This book will be of interest to specialists working on coffee/caffeine research and to physicians and anyone wishing to obtain objective information on the topic.

Silvio Garattini

Acknowledgments

Our thanks to the authors and to the secretarial staff, who helped organize the workshop and prepare the manuscript.

Caffeine, Coffee, and Health,
edited by S. Garattini.
Raven Press, Ltd., New York , 1993.

1

The Consumption of Coffee

Amleto D'Amicis and *Rinantonio Viani

*Human Nutrition Unit, National Institute of Nutrition, 00178 Rome, Italy; and
Nestec Ltd., 1800 Vevey, Switzerland

Coffee consumption, originally limited to the shores of the Red Sea, spread throughout the Arab world during the fifteenth century (1,2). By the end of the sixteenth century, European travellers had discovered the hot beverage, "black as ink" in the coffee houses of Cairo, Damascus, and Constantinople, and brought it across the Mediterranean to Genoa, Venice, and Marseille. Less than a century later, coffee drinking had spread throughout Europe, and to the colonies, encouraged by the popularity of the coffee houses.

From the start, coffee came under fire for alleged health risks and social effects. Governments, scared by the political impact of coffee houses, did not look at the increasing consumption with a benevolent eye. The introduction of coffee growing in the colonies destroyed the monopoly of Arabian traders, bringing in trade and taxes, while reducing price, so that finally the authorities' qualms as to the possible health effects finally vanished. Consumption has now increased to such a level that the coffee trade competes with wheat in global importance (3).

PRODUCTION

According to the Food Balance Sheets (FBS) established by the Food and Agriculture Organization (FAO) (4), coffee production was 6,058,000 metric tons in 1989. The major producing continent is South America with 42.0%, followed, in decreasing order, by Africa (20.4%), Asia (18.5%), North and Central America (17.9%), and Oceania (1.2%) (see Table 1). Total world coffee production increased by 214,000 metric tons over the period 1985 to 1989, even though South America reduced its production by 76,000 metric tons. In 1989, 99.8% of the total coffee production was obtained from the less developed countries (LDC)—some 6,057,000 metric tons.

Among the world's coffee producing countries in 1989 by continent, in South America Brazil was the major coffee producer, (1,532,000 metric tons);

TABLE 1. *Whole world coffee production according to continent*

Region	Production ×1,000 tons	% of total production	Aver. 1985–1989 ×1,000 tons
South America	2,546	42.0	2,622
Africa	1,237	20.4	1,220
Asia	1,118	18.5	895
North and Central America	1,086	17.9	1,047
Oceania	71	1.2	60
Total	6,058	100.0	5,844

Source: Food Balance Sheets 1989 (4).

in North and Central America, the main producer was Mexico (326,000 metric tons); the main producer in Africa was the Ivory Coast (239,000 metric tons); in Asia, Indonesia produced 411,000 metric tons, and Papua-New Guinea accounted for almost the total production in Oceania (70,000 metric tons). Table 2 gives the production in the top ten coffee producing countries in the world.

Although coffee production is widespread in several geographical regions—involving 55 countries in 1989—the majority (4,137,000 tons, or 68.5% of the total) was concentrated in a small number of countries.

CONSUMPTION

It is not easy to correctly assess the coffee consumption of a population or of individuals. It is possible, however, to obtain an estimate from (a) the FAO food balance sheets (disappearance), based on the algebraic sum of production, import, and export, and (b) food surveys, based on the intake at the individual or household level.

TABLE 2. *The top ten countries contributing to about 70% of world coffee production*

Country	Production ×1,000 metric tons	% of production
Brazil	1,532	25.3
Colombia	664	11.0
Indonesia	411	6.8
Mexico	326	5.4
Ivory Coast	239	4.0
Guatemala	220	3.6
India	215	3.6
Ethiopia	200	3.3
Uganda	174	2.9
Philippines	156	2.6
Total	4,137	68.5

Source: Food Balance Sheets 1989 (4).

Food Balance Sheets (Disappearance)

Food Balance Sheets (FBS) have the advantage of providing data for most of the countries in the world, of assessing trends, and, even though they have a low degree of precision, they permit an estimate of individual consumption. On the other hand, they do not discriminate between consumers and nonconsumers, and hence no analysis of coffee consumption in specific population groups is possible. Furthermore, this method does not consider waste. Other uses, such as confectionary, are insignificant. However, it is possible to obtain an overview of world coffee consumption and to compare consumption between countries.

In most of the coffee-producing countries, coffee represents the main source of income (5). Usually, when a product is a country's major source of foreign exchange, it is not widely consumed within that country. This is in fact the case for the majority of coffee-producing countries. Accordingly, coffee is generally produced by the LDCs but consumed by the developed countries.

Consumption by continent is shown in Table 3. First place is occupied by Europe with 4.6 kilograms of green coffee per person per year (assuming an average roasting loss of 16% to calculate the amount of roasted coffee actually consumed). That is 283.3% higher than the average figure of 1.2 kg/pp/yr. It is followed by North and Central America with 3.6 kg/pp/yr (+200%), Oceania and South America with 2.3 kg/pp/yr (+91.7%), then Africa, which consumes 50% less than average (0.6 kg/pp/yr) and Asia with 0.3 kg/pp/yr, which is 75% less than average. At a domestic level (see Table 4), 19 countries consume at least 4 kg/pp/yr, 14 of them in Europe with only 4 in the LDC category. The Nordic countries are the highest coffee consumers in the world with a figure of more than 10 kg/pp/yr.

During the period 1985 to 1988, small changes in consumption occurred within these countries, most of them tending to increased consumption and very few with a downward trend even among the major consumers (6). Fig.

TABLE 3. *Coffee consumption, expressed as kg/pp/year, per continent*

Region	Consumption kg/pp/year	% difference from the world average
Europe	4.6	+283.3
North and Central America	3.6	+200.0
Oceania	2.3	+91.7
South America	2.3	+91.7
Africa	0.6	−50.0
Asia	0.3	−75.0
World average	1.2	—

Source: Food Balance Sheets 1989 (4), adapted.

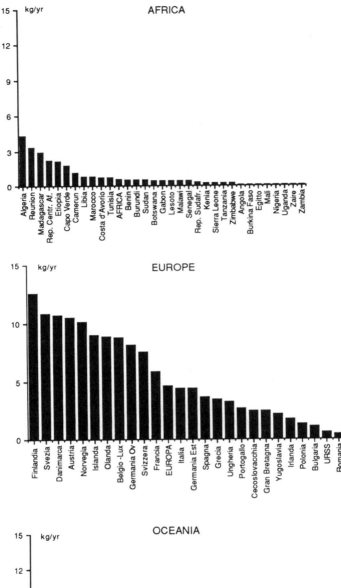

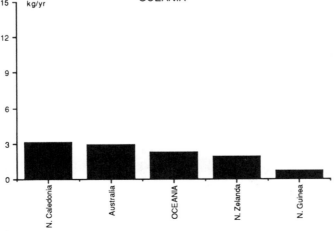

FIG. 1. Rank order of coffee consumption (kg/pp/yr) at Continential level.

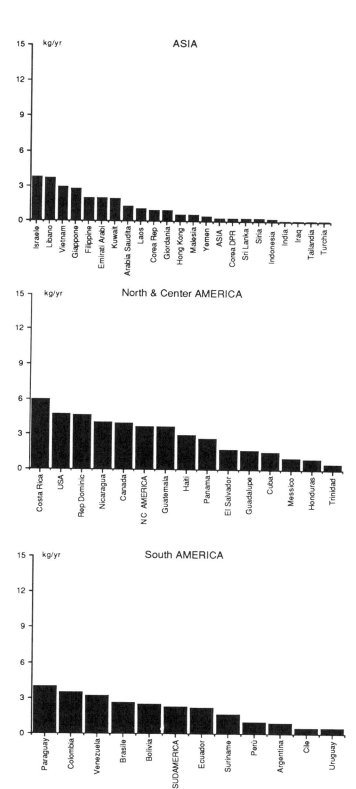

FIG. 1. (*Continued*).

COFFEE CONSUMPTION

TABLE 4. *Countries that consume four or more kg/pp/yr of green coffee*

Country	Consumption kg/pp/yr	Consumption kg/pp/avg 1985–1989	Change of Consumption kg/pp/yr	Consumption kg/pp/yr*
Finland	12.6	12.0	+0.6	12.9
Sweden	10.9	11.3	−0.4	11.9
Denmark	10.7	10.7	0	10.1
Austria	10.5	8.4	+2.1	10.6
Norway	10.2	10.2	0	10.3
Iceland	9.0	10.4	−1.4	—
Netherlands	8.9	10.0	−1.1	10.6
Belgium-Lux	8.8	8.4	+0.4	5.2
West Germany	8.2	7.8	+0.4	8.2
Switzerland	7.5	6.4	+1.1	—
Costa Rica	6.0	5.9	+0.1	—
France	5.8	5.6	+0.2	5.6
United States	4.7	4.5	+0.2	4.6
Dominican Republic	4.6	5.6	−1.0	—
East Germany	4.4	4.3	+0.1	—
Italy	4.4	4.5	−0.1	5.1
Algeria	4.3	3.4	+0.9	—
Nicaragua	4.0	2.5	+1.5	—
Paraguay	4.0	4.5	−0.5	—

Source: Food Balance Sheets 1989 (4).
* USDA (24)

1 shows coffee consumption in kg/pp/yr for 1989, on a country-by-country basis.

Besides FBS, there are other national and international sources of information on coffee consumption. The reports of the national coffee federations based on imports and trade of green coffee furnish useful data for evaluating consumption patterns in specific countries or areas. From the European Coffee Federation report (7), for example, we can draw information concerning the types of coffee consumed in Europe. The two major commercial varieties are arabica and robusta. Table 5 sets out the proportions (percent) of arabica, robusta, and other coffees consumed in Western European countries ("Other" often means unspecified and is either instant coffee or coffee imported as ground roasted or decaffeinated). On the basis of these data, an arbitrary classification of all consumer countries in three levels is possible: (a) where consumption of arabica accounts for more than 70%; (b) where consumption of arabica is around 50%; (c) where consumption of robusta predominates. Northern European countries (Sweden and Finland with 100% of arabica) are in the first group, while France, Italy, the Netherlands, and the United Kingdom fall in the second group. Portugal and Spain are in the third group. These considerations might be important because they also reflect caffeine consumption since, as reported in the chapter dealing with coffee composition (see the chapter by Viani), robusta contains almost double the amount of caffeine as arabica.

TABLE 5. *Proportion (%) of coffee species imported by some European countries*

Country	Species	1987	1988	1989
Austria	Arabicas	89	87	77
	Robustas	9	12	20
	Other	2	1	3
Denmark	Arabicas	84	80	76
	Robustas	14	17	22
Finland	Arabicas	99	99	100
	Robustas	—	1	—
	Other	1	—	—
Greece	Arabicas	94	94	93
	Robustas	5	5	7
	Other	1	1	—
Norway	Arabicas	98	97	96
	Robustas	1	2	2
	Other	1	1	2
Sweden	Arabicas	100	99	100
	Other	—	1	—
Switzerland	Arabicas	84	81	84
	Robustas	14	17	14
	Other	2	2	2
West Germany	Arabicas	92	89	86
	Robustas	8	10	11
	Other	—	1	3
France	Arabicas	43	45	47
	Robustas	55	54	53
	Other	2	1	—
Italy	Arabicas	51	52	52
	Robustas	49	48	48
Netherlands	Arabicas	75	68	62
	Robustas	23	27	27
	Other	2	5	6
United Kingdom	Arabicas	55	57	57
	Robustas	44	42	42
	Other	1	1	1
Portugal	Arabicas	n.a.	30	26
	Robustas	n.a.	62	62
	Other	n.a.	8	12

Surveys and Interviews

Food (population) surveys are an alternative to FBS for collecting information on individual coffee consumption. Surveys are more precise than FBS and permit an evaluation of individual consumption, however, they are usually very expensive and require a high degree of participation by the interviewees (8). They must be carried out by qualified, well-trained interviewers. The higher the degree of precision required, the lower the applicability of the method because of the greater participation required from the subject. Nonetheless, a well carried out survey ensures valid results even though, in view of the high costs and the length of time often required, it can be conducted only on a limited number of respondents.

Surveys are available that are less precise but more widely applicable, e.g., those based on a short personal interview (often by telephone) involving little time and trouble for the respondent, or by self-administered questionnaires constructed ad hoc. These less expensive surveys must be carried out on a larger number of respondents to give acceptable results. Normally the response rate is higher with telephone interviews than with self-administered questionnaires.

In the past few decades, systematic surveys of coffee consumption have only been done by this method in three countries: the United States, Japan, and West Germany. Based on their economic levels, these countries could be considered indicators of their respective geographic regions (9–11). These surveys give information on coffee consumption, trends and other relevant data, based on samples of 7,500 Americans, 4,500 Japanese, and 4,000 West Germans. They reported consumption of coffee both as "cups per person per day" and "cups per coffee drinker per day." The latter is, of course, higher than the former. The results of the surveys are shown mostly as cups per person per day (cups/pp/day), which allows an easy comparison with countries where consumption has not been measured directly and is given as "amount consumed per person."

In the United States, recent results indicate a mean coffee consumption of 1.75 cups/pp/day (9) and a continuous levelling off of consumption that began around 1985. But while the proportion of coffee drinkers in the long term has remained relatively constant (52.4%), the number of cups consumed daily by coffee drinkers has reached 3.41 in 1991, the highest level recorded in the last seven years.

In 1990 in Japan, the number of cups per day was 1.41 per person with 81.9% of people stating they enjoy coffee (10).

In West Germany, data for 1990 indicate a daily consumption of 3.87 cups per person; the percent of drinkers was 88.5%, and the number of cups per coffee drinker per day was 4.37 (11).

With respect to the popularity of coffee, the proportion of consumers is higher in West Germany and in Japan than in the United States, indicating more widespread consumption. In the U.S., soft drinks are more popular, particularly among young people, and the amount consumed is increasing. In West Germany, coffee is the most popular beverage followed by mineral water and beer. In Japan, green tea still remains the most popular beverage.

The different methods of conducting surveys mean that data are not directly comparable. In the United States and Germany, the surveys were based on consumption during the previous 24 hours (the day before), while in Japan the survey looked at the frequency of consumption. Age brackets were also different, thus making it difficult to compare consumption in the three countries, particularly among young people. Again, in each country, coffee consumption patterns are influenced by lifestyle, culture, tradition and behavior, so any comparison has to be considered merely approximate.

Details on coffee consumption in other countries are scanty. In France, Debry (12) reported the number of cups drunk per person per day as 1.47 in 1986 and the proportion of consumers as 80% of the population. In Switzerland, coffee consumption is estimated at 2.58 cups/pp/day (13). In the United Kingdom where tea still competes with coffee in popularity, coffee consumption is increasing, due mainly to the increased consumption of ground roasted, although most of the coffee drunk is still in the instant form (85–90%) (14).

In Italy, after a slow increase during the 1980s, consumption has now more or less levelled off with most coffee consumed at home (approximately 70%) (15) brewed in a mocha pot. In a nationwide survey on food consumption involving about 12,000 households carried out during 1980 to 1984 by the National Institute of Nutrition (16), home consumption of all types of coffee was 10.5 grams (g) per person per day. Highest consumption was observed in the northeast with a level of 11.2 g per person per day, followed by the northwest and central Italy with 10.6 g and finally the south with 10.0 g per person per day.

The figure 10.5 g per day (equivalent to 3.83 kg/pp/yr) corresponds to about 88% of the total consumption of coffee during 1982 to 1983 (respectively 4.33 and 4.34 kg/yr, given in the FBS (17). This figure suggests that 88% of coffee is consumed at home. However in Italy, as in some other countries, coffee consumed outside the home has increased slightly, mainly as increasing numbers of people take lunch in public places or company cafeterias (12). From the results of another Italian survey by the National Institute of Statistics (ISTAT) (18), where home consumption of coffee was investigated with the consumption of tea and other surrogates, the geographical pattern of consumption was still evident.

TREND IN CONSUMPTION

As mentioned, on the basis of disappearance (FBS), world coffee consumption is increasing. To evaluate whether this is due to an increase in the number of consumers or to an increase in the coffee actually consumed by habitual drinkers we can use data from the systematic surveys regularly carried out in the United States, Japan, and West Germany using different methods (9–11). These data enable us, for the period 1980 to 1991, to analyze the trend in consumption (see Table 6) and the percentage of consumers (see Table 7) within each country.

In the United States, consumption (measured as cups/pp/day), after a decrease in 1986, has stabilized during the last five years, almost as though a levelling off had occurred in the long-term downward trend in coffee consumption that began in the mid-1980s. At the same time, consumption in

TABLE 6. *Number of cups of coffee consumed per day in three different countries, based on the total population*

Year	1980	1983	1985	1986	1987	1988	1989	1990	1991
United States[a]	2.02	1.85	1.83	1.74	1.76	1.67	1.75	1.73	1.75
Japan[b]	1.06	1.23	1.29	—	1.36	—	—	1.41	—
West Germany[c]	4.03	—	4.00	3.89	4.18	4.08	4.11	3.87	—

[a]By telephone interview (population aged 10 yrs and over); [b] by questionnaire (population over high school age to 79 yrs); [c] by interview (population aged over 15 yrs).

Japan has been constantly increasing. In West Germany, consumption has been relatively stable during this decade, with some fluctuations around 1986.

The trend in coffee consumption (number of coffee drinkers) in all three countries shows wide fluctuations. In the last decade, the number of consumers has decreased by 2% in Japan and West Germany and 5% in the United States, while coffee consumption, in terms of cups/drinker/day, has increased in each country.

It is interesting to analyze the trends in relation to the consumers' ages. In all three countries, the younger groups show decreasing coffee consumption in cups/pp/day. This seems to be attributable (9) to the strong advertising strategy of the soft drink producers, as indicated by consumption of soft drinks, which has increased by 13.7% in the United States in the last decade. In older strata of the population, the trend is stable or increasing, with the exception of the population of Japan where the older age groups consume less than other age groups. This is probably because older people are unwilling to give up the traditional Japanese habit of tea drinking. The Japanese survey (10), in fact, showed that "people who drink least coffee are those that eat more rice for breakfast, and eat the same foods together as a family; most heavy coffee drinkers, on the other hand, eat bread for breakfast or do not eat breakfast at all, and if they do eat breakfast do so separately and/or eat different foods than the other members of their family." In addition, from the same survey one can conclude that "the higher the percentage of people with an urban lifestyle who have a high stress level and distinct preferences for gourmet food and drink, the more coffee drunk. Furthermore, they are closer to an *adult* style of health awareness and care than a *young* style."

TABLE 7. *Proportion of coffee consumers (drinkers), based on all types of coffee*

Year	1980	1983	1985	1986	1987	1988	1989	1990	1991
United States[a]	56.6	—	54.9	52.4	52.0	50.0	52.5	52.4	51.4
Japan[b]	77.5	83.9	82.7	—	82.9	—	—	81.9	—
West Germany[c]	90.9	—	89.2	87.7	89.2	—	—	88.5	—

[a] By telephone interview (population aged 10 yrs and over); [b] by questionnaire (population over high school age up to 79 yrs); [c] by interview (population aged over 15 yrs).

These observations seem to indicate a more marked "westernization" of food habits and lifestyle among Japanese people who drink more coffee.

CONSUMPTION AND METHODS OF PREPARATION

Brewing Techniques

Boiled coffee is prepared by boiling coarsely ground light-roasted arabica coffee in water (50–70 g/L) for about 10 minutes and is drunk without filtering off the grounds. This method has 75% caffeine extraction efficiency (19). Cup size is usually 150–190 ml. This method is used in the Nordic countries.

Espresso is prepared by brewing 6–7 g finely ground medium-to-dark roasted coffee in individual portions with water at 92–95°C and 8–12 bar for about 30 seconds, with 80% caffeine extraction efficiency (20). Cup size is 20–35 ml in Italy and 120–150 in other countries.

Filter coffee is prepared by pouring boiling water over medium-ground light-to-dark-roasted coffee (30–80 g/L) through a paper filter or automatic drip machine, for about 6.5 minutes; with 97–100% caffeine extraction efficiency (19). It is used in northern Europe with higher dosages and in the United States with lower dosages of light-roasted, elsewhere higher doses and medium-to-dark-roast. The usual cup size is 50–190 ml.

Greek/Turkish "mud" coffee is prepared by bringing to a gentle boil very finely ground medium-to-dark-roasted coffee (4–6 g/50–60 ml water) often with sugar (5–10 g). It is consumed mostly in the Middle East; the cup size is 30–50 ml.

Liquid coffee is a ready-to-drink coffee mixture usually containing additives, consumed either hot or cold, mainly in Japan and Korea. The cup size is 185–200 ml.

Mocha coffee is prepared by forcing just-overheated water through finely ground dark-roasted coffee (5–8 g/cup) for 1–2 minutes, with 92–98% caffeine extraction efficiency (19). It is consumed mainly in Italy and Spain. The usual cup size is 40–120 ml.

Percolated coffee is prepared by recirculating boiling brew through coarsely ground light-to-medium-roasted coffee (30–60 g/L) for 7.5 minutes (19), with 85% caffeine extraction efficiency. It is consumed in the United States and the English-speaking countries, and the usual cup size is 150–190 ml. Its use is declining with the introduction of automatic drip machines.

Soluble coffee is prepared by dissolving 1.5–3.0 g of soluble coffee powder in hot or cold water. It is used worldwide. The cup size is 80–190 ml.

Place of Consumption

The place where coffee is drunk can shed light on the reasons for consumption. Observational data from the surveys under consideration (9–11) indi-

TABLE 8. *Caffeine availability and caffeine content*

Country	Coffee species %[b]	Caffeine % in mixture	Caffeine availability mg/day[c]	Brewing methods (most widely used)	Ground coffee g/l
Finland	A 100	1.10	380	Boiled	50–70
				Filter	50–80
Sweden	A 100	1.10	329	Boiled	50–70
				Filter	50–80
Denmark	A 76	1.32	387	Filter	50–80
	R 22			Boiled	50–70
Austria	A 77	1.29	371	Filter	50–80
	R 20				
Norway	A 96	1.10	307	Boiled	50–70
	R 2			Filter	50–80
Netherlands	A 62	1.27	310	Filter	50–80
	R 27				
Belgium-Lux	—[f]	1.27	306	Filter	50–80
West Germany	A 86	1.19	267	Filter	50–80
	R 11				
Switzerland	A 84	1.23	253	Filter	50–80
	R 14			Instant	1.5–2.5[g]
				Espresso	6–7[g]
France	A 47	1.69	267	Filter	50–80
	R 53			Instant	2–3[g]
United States	A 74	1.23	158	Filter	30–60
	R 19			Percolated	30–60
Italy	A 52	1.63	196	Espresso	6–7[g]
	R 48			Mocha	5–8[g]
Canada	—[h]	1.23	131	Filter	30–60
				Percolated	30–60
United Kingdom	A 57	1.55	102	Instant	1.5–2.0[g]
	R 42			Percolated	30–60
Portugal	A 26	1.65	118	Espresso	6–7[g]
	R 62				

[a] Assuming that all the caffeine has been extracted. The efficiency of (caffeine) extraction, which is highest in drip filter coffee and lowest in boiled and espresso coffee, increases with fineness of grind (particle size 1.0–0.1 mm), water/coffee ratio (5:1–30:1), water temperature (90–100°C), and contact time (0.5–2.0 minutes).

[b] Proportion of arabica (A—1.1% caffeine), robusta (R—2.2% of caffeine) imported into each country. The difference from 100% indicates coffees imported as soluble, decaffeinated or roasted, without details of blend.

[c] Based on green coffee consumed per day per person.

[d] Calculated with smaller amount (ground coffee g/l) of coffee. These figures should be corrected for caffeine extraction efficiency.

cate that in 1990 most of the coffee appears to have been consumed in the home. Figures for the United States, West Germany, and Japan are respectively 72%, 70%, and 54%. The place of work comes next with 17%, 19%, and 24%, respectively, followed by other locations such as restaurants, coffee shops, bars, etc., with 11%, 11%, and 19%, respectively.

The high consumption of coffee at home suggests that coffee is mainly *in "a cup of coffee"^{a} in different countries*

Usual cup size ml	Caffeine mg/cup^d	Caffeine mg/ml^d	Caffeine mg/cup^e	Caffeine mg/ml^e	Caffeine extraction efficiency %
150–190	83–105	0.6	116–146	0.8	75
50–190	28–105	0.6	44–167	0.9	97–100
150–190	83–105	0.6	116–146	0.8	75
50–190	28–105	0.6	44–167	0.9	97–100
50–190	33–125	0.7	53–201	1.1	97–100
150–190	99–125	0.7	139–176	0.9	75
50–190	32–123	0.6	52–196	1.0	97–100
150–190	83–105	0.6	116–146	0.8	75
50–190	28–105	0.6	44–167	0.9	97–100
50–190	32–121	0.6	51–193	1.0	97–100
50–190	32–121	0.6	51–193	1.0	97–100
50–190	30–113	0.6	48–181	1.0	97–100
50–190	31–117	0.6	49–187	1.0	97–100
50–190	19	0.4–0.1	31	0.6–0.2	100
50–150	74	1.5–0.5	86	1.7–0.6	80
50–190	42–161	0.8	68–257	1.4	97–100
50–190	34	0.7–0.2	51	1.0–0.3	100
150–190	55–70	0.4	111–140	0.7	97–100
150–190	55–70	0.4	111–140	0.7	85
20–35	98	4.9–2.8	114	5.7–3.3	30–80
40–50	98	2.5–2.0	114	2.9–2.3	92–98
150–190	55–70	0.4	111–140	0.7	97–100
150–190	55–70	0.4	111–140	0.7	85
80–190	23	0.3–0.1	37	0.5–0.2	100
150–190	70–88	0.5	140–177	0.9	85
40–120	99	2.5–0.8	116	2.9–1.0	80

^{e} Calculated with larger amount (ground coffee g/l) of coffee. These figures should be corrected for caffeine extraction efficiency.

^{f} Data not available.

^{g} Data from the Netherlands (1.27% of caffeine) have been arbitrarily used for the calculation 7 g per cup. For instant coffee, a standard dose is taken as a 2 g.

^{h} Data not available. Data from the United States (1.23% of caffeine) have been arbitrarily used for the calculation.

drunk during or after meals, and thus considered "physiologically useful." The second preferred place of consumption in terms of quantity, the work place, suggests that coffee is considered a "pleasant occasion" to break working hours. The remainder is consumed mostly while eating out, which would reinforce the connection of coffee with meals. From these considerations, coffee consumption appears in general to have a positive image.

CAFFEINE CONSUMPTION

Regular coffee contains caffeine, but the caffeine intake from coffee cannot easily be estimated from the actual intake of coffee because of the wide range of caffeine content in a cup of coffee (21–23). Different amounts of ground coffee, the use of coffee mixtures with surrogates, and brewing methods all influence the caffeine content. According to a study in Canada (21), one

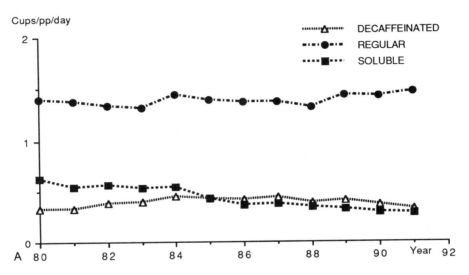

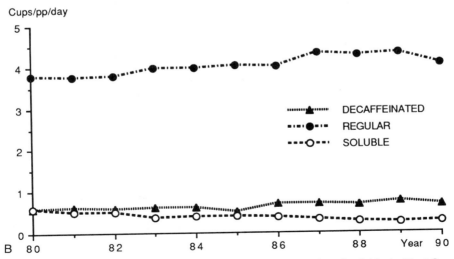

FIG. 2. Changes in coffee consumption, normal, decaffeinated, and soluble, in West Germany **(A)** and the United States **(B)** from 1980–1991.

household cup equals approximately 225 ml but can vary between 25 and 330 ml, with mean caffeine content of 84 mg per cup for drip, 71 for instant, and 82 for percolated coffee. In another study in Canada (22), cup size varied from 140 to 285 ml, with a caffeine content of 29–176 mg/cup for brewed and instant coffee. In the United States, mean caffeine contents were 115 mg (the range being from 60 to 180 mg) for a 150 ml cup of drip coffee, 80 mg (40–170 mg) for percolated coffee, and 65 mg (30–120 mg) for instant coffee (23).

Table 8 shows the theoretical caffeine content in "a cup" or "per milliliter" in several countries, for different mixtures, and for different brewing methods. These quantities could be used in the calculation of caffeine consumption for epidemiological purposes.

In some cases it is possible to assess the consumption of regular (with caffeine) and decaffeinated coffee. Both the percentage of consumers and the number of cups of decaffeinated coffee per day have decreased in the last decade in the United States, down 2.4% and 0.06 cups/person/day (9). In West Germany, however, consumption of decaffeinated coffee increased from 1980 to 1986, at which time it stabilized, but with a net increase of 2% over the decade (Fig. 2).

FLUID INTAKE

Coffee consumption, besides organoleptic pleasure and mild stimulation, is also an important way to introduce water into the diet during the day. In West Germany, Finland, and Switzerland coffee is the most popular drink and the largest source of water from beverages. Cup size, even if widely fluctuating as indicated in the section on brewing techniques (13), and the number of cups per day, permits an estimate of the average water intake per person at 600 ml in these countries.

ACKNOWLEDGMENT

We wish to thank Ms. Ruth Shalom Acheson for kindly revising our English.

REFERENCES

1. Hattox RS. *Coffee and coffee houses.* Seattle: University of Washington; 1988.
2. FoSAN. *de Coffea: Gruppo di studio sul caffè.* No 1. Est Edizioni, Torino; 1991.
3. Viani R. Coffee. *Ullmann's Encyclopedia of industrial chemistry*; vol A7. Weinheim, GFR: VCH Verlag; 1986;315–39.
4. FAO. *Food Balance Sheets 1989.* FAO, Rome; 1991.
5. King Communications Group, Inc. World Coffee up by five percent. *World-Food-Drink-Report* Jan 10, 1991.
6. FAO. *Food Balance Sheets, average 1985–1989.* FAO, Rome; 1991.

7. ECF. European Coffee Federation. *European Coffee report 1989.* Hans-G. Müller-Henniges, Bernhard Rothfos GmbH, May, 1990.
8. Ferro-Luzzi A. Meaning and constraints of energy-intake studies in free-living populations. In: Harrison GA, ed. Energy and Effort, *Symposia of the Society for the Study of Human Biology-22.* London: Taylor & Francis Ltd.; 1982;115–7.
9. National Coffee Association of USA. Coffee drinking study 1991. *NCA of USA* New York; 1991.
10. Nippon Research Center. A basic survey for monitoring trends in the demand for coffee 1991. *All Japan Coffee Association,* June, 1991.
11. ICO. International Coffee Organization. Federal Republic of Germany. Coffee Consumption habits trend data 1980 to 1990. *ICO. ED* PC-97/91 (E), July, 1991.
12. Debry G. Le Café: sa composition, sa consomation, ses incidences sur la santé. *Monographie n° 1 Centre de Nutrition Humaine.* Nancy; 1989.
13. Anon. Coffee. 1. Production and Use. In: IARC Working Group, eds. IARC Monographs on the evaluation of carcinogenic risk to humans. Vol 51. *WHO-International Agency for Research on Cancer (IARC);* 1991.
14. Nestlé. *Hot beverages report 1991. UK.* Nestlé, Vevey; 1991.
15. Anon. Coffee in Italy. (*Special Report No. 17. Marketing Europe* 1988;311:44–55.
16. Turrini A, Saba A, Lintas C. Study of the Italian total diet for monitoring food constituents and contaminants. *Nutr Res 11,* 1991;8:861.
17. Clarke RJ, Macrae R. *Coffee;* Vol 3. Physiology. London: Elsevier Applied Science; 1988.
18. Istituto Nazionale di Statistica (ISTAT). Consumi alimentari delle famiglie italiane 1989. In: *ISTAT* Annuario Italiano di Statistica, 1991.
19. Peters A. Brewing makes the difference. *Proceeding of the 14th International Conference on Coffee Science.* San Francisco (USA): July, 1991.
20. Petracco M. Physico-chemical and structural characterisation of "espresso" coffee brew. *Proceedings of 13th ASIC Colloquium.* Paipa (Colombia) 1989;246.
21. Stavric B, Klassen R, Watkinson B, Karpinski K, Stapley R, Fried P. Variability in caffeine consumption from coffee and tea: possible significance for epidemiological studies. *Food Chem Toxicol* 1988;26:111–8.
22. Gilbert RM, Marshman JA, Schwieder M, Berg R. Caffeine content of beverages as consumed. *Can Med Assoc J* 1976;114:205–8.
23. Lecos C. The latest caffeine scorecard. *FDA Consumer.* March 1984;14–6.
24. USDA *World coffee and tea.* September, 1991;16.

Caffeine, Coffee, and Health,
edited by S. Garattini.
Raven Press, Ltd., New York © 1993.

2

The Composition of Coffee

Rinantonio Viani

Nestec Ltd., 1800 Vevey, Switzerland

The two main commercial varieties of raw coffee, *Coffea arabica* L. (arabica coffee), and *Coffea canephora* Pierre ex Froehner (robusta coffee), are different in composition. Arabica contains more lipids and trigonelline, and robusta more caffeine and chlorogenic acids. Compounds typical of coffee have been identified, the main ones being cafestol and kahweol esters with fatty acids. Constituents specific to each species are also known, with kahweol and atractyligenin practically absent in robusta, 16-0-methylcafestol absent in arabica and 24-methylenecholesterol and Δ^5-avenasterol more important in robusta.

No change other than a 10- to 20-fold reduction in the caffeine content of the bean is caused by decaffeination. Many hundreds of compounds have been identified, particularly in the volatile fraction, most of which are formed during roasting, and their impact on the flavor is beginning to be understood.

The melanoidins, high molecular pigments, form the least known fraction both from the structural and organoleptic point of view.

INTRODUCTION

Of the more than 100 plant species known to contain methylxanthines, particularly caffeine, or 1,3,7-trimethylxanthine, human beings have chosen to use only a few, intrigued by their taste. Tea, cocoa, and coffee were all introduced to Europe around the seventeenth century, acquiring popularity with the creation of coffee houses. Tea, still the most popular hot beverage in the world with by far the longest documented history, has a taste in which astringency and bitterness are subtly modulated by the "umami" component. Bitter-tasting hot chocolate became the drink of the French upper classes during the Age of Enlightenment. Coffee, a sweetish-tasting berry, used as a pep-pill by travelers in the Horn of Africa, did not spread beyond the shores of the Red Sea until, around the fifteenth century. It was discovered that, after roasting the hard seeds contained in the coffee cherry, a hot

17

TABLE 1. *Attributes of coffee for the expert taster*

Attribute	Definition
Acidity	Sensory acidity is well correlated to titrated acidity, but bitterness and volatile aroma also contribute.
Body	Linked with the physical characteristics of the beverage, such as mouth-feel; however, viscosity of the cup alone is not sufficient to define it.
Aroma	The contribution of the volatile constituents in the overall appreciation.
Taste	Where bitterness plays an important role, taste is defined by a series of attributes, such as soft, clean, full, round, rich, etc.

aromatic brew was obtained with a strong, bitter, astringent and somewhat acid taste.

The quest for the components, which make the beverage so popular around the world, did not end in 1820 with the isolation by Runge of pure, crystalline caffeine from coffee. The search still continues to determine what it is in these caffeine-containing plants that makes them so special.

FROM THE CHERRY TO THE CUP

Coffee cherries do not ripen all at the same time, and the moment of harvesting is critical for the final flavor in the cup. Ripe cherries give a brew defined by professional tasters by its aroma, body, acidity, and taste (Table 1).

Immature, greenish cherries will give a harsh cup; overripe blackish cherries will impart an impure taste, and even perfectly ripe red cherries may develop fermented or musty notes if the delay before processing is too long. The expert taster is attentive to these defects and will select only flawless lots, rejecting defective beans. The main substances responsible for a less-than-perfect taste have now been identified (Table 2).

TABLE 2. *Main defects of coffee*

Defect	Organoleptic character: contaminant
Black bean	Black, astringent, woody taste
Immature bean	Greenish with no coffee taste: ratio between di- and mono-caffeoyl-quinic acids too high (1)
"Rioy" bean	Phenolic smell and taste: 2,4,6-trichloroanisole (TCA)[a] (2)
Musty bean	Pale to blackish: geosmin (2)
Earthy bean	Pale to normal: methylisoborneol (3)
Stinker bean	Pale to brown with impure smell and taste: fermentation with formation of aliphatic esters and acids, and of dimethyl sulphide and dimethyl disulphide (4)
"Peasy" bean	Flavor of fresh green peas: 2-isopropyl-3-methoxypyrazine (5)

[a] TCA, responsible for the "rioy" flavor, also imparts the taste of cork to wine and is one of the substances known in nature to which the human nose is the most sensitive (down to 0.001 ppb in the cup).

CHEMICAL COMPOSITION

Detailed information on the history, botany, culture, processing, and marketing of coffee, as well as on the chemistry and physiology of the infusion has recently been edited by Clarke and Macrae (6), and in a compact form by Viani (7). The proceedings of the conferences organized every second year by the *Association Scientifique Internationale du Café* contain a wealth of information on coffee chemistry, physiology, technology, and botany (8).

Raw (Green) Coffee

The two main commercial species of coffee, *Coffea arabica* L. (arabica coffee) and *C. canephora* Pierre ex Froehner (robusta coffee), show both quantitative and qualitative differences in their chemical compositions. Arabica contains more lipids and trigonelline, while robusta contains more caffeine and chlorogenic acids. Minor constituents specific to one species only have also been identified. The composition of raw (green) coffee beans is indicated in Table 3.

Green coffee beans, stored in appropriate dry conditions, are stable over several years, and aged, vintage coffees are appreciated in some cultures for their mild taste.

Roasted Coffee

The composition of the bean is dramatically altered by roasting. At the start, moisture is reduced by heating until the beans reach a temperature of about 160°C. Organic losses then begin with evolution of carbon dioxide, swelling of the beans, and reduction of their apparent density. Important chemical transformations occur, and many hundreds of volatile substances

TABLE 3. *Composition of raw coffee (% dry matter)[a]*

Component	Arabica	Robusta
Caffeine	1.2	2.2
Minerals (oxides)	4.2	4.4
—of which potassium	1.7	1.8
Lipids	16.0	10.0
Trigonelline	1.0	0.7
Proteins, amino acids	11.5	11.8
Aliphatic acids	1.4	1.4
Depsides (chlorogenic acids)	6.5	10.0
Glycosides	0.2	tr.
Carbohydrates (by difference)	58.0	59.5

[a] The water content of commercial raw coffee beans normally varies between 8 and 12%.

TABLE 4. *Composition of medium roasted coffee beans (% dry basis[a])*

Component	Arabica	Robusta
Caffeine	1.3	2.4
Minerals (oxides)	4.5	4.7
—of which potassium	1.8	1.9
Lipids	17.0	11.0
Trigonelline, niacin	1.0	0.7
"Proteins"	10.0	10.0
Aliphatic acids	2.4	2.5
Depsides (chlorogenic acids)	2.7	3.1
Carbohydrates	38.0	41.5
Volatile aroma	0.1	0.1
Melanoidins (by difference)	23.0	23.0

[a] The water content of commercial roasted coffee beans normally varies between 1 and 5%.

that make up the roast coffee aroma are formed together with polymeric brown pigments, the melanoidins, whose structures are only partially known. Above 200°C the reaction becomes exothermic and, at temperatures above 240°C, the beans become scorched and start to burn with the formation of soot. The roasting loss of commercial coffees, i.e., the reduction in weight due to the loss of water and organic matter, may vary between 13% in the Nordic countries, and 20% in Mediterranean countries. Unlike green coffee beans, roasted coffee, particularly after it has been ground, spoils in a few days if not protected from oxygen and moisture, with loss of volatile components and staling; however, if it is protected from light and oxygen—under vacuum in the dark—it may keep for many months without appreciable organoleptic losses. The composition of roasted coffee beans is given in Table 4.

The composition of the infusion varies as a function of the brewing technique applied, but no important chemical changes actually occur with brewing or during industrial extraction, other than a partial loss of the volatile aroma. If the infusion is heated for several hours, hydrolysis may occur with a consequent increase in acidity and a change in the volatile content.

COMPOUNDS IDENTIFIED IN RAW, ROASTED, BREWED, AND SOLUBLE COFFEES

Caffeine and the Minor Purine Alkaloids

Only caffeine, of which robusta contains almost double the amount found in arabica, differentiates raw coffee from common staple food items. The presence of caffeine is important and probably explains why caffeine-containing plants were selected for consumption wherever available: in Asia, tea, in South America, maté, guarana', cocoa, and in Africa, cola and coffee.

Caffeine is a bitter substance, with a taste threshold in water of 0.2–1.8 mM/L^{-1}, i.e., of the same order of magnitude as its concentration in a cup of regular coffee. Its role in the typical, bitter taste of coffee is, however, not unique; taste perception changes with the temperature of the beverage and is reduced in older people. Its contribution to the taste, however, must not be overlooked, as at levels below the taste threshold caffeine affects the taste of sweet, bitter, and salty substances. The caffeine content of a cup of coffee

i.	$R_1 = R_2 = R_3 = CH_3$	Caffeine
ii.	$R_1 = H,\ R_2 = R_3 = CH_3$	Theobromine
iii.	$R_1 = R_2 = CH_3,\ R_3 = H$	Theophylline
iv.	$R_1 = R_3 = CH_3,\ R_2 = H$	Paraxanthine

v.	$R_1 = R_2 = R_3 = R_4 = CH_3$	Theacrine

vi.	$R_1 = R_4 = CH_3,\ R_3 = H$	Liberine
vii.	$R_1 = R_3 = R_4 = CH_3$	Methylliberine

TABLE 5. *Purine alkaloids of green coffee (mg/kg db)*

Component	Arabica	Robusta
Caffeine (i)	9000–14000	15000–26000
Theobromine (ii)	36–40	26–82
Theophylline (iii)	7–23	86–344
Paraxanthine (iv)	3–4	8–9
Theacrine (v)	0	11
Liberine (vi)	5	7–110
Methylliberine (vii)	0	3

can vary from 1–5 mg for decaffeinated coffee (negligible from a pharmacological point of view), up to 50–150 mg for a cup of regular coffee.

The complex and subtle pharmacological activity of caffeine still eludes researchers, in spite of the many studies in the 170 years since its discovery. Questions arise even about its stimulating properties (9). Beside caffeine, small amounts of other purine alkaloids have been identified in the coffee bean and are present at higher levels in beans from cherries harvested unripe (10). Their amounts are given in Table 5.

Paraxanthine, 1,7-dimethylxanthine, present only in trace amounts in unripe beans, is the most important caffeine metabolite in humans. Traces of xanthine, hypoxanthine, adenine, and guanine in raw coffee have also been reported (11). It must be emphasized that all the effects attributed to caffeine are quite small at the doses commonly found in a cup of coffee. It is therefore unlikely that the psychopharmacological effects of caffeine are the only reason for drinking coffee and, in fact, many people feel that drinking a cup of coffee is in itself an agreeable olfactory and gustatory experience.

Caffeine is stable and only a small percentage is lost through sublimation during roasting. During decaffeination, no major transformation occurs in the composition of the raw coffee bean other than the selective removal of caffeine (see Appendix). The popularity of decaffeinated coffee provides further proof that coffee's success is not due to caffeine alone. It may be worth mentioning that no clinical or laboratory study has shown any specific pharmacological effect of decaffeination.

Minerals

Coffee contains about 4% of mineral constituents, with potassium amounting to 40% of the total. The level is slightly higher in dry-processed robusta (4.14–4.39%; potassium 1.84–2.00%) and arabica (4.11–4.27%; potassium 1.77–1.88%) than in wet-processed arabica (3.58–3.95%; potassium 1.63–1.70%). Up to 90% of the potassium goes into the brew, and practically all of it is extracted industrially, and contents between 3.5% for high-yield

TABLE 6. *Mineral content of raw coffee (% db)*

Potassium	1.63–2.00
Calcium	0.07–0.35
Magnesium	0.16–0.31
Phosphate	0.13–0.22
Sulphate	0.13

soluble coffee and 5.5% for a home brew have been measured (12). Species differences also exist among the other elements present. The main minerals found in raw coffee beans are indicated in Table 6.

Phosphate in the form of phosphoric acid, with citric acid, is one of the main contributors to the acidity of coffee according to Maier (13). Nitrate but not nitrite is present in raw coffee (14). The hydrogen peroxide content of brewed, ground, roasted, and soluble coffees increases on standing (15) and may be related to the oxidation of polyphenols by atmospheric oxygen. However, the levels measured in coffee by various authors may be linked to the analytical method used (16,17), and its presence in the brew may even be an analytical artifact (18).

Lipids

Lipids constitute 15–18% of arabica and 8–12% of robusta raw coffee. Most of them, the coffee oil, are located in the endosperm; the remaining 0.2–0.3%, the wax, are on the outer layer of the bean. Coffee oil is composed mainly of triglycerides of fatty acids, particularly linoleic (40–45%) and palmitic (25–35%), in proportions similar to those found in common edible vegetable oils. A relatively large unsaponifiable fraction, rich in free and mostly esterified diterpenes of the kaurane family, mainly cafestol (viii) and kahweol (ix), characteristic of coffee. Although there are only minor differences in the triglyceride fraction between arabica and robusta, the unsaponifiable fraction contains constituents typical of arabica, kahweol, absent (19) or present only in small proportions (20) in robusta and, in roasted coffee oil, atractyligenin (x) (21), or of robusta, 16-0-methyl-cafestol (xi) (22,23), mainly in the form of palmitate (24). Among the sterols, 24-methylenecholesterol (xii) and Δ^5-avenasterol (xiii) are more important in robusta than in arabica beans (25). The outer wax contains the 5-hydroxytryptamides (xiv) of six fatty acids, viz. arachidonic (C20), and behenic (C22) acids, and, in lesser amounts, of lignoceric (C24), stearic (C18), 20-hydroxyarachidonic and 22-hydroxybehenic acids (26). The presence of these substances in coffee has been claimed to indicate undefined "irritating substances," to which some people may be sensitive. Their removal by washing the beans with solvent

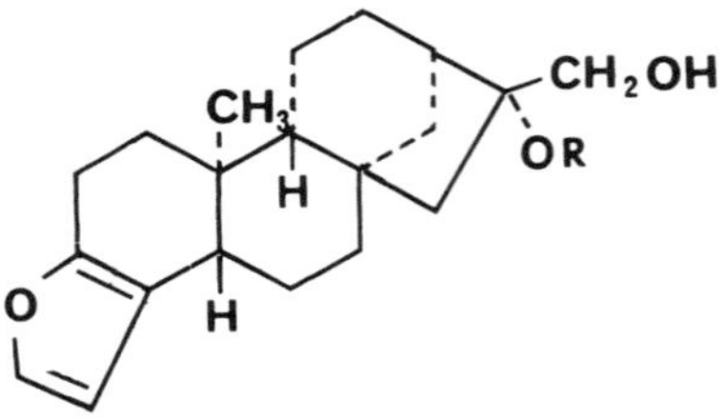

viii.　R=H　　　　Cafestol
xi.　　R=CH₃　　16-O-Methylcafestol

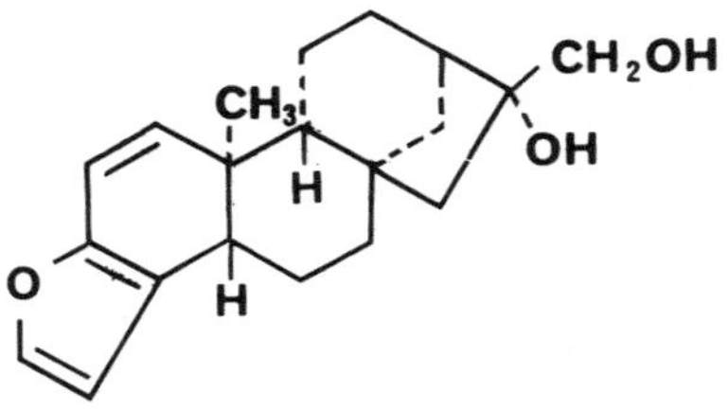

ix.　　Kahweol

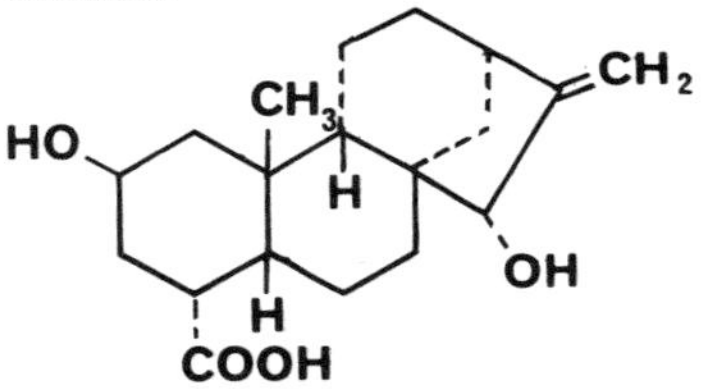

x.　　Atractyligenin

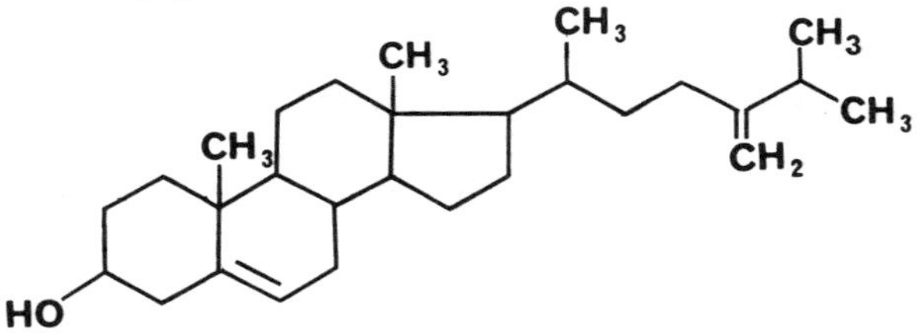

xii.　24-Methylenecholesterol

or by steaming should increase the wholesomeness of coffee. However, the relationship, if any, between the hydroxytryptamide content and any health effects of the brew has never been demonstrated. The composition of the lipid fraction of raw coffee is given in Table 7.

Some fatty acids, cafestol, and kahweol as well as their dehydro-derivatives are formed during roasting from the esters, and atractyligenin from

xiii. Δ^5-Avenasterol

xiv.   5-Hydroxytryptamides
R=CH$_3$, n=16,18,20,22
R=CH$_2$OH, n=18,20

glycosides, while the sterol fraction is unaffected (27,28); one-third of the 5-hydroxytryptamides is decomposed with formation of volatile compounds (29). During brewing and industrial extraction, most of the lipids remain in the spent ground and contribute only 1 to 40 mg per cup, depending on the fineness of the grind and on the filter device. Coffee lipids, present in higher proportions in boiled coffee than in filtered or soluble coffee, may contain a cholesterol-raising factor, "factor X" (30–32). The unknown substance(s) responsible for this effect may be present, in particular, in the unsaponifiable fraction of both arabica and robusta coffee oil. Cafestol and kahweol, present in the cup in amounts proportional to the oil content, are non-mutagenic (33) and have shown cancer-protective activity in animal experiments with relatively large doses (34,35).

TABLE 7. *Lipid fraction of raw coffee (% db)*

Triglycerides (mainly esters of linoleic and palmitic acids)	70–80
Free fatty acids	0.5–2.0
Diterpene esters (mainly cafestol and kahweol palmitate and linoleate)	15–18.5
Triterpene, sterols and methylsterol esters	1.4–3.2
Free diterpenes (mainly cafestol and kahweol)	0.1–1.2
Phospholipids	0.1
Hydrocarbons (mainly squalane and nonacosane)	tr.
5-hydroxytryptamides	0.3–1.0
Tocopherols (α, β, γ-isomers)	0.3–0.7

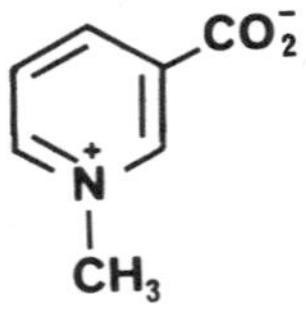

xv.   Trigonelline

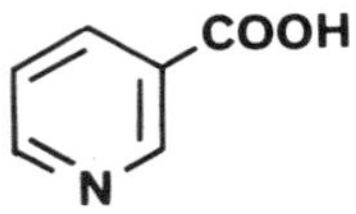

xvi.   Niacin

Trigonelline and Other Bases

Arabica and robusta raw coffees contain, respectively, 0.6–1.3% and 0.3–0.9% of trigonelline (xv), which during roasting is decomposed at temperatures above 180°C with the formation of volatile aroma components, mainly alkylpyridines (36), and of niacin (xvi). The cup content of trigonelline (itself a usable stored form of the vitamin [37]) and of niacin is given in Table 8.

Traces of betaine (below 0.1%) and choline (below 0.1% in raw beans, up to 1% in roasted beans from thermally degraded lecithins) have been measured (38), but the presence of histamine has not been confirmed (30).

Amino Acids, Peptides, and Proteins

Both free and bound amino acids are present in raw beans at levels estimated at 8.7–12.2%. The actual range may be smaller, and there are some

TABLE 8. Content of trigonelline and niacin in brewed and soluble coffee (mg/cup)

Product	Trigonelline	Niacin[a]
Brew[b]	40–55	0.03–0.06
Soluble coffee[c]	5–35	0.3–1.5

[a] Enzymatically as nicotinamide
[b] From 10 g of coffee
[c] 2 g of powder

TABLE 9. *Free and total aminoacids in raw coffee (% db)*

Amino acid	Free		Total protein
	Arabica	Robusta	
Alanine	0.05	0.09	0.5
Arginine	0.01	0.02	0.5
Aspartic acid	0.05	0.09	1.0
Asparagine	0.05	0.09	
Cysteine	0.001		0.3
Glutamic acid	0.13	0.08	1.9
Glycine	0.01	0.02	0.6
Histidine	0.01	tr.	0.2
3-Methylhistidine	tr.	tr.	
Isoleucine	0.01	0.02	0.4
Leucine	0.01	0.02	1.0
Gamma-aminobutyric acid	0.05	0.10	
Lysine	0.01	tr.	0.6
Methionine	0.004		0.2
Phenylalanine	0.02	0.04	0.7
Proline	0.03	0.04	0.6
Serine	0.03	0.04	0.5
Threonine	tr.	0.01	0.3
Tyrosine	0.01	0.02	0.4
Valine	0.01	0.02	0.5
Tryptophan	0.01	0.05	0.1
Total	0.5	0.8	10.3

qualitative and quantitative differences between arabica and robusta. Levels of 0.15–0.25% have been reported for free amino acids. Approximately half of the protein present is water soluble (albumin). The composition of total and free amino acids is given in Table 9 (38).

The free amino acids virtually disappear during roasting. Of those bound in proteins in the raw bean, all of the arginine and most of the cysteine disappear during roasting, while lysine, methionine, serine, threonine and tryptophan are somewhat reduced. The remaining acids can be recovered by hydrolysis of the brown pigments formed on roasting.

Aliphatic Acids, Depsides

The acidity of a coffee infusion is an important organoleptic character and is associated with the taste of the best high-grown arabicas, such as Kenyas. Maximum titratable acidity and lowest pH are reached at 11% roasting loss (39), while acid taste perception is strongest at roasting losses of about 15% (at higher roasting, rapid decomposition of the acids occurs, and the taste of the bitter substances formed masks the acid sensation). It is linked with the volatile aliphatic acids, particularly acetic acid, formed by pyrolysis of carbohydrates, and with the presence of the nonvolatile heat-labile acids, mainly citric. A major contribution also comes from phosphoric acid, which is stable. If the infusion is kept at high temperature, the acid taste increases because of hydrolysis of lactones and esters. The aliphatic acids present in raw and in a medium-roasted coffee are indicated in Table 10 (there are no major differences between arabica and robusta).

These acids pass almost completely into the brew, and the content in a cup prepared from 10 g of ground coffee has been estimated at 246–300 mg (40). Some of the volatile acids are lost during concentration and drying of industrial extracts. Various forms of quinic acid (xvii), liberated during roasting, are transformed into isomeric γ- and δ-lactones, and quinides (xviii, xix), which can revert to the acid if the infusion is maintained at high temperature (41,42).

The depsides of cinnamic, caffeic, ferulic and isoferulic acids with quinic acid, the chlorogenic acids, are common in the vegetable kingdom. 5-Caffeoylquinic acid (chlorogenic acid) is the most important component of the group in both green and roasted coffee and, with 5-feruloylquinic acid and 3,5-dicaffeoylquinic acid (dichlorogenic acid), is naturally present in the fresh bean as the potassium salt, probably as a 1:1 complex with caffeine. The other isomers and free acid moieties, caffeic, ferulic and quinic, present in roasted coffee mainly as its lactone quinide, may be formed only during processing of the beans (13). Many reactions occur on roasting with formation of volatile aromatic substances and high-molecular pigments. The chlorogenic acids of coffee are reported in Table 11.

The chlorogenic acids are unstable on roasting, as indicated in Table 12 (43).

On the basis of 10 g coffee per cup of brew and 85% recovery, a cup content of chlorogenic acids can be estimated at 15–325 mg. An average value of 190 mg/cup has been reported for American coffee (44). The chlorogenic acids content of a soluble coffee is given in Table 13 (45). A 2 g cup of soluble coffee contains 70–200 mg of chlorogenic acids.

Several isomeric (iso)feruloylquinic acid lactones, and (iso)feruloylquinides, tentatively identified in soluble coffee, might be the psychoactive substances with receptor binding activity resembling that of opiate antagonists,

TABLE 10. *Aliphatic acids in coffee (%, db)*

Component	Raw	Roasted
Formic acid	tr.	0.06–0.15
Acetic acid	0.01	0.25–0.34
C3–C10 acids	tr.	tr.–0.03
Lactic acid	tr.	0.02–0.03
Citric acid	0.7–1.4	0.3–1.1
Malic acid	0.3–0.7	0.1–0.4
Fumaric acid	tr.	0.01–0.03
Oxalic acid	0–0.2	?
Quinic acid and quinides	0.3–0.5	0.6–1.2

xvii.   Quinic acid
         (several isomers present in roasted coffee)

xviii.   γ-Quinides
         (several isomers present in roasted coffee)

xix.   δ-Quinides
         (several isomers present in roasted coffee)

R=H   Caffeoyl-
R=CH₃   Feruloyl-

xx.   R=H   Chlorogenic acid (5-caffeoylquinic acid)
xxi.   R=CH₃   5-Feruloylquinic acid

TABLE 11. *Chlorogenic acids of arabica and robusta raw coffees (% db)*

Component	Arabica	Robusta
5-Chlorogenic acid (xx)	3.0–5.6	4.4–6.5
4-Chlorogenic acid	0.5–0.7	0.7–1.1
3-Chlorogenic acid	0.3–0.7	0.6–1.0
Total	3.8–7.0	5.7–8.6
3,4-Dicaffeoylquinic acid	0.1–0.2	0.5–0.7
3,5-Dicaffeoylquinic acid	0.2–0.6	0.4–0.8
4,5-Dicaffeoylquinic acid	0.2–0.4	0.6–1.0
Total	0.5–1.2	1.5–2.5
3-Feruloylquinic acid	tr.	0.1
4-Feruloylquinic acid	tr.	0.1
5-Feruloylquinic acid (xxi)	0.3	1.0
5-Feruloyl-4-caffeoylquinic acid	0	tr.
Total	0.3	1.2

TABLE 12. *Chlorogenic acids content of arabica and robusta coffees in relation to degree of roasting (% db)*

Species	Raw	Light	Medium	Dark
Arabica	6.9	2.7	2.2	0.2
Robusta	8.8	3.5	2.1	0.2

TABLE 13. *Chlorogenic acids in soluble coffee*

Component	% db
5-Chlorogenic acid	0.7–1.9
4-Chlorogenic acid	0.8–2.3
3-Chlorogenic acid	1.0–3.5
Total	2.5–7.7
3-Feruloylquinic acid	0.3–0.8
4-Feruloylquinic acid	0.2–0.4
5-Feruloylquinic acid	0.2–0.4
Total	0.8–2.0
3,4-Dicaffeoylquinic acid	tr.–0.5
3,5-Dicaffeoylquinic acid	0.1–0.3
4,5-Dicaffeoylquinic acid	0.1–0.4
Total	0.2–1.2

which have been detected in coffee (46,47). The cancer-protective effect of the chlorogenic acids is certainly linked to their antioxidant properties, as shown by the inhibition of N-nitrosamine formation in humans after ingestion of nitrate and proline together with soluble decaffeinated coffee (48).

Amides of tryptophan and tyrosine with caffeic acid have been isolated from raw robusta coffee: the fate on roasting of N-β-caffeoyl-L-tryptophan (49), and N-E-caffeoyl-L-tyrosine, which is present only in Angolan robusta (50), has not yet been investigated.

Carbohydrates

Oligosaccharides and soluble and insoluble polysaccharides constitute about one-half of the raw bean dry matter, without major species differences. The soluble fraction is composed of sucrose and of polymers of galactose, arabinose, and mannose (the galactomannans and arabinogalactans). The insoluble cell constituents include "holocelluloses," which contain, in addition to some cellulose, the very hard β-1,4-mannan, and a small amount of "hemicellulose," mainly arabinogalactan (51,52). No lignine, as characterized by polymers of xylose, is present in the seed, and levels of xylose up to 0.2% found after acid hydrolysis can be attributed to residual "silverskin" remaining on the surface and in the central cut of the bean. Roasting strongly degrades the carbohydrates, with depolymerization and liberation of monosaccharides, which then further react with the amino acids to form brown polymers and aromatic constituents. During industrial extraction, further depolymerization occurs, with liberation of monomers and increased solubility. The carbohydrate composition of raw and roasted coffee is given in Tables 14 and 15.

These figures give only an approximation as the levels change with the degree of roasting and some carbohydrates are partially degraded and may be included as melanoidins. The carbohydrates in the soluble extract have been the topic of several studies. The levels of free carbohydrates and of

TABLE 14. *Carbohydrates in raw coffee (% db)*

Constituent	Arabica		Robusta
Monosaccharides		0.2–0.5	
Sucrose	6–9		3–7
Polysaccharides	43.0–45.0		46.9–48.3
Arabinose	3.4–4.0		3.8–4.1
Mannose	21.3–22.5		21.7–22.4
Glucose	6.7–7.8		7.8–8.7
Galactose	10.4–11.9		12.4–14.0
Rhamnose		0.3	
Xylose		0–0.2	

TABLE 15. *Carbohydrates in roasted coffee*

Constituent	% db
Monosaccharides	0–2.0
Glucose, fructose, arabinose	Disappear at high roasting
Galactose	Increases with roasting
Sucrose	0.4–2.8 decreases with roasting
Soluble polysaccharides	5.8–12.1
Holocelluloses	10–21
Phytate (inositol hexaphosphate)	0.1–0.2 (53)

total carbohydrates measured after acid hydrolysis are indicated in Table 16 (54,55).

Glycosides

Atractyloside (xxii) and the related glycosides, cofaryloside and cafestolone, have been identified in raw arabica coffee. Their respective aglycones have been identified in roasted coffee. The glucoronide of atractyligenin has been found in amounts in the order of 2–40 mg/day in the urine of coffee drinkers. The atractyligenin content has been estimated at 2.98–11.5 mg/cup of brewed arabica and at less than 1 mg/cup of soluble arabica coffee. Only

xxii.   Atractyloside

TABLE 16. *Carbohydrates of soluble coffee (% db)*

Component	Free	Total
Arabinose	0.75–2.01	2.35–5.80
Fructose	0.05–0.42	
Mannose	0.13–2.62	10.20–19.7
Glucose	0.00–0.54	0.57–1.74
Galactose	0.27–0.72	13.50–14.7
Sucrose	0.01–0.64	
Xylose		0.00–0.32
Inositol	0.20–1.03	
Mannitol	0.02–0.22	

trace levels of atractyligenin and its glycosides have been found in raw robusta beans (21).

Volatile Components

More than 700 volatile substances have been identified in roasted coffee, corresponding to around 0.1% of the total matter. The substances identified up to 1989 were listed by Maarse & Visscher (56) with some quantitative data, and a few new constituents have been reported since then (57–59). The chemical and aroma-impact characteristics of the volatile constituents were reviewed by Flament (60). Quantitative differences between the aromas of arabica and robusta coffees have been found, with "caramel-like" and "sweet-roasty" odor notes prevalent in arabica and "spicy" or "earthy-roasty" notes more intense in robusta beans and brews (61). The per capita intake of coffee aroma constituents from coffee consumption can be estimated by multiplying the average content present in coffee by the per capita coffee consumption (62).

The mutagenicity of about 40 roast coffee aroma constituents was measured in three Ames tester strains (17). Only aliphatic dicarbonyl compounds, particularly methylglyoxal, showed direct mutagenic activity in Ames tester strains TA100 and TA102. Very weak effects were seen with some N-heterocyclic compounds in strains TA98 after metabolic activation.

Melanoidins

This name is used to group a heterogeneous, poorly characterized class of brown to black polymeric material formed at roasting by reaction of free monosaccharides with chlorogenic acids (63) or amino acids. Partially depolymerized polysaccharides and proteins undergo similar reactions. These substances contribute to the bitter coffee taste with some phenolic notes (64). The various processes are schematized in Fig. 1 (7).

Melanoidins formed by Maillard reaction have been shown to have a demutagenic effect against heat-induced mutagens, probably by scavenging active oxygen (65,66). The determination of melanoidins as soluble dietary fibers (67), probably the metal chelating fraction of coffee (68), in brewed and soluble coffees yields figures of 10% and 22% of the total organic matter respectively. An active cholinomimetic compound of empirical formula $C_{19}H_{36}N_{20}O_{10}$ has been isolated among the browning reaction products from brewed and soluble regular and decaffeinated coffees. This substance has not yet been fully characterized (69).

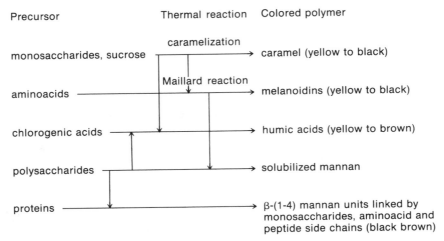

FIG. 1. Melanoidins formed at roasting by reaction of free monosaccharides with clorogenic acids or amino acids.

CONTAMINANTS

This chapter includes the endogenous contaminants, nitrosamines and heterocyclic amines, that might be formed during roasting, and the exogenous contaminants, paraffins, pesticides, and mycotoxins. Polycyclic hydrocarbons belong to both classes because they can be formed both by the fuel and by the coffee bean under suboptimal roasting conditions.

Paraffins

Agricultural material transported in jute and sisal sacks may be contaminated by paraffins used in the processing of the fiber ("batching") (70,71). For example, in green beans, 230 mg/kg of paraffin were measured in one sample. In roast beans, up to 150 mg/kg were measured with 100 mg/kg being average. In soluble coffee, less than 2 mg/kg of paraffin were measured.

Polycyclic Aromatic Hydrocarbons

The bulk of the analytical work has been done on the benzo-a-pyrene (BaP) content, but the proportions of the twelve polycyclic aromatic hydrocarbons (PAH) identified in roasted coffees and in commercial extracts do not change much (72). It can be concluded that coffee is a foodstuff poor in PAH, contributing less than 0.1% of the total dietary intake:

Green beans: 0.01–4.4 μ/kg, 0.37 μg/kg average as BaP.

Roast beans: light to medium roast less than 0.5 μg/kg as BaP, with a slight reduction from the amount present in the green bean, particularly in gas-fired direct roasters. The content increases in darker roasts, above 240°C and 20% roasting loss. Up to 5 μg/kg BaP have been measured in contact-roasted beans, particularly when charred.

Brew: 0.04–1.5 ng/cup, 0.5 ng/cup average. Transfers of 0.6–20%, average 5%, to the brew have been measured; the transfer is 4.6% at 50 g/L coffee strength and decreases with increasing cup strength, indicating saturation.

Instant coffee: 0–0.1 μg/kg, 0.03 μg/kg average, indicating a transfer of the order of 7% during industrial extraction (73). Cup contents of 0–0.2 ng, but only 0.06 ng average, have been measured.

Nitrosamines

Traces of N-nitrosopyrrolidine (NPYR) have been found both in roasted and in soluble coffee:

Roasted coffee: One sample out of six examined contained 0.4 ppb of NPYR (74).

Soluble coffee: NPYR was present in five out of ten samples at 0.3–1.4 parts per billion (ppb) (75), and in two samples out of seven at levels of 1.5 and 2.8 ppb (74).

Heterocyclic Amines

Mutagenic heterocyclic amines are formed in trace amounts in foods by reaction of amino acids and sugars during high-temperature heating. All the compounds identified so far have the amino acid creati(ni)ne, unknown in coffee, as one of the precursors (76). However, a group of authors have tentatively identified 2-amino-3,4-dimethylimidazo[4,5-*f*] quinoline (MeIQ) in one of six mutagenic fractions isolated from roasted coffee beans. The content of MeIQ was estimated at 16 ng/kg in regular hot-air roasted coffee, 32 ng/kg in charcoal-roasted coffee, and 150 ng/kg in high-temperature scorched coffee beans (77). The five other mutagenic fractions might also be heterocyclic amine-like substances (78). However, MeIQ was not detectable using a very sensitive method in either brewed or soluble coffees (79).

Pesticide Residues

In a survey of organochlorine and organophosphorus pesticide residues of raw coffee imported into Germany from 11 different countries, the level was lower than that permitted in 15 out of 17 samples. The residue was further reduced to insignificant amounts during roasting (80). The level of pesticides present on raw coffee beans has been decreasing over the last years, and Cetinkaya (81) could not detect either organochlorine or organophosphorus pesticide residues in 50 samples from coffee imported from 11 different countries. The level of contamination of the coffee imported into the United States is also diminishing. In addition, the contamination drops substantially during storage. Finally, roasting, brewing, and industrial extraction quantitatively eliminate the contaminants (82).

Mycotoxins

Coffee beans stored at high moisture levels in unsanitary conditions can be spoiled by fungal growth, with development of earthy and musty off-flavors, due to the formation of geosmin. All musty-tasting samples should be carefully analyzed for the presence of mycotoxins. Occasionally, ochratoxin A and, very rarely, aflatoxin B_1 have been found, particularly on decaffeinated beans. Rapid analytical procedures for the determination of ochratoxin A and aflatoxin B_1 have been developed (83,84). Both are almost completely destroyed during roasting and brewing (21,85,86).

APPENDIX: DECAFFEINATION TECHNIQUES (87)

The presence of water in the decaffeination process is necessary to dissolve the caffeine-potassium chlorogenate complex (88). In addition to water, the solvents and absorption materials used in decaffeination are dichloromethane (methylene chloride), ethyl acetate, fats and oils, supercritical carbon dioxide, and acid-treated active carbon, either as such or charged with sucrose. The techniques applied can be divided into two main groups according to the bean moisture level: at moisture levels below 40%, bean decaffeination, and at moisture levels above 60%, extract decaffeination. Decaffeination is usually done on the raw beans to avoid spoilage or loss of roasted coffee aroma.

Bean Decaffeination Processes

Raw coffee beans are swollen for up to 5 hours to 30–40% moisture using water and steam at 20–100°C. Decaffeination is done in either static or rotating drums with a water-saturated solvent selective for caffeine. Common solvents and operating conditions are indicated in Table 17.

Residual dichloromethane or ethyl acetate is removed from the decaffeinated beans by steam distillation at 100–110°C, during 1–4 hours (deodorization), and the solvent is recycled after purification. Supercritical carbon diox-

TABLE 17. *Solvent decaffeination*

Solvent	Conditions
Dichloromethane	40–100°C for 2–24 hours
Supercritical carbon dioxide (above 31.06°C and 73.8 bar)	40–80°C at 200–300 bar for 5–30 hours
Ethyl acetate	65–105°C for 2–24 hours
Fats and oils	95–105°C for 6–9 hours

ide is passed through active carbon, which retains the caffeine and the caffeine is removed from fats/oils through sublimation. The decaffeinated beans must then be dried to the original moisture level of 9–12%.

Extract Decaffeination Processes

Raw coffee beans are extracted with water at 70–100°C for 10 minutes to 2 hours and the extract is decaffeinated either by liquid–liquid extraction with any of the solvents indicated in Table 17 or by selective absorption of caffeine on acid-treated active carbon. Solvent extraction is carried out at 80–85°C for up to 10 hours followed by deodorization. In the adsorption processes, the extract at 60–100°C is passed for up to 8 hours through active carbon, which is used either as such or after loading with sucrose to reduce losses (89).

The adsorption processes, which do not use solvent to recover the caffeine from the extract, are commonly known as *water decaffeination*. The decaffeinated extract is either concentrated and re-incorporated in the pre-dried beans (Fig. 2), or recycled and used to decaffeinate new beans (Fig. 3).

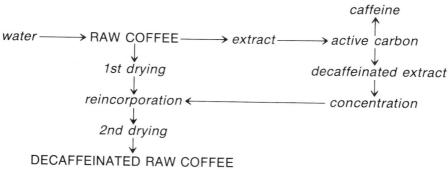

FIG. 2. Decaffeination using water as extraction medium.

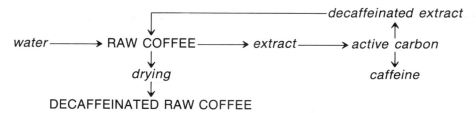

FIG. 3. Decaffeination using extract as extraction medium.

Soluble coffee is also decaffeinated as an extract, but suitable means to protect and recover the flavor need to be found.

REFERENCES

1. Clifford MN, Kazi T, Crawford S. The content and washout kinetics of chlorogenic acids in normal and abnormal green coffee beans. 12th ASIC Symp 1987;221–8.
2. Spadone JC, Takeoka G, Liardon R. Analytical investigation of rio off-flavor in green coffee. *J Agric Food Chem* 1990;38:226–33.
3. Vitzthum OG, Weisemann C, Becker R, Köhler HS. Identification of an aroma key compound in robusta coffees. *Café Cacao Thé* 1990;34(1):27–33.
4. Guyot B, Cochard B, Vincent JC. Détermination quantitative du diméthylsulfure et du diméthyldisulfure dans l'arôme de café. *Café Cacao Thé* 1991;35(1):49–56.
5. Becker R, Döhla B, Nitz S, Vitzthum OG. Identification of the "peasy" off-flavour note in Central African coffees. *12th ASIC Symp* 1987;203–15.
6. Clarke RJ, Macrae R, eds. *Coffee*; vols 1–5. London: Elsevier; 1985–1988.
7. Viani R. Coffee. *Ullmann's encyclopedia of industrial chemistry*; vol A7. Weinheim, GFR: VCH Verlag; 1986;315–39.
8. Association Scientifique Internationale du Café (ASIC). *Symposia proceedings*, vols. 1–14. Paris: ASIC; 1963–1991.
9. Dews PB, ed. *Caffeine perspectives from recent research*. Berlin: Springer Verlag; 1984.
10. Kappeler AW, Baumann TW. Purine alkaloid pattern in coffee beans. 11th ASIC Symp 1985;273–9.
11. Vitzthum OG. Chemie und Bearbeitung des Kaffees. In: Eichler O, ed. *Kaffee und Coffein*. Berlin: Springer Verlag; 1975.
12. Clarke RJ. Water and mineral content. In: Clarke RJ. Macrae R, eds. *Coffee*; vol 1: Chemistry. London: Elsevier; 1985;42–82.
13. Maier HG. Les acides du café. *Café Cacao Thé* 1987;31(1):49–57.
14. Amorim HV, Basso LC, Crocomo OJ, Teixeira AA. Polyamines in green and roasted coffee. *J Agric Food Chem* 1977;25:957–8.
15. Fujita Y, Wakabayashi K, Nagao M, Sugimura T. Implications of hydrogen peroxide in the mutagenicity of coffee. *Mutat Res* 1985;114:227–30.
16. Nagao M, Fujita Y, Wakabayashi K, Nukaya H, Kosuge T, Sugimura T. Mutagens in coffee and other beverages. *Environ Health Perspect* 1986;67:89–91.
17. Aeschbacher HU, Wolleb U, Löliger J, Spadone JC, Liardon R. Contribution of coffee aroma constituents to the mutagenicity of coffee. *Food Chem Toxicol* 1989;27:227–32.
18. Rinkus SJ, Taylor RT. Analysis of hydrogen peroxide in freshly prepared coffees. *Food Chem Toxicol* 1990;28:323–31.

19. Nackunstz B, Maier HG. Diterpenoide im Kaffee III. Cafestol und Kahweol. *Z Lebensm Unters Forsch* 1987;184:494–9.
20. Pettit BC. Identification of the diterpene esters in arabica and robusta coffees. *J Agric Food Chem* 1987;35:549–51.
21. Viani R. Physiologically active substances in coffee. In: Clarke RJ, Macrae R, eds. *Coffee*; vol 3: Physiology. London: Elsevier, 1988;1–31.
22. Speer K, Mischnick P. 16-O-Methylcafestol—ein neues Diterpen im Kaffee—Entdeckung und Identifizierung. *Z Lebensm Unters Forsch* 1989;189:219–22.
23. Speer K, Montag A. 16-O-Methylcafestol—ein neues Diterpen im Kaffee erste Ergebnisse: Gehalte in Rohund Röstkaffees. *Dtsch Lebesnm Rundsch* 1989;85:381–4.
24. Speer K, Tewis R, Montag A. 10-O-Methylcafestol—ein neues Diterpen im Kaffee—freies und gebundenes 16-O-Methylcafestol. *Z Lebensm Unters Forsch* 1991;192:451–4.
25. Mariani C, Fedeli E. Gli steroli della specie arabica e robusta del caffè. *Riv Ital Sostanze grasse* 1991;68:111–5.
26. Folstar P. Lipids. In: Clarke RJ, Macrae R, eds. *Coffee*; vol 1: Chemistry. London: Elsevier: 1985;203–22.
27. Ogawa M, Kamiya C. Iida Y. Contents of tocopherols in coffee beans, coffee infusions and instant coffee. *Nippon Shokuhin Kogyo Gakkaishi* 1989;36:490–494. C A 1989;111:193336f.
28. Saltor M, Duplatre A, Boatella J. Identification of coffee species on the basis of sterols. *An Bromatol* 1989;41:1–8. C A 1989;112:117458c.
29. Viani R, Horman I. Determination of trigonelline in coffee. 7th ASIC Symp 1975;273–8.
30. Van Dusseldorp M, Katan MB, van Vliet T, Demacker PNM, Stalenhoef AFH. Cholesterol-raising factor from boiled coffee does not pass a paper filter. *Arterioscler Thromb* 1991; 586–93.
31. Thelle DS. Coffee. An unexpected cholesterol-raising factor. 14th ASIC Symp 1991;81–5.
32. Ahola I, Juahiainen M, Aro A. The hypercholesterolaemic factor in boiled coffee is retained by a paper filter. *J Intern Med* 1991;230:293–7.
33. Pezzuto JM, Nanayakkara NPD, Compadre CM et al: Characterization of bacterial mutagenicity mediated by 13-hydroxy-ent-kaurenoic acid (steviol) and several structurally-related derivatives and evaluation of potential to induce glutathione S-transferase in mice. *Mutat Res* 1986;169:93–103.
34. Wattenberg LW. Inhibition of neoplasia by minor dietary constituents. *Cancer Res* (Suppl) 1983;43:2448s–53s.
35. Miller EG, McWhorter K, Rivera-Hidalgo F, Wright JM, Hirsbrunner P, Sunahara GI. Kahweol and cafestol: inhibitors of hamster buccal pouch carcinogenesis. *Nutr Cancer* 1991;15:41–6.
36. Viani R, Horman I. Thermal behavior of trigonelline *J Food Sci* 1974;39:1216–7.
37. Taguchi H. Biosynthesis and metabolism of trigonelline, and physiological action of the compound. *Vitamins* (Japan) 1988;62:549–57.
38. Macrae R. Nitrogenous components. In: Clarke RJ, Macrae R, eds. *Coffee*; vol 1: Chemistry. London: Elsevier; 1985;115–52.
39. Da Porto C, Nicoli MC, Severini C, Sensidoni A, Lerici CR. Study on physical and physico-chemical changes in coffee beans during roasting. Note 2. *Ital J Food Sci* 1991;3:197–207.
40. van der Stegen GHD, van Duijn J. Analysis of normal organic acids in coffee. 12th ASIC Symp 1987;238–46.
41. Hucke J, Maier HG Chinasäurelacton im Kaffee. *Z Lebensm Unters Forsch* 1985;180: 479–84.
42. Scholz BM, Maier HG. Isomers of quinic acid and quinide in roasted coffee. *Z Lebensm Unters Forch* 1990;190:132–4.
43. Trugo LC, Macrae R. A study of the effect of roasting on the chlorogenic acid composition of coffee using HPLC. *Food Chem* 1984;15:219–27.
44. Clinton WP. The chemistry of coffee. 11th ASIC Symp 1985;87–92.
45. Trugo LC, Macrae R. Chlorogenic acid composition of instant coffees. *Analyst* 1984;109: 263–6.
46. Boublik JH, Quinn MJ, Clements JA, Herington AC, Wynne KN, Funder JW. Coffee contains potent opiate receptor binding activity. *Nature* 1983;301:246–8.
47. Wynne KN, Familari M, Boublik JH, Drummer OH, Rae ID, Funder JW. Isolation of opiate receptor ligands in coffee. *Clin Exper Pharmacol Physiol* 1987;14:785–90.

48. Leaf C, Tannenbaum SR, Glogowski JA, Würzner HP. The effect of coffee on N-nitrosamine formation in human and in vitro. 14th ASIC Symp 1991;52–6.
49. Morishita H, Takai Y, Yamada H, et al. Caffeoyltryptophan from green robusta coffee beans. *Phytochemistry* 1987;26:1195–6.
50. Clifford MN, Kellard B, Ah-sing E. Caffeolytyrosine from robusta coffee beans. *Phytochemistry* 1989;28:1989–90.
51. Trugo LC. Carbohydrates. In: Clarke RJ, Macrae R, eds. *Coffee*; vol 1: Chemistry. London: Elsevier; 1985:83–114.
52. Bradbury AGW, Halliday DJ. Chemical structure of green coffee bean polysaccharides. *J Agric Food Chem* 1990;38:389–92.
53. Bos DK, Verbeck C, van Eeden CHP, Slump P, Wolters MGE. Improved determination of phytate by ion-exchange chromatography. *J Agric Food Chem* 1991;39:1770–2.
54. Blanc MB, Davis GE, Parchet JM, Viani R. Chromatographic profile of carbohydrates in commercial soluble coffees. *J Agric Food Chem* 1989;37:926–30.
55. Davis GE, Garwood VW, Barfuss DL, Husaini SA, Blanc MB, Viani R. Chromatographic profile of carbohydrates in commercial coffees. 2. Identification of mannitol. *J Agric Food Chem* 1990;38:1347–50.
56. Maarse H, Visscher CA, eds. Volatile compounds in food; vol 2. 6th ed. Zeist NL: TNO-CIVO, 1989.
57. Shimoda M, Shibamoto T. Isolation and identification of headspace volatiles from brewed coffee with an on-column GC/MS method. *J Agric Food Chem* 1990;38:802–4.
58. Nishimura O, Mihara S. Investigation of 2-hydroxy-2-cyclopenten-1-ones in roasted coffee. *J Agric Food Chem* 1990;38:1038–41.
59. Holscher W, Steinhart H. New sulfur-containing aroma-impact-compounds in roasted coffee. 14th ASIC Symp 1991;130–6.
60. Flament I. Coffee, cocoa, and tea. *Foods Revs Internl* 1989;5:317–414.
61. Blank I, Sen A, Grosch W. Aroma impact compounds of Arabica and Robusta coffee. Qualitative and quantitative investigations. 14th ASIC Symp 1991;117–29.
62. Stofberg J, Stoffelsma J. Consumption of flavoring materials as food ingredients and food additives. *Perfum Flav* 1980;5:19–35.
63. Nakabayashi T, Yamada K. Formation process of coffee brown pigments during roast. *Nippon Shokuhin Kogyo Gakkaishi* 1987;34:211–5.
64. Heinrich L, Baltes W. Vorkommen von Phenolen in Kaffee-Melanoidinen. *Z Lebensm Unters Forsch* 1987;185:366–70.
65. Hayase F, Hirashima S, Okamoto G, Kato H. Scavenging of active oxygens by melanoidins. *Agric Biol Chem* 1989;53:3383–5.
66. Jaccaud E, Aeschbacher HU. Inhibition of in vivo mutagenicity by Maillard reaction products and coffee. In: Aeschbacher HU, Finot PA, Hurrell RF, Liardon R, eds. *The Maillard reaction in food processing, human nutrition and physiology*. Basel: Birkhäuser Verlag; 1990;367–72.
67. Anon. Total dietary fiber in foods Method #985.29. In: Helrich K, ed. *Official methods of analysis of the AOAC*. 15th ed. Arlington VA: 1990;1105–17.
68. Homa S, Nakamura Y, Asakura T. Sekiguchi N, Murata M. Separation and characterization of metal chelating compounds in coffee. In: Aeschbacher HU, Finot PA, Hurrell RF, Liardon R, eds. *The Maillard reaction in food processing, human nutrition and physiology*. Basel: Birkhäuser Verlag; 1990;279–84.
69. Tse SYH. Coffee contains cholinomimetic compound distinct from caffeine. I: Purification and chromatographic analysis. *J Pharm Sci* 1991;80:665–9.
70. Grob K, Lanfranchi M, Egli J, Artho A. Determination of food contamination by mineral oil from jute sacks using coupled LC-GC. *J Assoc Off Anal Chem* 1991;74:506–12.
71. Grob K, Biedermann M, Artho A, Egli J. Food contamination by hydrocarbons from packaging materials determined by coupled LC-GC. *Z Lebensm Unters Forsch* 1991;193:213–9.
72. Maier HG. Teneur en composés cancérigènes du café en grains. *Café Cacao Thé* 1991;35:133–42.
73. Strobel RGK. Polycyclic aromatic hydrocarbon contaminants in coffee. In: Clarke RJ, Macrae R, eds. *Coffee*; vol 3: Physiology. London: Elsevier; 1985;321–64.
74. Sen NP, Seaman SW. Volatile N-Nitrosamines in dried foods. *J Assoc Off Anal Chem* 1981;64:1238–42.

75. Sen NP, Seaman SW, Weber D. Mass spectrometric confirmation of the presence of N-nitrosopyrrolidine in instant coffee. *J Assoc Off Anal Chem* 1990;73:325–7
76. Felton JS, Knize MG. Heterocyclic-amine mutagens/carcinogens in foods. In: Cooper CS, Grover PL, eds. *Chemical carcinogenesis and mutagenesis*; vol 1. Berlin: Springer Verlag; 1990;471–502.
77. Kikugawa K, Kato T, Takahashi S. Possible presence of 2-amino-3,4-dimethylimidazo[4,5-*f*]quinoline and other heterocyclic amine-like mutagens in roasted coffee beans. *J Agric Food Chem* 1989;37:881–6.
78. Kato T, Takahashi S, Kirugawa K. Generation of heterocyclic amine-like mutagens during the roasting of coffee beans. *Eisei Kagaku* 1989;35:370–6.
79. Gros GA, Wolleb U. 2-amino-3,4-dimethylimidazo[4,5-*f*]quinoline (MeIQ) is not detectable in commercial instant and roasted coffee. *J Agric Food Chem* 1991;39:2231–6.
80. Cetinkaya M, von Düszeln J, Thiemann W, Silwar R. Untersuchung von Organochlor-Pesticidrückständen in Roh- und Röstkaffee und deren Abbauverhalten beim Röst prozess. *Z Lebensm Unters Forsch* 1984;179:5–8.
81. Cetinkaya M. Organophosphor- und Organochlorpestizidrückstände in Rohkaffee. *Dtsch Lebensm Rundsch* 1988;84:189–90.
82. McCarthy JP, Adinolfi J, McMullin SL, et al. NCA survey of pesticide residues in brewed coffees. 14th ASIC Symp 1991;154–82.
83. Terada H, Tsubouchi H, Yamamoto K, Hisada K, Sakabe Y. Liquid chromatographic determination of ochratoxin-A in coffee beans and coffee products. *J Assoc Off Anal Chem* 1986;69:960–4.
84. Nakajima M, Terada H, Hisada K, et al. Determination of ochratoxin A in coffee beans and coffee products by monoclonal antibody affinity chromatography. *Food Agric Immunol* 1990;2:189–95.
85. Strobel RGK. Allergens and mould toxin contaminants. In: Clarke RJ, Macrae R, eds. *Coffee*; vol 3: Physiology. London: Elsevier; 1985;215–320.
86. Micco C, Miraglia M, Brera C, Desiderio C, Masci V. The effect of roasting on the fate of aflatoxin B1 in artificially contaminated green coffee beans. 14th ASIC Sympm 1991;183–9.
87. Viani R. Entkoffeinierung. In: Heiss R, ed. *Lebensmitteltechnologie*. 4th ed. Berlin: Springer Verlag; 1991;367–71.
88. Horman I, Viani R. The nature and conformation of the caffeine-chlorogenate complex of coffee. *J Food Sci* 1972;37:925–7.
89. Heimann W. A modified secoffex process for green bean decaffeination. 14th ASIC Symp 1991;349–56.

Caffeine, Coffee, and Health,
edited by S. Garattini.
Raven Press, Ltd., New York © 1993.

3

Metabolism of Caffeine and Other Components of Coffee

Maurice J. Arnaud

Nestec Ltd., Nestlé Research Centre, CH-1000 Lausanne 26, Switzerland

The metabolic pathways of caffeine, one of the most widely studied chemicals, and some other compounds that either characterize coffee brews or that even at trace levels may be responsible for its physiological or toxicological effects are described. The pharmacokinetics of caffeine are also described. Dose-dependent kinetics have now been reported in animals and humans, suggesting a saturation of metabolic transformations. In the neonatal period, elimination of caffeine is impaired in animals and humans, due to the immaturity of the hepatic enzyme systems. An age-dependent slowing of caffeine metabolism has been observed in the rat, but no such effect has yet been reported in humans. Caffeine can be detected in all body fluids and it passes through all biological membranes, including the blood-brain and placental barriers. No specific accumulation of caffeine or its metabolites has been observed in various organs or tissues. Its metabolic profile in plasma is characterized by the predominance of paraxanthine in humans, theophylline in the monkey, and similar amounts of each dimethylxanthine in the rat. In humans, only 0.5–2% of an ingested caffeine dose is excreted unchanged in the urine. Urinary caffeine concentrations are used as a disqualifying factor for athletes. Twenty-eight metabolites have been identified in the urine of animals and humans, and there are important species differences in the quantitative and qualitative pathways. No differences have been observed in the metabolic fate of caffeine between men and women although studies have suggested an effect of the menstrual cycle. Decreased elimination of caffeine and a change of metabolic pattern was reported in women using oral contraceptives and during the last trimester of pregnancy. Obesity and physical exercise modify caffeine pharmacokinetics and metabolite formation. Drugs taken simultaneously may impair caffeine elimination due to competitive inhibition at the hepatic microsomal level. Changes in caffeine elimination and in the metabolites excreted in urine are observed in cigarette smokers, and patients with liver disease have impaired elimination with no change in the metabolic profile.

In humans, chronic ingestion or restriction of caffeine intake does not modify its metabolism. The effect of some dietary constituents such as broccoli, alcohol, and vitamins have been studied. Genetic expression plays a role in caffeine elimination and metabolism in animals and in humans. However, the polymorphism of acetylator phenotype determined from urinary metabolite concentrations has no effect on caffeine clearance. Several other urinary concentration ratios constitute indexes of hepatic enzyme activities. This is the case of xanthine oxidase and the caffeine metabolic ratio that correlates with caffeine 3-demethylation, caffeine plasma clearance, and cytochrome P-450IA2 activity.

The metabolism of coffee constituents such as trigonelline, chlorogenic acid with its two components, caffeic and quinic acids, are also presented. Other aromatic compounds present in small amounts, guaiacol and eugenol or, even in trace amounts, benzo(a)pyrene, are described. A large number of Maillard reaction products and heterocyclic compounds are produced during roasting, and metabolic data are reported on methylfuran, hydroxymethylfuraldehyde, pyridines, maltol, quinolines, and naphthalene. The metabolism of methylglyoxal and several terpenes and sterols are reported. Finally, different coffee constituents with possible physiological effects including waxes, hydrogen peroxide, and unidentified factors with hypercholesterolemic, estrogenic, cholinomimetic, and opiate receptor antagonist activities are mentioned.

INTRODUCTION

The chemical composition of coffee cherries varies according to the species (*Coffea arabica, C. canephora, C. liberica*, and *C. dewevrei* being the most important) and to the climate and soil conditions. The successive operations necessary to transform harvested cherries into green and then roasted beans dramatically change the constituents originally present and can vary with ecological conditions and national or local taste. Finally, the composition of the beverage will depend on whether blends or pure varieties have been used and on the different brewing techniques: boiling, infusion, filtration, percolation, vaporization under pressure, and instant coffee. The metabolism of model compounds, which characterize coffee brews, will be described with no consideration of their concentrations, which vary according to the higher or lower extraction of soluble substances from roasted coffee.

Most investigations have been made on caffeine, and it is interesting to note that the earliest study on caffeine metabolism, carried out in 1850 (1), was performed before its chemical structure had been identified. The metabolic fate of other coffee constituents has not been so well investigated, except for several products detected in trace amounts, that are expected to have more toxic than physiological and pharmacological effects. Although hundreds of chemicals have been identified (2), there have been few metabolic studies on volatile compounds or on water-soluble macromolecules such as degraded polysaccharides and melanoidins. The metabolism of some other compounds present in coffee brews may already be known because larger amounts are found in other foodstuffs or because they are present in the human body as endogenous metabolites. This is the case for nutritional constituents such as minerals, vitamins, carbohydrates, lipids, and amino acids for which bioavailability and metabolic fate have been reported elsewhere (3).

ALKALOIDS

Caffeine

Absorption

Caffeine absorption from the gastrointestinal tract is rapid and complete in humans, with 99% of the administered dose absorbed in about 45 min (4–8). Orally administered caffeine is mainly absorbed from the small intestine although 20% has been reported to be absorbed from the stomach (4). Complete absorption has been demonstrated in animals using radiolabelled caffeine (9,10), with the exception of horses where the apparent bioavailability of an oral dose was only 39% (11). Pharmacokinetics were independent of the route of administration. After oral or intravenous doses, plasma concentration curves were superimposable, suggesting that there is no important hepatic first-pass effect in humans (12) or animals (13). The efficacy of percutaneous caffeine absorption has been demonstrated in vitro (14) in animals (15) and in premature infants treated for neonatal apnea. Caffeine plasma levels between 11 and 20 mg/l were obtained 48 hours after a loading dose divided into four abdominal applications at 12-hour intervals (16). Outward transcutaneous caffeine migration in adult volunteers was shown to be a linear function of the plasma AUC (area under the plasma caffeine–time curve), and sweating did not play a significant role in the flux of caffeine (17).

Pharmacokinetics

Peak plasma caffeine concentration is reached from 15 to 120 min after oral ingestion in humans, and for doses of 5–8 mg/kg the mean plasma values were 8–10 mg/L (6,18,19). Delayed gastric emptying due to the presence of dietary constituents and pathologies such as gastric stasis, explains the pharmacokinetic differences (4–6,19–21). The fraction of caffeine reversibly bound to plasma proteins varies from 10% to 30% in animals and humans. Caffeine is eliminated by apparently first order kinetics, described by a one-compartment open model system in humans (6) and in animals (22). Nonlinear kinetics, shown by a disproportionate increase in the dose-concentration relationship, indicates a limited capacity to absorb and/or metabolize caffeine in rats at doses higher than 10 mg/kg (13,22,23). At higher doses, the presence of two plasma peaks or a plateau indicates delayed intestinal absorption, and kinetic parameters cannot be determined accurately (23). In the rat, it is not known at which dose saturation of metabolic capacity occurs.

Until recently, the existence of dose-dependent kinetics in humans at levels of normal consumption was not shown by the results of several studies using a limited number of patients and a small range of doses: 2 to 10 mg/kg (6,7,24). However, in a case of acute intoxication in a ten-month-old infant, dose-dependent kinetics was observed when caffeine plasma levels were higher than 30 mg/l (25).

Dose-dependent kinetics have now been shown not only after very high intake but even at doses lower than 5 mg/kg. These new results obtained by different laboratories (26–29) indicate that some metabolic transformations must be rapidly saturated in the dose range of 1–4 mg/kg. This pathway could be the formation of paraxanthine as both caffeine and paraxanthine plasma concentrations are dependent on the 3-demethylation of caffeine (30), but a decrease in the clearance of paraxanthine has also been suggested (27). In the rat, paraxanthine is eliminated by a saturable process (31). The results in vitro did not suggest different mechanisms in the rat and humans. Microsomes prepared from human and rat liver present biphasic kinetics, indicating the potential participation of two different isozymes with different substrate affinities in the production of individual metabolites (32–34). At the concentrations reached in vivo, most demethylation activity is mediated by the high-affinity enzyme site with only a negligible contribution from the low-affinity site. The demethylation of paraxanthine, theophylline, and theobromine at high concentrations also show biphasic kinetics in the production of individual metabolites with human microsomes (33).

For doses lower than 10 mg/kg, caffeine's half-life ranges from 0.7–1.2 hours in the rat and mouse, 1–4 hours in rabbits, 3–5 hours in the monkey, 6 hours in beagle dogs, and 11 hours in baboons (35,36). Half-lives of 2.5–4.5 hours were observed in human volunteers receiving a 4 mg/kg caffeine dose (37).

The comparative pharmacokinetics in the young and the elderly show no significant differences in half-life suggesting that aging does not alter caffeine elimination in humans (8). In the rat, on the other hand, an age-dependent increase of caffeine half-life has been observed (38,39). In humans, a slight decrease in plasma caffeine binding has been reported in the elderly who have a significantly lower plasma albumin concentration (40).

Caffeine's half-life is increased in the neonatal period both in animals and humans due to the maturity of the hepatic enzyme systems (41). When ^{13}C-labelled caffeine was fed to premature neonates and to 1–19-month-old infants, the collection of expired $^{13}CO_2$ increased with postnatal age and correlated with caffeine plasma clearance (42). Similar results were reported in different animal species (43). Half-lives of 50–103 hours were found in premature and newborn infants but decreased rapidly to 14.4 hours and 2.6 hours in 3–5 month and 5–6 month infants, respectively (44–48). Unexplainedly longer caffeine half-lives were found in breast-fed than formula-fed infants (49). The clearance of 31 ml/kg/h in one-month-old infants increases to a maximum of 331 ml/kg/h in five- to six-month-old infants, compared with 155 ml/kg/h in adults (41).

Mean distribution volume was 0.7 l/kg (0.5–0.8 l/kg) in newborn infants, adult, and aged subjects. In different animal species, a similar distribution volume of 0.8 l/kg has been reported (22,36). These values are in agreement with the distribution of caffeine into the intracellular tissue water (50).

Distribution

Caffeine is sufficiently hydrophobic to pass through all biological membranes. No blood-brain barrier has been observed for caffeine in the adult or fetal animal (51–53), in contrast to its dimethylxanthine metabolites (30,54,55). In these experiments a 30-minute equilibrium period was allowed between brain tissue and blood, less when microdialysis was used (56). With an experimental protocol established to study a single passage through the cerebral circulation, a brain-to-plasma ratio of 0.80 for caffeine was found (57). In newborn infants, caffeine concentrations were similar in plasma and cerebrospinal fluid (58,59). In the human and animal models, no placental barrier prevents the passage of caffeine to the embryo (60) or fetus (51,61). Unusually high caffeine concentrations acquired transplacentally have been reported in a premature infant (62). Analysis of animal (63), human, and fetal gonads showed that their caffeine concentrations were the same as in plasma (64).

Caffeine has been detected in all body fluids. The concentration ratio between blood and semen is 1, and the decline after administration is similar (65,66). Since caffeine equilibrates rapidly with serum, an average milk-to-serum concentration ratio of 0.52 was found. A more recent study reported a ratio of 0.81 for the right and left breasts. As the binding of caffeine to constituents of serum and whole breast milk was 25.1% and only 3.2%, respectively, all the binding in breast milk was accounted for by the butter-fat content (67–71). Caffeine can also be detected in umbilical cord blood (72,73), bile (30,74), and saliva. The saliva concentrations are 65–85% of those in the plasma (75–80).

After ingestion of caffeine, metabolites such as theophylline, theobromine, and paraxanthine are detected in body fluids. Theophylline and theobromine plasma concentrations increase to a small and similar extent in humans. In contrast, the level of paraxanthine is ten times higher than theophylline and theobromine. Caffeine plasma concentrations decrease more rapidly than paraxanthine so that, in spite of important interindividual differences, paraxanthine concentrations become higher than caffeine within 8 to 10 hours of administration (81,6). This metabolic plasma profile characterizes all animal species. In monkeys, theophylline is the major caffeine metabolite in plasma (82), while in rats, paraxanthine, theophylline, and theobromine are present in similar amounts (22,83).

Because caffeine is submitted to 98% renal tubular reabsorption, only a small percentage—0.5–2% of the ingested dose in humans and 5% in the mouse and rat—is excreted unchanged in urine. In athletes participating in competitive sport, the presence of caffeine concentrations higher than 12 mg/l in urine is considered as a disqualifying factor by the International Olympic Committee (IOC). At caffeine intakes of 450 mg/day over six days, a good correlation was found between urinary and plasma caffeine concentrations, but there was marked interindividual variation in the urine with a 15.9-fold range. Because of this wide variability in individual caffeine pharmacokinetics, the authors concluded that the limit needs to be revised, or that athletes should be advised to limit their intake (84).

The results of a study on cyclotourists after the ingestion of 350 mg caffeine suggest a decreased catabolism of caffeine during exercise followed by an increase during the postexercise period (85). The reduction of caffeine elimination was also much greater in women than in men because of a larger decrease in urinary volume in women. All these uncontrolled variations of caffeine urine concentrations, the nature of the sport, sex, weight, and sampling time argue against the utility of this test.

At a caffeine intake of 1 g, another study found that the mean recovery of caffeine in urine was 0.74–0.91% of the dose and that a urinary concentration of 14 ml/l can be reached. However, the authors concluded that athletes would not attain these values by mere social intake of caffeine-containing beverages and foods (86).

The limited excretion of caffeine in urine indicates that its metabolism is the rate-limiting factor in its plasma clearance. No specific accumulation of caffeine and its metabolites is observed, in various organs or tissues, even after high doses (22). Recently, the kinetics of concentrations in blood, brain, liver, muscle, and fat was studied at two dose levels, 5 and 20 mg/kg, using microdialysis in the rat (56).

Physiological and Environmental Factors Influencing Pharmacokinetics

Caffeine clearance can be modified by exogenous and endogenous factors. Its clearance is stimulated by smoking (75,87–93), while cessation of cigarette smoking significantly reduced it (94) as well as changing the pattern of caffeine metabolism (95).

No difference in the metabolic fate of caffeine is observed between men and women (96,97). However, in healthy women, caffeine elimination was 25% longer (half-life 6.85 hours) in the luteal phase of the menstrual cycle compared with the follicular phase (half-life 5.54 hours) (98). The use of oral contraceptives can double the caffeine half-life (80,97–101). The half-life was also prolonged during the last trimester in pregnant women (96,102–106) and during the last half of gestation in the rabbit (107). The half-life returns to the pre-pregnant value a few weeks postpartum (105,106). In the rat, the effect of pregnancy on the pharmacokinetics of caffeine is not known as individual variations in rats taking caffeine during pregnancy were too large (83). Using a noninvasive breath test with [1,3,7-Me-^{14}C] caffeine from day 11 of pregnancy to day 7 after birth, a decrease of 25% in mean total demethylation was reported between days 19 to 21 of pregnancy followed by an immediate return 1 to 2 days after birth to the value observed in nonpregnant animals (108).

Caffeine is metabolized by hepatic microsomal enzyme systems (32,74,109), and no significant contribution by other organs has yet been demonstrated. The major role of the liver is indicated by the impaired elimination of caffeine in subjects with liver diseases (110–118), in whom caffeine half-lives may be increased up to 50 to 160 hours. In rats submitted to partial hepatectomy, caffeine clearance was considerably reduced (119). However, measurements of caffeine clearance in patients following orthotopic liver transplantation were of little use in the differential diagnosis of early postoperative complications, certainly on account of the heterogeneity of the patients because of sepsis, acute rejection, and antibiotic or immunosuppressive therapy (120).

Several animal studies have suggested that caffeine induces some forms of cytochrome P-450 and can thus induce its own metabolism. In fact, when doses as high as 100–150 mg/kg caffeine were used for pretreatment, microsomal induction was observed with different experimental protocols (121–126) with few exceptions (127). In contrast, all the studies using lower doses, 30–50 mg/kg, showed either induction (128), inhibition (129,130), or no effect (124,128). The effect of low doses of caffeine in microsomal enzyme activities is thus not clear, and some of the differences can be explained by the different experimental protocols (131).

In healthy volunteers, the daily ingestion of 480 mg caffeine for one week failed to alter caffeine pharmacokinetics and metabolism (132). Changes in caffeine kinetics were analyzed in healthy coffee drinkers before and after restriction of caffeine-containing foods and beverages to evaluate the effects of caffeine restriction on the activities of hepatic microsomal enzymes.

The 21-days restriction period produced a significant but small decrease in the elimination rate constant with wide interindividual variations in both directions. The authors concluded that their study does not provide any clear answer about the time required for de-induction to occur (133).

Induction of caffeine metabolism has been repeatedly demonstrated in animals pretreated with 3-methylcholanthrene and β-naphthoflavone (13,90,134–138). Phenobarbital had practically no effect on caffeine elimination (136). Similar effects of 3-methylcholanthrene and phenobarbital were reported in cultured human hepatocytes (139). The induction of demethylation by 3-methylcholanthrene, giving paraxanthine and theophylline, was significantly correlated but not for the formation of theobromine, suggesting that at least two isozymes of the P-450IA family are involved in the demethylation of caffeine. Another study found that caffeine 3-demethylation was catalyzed by human cytochrome P-450IA2, not by other P-450 (140). Caffeine was proposed as a safe probe for measuring relative P-450IA2 activity in humans, and it was demonstrated that this enzyme does not support the N-7 and N-1 demethylation of caffeine that is mediated, at least partly, by other P-450 enzymes (141).

Clinical studies report increasingly frequent drug interactions leading to impaired caffeine elimination. Decreased clearance of caffeine and its main metabolite, paraxanthine was observed (142), and these effects are explained by competitive inhibition at the hepatic microsomal level (143). However, in these in vitro systems, the rate of production of caffeine metabolites is very low compared with that expected from extrapolation of the in vivo elimination half-life of caffeine in the average adult human (32).

During neonatal development, experiments in vitro and in vivo show a progressive increase in the activity of the hepatic microsomal system (144,145). In the beagle puppy, the change in caffeine clearance was determined by the rate of maturation of caffeine 7-demethylation (146).

Dietary constituents may have an effect on drug metabolism (147,148), and impaired or increased elimination of caffeine was reported with alcohol (132,149) and broccoli (150), respectively. Increased elimination of caffeine was also observed in guinea pigs when the dietary vitamin C intake reached 7 mg/g diet (151).

In animals, aging increased the elimination half-life from 1 hour in 49-day-old rats, to 1.5 hour in 105-day-old rats, and 3 hours in 210-day-old rats (38). These results from a breath test agree with earlier in vivo plasma analysis and liver perfusion studies that indicated an age-related decline in the hepatic demethylation of caffeine in rats (39).

Only one study reported chronovariation in caffeine elimination. The effect was small (-25 to 16%) in most subjects. In one subject, saliva caffeine half-life was decreased by 80% (152).

In adult volunteers, the effects of one hour's moderate exercise (30% $\dot{V}O_2$ max) were studied immediately after the ingestion of a capsule containing 250 mg caffeine (153). Exercise caused a sharp rise in plasma caffeine concentrations from 7.28 mg/l at rest to 10.45 mg/l, a decrease in the distribution volume from 37 l to 20.9 l and a reduction of the half-life from 4.00 to 2.30 hours. These results however are not in agreement with a previous study showing no effect in lean, caffeine-naive, untrained, nonsmoking male volunteers (154). However, obese subjects with more than 30% body fat showed a decrease in the maximal serum concentration and area under the curve when exercising on a treadmill at 40% $\dot{V} O_2$ max. In these subjects, caffeine distribution volume was larger both at rest and when performing exercise (101 l and 103 l, respectively) than in lean subjects (43.2 l and 54.1 l). Significantly higher absorption rate constants, lower elimination rate constants, and a longer mean serum half-life (4.32 versus 2.59 hr) were also reported in obese subjects (154). A recent study in patients with decompensated Type I and Type II diabetes mellitus showed that caffeine half-life, apparent clearance, and distribution volume were similar to controls (155).

Genetic and/or environmental factors are suggested as an explanation for the larger variability of caffeine clearance when compared with hepatic galactose elimination in the same patients (120). Genetic expression was shown to play a role in experiments where mice of different strains received caffeine orally, and half-lives ranged from 0.58 hours for SWR/J mice to 1.67 hours for A/J mice. Significant differences in the quantitative formation and excretion of a metabolite specific to the species, the glucuronide of paraxanthine, were found for the different strains of mice studied (156). In the rabbit, polymorphism with rapid- and slow-metabolizing caffeine subpopulations was demonstrated, characterized by dose-dependent or dose-independent pharmacokinetics, respectively. Caffeine metabolism was inhibited when paraxanthine was co-administered to the dose-dependent animals (157). In humans, an acetylated uracil derivative (AFMU) is produced according to the polymorphism of the acetylator phenotype, but this pathway does not seem to play a role in the interindividual variations of caffeine pharmacokinetics (30).

Metabolism

Extensive reviews have been published on the discovery of the products of caffeine metabolism (3,158–160). Caffeine is eliminated by animals through liver biotransformation to dimethylxanthines, dimethyl and monomethyl uric acids, trimethyl and dimethylallantoin and uracil derivatives. The quantitative profile of urinary caffeine metabolites depends on their rate formation, body distribution, plasma concentration, and renal excretion. The metabolic pathways (Fig. 1) show multiple and separate demethylation, C-8 oxidation, and uracil formation in humans and rodents. These transformations occur in liver microsomes except for the C-8 oxidation of 1-methylxanthine into 1-methyluric acid, which is mediated by xanthine oxidase (161–164). The reverse biotransformation of theophylline into caffeine was first reported in premature infants treated in the management of apnea (165,166). In theophylline-treated babies, the accumulation of caffeine is due

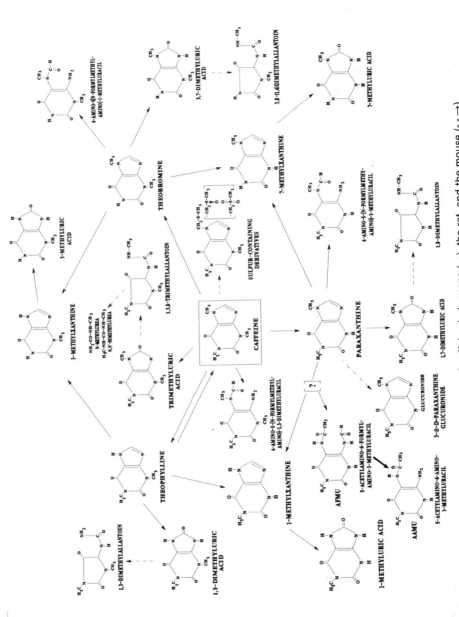

FIG. 1. Metabolic pathways of caffeine in humans (→), the rat, and the mouse (- - →).

to the immaturity of the hepatic microsomal enzymes that correspond only to one-third of the normal adult level (41). In adults, caffeine produced from the conversion of theophylline to caffeine is extensively metabolized and has been evaluated at 6% of the theophylline dose (81,158). The methylation of theophylline to caffeine has also been shown in the rat, but the quantitative importance of this pathway cannot be established (54).

The major metabolic difference between rodents and humans is that, in the rat, 40% of the caffeine metabolites are trimethyl derivatives but in humans they are less than 6% (10). Because of the importance of demethylation in humans, breath tests were developed using caffeine labelled on the methyl group with radioactive or stable isotopes to detect impaired liver function (89–91,113,167,168). Humans are characterized by the quantitative importance of 3-methyl demethylation leading to the formation of paraxanthine. This first metabolic step represents 72–80% of caffeine metabolism (3,19,26). The quantitative urinary excretion of caffeine metabolites in rat, mouse, and humans, expressed as a percentages of the administered dose, is shown in Table 1.

TABLE 1. Urinary excretion of caffeine and its metabolites in humans and rodents. Recoveries expressed as the percentage of the administered dose.

	Humans	Rat	Mouse
Caffeine	1.2	3	2
Trimethyluric acid	1.3	8	4
Trimethylallantoin	—	7	0.4
6-Amino-5-[N-formylmethylamino] 1,3-Dimethyluracil (1,3,7-DAU)	1.1	20	9
Paraxanthine	6	12	14
3-β-D-Paraxanthine glucuronide	—	—	19
Theophylline	1	6	0.7
Theobromine	2	8	4
1,7-Dimethyluric acid	6	5	6
1,3-Dimethyluric acid	2.5	4	7
3,7-Dimethyluric acid	0.8	traces	1
Dimethylallantoin	—	traces	traces
6-Amino-5-[N-formylmethylamino] 3-Methyluracil (1,7-DAU)	2.4	2.5	1.4
6-Amino-5-[N-formylmethylamino] 1-Methyluracil (3,7-DAU)	2	6	5
1-Methylxanthine	18	5	6
7-Methylxanthine	7	2	3
3-Methylxanthine	3	1	2
1-Methyluric acid	25	6	8
7-Methyluric acid	—	0.8	1
3-Methyluric acid	0.1	0.3	2
5-Acetylamino-6-formylamino-3-Methyluracil (AFMU)	15	—	—
α-[7-(1,3-dimethylxanthinyl)]methyl methylsulfoxide	—	traces	traces
α-[7-(1,3-dimethylxanthinyl)]methyl methylsulfide	—	—	traces
α-[7-(1,3-dimethylxanthinyl)]methyl methylsulfone	—	—	traces
N-Methylurea, NN'-Dimethylurea	—	traces	—

From refs. 6, 9, 10, 22, 78, 142.

The analysis of urinary caffeine metabolites shows quantitative and qualitative differences between the rat, Chinese hamster, and mouse where a new derivative of paraxanthine was quantitated (10) and identified as the β-N-glucuronide of paraxanthine (169). Trimethylallantoin has been found only in rodents (10,170) and was identified as 1,3,8-trimethylallantoin (171). Trace amounts of methylated ureas (9) and sulfur-containing derivatives (172,173) found in rat urine are produced by the intestinal flora. Uracil derivatives produced from caffeine, 6-amino-5-[N-formylmethylamino] 1,3-dimethyluracil (1,3,7-DAU), from theobromine, 6-amino-5-[N-formylmethylamino]-1-methyluracil (3,7-DAU), and from paraxanthine, 6-amino-5-[N-formylmethylamino]-3-methyluracil (1,7-DAU) were also found in human urine (174–176). The uracil metabolite of caffeine amounts to about 1% of the administered dose in the urine of adults, while its excretion increased in the urine of a premature infant after caffeine overload (177). In contrast, the acetylated uracil derivative, 5-acetylamino-6-formylamino-3-methyluracil (AFMU), one of the major caffeine metabolites in humans, has not been identified in other animal species. After identification of the acetylated urinary metabolites, AAMU (5-acetylamino-6-amino-3-methyluracil) and AFMU (78,178), their production and excretion rates were found to be related to the acetylation polymorphism (179) with a bimodal distribution of the general population into fast and slow acetylators (180).

Paraxanthine is the precursor of AFMU that accounts for 67% of paraxanthine clearance (3,37,142,181). The rate of AFMU production and clearance approximates and changes according to the rates of production of 1-methylxanthine and 1-methyluric acid (142,182), suggesting that it is formed through a common precursor of AFMU and 1-methylxanthine. This intermediate is not known. The other uracil derivatives identified are produced in vitro by rat liver microsomes, but the mechanism of their formation with a possible common precursor for trimethyl or dimethyluric acid has not yet been demonstrated (74,183).

The ratios of urinary concentrations of AFMU/1MX or AFMU/1MX + 1MU (184–186) or with the complete conversion of AFMU into AAMU, the ratios of AAMU/1MX or AAMU/1MX + 1MU (187–189), give markers of acetylator status in humans. In addition, the ratio of 1MU/1MX is an index of xanthine oxidase, 1,7DMU/1,7DMX of microsomal 8-hydroxylation, AFMU + 1MX + 1MU/1,7DMX of microsomal 7-demethylation (190), and the caffeine metabolic ratio (CMR), AFMU + 1MX + 1MU/1,7DMU reflects microsomal 3-demethylation and also systemic caffeine clearance as well as polycyclic aromatic hydrocarbon-inducible cytochrome P-450 activity (30,191,192). The molar ratio of paraxanthine to caffeine in urine taken 3 to 4 hours after caffeine administration was proposed as an alternate means of assessing hepatic cytochrome P-450IA2 activity (193). All these indexes of hepatic enzyme activity calculated from the urinary concentrations of paraxanthine metabolites are presented in Fig. 2.

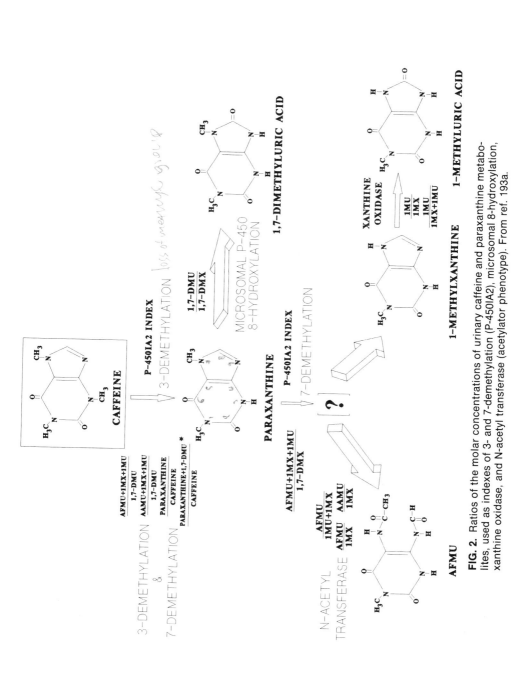

FIG. 2. Ratios of the molar concentrations of urinary caffeine and paraxanthine metabolites, used as indexes of 3- and 7-demethylation (P-450IA2), microsomal 8-hydroxylation, xanthine oxidase, and N-acetyl transferase (acetylator phenotype). From ref. 193a.

Physiological and Environmental Factors Influencing Metabolism

Administration of oral contraceptives increased the urinary excretion of caffeine, paraxanthine, and 1,7-dimethyluric acid at the expense of 1-methylxanthine, 1-methyluric acid, and the acetylated metabolites AFMU and AAMU (80). These results were confirmed by a recent report showing a 33% decrease in the caffeine metabolic ratio in women using oral contraceptives (194).

During pregnancy, the excretion of 1-methylxanthine and 1-methyluric acid was also increased (195). These results are in agreement with a caffeine study showing significantly increased hydroxylation activity during pregnancy. Late pregnancy was also characterized by a decrease in P-450IA2, xanthine oxidase, and acetyltransferase activities (196). In nonsmoking pregnant women and in smoking and nonsmoking women using oral contraceptives, the caffeine metabolic ratio was reduced by 29% and 20% respectively compared to a control group, indicating an inhibition of P-450IA2 (150). In the pregnant rat, urine analysis showed an increased excretion of dimethylxanthines correlated with a decrease in trimethyluric acid excretion (108).

Changes in the pattern of caffeine metabolites excreted in urine were evaluated in cigarette smokers after 3 or 4 days abstinence from smoking (95). During abstinence, 24-hour urine ratios of dimethylxanthines to caffeine and monomethylxanthines to dimethylxanthines were reduced, suggesting that cigarette smoking accelerates both demethylation steps. Less than 50% of the ingested dose was recovered in 24-hour urine.

A recent study reports the effects of smoking on caffeine urinary metabolites (197). In a population of 178 students including 19 smokers, analysis of the caffeine metabolic ratio showed a dose-effect relationship between the cytochrome index and the number of cigarettes smoked per day as well as the urinary nicotine levels. However, the highest enzyme indexes were more frequent in nonsmokers, suggesting that other unknown factors determine P-450IA2 activities. The ratio of urinary metabolites reflecting xanthine oxidase activity was increased in subjects smoking 1 to 9 and 10 or more cigarettes per day to 1.26 and 1.29, respectively, compared to 1.04 for control subjects. These results suggest that even light smoking increases xanthine oxidase activity (150).

After a one-month training period with 8 hours vigorous exercise per day, the caffeine metabolic ratio and the ratio for xanthine oxidase activity increased by 58% and 110%, respectively, while the ratio reflecting acetylation was unchanged. These results confirmed an inducing effect of physical exercise on cytochrome P-450 activity (150).

Cruciferous vegetables induce cytochromes P-450. The collection and analysis of urine samples of subjects fed a diet supplemented with either 500 g green beans or broccoli for ten days showed a 19% increase in the caffeine metabolic ratio corresponding to an induction of P-450IA2 activity by broccoli (150).

In a longitudinal study of 11 healthy male volunteers over several months, lifestyle factors, dose of caffeine, multivitamin, and ethanol intake had only modest effects on the caffeine metabolic ratio and no effect on xanthine oxidase index (194). These two indexes were not different between Chinese and European populations although individual metabolites differed, due to a higher proportion of rapid acetylators in the Asian compared with the European population. Within a log-normal distribution, the metabolic ratio showed a 6.3-fold range of variation and only a 1.7-fold range for the xanthine oxidase ratio.

The urinary metabolite profile of caffeine given either orally or intravenously at a dose of 5 mg/kg was compared in young and elderly males and the route of administration had no influence on the excretion of urinary metabolites (198). Significantly greater amounts of 1-methyluric acid, 7-methyluric acid and 1,7-dimethyluric acid were excreted in the urine of the elderly (69 ± 2 years). Other studies did not find significant age or sex-related changes (26,192).

The maturation of caffeine elimination in infancy was evaluated from the patterns of some urinary caffeine metabolites (199). Total demethylation, 3- and 7-demethylation increased exponentially with postnatal age to reach a plateau 120 days after birth while 8-hydroxylation was mature as early as one month of age. The ratio of AFMU/1MX did not change during infancy and was below 0.4 (200). This ratio appears to increase in fast acetylators between 6 and 12 months of age. Using the urinary metabolite ratio of 1MU/1MX, total xanthine oxidase activity was higher in premature infants with severe respiratory distress syndrome and in infants in severe acute clinical states (201).

Following one month of growth hormone therapy in growth-deficient children, caffeine 3-demethylation was decreased after the administration of [3-Me-^{13}C] caffeine (202). In hypophysectomized rats, human growth hormone treatment produced minor changes in the main caffeine metabolic pathways (203).

Many drugs taken simultaneously with caffeine competitively inhibit its metabolism through the first, most important metabolic transformation of caffeine in humans, 3-demethylation (204). These inhibitory effects on caffeine metabolism have also been demonstrated in vitro using human and rat liver microsomes (205). Furafylline, a highly selective inhibitor of P-450IA2, is a potent inhibitor of 3-demethylation in humans and to a lesser extent also of 1- and 7-demethylation. However, in the rat, 1000-times higher concentrations of furafylline were necessary to inhibit P-450IA2 to the same extent as the human isoenzyme. Quinolones also inhibit caffeine 3-demethylation (206). Some drugs such as allopurinol cause a dose-dependent inhibition of the conversion of 1-methylxanthine to 1-methyluric acid (142).

The urinary ratio of 1MU/1MX decreases from 0.8 to 1.0 in control subjects to 0.15 to 0.3 and 0.07 to 0.1 after 300 and 600 mg/day allopurinol treatment

(162). Wide human interindividual differences appear for caffeine 3-demethylation that varied 57-fold in a study using more than twenty human liver microsomal preparations (140). Another study using microsomal preparations confirmed the high degree of inter-liver variability in metabolic rate and showed a 20-fold range in paraxanthine demethylation rates (191). No sex differences in caffeine metabolism were observed from urinary metabolite patterns or metabolite ratios, and no correlation was found between age or weight of subjects (181). The excretion of caffeine metabolites and the different urinary ratios were measured in insulin-dependent diabetics receiving 200 mg caffeine (207). The results showed variations of the caffeine metabolism in patients with an uncontrolled diabetic state. These conclusions have been questioned (208) and need confirmation because they are based on large differences, 59% and 89%, in the recoveries of urinary metabolites in the two tests on the diabetic patients. Since the clearance of caffeine is not modified in diabetic patients, it is suggested that cytochrome P-450IA2 activity is not impaired (155).

A field biochemical study showed the effect of an environmental factor on caffeine 3-methyl demethylation and on the caffeine urinary metabolic ratio (209). The exposure of a rural population to polybrominated biphenyls (PBB) increased their values in comparison to not-exposed urban subjects. This induction was relatively small and the median value of smokers in the urban group was higher. The authors observed an unexplained lower induction in females than in males in the PBB-exposed group.

The recovery of caffeine metabolites in urine collected over 48 hours after oral administration of 400 mg of caffeine was studied in patients with compensated and decompensated cirrhosis (116). No significant differences were observed in the overall pattern of metabolite excretion between the control group and patients with decompensated cirrhosis except for a higher caffeine excretion (5% versus 2% of the dose). Further work is needed to clarify whether cirrhosis changes the pattern of caffeine metabolites as only very low-dose recoveries of 46–57% were reported.

Fecal Excretion of Metabolites

The use of radiolabelled caffeine has shown that fecal excretion after oral administrations amounts to 8–10% of the dose in rats and 2–5% in humans (9,78). The products identified in the feces of human volunteers were 1,7-dimethyluric acid, 1-methyluric acid, 1,3-dimethyluric acid, trimethyluric acid, and caffeine, which amounted to, respectively, 44, 38, 14, 6, and 2% of fecal radioactivity (78).

Trigonelline

Trigonelline, present at concentrations of 1% and 0.7% in dry arabica and robusta green coffee, is decomposed on roasting but around 0.2% is still present in roasted arabica coffee and 1.4% in dry instant coffee (2,160). The first study on the metabolism of trigonelline dates back to 1942 in rats (210). From a daily dose of 80 mg added to the diet, 56–86% was recovered unchanged in the urine. The metabolic balance of trigonelline labelled on the methyl group and injected intraperitoneally showed that 92–97% of the dose was recovered in the urine, 1% in feces and 0.1% in CO_2 (211). The urinary metabolites were not identified but previous results suggest that trigonelline is essentially excreted unchanged.

Trigonelline is transformed during roasting into nicotinic acid (niacin; vitamin PP), methyl nicotinate, and 3-methylpyridine (2). The metabolism of nicotinic acid has been extensively investigated in animals and the following metabolites were found with the unchanged product: nicotinuric acid, nicotinamide, N-methylnicotinamide, N-methyl-2-pyridone-5-carboxamide, N-methyl-4-pyridone-3-carboxamide, nicotinamide-N-oxide, 6-hydroxynicotinic acid, 6-hydroxynicotinamide and trigonelline (212–218). The excretion of trigonelline account for 3–5% of nicotinic acid administered to the rat (219).

AROMATIC COMPOUNDS

Chlorogenic Acids

Chlorogenic acids are the esters of caffeic and quinic acids. Their amount in coffee as a beverage depends on the degree and type of roasting of the green coffee beans. The most important is 5-caffeoylquinic acid (2%) and 3-caffeoylquinic acid, also called neochlorogenic acid (1%). The 4-caffeoylquinic isomer (0.2%) is also present as well as 3,4-,3,5-,4,5-dicaffeoyl (0.11%) and feruloylquinic acid (see also "Other compounds: opiate receptor"). The feruloylquinic and dicaffeoylquinic acids content is higher in robusta than in arabica coffee beans (2). The total percentage of chlorogenic acids in roasted coffee samples range from 0.2% to 4% and in dry instant coffee from 4% to 10%. Chlorogenic acids are drastically reduced (2) during roasting, and both quinic acid and caffeic acid are released (3,160). The quinic acid content increases from 1.3% in green beans to a maximum of 3.5% on roasting (2). In rats and humans, chlorogenic acid is hydrolyzed into caffeic and quinic acids (220).

Caffeic Acid

Caffeic acid is the precursor of m-hydroxyhippuric acid in human urine (221) where the glucuroconjugates of m-hydroxycoumaric acid and m-coumaric acid seemed to be the main metabolites. All the metabolites identified in the urine are presented in Fig. 3 (3). Caffeic acid, dihydrocaffeic, ferulic, dihydroferulic, vanillic, and m-coumaric acids as well as the glucuroconjugates of feruloylglycine and vanilloylglycine were identified in urine (3).

Intraperitoneal administration to the rat of one of these metabolites labelled with ^{14}C, [2-^{14}C] ferulic acid, showed that no radioactivity was incorporated into tissues while respectively 68% and 17% of the dose was recovered in urine and feces. m-Hydroxyphenylpropionic acid was identified in the urine and the excretion of unchanged ferulic acid was estimated at 25% of the dose administered (222).

A study of the choleretic effect after intraduodenal administration to rats showed that 20% of the dose of ferulic acid and less than 5% of caffeic acid or m-coumaric acid were recovered in biliary secretion (223). The role of intestinal bacteria on caffeic acid metabolism was demonstrated in humans by comparing control subjects with subjects treated with neomycin to suppress their gut flora (224). The same comparison was made in germfree and gnotobiotic rats (225,226). Dehydroxylation was due to bacteria. The specific roles of different bacteria of the flora in transforming caffeic acid into dihydrocaffeic acid, ferulic acid, dihydroferulic acid, m-hydroxyphenylpropionic acid, vinyl catechol, and ethyl cathechol in the host are now known. After the ingestion of 1 g caffeic acid by adult volunteers, only 10% of the dose was recovered, and the highest level of caffeic, vanillic, ferulic and isoferulic acids was identified and quantified in the urine samples collected in the first 4 hours (227).

Quinic Acid

The metabolic formation of an aromatic ring structure from quinic acid (1,3,4,5-tetrahydroxycyclohexane carboxylic acid) was reported before the beginning of this century (3). Hippuric acid was excreted in the urine after oral administration, but its formation was suppressed on parenteral injection of quinic acid in the guinea pig and after neomycin treatment in humans (228). The same results with neomycin were obtained in the rhesus monkey. The fate of quinic acid was investigated in 22 species of animals including humans where 60% of an oral dose of quinic acid was excreted as hippuric acid (229). In the rat, the "aromatization" of quinic acid does not appear to be enhanced upon chronic administration, and ranges from 17–27% and 0.7–2.0% of a 100 mg quinic acid dose were found as urinary hippuric acid and catechol, respectively. Neither protocatechuic acid nor vanillic acid was detected (230). "Aromatization" by the gut flora of another coffee component, shikimic acid, has also been demonstrated (231).

Guaiacol

Guaiacol (2-methoxyphenol) is a phenolic compound found at concentrations of 2–3 mg/kg and 8–10 mg/kg in arabica and robusta roasted coffees,

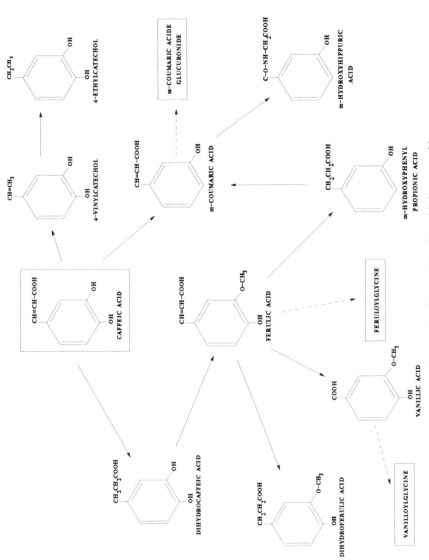

FIG. 3. Metabolic pathways of caffeic and ferulic acids in rats and humans.

respectively (160). The metabolism of guaiacol has been studied because it is used to esterify drugs such as ibuprofen to improve their gastrointestinal tolerance, and guaiacol glyceryl ether is also used as an expectorant. Two hours after oral administration in humans, the plasma concentrations of guaiacol reached a peak, followed by a plateau explained by delayed gastrointestinal absorption (232). One major metabolite, β-(methyoxyphenoxy)lactic acid, has been identified in humans (233).

Eugenol

Among the phenolic compounds, quantitative findings were reported for isoeugenol (4-propenyl-2-methoxyphenol) and only 0.1 mg/kg was found in roasted coffee (160). Eugenol (4-allyl-2-methoxyphenol), which was detected in coffee (2), is used as a food flavor particularly in the form of cloves and also as a fragrance agent. However, its pharmacological and toxicological properties, including its metabolism, were studied and reviewed recently because of its extensive use as a local anesthetic in dentistry (234). In female rats after administration by stomach tube of ^{14}C ring-labelled eugenol in the range of 0.5 to 1000 mg/kg, 10% of the dose was excreted in feces and 75–80% in urine. At all dose levels, half of the urinary metabolites was conjugated eugenol, but the nature of the conjugate was dependent upon the dose. At low doses, eugenol sulfate predominated while the glucuronide was the major metabolite at the highest dose. Sulfate and glucuronide conjugates of 4-propyl-2-hydroxyphenol (5–15%) and 4-propyl-2-methoxyphenol (1–3%) were also found, whereas 10% of the dose was uncharacterized acidic metabolites (235).

More than twenty metabolites of the methyl ether of eugenol and isoeugenol found in many plants were identified in the urine of rats (236). Figure 4 shows the metabolic pathways proposed for eugenol methyl ether. Although O-demethylation is quantitatively not as important for dimethoxy derivatives as for monomethoxy derivatives, the same metabolic pathways have been proposed for the monomethoxy derivatives (237).

Benzo(a)Pyrene

Polycyclic aromatic hydrocarbons (PAH), particularly benzo(a)pyrene, have been found in roasted coffee at concentrations of 0.1–4 μg/kg and below 1 μg/kg in soluble coffee (2). However, coffee consumption contributes to less than 0.1% of the total PAH inhaled or ingested from all sources (160). Benzo(a)pyrene has been considered as a prototype polycyclic hydrocarbon because of its powerful carcinogenic activity and its widespread presence in the environment.

The administration of benzo(a)pyrene in the jejunum of rats and analysis

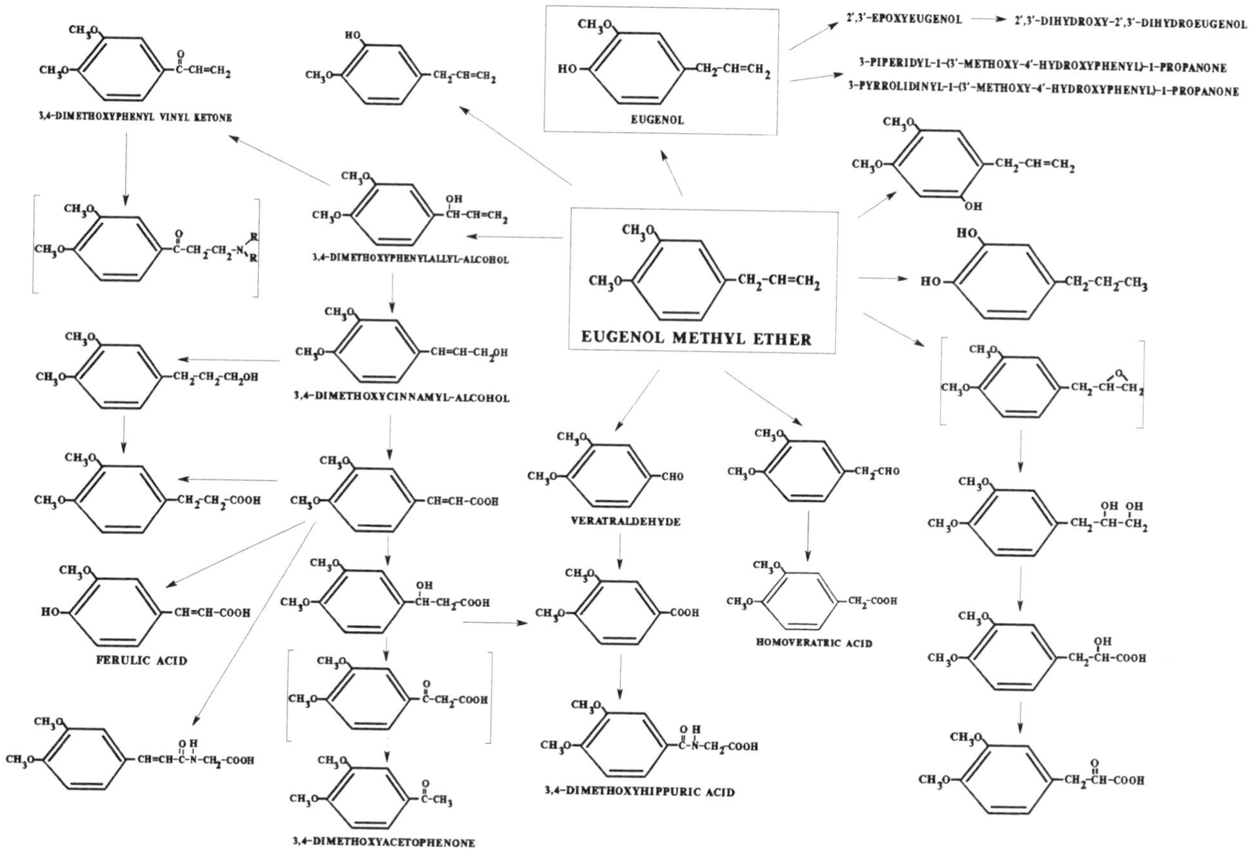

FIG. 4. Metabolic pathways of eugenol methyl ether and eugenol in rats.

of the portal blood showed an extensive metabolism by mucosal cells. The metabolites were not identified, but treatment with β-glucuronidase showed glucuronide conjugates (238). In a more recent study, these conjugates sensitive to β-glucuronidase and sulfatase appeared to be of no quantitative importance (239). Fecal excretion represents 85% of the dose of radiolabelled benzo(a)pyrene injected intraperitoneally in both conventional and germfree rats. This work suggests that the mercapturic acid pathway is quantitatively an important elimination route and shows an effect of intestinal flora. However, the method of extraction and chromatographic fractionation used allowed only the complex pattern of unidentified radioactive metabolites to be observed. Introduction of high pressure liquid chromatography for the separation of oxygenated benzo(a)pyrene metabolites allowed clean and quantitative separation that was not previously possible.

An extensive review has been published on the metabolic pathways of benzo(a)pyrene (Fig. 5) and the enzyme systems involved in its metabolism (240). For the detection of metabolites covalently bound to DNA, four hydroxylated benzo(a)pyrene metabolites: 3-hydroxy, 7,8-dihydro-7,8-dihydroxy, 7,8,9,10-tetrahydro-7,8,9-trihydroxy, and 7,8,9,10-tetrahydro-7,8,9, 10-tetrahydroxy-benzo(a)pyrene were analyzed by mass spectrometry (241).

HETEROCYCLIC COMPOUNDS

Maillard Reaction Products

Maillard reaction products are important constituents of roasted coffee. They correspond to 15–25% of dry, medium-roasted coffee, and 20–25% are soluble in hot water, giving the color of the beverage. In spite of their quantitative importance, they are poorly characterized as caramelized products of sucrose and condensation products of polysaccharides with proteins and other compounds. Among them, chlorogenic acid loss during roasting was correlated with its incorporation in browning products (2). With the application of industrial extraction processes to the preparation of instant coffee, higher percentage of melanoidins are extracted than in brewed coffee (160).

No Maillard product with known physiological properties is identified in coffee, and thus no metabolic study on a specific compound has yet been reported. In the evaluation of their nutritional effects, one study described the metabolic fate of radiolabelled "early" and "advanced" Maillard reaction products of casein and glucose given in a single meal to the rat (242). When casein was fed, 4% of the ingested dose was recovered in feces, and fecal excretion increased to 14% and 40–50% respectively with "early" and "advanced" Maillard casein. These results demonstrate the gastrointestinal

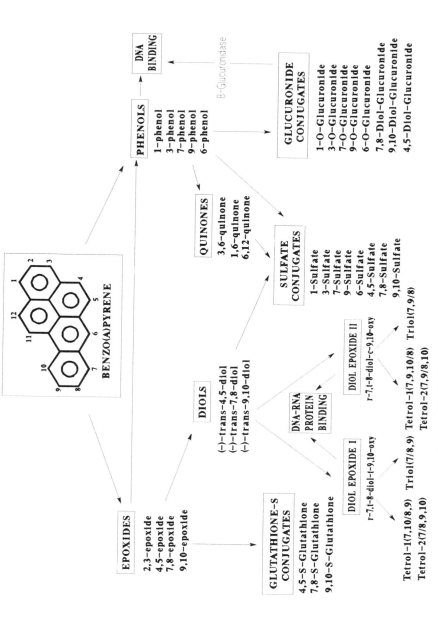

FIG. 5. Metabolic pathways of benzo(a)pyrene in rats.

malabsorption of Maillard reaction products. Even when absorbed, they are excreted from the body as shown by increases in urinary excretion of 10%, 15%, and 22%, respectively. Except for ε-deoxyfructosyllysine, the urinary metabolites have not been identified.

The fecal excretion of premelanoidins and melanoidins in the rat reaches 60–70% and 90–95% of the oral dose, respectively. The percentage of radio-activity excreted in urine from premelanoidin was 23–30%, but for melanoidins only 1% was recovered in both urine, labelled CO_2 and the carcass.

Extrapolation of these results to the metabolic fate of the Maillard reaction products found in coffee indicates that they transit through the gastrointestinal tract with absorption of only a few components. During their transit in mice, premelanoidins prepared by heating glycine and glucose inhibited nitrosourea formation and prevented genotoxic nitroso-compound-induced DNA damage in colon epithelial and bone marrow cells (243).

2-Methylfuran

2-Methylfuran is a naturally occurring furan found in many foods and detected in green and roasted coffee (2,244). An in vitro study demonstrated the metabolic activation of 2-methylfuran by the hepatic and pulmonary microsomal system to the reactive metabolite acetylacrolein (4-oxo-2-pentenal) that binds covalently to microsomal proteins (245). In vivo in the rat, the covalent binding to both protein and DNA was evaluated in the blood, liver, lungs, and kidney after intraperitoneal injection of 50–200 mg/kg body weight of 2-([^{14}C]methyl)furan. Maximal covalent binding was observed in the liver at 4 hours, but at all time points binding of the label was greatest in liver, followed by kidney, then blood and lung. In this study, liver glutathione levels were depressed after 2-methylfuran. The quantitative importance of metabolic activation in the formation of reactive metabolites was demonstrated by the increased covalent binding to protein and DNA with the phenobarbital pretreatment of rats, while covalent binding was decreased by the administration of N-octylimidazole, an inhibitor of cytochrome P-450 (246).

5-Hydroxymethyl-2-Furaldehyde

Aldehydes play an important role in the aroma of roasted coffee, and six furanoids have been identified. Furfural is found in quantities ranging from 55–80 mg/kg, 5-methylfurfural from 50–70 mg/kg, 5-hydroxymethyl-2-furfural from 10–35 mg/kg, and 2-furyl-acetaldehyde is present at a level of only 0.5 mg/kg (2,160).

Since hydroxymethylfuraldehydes are produced during advanced Maillard reactions through the dehydration of 3-deoxyhexosones and are thus detected not only in coffee but also in cooked foods as well as sterilized solutions for parenteral nutrition, the metabolism of 5-hydroxy-2-furaldehyde has been investigated as a model compound.

Metabolic balance studies in humans reported the excretion of 5-hydroxy-methyl-2-furoic acid and furan-2,5-dicarboxylic acid in urine. It is interesting to note that furan carboxylic acid is found in roasted coffee at a level of 55–80 mg/kg (2). These two metabolites account for only 50% of the dose given parenterally. This incomplete recovery supports the theory that most of the 5-hydroxymethyl-2-furaldehyde, described as a reactive substance, binds to tissue and accumulates in the body (247). However, this incomplete recovery might also be explained by the formation and excretion of unknown metabolites.

To identify other possible metabolic pathways, uniformly ^{14}C-labelled hydroxymethyl-2-furaldehyde was synthesized (248), and metabolic experiments were performed in the rat (249). About 85% of the oral dose was recovered 8 hours after administration and 95–100% after 24 hours. Identification of the metabolites in the rat confirmed the importance of the 5-hydroxymethyl-2-furoic acid found in humans but showed for the first time the presence of the conjugate N-(5-hydroxymethyl-2-fureoyl)glycine (Fig. 6). No accumulation of labelled compounds in tissues could be detected by whole body autoradiography 24 hours after administration.

Pyridines

Heterocyclic nitrogen and sulphur ring-containing compounds are important for the flavor of roasted coffee. A list of 68 pyrroles, 71 pyrazines, 11 quinoxalines, 4 quinolines, 5 indoles, 24 oxazoles, 26 thiazoles, 32 thiophenes, and 2 dithiolanes was reported. Twelve pyridine derivatives were detected (see also "Other compounds: cholinomimetic compound) and a concentration of 49 mg/kg pyridine was reported in roasted coffee (160).

Pyridine is a breakdown product of trigonelline formed during roasting (2). Before the beginning of this century, a first report showed the urinary excretion of methyl-pyridinum hydroxide in dogs after pyridine administration (250), and subsequent studies have confirmed the methylation of pyridine in humans and several animal species (251,252). Ring hydroxylation followed by glucuronic acid conjugation has also been reported in the rabbit (253). The metabolic N-oxidation of heteroaromatic nitrogen has not been extensively studied but was reported in 3-acetyl-pyridine (254) and quinoline (255). Pyridine-N-oxide was a quantitatively important metabolite when pyridine was given intraperitoneally to rats, mice, hamsters, guinea pigs, rabbits, and ferrets (255). This metabolite amounted to 10% of the dose in rats, 20% in rabbits, and about 40% in ferrets, hamsters, guinea pigs, and mice. In the case of 3-methylpyridine (β-picoline), 3-methylpyridine-N-oxide accounted for 4–7% of the dose for rats and mice and less than 1% for the other species.

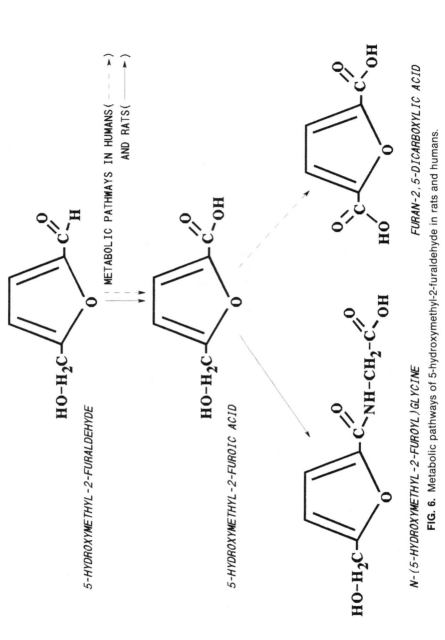

FIG. 6. Metabolic pathways of 5-hydroxymethyl-2-furaldehyde in rats and humans.

Maltol

Isomaltol (2-acetyl-3-hydroxyfuran) is one of the 111 furans detected in roasted coffee, and it was found in robusta and arabica coffees at levels of 1.5 and 8 mg/kg, respectively. Other heterocyclic oxygen ring-containing compounds are pyrones, but only three alkyl derivatives have been identified (160).

Maltol, the 2-methyl-3-hydroxy-1,4-pyrone, is found at a similar concentration of 40 mg/kg in both arabica and robusta roasted coffees (2) and is also a naturally occurring substance sold as a food flavor enhancing agent. The metabolism of maltol has been studied in beagle dogs after an intravenous dose of 10 mg/kg. The percentage of the administered dose recovered in urine varied widely, and the mean recovery of 58% (range 40–80%) obtained after 24 hours remained unchanged after three days of collection.

Maltol is rapidly and extensively metabolized and excreted as sulfate and glucuronide conjugates, and 88% of the total excretion occurred in the first 6 hours. No metabolite can be identified in feces, and both the wide variations and the incomplete recoveries may be explained by the inaccuracy of the analytical methods used (256).

Quinolines

Four benzo(b)pyridines (quinolines) have been detected in roasted coffee (160) and can be formed in the body from tryptophan metabolism (3).

The possible presence of 2-amino-3,4-dimethylimidazo[4,5-*f*] quinoline (MeIQ) and its estimated content have been recently reported (257). The level of 16 ng/kg in regular hot-air-roasted coffee beans was considered by the author to be relatively low and raised no question on the safety of coffee brews usually consumed. A recent publication described the development of a sensitive method for the isolation of MeIQ from instant coffee and home-brewed lyophilized coffee (258). The procedure was validated by the use of labelled MeIQ as a reference standard, and the detection limit was about 5–10 pg/g coffee. In spite of this very high sensitivity, MeIQ was not detectable in either instant or roasted coffee. Thus, the identification of MeIQ and other heterocyclic amine-like mutagenic material in roasted coffee needs confirmation and further investigation but excellent work on its metabolism and the formation of DNA adducts has already been done in animals and humans (259–262).

An association has been demonstrated between mutagenicity and the formation by rat liver microsomes of metabolites of [^{3}H] quinoline (263). Quinoline-2,3-epoxide was suggested as the active intermediate, and other studies have identified quinoline-1-oxide and 5,6-trans-dihydroxy-5,6-dihydroquinoline, while a third metabolite, 3-hydroxyquinoline, was also released from

DNA (264,265). In the rabbit, quinoline is hydroxylated then conjugated with glucuronic acid and to a lesser extent with sulfuric acid (253). Other unidentified water-soluble metabolites were glutathione, glucuronic acid, and sulfate conjugates.

Naphthalene

Naphthalene and six other derivatives, 1-methyl, 2-methyl, dimethyl, 2-ethyl, trimethyl, and tetramethylnaphthalene were identified in roasted coffee (2). They are present only in trace quantities in coffee, but the pathways of naphthalene metabolism have been extensively studied in vivo and in vitro (266,267) since naphthalene is a model compound for the study of aromatic polycyclic hydrocarbons. After intraperitoneal injection of [1-^{14}C]naphthalene in rats, the recovery of radioactivity in urine increased from 24% on the first day to 60% on the third day while fecal excretion amounted to 14% of the dose (268). After oral administration, more than 80% of the dose was recovered in urine after three days, 6.5% in feces and 2–6% in the carcass. In bile-duct-cannulated rats, no radioactivity appeared in feces or carcass, and only 27–34% of the dose was found in urine while 58–75% was secreted in bile (269).

The formation of a reactive epoxide, naphthalene 1,2-oxide, and its detoxification by several pathways has been demonstrated. Naphthalene oxide formation is the rate-limiting step in naphthalene metabolism. Incubation of ^{14}C-naphthalene with microsomes or isolated hepatocytes resulted in irreversible binding of radioactive material to cellular macromolecules (270,271). In the same experimental conditions, a considerable amount of protein-bound radioactivity was found with [^{14}C]1-naphthol, indicating the formation of reactive metabolites from 1-naphthol, a major metabolite of naphthalene (270). However, in the mouse and rat the toxicity of naphthalene did not appear to be mediated through 1-naphthol (272). At the same time, the in vitro mechanism for naphthol formation could not be substantiated by in vivo experiments in the rat (269). The results suggest that most of the naphthols are formed in vivo during enterohepatic circulation of a premercapturic acid pathway metabolite of naphthalene by a process mediated by the intestinal microflora. Inhibition of glucuronidation and sulfation causes a dramatic increase in the formation of reactive metabolites indicating that these reactions play an important role in naphthalene detoxification. When rats were maintained on a methionine-free diet for one week and then fed deuterated methionine, nine labelled methylthio-metabolites were observed in the urine. The fact that their formation was depressed in neomycin-treated rats confirmed the major role of intestinal microflora and the entero-hepatic circulation in naphthalene metabolism (269). The metabolism of naphthalene by rats results in the formation of 31 metabolites excluding conjugates (273). Figure 7 shows only the most important ones.

Other Compounds

Kahweolfuran is an unusual heterocyclic product of particular importance to flavor and is found in roasted coffee at a level of 0.45–2.0 mg/kg (2,160). No metabolic study has been reported.

ALIPHATIC COMPOUNDS

About 190 aliphatic compounds have been identified in green and roasted coffees (2). The complex carbohydrates of green beans decompose during roasting and generate 37 carboxylic acids present in amounts up to about 1.5%. The main acids found in significant quantities are malic, citric, lactic, succinic, and glycolic acids (160). In human liver, the direct conversion of endogenous glycolate to oxalate with the enzyme glycolic acid dehydrogenase has been proposed as a mechanism for primary hyperoxaluria (274). However, in goats, the infusion of ^{14}C-glycolic acid showed rapid oxidation with 44% recovered in $^{14}CO_2$ and 12% in urine after 5 hours. In milk, only 0.4% of the infused labelled glycolic acid was incorporated into casein, 0.08% into fat, and about 2% into lactose (275). More than ten of these acids are also present as 23 different esters and two ethers. The identification of trace amounts of 40 ketones and diketones, 20 alcohols and ketoalcohols, about 40 aliphatic hydrocarbons, 20 aldehydes, 14 sulphur- and 16 nitrogen-containing aliphatic compounds shows the complexity of the products formed during roasting. These products have no obvious physiological properties at such low concentrations, but they are particularly important as aroma constituents of the beverage.

The metabolism in the rat or humans of a number of these products is known, such as dimethylsulfoxide, dimethylsulfone (276–278), and formaldehyde (279), present at a level of 3.4–4.5 mg/L in brewed coffee (280).

Methylglyoxal

Other aldehydes have been more extensively investigated, particularly glyoxal and methylglyoxal. Methylglyoxal induces mutation in different in vitro tests. It was detected not only in coffee (281–283) but also in various other beverages such as black tea, whiskey, brandy (284), wine, beer, fruit juices, cola, and foods including bread, tomatoes, boiled potatoes, and soya sauce (160). No experiment on the metabolism and tissue distribution of methylglyoxal after oral ingestion in animal or human have been reported (3). It is still

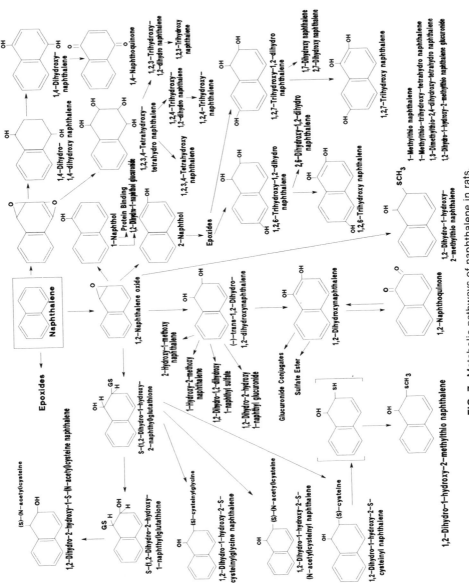

FIG. 7. Metabolic pathways of naphthalene in rats.

difficult to analyze methylglyoxal in tissues because of an active glyoxalase system (285), so our knowledge of its biosynthesis and degradation in animals is complicated and uncertain (286). Several groups of anaerobic bacteria in the human gut or isolated from feces produced methylglyoxal in vitro, and they may be one of the most important sources in humans (287). Methylglyoxal is a natural constituent of the liver and is produced in the liver cells of rats and other animal species through normal metabolic processes (288). It can be formed from acetoacetate and carbohydrate in glycolyzing tissues and from triose phosphates by nonenzymatic processes (289). In the liver, methylglyoxal is bound to protein (290), and different biosynthetic routes have been proposed (160,286). After oral administration, methylglyoxal can be detoxified by the glyoxalase system present in the mammalian intestine (291). In tissues, methylglyoxal is converted into D-lactic acid (292,293) and pyruvate and so contributes to glucose production (294).

LIPIDS

Palmitic acid and linoleic acid are the most important fatty acids present in roasted coffee, which contains approximately 11–16% w/w lipids in arabica and 4–11% in robusta. About 79% of these lipids are present as triglycerides along with unsaponifiables such as terpene esters (17%), while the remaining 4% are sterols, free terpenes, tocopherols, waxes, and unknown substances (160,2). During brewing, the majority of lipids are left in the spent grounds so the lipids are only a minor constituent of a cup of coffee.

Terpenes

Cafestol and kahweol are the main diterpenes specific to coffee. Kahweol and, to a lesser extent, cafestol increased glutathione S-transferase activity in mice when a dose equivalent to 20% powdered green coffee beans was added to the diet for 12 days (295). A 50% mixture of kahweol and cafestol in the diet of hamsters at a level of 2 g/kg produced a 35% reduction in tumor incidence induced by 7,12-dimethylbenz(a)anthracene in the buccal pouch (296). In spite of these demonstrations of physiological activities, no study has reported the metabolic fate of cafestol or kahweol.

Water-soluble diterpene glycosides of the kaurane and kaurene type have been found, particularly in arabica coffee. Atractyligenin is present in coffee both as the free compound and as the aglycone of three glycosides. The total atractyligenin content of roasted arabica coffees varies from 0.64 to 1.24 g/kg and free atractyligenin from 0.06 to 0.12 g/kg (297). Roasted robusta coffee contains only one-tenth or less atractyligenin and its derivatives. On roasting, total atractyligenin decreases by about 35% (298) with a concomitant 5- to 10-fold increase of free atractyligenin. It was also calculated that, respectively, 70% and 85% of the amount present in roast coffee is extracted in coffee brews and instant coffee (297). Atractyligenin has been found in the urine of coffee drinkers with two glucuronide conjugates of 2β-hydroxy-15-oxoatractylan-4α-carboxylic acid and dihydroatractyligenin, as shown in Fig. 8 (299,300). Between 2 and 40 mg of this carboxylic acid metabolite were found daily in human urine (299).

Several alicyclic compounds identified in roasted coffee are terpenes such as d-limonene, a monoterpene that has been studied in the rat (301), hamster, guinea pig, rabbit, dog, and humans (302). In the 24 hours after oral administration of ^{14}C-d-limonene, 25% of the dose appeared in bile while 60% was excreted in urine, 5% in feces, and 2% in expired CO_2. It was suggested that this incomplete balance of radioactivity was due to losses through volatile metabolites. Species differences in the metabolism of limonene were demonstrated, and, for example, two metabolites found in the rabbit were not excreted in the rat. Using rat liver microsomes, limonene epoxides were identified as the intermediates of glycol production (303). After a single 200 mg/kg dose, significant accumulation of ^{14}C from radiolabelled d-limonene was observed in the kidney cortex in male rats compared with that in female rats due to sex-specific nephrotoxic effects (304). All the metabolic pathways presented in Fig. 9 were reported earlier (3).

The metabolism of terpenoids in essential oils has been studied (305). The metabolic pathways of two monoterpenes identified in roasted coffee, myrcene, an aliphatic hydrocarbon, and p-cymene, an aromatic compound, were described. The experiments were done in rabbits, and the dose of monoterpene given by stomach tube corresponded to 400–700 mg/kg. Figures 10 and 11 show the metabolic pathways of myrcene and p-cymene. The metabolites produced from these monoterpenes demonstrate a large number of biotransformations including epoxidation, allylic oxidation, hydroxylation, reduction, hydration, and acetylation. In humans, a metabolic study was possible after suicidal ingestion of 400–500 ml pine oil (306). Pine oil contains four monoterpenes: the two isomers of pinene (65%), carene (26%), only 6% limonene, and other hydrocarbons (3%). Its lethal dose is in the range of 60 to 120 g for adults. From an analysis of blood and urine monoterpene concentrations, it was concluded that, after this large dose, monoterpenes were poorly absorbed from the gastrointestinal tract, and slowly metabolized; renal excretion of metabolites reached a peak only five days after ingestion.

Sterols

Various sterols are present in coffee oil and constitute about 5.4% of the total lipids. The most important sterols are β-sitosterol (53%), stigmasterol (21%), campesterol (11%), and cycloartenol (8%) (2,3). There is no evidence

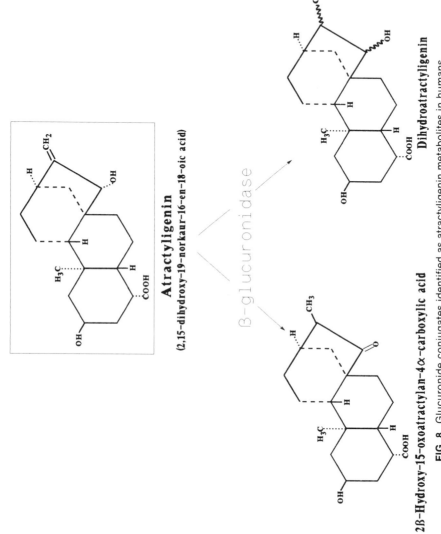

Atractyligenin
(2,15-dihydroxy-19-norkaur-16-en-18-oic acid)

β-glucuronidase

2β-Hydroxy-15-oxoatractylan-4α-carboxylic acid

Dihydroatractyligenin

FIG. 8. Glucuronide conjugates identified as atractyligenin metabolites in humans.

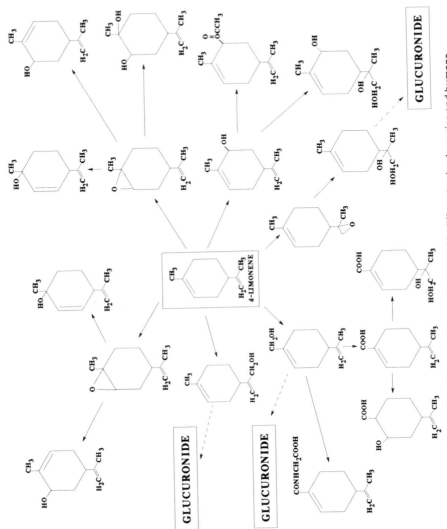

FIG. 9. Metabolic pathways of limonene reported in different animal species and humans.

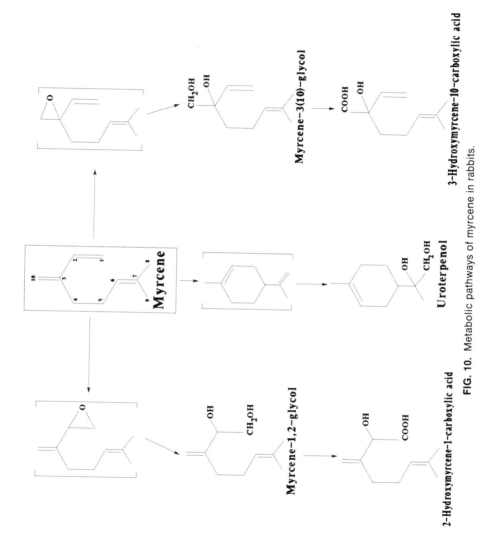

FIG. 10. Metabolic pathways of myrcene in rabbits.

77

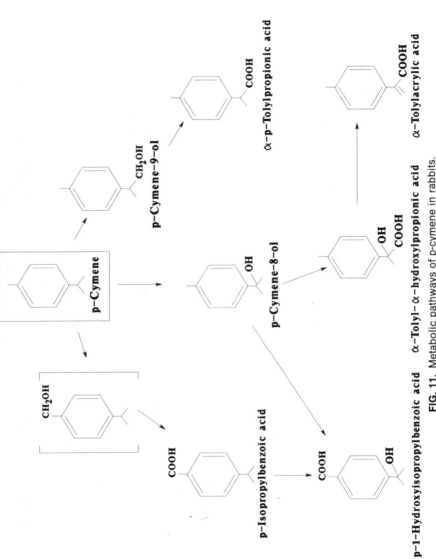

FIG. 11. Metabolic pathways of p-cymene in rabbits.

of sterols in brewed coffee (160), or rather they have been detected only in trace amounts. With the exception of potent and minor unidentified constituents, the sterols of coffee oil have no physiological effects on coffee drinkers. The total sterol intake of plant origin in the American diet has been estimated as 250 mg per day.

The absorption and metabolism of plant sterols, particularly campesterol, stigmasterol and β-sitosterol, which are the most common ones encountered in edible oils, have been studied in animals and humans. In humans, very small amounts of sitosterol were found in the tissues of patients fed a single dose of [³H]sitosterol (307). These results were confirmed using β-[¹⁴C]sitosterol in healthy subjects with ileostomies (308) where about 85% of the ingested dose was excreted through the ileostomy during the first 24 hours. These results demonstrated the suitability of β-sitosterol as a nonabsorbable marker of dietary lipid absorption in humans. Intravenous radioisotope studies showed the absorption of β-sitosterol in humans was 5% (309). However, increased sitosterol absorption in humans has been described in the inherited lipid storage disease "β-sitosterolemia and xanthmatosis" where considerable amounts of plant sterols, and sistosterol in particular, were found in the patients' plasma and tissues (310).

Animal studies on sitosterol absorption were done in rabbits and rats (311,312). Sitosterol was found in the plasma of rabbits fed a low-cholesterol diet containing 2% plant sterols for ten weeks. Stigmasterol was not detected but its dietary intake was ten times lower than that of sitosterol. In contrast, plasma campesterol was higher than plasma sitosterol although campesterol intake amounted to 34.5% of total plant sterol compared with 59.3% for sitosterol. Tissue distribution confirmed plasma analysis, and campesterol, in particular, accumulated in significant amounts in all tissues studied while stigmasterol was not detected. The comparative absorption of sitosterol, stigmasterol, and fucosterol in rats showed that these three sterols were very poorly absorbed, only 3–4% of the 50 mg dose administered. Inhibition of luminal cholesterol absorption (54%) was reported when either sitosterol or stigmasterol were fed simultaneously, but fucosterol had no such effect.

OTHER COMPOUNDS

Waxes

Coffee waxes represent 0.2–0.3% of the total lipids (313) and contain mainly 5-hydroxytryptamine derivatives of arachidonic, behenic, lignoceric, and stearic acids. Hydroxytryptamides partly decompose during roasting, and most of the residue remains in the spent grounds. Waxes of different plant origins are poorly absorbed, but they may have physiological effects along the gastrointestinal tract. The administration of regular and dewaxed coffee showed that waxes stimulate gastric acid secretion by enhanced gastrin release (314). The mechanisms and identity of the chemical(s) involved are unknown.

Hypercholesterolemic Factors

An epidemiological study showed the effect of coffee on serum cholesterol (315). Since this observation, several research teams tried to identify the specific effects of caffeine, and those of the blend and the degree of roasting, before drawing the conclusion that a hypercholesterolemic substance was either formed or extracted during preparation of boiled coffee (316). Boiled coffee contains more lipid material than drip filter coffee, and administration to volunteers of 1.3 g coffee lipid for six weeks showed the anticipated effect on serum cholesterol. The authors concluded that boiled coffee contains a lipid that raises cholesterol (317), and more recently it was demonstrated that this hypercholesterolemic factor is retained on paper filter (318,319).

Phytoestrogens

The first report on the presence of a compound with estrogenic activity from the unsaponified fraction of coffee oil was published in 1938 (320). A subsequent study showed that extracts from ethyl ether filtrates of green and roasted coffee beans and instant coffee powder have a very weak but notable binding affinity for uterine estrogen receptor proteins in vitro (321). Broad variations in estrogenic activity were observed in coffee samples. In addition, the estrogenic activity cannot be attributed to coumestrol or genistein, and the effect of cafesterol (322) was not studied. The weak estrogenic activity was confirmed in vivo where similar uterotropic responses were obtained with either a 17β-estradiol treatment or on feeding immature female mice the coffee extracts (323). The biologically active fractions isolated have a characteristic ultraviolet absorbance spectrum that excludes the presence of flavonoid, coumestan, or resorcyclic acid lactone compounds, generally regarded as the primary classes of phytoestrogens.

Opiate Receptor Antagonists

Experiments with rat brain membrane preparations showed that solutions of normal or decaffeinated instant coffee and coffee brews inhibit the in vitro binding of ^{3}H-labelled naxolone, an opiate antagonist (324). Preliminary characterization showed that the active compound is ether-extractable, heat-stable, not hydrolyzed with papain and has a molecular weight in the range of 1,000 to 3,500. This partially purified material acted as an opiate antagonist, blocking the effects of morphine in the guinea pig ileum in vitro. Further purification with a new isolation procedure showed that the opiate receptor activity of instant coffee was associated with one or more of the monoferuloyl or isoferuloyl esters of quinic acid lactone (325). The authors concluded that drinking coffee may be followed by effects mediated by opiate receptors as an average cup of coffee is five times the half-maximal effective dose. Drinking four cups of Italian-style espresso coffee did not appear to have any influence on anterior pituitary hormone secretion in healthy male volunteers (326). It is thus quite possible that the active substance is not absorbed or else is rapidly metabolized, and thus never gains access to the nervous system (327).

Cholinomimetic Compounds

A first report on the cholinomimetic activities of aqueous extracts of regular and decaffeinated coffees was published in 1977 (328). This effect has been confirmed using different in vitro experimental protocols. Recently, cardioactivities of aqueous extracts were tested with analysis of blood pressure and heart rate in the urethane-anesthetized rat model in order to purify bioactive fractions (329). The cardioactive compound was present only in roasted coffees and not in green coffee beans. Using solvent extractions and chromatographic separations, an 80-fold increase in pharmacological potency could be achieved. Although the complete chemical structure has not been elucidated, the author suggested from the UV spectrum and the formula weight of 452 that the major aromatic chromophore is a pyridine-related structure. NMR and IR analyses showed the presence of an enol group and an aliphatic substitution at the N-1 position on the pyridinium ring.

Phytate

Only one-third or half of the phytate present in coffee (1.2–5.4 mg/g) is water extractable (330), and their metabolism has already been described (3).

Hydrogen Peroxide

Hydrogen peroxide has been indirectly detected in coffee brews and instant coffee by oxygen measurement after the addition of excess catalase (331). The concentration of hydrogen peroxide increased when the coffee solution was allowed to stand at 37°C for at least 24 hours (284,331,332). This hydrogen peroxide generating system was confirmed but the concentration of hydrogen peroxide was 0.5 mg/kg coffee with the catalase method and

8–10 times higher with a polarographic method (283). Although continuous oral administration of high doses of hydrogen peroxide can induce gastroduodenal lesions in mice (333), the trace amounts of hydrogen peroxide present in coffee beverage should be rapidly inactivated by catalase.

CONCLUSIONS

Most of the large number of chemicals identified in coffee brews are detected in trace amounts and in consequence have no physiological effects at this level of consumption. However, many studies on decaffeinated coffee or on isolated coffee constituents have tried to demonstrate specific effects of compounds other than caffeine.

Intense research concerns the identification of hypercholesterolemic factor(s) and the hydrogen peroxide generating system. Although several physiological properties have been attributed to chlorogenic acids and their degradation products, their metabolism is not fully understood. The metabolic fate of cafestol and kahweol is not known although such knowledge could probably help in our understanding of the anti-tumor activity observed in animal experiments. The role of endogenous human metabolites such as methylglyoxal as a food constituent present not only in coffee but in other beverages and foods will be better evaluated with data pertaining to its oral metabolic fate.

Finally, the most important recent results for caffeine show dose-dependent kinetics not only in animals but also in humans in spite of species-specific differences in the metabolic pathways. In vitro studies on liver microsomes and the calculation of a caffeine metabolic ratio from the concentrations of urinary metabolites demonstrate the role of cytochrome P-450IA2 in caffeine 3-demethylation and in caffeine clearance. Other ratios serve as accurate indexes of hepatic enzyme activities with population studies showing human variability and the effects of genetics and environment. One of these ratios, based on the formation and excretion of an acetylated metabolite, provides the easiest and safest method of identifying acetylator phenotype in humans.

ACKNOWLEDGMENT

The author thanks Mrs. Ruth Shalom-Acheson for her helpful comments and corrections of the manuscript.

REFERENCES

1. Lehmann CG. In: Lehrbuch der physiologischen Chemie. 2nd ed. Leipzig: Verlag von Wilhelm Engelmann; 1850;367.

2. Spiller MA. The chemical components of coffee. In: The methylxanthine beverages and foods: chemistry, consumption, and health effects. New York: Alan R Liss, 1984;91–147.

3. Arnaud MJ. The metabolism of coffee constituents. In: *Coffee:* Vol. 3: Physiology; 1988; 33–55.

4. Chvasta TE, Cook AR. Emptying and absorption of caffeine from the human stomach. *Gastroenterology* 1971;61:838–43.

5. Marks V, Kelly JF. Absorption of caffeine from tea, coffee, and coca cola. *Lancet* 1973; 1:827.

6. Bonati M, Latini R, Galetti F, Young JF, Tognoni G, Garattini S. Caffeine disposition after oral doses. *Clin Pharm Ther* 1982;32:98–106.

7. Blanchard J, Sawers SJA. The absolute bioavailability of caffeine in man. *Eur J Clin Pharmac* 1983;24:93–8.

8. Blanchard J, Sawers SJA. Comparative pharmacokinetics of caffeine in young and elderly men. *J Pharmacokinetics Biopharmaceutics* 1983;11:109–26.

9. Arnaud MJ. Identification, kinetic and quantitative study of [2-^{14}C] and [1-Me^{14}C] caffeine metabolites in rat's urine by chromatographic separations. *Biochem Med* 1976;16:67–76.

10. Arnaud MJ. Comparative metabolic disposition of [1-Me^{14}C] caffeine in rats, mice, and chinese hamsters. *Drug Metab Dispos* 1985;13:471–8.

11. Greene EW, Woods WE, Tobin T. Pharmacology, pharmacokinetics, and behavioral effects of caffeine in horses. *Am J Vet Res* 1983;44:57–63.

12. Axelrod J, Reichental J. The fate of caffeine in man and a method for its estimation in biological material. *J Pharmac Exp Ther* 1953;107:519–23.

13. Aldridge A, Parsons WD, Neims AH. Stimulation of caffeine metabolism in the rat by 3-methylcholanthrene. *Life Sci* 1977;21:967–74.

14. Carver MP, Williams PL, Riviere JE. The isolated perfused porcine skin flap III. Percutaneous absorption pharmacokinetics of organophosphates, steroids, benzoic acid, and caffeine. *Toxicol Appl Pharmacol* 1989;97:324–37.

15. Carver MP, Riviere JE. Percutaneous absorption and excretion of xenobiotics after topical and intravenous administration to pigs. *Fundam Appl Toxicol* 1989;13:714–22.

16. Morisot C, Simoens C, Trublin F, et al. Efficacité de la caffeine transcutanée dans le traitement des apnées du prématuré. *Arch Fr Pediatr* 1990;47:221–4.

17. Conner DP, Millora E, Zamani K, et al. Transcutaneous chemical collection of caffeine in normal subjects: relationship to area under the plasma concentration-time curve and sweat production. *J Invest Dermatol* 1991;96;186–90.

18. Arnaud MJ, Welsch C. Caffeine metabolism in human subjects. Ninth Int Colloquium on the Science and Technology of Coffee, London. 1980;385–96.

19. Arnaud MJ, Welsch C. Theophylline and caffeine metabolism in man. In: Reitbrock N, Woodcock BG, Staib AH, eds. *Theophylline and other methylxanthines*. Friedr. Vieweg and Sohn. 1982;135–48.

20. Grab F. Factors influencing the absorption of caffeine. In University Microfilms Ltd. High Wycomb, England, Xerox Company, Ann Arbor, Michigan. 1968;2–110.

21. Brachtel D, Richter E. Effect of altered gastric emptying on caffeine absorption. *Z Gastroenterol* 1988;26:245–51.

22. Bonati M, Garattini S. Interspecies comparison of caffeine disposition. In: Dews PB, ed. *Caffeine*. Springer Verlag, Berlin: 1984;48–56.

23. Latini R, Bonati M, Castelli D, Garattini S. Dose-dependent kinetics of caffeine in rats. *Toxicology letters* 1978;2:267–70.

24. Newton R, Broughton LJ, Lind MJ, Morrisson PJ, Rogers HJ, Bradbrook ID. Plasma and salivary pharmacokinetics of caffeine in man. *Eur J Clin Pharmacol* 1981;21:45–52.

25. Jarboe CH, Hurst HE, Rodgers GC, Metaxas JM. Toxicokinetics of caffeine elimination in an infant. *Clinical Toxicology* 1986;24:415–28.

26. Kotake AN, Schoeller DA, Lambert GH, Baker AL, Schaffer DD, Josephs H. The caffeine CO_2 breath test: dose response and route of N-demethylation in smokers and nonsmokers. *Clin Pharmacol Ther* 1982;32:261–9.

27. Tang-Liu DDS, Williams RL, Reigelman S. Disposition of caffeine and its metabolites in man. *J Pharmacol Exp Ther* 1983;224:180–5.

28. Cheng WSC, Murphy TL, Smith MT, Cooksley WGE, Halliday JW, Powell LW. Dose-dependent pharmacokinetics of caffeine in humans: relevance as a test of quantitative liver function. *Clin Pharmacol Ther* 1990;47:516–24.

29. Denaro CP, Brown CR, Wilson M, Jacob P, Benowitz NL. Dose-dependency of caffeine metabolism with repeated dosing. *Clin Pharmacol Ther* 1990;48:277–85.
30. Arnaud MJ, Enslen M. The role of paraxanthine in mediating physiological effects of caffeine. 14th Intern Conf in Coffee Science, San Francisco, 14–19 July 1991, *Proceedings* ASIC, Paris, 1992;71–9.
31. Bortolotti A, Jiritano L, Bonati M. Pharmacokinetics of paraxanthine, one of the primary metabolites of caffeine, in the rat. *Drug Metab Dispos* 1985;13:227–31.
32. Grant DM, Campbell ME, Tang BK, Kalow W. Biotransformation of caffeine by microsomes from human liver. Kinetics and inhibition studies. *Biochem Pharm* 1987;36:1251–60.
33. Campbell ME, Grant DM, Inaba T, Kalow W. Biotransformation of caffeine, paraxanthine, theophylline and theobromine by polycyclic aromatic hydrocarbon-inducible cytochrome(s)P-450 in human liver microsomes. *Drug Metab Dispos* 1987;15:237–49.
34. Bonati M, Celardo A, Galletti F, Latini R, Tursi F, Belvedere G. Kinetics of caffeine metabolism in control and 3-methylcholathrene induced rat liver microsomes. *Toxicol Letters* 1984;21:53–8.
35. Christensen HD, Manio CV, Kling OR. Caffeine kinetics during late pregnancy. In: Soyka LF and Redmond GP, eds. *Drug metabolism of the immature human*. New York: Raven Press; 1981;163–81.
36. Bonati M, Latini R, Tognoni G, Young JF, Garrattini S. Interspecies comparison of in vivo caffeine pharmacokinetics in man, monkey, rabbit, rat, and mouse. *Drug Metabolism Reviews* 1984–85;15:1355–83.
37. Arnaud MJ. The pharmacology of caffeine. *Progr Drug Res* 1987;31:273–313.
38. Feely J, Kelleher P, Odumosu A. The effects of ageing on aminopyrine and caffeine breath tests in the rat. *Fundam Clin Pharmacol* 1987;1:409–12.
39. Latini R, Bonati M, Marzi E, Tacconi MT, Sadurska B, Bizzi A. Caffeine disposition and effects in young and one-year old rats. *J Pharm Pharmacol* 1980;32:596–9.
40. Blanchard J. Protein binding of caffeine in young and elderly males. *J Pharm Sci* 1982;71: 1415–8.
41. Aranda JV, Collinge JM, Zinman R, Watters G. Maturation of caffeine elimination in infancy. *Arch Dis Child* 1979;54:946–9.
42. Pons G, Blais J-C, Rey E, et al. Maturation of caffeine N-demethylation in infancy: a study using the $^{13}CO_2$ breath test. *Pediatr Res* 1988;23:632–6.
43. Krüger N, Helge H, Neubert D. CO_2 breath tests using ^{14}C-caffeine, ^{14}C-methacetin and ^{14}C-phenacetin for assessing postnatal development of monooxygenase activities in rats and marmosets. *Dev Pharmacol Ther* 1991;16:164–75.
44. Gorodischer R, Karplus M. Pharmacokinetic aspects of caffeine in premature infants with apnoea. *Eur J Cli Pharmac* 1982;22:47–52.
45. Parsons WD, Neims AH. Prolonged half-life of caffeine in healthy term newborn infants. *J Pediatr* 1981;98:640–1.
46. Aldridge A, Aranda JV, Neims AH. Caffeine metabolism in the newborn. *Clin Pharmac Ther* 1979;25:447–53.
47. Paire M, Van Lieferinghen P, Desvignes V, Dubray C, Raynaud EJ, Lavarenne J. Cinétique de la caféine au cours des premiers mois de la vie et implications pratiques. Sem Hôp Paris 1988;64:1813–7.
48. Pearlman SA, Duran C, Wood MA, Maisels MJ, Berlin CM.Caffeine pharmacokinetics in preterm infants older than 2 weeks. *Dev Pharmacol Ther* 1989;12;65–9.
49. Le Guennec JC, Billon B. Delay in caffeine elimination in breast-fed infants. *Pediatrics* 1987;79:264–8.
50. Burg AW, Werner E. Tissue distribution of caffeine and its metabolites in the mouse. *Biochem Pharmac* 1972;21:923–36.
51. Maikel R, Snodgrass W. Physicochemical factors in maternal-fetal distribution of drugs. *Toxic Appl Pharmacol* 1973;26:218–30.
52. Tanaka H, Nakazawa K, Arima M, Iwasaki S. Caffeine and its dimethylxanthines in fetal cerebral development in rat. *Brain Dev* 1984;6:355–61.
53. Lachance MP, Marlowe C, Waddel WJ. Autoradiographic disposition of [1-methyl-^{14}C]- and [2-^{14}C]caffeine in mice. *Toxicol Appl Pharmacol* 1983;71:237–41.
54. Arnaud MJ, Bracco I, Welsch C. Metabolism and distribution of labelled theophylline in the pregnant rat. Impairment of theophylline metabolism by pregnancy and absence of a blood-brain barrier in the fetus. *Pediatr Res* 1982;16:167–71.

55. Arnaud MJ, Getaz F. Postnatal establishment of a blood-brain barrier for theobromine in the rat. *Experientia* 1982;38:752.
56. Ståhle L, Segersvärd S, Ungerstedt U. Drug distribution studies with microdialysis. II. Caffeine and theophylline in blood, brain and other tissues in rats. *Life Sci* 1991;49: 1843–52.
57. McCall AL, Millington WR, Wurtman RJ. Blood-brain barrier transport of caffeine: dose-related restriction of adenine transport. *Life Sci* 1982;31:2709–15.
58. Somani SM, Khanna NN, Bada HS. Caffeine and theophylline: serum/CSF correlation in premature infants. *J Pediatr* 1980;96:1091–3.
59. Turmen T, Louridas TA, Aranda JV. Relationship of plasma and CSF concentration of caffeine in neonates with apnea. *J Pediatr* 1979;95:644–6.
60. Kimmel CA, Kimmel GL, White CG, Grafton TF, Young JF, Nelson CJ. Blood flow changes and conceptual development in pregnant rats in response to caffeine. *Fund and Appl Toxicol* 1984;4:240–7.
61. Ikeda GJ, Sapienza PP, McGinnis ML, Bragg LE, Walsh JJ, Collins TFX. Blood level of caffeine and results of fetal examination after oral administration of caffeine to pregnant rats. *J Appl Toxicol* 1982;2:307–14.
62. Khanna NN, Somani SM. Maternal coffee drinking and unusually high concentrations of caffeine in the newborn. *Clin Toxicol* 1984;22:473–83.
63. Aeschbacher HU, Milon H, Würzner HP. Caffeine concentrations in mice plasma and testicular tissue and the effect of caffeine on the dominant lethal test. *Mutation Res* 1978; 57:193–200.
64. Goldstein A, Warren R. Passage of caffeine into human gonadal and fetal tissue. *Biochem Pharmac* 1962;11:166–8.
65. Beach CA, Bianchine JR, Gerber N. The excretion of caffeine in the semen of men: comparison of the concentrations in blood and semen. *Proc West Pharmac Soc* 1982;25: 377–80.
66. Beach CA, Bianchine JR, Gerber N. The excretion of caffeine in the semen of men: pharmacokinetics and comparison of the concentrations in blood and semen. *J Clin Pharmac* 1984;24:120–6.
67. Tyrala EA, Dodson WE. Caffeine secretion into breast milk. *Arch Dis Child* 1979;54: 787–800.
68. Findlay JWA, Deangelis RL, Kearney MF, Welch RM, Findlay JM. Analgesic drugs in breast milk and plasma. *Clin Pharmac Ther* 1981;29:625–33.
69. Bailey DN, Welbert RT, Naylor AJ. A study of salicylate and caffeine excretion in the breast milk of two nursing mothers. *J Analyt Toxic* 1982;6:64–8.
70. Ryu JE. Caffeine in human milk and in serum of breast fed infants. *Devl Pharmac Ther* 1985;8:329–37.
71. Stavchansky S, Combs A, Sagraves R, Delgado M, Joshi A. Pharmacokinetics of caffeine in breast milk and plasma after single oral administration of caffeine to lactating mothers. *Biopharm Drug Dispos* 1988;9:285–99.
72. Parsons WD, Aranda JV, Neims AH. Elimination of transplacentally acquired caffeine in fullterm neonates. *Pediatr Res* 1976;10:333.
73. Van Thoff W. Caffeine in pregnancy. *Lancet* 1979;1:1020.
74. Arnaud MJ, Welsch C. Comparison of caffeine metabolism by perfused rat liver and isolated microsomes. In: Coon MJ, et al, eds. *Microsomes, drug oxidation and chemical carcinogenesis*. Academic Press, 1980;2:813–6.
75. Parsons WD, Neims AH. Effect of smoking on caffeine clearance. *Clin Pharmac Ther* 1978;24:40–5.
76. Cook CE, Tallent CR, Amerson EW, et al. Caffeine in plasma and saliva by a radioimmunoassay procedure. *J Pharmac Exp Ther* 1976;199:679–86.
77. Newton R, Broughton LJ, Lind MJ, Morrison PJ, Rogers HM, Bradbrook ID. Plasma and salivary pharmacokinetics of caffeine in man. *Eur J Clin Pharmac* 1981;21:45–52.
78. Callahan MM, Robertson RS, Arnaud MJ, Branfman AR, McComish MF, Yesair DW. Human metabolism of [1-methyl-^{14}C]- and [2-^{14}C]caffeine after oral administration. *Drug Metab Dispos* 1982;10:417–23.
79. Khanna N, Bada H, Somani S. Use of salivary concentrations in the prediction of serum caffeine and theophylline concentrations in premature infants. *J Pediatr* 1980;96:494–9.

80. Callahan MM, Robertson RS, Branfman AR, McComish MF, Yesair DW. Comparison of caffeine metabolism in three nonsmoking populations after oral administration of radiolabeled caffeine. *Drug Metab Dispos* 1983;11:211–7.
81. Tang-Liu DDS and Riegelman S. Metabolism of theophylline to caffeine in adults. *Res Commun in Chemical Pathol and Pharmacol* 1981;34:371–80.
82. Gilbert SG, So Y, Klassen RD, Geoffroy S, Stavric B, Rice DC. Elimination of chronically consumed caffeine in the pregnant monkey (*Macaca fascicularis*). *J Pharmacol Exp Ther* 1986;239:891–7.
87. Nakazawa K, Tanaka H, Arima M. The effect of caffeine ingestion on pharmacokinetics of caffeine and its metabolites after a single administration in pregnant rats. *Pharmacobio Dyn* 1985;8:151–60.
84. Birkett DJ, Miners JO. Caffeine renal clearance and urine caffeine concentrations during steady state dosing. Implications for monitoring caffeine intake during sport events. *Br J Clin Pharmac* 1991;31:405–8.
85. Duthel JM, Vallon JJ, Martin G, Ferret JM, Mathieu R, Videman R. Caffeine and sport: role of physical exercise upon elimination. *Med Sci Sports Exerc* 1991;23:980–5.
86. Van der Merwe PJ, Müller FR, Müller FO. Caffeine in sport. Urinary excretion of caffeine in healthy volunteers after intake of common caffeine-containing beverages. *S Afr Med J* 1988;74:163–4.
87. May DC, Jarboe CH, van Bakel AB, Williams WM. Effects of cimetidine on caffeine disposition in smokers and nonsmokers. *Clin Pharmac Ther* 1982;31:656–61.
88. Hart P, Farrell GC, Cooksley WGE, Powell LW. Enhanced drug metabolism in cigarette smokers. *Br Med J* 1976;2:147–9.
89. Arnaud MJ, Wietholtz H, Voegelin M, Bircher J, Preisig R. Assessment of the cytochromc P-448 dependent liver enzyme system by a caffeine breath test. In: Sato R, ed. *Microsomes drug oxidation and drug toxicity*. New York: Wiley Interscience; 1982;443–4.
90. Wietholtz H, Voegelin M, Arnaud MJ, Bircher J, Preisig R. Assessment of the cytochrome P-448 dependent liver enzyme system by a caffeine breath test. *Eur J Pharmacol* 1981;21:53–9.
91. Kotake AN, Schoeller DA, Lambert GH, Baker AL, Schaffer DD, Josephs H. The caffeine CO_2 breath test: dose response and route of N-demethylation in smokers and nonsmokers. *Clin Pharmac Ther* 1982;32:261–9.
92. Fraser HS, Dotson OY, Howard L, Grell GAC, Knight F. Drug metabolizing capacity in Jamaican cigarette and marijuana smokers and non-smokers. *West Indian Med J* 1983;32:207–11.
93. Joeres R, Klinker H, Heusler H, Epping J, Zilly W, Richter E. Influence of smoking on caffeine elimination in healthy volunteers and in patients with alcoholic liver cirrhosis. *Hepatology* 1988;8:575–9.
94. Murphy TL, McIvor G, Yap A, Cooksley WGE, Halliday JW, Powell LW. The effect of smoking on caffeine elimination: implication for its use as a semiquantitative test of liver function. *Clin Exp Pharm Phys* 1988;15:9–13.
95. Brown CR, Jacob P, Wilson M, Benowitz NL. Changes in rate and pattern of caffeine metabolism after cigarette abstinence. *Clin Pharmacol Ther* 1988;43:488–91.
96. Neims AH, Bailey J, Aldridge A. Disposition of caffeine during and after pregnancy. *Clin Res* 1979;27:A236.
97. Patwardhan RV, Desmond PV, Johnson RF, Schenker S. Impaired elimination of caffeine by oral contraceptive steroid. *J Lab Clin Med* 1980;95:603–8.
98. Balogh A, Irmisch E, Klinger G, Splinter F-K, Hoffmann A. Untersuchungen zur Elimination von Coffein und Metamizol im Menstruationszyclus der fertilen Frau. *Zent bl Gynäkol* 1987;109:1135–42.
99. Abernethy DR, Todd EL. Impairment of caffeine clearance by chronic use of low-dose estrogen-containing oral contraceptives. *Eur J Clin Pharmacol* 1985;28:425–8.
100. Balogh A, Liewald Th, Liewald S, et al. Zum Einfluß eines neuen Gestagens-Dienogest- und seiner Kombination mit Ethinylestradiol auf die Aktivität von Biotransformationsreaktionen. *Zent bl Gynäkol* 1990;112:735–46.
101. Meyer FP, Canzler E, Giers H, Walther H. Zeitverlauf der Hemmung der Coffeinelimination unter dem Einfluß des oralen Depotkontrazeptivum Deposiston. *Zent bl Gynäkol* 1991;113:297–302.

102. Aldridge A, Bailey J, Neims AH. The disposition of caffeine during and after pregnancy. *Semin Perinatol* 1981;5:310–4.
103. Knutti R, Rothweiler H, Schlatter C. Effect of pregnancy on the pharmacokinetics of caffeine. *Eur J Clin Pharmac* 1981;21:121–6.
104. Knutti R, Rothweiler H, Schlatter C. The effect of pregnancy on the pharmacokinetics of caffeine. *Arch Toxic* 1982;5:187–92.
105. Parsons WD, Pelletier JG. Prolonged half-life of caffeine in healthy term newborn infants. *J Pediatr* 1982;98:640–1.
106. Brazier JL, Ritter J, Berland M, Khenfer D, Faucon G. Pharmacokinetics of caffeine during and after pregnancy. *Dev Pharmacol Ther* 1983;6:315–22.
107. Dorrbecker SH, Raye JR, Dorrbecker BR, Kramer PA. Caffeine disposition in the pregnant rabbit. *Dev Pharmacol Ther* 1988;11:109–17.
108. Arnaud MJ, Gétaz F. Effect of pregnancy on [1,3,7-Me^{14}C] caffeine breath test in the rat. World Conference on Clinical Pharmacology, Stockholm; 1986.
109. Berthou F, Ratanasavanh D, Riche C, Picart D, Voirin T, Guillouzo A. Comparison of caffeine metabolism by slices, microsomes and hepatocyte cultures from adult human liver. *Xenobiotica* 1989;19:401–17.
110. Statland BE, Demas T, Danis M. Caffeine accumulation associated with alcoholic liver disease. *N Engl J Med* 1976;295:110–11.
111. Statland BE, Demas TJ. Serum caffeine half-lives. Healthy subjects vs. patients having alcoholic hepatic disease. *Am J Clin Path* 1980;73:390–3.
112. Desmond PV, Patwardhan RV, Johnson RF, Schenker S. Impaired elimination of caffeine in cirrhosis. *Dig Dis Sci* 1980;25:193–7.
113. Renner E, Wietholtz H, Huguenin P, Arnaud MJ, Preisig R. Caffeine: A model compound for measuring liver function. *Hepatology* 1984;4:38–46.
114. Sánchez-Alcaraz A, Ibáñez P, Sangrador G. Pharmacokinetics of intravenous caffeine in critically ill patients. *J Clin Pharmacy Ther* 1991;16:285–9.
115. Varagnolo M, Plebani M, Mussap M, Nemetz L, Paleari CD, Burlina A. Caffeine as indicator of metabolic functions of microsomal liver enzymes. *Clin Chim Acta* 1989;183:91–4.
116. Scott NR, Stambuk D, Chakraborty J, Marks V, Morgan MY. Caffeine clearance and biotransformation in patients with chronic liver disease. *Clin Sci* 1988;74:377–84.
117. Wang T, Kleber G, Stellaard F, Paumgartner G. Caffeine elimination: a test of liver function. *Klin Wschr* 1985;63:1124–8.
118. Jost G, Wahllander A, von Mandach U, Preisig R. Overnight salivary caffeine clearance: a liver function test suitable for routine use. *Hepatology* 1987;7:338–44.
119. Schaad H, Renner EL, Wietholtz H, Arnaud MJ, Preisig RR. Caffeine demethylation measured by breath analysis in experimental liver injury in the rat. *J Hepatol* 1992 (*submitted*).
120. Nagel RA, Dirix LY, Hayllar KM, Preisig R, Tredger JM, Williams R. Use of quantitative liver function tests-caffeine clearance and galactose elimination capacity-after orthotopic liver transplantation. *J Hepatol* 1990;10:149–57.
121. Mitoma C, Sorich TJ, Neubauer SE. The effect of caffeine on drug metabolism. *Life Sci* 1968;7:145–51.
122. Mitoma C, Lombrozo L, Le Valley SE, Dehn F. Nature of the effect of caffeine on the drug-metabolizing enzymes. *Arch Biochem Biophys* 1969:134:434–41.
123. Thithapandha A, Chaturapit S, Limlomwongse L, Sobhon P. The effects of xanthines on mouse liver cell. *Arch Biochem Biophys* 1974;161:178–86.
124. Aeschbacher HU, Würzner HP. Effect of methylxanthines on hepatic microsomal enzymes in the rat. *Toxic Appl Pharmac* 1975;33:575–81.
125. Govindwar SP, Kachole MS, Pawar SS. *In vivo* and *in vitro* effects of caffeine on hepatic mixed-function oxidases in rodents and chicks. *Fd Chem Toxic* 1984;22:371–5.
126. Gale GR, Atkins LM, Smith AB, Walker EM. Effects of caffeine on acetaminophen-induced hepatotoxicity in cadmium redistribution in mice. *Res Comm Chem Path Pharmac* 1986;51:337–50.
127. Govindwar SP, Kachole MS, Pawar SS. Effect of caffeine on the hepatic microsomal mixed function oxidase system during phenobarbital and benzo(a)pyrene treatment in rats. *Toxicol Lett* 1988;42:109–15.
128. Ahokas JT, Pelkonen O, Ravenscroft PJ, Emmerson BT. Effects of theophylline and caf-

feine on liver microsomal drug metabolizing mono-oxygenase in genetically AHH-responsive and non-responsive mice. *Res Commun Subst Abuse* 1981;2:277–90.

129. Cornish HH, Wilson CE, Abar EL. Effect of foreign compounds on liver microsomal enzymes. *Am Ind Hyg Ass J* 1970;31:605–8.

130. Khanna KL, Cornish HH. The effect of daily ingestion of caffeine on the microsomal enzymes of rat liver. *Food Cosmet Toxicol* 1973;11:11–7.

131. Arnaud MJ. Pharmacokinetics in animal chronic toxicological studies. *J Pharm Clin* 1985; 4:259–68.

132. George J, Murphy T, Roberts R, Cooksley WGE, Halliday JW, Powell LW. Influence of alcohol and caffeine consumption on caffeine elimination. *Clin Exp Pharmac Physiol* 1986; 13:731–6.

133. Caraco Y, Zylber-Katz E, Granit L, Levy M. Does restriction of caffeine intake affect mixed function oxidase activity and caffeine metabolism. *Biopharm Drug Dispos* 1990;11: 639–43.

134. Aldridge A, Neims AH. The effects of phenobarbital and β-naphthoflavone on the elimination kinetics and metabolic pattern of caffeine in the beagle dog. *Drug Metab Dispos* 1979; 7:378–82.

135. Willson RA, Hart FE. The comparison of *in vivo* plasma radioactivity clearance and $^{14}CO_2$ breath elimination of model drugs in the rat: a study in regional hepatocyte function. *Toxicol Appl Pharmacol* 1981;61:177–84.

136. Welch RM, Hsu SY, DeAngelis RL. Effect of aroclor 1254, phenobarbital, and polycyclic aromatic hydrocarbons on the plasma clearance of caffeine in rat. *Clin Pharmacol Ther* 1977;22:791–8.

137. Guaitani A, Abbruzzi R, Bastone A, et al. Metabolism of caffeine to 6-amino-5-[N-methyl-formylamino]-1,3-dimethyluracil in the isolated, perfused liver from control or phenobarbital-, β-naphthoflavone- and 3-methylcholanthrene-pretreated rats. *Toxicol Lett* 1987;38: 55–66.

138. Bonati M, Latini R, Marzi E, Cantoni R, Belvedere G. [2-^{14}C]caffeine metabolism in control and 3-methylcholanthrene induced rat liver microsomes by high pressure liquid chromatography. *Toxicol Lett* 1980;7:1–7.

139. Ratanasavanh D, Berthou F, Dreano Y, Mondine P, Guillouzo A, Riche C. Methylcholanthrene but not phenobarbital enhances caffeine and theophylline metabolism in cultured adult human hepatocytes. *Biochem Pharmacol* 1990;39:85–94.

140. Butler MA, Iwasaki M, Guengerich FP, Kadlubar F. Human cytochrome P-450PA (P-450IA2), the phenacetin O-deethylase, is primarily responsible for the hepatic 3-demethylation of caffeine and N-oxidation of carcinogenic arylamines. *Biochemistry* 1989;86: 7696–700.

141. Berthou F, Flinois J-P, Ratanasavanh D, Beaune P, Riche C, Guillouzo A. Evidence for the involvement of several cytochromes P-450 in the first steps of caffeine metabolism by human liver microsomes. *Drug Metab Dispos* 1991;19:561–7.

142. Lelo A, Kjellen G, Birkett DJ, Miners JO. Paraxanthine metabolism in humans: determination of metabolic partial clearances and effects of allopurinol and cimetidine. *J Pharmacol Exp Ther* 1989;248:315–9.

143. Joeres R, Klinker H, Heusler H, et al. Factors influencing the caffeine test for cytochrome P 448-dependent liver function. *Arch Toxicol* 1987;60:93–4.

144. Warszawski D, Ben-Zvi Z, Gorodischer R. Caffeine metabolism in liver slices during postnatal development in the rat. *Biochem Pharmacol* 1981;30:3145–50.

145. Warszawski D, Ben-Zvi Z, Gorodischer R, Arnaud MJ, Bracco I. Urinary metabolites of caffeine in young dogs. *Drug Metab Dispos* 1982;10:424–8.

146. Aldridge A, Neims AH. Relationship between the clearance of caffeine and its 7-N-demethylation in developing beagle puppies. *Biochem Pharmacol* 1980;29:1909–14.

147. Anderson KE, Conney AH, Kappas A. Nutritional influences on chemical biotransformations in humans. *Nutr Rev* 1982;40:161–71.

148. Vesell ES. Complex effects of diet on drug disposition. *Clin Pharmac Ther* 1984;36:285–96.

149. Mitchell MC, Hoyumpa AM, Schenker S, Johnson RF, Nichols S, Patwardhan RV. Inhibition of caffeine elimination by short-term ethanol administration. *J Lab Clin Med* 1983; 101:826–34.

150. Vistisen K, Loft S, Poulsen HE. Cytochrome P450IA2 activity in man measured by caf-

feine metabolism: effect of smoking, broccoli and exercise. In: Witmer, et al. eds. *Biological reactive intermediates* IV. New York: Plenum Press, 1990;407–11.

151. Blanchard J, Hochman D. Effects of vitamin C on caffeine pharmacokinetics in young and aged guinea pigs. *Drug Nutrient Interactions* 1984;2:243–55.

152. Levy M, Granit L, Zylber-Katz E. Chronopharmacokinetics of caffeine in healthy volunteers. *Annual Review Chronopharmacol* 1984;1:97–100.

153. Collomp K, Anselme F, Audran M, Gay JP, Chanal JL, Prefaut C. Effects of moderate exercise on the pharmacokinetics of caffeine. *Eur J Clin Pharmacol* 1991;40:279–82.

154. Kaminori GH, Somani SM, Knowlton RG, Perkins RM. The effects of obesity and exercise on the pharmacokinetics of caffeine in lean and obese volunteers. *Eur J Clin Pharmacol* 1987;31:595–600.

155. Zysset T, Wietholtz H. Pharmacokinetics of caffeine in patients with decompensated Type I and Type II diabetes mellitus. *Eur J Clin Pharmacol* 1991;41:449–52.

156. Arnaud MJ, Bracco I, Gétaz F. Synthesis of ring labelled caffeine for the study of metabolic and pharmacokinetics mouse interstrain differences in relation to pharmacologic and toxic effects. In: *Synthesis and applications of isotopically labelled compounds*. Baillie TA, Jones RJ, ed. Amsterdam: Elsevier Sci Publ BV; 1989;645–8.

157. Dorrbecker SH, Ferraina RA, Dorrbecker BR, Kramer PA. Caffeine and paraxanthine pharmacokinetics in the rabbit: concentration and product inhibition effects. *J Pharmacokinetics and Biopharmaceutics* 1987;15:117–32.

158. Arnaud MJ. Products of metabolism of caffeine. In: *Caffeine*. Dews PB, ed. Berlin: Springer-Verlag, 1984;3–38.

159. Arnaud MJ. The pharmacology of caffeine. *Progress in Drug Research* 1987;31:273–313.

160. Anon. *IARC Monographs on the evaluation of carcinogenic risks to humans, coffee, tea, maté, methylxanthines and methylglyoxal* 1991;51.

161. Bergmann F, Dikstein S. Studies on uric acid and related compounds. III Observation on the specificity of mammalian xanthine oxidase. *J Biol Chem* 1956;223:765–80.

162. Grygiel JJ, Wing LMH, Farkas J, Birkett DJ. Effects of allopurinol on theophylline metabolism and clearance. *Clin Pharmac Ther* 1979;26:660–7.

163. Manfredi RL, Vesell ES. Inhibition of theophylline metabolism by long-term allopurinol administration. *Clin Pharmac Ther* 1981;29:224–9.

164. Grant DM, Tang BK, Campbell ME, Kalow W. Effect of allopurinol on caffeine disposition in man. *Br J Clin Pharmac* 1986;21:454–58.

165. Bory C, Baltassat P, Porthault M, Bethenod M, Frederich A, Aranda JV. Metabolism of theophylline to caffeine in premature newborn infants. *J Pediatr* 1979;94:988–93.

166. Bada HS, Khanna NN, Somani SM, Tin AA. Interconversion of theophylline and caffeine in newborn infant. *J Pediatr* 1979;94:993–5.

167. Desmond PV, Patwardhan RV, Parker R, Schenker S, Speeg KV. Effect of cimetidine and other antihystamines on the elimination of aminopyrine, phenacetin and caffeine. *Life Sci* 1980;26:1261–8.

168. Arnaud MJ, Thelin-Doerner A, Ravussin E, Acheson KJ. Study of the demethylation of [1,3,7-Me-^{13}C]caffeine in man using respiratory exchange measurements. *Biomed Mass Spectrom* 1980;7:521–4.

169. Arnaud MJ, Richli U, Philippossian G. Isolation and identification of paraxanthine glucuronide as the major caffeine metabolite in mice. *Experientia* 1986;42:696.

170. Rao GS, Khanna KL, Cornish HH. Identification of two new metabolites of caffeine in the rat urine. *Experientia* 1973;19:953–5.

171. Arnaud MJ, Ben-Zvi Z, Yaari A, Gorodischer R. 1,3,8-Trimethylallantoin: a major caffeine metabolite formed by rat liver. *Res Comm Chem Path Pharmac* 1986;52:407–410.

172. Kamei K, Matsuda M, Momose A. New sulfur-containing metabolites of caffeine. *Chem Pharm Bull (Tokyo)* 1975;23:683–5.

173. Rafter JJ, Nilsson L. Involvement of the intestinal microflora in the formation of sulfur-containing metabolites of caffeine. *Xenobiotica* 1981;11:771–8.

174. Arnaud MJ and Welsch C. Metabolic pathway of theobromine in the rat and identification of two new metabolites in human urine. *J Agric Food Chem* 1979;27:524–7.

175. Arnaud MJ, Welsch C. Metabolism of [1-Me^{14}C]paraxanthine in the rat: identification of a new metabolite. *Experientia* 1979;35:34.

176. Latini R, Bonati M, Marzi E, Garattini S. Urinary excretion of an uracilic metabolite from caffeine by rat, monkey and man. *Toxicology Letters* 1981;7:267–72.

177. Gorodischer R, Zmora E, Ben-Zvi Z, et al. Urinary metabolites of caffeine in the premature infant. *Eur J Clin Pharmac* 1986;31:497–9.
178. Tang BK, Grant DM, Kalow W. Isolation and identification of 5-acetylamino-6-formylamino-3-methyluracil as a major metabolite of caffeine in man. *Drug Metab Dispos* 1983;11: 218–20.
179. Grant DM, Tang BK, Kalow W. Polymorphic N-acetylation of a caffeine metabolite. *Clin Pharmac Ther* 1983;33:355–9.
180. Evans DPA, White TA. Human acetylation polymorphism. *J Lab Clin Med* 1964;63: 394–403.
181. Grant DM, Tang BK, Kalow W. Variability in caffeine metabolism. *Clin Pharmac Ther* 1983;33:591–602.
182. Yesair DW, Branfman AR, Callahan MM. In: *The methylxanthine beverages and foods: chemistry, consumption and health effects.* New York: Alan R Liss Inc: 1984;215–233.
183. Ferrero JL, Neims AH. Metabolism of caffeine by mouse liver microsomes: GSH or cytosol causes a shift in products from 1,3,7-trimethylurate to a substituted diaminouracil. *Life Sci* 1983;33:1173–8.
184. Grant DM, Tang BK, Kalow W. A simple test for acetylation phenotype using caffeine. *Br J Clin Pharmacol* 1984;17:459–64.
185. Hardy BG, Lemieux C, Walter SE, Bartle WR. Interindividual and intraindividual variability in acetylation: characterization with caffeine. *Clin Pharmacol Ther* 1988;44:152–7.
186. Evans WE, Relling MV, Petros WP, Meyer WH, Mirro J, Crom WR. Dextromethorphan and caffeine as probes for simultaneous determination of debrisoquin-oxidation and N-acetylation phenotypes in children. *Clin Pharmacol Ther* 1989;45:568–73.
187. Tang BK, Zubovits T, Kalow W. Determination of acetylated caffeine metabolites by high-performance exclusion chromatography. *J Chromatogr* 1986;375:170–3.
188. Tang BK, Kadar D, Kalow W. An alternative test for acetylator phenotyping with caffeine. *Clin Pharmacol Ther* 1987;42:509–13.
189. Kilbane AJ, Silbart LK, Manis M, Beitins IZ, Weber WW. Human N-acetylation genotype determination with urinary caffeine metabolites. *Clin Pharmacol Ther* 1990;47:470–7.
190. Kalow W. Pharmacoanthropology: drug metabolism. *Fed Proc* 1984;43:2326–31.
191. Campbell ME, Grant DM, Tang BK, Kalow W. Biotransformation of caffeine, paraxanthine, theophylline and theobromine by polycyclic aromatic hydrocarbon-inducible cytochrome(s) P-450 in human liver microsomes. *Drug Metab Dispos* 1987;15:237–49.
192. Campbell ME, Spielberg SP, Kalow W. A urinary metabolic ratio that reflects systemic caffeine clearance. *Clin Pharmacol Ther* 1987;42:157–65.
193. Kadlubar FF, Talaska G, Butler MA, Teitel CH, Massengill JP, Lang NP. Determination of carcinogenic arylamine N-oxidation phenotype in humans by analysis of caffeine urinary metabolites. *Prog Clin Biol Res* 1990;340:107–14.
193a. Butler MA, Lang NP, Young JF, et al. Determination of CYP1A2 and acetyltransferase phenotypes in human populations by analysis of caffeine urinary metabolites. *Pharmacogenetics* 1992 (in press).
194. Kalow W, Tang B-K. Use of caffeine metabolic ratios to explore CYP1A2 and xanthine oxidase activities. *Clin Pharmacol Ther* 1991;50:508–19.
195. Scott NR, Chakraborty J, and Marks V. Urinary metabolites of caffeine in pregnant women. *Br J Clin Pharmac* 1986;22:475–8.
196. Bologa M, Tang B, Klein J, Tesoro A, Koren G. Pregnancy-induced changes in drug metabolism in epileptic women. *J Pharmacol Exp Ther* 1991;257:735–40.
197. Kalow W, Tang BK. Caffeine as a metabolic probe: exploration of the enzyme-inducing effect of cigarette smoking. *Clin Pharmacol Ther* 1991;49:44–8.
198. Blanchard J, Sawers SJA, Jonkman JHG, Tang-Liu D-S. Comparison of the urinary metabolite profile of caffeine in young and elderly males. *Br J Clin Pharmac* 1985;19:225–32.
199. Carrier O, Pons G, Rey E, et al. Maturation of caffeine metabolic pathways in infancy. *Clin Pharmacol Ther* 1988;44:145–51.
200. Pons G, Rey E, Carrier O, et al. Maturation of AFMU excretion in infants. *Fundam Clin Pharmacol* 1989;3:589–95.
201. Boda D, Németh I. Measurement of urinary caffeine metabolites reflecting the in vivo xanthine oxidase activity in premature infants with RDS and in hypoxic states of children. *Biomed Biochim Acta* 1989;48:S31–5.
202. Levitsky LL, Schoeller DA, Lambert GH, Edidin DV. Effect of growth hormone therapy

in growth hormone-deficient children on cytochrome P-450-dependent 3-N-demethylation of caffeine as measured by the caffeine $^{13}CO_2$ breath test. *Dev Pharmacol Ther* 1989;12: 90–5.

203. Bienvenu T, Pons G, Rey E, et al. Effect of growth hormone on caffeine metabolism in hypophysectomized rats. *Drug Metab Dispos* 1990;18:327–30.

204. Tarrús E, Cami J, Roberts DJ, Spickett RGW, Celdran E, Segura J. Accumulation of caffeine in healthy volunteers treated with furafylline. *Br J Clin Pharmac* 1987;23:9–18.

205. Sesardic D, Boobis AR, Murray BP, et al. Furafylline is a potent and selective inhibitor of cytochrome P-450IA2 in man. *Br J Clin Pharmac* 1990;29:651–63.

206. Fuhr U, Wolff T, Harder S, Schymanski P, Staib AH. Quinolone inhibition of cytochrome P-450-dependent caffeine metabolism in human liver microsomes. *Drug Metab Dispos* 1990;18:1005–10.

207. Bechtel YC, Joanne C, Grandmottet M, Bechtel PR. The influence of insulin-dependent diabetes on the metabolism of caffeine and the expression of the debrisoquin oxidation phenotype. *Clin Pharmacol Ther* 1988;44:408–17.

208. Denaro C, Benowitz N. Diabetic patients and hepatic drug metabolism. *Clin Pharmacol Ther* 1989;45:695–6.

209. Lambert GH, Schoeller DA, Humphrey HEB, et al. The caffeine breath test and caffeine urinary metabolite ratios in the Michigan cohort exposed to polybrominated biphenyls: a preliminary study. *Environ Health Perspect* 1990;89:175–81.

210. Handler P, Dann WJ. The inhibition of rat growth by nicotinamide. *J Biol Chem* 1942;146: 357–68.

211. McKennis H, Bowman ER, Horvath A, Bederka JP. Metabolic release of methyl groups from a series of N-methylpyridinium compounds. *Nature* 1964;202:699–700.

212. Komori Y, Sendju Y. Zur kenntnis der Vergleichenden Biochemie. III. Mitteilung. über das Verhalten der Nikotinsäure im Orgasnismus der Saugetiere und der Vogel. *J Biochem* (Tokyo) 1926;6:163–9.

213. Ackerman D. Über das Vorkommen von Trigonellin und Nikotinsäure im Harn nach Verfütterung von Nikotinsäure. *Z Biol* 1913;59:17–22.

214. Huff JW, Perlzweig WA. N-Methylnicotinamide, a metabolite of nicotinic acid in the urine. *J Biol Chem* 1943;150:395–400.

215. Knox WE, Grossman WI. A new metabolite of nicotinamide. *J Biol Chem* 1946;166:391–2.

216. WuChang ML, Johnson BC. N-Methyl-4-pyridone-5-carboxamide, a new major normal metabolite of nicotinic acid in rat urine. *J Biol Chem* 1959;234:1817–21.

217. Bonavita V, Narrod SA, Kaplan NO. Metabolites of nicotinamide in mouse urine: effects of azaserine. *J Biol Chem* 1961;236:936–9.

218. Lee YU, Gholson RK, Raica N. Isolation and identification of two new nicotinamide metabolites. *J Biol Chem* 1956;244:3277–82.

219. Mason JB, Kodicek E. The metabolism of niacytin in the rat. Trigonelline as a major metabolite of niacytin in the urine. *Biochem J* 1970;120:515–21.

220. Czok G, Walter W, Knoche K, Degener H. Über die Resorbierbarkeit von Chlorogensäure durch die Ratte. *Z Ernährungswiss* 1974;13:108–12.

221. Booth AN, Emerson OH, Jones TT, DeEds F. Urinary metabolites of caffeic and chlorogenic acids. *J Biol Chem* 1957;229:51–9.

222. Teuchy H, van Sumere CF. The metabolism of [1-^{14}C]phenylalanine, [3-^{14}C]cinnamic acid and [2-^{14}C]ferulic acid in the rat. *Arch Internat Physiol Biochim* 1971;79:589–618.

223. Westendorf J, Czok G. Die biliäre Ausscheidung choleretisch aktiver Zimtsäure-Derivate durch die Ratte. *Z Renährungswiss* 1983;22:255–70.

224. Shaw NKF, Gutenstein M, Jepson JB. Intestinal flora and diet in relation to m-hydroxyphenyl acids of human urine. In: Sissakian NM, ed. *Proc of the 5th Int Cong Biochem.* Moscow 1961. Oxford: Pergamon Press, 1963;5:427.

225. Scheline RR, Midtvedt T. Absence of dehydroxylation of caffeic acid in germ-free rats. *Experientia* 1970;26:1068–9.

226. Peppercorn MA, Goldman P. Caffeic acid metabolism by bacteria of the human gastrointestinal tract. *Proc Natl Acad Sci USA*; 1972;69:1413–5.

227. Jacobson EA, Newmark H, Baptista J, Bruce WR. A preliminary investigation of the metabolism of dietary phenolics in humans. *Nutr Rep Int* 1983;28:1409–17.

228. Cotran R, Kendrick MI, Kass EH. Role of intestinal bacteria in aromatization of quinic acid in man and guinea pig. *Proc Soc Exp Biol Med* 1960;104:424–6.

229. Adamson RH, Bridges JW, Evans ME, Williams RT. Species differences in the aromatization of quinic acid in vivo and the role of gut bacteria. *Biochem J* 1970;116:437–43.
230. Indahl SR, Scheline RR. Quinic acid aromatization in the rat. Urinary hippuric acid and catechol excretion following the singular or repeated administration of quinic acid. *Xenobiotica* 1973;3:549–56.
231. Asatoor AM. Aromatization of quinic acid and shikimic acid by bacteria and the production of urinary hippurate. *Biochem Biophys Acta* 1965;100:290–2.
232. Catanese B, Barillari G, Iorio E, Pini L. Studies on the oral absorption of ibuprofen guaiacol-ester in man. *Boll Chim Farm* 1982;121:567–72.
233. Vandenheuvel WJA, Smith JL, Silber RH. β-(2-Methoxyphenoxy)lactic acid, the major urinary metabolite of glyceryl guaiacolate in man. *J Pharm Sci* 1972;61:1997–8.
234. Anon. *IARC monographs on the evaluation of the carcinogenic risk of chemicals to humans. Allyl compounds, aldehydes, epoxides and peroxides* 1985;36:75–97.
235. Sutton JD, Sangster SA, Caldwell J. Dose-dependent variation in the disposition of eugenol in the rat. *Biochem Pharmacol* 1985;34:465–6.
236. Solheim E, Scheline RR. Metabolism of alkenebenzene derivatives in the rat. II. Eugenol and isoeugenol methyl ethers. *Xenobiotica* 1976;6:137–50.
237. Solheim E, Scheline RR. Metabolism of alkenebenzene derivatives in the rat I. p-Methoxyallylbenzene (Estragole) and p-methoxypropenylbenzene (Anethole). *Xenobiotica* 1973;3:493–510.
238. Bock KW, v. Clausbruch UC, Winne D. Absorption and metabolism of naphthalene and benzo(a)pyrene in the rat jejunum in situ. *Med Biol* 1979;57:262–4.
239. Egestad B, Pettersson P, Sjövall J, Rafter J, Hyvönen K, Gustafsson J-A. Studies on the chromatographic fractionation of metabolites of benzo(a)pyrene in faeces and urine from germfree and conventional rats. *Biomed Chromatogr* 1987;2:120–34.
240. Gelboin HV. Benzo(a)pyrene metabolism, activation, and carcinogenesis: role and regulation of mixed-function oxidases and related enzymes. *Physiological Reviews* 1980;60:1107–66.
241. Chess EK, Thomas BL, Hendren DJ, Bean RM. Mass spectral characteristics of derivatized metabolites of benzo(a)pyrene. *Biomed Environ Mass Spectrom* 1988;15:485–93.
242. Finot PA, Magnenat E. Metabolic transit of early and advanced Maillard products. *Prog Food Nutr Sci* 1981;5:193–207.
243. Aeschbacher HU, Jaccaud E. Inhibition by coffee of nitrosourea-mediated DNA damage in mice. *Fd Chem Toxic* 1990;28:633–7.
244. Maga JA. Furans in food. *CRC Crit Rev Food Sci Nutr* 1979;11:355–400.
245. Ravindranath V, Burka LT, Boyd MR. Reactive metabolites from the bioactivation of toxic methylfurans. *Science* 1984;224:884–6.
246. Ravindranath V, McMenamin MG, Dees JH, Boyd MR. 2-Methylfuran toxicity in rats—role of metabolic activation in vivo. *Toxicol Appl Pharmacol* 1986;85:78–91.
247. Jellum E, Borresen HC, Eldjarn L. The presence of furan derivatives in patients receiving fructose-containing solutions intravenously. *Clin Chim Acta* 1973;47:191–201.
248. Germond J-E, Arnaud MJ. Synthesis of [U-14C]-labelled 5-hydroxymethyl-2-furaldehyde. *J Lab Comp Radiopharm* 1987;24:343–8.
249. Germond J-E, Philippossian G, Richli U, Bracco I, Arnaud MJ. Rapid and complete urinary elimination of [14C]-5-hydroxymethyl-2-furaldehyde administered orally or intravenously to rats. *J Toxicol Environ Health* 1987:22;79–89.
250. His W. Über das Stoffwechselproduct des Pyridins. *Arch f Exper Path u Pharmacol* 1887;22:253–60.
251. Baxter JH, Mason MF. Studies on the mechanisms of liver and kidney injury: IV. A comparison of the effects of pyridine and methyl pyridinium chloride in the rat. *J Pharmacol* 1947;91:350–6.
252. Okuda Y. Studies on the methylation of pyridine compound in animal organisms. III. The methylation pattern of pyridine in dog organisms dosed with pyridine. *J Biochemistry* 1959;46:967–71.
253. Smith JN. The glucuronic acid conjugation of hydroxyquinolines and hydroxypyridines in the rabbit. *Biochem J* 1953;55:156–60.
254. Neuhoff V, Köhler F. Biochemische Analyse des Stoffwechsels von 3-Acetylpyridin—Isolierung und Identifizierung von 6 Metaboliten. *Naunyn-Schmiedebergs Arch Pharmak, u Exp Path* 1966;254:301–26.

255. Gorrod JW, Damani LA. The metabolic N-oxidation of 3-substituted pyridines in various animal species in vivo. *Eur J Drug Metabolism and Pharmacokinetics* 1980;5:53–7.
256. Rennhard HH. The metabolism of ethyl maltol and maltol in dog. *J Agr Food Chem* 1971; 19:152–4.
257. Kikugawa K, Kato T, Takahashi S. Possible presence of 2-amino-3,4-dimethylimidazo[4,5-*f*]quinoline and other heterocyclic amine-like mutagens in roasted coffee beans. *J Agric Food Chem* 1989;37:881–6.
258. Gross GA, Wolleb U. 2-Amino-3,4-dimethylimidazo[4,5-*f*] quinoline is not detectable in commercial instant and roasted coffees. *J Agric Food Chem* 1991;39:2231–6.
259. Sjödin P, Jägerstad M. A balance study of ^{14}C-labelled ^{3}H-imidazo[4,5-*f*]quinoline-2-amines (IQ and MeIQ) in rats. *Fd Chem Toxic* 1984;22:207–10.
260. Alexander J, Holme JA, Wallin H, Becher G. Characterization of metabolites of the food mutagens 2-amino-3-methylimidazo[4,5-*f*]quinoline and 2-amino-3,4-dimethylimidazo[4,5-*f*]quinoline formed after incubation with rat liver cells. *Chem-Biol Interact* 1989;72:125–42.
261. Hall M, Shé MN, Wild D, Fasshauer I, Hewer A, Phillips DH. Tissue distribution of DNA adducts in CFD1 mice fed 2-amino-3-methylimidazo[4,5-*f*]quinoline (IQ) and 2-amino-3,4-dimethylimidazo[4,5-*f*]quinoline (MeIQ). *Carcinogenesis* 1990;11:1005–11.
262. Aeschbacher HU, Turesky RJ. Mammalian cell mutagenicity and metabolism of heterocyclic aromatic amines. *Mutation Res* 1991;259:235–50.
263. Hollstein M, Talcott R, Wei E. Quinoline: conversion to a mutagen by human and rodent liver. *J Natl Cancer Inst* 1978;60:405–10.
264. Tada M, Takahashi K, Kawazoe Y, Ito N. Binding of quinoline to nucleic acid in a subcellular microsomal system. *Chem Biol Interactions* 1980;29:257–66.
265. Tada M, Takahashi K, Kawazoe Y. Metabolites of quinoline, a hepatocarcinogen, in a subcellular microsomal system. *Chem Pharm Bull* 1982;30:3834–7.
266. Jerina DM, Dalyl JW, Witkop B, Zaltzman-Nirenberg P, Udenfriend S. 1,2-Naphthalene oxide as an intermediate in the microsomal hydroxylation of naphthalene. *Biochemistry* 1970;9:147–55.
267. Bock KW, Van Ackeren G, Lorch F, Birke FW. Metabolism of naphthalene to naphthalene dihydrodiol glucuronide in isolated hepatocytes and liver microsomes. *Biochem Pharmacol* 1976;25:2351–6.
268. Chen K-C, Dorough HW. Glutathione and mercapturic acid conjugations in the metabolism of naphthalene and 1-naphthyl N-methylcarbamate (Carbaryl). *Drug and Chemical Toxicol* 1979;2:331–54.
269. Bakke J, Struble C, Gustafsson J-A, Gustafsson B. Catabolism of premercapturic acid pathway metabolites of naphthalene to naphthols and methylthio-containing metabolites in rats. *Proc Natl Acad Sci USA* 1985;82:668–71.
270. Hesse S, Mezger M. Involvement of phenolic metabolites in the irreversible protein-binding of aromatic hydrocarbons: reactive metabolites of [^{14}C]naphthalene and [^{14}C]1-naphthol formed by rat liver microsomes. *Mol Pharmacol* 1979;16:667–75.
271. Schwarz LR, Mezger M, Hesse S. Effect of decreased glucuronidation and sulfation on covalent binding of naphthalene in isolated rat hepatocytes. *Toxicology* 1980;17:119–22.
272. O'Brien KAF, Smith LL, Cohen GM. Differences in naphthalene-induced toxicity in the mouse and rat. *Chem Biol Interactions* 1985;55:109–22.
273. Horning MG, Stillwell WG, Griffin GW, Tsang W-S. Epoxide intermediates in the metabolism of naphthalene by the rat. *Drug Metab Dispos* 1980;8:404–14.
274. Fry DW, Richardson KE. Isolation and characterization of glycolic acid dehydrogenase from human liver. *Biochem Biophys Acta* 1979;567:482–91.
275. Peters JW, Beitz DC, Young JW. Metabolism of glycolic acid in lactating and nonlactating goats and in calf. *J Dairy Sci* 1971;54:1509–17.
276. Hucker HB, Ahmad M, Miller EA. Absorption, distribution and metabolism of dimethylsulfoxide in the rat, rabbit and guinea pig. *J Pharm Exp Ther* 1966;154:176–84.
277. Hucker HB, Miller JK, Hochberg A, Brobyn RD, Riordan FH, Calesnick D. Studies on the absorption, excretion and metabolism of dimethylsulfoxide (DMSO) in man. *J Pharm Exp Ther* 1967;155:202,309–17.
278. Willhite CC, Katz PI. Toxicology updates: dimethyl sulfoxide. *J Appl Toxicology* 1984;4:155–60.
279. Neely WB. The metabolic fate of formaldehyde-^{14}C intraperitoneally administered to the rat. *Biochem Pharmacol* 1964;13:1137–42.

280. Hayashi T, Reece CA, Shibamoto T. Gas chromatographic determination of formaldehyde in coffee via thiazolidine derivative. *J Assoc Anal Chem* 1986;69:101–5.
281. Kasai H, Kumeno K, Yamaizumi Z, et al. Mutagenicity of methylglyoxal in coffee. *Gann* 1982;73:681–3.
282. Hayashi T, Shibamoto T. Analysis of methyl glyoxal in foods and beverages. *J Agric Food Chem* 1985;33:1090–3.
283. Aeschbacher HU, Wolleb U, Löliger J, Spadone JC, Liardon R. Contribution of coffee aroma constituents to the mutagenicity of coffee. *Fd Chem Toxic* 1989;27:227–32.
284. Nagao M, Fujita Y, Wakabayashi K, Nukaya H, Kosuge T, Sugimura T. Mutagens in coffee and other beverages. *Environ Health Perspectives* 1986;67:89–91.
285. Brandt RB, Siegel SA. Methylglyoxal production in human blood. *Ciba Found Symp* 1979; 67:211–23.
286. Ohmori S, Mori M, Shiraha K, Kawase M. Biosynthesis and degradation of methylglyoxal in animals. *Prog Clin Biol Res* 1989;290:397–412.
287. Baskaran S, Rajan DP, Balasubramanian KA. Formation of methylglyoxal by bacteria isolated from human faeces. *J Med Microbiol* 1989;28:211–5.
288. Sato J, Wang Y, van Eys. Methylglyoxal formation in rat liver cells. *J Biol Chem* 1980; 255:2046–50.
289. Riddle V, Lorenz FW. Nonenzymatic, polyvalent anion-catalyzed formation of methylglyoxal as an explanation of its presence in physiological systems. *J Biol Chem* 1968;243: 2718–24.
290. Fodor G, Mujumdar R, Szent-Gyorgyi A. Isolation of methylglyoxal from liver. *Proc Natl Acad Sci USA* 1978;75:4317–9.
291. Baskaran S, Balasubramanian KA. Purification and active site modification studies on glyoxalase-I from monkey intestinal mucosa. *Biochem Biophys Acta* 1987;913:377–85.
292. Neuberg C. Weitere Untersuchungen über die biochemische Umwandlung von Methylglyoxal in Milchsäure nebst Bemerkungen über die Entstehung der verschiedenen Milchsäuren in der Natur. *Biochem Z* 1913;51:484–508.
293. Dakin HD, Dudley HW. On glyoxalase. *J Biol Chem* 1913;14:423–31.
294. Saez GT, Blay P, Vina JR, Vina J. Glucose formation from methylglyoxal in rat hepatocytes. *Biochem Soc Trans* 1985;13:945–6.
295. Lam LKT, Sparnins VL, Wattenberg LW. Isolation and identification of kahweol and cafestol palmitate as active constituents of green coffee beans that enhance glutathione S-transferase activity in the mouse. *Cancer Res* 1982;42:1193–8.
296. Miller EG, McWhorter K, Rivera-Hidalgo F, Wright JM, Hirsbrunner P, Sunahara GI. Kahweol and cafestol: inhibitors of hamster buccal pouch carcinogenesis. *Nutr Cancer* 1991;15:41–6.
297. Aeschbach R, Kusy A, Maier HG. Diterpenoide im Kaffee I. Atractyligenin. *Z Lebensm Unters Forsch* 1982;175:337–41.
298. Mätzel U, Maier HG Diterpenoide im Kaffee II. Glykoside des Atractyligenins. *Z Lebensm Unters Forsch* 1983;176:281–4.
299. Obermann H, Spiteller G, Hoyer G-A. Struktur eines Menschenharn isolierten C19-Terpenoids-2β-Hydroxy-15-oxoatractylan-4α-carbonsäure. *Chem Ber* 1973;106:3506–18.
300. Ludwig H, Obermann H, Spiteller G. Atractyligenin-ein wesentlicher Bestandteil gerösteter Kaffeebohnen. *Chem Ber* 1974;107:2409–11.
301. Igimi H, Nishimura M, Kodama R, Ide H. Studies on the metabolism of d-limonene (p-mentha-1,8-diene) I. The absorption, distribution and excretion of d-limonene in rats. *Xenobiotica* 1974;4:77–84.
302. Kodama R, Yano T, Furukawa K, Noda K, Ide H. Studies on the metabolism of d-limonene (p-mentha-1,8-diene) IV Isolation and characterization of new metabolites and species differences in metabolism. *Xenobiotica* 1976;6:377–89.
303. Watabe T, Hiratsuka A, Ozawa N, Isobe M. A comparative study on the metabolism of d-limonene and 4-vinylcyclohex-1-ene by hepatic microsomes. *Xenobiotica* 1981;11: 333–44.
304. Webb DR, Ridder GM, Alden CL. Acute and subchronic nephrotoxicity of d-limonene in Fischer 344 rats. *Fd Chem Toxic* 1989;27:639–49.
305. Ishida T, Asakawa Y, Takemoto T, Aratani T. Terpenoids biotransformation in mammals III: Biotransformation of α-pinene, β-pinene, pinane, 3-carene, carane, myrcene, and p-cymene in rabbits. *J Pharm Sci* 1981;70:406–15.

306. Köppel C, Tenczer J, Tönnesmann U, Schirop Th, Ibe K. Acute poisoning with pine oil: metabolism of monterpenes. *Arch Toxicol* 1981;49:73–8.
307. Gould RG, Jones RJ, LeRoy GV, Wissler RW, Taylor CB. Absorbability of β-sitosterol in humans. *Metabolism* 1969;18:652–62.
308. Newton DF, Mansbach CM. β-Sitosterol as a nonabsorbable marker of dietary lipid absorption in man. *Clin Chim Acta* 1978;89:331–9.
309. Salen G, Ahrens EH, Grundy SM. Metabolism of β-sitosterol in man. *J Clin Invest* 1970; 49:952–67.
310. Bhattacharyya AK, Connor WE. β-Sitosterolemia and xanthomatosis. A newly described lipid storage disease in two sisters. *J Clin Invest* 1974;53:1033–43.
311. Bhattacharyya AK, Lopez LA. Absorbability of plant sterols and their distribution in rabbit tissues. *Biochem Biophys Acta* 1979;574:146–53.
312. Vahouny GV, Connor WE, Subramaniam S, Lin DS, Gallo LL. Comparative lymphatic absorption of sitosterol, stigmasterol, and fucosterol and differential inhibition of cholesterol absorption. *Am J Clin Nutr* 1983;37:805–9.
313. Viani R. Coffee. In: *Ullmann's encyclopedia of industrial chemistry.* Weinheim Verlag Chemie, 1986;A7:333–4.
314. Corinaldesi R, De Giorgio R, Stanghellini V, et al. Effect of the removal of coffee waxes on gastric acid secretion and serum gastrin levels in healthy volunteers. *Current Ther Res* 1989;46:13–8.
315. Thelle DS, Arnesen E, Forde OH. The Tromso heart study. Does coffee raise serum cholesterol? *N Engl J Med* 1983;308:1454–7.
316. Aro A, Tuomilehto J, Kostiainen E, Uusitalo U, Pietinen P. Boiled coffee increases serum low density lipoprotein concentration. *Metabolism* 1987;36:1027–30.
317. Zock PL, Katan MB, Merkus M, Van Dusseldorp M, Harryvan JL. Effect of a lipid-rich fraction from boiled coffee on serum cholesterol. *The Lancet* 1990;335:1235–7.
318. Ahola I, Jauhiainen M, Aro A. The hypercholesterolaemic factor in boiled coffee is retained by paper filter. *J Intern Med* 1991;230:293–7.
319. Van Dusseldorp M, Katan MB, Van Vliet T, Demacker PNM, Stalenhoef AFH. Cholesterol-raising factor from boiled coffee does not pass a paper filter. *Arteriosclerosis and Thrombosis* 1991;11:586–93.
320. Slotta KH, Neisser K. Zur Chemise des Kaffees. Die Gewinnung von Cafesterol und anderen Verbindungen aus dem Unverschifbaren des Kaffeeöls. *Ber Deut Chem Gesel* 1938;71;1991–4.
321. Kitts DD. Competitive binding of phytoestrogens in coffee extracts with 17β-estradiol to uterine cytosol receptors. *Can Inst Food Sci Technol J* 1986;19:191–4.
322. Chakravorty PN, Wesner MM, Levin RH. Cafesterol. *J Am Chem Soc* 1943;65:929–32.
323. Kitts DD. Studies on the estrogenic activity of a coffee extract. *J Toxicol Environ Health* 1987;20:37–49.
324. Boublik JH, Quinn MJ, Clements JA, Herington AC, Wynne KN, Funder JW. Coffee contains potent opiate receptor binding activity. *Nature* 1983;301:246–8.
325. Wynne KN, Familari M, Boublik JH, Drummer OH, Rae ID, Funder JW. Isolation of opiate receptor ligands in coffee. *Clin Exp Pharmacol Physiol* 1987;14:785–90.
326. Zanoboni A, Zanoboni-Muciaccia W. Effects of naxolone and coffee on anterior pituitary hormones. *Drugs Exptl Clin Res* 1987;XIII:443–6.
327. Iverson LL. Another cup of coffee? *Nature* 1983;195:301.
328. Kalsner S. A coronary vasoconstrictor substance is present in regular and "decaffeinated" forms of both percolated and instant coffee. *Life Sci* 1977;20:1689–96.
329. Tse SYH. Coffee contains cholinomimetic compound distinct from caffeine. I: Purification and chromatographic analysis. *J Pharma Sci* 1991;80:665–9.
330. Harland BF, Oberleas D. Phytate and zinc contents of coffees, cocoas, and teas. *J Food Sci* 1985;50:832,833,842.
331. Fujita Y, Wakabayashi K, Nagoa M, Sugimura T. Implication of hydrogen peroxide in the mutagenicity of coffee. *Mutation Res* 1985;144:227–30.
332. Ariza RR, Dorado G, Barbancho M, Pueyo C. Study of the causes of direct-acting mutagenicity in coffee and tea using the Ara test in *Salmonella typhimurium*. *Mutation Res* 1988; 201:89–96.
333. Ito A, Naito M, Watanabe H. Induction and characterization of gastroduodenal lesions in mice given continuous oral administration of hydrogen peroxide. *Gann* 1982;73:315–22.

Caffeine, Coffee, and Health,
edited by S. Garattini. Published by
Raven Press, Ltd., New York 1993.

4

Mechanism of Action of Caffeine

John William Daly

Laboratory of Bioorganic Chemistry, National Institute of Diabetes, Digestive, and Kidney Diseases, National Institutes of Health, Bethesda, Maryland 20892

Caffeine has pharmacological effects on the function of cardiovascular, respiratory, renal, and nervous systems. It appears that blockade of adenosine receptors by caffeine has a significant role in pharmacology, but effects on calcium storage, phosphodiesterases, and perhaps other, undefined targets cannot be excluded. In particular, the effects of caffeine on behavior are complex and are not readily explained by blockade of A_1- and/or A_2-adenosine receptors alone. Caffeine appears to affect function of norepinephrine, dopamine, serotonin, acetylcholine, GABA, and glutamate systems in brain. The relevance of alterations in function of such systems and of adenosine systems to the tolerance that develops during chronic caffeine treatment requires further study, as does the basis for the withdrawal syndrome after chronic caffeine treatment. Adenosine receptors are upregulated during chronic treatment with caffeine, but this alone does not fully explain the tolerance to a receptor antagonist.

The trimethylxanthine caffeine and two dimethylxanthines, theophylline and theobromine, occur in a variety of plants, some of which have been used for centuries in the preparation of beverages. Coffee beans (*Coffea arabica* and *C. robusto*), tea leaves (*Camelia theca*), maté leaves (*Ilex paraguayensis*), African kola nuts (*Cola nitada*), and guarana vines (*Panela supana*) contain mainly caffeine, while cocoa beans (*Theobroma cacao*) and, hence, chocolate contain mainly theobromine. These xanthines, in particular caffeine, represent the central stimulants most widely used by humans. Caffeine also is used as a flavor enhancer in carbonated beverages and various foods and as an adjunct in certain medicinals, including the analgesic propoxyphene, non-narcotic analgesics such as aspirin and phenacetin, ergotamine for treatment of migraine headaches, certain diuretics and cold-allergy remedies and, finally, alone as a somnolytic. The pharmacological activities of the natural methylxanthines—caffeine, theophylline, and theobromine—have engendered extensive investigation of effects in humans and animals, of the underlying mechanisms, and of possible therapeutic applications. In addition, there has been synthesis and pharmacological evaluation of a wide range of unnatural xanthines related in structure to caffeine.

Caffeine itself continues to be used by humans worldwide, in beverages and as a central stimulant and somnolytic. Caffeine does not maintain self-administration as do classic addictive drugs, yet there do seem to be reinforcing effects of caffeine with respect to self-administration (1,2). Avoidance of caffeine is a well-recognized phenomenon, particularly by individuals in which dysphoric, anxiety-like effects occur. Indeed, caffeine appears to be a drug whose consumption in many individuals is "titrated" only to levels at which unpleasant effects are not manifest. There are therapeutic applications for caffeine in bronchial asthma, and in the apnea of preterm infants, where it is less likely than theophylline to cause tachycardia. Caffeine was formerly used in the treatment of narcolepsy. In veterinary medicine, caffeine has been used as a cardiac and respiratory stimulant, a diuretic, and to improve sperm motility in artificial insemination. It has also been used in treatment of dermatitis. The beneficial effects of caffeine on physical and mental performance and in treatment of hyperkinetic children remain controversial.

Theophylline, like caffeine, is an effective central stimulant. It is used in the treatment of bronchial asthma and pulmonary edema and of apnea in preterm infants and has been used both in humans and in veterinary medicine as a myocardial stimulant to increase coronary flow, for example, in congestive heart failure, and as a diuretic in congestive kidney failure. Theophylline also has potential as an anti-inflammatory. Although caffeine and theophylline can induce tremors, theophylline in low doses may have potential in the treatment of essential tremor (3).

Theobromine, the least active as a central stimulant of the three naturally occurring methylxanthines, has been used in the treatment of asthma, as a cardiac stimulant, as a diuretic, and in veterinary medicine as a vasodilator.

The mechanism(s) underlying the pharmacological effects of caffeine and theophylline have been and remain controversial. Three hypotheses have been advanced: (a) mobilization of calcium; (b) inhibition of phosphodiesterases; and, most recently, (c) antagonism of adenosine receptors. At present, it is generally conceded that antagonism of adenosine receptors, at least in part, underlies the pharmacological effects of low doses of caffeine and theophylline, while inhibition of phosphodiesterases and mobilization of calcium become more significant at higher doses. A wide range of pharmacological effects of caffeine/theophylline are presented in Table 1. In many instances adenosine or adenosine analogs have pharmacological effects opposite to those of the methylxanthines (Table 1). Much further research is nonetheless needed to clarify our understanding of how caffeine affects human beings. The rapid development of tolerance to most in vivo effects of caffeine in humans and animals remains an enigma.

TABLE 1. *Comparison of pharmacological effects of methylxanthines and adenosine analogs*

System	Effect of caffeine/theophylline	Effect of adenosine analog
Cardiovascular		
Heart	Positive ionotropic/	Negative ionotropic/
Vasculature	chronotropic	chronotropic
Coronary	Dilation	Dilation
Renal	Dilation	Constriction
Peripheral	Dilation	Dilation
Central	Constriction	Dilation
Respiratory	Bronchodilation	Bronchodilation or
	Stimulation of respiration	Constriction
		Inhibition of Respiration
Renal	Diuresis	Antidiuresis
	Stimulation renin release	Inhibition renin release
Gastrointestinal	Stimulation of gastric secretion	Inhibition of gastric secretion
Smooth muscle	relaxation	relaxation
Adipose	Stimulation lipolysis	Inhibition lipolysis
Platelet	Inhibition aggregation	Inhibition aggregation
Central nervous	Stimulation	Depression

PHARMACOKINETICS

In vivo, the pharmacological response to any agent is dependent not only on its potency and efficacy, but also on its pharmacokinetics, which include rates of uptake, barriers to diffusion, metabolism to inactive or active metabolites, and rates of clearance. Not only the peak levels, but the area under a curve plotting levels versus time are critical to the duration and magnitude of the effects of an agent—especially the chronic effects. Caffeine has been studied extensively in this regard and is a rather exceptional agent (4,5). Uptake on oral administration is rapid, with peak plasma levels attained within 1 to 2 hours or less. There is little barrier to diffusion of caffeine, which equilibrates almost completely with total body water. There is no long-term accumulation and there is a relatively low level of binding ($\approx$20%) to plasma proteins. The half-life of caffeine in most species is of the order of 2 to 4 hours and is closely linked to metabolism; i.e., very small amounts of a dose of caffeine are excreted prior to metabolism in most species. In humans, less than 4% of ingested caffeine is excreted unchanged. Since liver metabolism of caffeine is rate-determining for clearance, reduced rates of metabolism in infants and in the case of hepatic impairment can increase the half-life for caffeine to several days. Drugs that inhibit or induce cytochrome P-450 liver enzymes markedly alter the kinetics for clearance of caffeine. Chronic dosing with caffeine itself seems to have little effect on clearance rates. An oral dose of 1 mg/kg in humans, roughly the equivalent of a cup of coffee, yields plasma levels of 1 to 2 μg/ml or 5–10 μM. Lethal doses of caffeine require administration of at least 50 mg/kg, yielding plasma levels of at least 250 μM. Metabolism of caffeine yields the pharmacologically active demethylated products theophylline, paraxanthine, theobromine, and the monomethylxanthines. In addition, inactive ring oxidized (urates) and ring-opened (uracils) metabolites are formed. The metabolic routes for caffeine are remarkably dependent on species. In humans, 70% of metabolism yields paraxanthine, which is further metabolized to 1- and 7-methylxanthines. Theophylline and theobromine also are formed, while ring-oxidized and ring-opened products are minor (5%). In contrast to humans, theophylline can be the major metabolite in other species. Only 60% of metabolism is via demethylation in the rat, in contrast to 95% in humans. Theophylline, paraxanthine, and theobromine are all formed in the rat. In mice, demethylation yields theobromine>paraxanthine>theophylline. Guinea pigs apparently metabolize caffeine slowly; 20% of a dose of caffeine is excreted unchanged with demethylated products representing nearly all of the remainder of the dose. In most species, clearance of caffeine is first order, but, in rats, saturation kinetics occur at doses of 40 mg/kg and greater. Such varied pharmacokinetics for caffeine makes it likely that in vivo effects, particularly chronic effects, will vary considerably in different species. Furthermore, the ease of distribution of caffeine across diffusion barriers—such as the blood-brain barrier—makes comparison of in vivo potency to other xanthines, such as theophylline, theobromine, etc., that do not distribute as well, strongly dependent on this aspect of pharmacokinetics. Compared to caffeine, the pharmacokinetics of other xanthines has been studied only to a limited extent.

MOLECULAR PHARMACOLOGY OF CAFFEINE

Blockade of Adenosine Receptors

Two major classes of adenosine receptors occur in vertebrate tissues (6–8). These receptors have been studied extensively in recent years. Methylxanthines, including caffeine, are the classic antagonists for adenosine receptors.

The high-affinity A_1 class is inhibitory to adenylate cyclase via a guanyl nucleotide binding protein (G_1). Such A_1 receptors, or closely related adenosine receptors, can also link via guanyl nucleotide binding proteins to other effector systems (for a review see ref. 9). These systems include stimulation of potassium channels, inhibition of calcium channels, and either inhibition or stimulation of phosphoinositide breakdown. Caffeine and other xanthines antagonize all of these A_1-adenosine receptor-mediated responses. A_1-adenosine receptors occur at high levels throughout the brain and are also present in heart, trachea, kidney, and fat cells. A variety of adenosine analogs, many of them highly selective for A_1 receptors, have been developed. Xanthine antagonists that are highly selective for A_1 receptors have also been developed.

A_1 receptors, through stimulation of potassium channels in cardiac and neuronal tissues, will increase rates of reversal of action potentials and, through hyperpolarization, cause a reduction of excitability. It was suggested that the stimulatory effects of caffeine at 10 μM on evoked potentials in hippocampal slices were due to a decrease in potassium conductance (10), and are opposite to those of adenosine. Activation of A_1 receptors in synaptic terminals can be inhibitory to calcium channels or to calcium-dependent excitation-secretion coupling (11–13). In brain synaptosomes, however, adenosine analogs appear to stimulate potassium flux (14) and to have no effect on N-type calcium channels (15). It has been proposed that the synaptic adenosine receptors that inhibit transmitter release may represent, at least in the neuromuscular junction, an A_1 class (16). Adenosine, through a theophylline-sensitive receptor—presumably of the A_1 class—activates a chloride conductance in hippocampal neurons (17).

The A_1 receptors in some cells are inhibitory to the phospholipase C that breaks down phosphoinositides to yield inositol triphosphate and diacylglycerides (18). Such effects are antagonized by xanthines. In kidney slices, adenosine and analogs stimulate phosphoinositide breakdown (19). Caffeine not only antagonizes the adenosine responses in kidney slices, but at 10 μM it stimulates phosphoinositide breakdown itself. In brain, adenosine receptors can either augment or inhibit histamine-evoked stimulation of phosphoinositide breakdown (20,21). Both the inhibitory and stimulatory inputs via adenosine receptors in various tissues to phosphoinositide pathways are blocked by xanthines.

The A_2 class of adenosine receptors is stimulatory to adenylate cyclase via a guanyl nucleotide binding protein (G_s). Two subclasses of A_2 receptors occur in vertebrate tissues (22,23): the so-called *high affinity subclass* A_{2A} occurs in the limbic system of brain, in platelets, in liver, and presumably in adrenal chromaffin cells, and some other peripheral cell types. The so-called *low affinity subclass* occurs in all brain regions, in fibroblasts, and presumably in certain other peripheral cell types. Adenosine analogs (CGS 21680, APEC) have been developed, that allow easy indentification of A_{2A} and A_{2B} receptors coupled to adenylate cyclase. Their use should clarify the tissue distribution of such receptors. A xanthine-sensitive A_2-type receptor is responsible for relaxation of smooth muscle, but it remains unclear whether it is coupled to adenylate cyclase or another effective system (24–26). A xanthine-insensitive adenosine receptor also appears to be present in smooth muscle and can cause relaxation (27). Another relatively xanthine-insensitive adenosine receptor, similar in other regards to an A_2 receptor, occurs in mast cells and causes activation and release of histamine and serotonin (28–30). Certain methylxanthines, including 3-isobutyl-1-methylxanthine and theophylline but not caffeine, can interfere with antigen-elicited activation of mast cells (30). Although adenosine analogs that are highly selective for A_{2A} receptors have been developed, there are no xanthine or other antagonists with more than a modest selectivity for A_2 receptors.

Structures of caffeine and other xanthines that are adenosine receptor antagonists are presented in Fig. 1, while the affinities, based on inhibition of radioligand binding to brain A_1 and A_2 adenosine receptors are presented in Table 2. Structures of adenosine analogs that are very potent agonists and/ or highly selective for A_1 or A_2 receptors are presented in Fig. 2, while affinities for brain A_1 and A_2 receptors are presented in Table 3. Such compounds represent useful tools for the delineation of mechanisms involved in

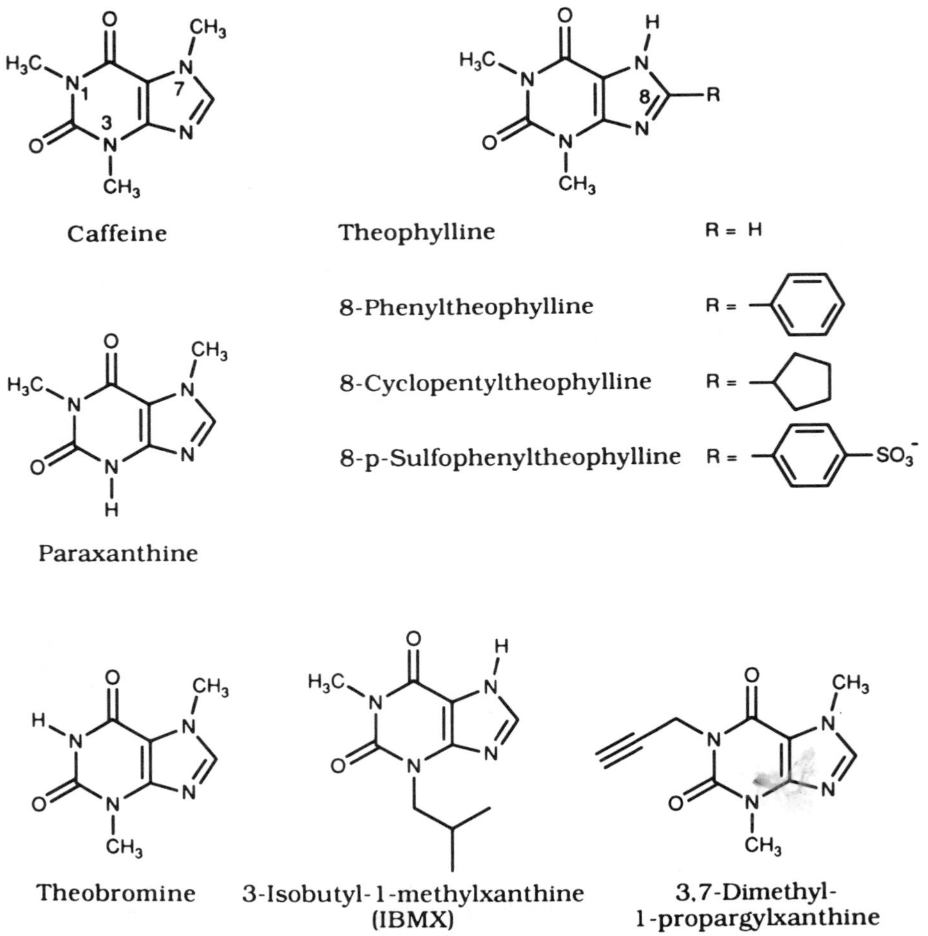

FIG. 1. Structures of caffeine, other natural xanthines, and synthetic xanthines: agents for the delineation of mechanism(s) involved in the actions of caffeine.

TABLE 2. *Affinities of xanthines for rat brain A_1 and A_2-adenosine receptors[a]*

Xanthine (X)[b]	K_1 (μM)[c]	
	A_1 Inhibition binding of [^{3}H]R-PIA rat brain membranes	A_{2A} Inhibition binding of [^{3}H]NECA rat striatal membranes
Caffeine	44 ± 16	40 ± 6
Theophylline	14 ± 3	22 ± 3
Theobromine	105 ± 6	40% Inhibition (250 μM)
Paraxanthine	33 ± 3	32 ± 3
Enprofylline (3-propylxanthine)	55 ± 6	137 ± 7
1,3,7-TripropylX	2.6 ± 0.4	13 ± 0.4
1,3,7-TripropargylX	3.0 ± 0.3	4.5 ± 0.7
3,7-Dimethyl-1-propargylX	45 ± 4	16 ± 4
IBMX (3-Isobutyl-1-methylX)	7 ± 2	16 ± 1
1,3-DipropylX	0.7 ± 0.3	6.6 ± 0.5
8-Cyclopentyltheophylline	0.024 ± 0.007	1.4 ± 0.2
8-Phenyltheophylline	0.40 ± 0.15	1.5 ± 0.1
8-p-Sulfophenyltheophylline	4.5 ± 0.5	6.1 ± 0.7

[a] Inhibition by xanthines of binding of [^{3}H]N^6-R-phenylisopropyladenosine (R-PIA) to A_1 receptors of rat brain membranes or of inhibition of binding of [^{3}H]N-ethylcarboxamidoadenosine (NECA) to A_{2A} receptors of rat striatal membranes in the presence N^6-cyclopentyladenosine to block A_1 receptors was assessed.
[b] For structures see Fig. 1.
[c] Values are means ± S.E.M. for published or unpublished data of our laboratory.

the actions of caffeine. Adenosine receptors exhibit somewhat different agonist and antagonist potencies in different species, but such differences are modest and should not prevent the potential use of various xanthines and adenosine analogs as tools to investigate the mechanism(s) underlying the in vivo pharmacology of caffeine. Caffeine is a relatively weak antagonist for adenosine receptors ($K_i \approx 40$–50 μM), and is virtually nonselective. Theophylline is at least twice as potent ($K_i \approx 15$ μM) but, again, is virtually nonselective. Theobromine is a very weak antagonist for adenosine receptors—more potent at A_1 ($K_i \approx 100$ μM) than at A_2 receptors. Paraxanthine, a major metabolite of caffeine, is somewhat more potent than caffeine at A_1 and A_2 receptors in humans and mice. A wide range of xanthines, analogous to caffeine but varying in the substituents at the 1-, 3- and 7-position, are available and, although some are much more potent adenosine receptor antagonists than caffeine, none are markedly selective for A_1 or A_2 receptors (31,32). The 8-cyclopentyl analogs of theophylline are highly selective for A_1 receptors (33,34); 1-propargyl-3,7-dimethylxanthine is somewhat selective for A_2 receptors (35); the 1,3,7-tripropargyl and 1,3,7-tripropyl analogs of caffeine are relatively potent adenosine antagonists (Table 2), but the former is a behavioral stimulant like caffeine, while the latter is a behavioral depressant (36). 3-Isobutyl-1-methylxanthine (IBMX) is a theophylline analog that is a behavioral depressant rather than a stimulant (36–38). The 8-p-sulfophenyl-

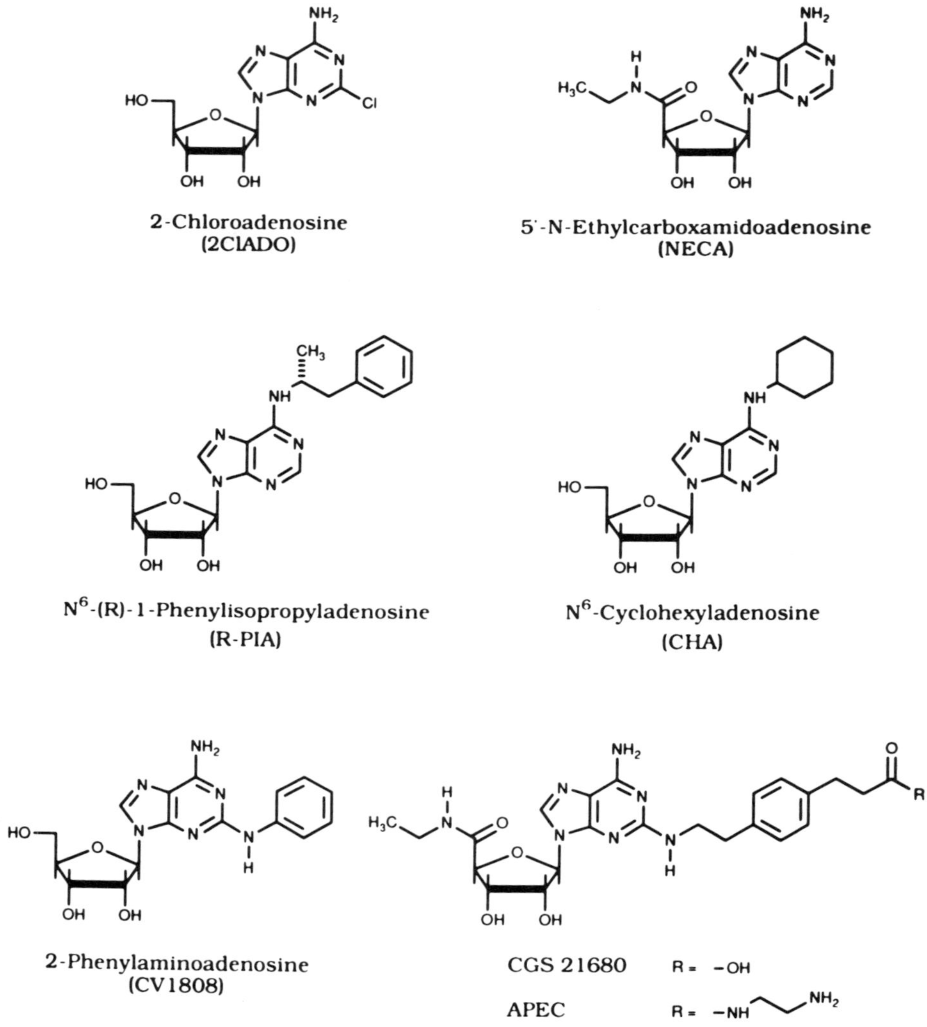

2-Chloroadenosine
(2ClADO)

5'-N-Ethylcarboxamidoadenosine
(NECA)

N^6-(R)-1-Phenylisopropyladenosine
(R-PIA)

N^6-Cyclohexyladenosine
(CHA)

2-Phenylaminoadenosine
(CV1808)

CGS 21680   R = —OH

APEC   R = —NH

FIG. 2. Structures of adenosine analogs: agents for the delineation of mechanism(s) involved in the actions of caffeine.

xanthines are active adenosine antagonists (39) that, because of the anionic sulfo group, will not penetrate into cells or across the blood-brain barrier (40) and therefore have minimal behavioral activity (37). There is extensive literature (22,23,31–34,39,41 and references therein) on structure activity relationships for xanthines at adenosine receptors.

The adenosine analogs that have been developed are metabolically more

TABLE 3. *Affinities of adenosine analogs for rat brain A_1 and A_2 adenosine receptors[a]*

Adenosine (Ado) Analog[b]	K_1 (nM)[c]	
	A_1 Inhibition binding [^{3}H]R-PIA	A_{2A} Inhibition binding [^{3}H]NECA
2-ChloroAdo	5.8 ± 1.0	69 ± 4
NECA	5.1 ± 0.3	12 ± 0.7
N^6-R-PhenylisopropylAdo	1.2 ± 0.1	160 ± 11
N^6-S-PhenylisopropylAdo	53 ± 8	6200 ± 360
N^6-CyclohexylAdo	0.85 ± 0.15	460 ± 40
N^6-CyclopentylAdo	0.32 ± 0.03	510 ± 120
2-PhenylaminoAdo (CV 1808)	300 ± 50	140 ± 19
CGS 21680	1800 ± 100	19 ± 10
APEC	99 ± 12	5.7 ± 0.5

[a] For binding protocols see legend, Table 2. Adenosine cannot be assayed because of the presence of adenosine deaminase in binding paradigms.
[b] For structures see Fig. 2.
[c] Values are means ± S.E.M. for published or unpublished data of our laboratory.

stable than adenosine and, in most cases, are not actively taken up into cells. The question of penetration of adenosine analogs into brain remains controversial: peripheral antagonists such as the 8-p-sulfophenylxanthines do not block behavioral depressant effects of adenosine analogs, indicating that such effects are centrally mediated (35,37,42). One study reports that uptake of N^6-R-phenylisopropyladenosine (PIA) is minimal (43), while another reports brain levels adequate to bind to a significant portion of A_1 receptors (38).

Caffeine and theophylline have many pharmacological activities in vivo that are opposite to those of adenosine and adenosine analogs (Table 1). Such opposite effects are suggestive of a tonic influence of endogenous adenosine in many tissues, which can be blocked by caffeine, theophylline, or other xanthines. The potencies of caffeine and theophylline at adenosine receptors in vitro are certainly consonant with a partial blockade of reception in vivo at doses of caffeine or theophylline that have pharmacological rather than toxicological effects. Pharmacologically active concentrations of caffeine and theophylline in plasma and brain range from a threshold of 5–10 μM for mild central stimulation to about 50 μM in the treatment of asthma or apnea. At such concentrations the function of adenosine receptors will be partially blocked by the xanthines.

The relationship of brain concentrations of caffeine and theophylline to spontaneous behavioral activity of rodents was first reported in 1972 (44). This study was also the first to document the biphasic effects of xanthines on behavior—namely on dose-dependent stimulation reaching a maximum and then declining as the concentration of xanthine is increased further. This decline was later (36) postulated to be caused by inhibition of phosphodiesterases. The biphasic nature of locomotor responses to caffeine, theophylline and a somewhat A_2 selective xanthine (3,7-dimethyl-1-propargylxanthine) is illustrated in Fig. 3. Other studies have shown triphasic effects of caffeine on locomotor activity: depression at very low doses, followed by stimulation, followed again by depressant effects (37,38,45). Convulsions with caffeine or theophylline occur at about 250 μM. Such toxological concentrations of xanthines are more consonant with their effects on mobilization of calcium or with actions at benzodiazepine receptors.

In 1980, a comparison was made between the threshold for stimulation of locomotor activity in mice for caffeine and ten other xanthines and the affinity of those xanthines for brain A_1 receptors (37). Penetration of the xanthines into brain was also assessed. A relatively good correlation was found between the behavioral activity and the receptor affinity (Table 4). A notable exception was IBMX, which caused an inhibition of locomotor activity. IBMX, in addition to being an antagonist at adenosine receptors, is a very potent phosphodiesterase inhibitor. It was proposed that the depression in behavior by IBMX was due to inhibition of brain phosphodiesterases. The stimulatory xanthines reversed the depressant effects of N^6-R-phenylisopropyladenosine (37). Remarkably, IBMX also reversed the depressant effects of the adenosine analog even though it was depressant by itself. An explanation for this anomaly has not been forthcoming. It should be noted that a

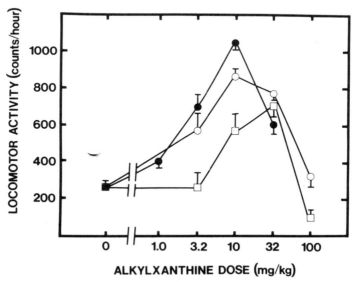

FIG. 3. Dose-dependent effects of xanthines on locomotor activity in mice. Caffeine (○); theophylline (□), 3,7-dimethyl-1-propargylxanthine (●). Activity measured by photocells in a circular arena for the 60-minute period following intraperitoneal injection of xanthine (35).

TABLE 4. Comparison of thresholds for stimulation of mouse locomotor activity by caffeine and other xanthines with their affinity for a brain A_1-adenosine receptor[a]

Xanthine	Penetration into brain (% of theory)			
	Threshold stimulation of locomotor activity (μmol/kg)	Threshold reversal depression of locomotor activity elicited by R-PIA (μmol/kg)	K_i (μM) Inhibition binding [^{3}H]cyclohexyladenosine to A_1 receptors rat brain membranes	Penetration into brain (% of theory)
7-(2-Chloroethyl) theophylline	2.5	10	5	19
Theophylline	10	5	12	58
Caffeine	25	5	25	63
Paraxanthine	20	10	15	26
7-(2-Hydroxyethyl) theophylline	30	10	50	32
Theobromine	250	250	75	29
3-Isobutyl-1-methylxanthine	Depression	2.5	25	15
8-Chlorotheophylline	Inactive	Inactive	250	13
1,9-Dimethylxanthine	Inactive	Inactive	Inactive	<10
Isocaffeine	Depression	Inactive	Inactive	11

[a] Values are from ref. 37, 38. See legend Fig. 4 for behavioral assay. Intraperitoneal injection of agents.

combination of either caffeine or theophylline with N^6-R-phenylisopropyladenosine not only reversed the depressant effects of the adenosine analog, but actually caused behavioral stimulation greater than that elicited by the xanthine alone as shown in Fig. 4. Combinations of low doses of N-ethylcarboxamidadenosine (NECA) with caffeine resulted in a stimulation of locomotor activity greater than that expected of caffeine alone (45). Further studies (38) demonstrated that those xanthines that had K_i values for A_1 receptors from 5–50 μM had thresholds for reversing the depressant effects of N^6-R-phenylisopropyladenosine ranging from 2.5 to 10 μmol/kg in mice (Table 4). IBMX was the most potent in this regard. The reversal of depression was greatest 30 to 60 minutes after injections. Caffeine was much more potent in reversing the depressant effects of an adenosine analog than in causing behavioral stimulation alone (38,45). Adenosine analogs, including N^6-R-phenylisopropyladenosine, N^6-cyclohexyladenosine and NECA, are very potent in causing reductions in locomotor activity (37,38,45–47). In addition to the anomalous behavioral super-stimulation by combinations of an adenosine analog and caffeine, combinations of depressant doses of IBMX and caffeine caused pronounced stimulation of locomotor activity (48). Thus, there appears a complex interplay of pathways or mechanisms underlying the pharmacology of xanthines and adenosine analogs in brain.

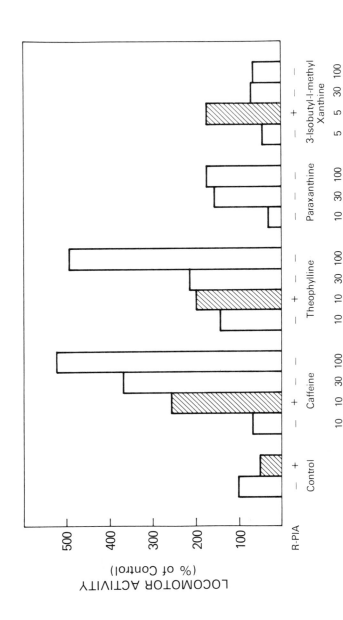

FIG. 4. Effects of xanthines alone and in combination with an adenosine analog on locomotor activity in mice. Activity measured by photocells in a square arena is plotted for the second 30-minute period following intraperitoneal injection of the xanthine and/or N[6]-R-phenylisopropyladenosine (R-PIA), the latter at 0.2 μmol/kg. Values derived from ref. 37 and 38. Note the depressant effects of the lowest dose of caffeine and paraxanthine and the stimulatory effect of R-PIA (hatched bars) in the presence of a low dose of a methylxanthine.

The early behavioral studies had been preceded by nearly a decade of research that showed that xanthines do block adenosine receptors, beginning with the geminal studies of Theodore W. Rall and coworkers with A_{2B}-adenosine receptors of brain slices (49,50). Antagonism of biological responses to an adenosine analog by a xanthine, usually theophylline, 8-phenyltheophylline, or 8-p-sulfophenyltheophylline, is now one criterion for the involvement of a membrane A_1 or A_2 adenosine receptor. The past 10 years have seen many studies supporting the adenosine hypothesis for the in vivo action of caffeine and other xanthines, but there also have been studies suggesting that other mechanisms also are involved (see below).

Inhibition of Phosphodiesterases and Other Effects on Nucleoside or Nucleotide Metabolism

The earlier hypothesis that caffeine and other methylxanthines owed their pharmacological activity to inhibition of phosphodiesterase stemmed from the ability of caffeine to augment glucagon-stimulated accumulation of a "heat-stable factor," later shown to be cyclic AMP (51). Potentiation of the action of a hormone by a methylxanthine became one of the criteria for an involvement of cyclic adenosine monophosphate (AMP). Caffeine and theophylline are relatively weak phosphodiesterase inhibitors, however, and had to be used at concentrations of 0.2 to 1 mM—concentrations not commensurate with the in vivo levels at which caffeine and theophylline exhibit most pharmacological actions. Furthermore, the augmentation of cyclic AMP accumulations by methylxanthines in certain tissues, most notably fat cells, were probably due to blockade of an A_1 receptor inhibitory to adenylate cyclase rather than to inhibition of phosphodiesterase. The inability of caffeine and theophylline to increase brain levels of cyclic AMP (52) is not strong evidence against a role for inhibition of phosphodiesterase in their neuropharmacology, since inhibition of a phosphodiesterase isozyme in certain morphological compartments could lead to an increase in cyclic AMP, undetectable when assessed in total brain homogenates. Other studies have shown increases in brain cyclic AMP after very high doses of caffeine or theophylline (53–55).

Stronger evidence that inhibition of phosphodiesterase by caffeine/theophylline does not underlie activities of xanthines as behavioral stimulants comes from the observation that nonxanthine phosphodiesterase inhibitors are behavioral depressants (56) and that, in a series of xanthines, those that are relatively potent inhibitors of a brain calcium-independent cyclic AMP-specific phosphodiesterase (rolipram-sensitive type IV subfamily, see ref. 57) were behavioral depressants even though they are adenosine receptor antagonists (36). The behavioral activities and potencies for a series of xanthines at A_1 and A_2 adenosine receptors and as inhibitors of the brain cyclic AMP-

TABLE 5. *Comparison of behavioral locomotor effects of xanthines with potencies at brain adenosine receptors and as inhibitors of a brain calcium-independent cyclic AMP-specific phosphodiesterase (PDE)*

Xanthine (X)	Locomotor activity mouse % of Control at 100 μmol/kg[a]	Affinity for brain receptors[b] Mouse A_1	Rat A_{2A} K_i, μM	Inhibition rat Ca^{2+}-independent PDE[c] IC_{50}, μM
Caffeine	220	59	40	480
Theophylline	280	15	22	670
3-Isobutyl-1-methylX	22	7	16	16
1,3,7-TripropylX	0	4	13	2
1,3,7-TripropargylX	260	4	5	97
1,7-Dimethyl-3-propargylX	250	20	46	220
3,7-Dimethyl-1-propargylX	200	22	16	200
1,3-Dipropyl-7-methylX	4	3	10	9
1,7-Dimethyl-3-propylX	81	18	40	73
1,3-Dimethyl-7-propylX	160	31	74	280
7-Benzyl-3-isobutyl-1-methylX	130	7	32	41
1,3-DipropylX	4	1.4	7	13
3-PropylX (Enprofylline)	120	55	137	180

[a] Values are from ref. 36. Intraperitoneal injection.
[b] For binding assay protocols see legend, Table 2. Values are from ref. 36 or are published or unpublished data from our laboratory.
[c] Values are from ref. 36.

specific phosphodiesterase are presented in Table 5. Rolipram, a nonxanthine-selective inhibitor of the cyclic AMP-specific phosphodiesterase, caused reduction in behavioral activity, as did high doses of theophylline and IBMX (58). Rolipram is now being evaluated as an antidepressant (59).

A xanthine denbufylline (1,3-dibutyl-7-(2′-oxopropyl)xanthine), that was highly active as an inhibitor of the cyclic AMP-specific phosphodiesterase, (60) enhanced excitability of hippocampal neurons as does IBMX (61,62). It is premature to conclude, however, that inhibition of phosphodiesterases by xanthines is the sole determinant of excitation in hippocampal slices. A very potent adenosine receptor and weak phosphodiesterase inhibitor, 8-phenyltheophylline, was much more potent than theophylline or IBMX in causing an increase in spontaneous spiking (63). 7-Benzyl-3-isobutyl-1-methylxanthine was inactive. A similar profile of activity pertained for reversal of the depressant effects of adenosine. Caffeine also causes excitation of hippocampal neurons (10) and at high concentrations causes epileptic-like discharges in hippocampal slices (64). High concentrations (1 mM) of theophylline and two other xanthines, propentofylline and pentoxyfylline, enhanced long-term potentiation in hippocampal slices (65).

Enprofylline (3-propylxanthine), a xanthine that is a relatively potent phosphodiesterase inhibitor with low activity as an antagonist of adenosine receptors (see Table 4), is not only not a behavioral stimulant, but does not cause seizures at very high doses (66). It seems unlikely, then, that inhibition of phosphodiesterases by caffeine or theophylline accounts for seizures.

There are two systems where phosphodiesterase inhibition may prove to be involved in the pharmacological activity of caffeine and theophylline: the cardiovascular system, and where relaxation of bronchioles occurs in the respiratory system. Nonxanthine inhibitors of cyclic GMP-inhibited phosphodiesterase (type III subfamily, see ref. 57), such as milrinone, are cardiac stimulants (67). However, enprofylline, a relatively potent xanthine inhibitor of certain phosphodiesterases, is not a potent cardiac stimulant (68), perhaps because of its low activity as an inhibitor of the cyclic GMP-inhibited Type III phosphodiesterase. Relaxation of vascular smooth muscle by xanthines underlies vasodilation and, again, inhibition of phosphodiesterases could have a role. In the respiratory system, relaxation of bronchioles by xanthines appears to involve inhibition of phosphodiesterases. Enprofylline is very effective as a bronchiole and tracheal relaxant, and it has been proposed that inhibition of phosphodiesterases has a significant role in these actions (69). In a recent study using guinea pig tracheal strips as a model, potencies of caffeine, theophylline and enprofylline analogs at adenosine receptors clearly did not correlate with ability to relax trachea (70). Instead, tracheal relaxation by xanthines appears to correlate better with ability to inhibit phosphodiesterases (69–72). Inhibition of phosphodiesterases is relevant to the treatment of asthma (73), and undoubtedly plays a role in the antiasthmatic activity of caffeine and theophylline (68).

Xanthines have other effects on nucleoside or nucleotide metabolism, but these are probably not relevant to the pharmacological activities of caffeine and theophylline, which include inhibition of $5'$-nucleotidase and alkaline phosphatase (74–76). Caffeine and theophylline are relatively weak inhibitors, with IC_{50} values of about 100 μM or higher. Xanthines can inhibit uptake of adenosine into cells (60,77–79). All of the xanthines, however, are very weak ($IC_{50}>200$ μM) in this regard.

Caffeine with an IC_{50} of 20 μM inhibits forskolin-stimulated cyclic AMP accumulations in rat brain slices (80–82). Theophylline, but not theobromine or IBMX, also inhibited the forskolin response. It was proposed (80,81) that blockade by caffeine of A_2-adenosine receptor stimulatory to adenylate cyclase in brain slices does not completely account for the caffeine-inhibition of the forskolin response. In contrast, in adipocyte membranes, xanthines, including IBMX, enhance activity of adenylate cyclase (83,84). It was suggested that xanthines increase adenylate cyclase activity by reducing a tonic G_i inhibitory input to adenylate cyclase. However, the inhibition correlates with the potency of the xanthines at A_1 receptors and has not been demonstrated in preparations that do not have A_1 receptors. It is possible that xanthines, by stabilizing an "antagonist conformation" of A_1 receptors, prevent an agonist-independent tonic input of an "agonist conformation" of A_1 receptors via G_i proteins to adenylate cyclase. Similarly, xanthines, by stabilizing an "antagonist conformation" of A_2 receptors in brain slices, may reverse an agonist-independent tonic input of an "agonist conformation" of A_2 receptors via G_s protein to adenylate cyclase and thereby reduce stimulation by forskolin, which is known to act synergistically with receptor-G_s input.

At high concentrations (K_i 0.9 mM), theophylline inhibits soluble guanylate cyclase (85). IBMX had minimal effects at 1 mM.

Mobilization of Calcium

The discovery of caffeine's ability to mobilize calcium from internal storage sites in cells stemmed from investigation of caffeine-induced contractures of skeletal and cardiac muscle (86,87). Caffeine at concentrations of 1 to 10 mM is now thought to cause release of calcium from a storage pool in the sarcoplasmic reticulum. This pool is probably the so-called *calcium-sensitive pool,* and distinct from the inositol trisphosphate-sensitive pool (88–91). Since concentrations of caffeine of 250 μM are the threshold for effects on calcium mobilization, it seems unlikely that such effects have any relevance to any effects of caffeine other than the toxic effects leading to seizures. The caffeine-sensitive storage pool of calcium is apparently required for oscillations in membrane potentials (91), and even minor effects on such oscillations might have significant effects on function in the central nervous system. Mobilization of calcium from internal sites by caffeine could be expected to have other effects besides the contracture observed in muscle cells. Such effects may underly transient inward fluxes of calcium (92) and apparent augmentation of sodium-calcium exchange mechanisms (93) elicited by caffeine. Stimulatory effects of high concentrations of caffeine on neuronal excitability (94) and on neurotransmitter release (95) also may be related to mobilization of internal calcium from storage sites.

There have been virtually no structure activity studies on the effects of xanthines on calcium mobilization. At 1.25 mM caffeine, theophylline, theobromine, IBMX, and 3,9-dimethylxanthine had similar stimulatory effects on efflux of calcium from sarcoplasmic reticulum vesicles prepared from rabbit skeletal muscle (96). Isocaffeine and 1,9-dimethylxanthine had minimal effects. Caffeine, theophylline, and theobromine had similar potencies in enhancing contractility in cardiac preparations (87). In frog oocytes, caffeine at 2 mM prevented inositol trisphosphate-induced oscillations in membrane potential, while IBMX did not, and IBMX, instead, caused a marked hyperpolarization, proposed to be due to an elevation of cyclic AMP (91).

Theophylline at 2 mM was stated to have effects similar to IBMX, rather than to caffeine.

BIOLOGICAL SYSTEMS AFFECTED BY CAFFEINE

Cardiovascular System

The effects of caffeine and theophylline on cardiac function are primarily stimulatory, with an accompanying increase in coronary blood flow. Adenosine analogs elicit the opposite response—a depressant effect on cardiac function, while also increasing coronary blood flow. Whether blockade of adenosine receptors by caffeine or theophylline is primarily responsible for their cardiovascular effects is unclear, but it appears unlikely. A comparison of the ability of theophylline, enprofylline, and 8-phenyltheophylline to reverse adenosine depression of guinea pig atrium (8-phenyltheophylline>theophylline>enprofylline) and to elicit positive inotropic/chronotropic responses (enprofylline>theophylline>8-phenyltheophylline) demonstrates that the cardiac stimulant effects of these three xanthines are not due to blockade of adenosine receptors (97). When tested in vivo in dogs, enprofylline ($EC_{50} \sim 2$ mg/kg) is a more potent cardiac stimulant than theophylline ($EC_{50} \sim 10$ mg/kg). 8-Phenyltheophylline has no significant effect. These and other results suggest that, although caffeine and theophylline can reverse cardiovascular effects of adenosine (cf., ref. 98), their intrinsic activities as cardiac stimulants and vasodilators are more likely due to inhibition of phosphodiesterases. There are results with other xanthines that are at variance with such a conclusion. Thus, 6-thiocaffeine, in spite of caffeine-like activity as a phosphodiesterase inhibitor, is a cardiac depressant (99). 6-Thiocaffeine did relax trachea. Interpretation of effects of xanthines on blood pressure and heart rate is complicated by the presence of xanthine-sensitive adenosine receptors, both in heart and vasculature as well as in the brainstem (100). Adenosine analogs have excitatory effects on respiration mediated through the carotid body; the profile of activities of adenosine analogs and xanthine antagonists indicated that an A_2-adenosine receptor was involved (101).

Adenosine can potentiate pressor (elevation of blood pressure, heart rate) responses to nicotine in rats via a peripheral caffeine-sensitive receptor (102). Caffeine enhances phencyclidine-elicited increases of blood pressure in rats (103).

Respiratory System

In the respiratory system, it remains uncertain to what extent caffeine and theophylline exert anti-asthmatic effects through blockade of adenosine receptors, and to what extent through phosphodiesterase inhibition. With respect to bronchodilation, inhibition of phosphodiesterase may prove of prime importance in view of the high activity of enprofylline, which is a potent phosphodiesterase inhibitor and a weak adenosine antagonist (69). As to the inflammatory component to asthma, adenosine-receptor mediated stimulation of release of histamine and serotonin from mast cells is relatively insensitive to blockade by xanthines (29,30). Theophylline at a concentration of 10 μM stimulates eosinophils as does 8-phenyltheophylline, a xanthine with little activity as a phosphodiesterase activator (104). Adenosine has the opposite effect. Thus, with regard to the role of eosinophils in inflammatory responses, theophylline may act via blockade of adenosine receptors. Bronchospasms can be elicited by adenosine analogs via a pathway, apparently involving the postganglionic cholinergic vagal nerves (105). It was not determined whether the response was sensitive to blockade by xanthines, but presumably it would be. In trachea, adenosine analogs can cause contraction via A_1 receptors, but the major effect in constricted muscles is to cause a relaxation (106–109). Relaxation is mediated both by a xanthine-sensitive A_2-adenosine receptor and a xanthine-insensitive adenosine receptor (27). Xanthines, including caffeine, antagonize both adenosine-elicited contraction and cause relaxation in smooth muscle (105,106). However, in one study the relaxation of guinea pig trachea by N^6-R-phenylisopropyladenosine was antagonized by theophylline and 8-phenyltheophylline, while the contraction was not (109).

Renal System

The effects of caffeine and theophylline on renal function, namely diuresis, increased blood flow, and stimulation of renin release, appear to be linked to blockade of adenosine receptors—adenosine analogs having the opposite effects to xanthines (cf., ref. 110). Xanthines, including theophylline and caffeine, reverse adenosine-mediated reduction in glomerular filtration, vasoconstriction, and inhibition of renin release (111–113). Enprofylline, a xanthine with low activity as an adenosine antagonist, has no diuretic activity (68).

There is some evidence indicating that generation of prostaglandins may be involved in xanthine-elicited diuresis. Indomethacin reduces theophylline-induced diuresis and excretion of prostaglandin E (114,115). Theophylline > caffeine = theobromine all stimulate prostaglandin production. Theophylline increases prostaglandin synthesis in rat kidney slices (116). The role of prostaglandins in the actions of xanthines in other biological systems has received little attention. Caffeine and theophylline were proposed to act as prostaglandin antagonists due to inhibition of phosphodiesterases in mesenteric arteries, while IBMX acted as a prostaglandin antagonist in ileum and uterine preparations (117).

Miscellaneous Systems

Caffeine is added to beverages and foods as a taste enhancer. It has been proposed that enhancement of taste of certain sweeteners and certain other agents by xanthines is due to blockade of an adenosine receptor (118,119). There is no great difference, however, in the efficacy of caffeine, theophylline, and theobromine.

Nausea and vomiting are major side effects in the use of theophylline as a bronchodilator. The emetic effects of a series of xanthines in ferrets (IBMX>enprofylline>theophylline>8-phenyltheophylline) was consonant with their potencies as phosphodiesterase inhibitors (120).

Sperm motility is increased by caffeine, theophylline, and IBMX and has been proposed to be due to inhibition of phosphodiesterases (121,122). Adenosine analogs can also stimulate sperm motility (123). Structure activity relationships, however, for adenosine analogs differed from that expected for A_1- or A_2-adenosine receptors. It now appears that effects on calcium by xanthines may underlie the stimulation of sperm motility. Methylxanthines stimulate calcium uptake into molluscan sperm with the following order of activity: IBMX>theophylline>theobromine>caffeine (124).

The effects of caffeine on plasma levels of various hormones have been reported, including decreases in thyroid stimulating hormone (TSH), growth hormone (GH), and thyroxine, and increases in corticosterone, catecholamines and endorphin, (125–128). The mechanisms involved are unclear, although it has been speculated that the changes are stress related. Theophylline and caffeine appeared more potent than theobromine and paraxanthine (127). Social stress in mice increases plasma levels of renin and corticosterone, and caffeine augments these changes (128).

Central Nervous System

The past decade of research on the central effects of xanthines has focused on the role of adenosine receptors through study of behavioral depressant effects of adenosine analogs and their reversal by xanthines. The A_1-adenosine receptors are inhibitory to neurotransmitter release, and, thus, blockade of such receptors by xanthines should have effects on function, turnover, and levels of biogenic amines, acetylcholine, and excitatory and inhibitory amino acids. The dopamine systems have received particular attention, since they appear closely linked to behavioral effects of adenosine analogs. Such an interrelationship may involve the A_{2A} receptors that coexist in the limbic system with dopamine receptors. The discovery that xanthines bind to benzodiazepine sites, albeit with low affinity, has focused attention on possible roles of the GABA-receptor in the central actions of xanthines. The well-known anxiety-producing effects and convulsive activities of xanthines have been further investigated. Interactions of xanthines and ethanol and other psychoactive drugs have also received attention. The soporific and hypothermic effects of adenosine find their converse in the somnolytic and hyperthermic effects of xanthines. Differences in sensitivity of inbred mouse strains to xanthines have been reported. Unlike the vasodilatory effects of xanthines in most blood vessels, caffeine and theophylline can cause vasoconstriction of cerebral vessels (129,130). The following subsections deal with these aspects of the central activity of caffeine, theophylline, and other xanthines, and the mechanisms involved.

Behavioral Activity

The effects of caffeine and other xanthines on spontaneous locomotor activity (36–38,45,131–134) continue to be investigated, since the initial studies in 1972 that correlated spontaneous locomotor effects rats with brain concentrations of caffeine and theophylline (44). Such studies have been extended to include effects of caffeine on exploratory activity (135), acquisition of conditioned responses (136–138), schedule-controlled responding (139–145), and on reinforced self-stimulation (146,147). Caffeine enhanced both degree and efficiency of tunnel maze exploration by rats (135). Caffeine had either no effect, enhanced, or retarded learning (136–138). N^6-R-phenylisopropyladenosine retarded acquisition of conditioned responses in rabbits, and both caffeine and theophylline, but not a phosphodiesterase inhibitor, rolipram, reversed the effect of the adenosine analog (138). In low doses (6–17 mg/kg), caffeine increases schedule-controlled responses in Harlan/Wistar rats, while higher doses (24 mg/kg) decrease responses (141). In Sprague-Dawley rats, caffeine and theophylline, at doses of 1 and 3 mg/kg, respectively, cause a slight increase in responses followed by marked decreases (142). The relative potencies were caffeine>theophylline>theobromine. The relative high potency of theobromine is not consonant with involvement of adenosine receptors. Caffeine causes greater reductions in responses in rats with lesions of the hippocampal system than in control rats (143). In squirrel monkeys, xanthines cause an increase in response rate with relative potencies as follows: IBMX>7-(2-chloroethyl)theophylline>caffeine (144), while the rank order of potencies in another study from the same laboratory was as follows: IBMX>8-cyclopentyltheophylline (a specific A_1 antagonist)>theophylline>8-phenyltheophylline>caffeine, with a range of ED_{50} values from 1.9 μmol/kg to 6.9 μmol/kg (132). Enprofylline had no effect except at the highest doses, when it reduced responding as did some of the other xanthines at their highest doses. The stimulatory activity of IBMX on responding in monkeys (144,145) is in marked contrast to its depressant effects on locomotor activity in rodents (36–38,58).

The dose-dependent elevations by xanthines in reinforcement thresholds for self-stimulation in rats correlates well with reported affinities of these xanthines for A_1 receptors (146). The following order was observed: 7-(2-chloroethyltheophylline>IBMX>paraxanthine = theophylline = caffeine >8-chlorotheophylline. The xanthines also decrease the response rate with a slightly different order of potency, as follows: IBMX>7-(2-chloroethyl)-theophylline > caffeine > theophylline > paraxanthine > 8-chlorotheo phylline. Increases in response rates were observed at the lower concentrations of all xanthines except IBMX and 8-chlorotheophylline. A general phosphodiesterase inhibitor, papaverine, increases the reinforcement threshold, while Ro 20-1724, a specific inhibitor of type IV phosphodiesterase, has nearly no effect on threshold. Both papaverine and Ro 20-1724 decrease the response rate. Although the increases in reinforcement thresholds by xanthines correlated well with affinities for A_1 receptors, neither N^6-R-phenylisopropyladenosine nor NECA significantly altered reinforcement thresholds (147). In squirrel monkeys, there also was a good correlation in rank order of potencies of 8-cyclopentyltheophylline, IBMX, theophylline, 8-phenyltheophylline, and caffeine for increasing responding rates, when compared to rank order of potencies for antagonizing the depressant effects of the adenosine analog NECA (145). In all cases, the xanthine was more potent in antagonizing NECA than in increasing rates alone. Although differing pharmacokinetics could be a factor, the results seem to suggest a major involvement of an A_1 receptor.

In discriminative stimulus studies, caffeine-treated rats acquired the ability to recognize caffeine (149–152). Theophylline showed the greatest generalization to caffeine, while paraxanthine, theobromine, and 8-phenyltheophylline generalized very poorly, and IBMX did not generalize (151). Adenosine analogs antagonized the recognition of caffeine. In other discriminative stimulus studies, theophylline, paraxanthine, and 3-methylxanthine generalized well to caffeine in rats trained to recognize caffeine (150,151). Theobromine did not generalize. Caffeine generalized, but only at relatively high concentrations, to theophylline in rats trained to recognize theophylline. Paraxanthine generalized only partially (~50%) at the two highest concentrations tested. Cross-generalization between low and high doses of caffeine were not complete (152), which is not surprising in view of the biphasic effects of caffeine on behavior.

The biphasic effects—first stimulatory, then depressant—of caffeine are manifest in neonatal rats even at day 1 (133). Oral caffeine stimulates both locomotor activity and social interactions in juvenile rats, while caffeine injections stimulate only locomotor activity (153). High doses of injected caffeine decrease the social interaction of juvenile male rats, referred to as "play soliciting" (154). Caffeine has either inhibitory or stimulatory effects on "play fighting" in juvenile rats, depending on length of exposure (155). Age-related effects of caffeine on various social behaviors in rats have been investigated (156). High doses of caffeine (60 mg/kg) in NIH Swiss mice are required to reduce locomotor activity and social interactions, although other aspects of social behavior are modified by lower doses (157). Effects of caffeine on social interactions might be related to its well-known anxiogenic properties. In a proposed social interaction test of anxiety, caffeine would appear to have anxiety-producing effects, since social interactions of male rats were reduced (158). Sustained high doses (150 mg/kg) of theophylline increase stereotypic movements, automutilation, and aggressive behavior in rats (159,160). The triggering of automutilation by high doses of caffeine is well known (161–163) and has been proposed as a model for Lesch-Nyhan syndrome.

Stimulation of spontaneous locomotor activity in mice has been reported for an A_1 selective xanthine, 8-cyclopentyltheophylline (164–166) and for two A_2 selective nonxanthine antagonists, the triazolopyrimidine CGS 21197 and the triazoloquinazoline CGS 22706 (167). Another A_1-selective antagonist, 2-thio-8-cyclopentyl-1,3-dipropylxanthine, does not cause locomotor stimulation but does reverse the locomotor depression elicited by the A_1 selective agonist N^6-cyclohexyladenosine (164). A related A_1 specific antagonist, 8-cyclopentyl-1,3-dipropylxanthine, also does not increase locomotor activity (168,169), nor does the potent A_1/A_2 antagonist (8-(4-N-dimethylaminoethylsulfonamidophenyl-1,3-dipropylxanthine (169). 8-Cyclopentyltheophylline markedly increases self-stimulation in rats (170). The selective A_1 antagonist 8-cyclopentyl-1,3-dipropylxanthine reduces the behavioral depressant effects of both N^6-R-phenylisopropyladenosine and, less effectively, of NECA (169). The A_1/A_2 antagonist 8-(4-N-dimethylaminoethylsulfonamidophenyl)-1,3-dipropylxanthine blocks the depressant effects of N^6-R-phenylisopropyladenosine, but not those of NECA.

Nonxanthine antagonists of adenosine receptors have behavioral effects. Carbamazepine, a somewhat selective A_1 antagonist (171), is a behavioral depressant (169) and anticonvulsant, probably due to mechanisms other than blockade of adenosine receptors. A nonselective nonxanthine antagonist, the triazoloquinoxaline CGS 15943A, causes a stimulation of locomotor activity (167,172). An A_2-selective nonxanthine antagonist, the triazoloquinoxaline CP 66-713, does not cause locomotor stimulation but does antagonize the locomotor depression elicited by an A_2-selective agonist, APEC (165).

Many of the results with these receptor antagonists are reminiscent of the fivefold greater potency of caffeine in reversing depressant effects of an adenosine analog than in causing behavioral stimulation alone (38). Thus, because of poor penetration into brain, some receptor antagonists may only reach concentrations sufficient to block depressant effects due to adenosine analogs, but not concentrations sufficient to cause locomotor stimulation alone. The dichotomy in the dose-dependency of these effects of xanthines alone and versus an adenosine analog raises questions as to the role of adenosine receptors in behavioral stimulation by caffeine and other xanthines.

An ex-vivo A_1-adenosine receptor binding assay was recently reported that allows estimates of the in vivo levels of adenosine receptor antagonists in brain (166).

The depressant effects of IBMX on spontaneous locomotor activity reported in the early eighties (37) have been proposed to be related to inhibition of a cyclic AMP-specific phosphodiesterase (36). Remarkably, a combination of a depressant adenosine analog with IBMX causes behavioral stimulation (see Fig. 4). A pretreatment of mice with intraperitoneal caffeine (32 mg/kg), which had no effect on locomotor activity, followed by IBMX at a dose that alone caused profound reduction in activity, now caused a 25-fold stimulation in activity (48, see also ref. 45). Obviously, the mechanisms involved in the central behavioral effects of xanthines and of adenosine analogs are multifaceted.

The effects of prenatal and neonatal exposure to caffeine on behavior in developing rats have been probed. Acute exposure to caffeine alters subsequent behavior of rat pups, both at one day and ten days (173). Prenatal exposure depresses subsequent activity in rat pups (174), and alterations in behavior remain even in adulthood (175–177). Postnatal administration to rats during the first week of life causes hypoactivity and subsequent impairment in a spatial learning task as adults (178). Of particular relevance to mechanisms underlying caffeine action is an acceleration in development of A_1 receptors in cerebral cortex of rats (179) and a delay in development of stimulatory effects of caffeine on locomotor activity (180) after neonatal exposure to caffeine. The development of the depressant effect of an adenosine analog was not altered significantly by prior exposure to caffeine. Others have reported effects of caffeine on locomotor activity in rat pups at day 1 (133). Chronic exposure of juveniles of a cichlid fish to caffeine solutions appeared to cause an increase in dendritic spines on midbrain neurons (181).

Differences in effects of xanthines on locomotor activity have been reported in four inbred strains of mice (182). These strains also show differences in sensitivity to toxic effects of caffeine (183). The strains differ in basal locomotor activity and in responses to the xanthines caffeine, theophylline, paraxanthine, and theobromine (182). In the most active strain, C57 BL/6J, caffeine and paraxanthine elicit the greatest increase in activity, while theophylline causes only a slight stimulation. Caffeine and theophylline have biphasic effects—first stimulating, then depressing activity. The threshold for all the stimulatory xanthines was similar. In the DBA/2J strain with an intermediate control activity, caffeine and paraxanthine elicit the greatest increase in activity, and theophylline is only slightly less efficacious. All three xanthines exhibit biphasic dose response curves. The threshold for stimulation was as follows: caffeine>theophylline>paraxanthine. Caffeine and theophylline elicit the greatest stimulation in the CBA/J strain, with paraxanthine causing a much smaller stimulation. All three xanthines exhibit biphasic dose response curves. The threshold for paraxanthine is lower than those for caffeine and theophylline. In the SWR/J strain with a basal locomotor activity, fully twofold less than the C57BL/6J strain, paraxanthine and theophylline elicit relatively low stimulation compared to the other strains, and have relatively high thresholds. Caffeine has only marginal effects. Curves are biphasic. Theobromine has either no effect or is inhibitory in all strains. The differences suggest that the mechanisms underlying locomotor stimulation by different methylxanthines are complex and not the same even for this limited set of compounds. In another study, caffeine caused more marked stimulation of locomotor activity in DBA mice than in C57 mice; the A_1-adenosine receptor levels in brain of these two strains did not differ significantly, nor did the depressant effects of N^6-R-phenylisopropyladenosine (184). Caffeine appeared to enhance performance in a visual discrimination paradigm for DBA and C57 mice, while reducing performance for BALB mice (137). Analysis of genetic determinants in the hybrids of the CBA/J (high responsiveness to caffeine and theophylline) and the SWR/J (low responsiveness to caffeine and theophylline) mouse strains suggest that the genes specifying caffeine-responsiveness differ from those encoding theophylline-responsiveness (185). Thus, behavioral effects of xanthines are, as expected, very complex, and attempted correlations using a variety of xanthines may prove futile. Genetic analysis of susceptibility to the toxic effects of caffeine in hybrids of CBA/J (sensitive) and SWR/J (resistant) strains indicate that an autosomal dominant trait is involved (186).

Behavioral Interactions of Xanthines and Adenosine Analogs

Behavioral depressant effects of adenosine analogs and their reversal by caffeine, theophylline and other xanthines have been well established since initial studies in the early 1980s. Assays have involved spontaneous locomotor activity (35–38,45,48,164–168,187), schedule-controlled responding (188–192) and self-stimulation (146,147). Caffeine, theophylline, and paraxanthine at 3 mg/kg antagonize decreases in responding elicited by N^6-R-phenylisopropyladenosine in rats, as does theobromine at 10 mg/kg (192). At 32 mg/kg, 3-methylxanthine and 7-methylxanthine antagonize the decrease in responding elicited by N^6-R-phenylisopropyladenosine, while 1-methylxanthine does not.

The nature of adenosine receptors involved in behavioral depression elicited by adenosine analogs is highly relevant to reversal by caffeine and other xanthines. At present it appears that activation of either A_1 or A_2 receptors can lead to reductions in locomotor activity and that there can be synergistic depressant effects upon activation of both A_1 and A_2 receptors (164,165). However, the rank order of potency of adenosine analogs—NECA>N^6-R-phenylisopropyladenosine>N^6-cyclohexyladenosine—in causing reductions in spontaneous behavioral activity, led to the proposal that primarily A_2

receptors were involved (193). On the other hand, the blockade of responses to the highly selective A_1-agonist N^6-cyclohexyladenosine by the highly selective A_1 specific antagonist 8-cyclopentyltheophylline—and not by an A_2 selective nonxanthine antagonist, the triazoloquinoxaline CP 66–713 (164,165)—indicates that, with some adenosine analogs, primarily A_1 receptors are involved in the reduction of locomotor activity. Even the effect of NECA, a mixed A_1/A_2 agonist, is blocked completely by the A_1 antagonist. Conversely, the behavioral depression elicited by the selective A_{2A} agonists 2-phenylaminoadenosine (CV 1808) and APEC is not blocked by the A_1 antagonist (165,170) and, at least in the case of APEC, is blocked by the A_2 selective antagonist CP 66-713 (165). Combinations of low doses of an A_1 selective agonist (N^6-cyclohexyladenosine) and an A_{2A} selective agonist (APEC) have greater than additive depressant effects on locomotor activity in mice (165). Caffeine is twofold less potent in antagonizing the locomotor depressant activity of N^6-cyclohexyladenosine compared to antagonism of NECA in mice (35), while theophylline is equipotent (35) (see Table 6). Remarkably, 3,7-dimethyl-1-propargylxanthine is about ten-fold more potent versus the mixed A_1/A_2 agonist NECA than versus the A_1 selective agonist N^6-cyclohexyladenosine. Similar results were obtained when the xanthines were studied as antagonists of N^6-cyclohexyladenosine and NECA-elicited hypothermia (35, see Table 6). However, 3,7-dimethyl-1-propargylxanthine is much more selective in the hypothermia assay, primarily because of a threefold lower potency versus N^6-cyclohexyladenosine-elicited hypothermia than versus N^6-cyclohexyladenosine-elicited locomotor depression. Caffeine and also theophylline are equally effective in reversing the locomotor depression and the hypothermia induced by the adenosine analogs (35). Theobromine, at doses that do not increase spontaneous locomotor activity,

TABLE 6. *Comparison of the in vivo potencies of caffeine, theophylline and 3,7-dimethyl-1-propargylxanthine (DMPX) as antagonists of adenosine analog-elicited locomotor depression and hypothermia*

| | Assay | |
| | Blockade of agonist-elicited locomotor depression IC_{50} μmol/kg[a] | |
Xanthine	versus N^6-Cyclohexyl-adenosine	versus NECA
Caffeine	14	8
Theophylline	29	20
DMPX	6	0.5
	Blockade of agonist-elicited hypothermia IC_{50} μmol/kg[a]	
Caffeine	17	8
Theophylline	22	21
DMPX	16	0.3

[a] IC_{50} values were determined versus ID_{50} values of N^6-cyclohexyladenosine or NECA (35). Intraperitoneal injection.

antagonizes N^6-cyclohexyladenosine-mediated locomotor depression but has no effect on NECA-mediated locomotor depression (165)—an effect opposite to the relative antagonistic effects of 3,7-dimethyl-1-propargylxanthine (Table 6). Theobromine antagonizes both N^6-cyclohexyladenosine and NECA-induced hypothermia. These two studies, both using DBA/25 mice, indicate that adenosine receptor pathways subserving locomotor depression and hypothermia differ, at least with respect to blockade by xanthines.

In toto, research findings on the mechanisms involved in the central behavioral activity of caffeine and related xanthines suggest that blockade of adenosine receptors is involved; but the functional roles of A_1, A_{2A} and A_{2B} adenosine receptors in different brain pathways remain to be defined. The following subsections concern effects or interactions of caffeine/theophylline on various neurotransmitters and drugs that may be associated with brain pathways modulated by adenosine receptors.

Xanthines and neurotransmitters

Adenosine, via interaction with xanthine-sensitive receptors, is inhibitory to release of many classes of neurotransmitters, including norepinephrine, dopamine, serotonin, acetylcholine, glutamate and GABA (7). Blockade of adenosine receptors by caffeine could therefore lead to increases in functional turnover of such neurotransmitters. Caffeine or theophylline in vivo can cause increases in turnover of norepinephrine, dopamine, and serotonin (194) and can block adenosine analog-elicited increases in acetylcholine levels (195,196). Combinations of caffeine and pentobarbital lower dopamine levels in mice, while caffeine has no effect alone (197). Denbufylline (1,3-dibutyl-7-(2-oxopropyl)xanthine), a potent phosphodiesterase inhibitor, decreases acetylcholine levels in vivo in rat striatum, cortex, and hippocampus (198); IBMX, another potent phosphodiesterase inhibitor, increases turnover of norepinephrine in vivo in rats (199). Such results suggest that either blockade of inhibitory A_1 adenosine receptors or inhibition of phosphodiesterase by xanthines can lead to enhanced turnover of central neurotransmitters. There is an extensive literature on effects of adenosine analogs and xanthines on neurotransmitter release and turnover in isolated preparations in vitro that is beyond the scope of the present treatise, since it is difficult to extrapolate from such in vitro results to pharmacological or physiological effects in vivo. Caffeine and other xanthines can inhibit the stimulated release of radioactive "adenosine" from brain slices (200). The significance of this observation to the in vivo pharmacology of xanthines is unknown. Xanthines are very weak inhibitors of adenosine uptake (60,77–79).

A variety of evidence suggests an involvement of dopamine systems in the central effects of caffeine. Caffeine can potentiate the behavioral stimulant responses to amphetamine (201–203) (which releases dopamine), responses to cocaine (which blocks reuptake of dopamine) (204), and responses to apomorphine, a directly acting dopaminergic agonist (203). Given in multiple injections over nine days, caffeine still enhances cocaine responses (205), while amphetamine- or methylphenidate-responses are attenuated with time after prior treatments with caffeine (202,206). In the early 1970s, caffeine was shown to potentiate the response to a combination of an α_2-adrenergic and a dopaminergic agonist in reserpinized mice (207). In contrast, apomorphine-elicited pecking in chickens is decreased by caffeine or theophylline (208). Neonatal or adult treatment with 6-hydroxydopamine, which markedly decreases dopamine levels (207,209), and inhibition of catecholamine synthesis by α-methyltyrosine (132) reduce caffeine stimulation of locomotor activity. Caffeine decreases levels of a dopaminergic metabolite in certain brain regions and increases it in other regions (210).

A single dose of caffeine can enhance self-administration of cocaine in rats (211). There are other studies that suggest that the behavioral stimulant effects of caffeine are not mediated solely through the dopaminergic systems activated by cocaine and amphetamine. For example, 6-hydroxydopamine lesions of the nucleus accumbens in rats block the locomotor stimulation elicited by amphetamine and enhance the response to apomorphine but have no significant effect on the response to caffeine (212–214). Coexistence of dopamine neurons and high affinity A_{2A} adenosine receptors in the limbic system provides evidence of a relationship between the dopamine and xanthine-sensitive adenosine systems. An A_{2A}-selective adenosine analog, CGS 21680, reduces the affinity of dopamine for D_2-dopamine receptors in rat striatal membranes (215).

Effects of adenosine analogs and xanthines on functional activity of striatal dopamine systems have been demonstrated in several paradigms using unilateral lesions or injections into dopaminergic areas. The results of these studies indicate that caffeine and theophylline enhance, and adenosine analogs inhibit, responses to the endogenous dopamine and to the agonist apomorphine, as evidenced by rotation of rats away from the side of greatest dopaminergic activity (216–224). The effects of the xanthines are consonant with blockade of A_2 receptors and the effects of adenosine analogs with the stimulation of adenylate cyclase via A_{2A} receptors. Both postsynaptic and presynaptic sites may be involved. Chronic treatment of rats with NECA—but not N^6-R-phenylisopropyladenosine—down-regulates A_{2A} receptors in striatum, with no significant effect on A_1 receptors (225). NECA also down-regulates D_1-dopamine receptors in striatum. Combinations of an intrastriatal adenosine analog and apomorphine in rats results in self-mutilation, while combinations of theophylline and apomorphine are very toxic (217).

In vivo in rats, caffeine increases activity of ventral tegmental dopaminergic neurons, that have projections to the frontal cortex and limbic structures, while having no effect on firing of substantia nigra dopaminergic neurons, that have projections to the striatum (226). The adenosine analog N^6-

R-phenylisopropyladenosine, the dopamine antagonist haloperidol, and the benzodiazepine diazepam all prevent the caffeine-induced increase in firing of dopamine neurons. In an earlier study, caffeine at low oral doses in rats increased firing of the reticular formation of the brain stem, without affecting firing in the visual cortex (227). The stimulatory effects of caffeine were antagonized by oral doses of nicotinic acid (niacin). Effects of high doses of caffeine on activity in medulla and spinal cord were suggested to be toxic sequelae. The cortical arousal pattern elicited by caffeine in cats is similar to that produced by direct stimulation of the reticular formation (228). Thus, both the ventral tegmentum and the reticular formation appear to be likely critical sites for behavioral activation by caffeine.

Consonant with an involvement of dopaminergic function in the behavioral stimulant effects of caffeine, reserpine reduces the behavioral effects of caffeine and amphetamine (229), as do other treatments (6-hydroxydopamine, α-methyltyrosine) that would also affect catcholamine levels (132,207,209). But lesions of the nucleus accumbens with 6-hydroxydopamine or the GABA agonist muscimol reduce amphetamine but not caffeine responses, leading to the conclusion that amphetamine and caffeine enhance locomotor activity via different circuitries (214). The dopamine antagonist pimozide antagonizes the locomotor stimulant effects of a low dose of caffeine, but not of a high dose (230). In another study, the dopamine antagonist flupenthixol, that readily blocks effects of amphetamine, was ineffective in blocking caffeine-elicited locomotor activity (214).

Comparison of effects of caffeine, amphetamine, and cocaine on schedule-controlled responding have not provided clear insights into interrelationships (231–233). Both caffeine and cocaine enhance the impairment of motor control elicited by the benzodiazepine midazolam (234).

In discriminative stimulus studies with caffeine-trained rats, cocaine generalizes completely to caffeine, while amphetamine only partially generalizes (148). Conversely, in amphetamine-trained rats caffeine (or ephedrine) only partially generalizes to amphetamine, while a combination of caffeine and ephedrin generalizes completely (235).

The dopaminergic antagonist haloperidol can cause catalepsy similar to symptoms in Parkinson's disease. Theophylline reduces haloperidol-induced catalepsy (236). This effect is not mediated via the adrenals and is accompanied by an increase in metabolic activity in striatum, but not hippocampus (237).

Paraxanthine—but not caffeine, theophylline or theobromine—was reported to inhibit binding of [^{3}H]SCH 23390, a selective antagonist, to D_1-dopamine receptors (238). A reduction in affinity of paraxanthine by GppNHp suggested that paraxanthine might be a D_1 dopaminergic agonist. The inhibition of binding of [^{3}H]CH 23390 by paraxanthine could not be confirmed in our laboratory (W.L. Padgett and J.W. Daly, unpublished results).

In view of a possible involvement of dopaminergic function in schizophrenia, the suggestion that excessive caffeine consumption induces or worsens psychosis (239,240) is noteworthy. Caffeine facilitates development of "neurotic" behavior in cats, using a conflict-induced paradigm (241). Caffeine and theophylline reverse the augmentation by an adenosine analog of swimming-induced immobility, an assay suggested to measure "depression" (242).

Serotoninergic pathways also have been proposed to be involved in caffeine-elicited stimulation of locomotor activity (243,244). However, in one study with mice, p-chlorophenylalanine, a specific serotonin depletor, decreased the caffeine response (243), while in other studies with rats it increased the caffeine response (126,244). The adrenergic antagonists propranolol and phenoxybenzamine do not reduce the caffeine response (243). Treatment of adult rats with 5,7-dihydroxytryptamine, which lowers brain serotinin levels, has no effect on stimulation of locomotor activity by caffeine, while neonatal treatment enhances the percent stimulation evoked by caffeine (209). Caffeine has greater effects on turnover and levels of serotonin in isolation-induced aggressive mice than in control mice (245). Further caffeine reduced aggression in the mice.

Xanthines can affect acetylcholine levels in rat brain (198), but there is little direct evidence to implicate central cholinergic systems in behavioral responses to caffeine. Comparisons of the effects of caffeine and nicotine on locomotor activity, rearing, and wheelrunning in rats led to the conclusion that different mechanisms are involved in their effects (246,247).

Effects of caffeine on the excitatory neurotransmitter glutamate have received little attention. Dizocilpine (MK-801), an antagonist at N-methyl-aspartate (NMDA) receptors, antagonizes caffeine-induced convulsions (248).

Interactions with Benzodiazepines

In view of the well-known anxiogenic effects of caffeine (2), interactions of caffeine and other xanthines with sites that bind the widely used anxiolytic benzodiazepines were not very surprising. However, the affinities of caffeine and theophylline ($K_1 > 300$ μM) for diazepam-binding sites associated with the $GABA_A$-receptor-channel are very low (249–251) and are more consonant with in vivo concentrations of caffeine and theophylline that cause convulsions rather than concentrations that cause anxiety. Convulsant activities of xanthines other than caffeine and theophylline are not well known. The potency order with respect to threshold for seizures for a limited series of xanthines administered intravenously was as follows: caffeine (160 mg/kg)>IBMX (230 mg/kg)>theophylline (500 mg/kg) (252). 8-Phenyltheophylline, enprofylline, and 8-p-sulfophenylxanthines did not cause seizures. Two very potent A_1 selective antagonists, however—xanthine amine congener

(XAC) and 8-(2-amino-4-chlorophenyl)1,3-dipropylxanthine—were very potent convulsants (40–60 mg/kg). On intraperitoneal injection, they did not cause convulsions, presumably because of insolubility in the peritoneal cavity.

Benzodiazepines have anxiolytic, muscle relaxant, anticonvulsant, and sedative activities. Benzodiazepines can either counteract the locomotor stimulant evoked by caffeine or potentiate it (38,253). Caffeine can antagonize several effects of benzodiazepines, including the muscle relaxant and anxiolytic activities of diazepam, where caffeine is a potent antagonist (254). Caffeine is much less effective in reversing the anticonvulsant activity of diazepam (254,255). In humans, caffeine also antagonizes diazepam-induced sedation and impairment of motor performance (256). Caffeine reduces the efficacy of a range of anticonvulsant drugs and can potentiate the action of convulsants (255). Theophylline ethylene diamine (aminophylline) at 20 and 40 mg/kg decreases the anticonvulsant activity of diazepam (257). Benzodiazepines antagonize caffeine-induced seizures with a rank order of potency commensurate with their affinity for benzodiazepine binding sites (258). However, the benzodiazepine antagonist Ro 15-1788 protects against caffeine-induced seizures much more effectively than diazepam (259). Although caffeine is a weak ligand in vitro for the benzodiazepine site (see above), in vivo studies suggest that caffeine at only 20 and 40 mg/kg affects channel function of the $GABA_A$ receptor-channel complex (260). In vitro at 50 μM, caffeine decreases chloride flux through the channel. These results suggest that the $GABA_A$ receptor complex must be considered a viable target for certain pharmacological effects of caffeine. Caffeine at 50 μM potentiates the depolarizing effects of GABA on frog spinal cord neurons (261).

Behaviorally, while a very low dose of caffeine reduces locomotor activity in mice, it has stimulatory effects on locomotor activity in the presence of a markedly depressant dose of diazepam (38). Diazepam potentiates the locomotor depressant effects of intracerebroventricular injections of adenosine but not of NECA (262). Doses of caffeine that stimulate locomotor activity in rats increased in vivo uptake of the benzodiazepine receptor ligand RO 15-1788 (263). In squirrel monkeys, caffeine, theophylline, 8-phenyl-theophylline, and IBMX augment the stimulatory effects of the benzodiazepine chlordiazepoxide on schedule-controlled responding (264). Adenosine analogs suppress the stimulatory effects of chlordiazepoxide. In rats, caffeine and chlordiazepoxide had generally additive effects on scheduled responding (136).

In discrimination paradigms, either an adenosine analog or chlordiazepoxide antagonize recognition of caffeine or theophylline in rats trained to recognize either caffeine or theophylline (265). The general phosphodiesterase inhibitor papaverine generalizes fairly well to caffeine when tested in caffeine-trained rats, suggesting that the caffeine cue may involve effects on cyclic AMP accumulation.

The "anxiogenic" effects of caffeine, as assessed by reductions in social interactions in rats, are reduced by chlordiazepoxide and propranolol but not by an adenosine analog or by clonidine (266). Caffeine had apparent anxiogenic effects in a social interaction paradigm with male rats (158). In another study, caffeine and yohimbine both had "anxiogenic-like" effects in social interaction, maze, and punished-response paradigms but had lesser effects in combination (267). Caffeine, like diazepam, increased punished responses in a food reinforcement schedule in mice (268). An adenosine agonist reverses responses to both caffeine and diazepam.

A wide range of results now indicates close relationships between central pharmacological activities of caffeine and benzodiazepines. Unlike the situation with caffeine and dopamine pathways, the relationship of GABA pathways to caffeine's action remains very poorly defined.

Genetic analysis of hybrid mice from the strain SWR/J, which is hyporesponsive to seizures induced by the benzodiazepine inverse agonist methyl 6,7-dimethoxy-4-ethyl-β-carboline-3-carboxylate (DMCM), and from the strain CBA/J, which is responsive, suggests that different genes encode DMCM susceptibility and caffeine susceptibility to seizures (269).

Adenosine analogs have anticonvulsant activity (7), so it is not surprising that the seizure-prolonging effects of caffeine/theophylline in kindled amygdaloid seizures appear to be due to antagonism of adenosine receptors (270,271).

Interactions with Ethanol

It is widely believed that caffeine can antagonize ethanol-induced depression and motor incoordination. Caffeine at less than 20 mg/kg intraperitoneally attenuates ethanol-induced incoordination in mice, while higher doses augmented the incoordination (272). In further studies, theophylline and 7-(2-chloroethyl)theophylline markedly attenuate ethanol-induced incoordination, while enprofylline has no effect (273,274). Adenosine analogs augment the ethanol-induced incoordination (273–275). It has been suggested that either an A_1- (274) or an A_2-adenosine receptor was involved (275). Caffeine and IBMX, but not theophylline, augment ethanol-induced ataxia (276). An ethanol-induced increase in locomotor activity is reduced only by a high dose (60 mg/kg) of caffeine (157). A lower dose (30 mg/kg) partially reverses ethanol-induced reduction in social interactions. Theophylline reduces ethanol-induced sleep and motor incoordination, but not hypothermia (277). Conversely, ethanol can alter responses to caffeine. Thus, ethanol antagonizes caffeine-induced convulsions in mice (276). The protective effect of theophylline was enhanced by adenosine and prevented by the benzodiazepine Ro 15-4513.

It is now apparent that release of adenosine is involved to some extent in the in vivo effects of ethanol. Thus, ethanol is metabolized in the liver in vivo to acetate, which is utilized as a source of acetyl coenzyme A in brain and other tissues. The conversion of acetate to acetyl coenzyme A requires ATP, and this leads to production of adenosine from the resulting 5'-AMP (278). Acetate-induced motor incoordination and reduction in locomotor activity are both reversed by 8-phenyltheophylline (278). These recent findings indicate that further, more-detailed studies on the interaction of caffeine and ethanol are needed.

Theophylline greatly increases activity as measured in a reduction in escape latency in ethanol-sensitive (long-sleep) mice, while it has no significant effect in ethanol-insensitive short-sleep mice (279). Both ethanol and an adenosine analog have greater sedative and hypothermic effects in the ethanol-sensitive mice.

Caffeine and ethanol clearly interact centrally, but no generalizations are possible. This is not unexpected, since both agents undoubtedly have many sites of central action, and both can be either behavioral stimulants or depressants, depending on the dose.

Analgesia

The role of caffeine in analgesia remains controversial. Caffeine is used as an adjuvant with analgesics, in particular with aspirin and acetaminophen, and appears to increase their effectiveness (280–282). Indeed, with respect to headaches, caffeine has independent, dose-dependent analgesic effects (282). Low doses of aspirin enhanced and prolonged caffeine-elicited stimulation of locomotor activity through an unknown mechanism (283).

Effects of caffeine on the activity of opioid analgetics have not been consistent. In one study, caffeine reduced stimulation of locomotor activity elicited by morphine but had no effect on morphine-elicited analgesia (284). Caffeine and theophylline have also been reported to inhibit morphine-elicited analgesia (285,286). On the other hand, both caffeine and theophylline can potentiate morphine-induced analgesia (287,288). Inhibition of phosphodiesterase by the xanthines does not seem to be involved in this potentiation, since phosphodiesterase inhibitors, including rolipram, IBMX and forskolin (which activates adenylate cyclase) inhibit morphine-elicited analgesia (289). Pretreatment of the rats with a phosphodiesterase inhibitor, however, results in an increase in morphine analgesia. 8-Phenyltheophylline, a potent adenosine antagonist with weak activity as a phosphodiesterase inhibitor, reverses morphine analgesia in the hot plate, but not the tail-flick assay (290). Prior treatment with 5,7-dihydroxytryptamine, to damage descending serotonin pathways, prevented the 8-phenyltheophylline effect. 6-Hydroxydopamine treatment did not. Morphine appears to release adenosine in spinal cord through a serotonergic pathway (291).

The inconsistent effects of caffeine/theophylline on morphine-analgesia may relate to the often biphasic effects of methylxanthines. They may also relate to different paradigms used to measure analgesia. Indeed, both theophylline and 8-phenyltheophylline cause hyperalgesia in the tail-flick assay (292), and both caffeine and theophylline decrease thresholds for pain responses in the Nielsen assay (293). It has been proposed that the motor and sensory pathways affected by morphine may be differentially affected by theophylline, with the ascending sensory pathways being less sensitive to the methylxanthine (294). Caffeine and theophylline potentiate the analgesic effects of the GABA, agonist baclofen (295).

The mechanisms involved in the analgesic or analgesic-enhancing effects of caffeine/theophylline are unclear. Adenosine analogs have potent analgesic effects, apparently mediated by A_1 adenosine receptors (292,296,297). Caffeine, theophylline and 8-phenyltheophylline, but not enprofylline, reduce the analgesic activity of adenosine analogs. The hyperalgesia of theophylline and 8-phenyltheophylline in one study (292) could have been the result of blockade of a tonic adenosine input to spinal pathways that subserve nociception. Morphine enhances adenosine release in rat cerebral cortical preparations (cf., ref. 298) and in spinal cord (291), indicating a role for adenosine in morphine analgesia. The adenosine analog N^6-R-phenylisopropyladenosine remains a potent analgesic, however, in morphine-tolerant mice (299). Caffeine is a more potent antagonist of the adenosine analog in the morphine-tolerant mice. Furthermore, N^6-R-phenylisopropyladenosine at low doses can potentiate morphine-elicited analgesia (286). At higher doses, adenosine analogs can decrease morphine-elicited analgesia (300).

Chronic treatment of mice with caffeine results in an increase in the analgesic potency of morphine and appears to reduce development of morphine-induced tolerance and dependence (301). Chronic treatment with an adenosine analog has no effect on morphine-induced responses.

Further research is needed to clarify the pathways and mechanisms involved in the effects of caffeine on nociception. It seems clear that opioid and adenosine pathways—probably descending pathways—are closely related, but unifying hypotheses are not obvious.

Sleep and Thermoregulation

The effect of caffeine on sleep is well known and unambiguous, while the hyperthermic effects of caffeine and theophylline, while unambiguous, are not as well known. Since neither of the two phenomena have been extensively studied, mechanisms and pathways are not well understood.

Caffeine had biphasic effects on sleep in rats (302). At lower doses, it increases wakefulness. Earlier studies showed a delay for several hours in the REM (rapid eye movement) sleep associated with dreaming (303). Similarly, theophylline can delay and perhaps consolidate the human sleep phase (304). The effects of caffeine on sleep were recently compared to those of the A_1-specific xanthine 8-cyclopentyltheophylline and the somewhat A_2-selective nonxanthine antagonist alloxazine (305). Both 8-cyclopentyltheophylline and alloxazine suppress sleep in a manner similarly to caffeine, but to a lesser degree. A combination of 8-cyclopentyltheophylline and alloxazine causes suppression of sleep equal to caffeine. Pharmacokinetics of these agents undoubtedly markedly influence their apparent efficacy and potency. The results suggest that agents that block A_1 adenosine receptors, and perhaps A_2 receptors will delay or suppress sleep. This is perhaps not unexpected in view of the sedative effects of adenosine analogs. Adenosine and adenosine analogs increase slow wave deep sleep, while caffeine increases wakefulness and decreases slow wave and REM sleep in rats (302).

Ethanol-induced sleep times in ethanol-sensitive (long-sleep) and ethanol-insensitive (short-sleep) mouse strains are increased by adenosine analogs and decreased by theophylline (306). The reduction by theophylline is more pronounced in ethanol-sensitive mice. Caffeine also decreases sleep in ethanol-sensitive mice but actually increases ethanol-induced sleep in ethanol-insensitive mice.

The hyperthermic effects of caffeine and other xanthines find a possible counterpart in the hypothermic effects of adenosine analogs (35,307,308). Xanthines antagonize the hypothermic effects of adenosine analogs. Nonselective antagonists, such as caffeine and theophylline, are nearly equally effective versus hypothermia elicited by the A_1-selective agonist N^6-cyclohexyladenosine as that elicited by the mixed A_1/A_2 agonist NECA (35, see Table 6). In contrast, the somewhat A_2-selective antagonist 3,7-dimethyl-1-propargylxanthine is nearly 60 times more potent versus NECA than versus N^6-cyclohexyladenosine, suggesting a major A_2 component in thermoregulation—at least for NECA. Theobromine, a xanthine with little activity as an adenosine receptor antagonist, reverses the hypothermic response to both N^6-cyclohexyladenosine and NECA (187). Theophylline does not reverse hypothermic responses to ethanol (277). However, the effects of xanthines alone on core body temperature may be more dependent on inhibition of calcium-independent phosphodiesterases than on blockade of adenosine receptors (309). In a series of five xanthines, the potency order for reducing body temperature in mice was as follows: 1,3-dipropyl-7-methylxanthine>IBMX>enprofylline≳theophylline = caffeine.

Theophylline increases cold resistance in rats and humans (310,311). This phenomenon, which involves increases in thermogenesis, appears to involve blockade of A_1 receptors in rats, based on the relative effectiveness of A_1 selective xanthines (312). The somewhat A_2 selective xanthine 3,7-dimethyl-1-propargylxanthine had no effect on thermogenic responses in cold-exposed rats.

Theories as to the mechanism involved in the somnolytic effects and hypothermic effects of caffeine seem simple: a blockade of adenosine receptors. But further studies are needed to define the site, pathways, and classes of adenosine receptors that are involved. The possibility remains that other mechanisms are involved.

EFFECTS OF CHRONIC TREATMENT WITH CAFFEINE

Chronic treatment with caffeine might be expected to engender homeo-static changes in the systems or pathways involved. In expectation of such insights, extensive studies on the chronic effects of caffeine on density and function of receptors have been conducted. Chronic treatment with caffeine has been reported to lead to virtually complete, insurmountable tolerance in some paradigms. This is a remarkable finding if pharmacological activity of caffeine is indeed due to *antagonist* activity at adenosine receptors, since upregulation of such receptors would not prevent higher concentrations of an antagonist (caffeine) from blocking them. Complete tolerance to caffeine would imply either agonist activity for the xanthine at an unknown receptor, or desensitization of receptors to an endogenous neurotransmitter, such as dopamine (whose activity in brain is augmented by caffeine) either through blockade of adenosine receptors or some other mechanism.

Chronic treatment with caffeine or theophylline results, not unexpectedly, in an "up-regulation" of brain adenosine receptors: densities of brain A_1-adenosine receptors are increased (313–334). In addition, the proportion of the high affinity state of the A_1 receptor, the levels of the guanyl nucleotide binding protein G_1, and the degree of inhibition of adenylate cyclase by an adenosine analog are increased (322,324). Elevated levels of A_1 receptors persist for at least 15 to 30 days after caffeine withdrawal (325,329). In one study, chronic caffeine and withdrawal had no effect on densities of cerebral cortical A_1-adenosine receptors (335). In this study, there was also no change in A_1-adenosine receptor-mediated inhibition of brain adenylate cyclase. Densities of striatal A_{2A}-adenosine receptors appeared to be increased by chronic caffeine in one study (280), while no change in striatal A_2 receptors was revealed by autoradiography in another study with theophylline (334). Almost all studies on upregulation of adenosine receptors are in rats, but at least one study used mice (330). Upregulation of A_1-adenosine receptors after chronic caffeine has also been reported for gerbils (336). The gerbil hippocampus exhibited less neuronal injury during ischemia after chronic caffeine.

There was no apparent effect of chronic caffeine in rats on A_1-adenosine receptor-mediated inhibition of lipolysis in fat cells, or on A_{2B}-adenosine receptor-mediated stimulation of cyclic AMP in brain slices (313,335). Another study with chronic caffeine revealed an increase in A_1 receptors in rat adipocytes but no change in inhibition of either lipolysis or adenylate cyclase activity by adenosine analogs (337). Stimulations of adenylate cyclase in rat platelets by NECA or prostaglandin E_1 are both increased after chronic caffeine, as are NECA- and prostaglandin-elicited inhibition of platelet aggregation (338). In humans, chronic caffeine appears to up-regulate A_2-adenosine receptors in platelets, as assessed by greater potency of NECA as an inhibitor of aggregation (338). Chronic caffeine increases the hypotensive effects of adenosine in rats (339).

The locomotor stimulant (at very low doses) and locomotor depressant effects of the adenosine analog N^6-R-phenylisopropyladenosine in rats appears unaltered after chronic caffeine (335,340–342). But in mice, N^6-R-phenylisopropyladenosine is more potent as a locomotor depressant after chronic treatment with caffeine (326). Chronic treatment with theophylline (by injection) enhances the inhibitory effects of adenosine on evoked potentials in hippocampal pyramidal neurons of hippocampal slices (328). In contrast to the many studies in which adenosine receptors or adenosine responses were augmented after chronic caffeine or theophylline, chronic theophylline resulted in a complete loss of the ability of adenosine to enhance depolarizing responses to N-methyl aspartate in mouse neocortical slices (343,344). The ability of isoproterenol to enhance responses also was lost, while that of serotonin was unaffected. GABA had no effect before theophylline-treatment, but potentiated the response after treatment.

Treatments other than caffeine that alter adenosine receptor densities or function should be mentioned. Chronic stress, like caffeine, causes an increase in rat brain A_1-adenosine receptors (317,319). Chronic morphine causes an increase in A_1-adenosine receptors without effect on the analgesic potency of an adenosine analog (299). Chronic carbamazepine, a putative adenosine receptor antagonist, causes an increase in rat brain A_1-adenosine receptors (327,345). In another study, chronic carbamazepine treatment slightly increased the behavioral depressant effects of N^6-R-phenylisopropyladenosine but not NECA and had no effect on the behavioral stimulant effects of caffeine (169). Chronic diazepam treatment of rats appeared to decrease levels of striatal A_{2A}-adenosine receptors, while having no significant effect on levels of brain A_1-adenosine receptors (346).

Benzodiazepine-binding sites are either unaffected (329) or slightly increased (325) after chronic caffeine. Stimulatory effects of GABA on binding of ligands to the benzodiazepine-site are reduced by chronic caffeine treatment (347). Seizure thresholds for convulsants are increased after chronic theophylline (332). Upregulation of A_1-adenosine receptors by chronic theophylline in rats, however, reversed in ten days, while the increase in seizure threshold to bicucculine required about 20 days to reverse (348).

β-Adrenergic receptor densities in brain are decreased by chronic caffeine treatment (322,349,350). Densities of α_1 or α_2-adrenergic receptors are unchanged. The reduction in β-receptors was proposed to be caused by a slight increase in apparent turnover of norepinephrine—but not dopamine—in rat forebrain (349). An adenosine analog has a greater inhibitory effect on electrically-stimulated release of norepinephrine in hippocampal slices from caffeine-treated rats (350). Chronic caffeine increases dopamine and serotonin in striatum, norepinephrine in frontal cortex, and serotonin and a norepinephrine metabolite in cerebellum (351). Other studies have reported no effects on amines after chronic caffeine or theophylline (352). Chronic caffeine alters levels of certain free amino acids in mouse brain (353). The increases in glutamate and decreases in GABA are perhaps noteworthy.

Levels of cholinergic receptors after chronic caffeine have not been assessed. Chronic caffeine has no effect on the ability of adenosine to inhibit release of acetylcholine from electrically-stimulated brain slices (320) but does reduce the excitatory effect of acetylcholine on rat cerebral cortical neurons (354).

The alterations in adenosine receptors or function observed after chronic caffeine or theophylline indicate that blockade of adenosine receptors is one significant action of the methylxanthines, while changes in the GABA receptor channel, in β-adrenergic receptors, and in acetylcholine function indicate that there are actions at these sites or pathways. Such actions might be indirect, as in an enhancement in the presence of chronic caffeine of inputs from GABAergic, noradrenergic, or cholinergic pathways. Further studies on dopamine, serotonin, and histamine and excitatory amino acid pathways are needed.

TOLERANCE AND WITHDRAWAL

Tolerance to the stimulatory effects of caffeine on locomotor activity has been reported for mice and rats (244,318,326,335,340–343,355–357). The tolerance develops rapidly (within one to three days), appears to be specific to xanthines, and is reversible within three to four days. In some cases, the tolerance appeared "insurmountable"; i.e., increasing doses of caffeine still evoked no stimulation of locomotor activity. The tolerance can be elicited by either chronic theophylline (341) or caffeine, and extends to other stimulatory xanthines (342), but not to responses to other stimulants, such as cocaine and amphetamine, nor to a variety of depressants, such as adenosine analogs, diazepam, and chlorpromazine (335,341,342). Pentobarbital, however, is less potent as a behavioral depressant in caffeine-treated rats (342). Chronic treatment of rats with a very low level of caffeine resulted in sensitization to caffeine-elicited locomotor stimulation (357).

Chronic treatment of mice by injection with N^6-R-phenylisopropyladenosine results in a decrease in the potency of the adenosine analog as a behavioral depressant and an increase in the potency of caffeine as a behavioral stimulant (326).

Chronic treatment with caffeine also causes the development of tolerance to effects of caffeine in schedule-controlled responding (142,340) and in discriminative stimulus paradigms (340). In contrast to the tolerance to locomotor stimulation, tolerance to caffeine in schedule-controlled responding and discrimination paradigms develops more slowly; it is surmountable by caffeine and, in the case of discriminative paradigms, extends to another stimulant methylphenidate (340). In rats, the biphasic curve for effects of caffeine—both stimulatory and inhibitory—on response rates can be left-shifted by chronic treatment with caffeine (142). Stimulation of wheelrunning was increased by caffeine during the course of repetitive daily injections to rats but this appeared linked to greater wheelrunning experience (358).

Evaluation of tolerance to caffeine is made more difficult by the biphasic nature of many of caffeine's effects. If this is the result of two independent mechanisms, it is possible that chronic caffeine will affect the mechanisms differently and that the stimulatory mechanism could then be masked by the inhibitory mechanism.

Chronic treatment with caffeine resulted in tolerance to other effects of caffeine. These included the stimulatory effect of caffeine on firing of neurons of the reticular formation of the mesencephalon (318). Chronic treatment of rats with theophylline had no effect on the convulsant action of theophylline (359), although chronic caffeine in rats in a different paradigm resulted in a lowering of sensitivity to other convulsants (321). Chronic theophylline also causes a reduction in seizure thresholds for several convulsants (342,348). Chronic caffeine appears to protect from ischemic damage to forebrain neurons in rats (360) and hippocampal neurons in gerbils (336). The biphasic stimulatory—then inhibitory—effects of caffeine on release of acetylcholine from electrically stimulated cerebral cortical slices are abolished after chronic caffeine (320). The ability of caffeine to elevate plasma corticosterone and thyroid-stimulating hormone is lost after chronic caffeine (127).

Withdrawal from caffeine in humans can elicit a variety of symptoms, including headache, irritability, nervousness, and reduction in energy (361,362). It will be difficult to define the basis for such symptoms in animals. Indeed, there have been no detailed mechanistic studies during withdrawal after chronic treatment with caffeine.

The development of tolerance to caffeine and the occurrence of withdrawal symptoms leads to the question of dependence and addiction. In animals, self-administration of caffeine is difficult to demonstrate (363–365, see also K. Bättig and H. Welzl, this volume).

SUMMARY

There has been an incredible amount of research relevant to the mechanism of action of caffeine. This chapter has attempted to provide an overview—albeit incomplete—of this literature. The emphasis has been on the behavioral effects of caffeine, a pharmacological action familiar to many humans. It would appear that antagonism of endogenous adenosine through blockade of adenosine receptors has a significant role in the behavioral effects of caffeine. The specific sites of such antagonism that are linked to the behavioral effects, however, are far from clear. Dopaminergic, GABAergic, serotoninergic, and cholinergic systems may all be affected. Furthermore, there are many observations on the behavioral effects of caffeine—both alone and in combination with other agents—that are not readily rationalized by a simplistic blockade of adenosine receptors. It would appear premature to conclude that calcium mobilization, direct effects on $GABA_A$ receptors, and even inhibition of phosphodiesterases do not also play a role in the central nervous system pharmacology of caffeine. The underlying mechanism of the rapidly developing tolerance to caffeine is probably complex and not linked solely to an upregulation of adenosine receptors. The field remains active, but it will undoubtedly be years before a satisfactory understanding of the complex mechanism of the action of caffeine is attained.

ACKNOWLEDGMENT

The support of the International Life Science Institute for our program on "Mechanism of Action of Caffeine and Theophylline" is gratefully acknowledged.

REFERENCES

1. Griffiths RR, Woodson PP. Reinforcing effects of caffeine in humans. *J Pharmacol Exp Therap* 1988;246:21–8.
2. Hughes JR, Higgins ST, Bickel WK, et al. Caffeine self-administration, withdrawal, and adverse effects. *Arch Gen Psychiatry* 1991;48:611–7.
3. Mally J, Stone TW. The effect of theophylline on essential tremor: The possible role of GABA. *Pharmacol Biochem Behav* 1991;39:345–9.
4. Neims AH, Von Borstel RW. Caffeine: Its metabolism and biochemical mechanisms of action. In: Wurtman RJ, Wurtman JJ, eds. *Nutrition and the Brain;* vol 6. New York: Raven Press, 1983;1–30.
5. Arnaud MJ. The pharmacology of caffeine. *Prog Drug Res* 1987;31:273–313.
6. Daly JW. Adenosine receptors: Targets for future drugs. *J Med Chem* 1982;25:197–207.
7. Williams M. Purine receptors in mammalian tissues: pharmacology and functional significance. *Ann Rev Pharmacol Toxicol* 1987;27:315–45.
8. Jacobson KA, van Galen PJM, Williams M. Adenosine receptors: pharmacology, structure activity relationships and therapeutic potential. *J Med Chem* 1992;35:407–22.
9. Linden J. Structure and function of A_1 adenosine receptors. *FASEB J* 1991;5:2668–76.
10. Greene RW, Haas HL, Hermann A. Effects of caffeine on hippocampal pyramidal cells in vitro. *Br J Pharmacol* 1985;85:163–9.
11. Dolphin AC, Forda SR, Scott RH. Calcium-dependent currents in cultured rat dorsal root ganglion neurons are inhibited by an adenosine analog. *J Physiol (London)* 1986;373:47–61.
12. Hu P-S, Fredholm BB. α_2-Adrenoceptor agonist-mediated inhibition of [^{3}H]noradrenaline release from rat hippocampus is reduced by 4-aminopyridine, but that caused by an adenosine analogue or w-conotoxin is not. *Acta Physiol Scand* 1989;136:347–57.

13. Silinsky EM. Adenosine derivatives and neuronal function. *The Neurosciences* 1989;1: 155–65.
14. Michaelis ML, Johe KK, Moghadam B, Adams RN. Studies on the ionic mechanism for the neuromodulatory actions of adenosine in the brain. *Brain Res* 1988;473:249–60.
15. Lundy PM, Frew R, Hamilton MG. Failure of adenosine analogues to affect N-type voltage sensitive Ca^{2+} channels in chick brain synaptosomes. *Biochem Pharmacol* 1990;40:651–4.
16. Ribeiro JA, Sebastião AM. Adenosine receptors and calcium: basis for proposing a third (A_3) adenosine receptor. *Prog Neurobiol* 1986;26:179–209.
17. Mager R, Ferroni S, Schubert P. Adenosine modulates a voltage-dependent chloride conductance in cultured hippocampal neurons. *Brain Res* 1990;532:58–62.
18. Delahunty TM, Cronin MJ, Linden J. Regulation of GH_3-cell function via adenosine A_1 receptors. Inhibition of prolactin release, cyclic AMP production and inositol phosphate generation. *Biochem J* 1988;255:69–77.
19. Narang N, Garg LC, Crews FT. Adenosine and its analogs stimulate phosphoinositide hydrolysis in the kidney. *Pharmacology* 1990;40:90–5.
20. Hollingsworth EB, Daly JW. Accumulation of inositol phosphates and cyclic AMP in guinea pig cerebral cortical preparations. Effects of norepinephrine, histamine, carbamycholine and 2-chloroadenosine. *Biochim Biophys Acta* 1985;847:207–16.
21. Alexander SPH, Hill SJ, Kendall DA. Is the adenosine receptor modulation of histamine-induced accumulation of inositol phosphates in cerebral cortical slices mediated by effects on calcium ion fluxes? *J Neurochem* 1990;55:1138–41.
22. Daly JW, Butts-Lamb P, Padgett W. Subclasses of adenosine receptors in the central nervous system: interaction with caffeine and related methylxanthines. *Cell Mol Neurobiol* 1983;1:67–80.
23. Bruns RF, Lu GH, Pugsley TA. Characterization of the A adenosine receptor labeled by [^{3}H]NECA in rat striatal membranes. *Mol Pharmacol* 1986;29:331–46.
24. Munshi R, Clanachan AS, Baer HP. 5′-Deoxy-5′-methylthioadenosine. A nucleoside which differentiates between adenosine receptor types. *Biochem Pharmacol* 1988;37: 2085–9.
25. Fenton RA, Bruttig SP, Rubio R, Berne RM. Effect of adenosine on calcium uptake by intact and cultured vascular smooth muscle. *Am J Physiol* 1982;242:H797–H804.
26. Cushing DJ, Brown GL, Sabouni MH, Mustafa SJ. Adenosine receptor-mediated coronary artery relaxation and cyclic nucleotide production. *Am J Physiol* 1991;261:H343–8.
27. Brackett LE, Daly JW. Relaxant effects of adenosine analogs on guinea pig trachea *in vitro*. Xanthine-sensitive and xanthine-insensitive mechanisms. *J Pharmacol Exp Therap* 1991;257:205–13.
28. Church MK, Hughes PJ. Adenosine potentiates immunological histamine release from rat mast cells by a novel cyclic AMP-independent cell-surface action. *Br J Pharmacol* 1985; 85:3–5.
29. Ali H, Cunha-Melo JR, Saul WF, Beaven MA. The activation of phospholipase C via adenosine receptors provide synergistic signals for secretion in antigen stimulated RBL-2H3 cells: Evidence for a novel adenosine receptor. *J Biol Chem* 1990;265:745–53.
30. Ali H, Müller CE, Daly JW, Beaven MA. Methylxanthines block antigen-induced responses in RBL-2H3 cells independently of adenosine receptors or cyclic AMP: Evidence for inhibition of antigen binding to IgE. *J Pharmacol Exp Therap* 1990;258:954–62.
31. Ukena D, Shamim MT, Padgett W, Daly JW. Analogs of caffeine: antagonists with selectivity for A_2 adenosine receptors. *Life Sci* 1986;39:743–50.
32. Daly JW, Hide I, Müller CE, Shamim M. Caffeine analogs: structure activity relationships at adenosine receptors. *Pharmacology* 1991;42:309–21.
33. Moos WH, Szotek DS, Bruns RF. N^6-Cycloalkyladenosines. Potent A_1-selective adenosine agonists. *J Med Chem* 1985;28:1383–4.
34. Shamim MT, Ukena D, Padgett WL, Daly JW. Effects of 8-phenyl and 8-cycloalkyl substitutents on the activity of mono-, di-, and trisubstituted alkylxanthines with substitution at the 1-, 3-, and 7-positions. *J Med Chem* 1989;32:1231–7.
35. Seale TW, Abla KA, Shamim MT, Carney JM, Daly JW. 3,7-Dimethyl-1-propargylxanthine: a potent and selective *in vivo* antagonist of adenosine analogs. *Life Sci* 1988;43: 1671–84.
36. Choi OH, Shamim MT, Padgett WL, Daly JW. Caffeine and theophylline analogues: corre-

lation of behavioral effects with activity as adenosine receptor antagonists and as phosphodiesterase inhibitors. *Life Sci* 1988;43:387–98.

37. Snyder SH, Katims JJ, Annau Z, Bruns RF, Daly JW. Adenosine receptors and behavioral actions of methylxanthines. *Proc Nat Acad Sci USA* 1981;78:3260–4.

38. Katims JJ, Annau Z, Snyder SH. Interactions in the behavioral effects of methylxanthines and adenosine derivatives. *J Pharmacol Exp Therap* 1983;227:167–73.

39. Daly JW, Padgett W, Shamim MT, Butts-Lamb P, Waters J. 1,3-Dialkyl-8-(*p*-sulfophenyl)-xanthines: potent water soluble antagonists for A_1- and A_2-adenosine receptors. *J Med Chem* 1985;28:487–92.

40. Heller LJ, Olsson RA. Inhibition of rat ventricular automaticity by adenosine. *Am J Physiol* 1985;248:H907–13.

41. Bruns RF. Adenosine antagonism by purines, pteridines and benzopteridines in human fibroblasts. *Biochem Pharmacol* 1981;30:325–33.

42. Durcan MJ, Morgan PF. NECA-induced hypomotility in mice: evidence for a predominately central site of action. *Pharmacol Biochem Behav* 1990;32:487–90.

43. Brodie MS, Lee K, Fredholm BB, Ståhle L, Dunwiddie TV. Central versus peripheral mediation of responses to adenosine receptor agonists: evidence against a central mode of action. *Brain Res* 1987;415:423–30.

44. Tithapanda A, Maling HM, Gillette JR. Effects of caffeine and theophylline on activity of rats in relation to brain xanthine concentrations. *Proc Soc Exp Biol Med* 1972;139:582–6.

45. Coffin VL, Taylor JA, Phillis JW, Altman HJ, Barraco RA. Behavioral interaction of adenosine and methylxanthines on central purinergic systems. *Neuroscience Lett* 1984;47:91–8.

46. Crawley JN, Patel J, Marangos PJ. Behavioral characterization of two long-lasting adenosine analogs: sedative properties and interactions with diazepam. *Life Sci* 1981;29:2623–30.

47. Barraco RA, Coffin VL, Altman HJ, Phillis JW. Central effects of adenosine analogs on locomotor activity in mice and antagonism of caffeine. *Brain Res* 1983;272:392–5.

48. Phillis JW, Barraco RA, Delong RE, Washington DO. Behavioral characteristics of centrally administered adenosine analogs. *Pharmacol Biochem Behav* 1986;24:263–70.

49. Kakiuchi S, Rall TW, McIlwain H. The effect of electrical stimulation upon the accumulation of adenosine 3',5'-phosphate in isolated cerebral tissue. *J Neurochem* 1969;16:485–91.

50. Sattin A, Rall TW. The effect of adenosine and adenine nucleotides on the adenosine 3',5'-phosphate content of guinea pig cerebral cortex slices. *Mol Pharmacol* 1970;69:13–23.

51. Rall TW, Sutherland EW. Formation of a cyclic adenine ribonucleotide by tissue particulates. *J Biol Chem* 1958;232:1065–76.

52. Sattin A. Increase in the content of adenosine 3',5'-monophosphate in mouse forebrain during seizures and prevention of the increase by methylxanthines. *J Neurochem* 1971;18:1087–96.

53. Breckenridge BM. The measurement of cyclic adenylate in tissues. *Proc Nat Acad Sci USA* 1964;52:1580–6.

54. Paul MI, Pauk GL, Ditzion BR. The effect of centrally acting drugs on the concentration of brain adenosine 3',5'-monophosphate. *Pharmacology* 1970;3:148–54.

55. Watanabe H, Passonneau JV. Cyclic adenosine monophosphate in cerebral cortex. Alterations following trauma. *Arch Neurol* 1975;32:181–4.

56. Beer B, Chasin M, Clody DE, Vogel JR, Horovitz ZP. Cyclic adenosine monophosphate phosphodiesterase in brain: effect on anxiety. *Science* 1972;176:428–30.

57. Beavo JA, Riefsnyder DH. Primary sequence of cyclic nucleotide phosphodiesterase isozymes and the design of selective inhibitors. *Trends Pharmacol Sci* 1990;11:150–5.

58. Wachtel H. Characteristic behavioral alterations in rats induced by rolipram and other selective adenosine cyclic 3',5'-monophosphate phosphodiesterase inhibitors. *Psychopharmacology* 1982;77:309–16.

59. Wachtel H. Potential antidepressant activity of rolipram and other selective cyclic adenosine 3',5'-monophosphate phosphodiesterase inhibitors. *Neuropharmacology* 1983;22:267–72.

60. Nicholson CD, Jackman SA, Wilke R. The ability of denbufylline to inhibit cyclic nucleotide phosphodiesterase and its affinity for adenosine receptors and the adenosine uptake site. *Br J Pharmacol* 1989;97:889–97.

61. Sutor B, Alzheimer C, Ameri A, Bruggencate GT. The low K_M-phosphodiesterase inhibitor

denbufylline enhances neuronal excitability in guinea pig hippocampus in vitro. *Naunyn-Schmiedeberg's Arch Phrmacol* 1990;342;349;356.

62. Gaal L, Schudt C, Illes P. Effects of phosphodiesterase inhibition on the excitability of hippocampal pyramidal neurons in vitro. *Eur J Pharmacol* 1991;202:117–20.

63. Dunwiddie TV, Hoffer BJ, Fredholm BB. Alkylxanthines elevate hippocampal excitability. Evidence for a role of endogenous adenosine. *Naunyn-Schmiedeberg's Arch Pharmacol* 1981;316:326–30.

64. Moraidis J, Bingmann D, Lehmenkühler A, Speckmann E-J. Caffeine-induced epileptic discharges in CA3 neurons of hippocampal slices of the guinea pig. *Neurosci Lett* 1991; 129:51–4.

65. Tanaka Y, Sakurai M, Goto M, Hayashi S. Effect of xanthine derivatives on hippocampal long-term potentiation. *Brain Res* 1990;522:63–8.

66. Persson CGA, Erjefält I. Seizure activity in animals given enprofylline and theophylline, two xanthines with partly different mechanisms of action. *Arch Int Pharmacodyn* 1982; 258:267–82.

67. Schmitz W, von der Leyen H, Meyer W, Neumann J, Scholz H. Phosphodiesterase inhibition and positive inotropic effects. *J Cardovasc Pharmacol* 1989;14 (suppl 3):S11–4.

68. Persson CGA, Erjefält I, Karlsson J-A. Adenosine antagonism, a less desirable characteristic of xanthine asthma drugs? *Acta Pharmacol Toxicol* 1981;49:317–20.

69. Persson CGA, Karlsson J-A, Erjefält I. Differentiation among bronchodilation and universal adenosine antagonism among xanthine derivatives. *Life Sci* 1982;30:2181–9.

70. Brackett LE, Shamim MT, Daly JW. Activities of caffeine, theophylline, and enprofylline analogs as tracheal relaxants. *Biochem Pharamcol* 1990;39:1897–904.

71. Ogawa K, Takagi K, Satake T. Mechanism of xanthine-induced relaxation of guinea pig isolated trachealis muscle. *Br J Pharmacol* 1989;97:542–6.

72. Polson JB, Krzanowski JJ, Szentvanyi A. Correlation between inhibition of a cyclic GMP phosphodiesterase and relaxation of canine tracheal smooth muscle. *Biochem Pharmacol* 1985;34:1875–9.

73. Torphy TJ, Undem BJ. Phosphodiesterase inhibitors: new opportunities for the treatment of asthma. *Thorax* 1991;46:512–23.

74. Fredholm BB, Hedqvist P, Vernet L. Effect of theophylline and other drugs on rabbit renal cyclic nucleotide phosphodiesterase, 5'-nucleotidase and adenosine deaminase. *Biochem Pharmacol* 1978;27:2845–50.

75. Fredholm BB, Lindgren E. Inhibition of soluble 5'-nucleotidase from rat brain by different xanthine derivatives. *Biochem Pharamcol* 1983;32:2832–4.

76. Croce MA, Kramer GL, Garbers DL. Inhibition of alkaline phosphatase by substituted xanthines. *Biochem Pharmacol* 1979;28:1227–31.

77. Belloni FL, Liang BC, Gerritsen ME. Effects of alkylxanthines and calcium antagonists on adenosine uptake by cultured rabbit coronary microvascular endothelium. *Pharmacology* 1987;35:1–15.

78. Fredholm BB, Lindström K. The xanthine derivative 1-(5'-oxohexyl)-3-methyl-7-propylxanthine (HWA 285) enhances the actions of adenosine. *Acta Pharmacol Toxicol* 1986;58: 187–92.

79. Wu PH, Barraco A, Phillis JW. Further studies on the inhibition of adenosine uptake into rat brain synaptosomes by adenosine derivatives and methylxanthines. *Gen Pharmacol* 1984;15:251–4.

80. Mante S, Minneman KP. Caffeine inhibits forskolin-stimulated cyclic AMP accumulation in rat brain. *Eur J Pharmacol* 1990;175:203–205.

81. Mante S, Minneman KP. Is adenosine involved in inhibition of forskolin-stimulated cyclic AMP accumulation by caffeine in rat brain? *Mol Pharmacol* 1990;38:652–9.

82. DeLapp HW, Eckols K. Forskolin stimulation of cyclic AMP in rat brain cortex slices is markedly enhanced by endogenous adenosine. *J Neurochem* 1992;58:237–42.

83. Ramkumar V, Stiles GL. A novel site of action of a high affinity A_1 adenosine receptor antagonist. *Biochem Biophys Res Commun* 1988;153:939–44.

84. Parsons WJ, Ramkumar V, Stiles GL. Isobutylmethylxanthine stimulates adenylate cyclase by blocking the inhibitory regulatory protein, G_i. *Mol Pharmacol* 1988;34:37–41.

85. Strinden ST, Stellwagen RH. Inhibition of guanylate cyclases by methylxanthines and papaverine. *Biochem Biophys Res Commun* 1984;123:1194–200.

86. Weber A, Herz R. The relationship between caffeine contracture of intact muscle and the effect of caffeine on reticulum. *J Gen Physiol* 1988;52:750–9.
87. Blinks JR, Olson CB, Jewell BR, Bravery P. Influence of caffeine and other methylxanthines on mechanical properties of isolated mammalian heart muscle. *Circ Res* 1972;30: 367–92.
88. Vigne P, Breittmayer J-P, Marsault R, Frelin C. Endothelin mobilizes Ca^{2+} from a caffeine- and ryanodine-insensitive intracellular pool in rat atrial cells. *J Biol Chem* 1990;265: 6782–7.
89. Matsumoto T, Kanaide H, Shogakiuchi Y, Makamura M. Characteristics of the histamine-sensitive calcium store in vascular smooth muscle. *J Biol Chem* 1990;265:5610–6.
90. Stauderman KA, McKinney RA, Murawsky MH. The role of caffeine-sensitive Ca^{2+} stores in agonist- and inositol 1,4,5-trisphosphate-induced Ca^{2+} release from bovine adrenal chromaffin cells. *Biochem J* 1991;278:643–50.
91. Berridge MJ. Caffeine inhibits inositol-trisphosphate-induced membrane potential oscillations in *Xenopus* oocytes. *Proc Royal Soc Lond B* 1991;244:57–62.
92. Clusin WT. Caffeine induces a transient inward current in cultured cardiac cells. *Nature* 1983;301:248–50.
93. Gupta MP, Makino N, Takeo S, Kaneko M, Dhalla MS. Cardiac sarcolemma as a possible site of action of caffeine in rat heart. *J Pharmacol Exp Therap* 1990;255:1188–94.
94. Kuba K, Nishi S. Rhythmic hyperpolarizations and depolarization of sympathetic ganglion cells induced by caffeine. *J Neurophysiol* 1976;39:547–63.
95. Poisner AM. Caffeine-induced catecholamine secretion: similarity to caffeine-induced muscle contraction. *Proc Soc Exp Biol Med* 1973;142:102–5.
96. Rousseau E, Ladine J, Liu Q-Y, Meissner G. Activation of the CA^{2+} release channel of skeletal muscle sarcoplasmic reticulum by caffeine and related compounds. *Arch Biochem Biophys* 1988;267:75–86.
97. Collis MG, Keddie JR, Torr SR. Evidence that the positive inotropic effects of alkylxanthines are not due to adenosine receptor blockade. *Br J Pharmacol* 1984;81:401–7.
98. Evoniuk G, Von Borstel RW, Wurtman RJ. Antagonism of the cardiovascular effects of adenosine by caffeine or 8-(p-sulfophenyl)theophylline. *J Pharmacol Exp Therap* 1987; 240:428–32.
99. Fassina G, Gaion RM, Caparrotta C, Carpenedo F. A caffeine analogue (1,3,7-trimethyl-6-thioxo-2-oxopurine) with a negative inotropic and chronotropic effect. *Naunyn-Schmiedeberg's Arch Pharmacol* 1985;330:222–36.
100. Tseng C-J, Biaggioni I, Appalsamy M, Robertson D. Purinergic receptors in the brainstem mediate hypotension and bradycardia. *Hypertension* 1988;11:191–7.
101. Ribeiro JA, Monteiro EC. On the adenosine receptor involved in the excitatory action of adenosine on respiration: antagonist profile. *Nucleosides Nucleotides* 1991;10:945–53.
102. Von Borstel RW, Evoniuk GE, Wurtman RJ. Adenosine potentiates sympathomimetic effects of nicotinic agonists *in vivo*. *J Pharmacol Exp Therap* 1986;236:344–9.
103. Malave A, Eberhard NK, Yim GKW. Caffeine potentiation of positive inotropic and pressor effects of phencyclidine. *Res Commun Substances Abuse* 1982;3:279–82.
104. Yukawa T, Kroegel C, Charez P, et al. Effect of theophylline and adenosine on eosinophil function. *Am Rev Respiratory Dis* 1989;140:327–33.
105. Manzini S, Ballati L. 2-Chloroadenosine induction of vagally-mediated and atropine-resistant bronchomotor responses in anaesthetized guinea-pigs. *Br J Pharmacol* 1990;100: 251–6.
106. Ghai G, Zimmerman MB, Hopkins MF. Evidence for A_1 and A_2 adenosine receptors in guinea pig trachea. *Life Sci* 1987;41:1215–24.
107. Farmer SG, Canning BJ, Wilkins DE. Adenosine receptor-mediated contraction and relaxation of guinea-pig isolated tracheal smooth muscle: effects of adenosine antagonists. *Br J Pharmacol* 1988;95:371–8.
108. Ahlijanian MK, Takemori AE. Effects of caffeine and 8-phenyl-theophylline on the actions of purines and opiates in the guinea-pig ileum. *J Pharmacol Exp Therap* 1986;236:171–6.
109. Caparrotta I, Cillo F, Fassina G, Gaion RM. Dual effect of $(-)$-N^6-phenylisopropyladenosine on guinea-pig trachea. *Br J Pharmacol* 1984;83:23–9.
110. Spielman WS, Arend LJ. Adenosine receptors and signalling in the kidney. *Hypertension* 1991;17:117–30.

111. Spielman WS. Antagonistic effect of theophylline on the adenosine-induced decrease in renin release. *Am J Physiol* 1984;247:F246–51.
112. Tofovic SP, Branch KR, Oliver RD, Magee WD, Jackson EK. Caffeine potentiates vasodialtor-induced renin release. *J Pharmacol Exp Therap* 1991;256:850–60.
113. Rossi NF, Churchill PC, Jacobson KA, Leahy AE. Further characterization of the renovascular effects of N^6-cyclohexyladenosine in the isolated perfused rat kidney. *J Pharmacol Exp Therap* 1987;240:911–15.
114. Oliw E, Auggard E, Fredholm BB. Effect of indomethacin on the renal actions of theophylline. *Eur J Pharmacol* 1972;43:9–16.
115. Takeuchi K, Kogo H, Aizawa Y. Effects of methylxanthines on urinary prostaglandin E secretion in rats. *Japan J Pharmacol* 1980;31:253–9.
116. Takeuchi K, Kogo H, Aizawa Y. Effect of theophylline on the release and contents of prostaglandins E and F in rat renal medulla. *Japan J Pharmacol* 1981;31:477–9.
117. Horrobin DF, Manku MS, Franks DJ, Hamet P. Methylxanthine phosphodiesterase inhibitors behave as prostaglandin antagonists in a perfused rat mesenteric artery preparation. *Prostaglandins* 1977;13:33–40.
118. Schiffman SS, Gill JM, Diaz C. Methylxanthines enhance taste: evidence for modulation of taste by adenosine receptor. *Pharmacol Biochem Behav* 1985;22:195–203.
119. Schiffman SS, Diaz C, Becker TG. Caffeine intensifies taste of certain sweeteners: role of adenosine receptor. *Pharmacol Biochem Behav* 1986;24:429–32.
120. Howell RE, Muchsam WT, Kinnier WJ. Mechanism for the emetic side effect of xanthine bronchodilators. *Life Sci* 1990;46:563–8.
121. Garbers DL, Lust WD, First NL, Hardy HA. Effects of phosphodiesterase inhibitors and cyclic nucleotides on sperm respiration and motility. *Biochemistry* 1971;10:1825–31.
122. Jiang CS, Kilfeather SA, Pearson RM, Turner P. The stimulatory effects of caffeine, theophylline, lysine-theophylline and 3-isobutyl-1-methylxanthine on human sperm motility. *Br J Clin Pharmacol* 1984;18:258–62.
123. Vijayaraghauan S, Hoskins DD. Regulation of bovine sperm motility and cyclic adenosine 3',5'-monophosphate by adenosine and its analogues. *Biol Reprod* 1986;34:468–77.
124. Kopf GS, Lewis CA, Vacquier VD. Characterization of basal and methylxanthine-stimulated Ca^{2+} transport in abalone spermatozoa. *J Biol Chem* 1984;259:5514–20.
125. Spindel E, Arnold M, Cusack B, Wurtman RJ. Effects of caffeine on anterior pituitary and thyroid function in the rat. *J Pharmacol Exp Therap* 1980;214:58–62.
126. Arnold MA, Carr DB, Togasaki DM, Piar MC, Martin JB. Caffeine stimulates β-endorphin release in blood but not in cerebrospinal fluid. *Life Sci* 1982;31:1017–24.
127. Spindel E, Griffith L, Wurtman RJ. Neuroendocrine effects of caffeine. II. Effects on thyrotropin and corticosterone secretion. *J Pharmacol Exp Therap* 1983;225:346–50.
128. Henry JP, Stephens PM. Caffeine as an intensifier of stress-induced hormonal and pathophysiologic changes in mice. *Pharmacol Biochem Behav* 1980;13:719–27.
129. Moyer JH, Tashnek AB, Miller SI, Snyder H, Bowman RO. The effect of theophylline with ethylenediamine (aminophylline) and caffeine on cerebral hemodynamics and cerebrospinal fluid pressure in patients with hypertension headaches. *Am J Med Sci* 1952;244:377–85.
130. Nehlig A, de Vascoucelos P, Boyet S. Effects of caffeine and/or L-phenylisopropyladenosine (LPIA) on local cerebral blood flow and glucose utilization in the rat. *Nucleosides Nucleotides* 1991;10:1225–26.
131. Kaplan GB, Tai NT, Greenblatt DJ, Shader RI. Caffeine-induced behavioral stimulation is dose- and concentration-dependent. *Br J Pharmacol* 1991;160:435–40.
132. White BC, Simpson CC, Adams JE, Harleins Jr D. Monoamine synthesis and caffeine-induced locomotor activity. *Neuropharmacology* 1978;17:511–3.
133. Holloway Jr WR, Thor DH. Caffeine sensitivity in the neonatal rat. *Neurobehav Toxicol Teratol* 1982;4:331–3.
134. Hughes RN, Greig AM. Effects of caffeine, methamphetamine and methylphenidate on reactions to novelty and activity in rats. *Neuropharmacology* 1976;15:673–6.
135. Oettinger R, Martin JR, Rosenberg E, Bättig K. Effects of tunnel/maze complexity on caffeinic hyperactivity in the rat. *Pharmacol Biochem Behav* 1985;23:85–90.
136. Castellano C. Effects of caffeine on discrimination, learning consolidation, and learned behavior in mice. *Psychopharmacology* 1976;48:255–60.

137. Castellano C. Effects of pre- and post-trial caffeine administrations on simultaneous visual discrimination in three inbred strains of mice. *Psychopharmacology* 1977;51:255–8.
138. Winsky L, Harvey JA. Effects of N⁶-(L-phenylisopropyl)adenosine, caffeine, theophylline and rolipram on the acquisition of conditioned responses in the rabbit. *J Pharmacol Exp Therap* 1987;241:223–9.
139. McKim WA. The effect of caffeine, theophylline and amphetamine on operant responding of the mouse. *Psychopharmacology* 1980;68:135–8.
140. Sanger DJ. The effects of caffeine on timing behavior in rodents. Comparisons with chlordiazepoxide. *Psychopharmacology* 1980;68:305–9.
141. Meliska CJ, Brown RE. Effects of caffeine on schedule-controlled responding in the rat. *Pharmacol Biochem Behav* 1982;16:745–50.
142. Carney JM. Effects of caffeine, theophylline, theobromine on scheduled controlled responding in rats. *Br J Pharmacol* 1982;75:451–4.
143. Shull RN, Holloway FA. Effects of caffeine and L-PIA on rats with selective damage of the hippocampal system. *Pharmacol Biochem Behav* 1985;22:449–59.
144. Coffin VL, Spealman RD. Psychomotor-stimulant effects of 3-isobutyl-1-methylxanthine; comparison with caffeine and 7-(2-chloroethyl)-theophylline. *Eur J Pharmacol* 1989;170:35–40.
145. Spealman RD. Psychomotor stimulant effects of methylxanthines in squirrel monkeys: Relationship to adenosine antagonism. *Psychopharmacology* 1988;95:19–24.
146. Mumford GK, Holtzman SG. Methylxanthines elevate reinforcement threshold for electrical brain stimulation: role of adenosine receptors and phosphodiesterase inhibition. *Brain Res* 1990;528:32–8.
147. Mumford GK, Holtzman SG. Do adenosinergic substrates mediate methylxanthine effects upon reinforcement thresholds for electrical brain stimulation in the rat. *Brain Res* 1991;550:172–8.
148. Holtzman SG. Discriminative-stimulus properties of caffeine in the rat: noradrenergic mediation. *J Pharmacol Exp Therap* 1986;239:706–14.
149. Modrow HE, Holloway FA, Carney JM. Caffeine discrimination in the rat. *Pharmacol Biochem Behav* 1981;14:683–8.
150. Modrow HE, Holloway FA. Drug discrimination and cross generalization between two methylxanthines. *Pharmacol Biochem Behav* 1985;23:425–9.
151. Carney JM, Holloway FA, Modrow HE. Discriminative stimulus properties of methylxanthines and their metabolites in rats. *Life Sci* 1985;36:913–20.
152. Mumford GK, Holtzman SG. Qualitative differences in the discriminative stimulus effects of low and high doses of caffeine in the rat. *J Pharmacol Exp Therap* 1991;258:857–65.
153. Holloway Jr WR, Thor DH. Caffeine and social investigation in the adult male rat. *Neurobehav Toxicol Teratol* 1983;5:119–25.
154. Thor DH, Holloway Jr WR. Play soliciting in juvenile male rats: effects of caffeine, amphetamine and methylphenidate. *Pharmacol Biochem Behav* 1983;19:725–7.
155. Holloway Jr WR, Thor DH. Acute and chronic caffeine exposure. Effects on playfighting in the juvenile rat. *Neurobehav Toxicol Teratol* 1984;6:85–91.
156. Holloway Jr WR, Thor DH. Caffeine: effects on the behaviors of juvenile rats. *Neurobehav Toxicol Teratol* 1983;5:127–34.
157. Hilakivi LA, Durcan MJ, Lister RG. Effects of caffeine on social behavior, exploration and locomotor activity: interactions with ethanol. *Life Sci* 1989;44:543–53.
158. File SE, Hyde JRG. A test of anxiety that distinguishes between the actions of benzodiazepines and those of other minor tranquilizers and of stimulants. *Pharmacol Biochem Behav* 1979;11:65–9.
159. Sakata T, Fuchimoto H. Stereotyped and aggressive behavior induced by sustained high dose of theophylline in rats. *Japan J Pharmacol* 1973;23:781–5.
160. Sakata T, Fuchimoto H. Further aspects of aggressive behavior induced by sustained high dose of theophylline in rats. *Japan J Pharmacol* 1973;23:787–92.
161. Lloyd HGE, Stone TW. Chronic methylxanthine treatment in rats: a comparison of Wistar and Fischer 344 strains. *Pharmacol Biochem Behav* 1981;14:827–30.
162. Mueller K, Saboda S, Palmour R, Nyhan WL. Self-injurious behavior produced in rats by daily caffeine and continuous amphetamine. *Pharmacol Biochem Behav* 1982;17:613–7.
163. Miñana MD, Portolés M, Jordá A, Grisolía S. Lesch-Nyhan syndrome, caffeine model: increase of purine and pyrimidine enzymes in rat brain. *J Neurochem* 1984;43:1556–60.

164. Nikodijevic O, Daly JW, Jacobson KA. Characterization of the locomotor depression produced by an A_2-selective adenosine agonist. *FEBS Lett* 1990;261:67–70.
165. Nikodijevic O, Sarges R, Daly JW, Jacobson KA. Behavioral effects of A_1- and A_2-selective adenosine agonists and antagonists: evidence for synergism and antagonism. *J Pharmacol Exp Therap* 1991;259:286–94.
166. Baumgold J, Nikodijevic O, Jacobson KA. Penetration of adenosine antagonists into mouse brain as determined by ex-vivo binding. *Biochem Pharmacol* 1992;43:889–94.
167. Griebel G, Misslin R, Vogel E. Behavioral effects of selective A_2 adenosine receptor antagonists CGS 21197 and CGS 22706 in mice. *Neuroreport* 1991;2:139–40.
168. Griebel G, Saffroy-Spittler M, Misslin R, Remmy D, Vogel E, Bourguignon J-J. Comparison of the behavioral effects of an adenosine A_1/A_2- receptor antagonist, CGS 15943A, and an A_1 selective antagonist, DPCPX. *Psychopharmacology* 1991;103:541–4.
169. Elphick M, Taghavi Z, Powell T, Godfrey PP. Chronic carbamazepine down-regulates adenosine A_2 receptors: studies with the putative selective adenosine antagonists PD115,119 and PD116,948. *Psychopharmacology* 1990;100:522–9.
170. Bruns RF, Davis RE, Ninteman FW, Poschel BPH, Wiley JM, Heffner TG. Adenosine antagonists as pharmacological tools. In: Paton DM, ed. *Adenosine and adenine nucleotides: physiology and pharmacology*. Taylor and Francis, 1988:39–50.
171. Clark M, Post RM. Carbamazepine, but not caffeine, is highly selective for adenosine A_1 binding sites. *Eur J Pharmacol* 1989;169:399–406.
172. Holtzman SG. CGS 15943, a nonxanthine adenosine receptor antagonist: effects on locomotor activity of nontolerant and caffeine-tolerant rats. *Life Sci* 1991;49:1563–70.
173. Holloway Jr WR. Caffeine: effects of acute and chronic exposure on the behavior of neonatal rats. *Neurobehav Toxicol Teratol* 1982;4:21–32.
174. Concannon JT, Braughler JM, Schecter MD. Pre- and postnatal effects of caffeine on brain biogenic amines, cyclic nucleotides and behavior in developing rats. *J Pharmacol Exp Therap* 1983;226:673–9.
175. Sinton CM, Valatx JL, Jouvet M. Gestational caffeine modifies offspring behavior in mice. *Psychopharmacology* 1981;75:69–74.
176. Nakamoto T, Roy G, Gottschalk SB, Yazdani M, Rossowska M. Lasting effects of early chronic caffeine feeding on rats behavior and brain in later life. *Physiol Behav* 1991;49: 721–7.
177. Hughes RN, Beveridge IJ. Sex and age dependent effects of prenatal exposure to caffeine on open field behavior, emergence latency and adrenal weights in rats. *Life Sci* 1990;47: 2075.
178. Zimmerberg B, Carr KL, Scott A, Lee HH, Weider JM. The effects of postnatal caffeine on growth, activity and learning in rats. *Pharmacol Biochem Behav* 1991;39:883–8.
179. Guillet R, Kellogg C. Neonatal exposure to therapeutic caffeine alters the ontogeny of adenosine A_1 receptors in brain of rats. *Neuropharmacology* 1991;30:489–96.
180. Guillet R. Neonatal caffeine exposure alters adenosine receptor control of locomotor activity in the developing rat. *Dev Pharmacol Ther* 1990;15:94–100.
181. Burgess JW, Monachello MP. Chronic exposure to caffeine during early development increases dendritic spine and branch formation in midbrain optic tectum. *Dev Brain Res* 1983;6:123–9.
182. Logan L, Seale TW, Carney JM. Inherent differences in sensitivity to methylxanthines among inbred mice. *Pharmacol Biochem Behav* 1986;24:1281–6.
183. Seale TW, Johnson P, Carney JM, Rennert OM. Interstrain variation in acute toxic response to caffeine among inbred mice. *Pharmacol Biochem Behav* 1984;20:567–73.
184. Buckholtz NS, Middaugh LD. Effects of caffeine and L-phenylisopropyladenosine on locomotor activity of mice. *Pharmacol Biochem Behav* 1987;28:179–85.
185. Seale TW, Roderick TH, Johnson P, Logan L, Rennert OM, Carney JM. Complex genetic determinants of suceptibility to methylxanthine-induced locomotor activity changes. *Pharmacol Biochem Behav* 1986;24:1333–41.
186. Seale TW, Johnson P, Roderick TH, Carney JM, Rennert OM. A single gene difference determines relative susceptibility to caffeine-induced lethality in SWR and CBA inbred mice. *Pharmacol Biochem Behav* 1985;23:275–8.
187. Carney JM, Cao W, Logan L, Rennert OM, Seale TW. Differential antagonism of the behavioral depressant and hypothermic effects of 5'-(N-ethylcarboxamide)adenosine by theobromine. *Pharmacol Biochem Behav* 1986;25:769–73.

188. Glowa JR, Spealman RD. Behavioral effects of caffeine, N^6-(L-phenylisopropyl)adenosine and their combination in the squirrel monkey. *J Pharmacol Exp Therap* 1984;231:665–70.
189. Glowa JR, Sobel E, Malaspina S, Dews PB. Behavioral effects of caffeine, (−)-N-[(R)-1-methyl-2-phenylethyl]adenosine (PIA), and their combination in the mouse. *Psychopharmacology* 1985;87:471–74.
190. Goldberg SR, Prada JA, Katz JL. Stereoselective behavioral effects of N^6-phenylisopropyladenosine and antagonism by caffeine. *Psychopharmacology* 1985;87:272–7.
191. Spencer Jr DG, Lal H. Discriminative stimulus properties of L-phenylisopropyladenosine: blockade by caffeine and generalization to 2-chloroadenosine. *Life Sci* 1983;32:2329–33.
192. Logan L, Carney JM. Antagonism of the behavioral effects of L-phenyl-isopropyladenosine (L-PIA) by caffeine and its metabolites. *Pharmacol Biochem Behav* 1984;21:375–9.
193. Durcan MJ, Morgan PF. Evidence for adenosine A_2 receptor involvement in hypomobility effects of adenosine analogues in mice. *Eur J Pharmacol* 1989;168:285–90.
194. Hadfield MG, Milio C. Caffeine and regional brain monoamine utilization in mice. *Life Sci* 1989;45:2637–44.
195. Murray TF, Blaker WD, Cheney DL, Costa E. Inhibition of acetylcholine turnover rate in rat hippocampus and cortex by intraventricular injection of adenosine analogs. *J Pharmacol Exp Therap* 1982;222:550–4.
196. Forloni G, Fisone G, Consolo S, Ladinsky H. Qualitative differences in the effects of adenosine analogs on the cholinergic systems of rat striatum and hippocampus. *Naunyn-Schmiedeberg's Arch Pharmacol* 1986;334:86–91.
197. Waldeck B. On the interaction between caffeine and barbiturates with respect to locomotor activity and brain catecholamines. *Acta Pharmacol Toxicol* 1975;36:1–9.
198. Katsura H, Hashimoto T, Kuriyama K. Effect of 1,3-di-n-butyl-7-(2-oxopropyl)-xanthine (denbufylline) on metabolism and function of cerebral cholinergic neurons. *Japan J Pharmacol* 1991;55:233–40.
199. Galloway MP, Roth RH. Neuropharmacology of 3-isobutylmethylxanthine: effects on central noradrenergic systems *in vivo*. *J Pharmacol Exp Therap* 1983;227:1–8.
200. Stone TW, Hollins C, Lloyd H. Methylxanthines modulate adenosine release from slices of cerebral cortex. *Brain Res* 1981;207:421–31.
201. Schechter MD. Caffeine potentiation of amphetamine: implications for hyperkinesis therapy. *Pharmacol Biochem Behav* 1977;6:359–61.
202. White BC, Keller III GE. Caffeine pretreatment: enhancement and attenuation of d-amphetamine-induced activity. *Pharmacol Biochem Behav* 1984;20:383–6.
203. Klawans HL, Moses III H, Beaulieu DM. The influence of caffeine on d-amphetamine- and apomorphine-induced stereotyped behavior. *Life Sci* 1974;14:1493–500.
204. Misra AL, Vadlamani NL, Pontani RB. Effect of caffeine on cocaine locomotor stimulant activity in rats. *Pharmacol Biochem Behav* 1986;24:761–4.
205. Holtzman SG. Discriminative stimulus effects of caffeine: Tolerance and cross-tolerance with methylphenidate. *Life Sci* 1987;40:381–9.
206. Schenk S, Horger B, Snow S. Caffeine preexposure sensitizes rats to the motor activating effects of cocaine. *Behav Pharmacol* 1989–1990;1:447–51.
207. Waldeck B. Sensitization by caffeine of central catecholamine receptors. *J Neural Transmission* 1973;34:61–72.
208. Zarrindast MR, Nasir T. Methylxanthine-induced attenuation of pecking in chickens. *Brit J Pharmacol* 1991;104:327–30.
209. Erinoff L, Snodgrass SR. Effects of adult or neonatal treatment with 6-hydroxydopamine or 5,7-dihydroxytryptamine on locomotor activity, monoamine levels, and response to caffeine. *Pharmacol Biochem Behav* 1986;24:1039–45.
210. Govoni S, Petkov VV, Montefusco O, et al. Differential effects of caffeine on dihydroxyphenylacetic acid concentrations in various rat brain dopaminergic structures. *J Pharm Pharmacol* 1984;36:458–60.
211. Horger BA, Wellman PJ, Morien A, Davies BT, Schenk S. Caffeine exposure sensitizes rats to the reinforcing effects of cocaine. *Neuroreport* 1991;2:53–6.
212. Swerdlow NR, Koob GF. Separate neural substrates of the locomotor-activating properties of amphetamine, heroine, caffeine and corticotropin releasing factor (CRF) in the rat. *Pharmacol Biochem Behav* 1985;23:303–7.
213. Joyce EM, Koob GF. Amphetamine-, scopolamine- and caffeine-induced locomotor activ-

ity following 6-hydroxydopamine lesions of the mesolimbic dopamine system. *Psychophar-macology* 1981;73:311–3.

214. Swerdlow NR, Vaccarino FJ, Amalric M, Koob GF. The neural substrates for the motor-activating properties of psychostimulants: a review of recent findings. *Pharmacol Biochem Behav* 1986;25:233–48.
215. Ferré S, von Euler G, Johansson B, Fredholm BB, Fuxe K. Stimulation of high-affinity adenosine A_2 receptors decreases the affinity of dopamine D_2 receptors in rat striatal membranes. *Proc Natl Acad Sci USA* 1991;88:7238–41.
216. Fuxe K, Ungerstedt U. Action of caffeine and theophyllamine on supersensitive dopamine receptors: Considerable enhancement of receptor response to treatment with dopa and dopamine receptor agonists. *Med Biol* 1974;52:48–54.
217. Green RD, Proudfit HK, Yeung S-MH. Modulation of striatal dopaminergic function by local injection of 5′-N-ethylcarboxamide adenosine. *Science* 1982;218:58–61.
218. Fredholm BB, Fuxe K, Agnati L. Effect of some phosphodiesterase inhibitors on central dopamine mechanisms. *Eur J Pharmacol* 1976;38:31–8.
219. Fredholm BB, Herrara-Marschwitz M, Jonzon B, Lindstrom K, Ungerstedt U. On the mechanism by which methylxanthines enhance apomorphine-induced rotation in the rat. *Pharmacol Biochem Behav* 1983;19:535–54.
220. Herrera-Marschitz M, Casas M, Ungerstedt U. Caffeine produces contralateral rotation in rats with unilateral dopamine denervation: comparisons with apomorphine-induced responses. *Psychopharmacology* 1988;94:38–45.
221. Casas M, Ferré S, Cobos A, Grau JM, Jané F. Relationship between rotational behavior induced by apomorphine and caffeine in rats with unilateral lesion of the nigrostriatal pathway. *Neuropharmacology* 1989;28:407–9.
222. Brown SJ, Gill R, Evenden JL, Iversen SD, Richardson PJ. Striatal A_2 receptor regulates apomorphine-induced turning in rats with unilateral dopamine denervation. *Psychophar-macology* 1991;103:78–82.
223. Josselyn SA, Beninger RJ. Behavioral effects of intrastriatal caffeine mediated by adeno-sinergic modulation of dopamine. *Pharmacol Biochem Behav* 1991;39:97–103.
224. Carey RJ. Reinstatement by caffeine of an extinguished conditioned dopaminergic drug response. *Pharmacol Biochem Behav* 1990;36:127–32.
225. Porter NM, Radulovaki M, Green RD. Desensitization of adenosine and dopamine recep-tors in rat brain after treatment with adenosine analogs. *J Pharmacol Exp Therap* 1988; 244:218–25.
226. Stoner GR, Skirboll LR, Werkman S, Hommer DW. Preferential effects of caffeine on limbic and cortical dopamine systems. *Biol Psychiatry* 1988;23:761–8.
227. Foote WE, Holmes P, Pritchard A, Hatcher C, Mordes J. Neurophysiological and pharma-codynamic studies on caffeine and on interactions between caffeine and nicotinic acid in the rat. *Neuropharmacology* 1978;17:7–12.
228. Schallek W, Kuehn A. Effects of drugs on spontaneous and activated EEG in the rat. *Arch Int Pharmacodyn Therap* 1959;120:319–33.
229. Finn IB, Iuvone PM, Holtzman SG. Depletion of catecholamines in the brain of rats differentially affects stimulation of locomotor activity by caffeine, D-amphetamine and methylphenidate. *Neuropharmacology* 1990;29:625–31.
230. Estler C-J. Influence of pimozide on the locomotor hyperactivity produced by caffeine. *J Pharm Pharmacol* 1979;31:126–7.
231. Logan L, Carney JM, Holloway FA, Seale TW. Effects of caffeine, cocaine and their combination on fixed-interval behavior in rats. *Pharmacol Biochem Behav* 1989;33:99–104.
232. Glowa JR. Some effects of d-amphetamine, caffeine, nicotine and cocaine on schedule-controlled responding of the mouse. *Neuropharmacology* 1986;25:1127–35.
233. Evans EB, Wenger GR. The acute effects of caffeine, cocaine and d-amphetamine on the repeated acquisition responding of pigeons. *Pharmacol Biochem Behav* 1990;35:631–6.
234. Falk JL, Lau CE. Synergism by caffeine and by cocaine of the motor control deficit produced by midazolam. *Pharmacol Biochem Behav* 1991;39:525–9.
235. Holloway FA, Michaelis RC, Huerta PL. Caffeine-phenethylamine combinations mimic the amphetamine discriminative cue. *Life Sci* 1985;36:723–30.
236. Casas M, Ferrè S, Guix T, Janè F. Theophylline reverses haloperidol-induced catalepsy in the rat. Possible relevance to the pharmacological treatment of psychosis. *Biol Psych* 1988;24:642–8.

237. Dijk S, Krugers HJ, Korf J. The effect of theophylline and immobilization stress on halo-peridol-induced catalepsy and on metabolism in the striatum and hippocampus, studied with lactography. *Neuropharmacology* 1991;30:469–73.
238. Ferré S, Guix T, Sallés J, et al. Paraxanthine displaces the binding of [^{3}H]SCH 23390 from rat striatal membranes. *Eur J Pharmacol* 1990;179:295–9.
239. Mikkelsen EJ. Caffeine and schizophrenia. *J Clin Psychiatry* 1978;39:732–6.
240. Shoul PW, Farrell MK, Maloney MJ. Caffeine toxicity as a cause of acute psychosis in anorexia nervosa. *J Pediatr* 1984;105:493–5.
241. Yen-Koo HCY, Krop S, Mendez HC. Antagonism of caffeine-facilitated conflict-induced behavior by depressants in cats. *Pharmacology* 1982;25:111–5.
242. Kulkarni SK, Mehta AK. Purine nucleoside-mediated immobility in mice: reversal by antidepressants. *Psychopharmacology* 1985;85:460–3.
243. Estler C-J. Effect of α- and β-adrenergic blocking agents and parachlorophenylalanine on morphine- and caffeine-stimulated locomotor activity of mice. *Psychopharmacologia* 1973; 28:261–8.
244. Ray SK, Poddar MK. Role of central serotonin in caffeine-induced stimulation of locomotor activity in rat. *Biogenic Amines* 1990;7:153–64.
245. Valzelli L, Baernasconi S. Behavioral and neurochemical effects of caffeine in normal and aggressive mice. *Pharmacol Biochem Behav* 1973;1:251–4.
246. Meliska CJ, Loke WH. Caffeine and nicotine: differential effects on ambulation, rearing and wheelrunning. *Pharmacol Biochem Behav* 1984;21:871–5.
247. Lee EHY, Isai MJ, Tank YP, Chai CY. Differential biochemical mechanisms mediate locomotor stimulation effects by caffeine and nicotine in rats. *Pharmacol Biochem Behav* 1987;26:427–30.
248. Toray SN, Kulkarni SK. Antagonism of caffeine-induced convulsions by ethanol and di-zocilpine (MK-801) in mice. *Meth Find Exp Clin Pharmacol* 1991;13:413–7.
249. Marangos PJ, Pand SM, Parma AM, Goodwin FK, Syapin P, Skolnick P. Purinergic inhibi-tion of diazepam binding to rat brain (*in vitro*). *Life Sci* 1979;24:851–8.
250. Boulenger J-P, Patel J, Marangos PJ. Effects of caffeine and theophylline on adenosine and benzodiazepine receptors in human brain. *Neurosci Lett* 1982;30:161–6.
251. Skerritt JH, Chow SC, Johnston GAR, Davies LP. Purines interact with 'central' but not 'peripheral' benzodiazepine binding sites. *Neurosci Lett* 1982;34:63–8.
252. Morgan PF, Deckert J, Jacobson KA, Marangos PJ, Daly JW. Potent convulsant actions of the adenosine receptor antagonist, xanthine amine congener (XAC). *Life Sci* 1989;45: 719–28.
253. De Angelis L, Bertolissi M, Nardini U, Trasvesa U, Vertua R. Interaction of caffeine with benzodiazepines: Behavioral effects in mice. *Arch Int Pharmacodyn* 1982;255:89–102.
254. Pole P, Bonetti EP, Pieri L, et al. Caffeine antagonizes several central effects of diazepam. *Life Sci* 1981;28:2265–75.
255. Czuczwar SJ, Gasior M, Janusz W, Czczepanik B, Wlodarczyk D, Kleinrok Z. Influence of different methylxanthines on the anticonvulsant activity of common antiepileptic drugs in mice. *Epilepsia* 1990;31:318–23.
256. Roache JD, Griffiths RR. Interactions of diazepam and caffeine: behavioral and subjective dose effects in humans. *Pharmacol Biochem Behav* 1987;26:801–12.
257. Czuczwar SJ, Turski WA, Ikonomidou C, Turski L. Aminophylline and CGS 8216 reverse the protective action of diazepam against electroconvulsions in mice. *Epilepsia* 1985;26: 693–6.
258. Marangos PJ, Martino AM, Paul SM, Skolnick P. The benzodiazepines and inosine antago-nize caffeine-induced seizures. *Psychopharmacology* 1981;72:269–73.
259. Velluci SV, Webster RA. Antagonism of caffeine-induced seizures in mice by Ro 15-1788. *Eur J Pharmacol* 1984;77:289–93.
260. Lopez F, Miller LG, Greenblatt DJ, Kaplan GB, Shader RI. Interaction of caffeine with the GABA$_A$ receptor complex: alterations in receptor function but not ligand binding. *Eur J Pharmacol* 1989;172:453–9.
261. Nistri A, Berti C. Caffeine-induced potentiation of GABA effects on frog spinal cord: an electrophysiological study. *Brain Res* 1983;258:263–70.
262. Barraco RA, Phillis JW, Delong RE. Behavioral interaction of adenosine and diazepam in mice. *Brain Res* 1984;323:159–63.

263. Kaplan KB, Greenblatt DJ, Leduc BW, Thompson ML, Shader RI. Relationship of plasma and brain concentrations of caffeine and metabolites to benzodiazepine receptor binding and locomotor activity. *J Pharmacol Exp Therap* 1989;248:1078-83.
264. Coffin VL, Spealman RP. Modulation of the behavioral effects of chlordiazepoxide by methylxanthines and analogs of adenosine in squirrel monkeys. *J Pharmacol Exp Therap* 1985;235:724-8.
265. Holloway FA, Modrow HE, Michaelis RC. Methylxanthine discrimination in the rat: possible benzodiazepine and adenosine mechanisms. *Pharmacol Biochem Behav* 1985;22: 815-24.
266. Baldwin HA, File SE. Caffeine-induced anxiogenesis: the role of adenosine, benzodiazepine and noradrenergic receptors. *Pharmacol Biochem Behav* 1989;32:181-6.
267. Baldwin HA, Johnston AL, File SE. Antagonistic effects of caffeine and yohimbine in animal tests of anxiety. *Eur J Pharmacol* 1989;159:211-5.
268. Haraguchi H, Kuribara H. Behavioral effects of adenosine agonists: evaluation by punishment, discrete shuttle avoidance and activity tests in mice. *Japan J Pharmacol* 1991;55: 303-10.
269. Seale TW, Abla KA, Roderick TH, Rennert OM, Carney JM. Different genes specific hyporesponsiveness to seizures induced by caffeine and the benzodizepine inverse agonist, DMCM. *Pharmacol Biochem Behav* 1987;27:451-6.
270. Albertson TE, Joy RM, Stark LG. Caffeine modification of kindled amygdaloid seizures. *Pharmacol Biochem Behav* 1983;19:339-43.
271. Dragunow M. Adenosine receptor antagonism accounts for the seizure-prolonging effects of aminophylline. *Pharmacol Biochem Behav* 1990;36:751-5.
272. Dar MS. The biphasic effects of centrally and peripherally administered caffeine on ethanol-induced motor incoordination in mice. *J Pharm Pharmacol* 1988;40:482-7.
273. Clark M, Dav MS. Mediation of acute ethanol-induced motor disturbances by cerebellar adenosine in rats. *Pharmacol Biochem Behav* 1988;30:155-61.
274. Dar MS. Central adenosinergic system involvement in ethanol-induced motor incoordination in mice. *J Pharmacol Exp Therap* 1990;255:1202-9.
275. Dar MS. Functional correlation between subclasses of brain adenosine receptor affinities and ethanol-induced motor incoordination in mice. *Pharmacol Biochem Behav* 1990;37: 747-57.
276. Dar MS, Jones M, Close G, Mustafa SJ, Wooles WR. Behavioral interactions of ethanol and methylxanthines. *Psychopharmacology* 1987;91:1-4.
277. Dar MS, Mustafa SJ, Wooles WR. Possible role of adenosine in the CNS effects of ethanol. *Life Sci* 1983;33:1363-74.
278. Carmichael FJ, Israel Y, Crawford M, et al. Central nervous system effects of acetate: contribution to the central effects of ethanol. *J Pharmacol Exp Therap* 1991;259:403-8.
279. Proctor WR, Dunwiddie TV. Behavioral sensitivity to purinergic drugs parallels ethanol sensitivity in selectively bred mice. *Science* 1984;224:519-21.
280. Vinegar R, Truax JF, Selph JL, Welch RM, White HL. Potentiation of the anti-inflammatory and analgesic activity of aspirin by caffeine in the rat. *Proc Soc Exp Biol Med* 1976; 151:556-60.
281. Laska EM, Sunshine A, Mueller F, Elvers WB, Siegel C, Rubin A. Caffeine as an analgesic adjuvant. *J Am Medical Assoc* 1984;251:1711-8.
282. Ward N, Whitney C, Avery D, Dunner D. The analgesic effects of caffeine in headache. *Pain* 1991;44:151-5.
283. Collins C, Laird RI, Richards PT, Stormer GA, Weyraugh S. Aspirin-caffeine interaction in the rat. *J Pharm Pharmacol* 1979;31:611-4.
284. Oliverio A, Castellano C, Parone F, Vetulani J. Caffeine interferes with morphine-induced hyperactivity but not analgesia. *Polish J Pharmacol Pharm* 1983;35:445-9.
285. Ho IK, Loh HH, Way EL. Cyclic adenosine monophosphate antagonism of morphine analgesia. *J Pharmacol Exp Therap* 1973;185:336-46.
286. Ahlijanian MK, Takemori AE. Effects of (-)-N^6-(R-phenylisopropyl)adenosine (PIA) and caffeine on nociception and morphine-induced analgesia, tolerance and dependence in mice. *Eur J Pharmacol* 1985;112:171-9.
287. Misra AL, Pontani RB, Vadlamani NL. Potentiation of morphine analgesia by caffeine. *Br J Pharmacol* 1985;84:789-91.

288. Paalzov G. Naloxone antagonizes theophylline-induced potentiation of morphine-inhibition of a nociceptive reaction in rats. *Psychopharmacology* 1979;62:235–9.
289. Nicholson D, Reid A, Sawynok J. Effects of forskolin and phosphodiesterase inhibitors on spinal antinociception by morphine. *Pharmacol Biochem Behav* 1991;38:753–8.
290. Sawynok J, Espey MJ, Reid A. 8-Phenyltheophylline reverses the antinociceptive action of morphine in the periaqueductal gray. *Neuropharmacology* 1991;301:871–7.
291. Sweeney MI, White TD, Sawynok J. Intracerebroventricular morphine releases adenosine and adenosine 3′,5′-cyclic monophosphate from the spinal cord via a serotonergic mechanism. *J Pharm Exp Therap* 1991;259:1013–8.
292. Sawynok J, Sweeney MI, White TD. Classification of adenosine receptors mediating antinociception in the rat spinal cord. *Br J Pharmacol* 1986;88:923–30.
293. Paalzow G, Paalzow L. The effects of caffeine and theophylline on nociceptive stimulation in the rat. *Acta Pharmacol Toxicol* 1973;32:22–32.
294. Jurna I. Aminophylline differentiates between the depressant effects of morphine on the spinal nociceptive reflex and on the spinal ascending activity evoked from different C fibres. *Eur J Pharmacol* 1981;71:393–400.
295. Sawynok J. Theophylline-induced potentiation of the antinociceptive action of baclofen. *Br J Pharmacol* 1983;78:353–7.
296. Holmgren M, Hedner J, Mellstrand T, Nordberg G, Hedner Th. Characterization of the antinociceptive effects of some adenosine analogues in the rat. *Naunyn-Schmiedeberg's Arch Pharmacol* 1986;334:290–3.
297. Harrick-Davis K, Chippari S, Lattinger D, Ward SJ. Evaluation of adenosine agonists as potential analgesics. *Eur J Pharmacol* 1989;162:365–9.
298. Wu PH, Phillis JW, Yuen H. Morphine enhances the release of ^{3}H-purines from rat brain cerebral cortical prisms. *Pharmacol Biochem Behav* 1982;17:749–59.
299. Ahlijanian MK, Takemori AE. Changes in adenosine receptor sensitivity in morphine-tolerant and -dependent mice. *J Pharmacol Exp Therap* 1986;236:615–20.
300. Mantegazza P, Tammiso R, Zambotti, Zecca L, Zonta N. Purine involvement in morphine antinociception. *Br J Pharmacol* 1084;83:883–8.
301. Ahlijanian MK, Takemori AE. The effect of chronic administration of caffeine on morphine-induced analgesia, tolerance and dependence in mice. *Eur J Pharmacol* 1986;120:25–32.
302. Yanik G, Glaum S, Radolovacki M. The dose response effects of caffeine on sleep in rats. *Brain Res* 1987;403:177–80.
303. Radulovacki M, Walovitch R, Yank G. Caffeine produces REM sleep rebound in rats. *Brain Res* 1980;201:497–500.
304. Okudaira N, Kripke DF, Mullaney DJ. Theophylline delays human sleep phase. *Life Sci* 1984;34:933–8.
305. Virus RM, Ticho S, Pilditch M, Radulovacki M. A comparison of the effects of caffeine, cyclopentyltheophylline, and alloxazine on sleep in rats. Possible roles of central nervous system adenosine receptors. *Neuropsychopharmacology* 1990;3:243–9.
306. Smolen TN, Smolen A. Purinergic modulation of ethanol-induced sleep time in long-sleep and short-sleep mice. *Alcohol* 1991;8:123–30.
307. Lin MT, Chandra A, Lui GG. The effects of theophylline and caffeine on thermoregulatory functions of rats at different ambient temperatures. *J Pharm Pharmacol* 1980;32:204–8.
308. Wager-Srdav SA, Oken MM, Morley JE, Levine AS. Thermoregulatory effects of purines and caffeine. *Life Sci* 1983;33:2431–8.
309. Durcan MJ, Morgan PF. Hypothermic effects of alkylxanthines: Evidence for a calcium-independent phosphodiesterase action. *Eur J Pharmacol* 1991;204:15–20.
310. Wang LCH, Man SFP, Belcastro AN. Metabolic and hormonal responses in theophylline-increased cold resistance in males. *J Appl Physiol* 1987;63:589–96.
311. Wang LCH, Jourdan ML, Lee TF. Mechanisms underlying the supramaximal thermogenesis elicited by aminophylline in rats. *Life Sci* 1989;44:927–34.
312. Lee TF, Li DJ, Jacobson KA, Wang LCH. Improvement of cold tolerance by selective A_1 adenosine receptor antagonists in rats. *Pharmacol Biochem Behav* 1990;37:107–12.
313. Fredholm BB. Adenosine actions and adenosine receptors after 1 week treatment with caffeine. *Acta Physiol Scand* 1982;115:283–6.
314. Murray TF. Up-regulation of rat cortical adenosine receptors following chronic administration of theophylline. *Eur J Pharmacol* 1982;82:113–4.

315. Boulenger J-P, Patel J, Post RM, Parma AM, Marangos PJ. Chronic caffeine consumption increases the number of brain adenosine receptors. *Life Sci* 1983;32:1135–42.
316. Marangos PJ, Boulenger J-P, Patel J. Effects of chronic caffeine on brain adenosine receptors: regional and ontogenetic studies. *Life Sci* 1984;34:899–907.
317. Boulenger J-P, Marangos PJ, Patel J, Uhde TW, Post RM. Central adenosine receptors: possible involvement in the chronic effects of caffeine. *Psychopharmacol Bull* 1984;20: 431–5.
318. Chou DT, Khan S, Forde J, Hirsh KR. Caffeine tolerance: behavioral, electrophysiological and neurochemical evidence. *Life Sci* 1985;36:2347–58.
319. Boulenger J-P, Marangos PJ, Zander KJ, Hanson J. Stress and caffeine: effects on central adenosine receptors. *Clin Neuropharmacol* 1986;9:79–83.
320. Corradetti R, Pedata F, Pepeu G, Vannuchi MG. Chronic caffeine treatment reduces caffeine but not adenosine effects on cortical acetylcholine release. *Br J Pharmacol* 1986;88: 671–6.
321. Szot P, Sanders RC, Murray TF. Theophylline-induced upregulation of A_1-adenosine receptors associated with reduced sensitivity to convulsants. *Neuropharmacology* 1987;26: 1173–80.
322. Green RM, Stiles GL. Chronic caffeine ingestion sensitizes the A_1 adenosine receptor-adenylate cyclase system in rat cerebral cortex. *J Clin Invest* 1986;77:222–7.
323. Hawkins M, Dugich MM, Porter NM, Urbancic M, Radulovacki M. Effects of chronic administration of caffeine on adenosine A_1 and A_2 receptors in rat brain. *Brain Res Bull* 1988;21:479–82.
324. Ramkumar V, Bumgarner JR, Jacobson KA, Stiles GL. Multiple components of the A_1 adenosine-adenylate cyclase system are regulated in rat cerebral cortex by chronic caffeine ingestion. *J Clin Invest* 1988;82:242–7.
325. Wu PH, Coffin VL. Up-regulation of brain [^{3}H]diazepam binding sites in chronic caffeine-treated rats. *Brain Res* 1984;294:186–9.
326. Ahlijanian MK, Takemori AE. Cross-tolerance studies between caffeine and $(-)$-N^6-(phenylisopropyl)adenosine (PIA) in mice. *Life Sci* 1986;88:577–88.
327. Daval JL, Deckert J, Weiss SRB, Post RM, Marangos PJ. Upregulation of adenosine A_1 receptors and forskolin binding sites following chronic treatment with caffeine or carbamazepine: a quantitative autoradiographic study. *Epilepsia* 1989;30:26–33.
328. Lupica CR, Jarvis MF, Berman RF. Chronic theophylline treatment in vivo increases high affinity adenosine A_1 receptor binding and sensitivity to exogenous adenosine in the in vitro hippocampal slice. *Brain Res* 1991;542:55–62.
329. Boulenger J-P, Marangos PJ. Caffeine withdrawal affects central adenosine receptors but not benzodiazepine receptors. *J Neural Transm* 1989;78:9–19.
330. Zielke CL, Zielke HR. Chronic exposure to subcutaneously implanted methylxanthines. Differential elevation of A_1-adenosine receptors in mouse cerebellar and cerebral cortical membranes. *Biochem Pharmacol* 1987;36:2533–8.
331. Sanders RC, Murray JF. Chronic theophylline exposure increases agonist and antagonist binding to A_1 adenosine receptors in rat brain. *Neuropharmacology* 1988;27:757–60.
332. Szot P, Sanders RC, Murray TF. Theophylline-induced upregulation of A_1-adenosine receptors associated with reduced sensitivity to convulsants. *Neuropharmacology* 1987;26: 1173–80.
333. Fastbom J, Fredholm BB. Effects of long-term theophylline treatment on adenosine A_1-receptors in rat brain: autoradiographic evidence for increased receptor number and altered coupling to G-proteins. *Brain Res* 1990;507:195–9.
334. Lupica CR, Berman FR, Jarvis MF. Chronic theophylline treatment increases adenosine A_1, but not A_2, receptor binding in the rat brain; an autoradiographic study. *Synapse* 1991; 9:95–102.
335. Holtzman SG, Mante S, Minneman KP. Role of adenosine receptors in caffeine tolerance. *J Pharmacol Exp Therap* 1991;256:62–68.
336. Rudolphi KA, Keil M, Fastbom J, Fredholm BB. Ischaemic damage in gerbil hippocampus is reduced following upregulation of adenosine (A_1) receptors by caffeine treatment. *Neurosci Lett* 1989;103:275–80.
337. Zhang Y, Wells JN. Effects of chronic caffeine administration on peripheral adenosine receptors. *J Pharmacol Exp Therap* 1990;254:270–6.

338. Biaggioni I, Paul S, Puckett A, Arzubiaga C. Caffeine and theophylline as adenosine receptor antagonists in humans. *J Pharmacol Exp Therap* 1991;258:588–93.

339. Von Borstel RW, Wurtman RJ, Conlay LA. Chronic caffeine consumption potentiates the hypotensive action of circulating adenosine. *Life Sci* 1983;32:1151–8.

340. Holtzman SG, Finn IB. Tolerance to behavioral effects of caffeine in rats. *Pharmacol Biochem Behav* 1988;29:411–8.

341. Finn IB, Holtzman SG. Tolerance and cross-tolerance to theophylline-induced stimulation of locomotor activity in rats. *Life Sci* 1988;42:2475–82.

342. Finn IB, Holtzman SG. Pharmacologic specificity of tolerance to caffeine-induced stimulation of locomotor activity. *Psychopharmacology* 1987;93:428–34.

343. Mally J, Connick JH, Stone TW. Theophylline down regulates adenosine receptor function. *Brain Res* 1990;509:141–4.

344. Mally J, Connick JH, Stone TW. Changes in neurotransmitter sensitivity in the mouse neocortical slice following propranolol and theophylline administration. *Br J Pharmacol* 1991;102:711–7.

345. Marangos PJ, Weiss SRB, Montgomery et al. Chronic carbamazepine treatment increases brain adenosine receptors. *Epilepsia* 1985;26:493–8.

346. Hawkins M, Pan W, Stefanovich P, Radulovacki M. Desensitization of adenosine A_2 receptors in the striatum of the rat following chronic treatment with diazepam. *Neuropharmacology* 1988;27:1131–40.

347. Roca DJ, Schiller GD, Farb DH. Chronic caffeine or theophylline exposure reduces γ-aminobutyric acid/benzodiazepine receptor site interactions. *Mol Pharmacol* 1988;30:481–5.

348. Sanders RC, Murray TF. Temporal relationship between A_1 adenosine receptor upregulation and alterations in bicuculline seizure susceptibility in rats. *Neurosci Lett* 1989;101:325–30.

349. Goldberg MR, Curatolo PW, Tung C-S, Robertson D. Caffeine down-regulates β adrenoreceptors in rat forebrain. *Neuroscience Lett* 1982;31:47–52.

350. Fredholm BB, Jonzon B, Lindgren E. Changes in noradrenaline release and in beta receptor number in rat hippocampus following long-term treatment with theophylline or L-phenylisopropyladenosine. *Acta Physiol Scand* 1984;122:55–9.

351. Kirch DG, Taylor TR, Gerhardt GA, Benowitz NL, Stephen C, Wyatt RJ. Effect of chronic caffeine administration on monoamine and monoamine metabolite concentrations in rat brain. *Neuropharmacology* 1990;19:599–602.

352. Zielke MR, Zielke CI. Lack of a sustained effect on catecholamines or indoles in mouse brain after long-term subcutaneous administration of caffeine and theophylline. *Life Sci* 1986;39:565–72.

353. Wajda IJ, Banay-Schwartz M, Lajtha A. The effect of caffeine on some mouse brain free amino acid levels. *Neurochemical Res* 1989;14:317–20.

354. Lin Y, Phyllis JW. Chronic caffeine exposure reduces the excitant action of acetylcholine on cerebral cortical neurons. *Brain Res* 1990;524:316–8.

355. Holtzman SG. Complete, reversible drug-specific tolerance to stimulation of locomotor activity by caffeine. *Life Sci* 1983;33:779–87.

356. Finn IB, Holtzman SG. Tolerance to caffeine-induced stimulation of locomotor activity in rats. *J Pharmacol Exp Therap* 1986;238:542–5.

357. Meliska CJ, Landrum RE, Landrum TA. Tolerance and sensitization to chronic and subchronic oral caffeine: effects on wheelrunning in rats. *Pharmacol Biochem Behav* 1990;35:477–9.

358. Meliska CJ, Landrum RE, Loke WH. Caffeine effects: interaction of drug and wheelrunning experience. *Pharmacol Biochem Behav* 1985;23:633–5.

359. Ramzan JM, Levy G. Chronic theophylline administration has no apparent effect on theophylline concentrations required to produce seizures in rats. *Proc Soc Exp Biol Med* 1986;182:176–80.

360. Sutherland GR, Peeling J, Lesiuk HJ, et al. The effects of caffeine on ischemic neuronal injury as determined by magnetic resonance imaging and histopathology. *Neuroscience* 1991;42:171–82.

361. Griffiths RR, Bigelow GE, Liebson IA. Human coffee drinking: reinforcing and physical dependence producing effects of caffeine. *J Pharm Exp Therap* 1986;239:416–25.

362. Griffiths RR, Evans SM, Heishman SJ, et al. Low-dose caffeine physical dependence in humans. *J Pharm Exp Therap* 1990;255:1123–32.
363. Hoffmeister F, Wuttke W. Self-administration of acetylsalicylic acid and combinations with codeine and caffeine in rhesus monkeys. *J Pharm Exp Therap* 1973;186:266–75.
364. Collins RJ; Weeks JP, Cooper MM, Good PI, Russell RR. Prediction of abuse liability of drugs using IV self-administration by rats. *Psychopharmacology* 1984;82:6–13.
365. Griffiths RR, Woodson PP. Reinforcing properties of caffeine: studies in humans and laboratory animals. *Pharmacol Biochem Behav* 1988;29:419–27.

Caffeine, Coffee, and Health,
edited by S..Garattini.
Raven Press, Ltd., New York © 1993.

5

Metabolic Effects of Coffee and Caffeine Intake on the Cardiovascular System

Dag S. Thelle

*Department of Epidemiology, Nordic School of Public Health,
S-402 42 Göteborg, Sweden*

It is likely that coffee exerts an effect upon the cardiovascular system by affecting the clotting system, blood pressure, and lipid metabolism. The results of studies are not consistent, but based upon the available reports, it can be concluded that coffee consumption exerts only a minor and probably negligible effect upon systolic and diastolic blood pressure. Unfiltered coffee however has a considerable cholesterol-raising effect. The subsequent increase in cardiovascular risk by this increase in total cholesterol may be partially reduced by the possible reduction of fibrinolytic time by caffeine. Given the widespread consumption of coffee, both long-term epidemiological studies and experiments should be encouraged to determine the true effect on cardiovascular health.

BACKGROUND

Among the more than a hundred active chemicals in coffee, caffeine is by far the best known (1). Still, its physiological effects on human beings are difficult to disentangle from the overall effects of coffee drinking, as coffee is the most important source of caffeine. When assessing the evidence of a physiological effect of any external factor, including a dietary one, we are faced with the etiological question: Is there a causal relationship between factor and effect? and the medical or public health related question: Is it important?

The evidence of a causal association may stem from different sources. Some evidence will be available from so-called *natural experiments* in which populations or individuals are exposed or not exposed to the factor in question but without the persons themselves really being in control. Such uncontrolled or natural experiments are scarce with regard to coffee or caffeine, even if some particular religious groups abstaining from coffee may give hints with regard to possible detrimental effects of coffee (2). Still, these findings can generate only hypotheses that later must be tested in planned surveys or experiments.

This paper discusses some of the physiological effects of coffee on the cardiovascular system, especially on clotting and coagulation, lipid metabolism, and blood pressure.

COFFEE, CAFFEINE, AND HEMOSTASIS

It is seemingly a paradox that populations with a high incidence of cerebral hemorrhages have a low incidence of myocardial infarctions, especially when considering that increased blood pressure is associated with both these manifestations of cardiovascular disease (3). It is likely that a number of factors are operating in different directions, influencing either the risk for atherosclerosis and clotting, or having an effect on fibrinolysis. Thus when a product such as coffee, with so many active substances, is examined, one must keep in mind that the final result, the overt clinical disease, may not occur because of protective factors overriding the detrimental ones. Therefore, the lack of a relationship between clinical disease and coffee consumption does not necessarily indicate a lack of physiological effects of one or more substances, but may reflect an interaction of these substances operating in opposite directions.

When considering hemostasis, we will assess the effects on clotting or coagulation fibrinolysis and thrombosis or platelet activation. Relatively few studies of the effects of coffee or caffeine upon coagulation factors have been published, and our knowledge of the importance of these factors on the incidence of cardiovascular disease is also relatively scanty (4–6). A cross-sectional study in Finland showed a weak association between fibrinogen and coffee consumption, but the possible confounding effect of cigarette smoking cannot be excluded (4). Only one study published so far has examined the effects of coffee intake on fibrinogen, factor VII and the protein C–protein S system in an experimental setting, but no effects were observed (6). The same group of researchers also examined the effects of caffeine on fibrinogen and factor VII but, again, with inconclusive results.

The other side of the clotting coin is the fibrinolytic system. It has been known for a long time that reduced fibrinolysis is associated with an increased risk of coronary artery disease (7). The possible relationship between triglycerides, Lp(a) and fibrinolysis, as well as better laboratory procedures for assessing this activity, have led to increased interest in this issue. In two experiments a shortening of fibrinolysis time was observed, indicating an activation of the fibrinolytic system (8,9). This was most likely due to caffeine, because the effect was not seen after consumption of decaffeinated coffee. The possible mechanism might be a reduction of plasminogen activator/inhibitor, but these results must be considered preliminary, and no firm conclusions can be drawn. The finding only illustrates that caffeine may have effects that counteract other physiological effects of coffee. The increased risk of coronary heart disease associated with the consumption of decaffeinated coffee observed in a U.S. study may be an indication that there is a relationship between fibrinolysis and caffeine intake (10).

Thrombus formation is closely related to platelet activation. This involves both platelet aggregation and the release of platelet constituents. A number of studies, both experimental and cross-sectional, have examined this issue. The results are inconsistent and, because the studies comprise few people, are often open and uncontrolled for other factors, no firm conclusions can be drawn from them with regard to coffee, platelet aggregation, or thrombus formation (5,11–14).

COFFEE, CAFFEINE, AND BLOOD PRESSURE

In their cross-sectional study of almost 30,000 middle-aged men and women, Stensvold et al. showed that drinking more than one cup of coffee per day was inversely associated with both systolic and diastolic blood pressure (15). They calculated that the decrease in blood pressure with increasing coffee consumption might partially outweigh the increased risk of cardiovascular disease by the cholesterol-raising effect of coffee that was also observed in this study.

The literature is not consistent with regard to coffee, caffeine, and blood pressure. Originally caffeine was thought to lower blood pressure, and Stensvold et al. agree with that view (16). Short-term studies, however, have shown an immediate rise in blood pressure with coffee or caffeine (17). The increase is of short duration, usually less than four hours, and is often accompanied by a modest decrease in heart rate (18,19).

This cardiovascular response does not seem to last long, as tolerance usually develops within a couple of days. This is further supported by numerous experiments that show a negative effect of coffee on blood pressure, but most of these trials are of short duration (20,21).

One long-term experiment recently assessed the effects of coffee brewed according to different methods (17). In this study, 107 subjects aged 18 to 33 years took part in a 12-week trial. After nine weeks, those on boiled, unfiltered coffee and those drinking filtered drip-brew coffee showed no change in blood pressure. This was in contrast to those who abstained from coffee who showed a decline of 6.1 mm Hg in systolic blood pressure. Part of the decrease could be due to weight loss in the coffee-abstaining group, but there remained an unexplained decline of 4.9 mm Hg. There are no previous reports of a decline in blood pressure after abstaining from coffee, but the seemingly conflicting results between the cross-sectional study in Norway and this Dutch experiment warrant further research on the effects of coffee on blood pressure.

COFFEE, CAFFEINE, AND BLOOD LIPIDS

The report from northern Norway in 1983 brought coffee back onto the cardiovascular agenda as a possible cholesterol-increasing factor (22). The first time an experiment on coffee and cholesterol is mentioned in the literature is in 1970. Egede-Nissen reported on the effect of abstaining from coffee on total cholesterol in hypercholesterolemic subjects. This was an uncontrolled observation, but the author claimed that refraining from coffee reduced the total cholesterol level by 17% (23). Four years later, Bjelke reported on the association between total cholesterol and coffee, and he also suggested that bile acids production and secretion could have something to do with this association (24).

A review of the cross-sectional studies published so far illustrates large inconsistencies. Ten of the studies, involving nearly 110,000 subjects, report a significant positive relationship between coffee consumption and serum cholesterol for both sexes (25). Included in this group was a Finnish study (26) in which people aged 25 to 44 years showed a linear increase in serum cholesterol with coffee consumption, irrespective of sex. Serum cholesterol in people aged 45 to 64 years was highest in those drinking 4 to 6 cups of coffee a day, mean cholesterol levels being 0.3 mmol/l higher in these people than in age-matched noncoffee drinkers. This can be compared with the Norwegian observations where those drinking 5 to 8 cups per day had 0.51 mmol/l higher total cholesterol levels than those consuming less than one cup of coffee per day (22). In the remaining studies, the evidence of a link between coffee and cholesterol was less clearcut.

The discrepancies between the studies suggests that confounding factors such as brewing methods were distorting the relationship between coffee and cholesterol. That different brewing methods might be important for the cholesterol-raising effect of coffee was the main area of interest in a doctoral thesis in Rotterdam in 1990 (17). In an extensive meta-analysis including 24 cross-sectional studies, Bak showed that the beta-coefficient or increase in total cholesterol per cup of coffee was 0.008 mmol/l in populations consuming filtered brews; whereas the corresponding figure was 0.038 mmol/l for those drinking unfiltered (boiled) coffee. This observation has been confirmed by experiments in Nordic countries and the Netherlands (27–29). Brewing methods involving filtering resulted in only a very slight increase, if at all, in cholesterol levels compared to the unfiltered brew. The intake of 4 to 6 cups of unfiltered coffee per day was associated with an increase in total cholesterol of 0.5 mmol/l, which corresponds with the results of the cross-sectional studies.

The idea that coffee contained a lipid-raising factor was further taken up by Zock et al. in Wageningen (30). They heated 1,350 kg of water to boiling in 150 kg batches with 15 kg of coarsely ground coffee per batch. After centrifugation a supernatant was visible. This supernatant was lipid rich, and the enrichment was ten times that of boiled coffee. It was given to 10 volunteers and taken with their daily meals for 42 days, corresponding to drinking approximately 6 to 7 cups of unfiltered (boiled) coffee per day. During the trial, LDL-cholesterol increased by 0.85 mmol/l, which again is consistent with what has been observed in experiments exposing people to boiled nonfiltered coffee. Zock et al. concluded that this lipid-raising factor must be a powerful, naturally occurring substance.

It is reasonable to conclude that filtering might retain this substance as the brewing methods seem to be of such importance. This finding—that brewing methods really do play a role—may explain why there are national and regional differences in the cholesterol-raising effect of coffee. The exact nature of the lipid-raising factor is still unknown, as is the mechanism by which this naturally occurring substance exerts its effect. Salonen et al. ascribed a substantial proportion of the decline in total cholesterol levels in Finland over the last 15 years to the change in coffee brewing methods (31).

Thus as long as one prepares coffee by methods that include filtering the brew, one may continue enjoying this popular beverage which, even though it has no known nutritional value, remains one of our most stimulating drinks.

REFERENCES

1. Dews PB, ed. *Caffeine*. Berlin, Heidelberg: Springer Verlag 1984.
2. Fönnebö V. The Tromsö Heart Study; coronary risk factors in Seventh-Day Adventists. *Am J Epidemiol* 1985;122:789–93.
3. Gordon T. Mortality experience among the Japanese in the United States, Hawaii and Japan. Public Health Rep 1957;72:543.
4. Happonen P, Salonen JT, Seppanen K, Rauramaa R. Association of coffee consumption with plasma lipoproteins, fibrinogen and platelet aggregability in middle-aged men. *Proceedings of the meeting of the International Epidemiological Association*. Finland 1987.
5. Naismith DJ, Akinyaniu PA, Szanto S, Yudkin J. The effect in volunteers of coffee and decaffeinated coffee on blood glucose, insulin, plasma lipids and some factors involved in blood clotting. *Nutr Metab* 1970;12:144–51.
6. Bak AAA, Van Vliet HHDM, Grobbee DE. Coffee, caffeine and hemostasis; results from two randomized studies. *Atherosclerosis*. In press.
7. Chakrabarti R, Fearnley GR, Hocking ED, Delitheos A, Clarke GM. Fibrinolytic activity and coronary artery disease. *Lancet* 1966;i;573.
8. Al Samarrae W, Truswell AS. Short-term effect of coffee on blood fibrinolytic activity in healthy adults. *Atherosclerosis* 1977;26:255–60.
9. Wojta J, Kirchheimer JC, Peska MG, Binder BR. Effect of caffeine ingestion on plasma fibrinolytic potential. *Thromb Haemost* 1988;59:337–8.
10. Grobbee DE, Rimm EB, Giovannucci E, Colditz G, Stampfer M, Willett W. Coffee, caffeine, and cardiovascular disease in men. *N Engl J Med* 1990;323:1026–32.
11. Ammaturo V, Perricone C, Canazio A, et al. Caffeine stimulates in vivo platelet reactivity. *Acta Med Scand* 1988;224:245–7.
12. Paoletti R, Corsini A, Tremoli E, Fumagalli R, Catapano AL. Effects of coffee on plasma lipids, lipoproteins and apolipoproteins. *Pharm Res* 1989;21:27–38.

13. Aro A, Kostiainen E, Huttunen JK, Seppala E, Vapaatalo H. Effects of coffee and tea on lipoproteins and prostanoids. *Atherosclerosis* 1985;57:123–8.
14. Bydlowski SP, Yunker RL, Rymaszewski Z, Subblah MTR. Coffee extracts inhibit platelet aggregation in vivo and in vitro. *Int J Vitam Nutr Res* 1987;57:217–23.
15. Stensvold I, Tverdal A, Foss OP. The effect of coffee on blood lipids and blood pressure. Results from a Norwegian cross-sectional study, men and women, 40–42 years. *J Clin Epidemiol* 1989;42:877–84.
16. Robertson D, Curatolo PW. In Dews PB, ed. *Caffeine.* Berlin, Heidelberg: Springer Verlag 1984.
17. Bak AAA. Coffee and cardiovascular risk: an epidemiological study. Rotterdam: Thesis; 1990.
18. Conrad KA, Blanchard J. Trang JM. Cardiovascular effects of caffeine in elderly men. *J Am Geriatr Soc* 1982;30:267–72.
19. Whitsett TL, Manion CV, Christensen HD. Cardiovascular effects of coffee and caffeine. *Am J Cardiol* 1984;53:918–22.
20. Robertson D, Wade D, Workman R, Woosley L, Oates JA. Tolerance to the humoral and hemodynamic effects of caffeine in man. *J Clin Invest* 1981;67:1111–7.
21. Ammon HPT, Bieck PR, Mandalaz D, Verspohl EJ. Adaption of blood pressure to continuous heavy coffee drinking in young volunteers. A double-blind crossover study. *Br J Clin Pharm* 1983;15:701–6.
22. Thelle DS, Arnesen E, Förde OH. The Tromsö Heart Study. Does coffee raise serum cholesterol? *N Engl J Med* 1983;308:1454–7.
23. Egede-Nissen A. Kolesterol og kaffe. En obervasjion fra praksis. *Tdnlf* 1970;90:1506–7.
24. Bjelke E. Colon cancer and blood-cholesterol. *Lancet* 1974;i:116–7.
25. Thelle DS, Heyden S, Fodor JG. Coffee and cholesterol in epidemiological and experimental studies. *Atherosclerosis* 1987;67:97–103.
26. Tuomilehto J, Tanskanen A, Pietinen P, et al. Coffee consumption is correlated with serum cholesterol in middle-aged Finnish men and women. *J Epidemiol Community Health* 1987; 41:237–42.
27. Förde OH, Knutsen SF, Arnesen E, Thelle DS. The Tromsö Heart Study: coffee consumption and serum lipid concentrations in men with hypercholesterolaemia. A randomized intervention study. *Br Med J* 1985;290:893–5.
28. Aro A, Tuomilehto J, Kostianien E, Uusitalo U, Pietinen P. Boiled coffee increases serum low-density lipoprotein concentration. *Metabolism* 1987;36:1027–30.
29. Bak AAA, Grobbee DE. The effect on serum cholesterol levels of coffee brewed by filtering or boiling. *N Engl J Med* 1989;321:1432–7.
30. Zock PL, Katan MB, Merkus MP, van Dusseldorp M, Harryvan JL. Effect of a lipid-rich fraction from boiled coffee on serum cholesterol. *Lancet* 1990;335:1235–7.
31. Salonen JT, Happonen P, Salonen R, et al. Inter-dependence of associations of physical activity, smoking, and alcohol and coffee consumption with serum high-density lipoprotein and non-high-density lipoprotein cholesterol—a population study in Eastern Finland. *Prev Med* 1987;16:647–58.

Caffeine, Coffee, and Health,
edited by S. Garattini.
Raven Press, Ltd., New York © 1993.

6

The Cardiovascular Effects of Caffeine

*†Rogelio Mosqueda-Garcia, *†‡David Robertson, and
*Rose Marie Robertson

*Departments of *Medicine, †Pharmacology, and ‡Neurology, Vanderbilt
University Medical Center, Nashville, Tennessee 37232*

Clinical research during the last decade has greatly increased our understanding of the cardiovascular effects of caffeine, one of the major constituents of coffee. Acute administration of caffeine in coffee-naive subjects results in a modest pressor effect, with biphasic changes in heart rate and significant increases in plasma catecholamines and sympathetic nerve activity. Inhibition of baroreflex activity plays an important role in these effects. This inhibition was clarified in normotensive subjects, in whom acute caffeine administration significantly reduced the reflex bradycardia evoked by a vasopressor agent. The exact mechanism of these hemodynamic effects is likely to involve an antagonism of adenosine receptors within the central nervous system. Whereas adenosine infusion in conscious humans increases blood pressure, its administration in the central nervous system results in hypotension and bradycardia. More relevant, administration of minute doses of caffeine or related methylxanthines in the brainstem causes marked inhibition of baroreflex activation. Finally, concerns have been expressed about the possible health consequences of caffeine's pressor effects. Our group, along with a number of others, has consistently documented, however, that tolerance rapidly develops to most of the cardiovascular effects of caffeine. This may well explain the disparity between the acute effects of caffeine and the relative absence of deleterious cardiovascular consequences of coffee reported in many epidemiological studies. There is a lack of information, on the other hand, concerning the long-term cardiovascular effects of occasional but cyclic coffee drinking in subjects who have not developed tolerance. Future research should focus, as well, on whether a possible interaction between stress and caffeine consumption results in significant pressor effects that might pose a health risk.

INTRODUCTION

Interest in the effect of caffeine on the cardiovascular system has been manifest for more than 100 years. A considerable number of studies were already available when Bock (1) and Eichler (2) revised the literature in 1920 and 1938, respectively. Many studies were carried out in vitro and in animal models, but studies of the human pharmacology of caffeine, increased in the 1970s and 1980s. We will concentrate on studies of caffeine itself, as coffee has many other constituents that may complicate the responses. We will include some data from animal studies but primarily concentrate on effects in humans.

Studies in isolated tissues, perfused organs or whole animal preparations have clearly demonstrated an increase in myocardial contractility with caffeine (3–5) as well as with other methylxanthines such as theophylline (5). The effect on heart rate has been more variable, depending on the dose and route of administration. Bradycardia mediated by parasympathetic activation is seen with modest doses (6), while larger doses can increase heart rate. Blood pressure is increased by intravenous caffeine at doses of 2.5 to 10 mg/kg, although there is a transient initial depressor effect (6) that is not seen when the agent is given by mouth.

CLINICAL STUDIES IN NORMAL SUBJECTS

Early data were often contradictory in humans: a depressor, tachycardiac effect was described by Sollman and Pitcher (7), a pressor, bradycardic effect by Horst (8), while no effect was seen by Starr (9). These discrepancies can be at least partially explained by the subsequent realization that the responses of habitual and nonhabitual consumers are quite different. The controversy led us, in 1978, to undertake a series of investigations of the clinical pharmacology of caffeine in caffeine-naive subjects. We first studied the effect of a single oral dose of caffeine (250 mg; equivalent to 2.1 cups of coffee in the United States) on blood pressure, heart rate, plasma catecholamines, and plasma renin activity (10). We chose nine healthy, noncoffee drinkers who also abstained from tea, chocolate, and caffeine-containing drinks for three weeks prior to the study. Subjects were brought into sodium balance and studied in a double-blind, randomized, cross-over protocol.

Caffeine significantly increased plasma renin activity by 57% (Fig. 1), plasma norepinephrine by 75% (Fig. 2), and plasma epinephrine by 207%, with a rise in plasma caffeine levels from 0 to 11 (range 4.2–26) μg/ml (Fig. 3). Blood pressure increased a maximum of 14/10 mmHg at 60 minutes after caffeine (p < 0.05) and had returned essentially to baseline by three hours after caffeine (Fig. 4). Heart rate fell slightly but significantly (from 66 to 60 bpm) during the period of peak blood pressure rise (45–75 minutes after caffeine) but then rose above baseline (70–72 bpm) during the next 90 minutes (Fig. 4). The elevation in plasma renin activity caused by caffeine in these subjects was of particular interest. If renin samples had been drawn for the purpose of classifying these patients in terms of renin status, several of these

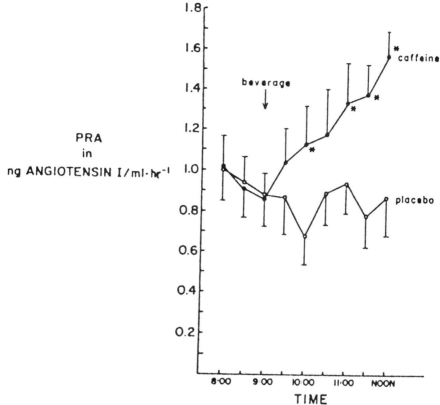

FIG. 1. The effect of 250 mg caffeine (•) or placebo beverage (○) on plasma renin activity (PRA) in 9 normal, noncoffee-drinking subjects. PRA increased by 57% over the three hours after caffeine ingestion, while placebo had no effect. (From Robertson D et al., ref. 10, with permission.)

normotensive subjects might have fallen into a high-renin category. Knowledge of prior caffeine ingestion can be quite important for these classifications.

We felt it was important to place these data in the perspective of prior studies that had included coffee drinkers. It may be even more important to examine more chronic pharmacological effects, in view of the fact that, in some studies, ''noncoffee drinkers'' included persons who ingested as much as 100 mg of caffeine each day. For this reason we used 18 coffee drinkers who had abstained from coffee, colas, tea, and chocolate for three weeks prior to this study (11). Subjects were again studied in sodium balance in a double-blind protocol with random assignment to Group I, which received placebo beverage with each meal, and Group II, which received placebo for

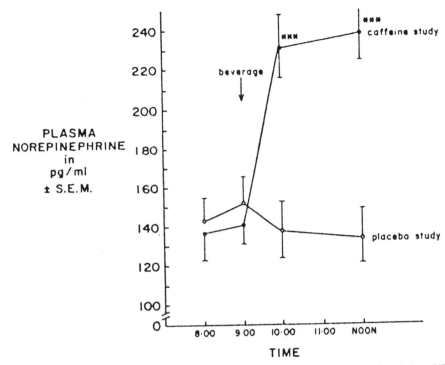

FIG. 2. The effect of 250 mg caffeine (•) or placebo (○) on plasma norepinephrine (NE) levels, sampled sequentially in 9 normal, noncoffee-drinking subjects in sodium balance, who remained supine after beverage ingestion. The rise in NE levels was equivalent to that seen after assuming the upright position. (From Robertson D et al., ref. 10, with permission.)

the first three days, then caffeine (250 mg) with each meal for seven days, and placebo again for four days.

While caffeine levels were slightly higher with each dose after several days of administration, the hemodynamic response demonstrated considerable tolerance (Fig. 5). The acute response to caffeine on day 1 was similar to our prior study, with a rise in systolic pressure of 11.2 ± 2.5 mmHg ($p < 0.01$). However, while the increase in blood pressure after dosing was still significant on day 2 of caffeine administration, by the fourth day there was no effect of caffeine on blood pressure, and this tolerance to an acute dose of 250 mg persisted for the seven days of caffeine administration and throughout the subsequent four days of placebo. Heart rate also showed no response to caffeine during chronic administration.

Catecholamines also exhibited tolerance. The response of both norepinephrine and epinephrine to an acute dose of caffeine was not different from the response to placebo on the seventh day of caffeine administration (Fig. 6).

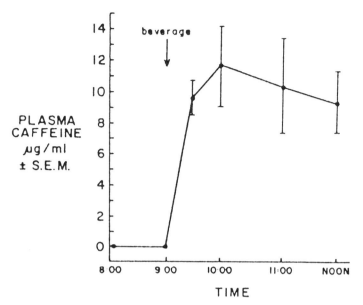

FIG. 3. Plasma caffeine levels in the 9 noncoffee-drinking subjects depicted in Figs. 1 and 2. No subject had ingested other methylxanthines for three weeks prior to the study. (From Robertson D et al., ref. 10, with permission.)

Baseline plasma renin activity was not elevated after seven days of caffeine administration, and the response to the acute dose of caffeine was abolished by chronic caffeine administration (Fig. 7). Thus, this study not only confirmed the modest pressor effect of caffeine but, more important, it demonstrated rapid and essentially complete tolerance to the hemodynamic and neurohumoral effects over as short a period as three to four days.

EFFECTS IN HYPERTENSIVES

Because of the increase observed in plasma renin activity in both these studies, we felt it was essential to assess the effects of caffeine in hypertensive subjects in addition to our previously studied normal subjects (12). We enlisted 18 subjects with mild hypertension (diastolic pressure 90–105 mmHg) and no renal or endocrine dysfunction. All were coffee or tea drinkers, but all abstained from caffeine and other methylxanthines prior to study. Seven men and 11 women, aged 20 to 44 years, were included, and all were studied in sodium balance. As in our previous study, the response to an acute dose of 250 mg of caffeine was tested while subjects were receiving either placebo for three days, caffeine (250 mg po tid) for eight days, and placebo for four days (Group 1) or placebo throughout (Group II). Blood pressure

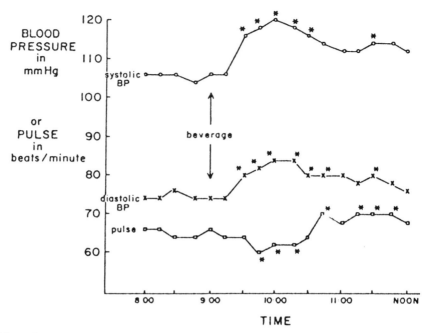

FIG. 4. The effect of 250 mg caffeine on blood pressure (o, x) and heart rate (o). There is an initial, slight rise in both systolic and diastolic pressure, accompanied by a fall in heart rate, but heart rate then rises above baseline values while the blood pressure remains slightly elevated. By three hours after caffeine ingestion, all effects have essentially returned to baseline. (From Robertson D et al., ref. 10, with permission.)

and heart rate were also measured in both the supine and upright postures before and after breakfast and lunch each day. In these mild hypertensives, there was again a modest but significant increase in systolic blood pressure (9.2 ± 3.4 mmHg peak response) after the first dose of caffeine but no significant rise in diastolic pressure (Fig. 8). This effect was accompanied by a fall in heart rate (72 ± 3.4 bpm) after the first dose of caffeine. Chronically, we found that the average blood pressure (a mean of 8 determinations/day) was significantly ($p < 0.05$) elevated above baseline only on the first day of caffeine administration. There was no acute response of either systolic or diastolic blood pressure to caffeine after the first day of caffeine administration.

In contrast to our results in normal subjects (10), in these mild hypertensives there was no significant rise in plasma renin activity with either acute or chronic caffeine administration (Fig. 9). Angiotensin I and II levels were likewise impervious to caffeine. While there was a slight rise in plasma norepinephrine after the first dose, this rise was not significant and was even less after seven days of caffeine. Plasma epinephrine did not respond to either

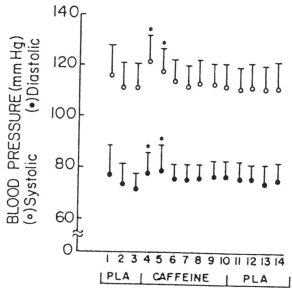

FIG. 5. The blood pressure response to caffeine. Numbers on the horizontal axis indicate the day of the study. On days 1–3, subjects were given placebo beverage with each meal. On days 4–10, they received 250 mg caffeine with each meal. On days 11–14, they again received placebo. Each point represents the mean of six upright and six supine sphygmo-manometric systolic (○) and diastolic (●) blood pressure determinations. *p < 0.05.
(From Robertson D et al., ref. 11, with permission.)

acute dosing or after one week of caffeine. Overall, the hemodynamic response to acute caffeine dosing was not greater, but rather somewhat less in hypertensive subjects than in normal controls. Again, tolerance developed rapidly and completely.

ADENOSINE

A number of studies from our laboratory and others have suggested that the major effects of caffeine in humans are exerted via antagonism of adenosine receptors (13,14). We therefore investigated the cardiovascular effects of intravenous adenosine in humans in a series of studies (15,16). In normotensive subjects, adenosine infusion produced a transient increase (15/13 mmHg) in blood pressure, followed by a reduction in pressure (− 12/16 mmHg) below baseline. Heart rate increased during the trough of the depressor response.

We subsequently established that these pressor and tachycardiac responses are mediated through reflex sympathetic activity, as they are not seen in patients with severe sympathetic dysfunction. In addition, infusion of adenosine in the proximal aortic arch replicated the intravenous findings,

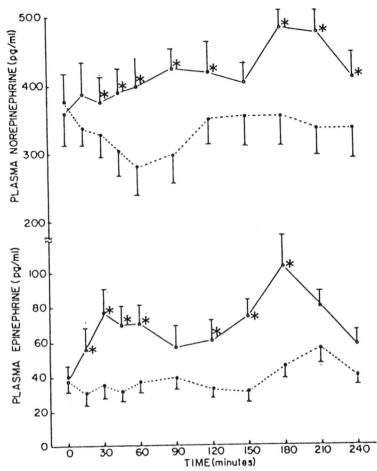

FIG. 6. The response of plasma epinephrine and norepinephrine to acute ingestion of 250 mg caffeine on the first day of continuous, regular caffeine ingestion (•) and on the final day of caffeine (○).
* $p < 0.05$.
(From Robertson D et al., ref. 11, with permission.)

while infusion distal to the carotids and their chemoreceptors produced only a depressor effect (16). This strongly suggested that, in humans, as had previously been demonstrated in animals, adenosine can increase sympathetic outflow via the carotid chemoreceptor. Since then, we have directly measured sympathetic nerve traffic in response to adenosine (using microneurography) and confirmed this concept (17).

More recent studies carried out at our institute have suggested that there is an important relationship between adenosine, renin, and caffeine in cardio-

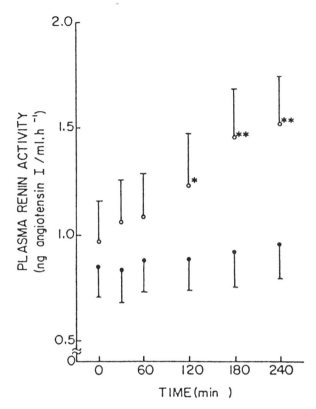

FIG. 7. Urinary norepinephrine before, during, and after the week of caffeine administration, 250 mg with each meal. Data from subjects receiving placebo throughout the 14 days of the study are not shown.
* $p < 0.05$. ** $p < 0.01$.
(From Robertson D et al., ref. 11, with permission.)

vascular control (18,19). Specifically, it was found that adenosine levels were quite elevated in the 2-kidney, 1-clip renovascular hypertensive rat. We speculated that this elevation of adenosine might be providing a partial compensation for the elevated renin activity. When these animals are given caffeine in their drinking water from an early age, not only does tolerance not develop, but blood pressure rises far more than when they are raised without caffeine. In fact, malignant hypertension develops in a high proportion, and mortality is quite high. While clinical studies remain to be done, the possibility exists that there will be subsets of hypertensive subjects whose responses to caffeine will be more impressive than those we have seen in normal subjects or in mild to moderate, non-high renin hypertensives. Although renovascular hypertension is not common, avoidance of caffeine might be very important

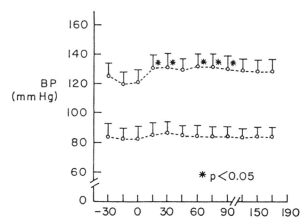

FIG. 8. Effects of short-term caffeine administration on blood pressure in subjects with borderline hypertension. These observations were carried out on day 4 of the study. Systolic and diastolic blood pressures are shown with standard deviations. The x-axis is time in minutes before or after the administration of 250 mg of caffeine in a rye-barley beverage. (From Robertson D et al., ref. 12, with permission.)

in its therapy if patients' responses and lack of tolerance paralleled those of renovascular hypertensive rats. This would be a significant exception to our general finding that caffeine does not exert a significant long-term pressor effect in humans.

EFFECTS OF CAFFEINE ON BAROREFLEX FUNCTION

In addition to studying the effects of caffeine on blood pressure and heart rate, we have recently characterized the action of this and other methylxanthines on the reflex control of the circulation. The short term modulation of blood pressure is accomplished by integration of systemic and central

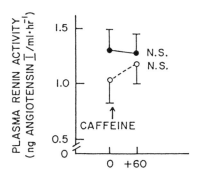

FIG. 9. Effect of short-term caffeine administration on plasma renin activity in subjects with borderline hypertension. Plasma renin activity was not significantly raised 60 minutes following caffeine administration in subjects with borderline hypertension (○) nor was short-term caffeine administration effective in raising plasma renin activity after seven days of caffeine administration (●). (From Robertson D et al., ref. 12, with permission.)

regulatory mechanisms (20). Sudden changes in blood pressure affect the activity of stretch receptors. These structures, also called baroreceptors, are located in different hemodynamic areas including the aortic arch, carotid sinus, lungs, and heart (21). Information from the baroreceptors is relayed to the central nervous system through the glossopharyngeal and vagus nerves. Fibers from these nerves terminate, within the central nervous system, in the nucleus of the solitary tract (NTS) (22). In the NTS, neuronal cell groups regulate reflex cardiovascular activity through changes in sympathetic and parasympathetic tone (20–22). The integrated function of baroreceptors, central brain nuclei, and systemic effectors evoke cardiovascular changes, which are in general referred to as the *baroreflex,* or *baroreceptor reflex.* The baroreflex can effectively maintain blood pressure within narrow limits. For instance, acute elevation of blood pressure is compensated by a baroreflex-mediated bradycardia. The sudden elevation of blood pressure increases firing of the baroreceptors, and this affects the activity of cardiovascular neurons in the NTS. This results in increased parasympathetic tone (reflex bradycardia) with concomitant inhibition of sympathetic outflow (decrease in norepinephrine release and decrease in vascular peripheral resistance). These actions oppose vasopressor effects and attempt to restore previous blood pressure levels. Conversely, a sudden drop in blood pressure will trigger reflex-mediated tachycardia, due to decreased firing of the baroreceptors and centrally mediated increased sympathetic outflow.

The possibility that caffeine affects baroreflex function was suggested by our earlier observations (10). We reported a biphasic response in heart rate after an oral acute dose of 250 mg of caffeine in normotensive subjects. During the initial increase in blood pressure, we observed a slight decrease in heart rate, suggesting normal activity of the baroreflex. In the subsequent phase, however, the heart rate increased even though the blood pressure remained elevated. This response suggested a significant alteration of baroreflex function.

In recent studies (23), we decided to directly assess the effects of caffeine on baroreflex function. Ten healthy male volunteers were asked to abstain from methylxanthine-containing food and beverages for at least seven days before the study. An intra-arterial line was placed in the radial artery for continuous monitoring of blood pressure. Intravenous lines were placed in antecubital veins for drug administration and blood sampling. We evaluated baroreflex sensitivity with a bolus intravenous dose of the vasopressor agent phenylephrine. The effects of phenylephrine administration on blood pressure and heart rate were analyzed from the onset of the rise in systolic pressure until commencement of the fall in blood pressure. Baroreflex sensitivity was calculated by plotting each RR interval against the preceding systolic blood pressure. The slope of the derived linear regression line for these points was taken to indicate baroreflex sensitivity (milliseconds [ms] per milliliters of mercury [mmHg]). The steeper the slope of the regression line, the more sensitive the baroreflex function with respect to control of heart rate.

Subjects (21 ± 0.58 years) were admitted to a group that received caffeine (250 mg, n = 6), or to a placebo control group (21.3 ± 0.61 years, n = 4) in a single blind protocol. Baroreflex response was evaluated 10 minutes before and 30, 60, 120, and 180 minutes after caffeine or placebo. In a later study, the effect of repeated caffeine administration on baroreflex activation was assessed in the same group of subjects and compared to the effects of similarly administered placebo in the control group. The subjects in the experimental group received 250 mg of caffeine three times a day for seven days. Baroreflex determinations were done after seven days of caffeine or placebo treatment (after the last dose), as described above.

The acute administration of 250 mg of caffeine significantly affected baroreflex activity. At 30 minutes after caffeine ingestion, blood pressure rose from control values of 127 ± 8/57 ± 4 mmHg (systolic/diastolic) to 136 ± 3/68 ± 5 mmHg ($p < 0.05$). Although heart rate did not change, baroreflex slope decreased markedly (from 31 ± 7 msec/mmHg to 11.6 ± 2 msec/mmHg, $p < 0.01$, Fig. 10). Baroreflex sensitivity remained inhibited for the rest of the study period despite the blood pressure returning to basal levels. Interestingly, the maximal effects of caffeine on the baroreflex and blood pressure did not occur concomitantly. The peak pressor effect was evident at 60 minutes (139 ± 7/70 ± 5 mmHg), while the maximal baroreflex inhibi-

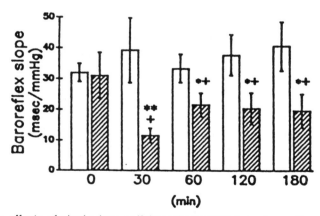

FIG. 10. The effects of single-dose caffeine administration on baroreflex sensitivity in normotensive healthy volunteers. Baroreflex response (slope) was evaluated with phenylephrine before (10 minutes) and after 30, 60, 120, and 180 minutes of oral single-dose placebo (*open bars;* n = 4) or caffeine administration (250 mg, *hatched bars;* n = 6). *Vertical bars* represent 2 × SE. Asterisks (*) indicate significant differences from corresponding values in the placebo group (* $p < 0.05$, ** $p < 0.01$) and *crosses* (+) indicate a significant difference from its own control ($p < 0.05$). (From Mosqueda-Garcia R et al., ref. 23, with permission.)

tion was present 30 minutes earlier. In the placebo group, no significant changes were observed in blood pressure, heart rate, or baroreflex slope.

Different hemodynamic effects were seen during the chronic phase of the study. Blood pressure and heart rate at the end of the period with chronic caffeine were not different from controls or baseline. Similarly, the last dose of chronic caffeine failed to increase blood pressure or to demonstrate an attenuation of baroreflex activity (Fig. 11).

These results indicate that single doses of caffeine affect the reflex control of the circulation, and this may contribute to the pressor effect of coffee. On the other hand, the action of caffeine on relevant baroreceptor mechanisms is overcome by either central or peripheral changes that restore initial hemodynamic conditions when tolerance develops.

It is important to elucidate the site and mechanism of action by which caffeine inhibits baroreflex function. As discussed by Daly (this volume), various actions may explain the effects of caffeine, including inhibition of phosphodiesterases (24), effects on intracellular calcium (25), and/or adenosine-receptor antagonism (26). We did not investigate the role of the first two possibilities because the plasma concentrations of caffeine in our study were below the threshold described for these effects in other studies. On the other hand, we explored whether caffeine and other adenosine receptor antagonists inhibit baroreflex activity when administered in the central nervous system (27).

We studied the effects of intracisternal administration of caffeine on baro-

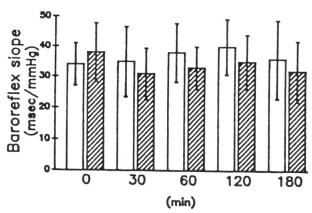

FIG. 11. Effects of repeated caffeine or placebo administration on baroreflex sensitivity. Subjects received either 250 mg caffeine t.i.d. (n = 6) or placebo (n = 4) during seven days. The day of the experimental procedure, baroreflex response was elicited by phenylephrine immediately before the last dose of placebo (*open bars*) or caffeine (*hatched bars*). Baroreflex evaluation was repeated at 30, 60, 120, and 180 minutes. Note the absence of significant effects of baroreflex slope by either caffeine or placebo, contrasting with the data shown in Fig. 10. (From Mosqueda-Garcia R et al., ref. 23, with permission.)

reflex function (27) in urethane-anesthetized rats. The reflex bradycardiac response to pressor doses of phenylephrine was evaluated before and after intracisternal administration of either caffeine (6 μg/10 μl) or artificial cerebrospinal fluid (CSF, 10 μl). Baroreflex sensitivity in the control period (3.9 ± 1.2 msec/mmHg, n = 5) was not altered in the CSF-treated group (3.6 ± 0.5 msec/mmHg, n = 4). Intracisternal administration of caffeine did not change basal blood pressure or heart rate, but, when baroreflex activation was retested, a significant inhibition was observed (1.5 ± 0.8 msec/mmHg; $p < 0.05$, Fig. 12). In contrast, no significant change was observed in the CSF-treated rats (3.8 ± 0.7 msec/mm Hg). Similar effects on baroreflex activation were observed after systemic administration of caffeine (Fig. 12).

To evaluate the possible interference of anesthesia with the baroreflex effects of caffeine, we studied a group of conscious-instrumented animals (27). The pressor effects of phenylephrine without caffeine were similar to those in anesthetized animals, but the reflex bradycardia was more pronounced. Consequently, the slope of the baroreflex curve was greater in conscious than in anesthetized animals. In contrast to CSF, which did not significantly affect baroreflex slope (7.8 ± 2 mmHg), the intracisternal administration of caffeine inhibited the reflex bradycardia and decreased the baroreflex slope (4.3 ± 1.2 msec/mmHg; $p < 0.05$). The effects on baroreflex function lasted up to 90 minutes after caffeine administration.

The strongest evidence that the effects of caffeine on baroreflex activity are related to antagonism of adenosine receptors comes from studies where

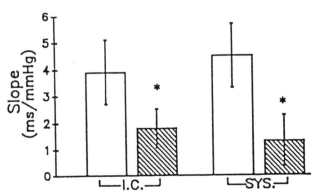

FIG. 12. Effects of central or systemic administration of caffeine on baroreflex sensitivity in urethane anesthetized rats. Baroreflex response was evaluated before (I.C., *open bar*) and after the intracisternal administration of 6 μg/10 μl of caffeine (I.C., *hatched bar*) in 5 animals or after chronic administration of caffeine (0.1% in drinking water during 7 days (SYS, *hatched bar*, n = 6), or no treatment (SYS, *open bar*, n = 4) in different groups of animals. *Vertical bars* represent 2 X S.E.,* indicates significant difference from corresponding control ($p < 0.05$ by paired T test in the I.C. group or by unpaired T test in the SYS group).

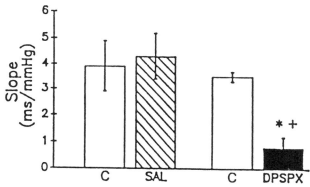

FIG. 13. The effect of intra-NTS administration of the adenosine antagonist dipropyl-8-p-sulphenylxanthine (DPSPX) on baroreflex sensitivity in anesthetized rats. Baroreflex response (Slope) was evaluated with phenylephrine before (c, *open bars*) and after 60 nl of intra-NTS saline (SAL, *hatched bar*, n = 4) or 0.92 nmol intra-NTS DPSPX (*solid bar*, n = 6). All the values represent the mean + S.E. of at least three determinations, carried out in the same animal after each experimental treatment. *Vertical bars* represent 2 XS.E., and * or + indicates significant difference from its own control or from the saline treated group, respectively ($p < 0.01$), when compared with a two-way analysis of variance followed by the Duncan's test.

we used the adenosine receptor antagonist 1,3-dipropyl-8-p-sulphenylxanthine (DPSPX). We have previously demonstrated that DPSPX is a selective receptor antagonist of the central cardiovascular effects of adenosine (28). In a subsequent study, urethane-anesthetized rats were instrumented for direct microinjections of drugs in the NTS. Microadministration of saline (60 nl) into the NTS did not modify the reflex bradycardia elicited by phenylephrine or, consequently, the slope of the baroreflex curve (3.9 ± 1 and 4.0 ± 0.9 msec/mmHg for control and saline, respectively). In contrast, after microinjection of DPSPX (0.92 nmol/60 nl), similar increases in blood pressure elicited less bradycardia with a significant inhibition of the baroreflex slope (from 3.5 ± 0.2 to 0.8 ± 0.4 msec/mmHg, n = 6). Like intracisternal caffeine, the administration of DPSPX into the NTS did not modify resting blood pressure or heart rate, and it had remarkably similar effects on the reflex bradycardic response (27) (Fig. 13).

These results further support the theory that caffeine affects baroreflex function through antagonism of adenosine receptors in the central nervous system. Whether the NTS is the primary site of the actions of caffeine remains to be elucidated.

EFFECTS OF CAFFEINE ON CENTRAL SYMPATHETIC TONE

The inhibition of the baroreflex by caffeine is also compatible with activation of central sympathetic tone. We and others have previously documented increases in both plasma norepinephrine and epinephrine in association with the acute increase in blood pressure after caffeine administration in caffeine-naive subjects (10,29,30). The pressor effect would be expected to increase parasympathetic tone and to decrease sympathetic outflow if the baroreflex were intact. Caffeine impairs this response, and it could lead to a relative increase in central sympathetic function.

Controversy exists, however, regarding the effects of caffeine on sympathetic activity. In our studies, for instance, there was no clear relationship between the rise in blood pressure and the rise in norepinephrine (10). Furthermore, in patients with severe autonomic dysfunction, whose norepinephrine storages are importantly depleted, there was a rise in blood pressure with caffeine similar to the one present in subjects with intact autonomic function (31). Other authors have failed to observe increases in plasma norepinephrine (32,33). Izzo et al. (32), for example, were unable to document changes in plasma norepinephrine, renin activity, and vasopressin values at caffeine concentrations between 5 to 8 μg/ml. Another group demonstrated an increase in metabolic rate and lipolysis with unchanged plasma catecholamines (34). Several factors should be considered, however, when inferring sympathetic function from plasma catecholamine values (35). Apart from methodological problems (inter- and intra-assay variability and sensitivity), kinetic and physiological factors determine the final plasma values of norepinephrine. Plasma norepinephrine, for example, is the ratio of the spillover rate into the bloodstream and clearance. In addition, sympathetic outflow and changes in bloodflow during experimental manipulations may vary from one vascular bed to another. Finally, modulation of norepinephrine release by presynaptic systems as well as multiple removal processes for this catecholamine also determine the cleft-plasma concentration gradient of norepinephrine. If these factors are not carefully considered, peripheral venous blood catecholamine levels can be, at best, an insensitive index of sympathetic activity.

A technique for directly assessing human sympathetic activity (without reference to neurotransmitter release and clearance) was recently developed (36). This technique—microneurography—adds greatly to clarifying the effects of caffeine on neural sympathetic action. We have evaluated the effects of caffeine on sympathetic function (37) in preliminary studies using microneurography.

Nine male normotensive volunteers abstained from coffee and methylxanthines for at least seven days prior to study. Three subjects were randomly allocated to a group that received placebo and six to a group that received 250 mg of caffeine. All the subjects were instrumented with a radial arterial line for continuous recording of blood pressure. Microneurographic recordings were done according to the method of Wallin and collaborators (36). We placed the recording electrode in the right peroneal nerve to record muscle sympathetic nerve activity. We filtered (bandwidth = 700–2,000 Hz) and integrated the recording signal with a time constant of 0.1 seconds. The mean voltage of the integrated signal was used to measure nerve traffic. Sympathetic activity was expressed as bursts/minute × mean burst amplitude. Since voltage amplitude varies between subjects, we reported data as percent changes from a baseline period just prior to the intervention.

In agreement with our earlier reports (10,23), blood pressure increased from $134 \pm 2/69 \pm 3$ to $143 \pm 3/75 \pm 4$ mm Hg ($p < 0.01$) at 30 minutes after caffeine. Heart rate remained unchanged. We recorded a modest increase in venous plasma norepinephrine (11.2%) and epinephrine (24%) using a very sensitive HPLC assay for catecholamines. In contrast, muscle sympathetic nerve activity increased by 79% during the same period. Blood pressure was still elevated ($144 \pm 3/71 \pm 2$ mmHg) at 120 minutes after caffeine administration, and muscle sympathetic nerve activity was maximally increased (by 138%). Plasma norepinephrine failed to increase further, whereas epinephrine increased by 66% (37).

These results indicate that caffeine has important effects on central sympathetic activity. These changes, however, are not entirely reflected by plasma norepinephrine concentrations. The reason for this discrepancy is not clear. In addition to central sympathetic activation, caffeine may also affect other mechanisms that decrease plasma levels of norepinephrine. Whether this is a presynaptic action (on adenosine receptors) or an effect on clearance processes for norepinephrine is unknown and remains to be elucidated.

HEALTH CONSEQUENCES OF BAROREFLEX IMPAIRMENT AND SYMPATHETIC ACTIVATION BY CAFFEINE

Concern about the pressor and autonomic effects of caffeine seems to be diminishing (38–41). We have demonstrated, along with others, that tolerance develops with continuous coffee use (11,32,42). The development of tolerance may explain the apparent disparity between the acute effects of caffeine and the relative absence of deleterious consequences of coffee that has been documented in a number of epidemiologic studies (43). The effects of caffeine on baroreflex function seem to follow a similar pattern. After continuous caffeine administration, baroreflex function was unaffected (23). Although we have not studied the effects of chronic caffeine on sympathetic nerve activity, it is likely that tolerance develops similar to what we have observed for plasma catecholamines. What, then, would be the medical significance of the baroreflex inhibition and sympathetic activation of caffeine consumption?

Caffeine ingestion can have a significant clinical effect in some situations. Caffeine ingestion may be begun by nonregular coffee drinkers or increased by coffee drinkers during periods of stress. An increase in coffee consumption is observed during heightened occupational demand or during conflicting emotional settings. In addition, it is important to consider that another well-recognized pressor stimuli is mental stress (44,45). Blood pressure usually increases about 15 mmHg without significant reflex bradycardia in normal subjects, when confronted with a mental numerical problem or emotional stimuli. The combination of these two factors (stress and coffee) could have an effect, particularly in nonregular coffee drinkers.

The study of the cardiovascular effects of coffee ingestion and stress, however, has only recently been investigated (46–50). The few reports available have indicated an additive pressor effect with the combination of caffeine consumption and stress (46–50). Pincomb and collaborators (49), for instance, demonstrated that the pressor effects of caffeine were additive to those of a behavioral task. More important, the combination of these two factors increased the number of subjects whose blood pressure reached hypertensive levels (49). There were similar findings in another study, when the administration of 250 mg of caffeine was combined with a mental arithmetic task (50). Interestingly, this last study was done in regular coffee drinkers with an abstinence period of no more than 12 hours (50). On the other hand, there is no clinical or epidemiologic data supporting a significant deleterious effect of caffeine and stress. If one extrapolates from the studies in myocardial infarction, even the combination of caffeine and stress may only rarely have a significant clinical impact.

We have no information at present about the long-term cardiovascular effects of occasional, but cyclic, ingestion of coffee during periods of stress, nor do we know whether tolerance is overcome in moderate coffee drinkers by increasing the amounts of caffeine and whether this results in a more pronounced pressor effect during stressful situations. Epidemiological studies should also attempt to characterize the cardiovascular risks of occasional coffee drinkers and whether this has been a confounding factor in previous studies. More research is clearly needed to assess the potential cardiovascular effects of the coffee-stress interaction.

REFERENCES

1. Bock J. Die Purinderivate. In: Heffter A, Heubner W, eds. *Handbuch der experimentellen Pharmacologie,* Berlin: Springer, 1920:508–98.
2. Eichler O. *Kaffee und coffein.* Springer Berlin 1938.
3. Degubareff T, Sleator W Jr. Effects of caffeine on mammalian atrial muscle and its interaction with adenosine and calcium. *J Pharmacol Exp Ther* 1965;148:202–14.
4. Chapman RA, Miller DJ. The action of caffeine on frog myocardial contractility. *J Physiol (Lond)* 1971;217:64p–6p.
5. Rall TW. The xanthines. In: Gilman AG, Goodman LS, Gilman A, eds. *The pharmocological basis of therapeutics.* New York: Macmillan, 1986:592–607.
6. Raff WK. Wirkung des Coffeins auf Herz und Kreislauf. *Arzneimittelforsch* 1971;21:1177–9.
7. Sollman T, Pilcher D. The actions of caffeine on the mammalian circulation. *J Pharmacol Exp Ther* 1971;3:19–92.
8. Horst K, Wilson RJ, Smith RG. The effect of coffee and decaffeinated coffee on oxygen consumption, pulse rate and blood pressure. *J Pharmacol Exp Ther* 1936;58:294–304.

9. Starr I, Gamble CJ, Margolies A. A clinical study of the action of 10 commonly used drugs on cardiac output, work and size: on respiration, on metabolic rate, and on the electrocardiograms. *J Clin Invest* 1937;16:799–823.
10. Robertson D, Frolich JC, Carr RK, et al. Effects of caffeine on plasma renin activity, catecholamines and blood pressure. *N Engl J Med* 1978;298:181–6.
11. Robertson D, Wade D, Workman R, Woosley RL, Oates JA. Tolerance to the humoral and hemodynamic effects of caffeine in man. *J Clin Invest* 1981;67:1111–7.
12. Robertson D, Hollister AS, Kincaid D, et al. Caffeine and hypertension. *Am J Med* 1984; 77:54–60.
13. Fredholm BB, Persson CGA. Xanthine derivatives as adenosine receptor antagonists. *Eur J Pharmacol* 1982;81:673–6.
14. Curatolo PW, Robertson D. The health consequences of caffeine. *Ann Int Med* 1983;98: 641–53.
15. Biaggioni I, Olafsson B, Robertson RM, Hollister AS, Robertson D. Cardiovascular effects of adenosine infusion in man and their modulation by dipyridamole. *Life Sci* 1986;39: 2229–36.
16. Biaggioni I, Olafsson B, Robertson RM, Hollister AS, Robertson D. Cardiovascular and respiratory effects of adenosine in conscious man: evidence for chemoreceptor activation. *Circ Res* 1987;61:779–86.
17. Biaggioni I, Killian TJ, Mosqueda-Garcia R, Robertson RM, Robertson D. Adenosine increases sympathetic nerve traffic in humans. *Circulation* 1991;83:1668–75.
18. Ohnishi A, Branch RA, Jackson K, Biaggioni I, Deray G, Jackson EK. Chronic caffeine administration exacerbates renovascular but not genetic hypertension in rats. *J Clin Invest* 1986;78:1045–50.
19. Ohnishi A, Li P, Branch RA, Biaggioni I, Jackson E. Role of adenosine in renin-dependent renovascular hypertension in rats. *Hypertension* 1988;12:152–61.
20. Palkovits M, Zaborszky L. Neuroanatomy of central cardiovascular control. Nucleus tractus solitarii: afferent and efferent neuronal connections in relation to the baroreceptor reflux arc. *Prog Brain Res* 1977;47:9–34.
21. Spyer KM. Neural organization and control of the baroreceptor reflex. *Physiol Biochem* 1981;88:23–124.
22. Seller H, Illert M. The localization of the first synapse in the carotid sinus baroreceptor reflex pathway and its alteration of afferent input. *Pflug Arch* 1969;306:1–19.
23. Mosqueda-Garcia R, Tseng CJ, Biaggioni I, Robertson RM, Robertson D. Effects of caffeine on baroreflex activity in man. *Clin Pharmacol Ther* 1990;48:568–74.
24. Beavo JA, Rogers NL, Crofford OB, Hardman JG, Sutherland EW. Effects of xanthine derivatives on lipolysis and on adenosine 3'5'-monophosphate phosphodiesterase activity. *Molecular Pharmacology* 1970;6:597–603.
25. Lin CI, Vassalle M. Role of calcium in the inotropic effects of caffeine in cardiac Purkinje fibers. *Int J Cardiol* 1983;3:421–34.
26. Fredholm BB. On the mechanism of action of theophylline and caffeine. *Acta Medica Scandinavica* 1985;217:149–53.
27. Mosqueda-Garcia R, Tseng C-J, Appalsamy M, Robertson D. Modulatory effects of adenosine on baroreflux activation in the brainstem of normotensive rats. *Eur J Pharmacol* 1989; 174:119–22.
28. Tseng C-J, Biaggioni I, Appalsamy M, Robertson D. Purinergic receptors in the brainstem mediate hypotension and bradycardia. *Hypertension* 1988;11:191–7.
29. Whitsett TL, Manion CV, Christensen HD. Cardiovascular effects of coffee and caffeine. *Am J Cardiol* 1984;53:918–22.
30. Smits P, Hofman H, Thien T, Houben H, Van't Laar A. Hemodynamic and humoral effects of coffee after beta-selective and nonselective beta-blockade. *Clin Pharmacol Ther* 1983; 34:153–8.
31. Onrot J, Goldberg MR, Biaggioni I, Hollister AS, Kincaid D, Robertson D. Hemodynamic and humoral effects of caffeine in human autonomic failure: therapeutic implications for postprandial hypotension. *N Engl J Med* 1985;313:549–54.
32. Izzo JL, Ghosal A, Kwong T, Freeman RB, Jaenike JR. Age and prior caffeine use alter the cardiovascular and adrenomedullary responses to oral caffeine. *Am J Cardiol* 1983;52: 769–73.

33. Myers MG. Effects of caffeine on blood pressure. *Arch Intern Med* 1988;148:1189–93.
34. Jung RT, Shetty PS, James WPT, Barrand MA, Callingham BA. Caffeine: its effect on catecholamines and metabolism in lean and obese humans. *Clin Sci* 1981;60:527–35.
35. Goldstein DS, Eisenhofer G. Plasma catechols. What do they mean? *News in Physiological Sciences* 1988;3:138–44.
36. Valbo AB, Hagbarth KE, Torebjork HE, Wallin BG. Somatosensory, proprioceptive, and sympathetic activity in human peripheral nerves. *Physiol Rev* 1979;59:919–57.
37. Mosqueda-Garcia R, Killian TJ, Haile V, Tseng C-J, Robertson RM, Robertson D. Effects of caffeine on plasma catecholamines and muscle sympathetic nerve activity in man. *Circulation* 1990;82:III-335 (abs).
38. Heyden S, Tyroler HA, Heiss G, Hames CG, Bartel A. Coffee consumption and mortality. Total mortality, stroke mortality, and coronary heart disease morality. *Arch Int Med* 1978; 138:1472–5.
39. Dawber TR, Kannel WB, Gordon T. Coffee and cardiovascular disease. Observations from the Framingham Study. *N Engl J Med* 1974;291:871–4.
40. Wilson PWF, Garrison RJ, Kannel WB, McGee DL, Castelli WP. Is coffee consumption a contributor to cardiovascular disease? Insights from the Framingham Study. *Arch Int Med* 1989;149:1169–72.
41. Grobbee DE, Rimm EB, Giovannucci E, Colditz G, Stampfer M, Willett W. Coffee, caffeine and cardiovascular disease in man. *N Engl J Med* 1990;323:1026–32.
42. Ammon HPT, Bieck PR, Mandalaz D, Verspohl EJ. Adaptation of blood pressure to continuous heavy coffee drinking in young volunteers. A double-blind, crossover study. *Br J Clin Pharmacol* 1983;15:701–6.
43. Bertrand CA, Pomper I, Hillman G, Duffy JG, Micheli I. No relation between coffee and blood pressure. *N Engl J Med* 1978;299:315–6.
44. Robertson D. Clinical Pharmacology: assessment of autonomic function. In: Baughman KL, Greene BM, eds. *Clinical Diagnostic Manual for the House Officer.* Baltimore: Williams & Wilkins, 1981:86–101.
45. McLeod JG, Tuck RR. Disorders of the autonomic nervous system: Part 2: Investigation and treatment. *Ann Neurol* 1987;21:519–29.
46. Lane JD. Caffeine and cardiovascular responses to stress. *Psychosom Med* 1983;45:447–51.
47. Lane JD, Williams RB. Caffeine affects cardiovascular responses to stress. *Psychophys* 1985;22:648–55.
48. Pincomb GA, Lovallo WR, Passey RB, Brackett DJ, Wilson MF. Caffeine enhances the physiological response to occupational stress in medical students. *Health Psychology* 1987; 6:101–12.
49. Pincomb GA, Lovallo WR, Passey RB, Wilson MF. Effects of behaviour state on caffeine's ability to alter blood pressure. *Am J Cardiol* 1988;61:798–802.
50. France C, Ditto B. Caffeine effects on several indices of cardiovascular activity at rest and during stress. *J Behav Med* 1988;11:473–82.

Caffeine, Coffee, and Health,
edited by S. Garattini.
Raven Press, Ltd., New York © 1993.

7

Coffee and Cardiovascular Diseases

A Personal View After 30 Years of Research

Siegfried Heyden

*Department of Community and Family Medicine, Duke University Medical
Center, Durham, North Carolina 27710*

In a comprehensive review spanning 30 years (1961–1991) of personal experience with community surveys, epidemiological studies, animal experiments and, most important, with a prospective study in a large hypertensive population, the suspected association between coffee and cardiovascular diseases was dismissed. Likewise, all-cause mortality rates in (a) high coffee consumers in comparison to (b) low or (c) no coffee consumers were evenly distributed in these three groups. In view of these negative findings in humans, results of animal experiments were irrelevant; it was reassuring, however, that in rabbits, rhesus monkeys, and rats, caffeine feeding experiments and caffeine injections, both subcutaneous and intravenous, resulted in lower cholesterol levels in the experimental animals and either the same or lower grades of aortic atheromatosis compared to control animals. Historically, it is difficult to understand why coffee was suspected of causing cardiovascular diseases. We are reminded of an editorial in the *British Medical Journal*[1]: "What is it in man's devious make-up that makes him round on the seemingly more wholesome and pleasurable aspects of his environment and suspect them of being causes of his misfortunes? Whatever it is, stimulants of all kinds (and especially coffee and caffeine) maintain a position high on the list of suspicion despite a continuing lack of real evidence of any hazard to health."

INTRODUCTION

Coffee and caffeine have long been suspected of causing illnesses ranging from myocardial infarction, arrhythmias, hypertension, hyperlipidemia, gout and anxiety, to fibrocystic breast disease, various cancers and birth defects, and osteoporosis. No other agent in the human environment has been as

---

[1] Editorial, *Br. Med. J.* 1976, 1:1031.

frequently associated with such a variety of chronic-degenerative, even malignant diseases as coffee.

Acute administration of caffeine in volunteers has resulted in temporary increases in blood pressure, serum catecholamine levels, plasma renin activity, serum free fatty acid levels, urine production and gastric acid secretion (1). Chronic caffeine consumption, however, does not produce these physiological responses. Older caffeine users showed no increase in blood pressure or heart rate (2), and "continuous heavy coffee ingestion does not involve a risk of the development of hypertension" (3). Chronic caffeine consumption has no effect on plasma catecholamine levels (3), plasma renin activity, blood cholesterol or glucose levels, or urine production (1). Gout and osteoporosis cannot be discussed seriously, since the little evidence that has been offered by few authors lacks scientific credibility.

Recent literature appears to negate most of the assertions previously alluded to, notably in regard to myocardial infarction, kidney and bladder cancers (1), pancreatic cancer (4), anxiety (5), fibrocystic breast disease (6,7), maternal coffee consumption and pregnancy outcome (1,8,9), and hyperlipidemia (10).

Positive effects of coffee are being increasingly reported. Coffee has been shown, for instance, to be an effective bronchodilator in young patients with asthma (11), a good source of potassium (12), and as a booster of pain-free walking time for patients with chronic stable angina (13,14). Ingestion of one and two cups of coffee increased the exercise duration until onset of angina by 8% and 12%, respectively, whereas decaffeinated coffee had no effect. Caffeine "may be effective as a topical treatment of atopic dermatitis and as systemic therapy for neonatal apnea" (1) and was recently praised as "an analgesic adjuvant" (15). The positive effects of coffee in the prevention of postprandial hypotension, particularly after breakfast and mainly in the elderly, has been shown experimentally (16). Patients with "autonomic failure are advised to drink two cups of coffee (approximately 200–250 mg. of caffeine)." The only remaining uncertainty is whether arrhythmias are induced in susceptible patients with two cups of coffee or equivalent caffeine (17). Even this finding was challenged: "What is not yet appreciated is that ventricular premature beats are innocuous in the overwhelming majority of persons. They no more augur against sudden death than a sneeze portends pneumonia" (18).

CHRONIC COFFEE AND CAFFEINE CONSUMPTION AMONG 10,000 HYPERTENSIVES[2]: MORTALITY RATES IN A FOUR-YEAR FOLLOW-UP

In the light of the medical and paramedical literature presenting a negative image of coffee as regards the health of regular coffee consumers and the

---

[2] The full report was published in 1988: Martin J.B., Annegers JF, Curb JD, Heyden S, Howson C, Lee ES, Lee M. Mortality patterns among hypertensives by reported level of caffeine consumption. *Prev. Med.* 17:310–320, 1988.

obvious contradictions posed by more recent publications, a large prospective study was needed to investigate the effect of coffee and caffeine on the hardest endpoint of any study—mortality from all causes. While several epidemiological studies had already shown an absence of any effect of coffee consumption on mortality in total communities (19–25), there has never been, with the exception of MR FIT, a representative prospective study of an important segment of the general population—hypertensive men and women. The prospective MR FIT Study admitted 12,000 hypercholesterolemic men, most of them mildly hypertensive, into the six-year trial. Caggiula et al. (26) concluded: "The results of this large, carefully evaluated longitudinal study do not support a relationship between coronary heart disease events or total mortality and coffee consumption in these high risk men." A coffee-cholesterol link was not discussed in this study, since 83% of the men were hypercholesterolemic at baseline. As many as 65 million Americans may have mild to moderate or severe hypertension.

This chapter will focus on the mortality data from the largest American hypertension intervention trial in 14 centers, the Hypertension Detection and Follow-up Program (27), in which the author was Co-principal Investigator in the Evans County, Georgia, center from 1973 to 1981. The purpose of this report is to examine mortality rates from all causes as well as specific causes among more than 10,000 hypertensive patients over a four-year period and to relate these rates to coffee consumption during lifetime. If this study had revealed a higher all-cause death rate in addition to the cardiovascular and cerebrovascular death rate among heavy or moderate coffee drinkers, as compared to nonusers of caffeine, this would have been an important argument to limit coffee consumption among hypertensive patients.

Methodology

The Hypertension Detection and Follow-up Program (HDFP) was a community-based, five-year (1974–1979) collaborative trial of antihypertensive treatment (27). Participants between ages 30 to 69 years were recruited from 14 population groups throughout the United States. A total of 10,064 individuals with diastolic blood pressure of 90 mm Hg or above were enrolled, after appropriate screening at home and clinics. The type of treatment for hypertension is irrelevant as far as this report is concerned. At the first home visit—at the end of year 1—the HDFP participants were classified on the basis of their caffeine intake from both beverages and medication, according to their answers to standardized questions. Caffeine consumption data were collected at the follow-up visits—in year 2 and year 5—using a slightly modified questionnaire. Changes in the questionnaire included a distinction between regular coffee and decaffeinated coffee, the addition of a question

TABLE 1. *Equivalency of caffeine consumption per day and distribution of study cohort by level of caffeine consumption[a] in the hypertension detection and follow-up program (HDFP) population*

Equivalency	Level of caffeine consumption			
	None	Low	Medium	High
Total caffeine consumed/day[b] (mg)	0	0.1–214	214–428	428
No. of cups of coffee consumed/ day equivalent	0	0.1–2	2.1–4	4
Distribution				
Participants (n)	1425	4164	2650	1825
Distribution (%)	14	41	26	18

[a] Level of caffeine consumption was fairly stable over the four-year study period.
[b] Beverages and medication caffeine sources.

concerning cola consumption, and a deletion of the question on medication. These data were used to evaluate the validity of the baseline caffeine-consumption data.

The total daily milligrams of caffeine consumed from all selected sources were converted to the equivalent of cups of coffee per day. The conversion averaged the daily caffeine consumption at 317 mg (275 mg from coffee, 26 mg from tea, and 16 mg from medication). The 10,064 men and women were stratified into four caffeine consumption groups (Table 1).

Among the potentially confounding factors, age, race, sex, and smoking habits were found to be associated with both caffeine consumption and the outcome variable, death. The analyses of the data were stratified according to age, sex, and race categories to control for confounding. Smoking status classified the cohort into two groups: current smokers (37%) and nonsmokers. Ex-smokers (2%) were combined with persons who reported never having smoked (61%). For the 592 cases of death that occurred between year 1 and year 5, death certificates were coded by a nosologist, using the Eighth Revision of the International Classification of Diseases Adapted (ICDA) Code.

Rate ratios were calculated to compare mortality rates within the study population by level of caffeine intake. Rate ratios were summarized over sex, race, and 10-year age bands. Standardized mortality ratios (SMR) were calculated to compare the mortality rates of hypertensives by level of caffeine consumption to the mortality rates of the general population. Death rates for the United States in 1975 were used as the standard population rates.

Results

Table 2 shows no association between caffeine consumption and all-cause mortality. Using the noncaffeine consumption group as the reference group,

TABLE 2. Mortality rate ratios[a] over four-year follow-up by level of caffeine intake in the hypertension detection and follow-up program (HDFP) population

Mortality (n = 592)	Caffeine consumption group			
	None	Low	Medium	High
All-cause	1.00	0.82	0.82	0.90
Cerebrovascular	1.00	0.73	0.61	1.30
All other cardiovascular	1.00	0.93	0.81	0.80
Cancer	1.00	0.98	0.95	1.05

[a] Standardized by race, sex, and across five 10-year age groups.

the rate ratio for all-cause mortality was 0.82 for low, 0.82 for medium, and 0.90 for high caffeine consumption.

There was no association between the three cause-specific mortality groupings and caffeine consumption. In the category of cerebrovascular deaths, neither the apparently low rate of 0.61 for medium nor the slightly increased rate of 1.30 for high caffeine consumer groups are significantly different from the noncaffeine consumer group. "All other cardiovascular diseases" comprises mainly myocardial infarct, chronic coronary heart disease, and a few cases of congestive heart failure.

In an attempt to investigate the cancer mortality in greater detail, the 102 site-specific cancer deaths that occurred over the four years' observation period were divided into the four caffeine consumption groups. Analyses by 12 different cancer sites showed no accumulation of cases at any one site, and cancer mortality was distributed uniformly in all four groups with an incidence varying between 0.8% in the medium caffeine consumption, 1.1% in the low caffeine consumption group, and 1% in the abstainers.

Cigarette smoking and coffee drinking were strongly associated in this study population. The proportion of current smokers increased with the four levels of caffeine consumption.

As expected, smokers had a significantly higher mortality than nonsmokers. However, the mortality from cerebrovascular, other cardiovascular diseases (mainly coronary heart disease), and cancer was not increased among smokers with "medium" or "heavy" intake of caffeine as compared with smokers with "no caffeine" or "low" caffeine consumption (Tables 3 and 4).

Discussion

The most important result of this study was the absence of any association between caffeine consumption and mortality among hypertensive patients. *The major strength of this study rests with the uniquely comprehensive follow-up of deaths (99.9%) that HDFP was able to achieve.* The consistency

TABLE 3. *Standardized mortality rate ratios by caffeine consumption group and cigarette smoking status in the hypertension detection and follow-up program (HDFP) population*

Mortality and smoking status	Caffeine consumption group			
	None	Low	Medium	High
All-cause mortality				
Nonsmoking	0.94	0.79	0.85	0.78
(n)[a]	(50)	(134)	(84)	(36)
Smoking	1.97	1.46	1.25	1.38
(n)[a]	(46)	(121)	(63)	(55)
Cerebrovascular				
Nonsmoking	1.30	1.01	0.67	2.32
(n)[a]	(6)	(16)	(5)	(7)
Smoking	1.56	1.65	2.34	1.91
(n)[a]	(4)	(12)	(9)	(5)

[a] Number of deaths.

of the findings in all-cause and cause-specific mortality, including cancer, corroborates evidence provided by prospective epidemiological studies with the same results, for all-cause mortality, namely the largest prospective study of 45,000 men (23), MR FIT (26), Framingham (21,22), Evans County (20), and Gothenburg, Sweden (24,25). In studying cancer mortality and habitual coffee intake, however, this report represents what is probably the first prospective study to follow such a large number of people between 30 and 69 years of age for four years. In the literature, one frequently finds reports linking coffee consumption with a variety of cancer sites beginning with stomach, colon, and prostatic cancer, followed by kidney and bladder cancer, and the more recent allegations of an association with pancreatic, ovarian, and breast cancer. In view of the present report, it is reassuring that

TABLE 4. *Standardized mortality rate ratios by caffeine consumption group and cigarette smoking status in the hypertension detection and follow-up program (HDFP) population*

Mortality and smoking status	Caffeine consumption group			
	None	Low	Medium	High
All other cardiovascular				
Nonsmoking	1.22	0.94	1.21	0.79
(n)[a]	(24)	(61)	(48)	(15)
Smoking	2.60	1.55	1.35	1.87
(n)[a]	(20)	(49)	(26)	(29)
Neoplastic				
Nonsmoking	0.70	0.62	0.44	0.59
(n)[a]	(9)	(26)	(11)	(7)
Smoking	1.12	1.04	0.96	1.28
(n)[a]	(6)	(21)	(12)	(13)

[a] Number of deaths.

several cancer sites were already eliminated in later epidemilogical studies as well as in several experimental observations in animal models.

If there never was any real concern among scientists about coffee consumption in *normotensive persons,* this report addressed for the first time the age-old notion shared by some health officials and para-medical personnel that coffee may raise blood pressure and, consequently, hypertensives should drink less coffee or even abstain from it. "It now seems quite certain that although the acute ingestion of caffeine alters many hemodynamic variables, the chronic ingestion of caffeine has little or no effect on blood pressure, heart rate, plasma catecholamine levels, and plasma renin activity in normal subjects" (1). Obviously, in the HDFP population we are dealing with habitual caffeine consumers and "it seems unlikely that the habitual consumption of caffeine would significantly alter cardiac output or stroke volume" (1). The tolerance to caffeine's effect on hemodynamic variables has been frequently overlooked in previous short-term experiments with caffeine-naive volunteers.

The level of caffeine consumption by the study cohort was fairly stable throughout the four years. The average caffeine consumption from cola was 19 mg per day and remained unchanged throughout the two to five year follow-up home visits. If an adjustment was made to the year 1 data for a possible inclusion of decaffeinated coffee, the average daily caffeine consumption from coffee decreased slightly from 228 mg in year 1 to 201 mg in year 5 and from tea from 26 mg in year 1 to 24 mg in year 5.

Finally, the cholesterol levels of the coffee consumers increased moderately with increasing number of cups of coffee per day (Table 5). The percentage distribution for number of cups of coffee per day was a follows: <1 cup, 38.8%; 1–4cups, 49.9%; 5–8 cups, 9.1%, and ≥9 cups, 2.2%. The age-adjusted means for serum cholesterol were, respectively, 228.0, 230.0, 232.7, and 235.1 mg/dl. These differences were statistically significant as determined by analysis of covariance ($p < .006$). Multiple linear regression of total serum cholesterol on number of cups of coffee consumed, age, sex, race, percent ideal weight, physical activity, smoking status, diastolic blood pressure, and diuretic therapy status yielded a regression coefficient for coffee that was significantly different from zero ($p < .01$). In this hypertensive

TABLE 5. *Mean levels and age-adjusted mean levels of total serum cholesterol according to coffee consumption in the HDFP population*

Cups per day	Means mg/dl	Age-adjusted means mg/dl
<1	227.7	228.0
1–4	230.3	230.0
5–8	232.1	232.7
9 +	233.7	235.1
Totals	229.5	229.5

population, coffee consumption is apparently positively associated with the level of serum total cholesterol on diuretic therapy (28).

Sex differences in cholesterol and lipoprotein levels were demonstrated among coffee drinkers in the Framingham Heart Study: Significant *negative* associations between coffee and total cholesterol and VLDL-C were found in men, whereas *positive* associations with LDL-C were observed in women. "Although inconsistent effects on the lipid profiles were seen, no increase in primary or secondary cardiovascular disease was seen with coffee drinking" (22). Therefore, these two prospective studies are among the few that demonstrate *some* cholesterol changes under the influence of coffee, however *without any effect on incidence of coronary heart disease*. In conclusion, there is no evidence from this large study to support the hypothesis that the level of caffeine consumption is related to the death rates from all causes: strokes, coronary heart disease, or cancer in hypertensive patients.

COFFEE CONSUMPTION AND CARDIOVASCULAR MORTALITY IN A COMMUNITY

The Evans County Study in Evans County, Georgia, was one of the 14 centers of the HDFP, and the exclusively hypertensive patients in the program were *not* part of the community-wide survey to be reported here. It seems important to investigate the alleged association between coffee and cardiovascular causes of death in an unselected population with life-long coffee-drinking habits. The three time periods of our study protocol point out the difficulties in carrying out community research.

Methodology

A prevalence survey in Evans County was conducted during 1960–1962, and the study population was reexamined between 1967 and 1969. During this second study of 2,530 adults (60% white, 40% black), the examining physicians asked each person a few standard questions concerning coffee consumption. Persons who gave a history of drinking 5 cups of coffee or more per day regularly, i.e., during summer and winter, were placed in the high coffee-consuming group. All others were classified as low consumers or nonconsumers. The population was followed annually for $4\frac{1}{2}$ years with questionnaires. Between July 31, 1969, and January 1, 1974, a total of 339 deaths occurred. Of these, 130 (38%) were confidently attributed to cardiovascular and cerebrovascular causes. They were confirmed by autopsy reports, hospital records, and reviews of all available information by a neurologist and a cardiologist, including interviews of family and/or co-workers in cases of sudden death. "Possible" cardiovascular and cerebrovascular deaths were classified with all other causes of death, such as accidents, postoperative complications, pneumonia, and cancer. Age adjustment within each race-sex group was used to avoid possible confounding in the analysis stemming from the well-known observation that older people tend to drink less coffee than middle-aged people.

The choice of mortality as the endpoint for this study was made because our cross-sectional study from 1967 to 1969, which analyzed coffee drinking in relation to coronary heart disease (CHD) and stroke, had not disclosed any differences in high or low coffee-consuming groups. At that time we pointed out the disadvantage of the study, which is the one implicit in a prevalence survey: the study is automatically limited to survivors of the diseases under consideration. The manifestations of ischemic heart disease, death from myocardial infarction, and sudden death, as well as stroke deaths, thus escape a cross-sectional study. If it were assumed that the heavy coffee drinkers had all died of ischemic heart disease or stroke prior to our 1967–1969 survey, we would indeed have missed these important manifestations of CHD and cerebrovascular disease (CVD).

Results

Mortality from all causes in this total community was not significantly different for white men, white women, or black men, regardless of high coffee consumption (≥ 5 cups/day) or little or no coffee consumption (Table 6). There was a suggestion of lower total mortality among black women who drank five cups or more. However, despite statistical significance ($p < .02$), this result must be considered tentative because of the small number observed.

Total mortality, therefore, was not influenced by the coffee-drinking habit. If anything, the group of high coffee consumers appeared slightly favored by a lower mortality compared to low consumers or nonconsumers.

TABLE 6. *Risk of mortality in the Evans county population from all causes adjusted for age, coffee consumption, and smoking habits[a]*

Race and sex	Coffee consumption <5 cups/day			Coffee consumption ≥5 cups/day		
	Adjusted			Adjusted		
	PAR/cases	Mortality, %	SMR	PAR/cases	Mortality, %	SMR
White						
Men	556/72	12.9	1.0	94/10	11.3	0.9
Women	639/53	8.3	1.0	134/9	8.9	1.1
Black						
Men	323/53	16.4	1.0	18/3	19.8	1.2
Women	427/52	12.2	1.0	32/1	3.6	0.3

[a] Indirect method
PAR, population at risk; SMR, standardized mortality ratio.

Mortality from CVD showed differences between the two coffee-drinking groups. While stroke deaths were found more often in white and black men who had reported low lifetime coffee intake or no coffee intake, white and black women who were heavy consumers of coffee had a somewhat higher age-adjusted stroke mortality than low consumers or nonconsumers.

Mortality from CHD did not show any consistent differences between the heavy coffee drinkers and the light coffee drinkers or the nondrinking persons. White men who drank five cups of coffee or more had a slightly higher CHD mortality. White women in the five-cup-a-day group had a marginally lower CHD mortality than white women who did not drink coffee. The CHD mortality for blacks, though higher for those with low coffee consumption, cannot be seriously considered because of the small number of blacks who were high coffee consumers. Since there were no major differences in CHD rates among the coffee-consuming groups, no adjustment for cigarette smoking was necessary.

Lack of systematic differences in vascular mortality among the four race-sex groups led us to the conclusion that there was no evidence of an association between coffee-drinking habits and mortality either from all causes or from specific vascular diseases. To assume there was a higher CHD death rate among heavy coffee drinkers, one would have to explain a "protective" effect of coffee for other causes of death, since all causes of death (total mortality) were equally distributed between high coffee consumers and low consumers or nonconsumers (Table 6).

Our strict criteria for the diagnosis of death due to CHD or stroke may have favored somewhat the category "other causes of death." The theoretical possibility exists, therefore, that we may have misplaced a CHD death into the "mortality from other causes" category. In this eventuality, the chances are that this rare instance would have occurred among the lower socioeconomic group, having less documentation by either ECG, hospital records, or autopsy reports.

Discussion

While the commonly accepted risk factors were unrelated to coffee use, it is well documented that cigarette smoking is highly significantly related to coffee drinking (29). Only the Boston Collaborative Drug Surveillance Program (30)—which, incidentally, had shown an association between coffee drinking and myocardial infarction (MI) in hospitalized patients—did not find this strong correlation between smoking and coffee intake. There was an unusually small difference in proportions of cigarette smokers between the MI group and the control group. The authors suggested that the controls may have had a high proportion of smokers because many have had tobacco-

associated diseases. For this reason alone, the results from community studies are preferable to hospital studies.

The 1967–1969 cross-sectional study in Evans County, Georgia, did not
demonstrate an increase in any of the common risk factors predisposing to
ischemic heart disease among heavy coffee drinkers, with the exception of
cigarette smoking. Cigarette smoking was strongly correlated with heavy
coffee consumption. If there was a high CHD incidence among heavy coffee
drinkers compared to nonconsumers or low consumers, it could be explained
on the basis of the strong correlation between the two habits, as was consistently shown by three earlier studies: the Chicago Electrical Workers Study
(31), the Gothenburg Study (32), and the National Research Council Study
(33). The Framingham Study, as well as the Chicago Western Electric Study,
the Kaiser-Permanente Study, and the Florida Community (death certificate)
Study (34), refuted an association between heavy coffee consumption per se
and the incidence of myocardial infarction or death from ischemic heart
disease. To prove the absence of an association is one of the most challenging
tasks in nonexperimental research, and one that places costly demands on
study design and sample size. The $4\frac{1}{2}$-year mortality follow-up study in
Evans County (20) showed no differences in CHD deaths among heavy consumers and nondrinkers or low-consumption coffee drinkers and adds findings of a prospective nature to the reported observations that consistently
point to a lack of association between coffee consumption and cardiovascular
mortality.

Conclusion

Total mortality showed no association with coffee usage in the four race-
sex groups of Evans County, Georgia. Deaths from coronary heart disease
(CHD) in white men and women and black men showed no statistically significant difference between high and low coffee consumers. In an area that has
been designated the "Stroke Belt" of the United States, neither CHD nor
cerebrovascular death rates seem related to coffee-drinking habits. To refute
or confirm the allegations of a detrimental influence of high coffee intake,
however, larger samples are needed. Nevertheless, our finding that mortality
from all causes is not increased in the high coffee-consuming group means
that a finding of increased CHD mortality with high coffee consumption
would have to be compensated by a protective lower rate for other causes
of death.

ANIMAL EXPERIMENTS

A review of the vast amount of literature that has accumulated over the
past 30 years on coffee and caffeine in relation to both cholesterol metabolism

and CHD leaves the observer convinced that there can be no seriously relevant cause-and-effect association between coffee consumption and either lipid levels or heart attacks. Definitive proof is generally impossible, but some misgivings about the few reports of a positive association between coffee intake and the incidence of CHD arose from two prospective epidemiological studies that reversed their findings from positive to negative and back again (Chicago Western Electric Study), or from negative to positive association (Kaiser Permanente Study).

The prospective Chicago Western Electric Study (35) followed 1,873 men who were 41 to 57 years old and free of CHD in 1959. Follow-up until 1983 demonstrated that men who reportedly consumed ≥6 cups of coffee per day compared with those who consumed <6 cups had a 5.6 mg/dl increase in total cholesterol, twice the incidence of first major coronary events during eight years of follow-up, and 1.5 times the risk of coronary death during 21 years of follow-up. The authors stated that the "increased risk of CHD is absent in men with serum cholesterol levels <230 mg/dl but may be significant for strong coffee drinkers with cholesterol levels >230 mg/dl."

It will not have escaped the reader that this paper (a) represents the third interpretation of the same study: the first report by Paul (36) in 1963 on the Chicago Western Electric Study placed the blame for CHD solely on coffee. This association was later discussed, in the second interpretation, in conjunction with intake of sugar in the coffee; ultimately, the association between coffee use and cigarette smoking vindicated coffee at least temporarily (37).

The Kaiser Permanente Study so far has offered three versions. In 1973, it stated: "Coffee drinking is not an established risk factor for myocardial infarction" (38). In 1985, a positive association between increased coffee intake and higher cholesterol levels was found (39). In 1990, the same authors concluded from a new cohort study that coffee consumption presents risk for acute myocardial infarction *independent* of a coffee-cholesterol link (40).

Thus, in addition to the remaining issues stemming from a few epidemiological observational studies reporting positive and a larger number of studies showing negative results, we are faced with the same unsatisfactory inconsistencies of results from *within* the same study centers: The Western Electric Studies seem to show a link between coffee and CHD via cholesterol, and the Kaiser Permanente Studies apparently deny the cholesterol link but now associate coffee consumption with CHD. These paradoxes lead the practitioner to the simple question: When do we get the next interpretation and which are we supposed to apply to our patients?

When neither observational, cross-sectional prevalence studies nor prospective studies of populations permit a final, definite conclusion on causality between coffee and CHD, one can—reluctantly—resort to animal experiments to look for possible clues.

Overview of 30 Years of Animal Experiments

The association of coffee and cholesterol was tested first in the animal model over 30 years ago. Surprising as it may be for us today, results from animal experiments reported neither an influence of caffeine on cholesterol levels nor on the development of aortic atheromatosis.

Myasnikov (1958) (41) had conducted experiments with rabbits and found no difference in the serum cholesterol levels between the animals that had received cholesterol alone and those that had received caffeine in addition to the cholesterol diet. Atheromatosis was quite pronounced in both groups.

Czochra-Lysanowicz et al. (1961) (42) (University of Lublin) found a negative effect of caffeine on the development of aortic atheromatosis, induced by cholesterol feeding. Her experiments lasted 100 days. In animals given a daily regimen of 1 g of cholesterol (dissolved in rapeseed oil), she observed increases of mean cholesterol levels from 56.6 to 1,295 mg/100 ml in the control group. Likewise, in the control animals, the degree of aortic atheromatosis at the end of the experiment was graded as 2.5. The experimental group also received 1 g of cholesterol and, in addition, received 0.02 g caffeine i.v. daily for 3 months. The results in the experimental group were striking—the cholesterol levels rose from a mean of 56.7 to 849.7 mg/100 ml only (Table 7). Atheromatosis changes were seen in the aorta of all animals, but to a lesser degree than in the control animals (grade 2.0).

The rabbit experiments were repeated by the same group in 1967 (Kedra et al.) (43), this time feeding caffeine benzoate by mouth. They summarized

TABLE 7. *Comparison of results from two experiments with caffeine in Zurich and Lublin on rabbits that were fed 1 g of cholesterol daily for 100 days*

Caffeine group	Zurich	Lublin	Average cholesterol level
Cholesterol levels at the start	81.5 (mg/100 ml) (10 rab)	56.7 (mg/100 ml) (7 rab)	71.3 (mg/100 ml)
At termination of the experiments	885.0 (mg/100ml) (8 rab)	878.2 mg.% (7 rab)	882.2 (mg/100 ml)
Cholesterol increment	803.5 (mg/100 ml) (10 rab)	822.5 (mg/100 ml) (7 rab)	810.9 (mg/100 ml)

Control group[a]	Zurich	Lublin	Average cholesterol level
Cholesterol levels at the start	86.2 (mg/100 ml) (8 rab)	55.6 (mg/100 ml) (10 rab)	60.9 (mg/100 ml)
At termination of the experiments	1350.0 (mg/100 ml) (8 rab)	1295.1 (mg/100 ml) (19 rab)	1320.9 (mg/100 ml)
Cholesterol increment	1263.8 (mg/100 ml) (8 rab)	1239.5 (mg/100 ml) (10 rab)	1260.0 (mg/100 ml)
Group difference	460.3 (mg/100ml)	417.0 (mg/100 ml)	449.1 (mg/100 ml)

[a] The control group did not receive caffeine from either form, p.o. (Zurich) or i.v. (Lublin).

their second 3-month experiment with 18 rabbits receiving 1 g of cholesterol plus 80 mg of caffeine benzoate in water per day (17 control animals received the same amount of cholesterol without caffeine). "This study showed that 'atherosclerosis' is more extensive in cholesterol-fed rabbits (mean index 2.32) than in those simultaneously treated with cholesterol and caffeine (mean index 1.61). However, the difference is not statistically significant. . . . It is a fact that the rabbits of this group (cholesterol plus caffeine) exhibited a lower level of total lipids, cholesterol and lipoproteins than those of the control group. Again the differences are statistically insignificant" (43).

We conducted our own experiments on rabbits (44), also for 100 days, using Nescafé that was fed to one group by mouth, plus 1 g of cholesterol, while the control group received 1 g of cholesterol only (dissolved in rapeseed oil and mixed with oatmeal). The results are shown in Table 7 and compared with the results obtained by our Polish colleagues. They clearly demonstrate lower cholesterol levels in the caffeine-treated animals than in the control animals.

In a second experiment, also lasting three months (45) the experimental group received daily subcutaneous injections of 0.22 ml caffeine benzoate (25 mg caffeine). Again, both groups of rabbits were fed the cholesterol-enriched diet, containing 1 g of cholesterol per day. At the termination of the experiment, cholesterol levels were lower in the experimental group than in the control group, but the difference was statistically insignificant.

There was no significant difference in the degree of atheromatosis of the aorta between the caffeine-treated group and the control group, with only a few more control animals showing more extensive atheromatosis of the aorta. There was also a lower degree of coronary atherosclerosis in the caffeine-treated animals. However, the differences between the experimental animals and control animals did not reach statistical significance.

The observation of higher individual cholesterol and higher mean cholesterol levels in the control group compared to the caffeine-treated group has to be evaluated in the light of two facts: (a) The rabbit is known to have a species-specific susceptibility to hypercholesterolemia and its sequelae. If caffeine did indeed have a hypercholesterolemia-enhancing effect, we would have expected a higher mean cholesterol level in the caffeine-treated group than in the control group. (b) The dosage of daily caffeine injections for rabbits can be compared with a very high coffee consumption in humans. At the onset of the experiment, the rabbits weighed 1.5–2 kg, therefore the daily caffeine dosage on the basis of body weight was 12.5–16.7 mg. The average cup of coffee contains about 100 mg of caffeine, and, in a 70 kg man, this is about 1.4 mg of caffeine per kg of body weight. This translates the rabbit dose to a daily human coffee intake equivalent of 9 to 12 cups. Although it could be argued that such an intake is excessive, it is certainly not implausible. Furthermore, our concern, if any, would be for individuals who consume this amount of coffee. Caffeine levels that might be considered high in relation to average human consumption thus had no exacerbating effects on serum cholesterol or atheromatosis in rabbits.

More recently, Haffner et al. (46) reviewed the results of animal experiments. One was conducted on rats, whose serum cholesterol rose acutely over 7 days, but not after 25 days of caffeine feeding. This finding was associated with an increase in fecal excretion of neutral steroids. Interestingly, Hostmark et al. (47) also observed "caffeine's pronounced hypolipemic effect in rats," but suggested that "plasma lipid regulation by neutral sterol and bile acid excretion is not of major significance in explaining the hypolipemic effect of coffee in the rat." Callahan et al. (48) used rhesus monkeys, giving the control group water, while the experimental animals received 50% of their fluids as coffee. The investigators found no consistent coffee-induced changes in serum lipoproteins or in aortic fatty streaks examined postmortem.

REFERENCES

1. Curatolo PW, Robertson D. The health consequences of caffeine. *Ann Int Med* 1983;98: 641–53.
2. Izzo JL, Ghosal A, Kwong T, Freeman RB, Jaenike JR. Age and prior caffeine use alter the cardiovascular and adrenomedullary responses to oral caffeine. *Am J Cardiol* 1983;52: 767–73.
3. Ammon HPT, Bieck PR, Mandalaz D, Verspohl EJ. Adaptation of blood pressure to continuous heavy coffee drinking in young volunteers. A double-blind crossover study. *Br J Clin Pharmac* 1983;15:701–6.
4. Wynder EL, Hall NEL, Polansky M. Epidemiology of coffee and pancreatic cancer. *Cancer Res* 1983;43:3900–6.
5. Eaton WW, McLeod J. Consumption of coffee or tea and symptoms of anxiety. *Am J Publ Hlth* 1984;74:66–8.
6. Heyden S, Muhlbaier LH. Prospective study of 'fibrocystic breast disease' and caffeine consumption. *Surgery* 1984;96:479–84.
7. Heyden S, Fodor JG. Coffee consumption and fibrocystic breasts: an unlikely association. *Canad J Surg* 1986;29:208–11.
8. Kurppa K, Holmberg PC, Kuosma E, Saxen L. Coffee consumption during pregnancy and selected congenital malformations: a nationwide case-control study. *Am J Publ Hlth* 1983; 73:1397–9.
9. Martin JC. An overview: maternal nicotine and caffeine consumption and offspring outcome. *Neurobehav Toxicol Teratol* 1982;4:421–7.
10. Heyden S, Heiss G, Manegold C, et al. The combined effect of smoking and coffee drinking on LDL and HDL cholesterol. *Circulation* 1979;60:22–5.
11. Becker AB, Simons KJ, Gillespie CA, Simons FER. The bronchodilator effects and pharmacokinetics of caffeine in asthma. *N Engl J Med* 1984;310:743–6.
12. Gillies ME, Birkbeck JA. Tea and coffee as sources of some minerals in the New Zealand diet. *Am J Clin Nutr* 1983;38:936–42.
13. Piters KM. Coffee boosts pain-free walking time for patients with chronic stable angina. Presented to the Western Section, American Federation for Clinical Research, Carmel, CA, February, 1984. *Med Wrld News* 1984;(March 12):137.
14. Piters KM, Colombo A, Olson HG. Effect of coffee on exercise-induced angina pectoris due to coronary artery disease in habitual coffee drinkers. *Am J Cardiol* 1985;55:277–80.
15. Laska EM, Sunshine A, Mueller F, Elvers WB, Siegel C, Rubin A. Caffeine as an analgesic adjuvant. *JAMA* 1984;251:1711–33.

16. Onrot J, Goldberg MR, Biaggioni I, Hollister AS, Kincaid D, Robertson D. Hemodynamic and humoral effects of caffeine in autonomic failure. Therapeutic implications for postprandial hypotension. *N Engl J Med* 1985;313:549–54.
17. Dobmeyer DI, Stine RA, Leier CV, Greenberg R, Schaal SF. The arrhythmogenic effects of caffeine in human beings. *N Engl J Med* 1983;308:814–6.
18. Graboys TB, Lown B. Coffee, arrhythmias, and common sense. *N Engl J Med* 1983;308: 835–6.
19. Yano K, Rhoads GC, Kagan A. Coffee, alcohol and risk of coronary heart disease among Japanese men living in Hawaii. *N Engl J Med* 1977;297:405–9.
20. Heyden S, Tyroler HA, Heiss G, Hames CG, Bartel A. Coffee consumption and mortality. Total mortality, stroke mortality, and coronary heart disease mortality. *Arch Int Med* 1978; 138:1472–5.
21. Dawber TR, Kannel WB, Gordon T. Coffee and cardiovascular disease. Observations from the Framingham Study. *N Engl J Med* 1974;291:871–4.
22. Wilson PWF, Garrison RJ, Kannel WB, McGee DL, Castelli WP. Is coffee consumption a contributor to cardiovascular disease? Insights from the Framingham Study. *Arch Intern Med* 1989;149:1169–72.
23. Grobbee DE, Rimm EB, Giovannucci E, Colditz G, Stampfer M, Willett W. Coffee, caffeine, and cardiovascular disease in men. *N Engl J Med* 1990;323:1026–32.
24. Tibblin G, Wilhelmsen L, Werko L. Risk factors for myocardial infarction and death due to ischemic heart disease and other causes. *Am J Cardiol* 1975;35:514–22.
25. Wilhelmsen L, Tibblin G, Elmfeldt D, Wedel H, Werko L. Coffee consumption and coronary heart disease in middle-aged Swedish men. *Acta Med Scand* 1977;201:547–52.
26. Caggiula AW, Tillotson J, Grandits TD, Kuller LH, Ockene J, (for the MR FIT Group). Coffee drinking, coronary heart disease and total mortality. Presented at X World Congress of Cardiology, September 14–19, 1986, Washington, DC.
27. Hypertension Detection and Follow-up Program Cooperative Group. Five-year findings of the Hypertension Detection and Follow-up Program. I. Reduction in mortality of persons with high blood pressure, including mild hypertension. *JAMA* 1979;242:2562–71.
28. Davis BR, Curb JD, Borhani NO, Prineas RJ, Molteni A. Coffee and serum cholesterol in the Hypertension Detection and Follow-up Program. Cardiovascular Disease (CVD) Epidemiology Newsletter, American Heart Association. No. 37, January, 1985. Abstract for the 25th Conference on CVD-Epidemiology.
29. Klatsky AL, Friedman GD, Siegelaub AB. Coffee drinking prior to myocardial infarction: results from Kaiser-Permanente epidemiological study of myocardial infarction. *JAMA* 1973;226:540–3.
30. Report from the Boston Collaborative Drug Surveillance Program. Coffee drinking and acute myocardial infarction. *Lancet* 1972;2:1278–81.
31. Paul O. Stimulants and coronaries. *Postgrad Med* 1968;44:196–9.
32. Wilhelmsen L, Wedel H, Tibblin G. Multivariate analysis of risk factors for coronary heart disease. *Circulation* 1973;48:950–8.
33. Hrubec Z. Coffee drinking and ischemic heart-disease. [Letter]. *Lancet* 1973;1:548.
34. Hennekens CH, Drolette ME, Jesse MJ, et al. Coffee drinking and death due to coronary heart disease. *N Engl J Med* 1976;294:663–6.
35. Shekelle RB, Dyer AR, Stamler J. Coffee and risk of coronary heart disease in a population of employed, middle-aged men: The Western Electric Study. Presented at Workshop on Coffee, Plasma Lipids and Coronary Heart Disease, Goteborg, Sweden, May 8–10, 1989.
36. Paul O, Lepper MH, Phelan WH, et al. A longitudinal study of coronary heart disease. *Circulation* 1963;28:20–6.
37. Paul O, MacMillan A, McKean H, Park H. Sucrose intake and coronary heart disease. *Lancet* 1968;2:1049–51.
38. Klatsky AL, Friedman GD, Siegelaub AB. Coffee drinking prior to acute myocardial infarction: Results from the Kaiser-Permanente Epidemiologic Study of myocardial infarction. *JAMA* 1973;226:540–3.
39. Klatsky AL, Petitti DB, Armstrong MA, Friedman GD. Coffee, tea and cholesterol. *Am J Cardiol* 1985;(Feb):577–8.
40. Klatsky AL, Friedman GD, Armstrong MA. Coffee use prior to myocardial infarction restudied: heavier intake may increase the risk. *Am J Epidemiol* 1990;132:479–88.

41. Myasnikov AL. Influence of some factors on development of experimental cholesterol atherosclerosis. *Circulation* 1958;17:99–103.
42. Czochra-Lysanowicz A, Gorski M, Kendra M. The effect of nicotine and caffeine on the development of arteriosclerosis in rabbits. *Nadbitka Biuletynu* 1961;1:83–7.
43. Kedra M, Chibowski D, Poleszak J. Effect of caffeine on the development of atherosclerosis in cholesterol-fed rabbits. *Pol Med J* 1967;352–8.
44. Heyden S, Ruttner J. Die Beeinflussung des Cholesterins-spiegels durch Coffein im Tierversuch. *Pathol Microbiol* 1966;29:291–6.
45. Heyden S, DeMaria W, Johnston WW, O'Fallon WM. The influence of caffeine on cholesterol levels and the development of atherosclerosis in rabbits. *J Chron Dis* 1969;21:677–85.
46. Haffner SM, Knapp JA, Stern MP, Hazuda HP, Rosenthal M, Franco LJ. Coffee consumption, diet, and lipids. *Am J Epidemiol* 1985;122:1–2.
47. Hostmark AT, Lystad E, Haug A, Bjerkedal T, Eilertsen E. Effect of boiled and instant coffee on plasma lipids and fecal excretion of neutral sterols and bile acids in the rat. *Nutr Rep Internatl* 1988;38:859–64.
48. Callahan MM, Rohovsky MW, Robertson RS, Yesair DW. The effect of coffee consumption on plasma lipids, lipoproteins, and the development of aortic atherosclerosis in rhesus monkeys fed an atherogenic diet. *Am J Clin Nutr* 1979;32:834–45.

Caffeine, Coffee, and Health,
edited by S. Garattini.
Raven Press, Ltd., New York © 1993.

8

Coffee and Myocardial Infarction

Review of Epidemiological Evidence

Silvia Franceschi

Epidemiology Unit, Aviano Cancer Center, 33081 Aviano (PN), Italy

Since the possibility was raised that high coffee intake enhances the risk of coronary heart disease (CHD) and acute myocardial infarction (AMI), at least eight articles from six case-control studies and eleven articles from ten prospective investigations have provided estimates of the relative risk (RR) of CHD or AMI in individuals with different levels of consumption of coffee and other similar beverages, including tea and decaffeinated coffee. Significant, approximately twofold elevated risks were found in individuals in the highest category of intake in eight out of sixteen of the most updated analyses of epidemiological studies on coffee and CHD or AMI. Positive findings tend to be more common (5 of 6 versus 4 of 10) in case-control studies than in prospective investigations and occur more frequently in studies that are able, because of high local levels of coffee consumption, to single out a category of habitual drinkers of large amounts of coffee.

Some of the limitations of epidemiological studies on coffee and risk of AMI or CHD (e.g., nondifferential misclassification of coffee or caffeine intake, lack of assessment of consumption in the most appropriate point in time, etc.) tend to attenuate a potential positive association. The opposite must be said for the most worrisome confounding factor, cigarette smoking. Smoking is so strongly correlated with heavy coffee drinking and CHD that the possibility of some underadjustment in the studies linking coffee with CHD or AMI is difficult to discard.

INTRODUCTION

The possibility that high coffee intake enhances the risk of coronary heart disease (CHD) and, particularly, acute myocardial infarction (AMI) has become an important issue in the epidemiological debate on lifestyle and health since the early 1970s, following the first reports from a multidisease case-control surveillance program (1,2). Since then, at least eight articles from six case-control studies (2–9) and eleven articles from ten prospective investigations (10–20) have provided one or more series of estimates of the RR and CHD or AMI in individuals with different consumption levels of coffee and other similar beverages, including tea and decaffeinated coffee.

The above-mentioned studies included substantial numbers of individuals of both sexes from different countries (various parts of the United States, Canada, Italy, Israel, and Norway) and ethnic groups (whites, blacks, Japanese). Thus they offered the opportunity to compare the existence and the magnitude of the association across geographic areas characterized not only by different levels of coffee consumption (per capita intake in some northern European countries [21] is two or three times higher than in North America and other European countries) but also by large variability in lifestyle (and thus potential correlates of heavy coffee drinking at an individual level).

The bulk of epidemiological evidence that has accumulated on coffee and CHD and/or AMI raises a number of methodological issues, largely shared by studies on the association (either direct or inverse) between life-style factors and risk of chronic-degenerative diseases. Some of these problems of classification, bias, and confounding have been encountered and widely discussed also in the context of research on coffee and cancer (21 and the Chapter by La Vecchia, this volume).

More important, according to a widely held view, epidemiological studies, in addition to biochemical and clinical data, suggest that coffee should not be considered a single exposure (21) but a complex combination of multiple, and still partly unknown, exposures. The type and preparation of coffee and similar beverages (in addition, obviously, to total amount consumed) interact substantially with the eventual effect of this habit on human health, particularly on the development of some precursors of cardiovascular disease and, consequently, AMI itself (22,23).

The present knowledge on the mechanisms potentially implicated in the relationship between coffee drinking and the probability of developing various diseases is considered in other parts of the present book. This chapter will concentrate on epidemiological investigations and will try to establish the present state of the art on coffee and CHD and AMI as it emerges from human data.

SUBJECTS AND METHODS

The results of six case-control studies (1–9) and ten prospective studies (10–20) carried out between 1970 and 1991, some of them published repeatedly at different phases of data collection, will be reviewed in chronological order.

A certain number of earlier publications and/or investigations whose primary focus was not on coffee or that did not express the association between coffee and CHD in terms of estimates of RR (24–36) will also be considered but not shown in detail because they did not contribute substantially to the quantitative assessment of the independent effect of coffee, which is the aim of the present review.

Some general characteristics of eight published reports derived from case-control investigations on coffee and AMI are summarized in Table 1. Five studies included hospital controls, while one was population based and recruited controls from the same neighborhood to which the AMI cases belonged. The overall association between nonfatal and/or fatal AMI and consumption of coffee can be assessed in more than 4,000 cases and 17,000 control subjects.

The prospective studies include eleven reports from ten different cohort investigations, covering over 230,000 subjects followed for periods ranging from 2 to 35 years (Table 2).

As concerns the measure of the association between coffee and AMI or CHD, odds ratios (OR) or RR and their respective 95% confidence intervals (CI) are provided. Allowance has been made in each study for various potential distorting factors, as shown in Tables 1 and 2. The OR and RR, adjusted for as many potential confounding factors as possible, were chosen for presentation to provide the best estimate of the independent effect of coffee consumption. This adjustment was especially important when it concerned cigarette smoking, which was strongly and positively correlated with intake of coffee in most of the investigations. Overall OR or RR, shown in Tables 1 and 2, will be discussed as often as possible except when separate analyses of different population strata—generally according to age, sex, or race—are provided. These partial results will be also commented on when significant and/or suggestive interactions between the effect of coffee and other characteristics and/or habits seem to emerge in the patients.

Although the present review deals chiefly with coffee and AMI, the effect of other similar beverages such as decaffeinated coffee and tea (or total caffeine intake) will also be shown and discussed, as a possible way of disentangling the role of different substances contained in coffee.

Finally, somewhat different cardiovascular endpoints (AMI or CHD) and criteria for diagnostic validation were adopted in the various investigations. Wherever possible, the following analysis will concentrate on AMI.

RESULTS

Table 1 concerns the most important features and findings of eight publications from six case-control studies on coffee and risk of AMI. In the study from the Boston Collaborative Drug Surveillance Program (2), patients with nonfatal AMI were found to drink appreciably more coffee than matched controls, while no difference emerged in the quantity of tea ingested.

This positive result was replicated in a similar but larger investigation (3),

TABLE 1. *Case-control studies on risk of acute myocardial infarction*

Reference	Year	Country	Number of cases: number of controls	Type of controls
Boston Collaborative Drug Surveillance Program (2)	1972	United States Canada Israel	276:1,104	Hospital controls
Jick et al. (3)	1973	United States	440:12,759	Hospital controls
Hennekens et al. (4)	1976	United States	649:649	Neighborhood controls
Rosenberg et al. (5)	1980	United States	487:980	Hospital controls
Rosenberg et al. (6)	1987	United States	491:1,119	Hospital controls
Rosenberg et al. (7)	1988	United States	1,873:1,161	Hospital controls
La Vecchia et al. (8)	1989	Italy	262:519	Hospital controls
Gramenzi et al. (9)	1990	Italy	286:649	Hospital controls

*95% confidence limits do not include 1.

(AMI) and consumption of coffee, decaffeinated coffee, and tea

	Intake (cups/day)	Odds ratio (OR)	Allowance for distorting factors	Comments
Coffee:	0	1	Age, sex and smoking	Consistent association
	1.5	1.3		across different sexes
	≥6	2.1*		and countries
Tea:	0	1		
	1–5	0.9		
	≥6	0.7		
Coffee:	0	1	Age, sex, past coronary heart disease, hypertension, congestive heart failure, obesity, occupation, smoking and sugar	
	1–5	1.6		
	≥6	2.2*		
Tea:	no association			
Coffee:	0	1	Age, sex, history of AMI, diabetes, angina, congestive heart failure, religion, smoking, hospital	Fatal cases, interview to wives
	1–5	1.2		
	≥6	1.0		
Coffee:	0	1	Age, smoking, weight, diabetes, hypertension, blood lipids, oral contraceptives (OCs), hospital, medical access	Women <50 years of age Association was greater when controls with chronic conditions were used
	1–4	1.0		
	≥5	2.0*		
Decaffeinated coffee:	0	1		
	1–4	1.0		
	≥5	1.2		
Tea:	0	1		
	1–4	0.7		
	≥5	0.9		
Coffee:	0	1	Age, body mass index, smoking, diabetes, hypertension, cholesterolemia, OCs, geographic area, medical access	Update of Rosenberg et al., 1980 (5)
	1–4	1.4		
	≥5	2.0*		
Coffee:	0	1	Age, smoking, hypertension, diabetes, body mass index, personality type (A/B), physical activity, religion, alcohol, education, geographical area, medical access	Men <55 years of age
	1–2	1.4		
	3–4	1.6*		
	5–9	1.8*		
	≥10	2.9*		
Decaffeinated coffee:	0	1		
	1–2	0.9		
	3–4	1.7		
	≥5	1.8		
Tea:	0	1		
	1–2	1.2		
	3–4	0.5		
	≥5	1.7		
Coffee	0	1	Age, education, smoking, hypertension, diabetes, hyperlipidemia, alcohol, body mass index, OCs	Women <70 years of age High OR (7.6) in hyperlipidemic women
	1	0.8		
	2	0.9		
	3	1.0		
	≥4	1.7*		
Decaffeinated coffee:	0	1		
	≥1	0.9		
Coffee:	Low tertile	1	Age, area of residence, education, smoking, hyperlipidemia, diabetes, hypertension, body mass index and intake of selected food item	Update of LaVecchia et al., 1989. Allowance for dietary habits slightly lowered OR for heavy coffee drinking (from 1.8 to 1.6)
	Intermediate tertile	1.0		
	High tertile	1.6		

where it was also made clear that the association between coffee and AMI could not be explained by the use of sugar with coffee, as has been previously suspected (25).

Hennekens et al. (4) questioned wives of patients who had died of CHD within 24 hours of onset of symptoms about their husbands' coffee consumption and reported multivariate OR very close to 1. This study, however, also included a restricted analysis of patients in the age range 40 to 69 and with a more limited set of confounding variables (e.g., smoking was allowed for more crudely, without the specification of number of cigarettes) that achieved different results (i.e., OR for $\geq$ 6 versus 0 cups of coffee/day = 1.9), that were very similar to the findings of two other studies (2,3).

A study on coffee and nonfatal AMI in young and middle-aged women was first published in 1980 (5) and updated, but with very similar results, in 1987 (6). Coffee drinking and nonfatal AMI were associated overall and in various subgroups of patients, albeit weakly. Rosenberg et al. (37) were also among the authors who first drew attention to the fact that frequency of coffee drinking was greater among controls whose admissions were for acute emergencies, whereas subjects admitted for chronic conditions tended to selectively avoid coffee.

The relationship between coffee intake and AMI was also considered with the same study design in young and middle-aged men (7). Again, the results suggested that caffeine-containing coffee at least enhances the risk of AMI, and that men who drink five cups or more daily can as much as double their risk. The association was apparent in each age group and in both smokers and nonsmokers.

Finally, two articles examined the data on coffee and nonfatal AMI in women below age 70 from an Italian hospital-based case-control study (8,9). There was a still-positive association between heavy coffee drinking and AMI after allowance for several relevant covariates including a few indicator foods (i.e., fish, carrots, green vegetables, fresh fruit, meat, ham, salami, butter, and alcohol) that emerged as risk factors (9).

Eleven articles from ten prospective studies that gathered information on consumption of caffeine-containing or decaffeinated beverages and subsequent development of CHD or AMI are presented in Table 2. Observations from the Framingham studies, first in 1974 (10) and later in 1989 (17), reached the conclusion that coffee drinking as engaged in by the general population is not a factor in the development of atherosclerotic cardiovascular disease. Analyses to test the association between coffee intake with first and second occurrence of cardiovascular disease separately were attempted (17), but the comparison was restricted to all coffee drinkers (1 cup per day or more) versus non-coffee drinkers.

In the study from Evans County, Georgia (11), an area designated as the "Stroke Belt," neither CHD nor cerebrovascular death rates seemed related to coffee-drinking habits. Again, however, the comparison was restricted to only two groups of coffee consumption (i.e., <5 versus ≥5 cups per day) (11).

The Lutheran Brotherhood Study (12) found no association between coffee intake and mortality from ischemic heart disease but put emphasis on an inverse association between coffee and mortality from other diseases. This inverse association was limited to the first four years of follow-up and was chiefly observed for deaths from non-neoplastic digestive diseases.

Conversely, the findings of the Precursors Study (13) supported an independent dose-related association of coffee consumption with clinically evident CHD. This association was consistent with a twofold to threefold elevated risk for heavy coffee drinkers and was strongest when the time between the report of coffee intake and CHD was shortest (13). These findings were based on only 51 cases of CHD, however, which also included 21 cases of angina pectoris.

A similar, albeit somewhat weaker, relationship emerged from the Chicago Western Electric Company Study (14). While the increased risk of death from CHD in heavy drinkers was similar in smokers and nonsmokers, mortality from all causes was greatest in the highest and lowest coffee intake groups (14). Yano et al. (15) updated the only data set on a large number of subjects of Japanese ancestry living in Hawaii in 1987 (34). Age-adjusted incidence rates of both total CHD and definite CHD (AMI) were significantly higher among coffee drinkers (≥1 cup/day) than nondrinkers. However, no clear dose-response relation was observed and allowance for smoking reduced the association (15).

The effect of caffeine consumption on mortality was evaluated in a cohort study of 10,064 diagnosed hypertensive individuals participating in the Hypertension Detection and Follow-up Program from 1973 to 1976 (16). No evidence was found to support an association between increased levels of caffeine consumption and increased all-cause mortality or cardiovascular disease mortality during the four years following interview of the patients (16).

The Health Professionals Follow-up Study (18) obtained some unexpected results. Although higher levels of consumption of caffeinated coffee were not associated with higher risks of CHD, heavy intake of decaffeinated coffee was associated with a marginally significant risk increase (18). This study, with that by Gramenzi et al. (9), is the only one in which allowance for selected eating habits was possible.

In a large prospective study conducted in three Norwegian counties, coffee was claimed to affect mortality from CHD over and above its effect in raising cholesterol concentrations (19). This investigation allowed, because of high coffee consumption in Norway, the identification of a sufficiently large group of very heavy coffee drinkers (≥9 cups/day) in both sexes, whose risk of death from CHD was more than doubled (19).

TABLE 2. *Prospective studies on risk of acute myocardial infarction (AMI) or coronary*

Reference	Year	Country	Cohort Size	Follow-up (years)		Intake (cups/day)
Dawber et al. (10)	1974	United States	1,992 men 2,500 women (35–69 years)	12	Coffee:	Total 0 1 2 3 4 5 6 ≥6
Heyden et al. (11)	1978	United States	2,530 (60% white, 40% black)	4½	Coffee:	≥5 vs <5 white males white women
Murray et al. (12)	1981	United States	16,911	11½	Coffee:	0 <1 1–2 3–4 5–6 ≥7
LaCroix et al. (13)	1986	United States	1,130 male medical students	19–35	Coffee:	0 1–2 3–4 ≥5
Le Grady et al. (14)	1987	United States	1,910 white males (40–56 years)	19	Coffee:	≤1 2–3 4–5 ≥6
Yano et al. (15)	1987	Hawaii United States	7,194 Japanese males	15	Coffee:	0 ≥1
Martin et al.,(16)	1988	United States	10,940 hypertensive individuals	5	Coffee equivalents:	0 ≤2 3 ≥4
Wilson et al., (17)	1989	United States	2,648 males and 3,566 females	20	Coffee: (drinkers vs. nondrinkers) Smokers males: females: Nonsmokers males: females:	
Grobbee et al., (18)	1990	United States	45,589 males, (40–75 years)	2	Coffee:	0 <1 2–3 ≥4
					Decaffeinated coffee:	0 ≤1 2–3 ≥4
					All caffeine (mg/day):	<75 75–148 149–285 286–491 492–1780
Tverdal et al. (19)	1990	Norway	19,398 males 19,166 women (35–54 years)	6.4	Coffee:	<1 ≥9
Klatsky et al. (20)	1990	United States	101,774 males and females, white and black	7	Coffee:	0 <1 1–3 ≥4
					Tea:	0 <1 ≥1

*95% confidence limits do not include 1.

Relative Risk (RR)	Allowance for distorting factors	Comments
1	Smoking	From Framingham study. Upward trends in risk of AMI, sudden death, angina pectoris and total deaths disappeared after allowance for smoking
0.9		
0.9		
1.1		
1.2		
0.6		
1.3		
1.4		
0.7		
	Age	From the Evans County Study. No association between coffee and stroke
2.0		
0.6		
1.0	Age, smoking, rural/urban residence	From Lutheran Brotherhood Study. Consistent lack of association across four-year periods. Negative association between coffee and digestive diseases (other than cancer)
0.7		
1.0		
1.0		
1.0		
0.9		
1	Age, smoking, cholesterolemia, hypertension	From the Precursors Study. The association was strongest when the time between the reports of coffee intake and coronary events was shortest
1.4		
2.0		
2.8*		
1	Age, diastolic pressure, cholesterolemia, smoking	From Chicago Western Electric Company Study. Fatal CHD.
0.9		
1.0		
1.7*		
1	Age and smoking	From Honolulu Heart Program Study. Fatal and nonfatal AMI. No dose-response relation
1.2		
1	Age, race, and sex	From the Hypertension Detection and Follow-up Cooperative Group. No associations when smokers and nonsmokers were analyzed separately, or with all-cause, and neoplastic mortality.
0.9		
0.8		
0.8		
	Age, smoking, systolic pressure, body mass index, cholesterol	From the Framingham Study. The association between coffee intake and subsequent cardiovascular diseases was negative in males and positive in females
1.0		
1.0		
1.0		
1.0		
1	Age, smoking, alcohol intake, family history of AMI, diabetes, occupation, quintile of intake of energy, cholesterol, and various types of fat	From the Health Professionals Follow-up Study. Clinical validation of all death certificates; no significant association with stroke
0.9		
1.0		
0.8		
1		
1.1		
1.0		
1.6*		
1		
1.2		
1.1		
1.1		
1.2		
1	Age, systolic pressure, smoking, cholesterolemia, high density lipoproteins (HDL)	The association with death from CHD was strongest in the high risk part of the range of HDL and in the low risk part of systolic pressure; elevated risk in different cholesterol level strata
2.2* (males)		
5.1 (females)		
1	Age, sex, race, smoking, alcohol, education and baseline disease	From Kaiser Permanente Medical Care Program. Consistent increased RR of hospitalization for AMI in different strata of cholesterol level
0.8		
1.2		
1.4*		
1		
1.1		
1.0		

TABLE 3. *Coffee and acute myocardial infarction: summary results[a]*

Reference	Year	Study design	Highest intake category (cups of coffee/day)	Relative risk estimate	Allowance for smoking
Boston Collaborative Drug Surveillance Program (2)	1972	Case-control	≥6	2.1[b]	Yes
Jick et al. (3)	1973	Case-control	≥6	2.2[b]	Yes
Hennekens et al. (4)	1976	Case-control	≥6	1.0	Yes
Heyden et al. (11)	1978	Prospective	≥5 vs <5	White males 2.0 White females 0.6 Black males 0.0 Black females 0.0	No
Murray et al. (12)	1981	Prospective	≥7	0.9	Yes
La Croix et al (13)	1986	Prospective	≥5	2.8[b]	Yes
Le Grady et al. (14)	1987	Prospective	≥6	1.7[b]	Yes
Rosenberg et al. (6)	1987	Case-control	≥5	2.0[b]	Yes
Yano et al. (15)	1987	Prospective	≥1	1.2	Yes
Martin et al. (16)	1988	Prospective	≥4	0.8	Yes
Rosenberg et al. (7)	1988	Case-control	≥10	2.9	Yes
La Vecchia et al. (8)	1989	Case-control	≥4	1.7[b]	Yes
Wilson et al. (17)	1989	Prospective	per cup of coffee/day	1.0	Yes
Grobbee et al. (18)	1990	Prospective	≥4	0.8	Yes
Tverdal et al. (19)	1990	Prospective	≥9	2.2[b] (males) 5.1 (females)	Yes
Klatsky et al. (20)	1990	Prospective	≥4	1.4[b]	Yes

[a] From Tables 1 and 2, only most updated results.
[b] 95% confidence limits do not include 1.

Finally, the use of coffee, but not tea, was also associated with higher risk of hospitalization for AMI in the data derived from the Kaiser Permanente Medical Care Program (20). Again, the risk increase did not seem to be mediated by an effect on blood cholesterol (20).

Table 3 summarizes the main results from the most recent analysis of the above-mentioned studies and indicates, in addition to the instances in which a significant positive association between coffee intake and risk of CHD has been found, the highest coffee intake category that each investigation was able to identify.

DISCUSSION

From the summary results in Table 3, it seems that, in eight out of sixteen of the most updated analyses of epidemiological studies on coffee drinking habit and occurrence of CHD or AMI, significantly elevated risks were found in individuals in the highest category of coffee intake. Positive findings tend to be more common (4/6 versus 4/10), but not exclusive, in case-control studies as compared to prospective investigations and occur more frequently in those studies that were able, thanks to high local levels of coffee consumption, to single out a category of habitual drinkers of large amounts of coffee

(7,19). Cigarette smoking, by far the most important correlate of coffee drinking that can contribute to the apparent positive association with CHD risk, has been almost always (15/16) allowed for in the estimation of RR.

If there are strong reasons to believe that moderate coffee consumption (≤ 4 cups/day) does not constitute a public health problem (Table 1,2), it is impossible, for the time being, to draw a similar conclusion on the total safety of more substantial levels of chronic coffee intake. The remaining uncertainties are partly of an epidemilogical nature (i.e., problems of imprecision in measurement of the relevant exposure and temporal relationship, bias, and confounding). These uncertainties also stem from the lack of knowledge of the mechanisms of the alleged relationship between coffee intake and CHD risk, especially the implicated coffee constituent(s) (e.g., caffeine, etc.) and the intermediate steps of a potential causal association (e.g., hypercholesterolemia, etc.).

The possible ways in which coffee drinking can influence the risk of developing CHD (e.g., hypercholesterolemia, hypertension, and cardiac arrhythmia) have been reviewed elsewhere (21,38–40) and are also considered in other chapters of this book. The following discussion will thus concentrate on the limitations intrinsic to the epidemiological studies to date on coffee and CHD.

Imprecision

Some degree of imprecision can occur either in the measurement of exposure and/or in the classification of the disease of interest. When the imprecision in the measurement of coffee intake is independent from the disease status, as it probably is in the present case, and the imprecision in the classification of CHD on the other hand, is independent of the amount of coffee ingested, this type of imprecision is called *undifferential* or *random misclassification*. Although imprecision in CHD diagnosis does occur in epidemiological studies, only random misclassification of coffee consumption will be discussed here.

A study of a random sample of 2,714 adults in the United States (41) disclosed a considerable misclassification of total coffee intake when the estimates were limited to the number of cups of coffee consumed, which is the most common practice in epidemiological investigations. The amount of coffee consumed both on weekdays and on weekends, the size of the container used, and the variability of coffee drinking habits between seasons and over time, while generally overlooked, turned out to be important aspects (41).

An even more important source of imprecision in the study of the relationship between coffee and CHD is the lack of certainty about the implicated active substance(s). Caffeine is a natural candidate because of its important stimulant properties; it can induce alterations in mood and sleep patterns, alter myocardial function, induce hypertension and arrythmia, and increase plasma catecholamine levels and plasma serum activity, especially when administered to nonhabitual users (39). If caffeine, and not coffee, is considered the exposure of interest, then the problem of imprecision is substantially amplified (41). Caffeine-containing beverages (chiefly coffee, tea, chocolate, and soft drinks), foods, and nonprescription drugs are numerous and widely spread among all population strata. Furthermore, the amount of caffeine crucially depends on whether caffeinated or decaffeinated coffee is consumed and the method used to brew coffee or tea. Five surveys using a high-performance liquid chromatography procedure to measure caffeine concentrations indicated considerable variations between different coffees, brands of coffees, and day-to-day variations in coffee samples from commercial coffee shops (42).

Finally, other constituents of caffeine-containing beverages have not been excluded as potential contributors to the alleged adverse effects of coffee in the development of CHD (23,43,44). Indeed, replacement of regular coffee by decaffeinated coffee did not seem beneficial, particularly concerning the cholesterol-raising effect (45), while the especially marked lipid-raising effect of boiled, unfiltered coffee led to the incrimination of some substance other than caffeine that is removed by filtering (43,44). Another largely overlooked factor, that may account for differences in the effect of coffee according to brewing method is contact time between coffee grounds and water.

It is obvious that the imprecision in the measurement of any exposure is maximal when the etiological hypothesis is ill-defined and that these limitations would have the effect of obscuring the dose-response relationship to disease incidence and eventually underestimate the real impact of coffee on the risk of CHD.

Bias and Confounding

Apart from the above-mentioned problems of measurement, responders' estimates of coffee intake should be accurate and not subject to any important bias, since there is no social stigma, except in some restricted groups of the population, against coffee use.

The choice of the reference category is an interesting methodological issue. Since the reference group was made up of individuals who abstained from consuming any amount of coffee and/or caffeine in virtually every study (Table 1 and 2), this choice is open to criticism based on the peculiarity of this group. Using light coffee-drinkers as the reference group is an alternative, as has been proposed or done for other lifestyle habits (e.g., alcoholic beverages, oral contraceptives, etc.). A dose-response relationship is an important proof of causality, and it emerges more convincingly when the analysis is restricted to exposed individuals (i.e., excluding those who totally abstain from common habits, possibly for health-related reasons).

The most serious issue is perhaps that of confounding variables that could explain the alleged relationship of coffee or caffeine intake to CHD. Coffee drinking may be a marker for an atherogenic diet (46), sedentary life, or, most important, cigarette smoking, rather than an etiologic factor in CHD. Clustering of atherogenic behaviors in coffee drinkers have been reported in young (47,48) as well as middle-aged and elderly populations (4,49).

The aforementioned study of 2,714 white adults in the United States showed that, of 32 risk factors analyzed by linear and logistic regression, only sex and cigarette smoking were found to be important potential confounders of caffeine and coffee intake (50). Other variables that may deserve to be included in the study design and analyzed as potential confounders (since they are risk factors for CHD as well) are dietary fat intake, vitamin C intake, and body mass index for men, and vitamin use, alcohol intake, stress and perceived health status for women (50).

Tables 1–3 show that smoking habit has been incorporated in the vast majority of epidemiological studies but some problem of underadjustment may well have remained, however, and thus account for at least part of the positive association that emerged in some investigations.

It is a common practice to include terms for variables such as *serum lipid levels, hypertension,* and other cardiovascular disorders that may be intermediate steps in the relationship between coffee or caffeine and AMI, rather than confounding factors, in the multiple logistic regression analysis (Table 1 and 2). This aspect of the issue of confounding would, however, go in the opposite direction (i.e., decrease of real positive association).

Temporal Relationship

One important factor that must be considered when assessing the relationship between coffee consumption and CHD is the temporal relationship between the presumed cause and the effect (51). In the investigations presented in Tables 1 and 2, the time span between the assessment of coffee consumption and coronary events varied from a few weeks (in the instance of case-control studies) to several years—sometimes decades—in prospective studies, when baseline participants' characteristics and habits were assessed only at the beginning. The importance of this variable is evident, particularly since it is known that coffee intake peaks between the ages of 40 to 49 and then declines with advancing age (51). Consequently, the assessment of coffee consumption 5, 10, or 20 years prior to the development of CHD may represent a rather poor indicator of more recent consumption. Again, as in the quantitative assessment of relevant exposure, the lack of conclusive understanding of the mechanism of the action of coffee on the cardiovascular system (i.e., acute versus chronic effect) undermines the possibility of exploring the most relevant exposure time and so leads to an underestimation of the strength of a potential relationship. Experimental data, however, suggest that caffeine exerts an acute rather than chronic effect on the cardiovascular system. At least one prospective study (13) found that the association between coffee consumption and CHD increased as the time between the reporting and the coronary event decreased.

This suggests that most prospective investigations underestimate the risk imposed by heavy coffee consumption, while case-control studies provide a more accurate reflection of the effect of coffee or caffeine as a precipitor of AMI (51).

CONCLUSIONS

The importance of demonstrating the safety of coffee consumption can be easily understood by reviewing some figures: more than five million tons are produced annually in some 50 coffee-growing countries, and coffee is second only to oil in international trade (52); green coffee is the second most important food commodity in the world after wheat (52); approximately 1.5 billion cups of coffee are drunk everyday throughout the world, and in countries that show the heaviest per capita consumption it amounts to an average of 4 to 5 cups per person per day. Major constituents of coffee, especially caffeine, are also present in many other popular beverages (tea, cola-containing soft drinks) and nonprescription pharmaceutical preparations (21).

Along the same line, CHD can be singled out as the most important cause of death in males in industrialized countries (53). Although declining trends in mortality from cardiovascular disease have been recorded over the last two decades in most rich countries, trends are less favorable in males than in females and increases of CHD mortality have still been observed in recent years in some countries, especially in Eastern Europe (53).

The fact that most epidemiological studies cannot rule out heavy coffee consumption as a significant risk factor in CHD incidence and mortality therefore remains a source of concern. As already discussed by Christensen and Murray (51) and further emphasized in the updated list of studies in Table 3, 50% of the recent case-control and prospective studies produced results indicating that coffee consumption has a moderate but significant unfavorable influence on the risk of developing AMI or CHD. One study showed a not-significantly increased risk, while three others suggested a complete lack of association. RR slightly below unity (i.e., 0.9, 0.8, and 0.8), but not significant, were found in three investigations. Therefore it seems that slightly more studies revealed a positive trend and fewer an inverse trend than would have been expected. Furthermore, the limitations of epidemiological studies on coffee and risk of AMI or CHD (e.g., nondifferential misclassification of coffee or caffeine intake, lack of assessment of consumption at the most appropriate point in time, etc.) go, if anything, in the direction of attenuating a potential positive association. The opposite must be said, however, for the most disturbing confounding factor, cigarette smoking. Smoking is so strongly correlated with heavy coffee drinking (50) and CHD (54) that the possibility of some underadjustment in the studies that linked coffee with CHD or AMI is difficult to confidently discard.

ACKNOWLEDGMENTS

I am grateful to Mrs. Judy Baggott, Mr. Lewis McClellan, Mrs. Anna Redivo, and Mrs. Ilaria Calderan, who provided editorial assistance.

REFERENCES

1. Jick H, Miettinen OS, Shapiro S, Lewis GP, Siskind V, Slone D. Comprehensive drug surveillance. *J Am Med Assoc* 1970;213:1455–60.
2. Report from the Boston Collaborative Drug Surveillance Program. Coffee drinking and acute myocardial infarction. *Lancet* 1972;ii:1278–81.
3. Jick H, Miettinen OS, Neff RK, Shapiro S, Heinonen OP, Slone D. Coffee and myocardial infarction. *N Engl J Med* 1973;289:63–7.
4. Hennekens CH, Drolette ME, Jesse MJ, Davies JE, Hutchinson GB. Coffee drinking and death due to coronary heart disease. *N Engl J Med* 1976;294:633–6.
5. Rosenberg L, Slone D, Shapiro S, Kaufman DW, Stolley PD, Miettinen OS. Coffee drinking and myocardial infarction in young women. *Am J Epidemiol* 1980;111:675–81.
6. Rosenberg L, Werler MM, Kaufman DW, Shapiro S. Coffee drinking and myocardial infarction in young women: an update. *Am J Epidemiol* 1987;126:147–9.
7. Rosenberg L, Palmer JR, Kelly JP, Kaufman DW, Shapiro S. Coffee drinking and nonfatal myocardial infarction in men under 55 years of age. *Am J Epidemiol* 1988;128:570–8.
8. La Vecchia C, Gentile A, Negri E, Parazzini F, Franceschi S. Coffee consumption and myocardial infarction in women. *Am J Epidemiol* 1989;130:481–5.
9. Gramenzi A, Gentile A, Fasoli M, Negri E, Parazzini F, La Vecchia C. Association between certain foods and risk of acute myocardial infarction in women. *BMJ* 1990;300:771–3.
10. Dawber TR, Kannel WB, Gordon T. Coffee and cardiovascular disease. Observation from the Framingham Study. *N Engl J Med* 1974;291:871–4.
11. Heyden S, Tyroler HA, Heiss G, Hames CG, Bartel A. Coffee consumption and mortality. Total mortality, stroke mortality, and coronary heart disease mortality. *Arch Intern Med* 1978;138:1472–75.
12. Murray SS, Bjelke E, Gibson RW, Shuman LM. Coffee consumption and mortality from ischemic heart disease and other causes: results from the Lutheran Brotherhood Study, 1966–1978. *Am J Epidemiol* 1981;113:661–7.
13. LaCroix AZ, Mead LA, Liang K-Y, Bedell Thomas C, Pearson TA. Coffee consumption and the incidence of coronary heart disease. *N Engl J Med* 1986;315:977–82.
14. LeGrady D, Dyer AR, Shekelle RB, et al. Coffee consumption and mortality in the Chicago Western Eletric Company Study. *Am J Epidemiol* 1987;126:803–12.
15. Yano K, Reed DM, MacLean CJ. [Letter] *N Engl J Med* 1987;316:946.
16. Martin JB, Annegers F, Curb JD, et al. Mortality patterns among hypertensives by reported level of caffeine consumption. *Prev Med* 1988;17:310–20.
17. Wilson PWF, Garrison RJ, Kannel WB, McGee DL, Castelli WP. Is coffee consumption a contributor to cardiovascular disease? Insights from the Framingham Study. *Arch Intern Med* 1989;149:1169–72.

18. Grobbee DE, Rimm EB, Giovannucci E, Colditz G, Stampfer M, Willett W. Coffee, caffeine, and cardiovascular disease in men. *N Engl J Med* 1990;323:1026–32.
19. Tverdal A, Stensvold I, Solvoll K, Foss OP, Lung-Larsen P, Bjartveit K. Coffee consumption and death from coronary heart disease in middle aged Norwegian men and women. *BMJ* 1990;300:566–9.
20. Klatsky AL, Friedman GD, Armstrong MA. Coffee use prior to myocardial infarction restudied: heavier intake may increase the risk. *Am J Epidemiol* 1990;132:479–88.
21. IARC Working Group on the Evaluation of Carcinogenic Risks to Humans. IARC Monogr Eval Carcinog Risks Hum. *Coffee, tea, maté, methylxanthines and methylglyoxal.* Vol 51. Lyon:IARC, 1991.
22. Thelle DS, Heyden S, Fodor JG. Coffee and cholesterol in epidemiological and experimental studies. *Atherosclerosis* 1987;67:97–103.
23. Thelle DS. Coffee, cholesterol, and coronary heart disease. *BMJ* 1991;302:804.
24. Brown A. Coronary thrombosis: an environmental study. *BMJ* 1962;2:567–73.
25. Paul O, Lepper MH, Phelan WH, et al. A longitudinal study of coronary heart disease. *Circulation* 1963;28:20–31.
26. Yudkin J, Roddy J. Levels of dietary sucrose in patients with occlusive atherosclerotic disease. *Lancet* 1964;ii:6–8.
27. Yudkin J, Morland J. Sugar intake and myocardial infarction. *Am J Clin Nutr* 1967;20: 503–6.
28. Paul O, MacMillan A, McKean H, Park H. Sucrose intake and coronary heart disease. *Lancet* 1968;ii:1049–50.
29. Palotas G. Coffee and myocardial infarction. *N Engl J Med* 1973;289:979.
30. Nichols AB. Coffee drinking and acute myocardial infarction. *Lancet* 1973;i:480–1.
31. Klatsky AL, Freidman GD, Siegelaub AB. Coffee drinking prior to acute myocardial infarction. Results from the Kaiser-Permanente Epidemiologic Study of Myocardial Infarction. *JAMA* 1973;226:540–3.
32. Mann JI, Thorogood M. Coffee-drinking and myocardial infarction. *Lancet* 1975;ii:1215.
33. Wilhelmsen L, Tibblin G, Elmfeldt D, Wedel H, Werkö L. Coffee consumption and coronary heart disease in middle-aged Swedish men. *Acta Med Scand* 1977;201:547–52.
34. Yano K, Rhoads GG, Kagan A. Coffee, alcohol and risk of coronary heart disease among Japanese men living in Hawaii. *N Engl J Med* 1977;297:405–9.
35. Vandenbroucke JP, Kok FJ, Van't Bosch G, Van Den Dungen PJC, Van Der Heide-Wessel C, Van Der Heide RM. Coffee drinking and mortality in a 25-year follow-up. *Am J Epidemiol* 1986;123:359–61.
36. Schwarz B, Bischof H-P, Kunze M. Coffee and cardiovascular risk: epidemiological findings in Austria. *Int J Epidemiol* 1990;19:894–8.
37. Rosenberg L, Slone D, Shapiro S, Kaufman DW, Miettinen OS. Case-control studies on the acute effects of coffee upon the risk of myocardial infarction: problems in the selection of a hospital control series. *Am J Epidemiol* 1981;113:646–52.
38. Wennmalm Å, Wennmalm M. Coffee, catecholamines and cardiac arrhythmia. *Clin Physiol* 1989;9:201–6.
39. Barone JJ, Grice HC. Sixth International Caffeine Workshop, Hong Kong, 7–10 August 1989. *Fd Chem Toxic* 1990;28:279–83.
40. Bak AAA, Grobbee DE. Caffeine, blood pressure, and serum lipids. *Am J Clin Nutr* 1991; 53:971–5.
41. Schreiber GB, Maffeo CE, Robins M, Masters MN, Bond AP. Measurement of coffee and caffeine intake: implications for epidemiological research. *Prev Med* 1988;17:280–94.
42. Stavric B, Klassen R, Watkinson B, Karpinski K, Stapley R, Fried P. Variability in caffeine consumption from coffee and tea: possible significance for epidemiological studies. *Fd Chem Toxic* 1988;26:111–8.
43. Piettinen P, Geboers J, Kesteloot H. Coffee consumption and serum cholesterol: an epidemiological study in Belgium. *Int J Epidemiol* 1988;17:98–104.
44. Bak AAA, Grobbee DE. The effect on serum cholesterol levels of coffee brewed by filtering or boiling. *N Engl J Med* 1989;321:1432–7.
45. Vandusseldorp M, Katan MB, Demacker PNM. Effect of decaffeinated versus regular coffee on serum lipoproteins. A 12-week double-blind trial. *Am J Epidemiol* 1990;132:33–40.
46. Solvoll K, Selmer R, Loken EB, Foss OP, Trygg K. Coffee, dietary habits, and serum cholesterol among men and women 35–49 years of age. *Am J Epidemiol* 1989;129:1277–88.

47. Hemminki E, Rahkonen O, Rimpelä M. Selection to coffee drinking by health—who becomes an adolescent coffee drinker? *Am J Epidemiol* 1988;127:1088–90.
48. Hemminki E, Rahkonen O, Rimpelä A, Rimpelä M. Coffee drinking among Finnish youth. *Soc Sci Med* 1988;26:259–64.
49. Puccio EM, McPhillips JB, Barrett-Connor E, Ganiats TG. Clustering of atherogenic behaviors in coffee drinking. *Am J Public Health* 1990;80:1310–13.
50. Schreiber GB, Robins M, Maffeo CE, Masters MN, Bond AP, Morganstein D. Confounders contributing to the reported associations of coffee or caffeine with disease. *Prev Med* 1988; 17:295–309.
51. Christensen L, Murray T. A review of the relationship between coffee consumption and coronary heart disease. *J Community Health* 1990;15:391–408.
52. Viani R. Coffee. In: *Ullman's Encyclopedia of Industrial Chemistry,* vol. A7. Weinheim, VCH Verlagsgesellschaft, 1986;315–39.
53. Uemura K, Pisa Z. Trends in cardiovascular disease mortality in industrialized countries since 1950. *World Health Stat Q* 1988;41:155–78.
54. A report of the Surgeon General. The health consequences of smoking: cardiovascular disease. Rockville, Md.: Office on Smoking and Health, 1983.

Caffeine, Coffee, and Health,
edited by S. Garattini.
Raven Press, Ltd., New York, 1993.

9

Psychopharmacological Profile of Caffeine

Karl Bättig and Hans Welzl

Behavioral Biology Laboratory, Swiss Federal Institute of Technology, CH-8092 Zürich, Switzerland

Considering the actual state of research on behavioral effects of caffeine, one may distinguish between studies pursuing traditional topics, studies addressing new issues, and questions that so far have more or less escaped scientific interest. The continuation of traditional questions confirms that the effects of caffeine on different types of performance are mostly transient, subtle, and poorly dose dependent, but beneficial in nature. Effects on sleep are dose dependent and longer lasting, and a similar conclusion seems justified for the impairments of fine motor control, except that this necessitates rather high doses.

The question whether coffee drinking represents a caffeine-seeking behavior comparable to other drug-seeking behaviors has only recently encountered scientific interest. Aside from the fact that coffee drinking occurs in most people at rather regular high or low frequencies, the arguments for coffee drinking as a dependence behavior are rather fragmentary. The subjective recognition of caffeinic effects is rather poor except for high doses, self-titration for the caffeine content of any preparation is nearly absent, and self-application paradigms in both animals and humans distinguish this substance clearly from the different substances of abuse. Caffeine withdrawal discomfort is modest, transient, and includes slight fatigue, a reduction in activity, and in some subjects slight headache.

The importance of caffeine tolerance for the behavioral effects of caffeine remains poorly delineated so far. It may well be that most people adjust their coffee intake to doses within the limits of their individual tolerance, thereby avoiding doses that would induce the negative effects of sleep disturbance, loss of fine motor control, nervousness, and anxiety. The positive effects might also be modest, as they have been verified so far in the laboratory mostly only at dose levels that exceed daily-life dosages. On the other hand, the important roles of taste, social settings, and habit formation for the reward value of coffee have, up to now, hardly been touched by systematic research.

INTRODUCTION

Reasons for the widespread use of coffee can be seen in its aromatic qualities (taste, olfaction) as well as in its moderate stimulant or at least refreshing effects. A number of reviews can be recommended to the reader interested in the historical development of research in this area (1–7). Medically, caffeine is widely used in combination with analgesics in over-the-counter pain-killing preparations, but clinically it is used much less than theophylline, another methylxanthine. Although caffeine is commonly classified in textbooks as a psychostimulant substance (like amphetamine and cocaine), there are no doubts that its stimulant properties are modest. This was noted already in the review by Weiss and Laties (1) in comparisons with amphetamine, and even more recently, Dews (5) questioned whether caffeine should be considered as a stimulant drug at all or rather as a stabilizer of freshness.

GENERAL ASPECTS

Even under well-controlled laboratory conditions and when using high dosages of caffeine equivalent to four or more cups of coffee, only subtle behavioral effects of caffeine can be observed. Due to the small extent of caffeine-induced changes, it is especially important for a critical interpretation of experimental results to know in what way several pharmacological and nonpharmacological factors influence caffeine's action. These general aspects related to caffeine's effects on behavior are briefly discussed below.

Interaction with Different Neurotransmitter Systems

The pharmacological basis of caffeine's action on the central nervous system is mainly attributed to an interaction with the adenosinergic system (for discussion, see Daly, this volume). Caffeine and other methylxanthines are competitive inhibitors at adenosine receptors in the brain with relative affinities that correlate with relative potencies for stimulating locomotor activity in mice (8,9). Only high doses of caffeine also inhibit the enzyme phosphodiesterase (10,11). Especially at higher doses, caffeine also interacts with a number of different neurotransmitter systems.

Pharmacological, physiological, and behavioral studies suggest that caffeine acts on the synthesis and turnover of catecholamines. Caffeine increases noradrenaline synthesis and turnover in the brain of rats [e.g., (12)]. The effect on the dopaminergic system needs a rather high concentration of caffeine (13). Recently, caffeine (100.0 and 200.0 mg/kg, 30 minutes, i.p.) has been shown to increase serotonin, noradrenaline, and dopamine utilization in brains of mice with the most dramatic change in the serotonin utilization in the olfactory bulbs (14).

Further, caffeine antagonized several central effects of diazepam (15). The doses of caffeine necessary to effectively antagonize the different electrophysiological and behavioral effects of diazepam varied greatly. Whereas only 0.3 to 0.6 mg/kg p.o. caffeine were necessary to antagonize the anticonflict and muscle relaxant effects of diazepam in rats, 160 mg/kg (i.p.) caffeine were necessary to antagonize diazepam's anticonvulsant effects in mice.

However, caffeine has only a weak affinity to benzodiazepine receptors. The maximal inhibitory concentrations (IC_{50}) for diazepam binding in crude synaptosomal P2 fraction from human frontal cortex were 448 μM caffeine compared to that for adenosine receptor ligand binding, which was between 65 and 203 μM (16). In rats, the IC_{50} values for diazepam binding in the brain were 800 μM compared with 50 μM for adenosine receptors (9). Since the locomotor activity stimulating effects of caffeine could be seen already with brain concentrations of 63 μM, it is not likely that a direct action of caffeine on benzodiazepine receptors causes its locomotor activity stimulating effects. However, pretreatment with 30 mg/kg caffeine (i.p.) increased benzodiazepine binding in the rat (17).

Caffeine also potentiates the inhibitory activity of GABA in the frog spinal cord [e.g., (18)]. Chronic exposure of embryonic neurons to caffeine or theophylline reduced the ability of GABA to potentiate the binding of a benzodiazepine receptor agonist to the $GABA_A$/benzodiazepine receptor (19). This action can be blocked with the adenosine receptor agonist chloroadenosine. Very little or no information is available on possible effects of caffeine on other transmitter systems such as acetylcholine and the excitatory amino acids, and the same holds for possible interactions with the numerous different neuropeptides.

Central and Peripheral Action

Most of the behavioral effects of caffeine are thought to be due to its effects on central nervous system sites. However, caffeine also influences the peripheral nervous system controlling the function of the renal, cardiovascular, and respiratory systems [for review, see Mosqueda-Garcia and Robertson, this volume (6)]. Therefore, an effect of caffeine on behavior via the peripheral nervous system still has to be taken into consideration.

Development of Tolerance

When interpreting the effects of caffeine on behavior, it is important to know the history of caffeine exposure of the experimental subject. As with other drugs, prolonged exposure to caffeine leads to the development of tolerance to some of the specific drug effects. For example, even after one to three days, a given dose of caffeine is less effective in eliciting locomotor activity in rodents than when given the first time (20). This tolerance is probably based on the observed upregulation in the number of adenosine receptors after repeated caffeine treatment (21). Systematic studies on the impact of tolerance to the central nervous system effects in humans are missing so far, in contrast to recent work demonstrating its importance for the cardiovascular effects of the substance.

Application, Plasma Levels, and Metabolism of Caffeine

An average cup of coffee contains about 50 to 80 mg caffeine. It has become standard practice in experiments with human subjects to apply somewhere around 3 mg/kg caffeine, a dose approaching roughly the total daily caffeine intake of average coffee drinkers. The serum caffeine levels, after a single cup of coffee, are approximately 5 μM (6). In mice and rats, behaviorally active doses of caffeine (5 to 20 mg/kg) that increase locomotor activity result in considerably higher brain caffeine concentrations in the range of 50 to 70 μM (9,22).

Several studies suggest that caffeine plasma concentrations may not predict brain levels. Plasma levels seem to decline more rapidly than brain levels (22). The decline in caffeine levels in the brain also differs between brain regions (23). The metabolic half life of caffeine lies between 2 and 4 hours in most species and follows first-order kinetics; saturation kinetics occurs in rats for doses greater than 40 mg/kg (see Daly, this volume).

Application of caffeine in mice via subcutaneous implantation of silastic tubing filled with powdered caffeine led to a marked variance in serum caffeine concentrations (24). Oral application of caffeine seems to lead to only low tissue concentrations (25).

Individual Variation

Internal factors of the subject tested exert a strong influence on the psychopharmacological profile of caffeine. Personality in humans or the strain of rats or mice investigated can determine the behavioral effects of caffeine. Another factor determining caffeine's behavioral effects is age. Differences in the degree of behavioral changes after systemic caffeine can be seen whether children, adults, or elderly persons are used as subjects. Similar observations can be made in animals. Further, caffeine's behavioral effects depend on the subject's motivational and/or emotional state and activity.

MOTOR AND SENSORY SYSTEMS

Older studies have investigated effects of caffeine at high dose levels on isolated muscle preparations. Fewer studies were done on effects of caffeine on muscular performance in the intact organism, and research on sensory functions was concentrated mainly on possible analgesic effects.

Muscle Activity and Reflexes

Although caffeine tends to increase the contraction of isolated muscles, the doses necessary to induce an increase exceed those reached with daily intake by several orders of magnitude, as reviewed earlier (3). Investigations in humans were done in the past on the performance of single groups of muscles and reflexes and, in part, on different types of athletic performance. Earlier studies suggest that the potential ergogenic benefits of caffeine might be indirectly due to increases in motivation or decreases in subjective fatigue rather than to effects on any part of the motor system per se.

One of the first pharmacological experiments with caffeine investigated its effect on reflex activity. In 1913, Storm van Leeuwen (26) reported that caffeine increased spinal reflexes in decerebrate cats. In rabbits, caffeine first stimulated and then inhibited labyrinthine and body reflexes (27). Several authors observed an increase in the patellar response in humans [for references, see (28)]. However, others (29) were later unable to find any effect of caffeine on the patellar reflex. Further, the polysynaptic reflex evoked by stimulation of the sural nerve in spinal cats showed a marked increase with a minimum effective dose of approximately 5.0 mg/kg (28). The same authors found no consistent effects of caffeine (up to 100.0 mg/kg) on the monosynaptic reflex evoked by stimulating the biceps-semitendinosus nerves.

Jacobsen and Edgley (30) observed that raising the arm from a hanging to an upright position was both prompter, with shorter reaction times, and faster with 300 mg caffeine than with 600 mg or placebo. Tarnopolsky et al. (31) found no evidence of direct effects on the motor system, in terms of the maximal voluntary strength, peak twitch torque, and electrophysiological motor unit activation.

The reported effects on athletic performance also remain equivocal in the more recent literature. Positive effects on endurance performance have been discussed recently in the reviews by Brooks and Fahey (32) and Delbeke and Debackere (33). However, there are also reports of no effects, such as those by Ben-Ezra and Vaccaro (34) and Knapik et al. (35) or even reports of negative effects by Casal and Leon (36) and by Gaesser and Rich (37).

Another possibility through which caffeine could affect motor output would be through improvements of metabolic energy mobilization. However, although it was occasionally reported that caffeine increased blood glucose levels and, more frequently, increased the levels of free fatty acids and lowered the respiratory exchange ratio, these effects may be too modest in magnitude to explain improvements in performance, as suggested recently by the studies done by Gaesser and Rich (37) and by Casal and Leon (36), who also discussed the relevant findings of several other experiments.

Spontaneous Motor Activity

Spontaneous motor activity, which has been studied in many experiments with rodents, has so far hardly been assessed with caffeine in humans. Elkins et al. (38) measured the effects of 3 and 10 mg/kg caffeine against placebo in 19 prepubertal boys. The amount of activity was measured with an acceleration-sensitive device worn by the children in a vest pocket for 2 hours starting half an hour after drinking the test beverages. The lower dose produced a significant elevation of activity, by about 15%. In the same laboratory, this effect was also investigated in adult men by Rapoport et al. (39); the effect differentiated in an interesting fashion between low and high coffee consumers. There was no effect in the low consumers but an increase with 10 mg/kg in the high consumers. This increase, however, was perhaps a consequence of particularly low placebo values that could have been a consequence of caffeine withdrawal, as the subjects had to abstain from all caffeine sources for 48 hours before the experiments. Given these reports, it would certainly be interesting to use actometers over prolonged periods to assess any possible effects of caffeine as well as of caffeine withdrawal. The investigation of this aspect would also merit more interest, as it would allow direct comparisons with the numerous studies in laboratory rodents.

As a phenomenon closely related to spontaneous activity, one may see a decrease in hand steadiness often reported after the consumption of caffeine. This effect has been investigated less often in recent years. Calhoun (40), reviewing 10 studies and referring to earlier reviews on this matter by Weiss and Laties (1) and Nash (41), concluded that a decrease in hand steadiness is due to the effects of caffeine and agreement is greater than for most other behavioral effects of the substance. Even in early studies it was noted that this effect seems to last quite a long time after ingestion. Only a few studies have been done in recent years, and among them the one by Ghoneim et al. (42) merits particular attention because caffeine plasma levels as well as various behavioral functions were measured with hand steadiness across a period of 3^1w4.5_2 hours after 6 mg/kg caffeine. The decrease in hand steadiness reached its maximum shortly after ingestion but did not decline thereafter until the end of the measurement period, in contrast to the generally more modest, but positive, effects on the efficiency of digit cancellation and tapping. Interestingly, the decreases in hand steadiness were not significantly antagonized by diazepam, as was also the case in a study by Loke et al. (43), who observed decreased hand steadiness with 6 mg/kg but not with 3 mg/kg caffeine. It appears therefore that the effect is not only long lasting but also dependent on dose levels in the upper range of acute studies, which may be of less importance for daily-life dosages. In parallel to these objective measurements, subject-rated restlessness was also seen by Roache and Griffiths (44) only after the high dose of 600 mg.

Another approach was taken recently by Hasenfratz et al. (45), who measured the motor unrest of the subjects seated on an experimental chair with physical force transducers. Before and after ingesting 250 mg caffeine, the subjects had a preparatory relaxation period, then performed a video screen task followed by a final relaxation period. Motor unrest on the chair increased significantly after caffeine only for the preparatory relaxation period, whereas EMG activity of the frontal muscle increased for all three periods. Taken together, such findings suggest that high doses of caffeine in some way decrease the inhibitory modulation of the motor output systems.

Locomotor activity (LA) in rats or mice can be measured using a variety of test apparatuses that, however, do not always measure the same type of LA. Spontaneous LA, whose increase without apparent purpose might be the equivalent of human "restlessness," can be best measured as wheelrunning or activity in a simple runway apparatus. Increased spontaneous LA after drug injections usually decreases with fading stimulatory drug action and/or fatigue of the animal. Exploratory activity, i.e., LA that is elicited by exposure to a complex environment, can be measured in an open field (with or without specific objects to investigate such as holes in the holeboard apparatus) or in complex mazes. Novel stimuli are especially effective in eliciting exploratory activity. Thus, exploratory activity also includes a cognitive aspect, i.e., recognizing a situation as being novel (46). LA as measured in these apparatuses usually decreases due to habituation to the stimulus situation. Without careful planning of the experimental design, it is not always easy to attribute changes in LA either to changes in spontaneous LA or to changes in exploratory activity.

Caffeine given systemically has consistently been shown to increase LA up to 500% in mice [e.g., (8,9,47–53)] and rats [e.g., (54–57)]. This effect is dose dependent, with very low doses (1.9 mg/kg) (8) and high doses being ineffective or even decreasing LA in mice. Doses as low as 5.8 mg/kg in mice (9) or 5 mg/kg in rats (55) have been shown to increase LA substantially. Injecting i.p., a low (20 mg/kg) or a high (40 mg/kg) dose of caffeine in mice was associated 1 hour after treatment with brain concentrations of caffeine of 13 and 29.6 μg/g, respectively (58). Mice treated with the low dose were more active than those treated with the high dose. Only later (150 minutes after injection), the high dose stimulated LA more than the low dose. By then the brain caffeine concentrations in animals injected with the high dose had fallen to approximately 10 μg/g. The effective caffeine doses to maximally increase motor activity in rodents differ widely among investigators and are reported to lie between 10 and 200 mg/kg (for review see ref. 4).

These greatly differing effective doses are, among other factors, due to the great variety of apparatuses used to measure motor activity.

The effect of caffeine on activity also seems to depend on the route of administration. Whereas subcutaneous injections of caffeine (20 mg/kg) increased gross LA in rats threefold, more than four weeks of drinking a caffeine solution (0.125 or 0.5 mg/ml) did not change activity (59). This difference might be due to low plasma levels of caffeine when the drug is administered via the drinking water.

The stimulatory effect of caffeine on activity is not only dependent on the dose injected and the route of administration. Other factors such as the type of activity measured and the design of the test apparatus can determine whether a stimulatory or depressant effect of caffeine can be found. In rats, doses of 5 to 20 mg/kg caffeine increased LA in an open field but did not increase rearing, whereas metamphetamine (1 to 4 mg/kg) increased both, LA and rearing (60). The authors viewed LA and rearing as representative for horizontal and vertical activity, respectively. No explanation for why caffeine selectively increased LA was given. In contrast to these results, Meliska and Loke (56) observed enhanced LA and rearing in rats after injection of caffeine (5 and 15 mg/kg i.p.). In this context, it is interesting to note that selective A2 adenosine receptor antagonists also increased rearing (61). Similar to amphetamine (1 to 16 mg/kg s.c.), caffeine (12 to 50 mg/kg) increased activity of rats in a treadmill but not in a Y-maze (62). Caffeine (20 mg/kg i.p.) also failed to increase, or even decreased, exploratory activity (number of holes inspected) in mice in a holeboard apparatus (63). In mice, Hilakavi and colleagues (64) observed that caffeine (15 and 30 mg/kg i.p.) induced LA but not exploratory activity in a holeboard apparatus; injecting a high dose (60 mg/kg) decreased LA. File and colleagues (65) reported an increase in LA and a decrease in exploratory activity in rats injected pre-trial with caffeine (20 or 40 mg/kg).

Further, caffeine's stimulatory effect was dependent on the complexity of the maze used to measure LA (57). When the dark tunnel maze, which elicits exploration in rats, was reduced to a circular runway, caffeine (16 mg/kg i.p.) significantly increased LA. When more complex configurations such as a radial maze configuration were selected, only a small or no increase in LA after the same dose of systemic caffeine was observed. The data by Oettinger and colleagues (57) also suggest that whereas control rats show habituation, i.e., a decrease in LA over a 30 minute test period in the maze, caffeine-injected animals decreased their LA to a much smaller extent. Therefore with increased habituation of the control rats, the difference in LA between control and caffeine-treated animals became more pronounced. These results suggest that in simple or very familiar environments that do not elicit exploration, the stimulatory effects of caffeine on LA become evident. However, when a complex novel test apparatus elicits exploratory activity in undrugged rats, caffeine's stimulatory effects on activity are often no longer visible.

Other factors influencing LA are the motivational and/or emotional state of the animal. Caffeine more effectively increased LA in rats with a low motivation to run than in those with a high motivation (66). Rats, running through an alley to collect a sweetened food pellet in a goal box, increased their running speed when injected with caffeine (10 and 20 mg/kg i.p.). No increase in running speed after injection of the same doses of caffeine could be detected after increasing the motivation to run through the alley by adding aversive stimuli (strong light source, ventilator) in the area around the start box.

Caffeine (20 mg/kg) was more effective in decreasing exploratory activity in grouped than in isolated mice (63). However, isolated mice already showed a low baseline exploratory activity that could probably not be decreased further. Caffeine (5 and 40 mg/kg orally) also more effectively stimulated LA during daytime than during nighttime when LA in all animals was already high (67). The effectiveness of caffeine in inducing LA also depended on the strain of mice used. C57 mice were more sensitive to the stimulating effect of caffeine than DBA mice (68). Caffeine injected directly into the lateral ventricle of mice reduced LA at the lowest dose used (69). Higher doses did not change LA.

A tolerance to the locomotor stimulant effects of caffeine developed in rats when caffeine was added to their drinking water [0.5 or 1 mg/ml; e.g., (20,65,70)]. Tolerance could be demonstrated even after 1 to 3 days of treatment and was lost 3 to 4 days after the cessation of drug treatment (20). Tolerance to the LA stimulating effect of caffeine was accompanied by an increase in the number of adenosine receptors in the reticular formation (21). Other brain areas were not investigated. A cross-tolerance developed to the locomotor activity stimulating effect of other xanthines [theophylline, 7-(2-chloroethyl) theophylline] but not to the nonxanthine stimulants cocaine, methylphenidate, and d-amphetamine (70,71). The dose-effect curves for the LA depressant effect of adenosine analogues $(R)(-)$-phenylisopropyladenosine (PIA), N-ethylcarboxamidoadenosine (NECA) was shifted to the right in caffeine-tolerant rats (71).

When caffeine (15 mg/kg i.p.) was given subchronically (72-hour intervals), its ability to increase wheelrunning increased with reference to chronic caffeine or saline treatment (72). Thus, it appears that depending on the frequency of caffeine treatment, the drug can lead either to tolerance or sensitization. Similar results were obtained with subchronic oral administration of caffeine (0.5 mg/ml) (73). During withdrawal from caffeine, LA is depressed in mice (74).

In summary, these observations in rodents demonstrate the subtleties of the caffeinic effects. Although they are mostly stimulant, they can also be absent or even depressant, depending on dosage, tolerance, the route of administration, species and strain, and, most important, on the type of testing apparatus and on the emotional and/or circadian state of the animals.

Pain and Analgesia

A relationship between caffeine, pain, and analgesia might be seen in the fact that most over-the-counter headache and pain pills contain caffeine. Through carefully conducted experiments such as the ones by Haslam (75), who used the technique of local skin heating, it was revealed quite early that caffeine per se has hardly any effect on pain. Whether caffeine might have an effect on the analgesic properties of phenacetin and aspirin is less clear. No such effects were seen by Cass and Frederick (76) for chronic pain or by Baptisti et al. (77) in postpartum patients, whereas Lasagna (78) and Lim et al. (79) found evidence for a small potentiation of analgesic effects by caffeine.

However, under conditions of pain, caffeine could have an indirect beneficial effect by elevating mood and clear-headedness. A recent study by Lieberman et al. (80) tested a series of behavioral functions after 800 mg aspirin given either alone or in combination with 64 mg caffeine, a dosage quite adequate for comparison with over-the-counter analgesics. Mood as well as vigilance and self-reported efficiency were in fact improved with caffeine alone and with the caffeine-aspirin combination in comparison with both placebo and aspirin alone. Effects of caffeine on sensory functions other than pain, such as vision, hearing, taste and olfaction, have been considered only rarely in past research and were reviewed by Eichler (3). Effects were generally small or absent and not consistent across the studies. It is not unlikely that the improvements occasionally seen with caffeine were an indirect consequence of the central effects on general mood and freshness, as suggested above for the case of pain.

Furthermore, it cannot be excluded that caffeine might have analgesic effects only for specific target organs or specific types of pain. A recent study by Ward et al. (81) suggests that this could be the case for headache. In 53 nonmigrainous headache patients, caffeine significantly and dose dependently alleviated subjectively reported pain under double-blind conditions. The effect was similar to that of acetaminophen (which is frequently combined with caffeine), and it was independent of the effects of caffeine on mood as well as of the prior coffee consumption of the subjects.

Studies in animals have been done mostly in connection with the questions of interactions with other substances and are discussed in this context in the chapter by J. Daly. Caffeine (25.0, 50.0 and 100.0 mg/kg) decreased the thresholds for motor response (tail withdrawal and hindquarters movement) and vocalization response to pain (induced by electrical stimulation) in rats in a dose-dependent manner (82). Caffeine antagonized the dose-related increase in reaction times in a hot plate test after intracisternally injected adenosine agonists in mice (83).

PSYCHOMOTOR AND MENTAL PERFORMANCE

Complex performance is certainly at the center of interest in the actions of caffeine. It can be viewed in the light of the action of the complex functions of arousal on one hand and sleepiness on the other. The concept of the effects on performance through action on the nonspecific mesocortical arousal system is discussed in this volume by Snel, and the possibility of action through changes of the epinephrine and norepinephrine levels in plasma and urine has been reviewed by Fernstrom and Fernstrom (84).

An ideal approach for studying the effects of caffeine on arousal would include simultaneous measurements of the EEG, the appropriate behavioral functions, and catecholaminergic activity, although the latter could be approached in humans for the peripheral systems only, as plasma and urinary levels do not necessarily represent catecholaminergic brain states. However, so far one has to rely mainly on studies that have considered just one of these functions.

Arousal and EEG

The earliest report on effects of caffeine on the EEG was presented by Goldstein et al. (85). In this early study, the energy content of the EEG was summed across all frequency bands and was seen to decrease 90 to 180 minutes after the consumption of 200 mg caffeine. Presumably, this observation was due to increased desynchronization and would therefore be indicative of increased cortical arousal. Šulc et al. (86) used a power spectral analysis and observed increases in power in the upper part of the alpha band and decreases in power in the lower part of the alpha band and in the upper part of the theta band. This result comes closer to the profile of EEG changes proposed by Saletu (87) as a typical effect of psychostimulants and that would be characterized by decreases of power in the slow delta and theta bands and in the upper part of the fast beta band and by increases of power in the alpha band and in the lower part of the beta band.

As opposed to this picture, Clubley et al. (88) reported an increase of delta power after 100 mg of caffeine, which would indicate sedation rather than stimulation. In contrast to the other studies, Pollock et al. (89) did EEG between 30 and 50 minutes after the application of 200 mg caffeine, thus in the period when both the plasma levels and the cardiovascular effects of the substance are peaking, whereas the earlier studies measured the EEG much later after application. As a general result, EEG power was found to be reduced, and this effect reached significance for the 10 Hz (medium alpha) and the 15 Hz (low beta) bins.

Künkel (90) observed with 250 mg caffeine a result that approaches the profile suggested by Saletu for psychostimulants, with decreases of power in the theta and alpha bands and increases of the dominant frequencies in the alpha and beta bands. He further observed not only considerable individual differences in the magnitude of this response but also topographical differences across different leads.

A recent study done in our laboratory by Hasenfratz and Bättig (45) differed from several of the previous studies by measuring EEG both immediately before and 30 minutes after drinking coffee with 250 mg caffeine in order to evaluate the EEG changes. Furthermore, the changes were compared with those obtained after smoking a cigarette. The effects of smoking and caffeine on the EEG were additive and no interactions were obtained. Caffeine produced decreases of theta power and increases of beta power at parietal recording sites. Smoking produced the same changes in a more pronounced fashion both for parietal and vertex recordings. In addition, smoking also increased the peak frequency within the alpha band and decreased delta power for all recording sites. These findings suggest, therefore, that the effects of caffeine on the EEG are modest, at least when compared to those obtained after smoking between one and two cigarettes, depending on the individual smoking need. This slight action of caffeine in altering EEG parameters might partly explain the conflicting results obtained so far.

Reaction Time

Up until now, caffeine's effects on reaction times have hardly been consistent, and Estler (4) as well as James (91) came to the conclusion that a series of intervening conditions may determine the outcome of the measurements. Among these, the sensory modality involved, the type of motor response required, the levels of attention and arousal, and stimulus intensity might all be similarly important. With respect to the substance per se, dosage and habituation represent additional factors, as it has often been suggested that medium doses might produce improvements and high doses impairments or no effects (30,44). In addition, it should be considered that "optimal dose" levels may be different between high and low users of caffeine.

Another aspect can be seen in the implications of the methodological design and the procedure of measuring reaction times. Comparisons of pre- and posttreatment measurements and within (rather than between) subject designs are certainly more promising for detecting the subtle changes to be expected with caffeine as a "minor stimulant." Finally, it should not be overlooked that the technical developments in computerized methods of measuring reaction times provide considerable advantage over the procedures used in the early studies.

Using such techniques, Kerr et al. (92) obtained significant shortenings of the reaction times with a choice task after the application of 300 mg caffeine. Hasenfratz and Bättig (45), who investigated reaction times to the conflicting and nonconflicting stimuli of the Stroop task, observed that the outcome of the measurements was critically dependent on the presentation rate. The generally observed shortenings of the reaction times after 250 mg caffeine given in decaffeinated coffee reached significance only when the stimuli were presented with a 1-second delay but not when they were presented in immediate succession.

Sleep

The effects of caffeine on sleep are discussed in detail in the chapter by Snel. However, in this chapter they are considered in the light of the differences in the effects of caffeine on night sleep, on daytime sleepiness, and on performance efficiency. Although individual differences and habituation to caffeine have an influential role in the sleep-disturbing effects of caffeine, this effect is certainly more robust and dose dependent than the daytime effects of caffeine.

Usually subjects complaining about sleep quality after drinking coffee that is too strong report not only difficulties in falling asleep but also poor sleep quality for the entire night. In the last few years, the effects of caffeine on sleep have been increasingly investigated using the EEG-based criterion of the Multiple Sleep Latency Test (MSLT).

Using this technique, Walsh et al. (93) measured sleep latency repeatedly throughout the night after giving 4 mg/kg caffeine to the subjects in the evening, and they observed that these latencies maintained prolonged to a similar extent until 7 A.M. the next morning. This result is astonishing, as it was expected that the plasma caffeine would have decreased substantially by morning.

In contrast, effects of caffeine on subjective mood ratings and objective performance measures obtained during the day are less durable. This raises the question as to whether caffeine might exert its effects on objectively measured EEG sleep latency and on subjective mood and/or performance through different mechanisms. The relevance of this question is indicated by Johnson et al. (94), who investigated the morning caffeine effects after a previous evening diazepam medication and observed that the prolongation of sleep latencies (MSLT) after caffeine disappeared within a few hours and that it failed to correlate with mood and performance measures.

Few studies investigated the effects of caffeine on sleep in animals. Rats systemically injected with high doses of caffeine spent more time in a waking state (95). Rapid eye movement (REM)-rebound in REM-deprived rats was suppressed by caffeine (96). Caffeine (12.5 and 25.0 mg/kg) increased wakefulness and decreased sleep (slow wave sleep-1 and -2, REM sleep, total sleep time) in rats (97,98). Lower doses (0.125 and 1.25 mg/kg) increased slow wave sleep-1 at the expense of slow wave sleep-2 but did not affect total sleep time.

Vigilance

Vigilance, the ability to maintain attention and responsiveness in prolonged tasks, has in the past been considered by most reviewers as a relatively reliable indicator of caffeinic improvements. However, in this respect the results may vary as a function of the particular tasks that are used. The lengthy Wilkinson Auditory Vigilance task was seen, in two studies by Lieberman et al. (80,99), to be significantly facilitated by the low doses of 32 and 64 mg caffeine. With the same task, Fagan et al. (100) noted that the significant improvements obtained with 200 mg were mainly due to improvements during the second part of the 1-hour sessions. This calls for the interpretation that the improvement was critically due to an offset of fatigue, a view that is also rather frequently encountered in earlier reviews.

Classical tests of vigilance require the subjects to respond to infrequent target stimuli that differ only modestly from the frequent nontarget stimuli. Recently, the Bakan test (101), another paradigm of continuous attention, has also been used in several versions in different studies. In this task, target stimuli are defined by the previous stimulus, as would be the case with the instruction to press a button for the letter B (in a random sequence of letters) every time it was preceded by the letter X.

One frequently employed version, which has been seen to be particularly sensitive to nicotine obtained through smoking, requires subjects to attend the random presentation of single digits and to press a button after every triad of odd or even digits. The task was used recently by Frewer and Lader (102), and, using a constant stimulus presentation rate, they observed smaller intrasession declines in performance with 250 and 500 mg caffeine than with placebo.

The interpretation that the beneficial effect of caffeine was due to an offset of fatigue can, however, be challenged by studies using a subject-paced rather than a fixed-paced presentation of the stimuli. In a study by Bättig and Buzzi (103), the interstimulus interval was increased after each error and decreased after each correct response. One thereby obtains a measure of processing rate rather than of errors as the parameter of performance. In this study, the processing rate was dose dependently increased with 150 and 450 mg caffeine similarly for each successive 10-minute block of a session. This result would indicate that caffeine can improve performance beyond a mere offset of fatigue. The same result was obtained by Hasenfratz et al. (104) in two other experiments with 250 mg caffeine.

Another variable that might be important for the outcome of experiments with this paradigm is task difficulty. Particularly easy versions were employed by Lieberman et al. (99), who required the subjects to respond to every *4* preceded by a *6*, and by Fagan et al. (100), who presented simple geometrical symbols and required responses for every repetition of a stimulus. Both experiments observed no significant effects of caffeine at any dose level.

Operant Behavior in Animals

Measurements of reaction times or vigilance would be difficult to assess in animals in a manner corresponding to the procedures available in human subjects. Some analogies to such behaviors can be seen, however, in operant behaviors that are highly popular in animal research. In such tasks, animals are rewarded by food or punishment termination for adequate activation of response levers. The effects of caffeine also vary considerably in such situations, depending on different methodological factors.

In several studies with squirrel monkeys, caffeine as well as amphetamine increased responding on fixed-ratio (FR) and fixed-interval (FI) schedules with food or shock termination as reinforcements (105–108). On the other hand, Stinnette and Isaac (109) found a reduction in response rate (FI-80) in squirrel monkeys after injection of caffeine (2.0 and 4.0 mg/kg but not 8.0 mg/kg). When animals were tested in the dark, 8.0 mg/kg caffeine also depressed response rate. The effect of caffeine depended primarily on the response rates, which are a consequence of the type of reward schedule, and was highly independent of whether food or stimulus-shock termination were used as reinforcement (110). High responding under an FR schedule was depressed by caffeine in a dose-dependent manner (1.0 to 56.0 mg/kg). Moderate response rates maintained under an FI schedule were slightly increased by caffeine (3.0 to 10.0 mg/kg) whereas higher doses decreased responding. Caffeine (3.0 to 30.0 mg/kg) markedly increased responding, even when an FI schedule of stimulus-shock termination responding was concurrently depressed by response-produced shock.

In mice, low doses of caffeine (1.0, 3.0, and 10.0 mg/kg) increased and a high dose (100.0 mg/kg) decreased response rate on a multiple FR-30 FI-600 schedule (111). The increases were smaller than those induced by amphetamine. Direction and amount of change in response rate produced by amphetamine and caffeine were dependent on the control rate of responding. The drugs increased low rates and decreased high rates.

Caffeine (2.5 to 60.0 mg/kg) increased response rate under an FI-30 and FR-45 schedule with two levers and food as reinforcement in rats (112). Caffeine was more effective than amphetamine in increasing rate of responding in the FR-45 schedule, whereas amphetamine was more effective in the FI-45 schedule. An increase of response rate after injection of a low dose of caffeine (10.0 mg/kg) during an FI-300 task was observed by Logan and colleagues (113), whereas a higher dose (32.0 mg/kg) decreased response rate. The effects of caffeine were also reported to be dependent on response rate.

Caffeine (10.0 and 32.0 mg/kg) as well as amphetamine also decreased operant responding with a variable interval (VI) reward schedule (VI-30) for food in rats (114). A tolerance developed to this rate decreasing effect of caffeine resulting in a rightward shift of the dose-effect curve. McMillan (115) also observed a decrease in lever pressing under an FI-90 schedule for food reinforcement with high doses of caffeine (56.0 and 100.0 mg/kg) or amphetamine. In this study, the rate decreasing effect was dependent on the initial rate of lever pressing: the higher the rate of lever pressing, the smaller the rate decreasing effect of caffeine. Finally, Glowa (116) reported a decrease in responding under an FR-30 schedule in rats after injection of intermediate doses of caffeine (3.0 and 10.0 mg/kg). In contrast, these doses of caffeine had little effect on FI-60 responding. When responding under the FI-60 schedule was reduced by punishment, caffeine increased responding. Higher doses (30.0 and 100.0 mg/kg) suppressed responding under all conditions. Using rather high doses of caffeine (30.0 to 100.0 mg/kg), Harris and colleagues (117) observed a response rate decreasing effect with both an FR-30 and FI-120 schedule.

The time between drug injection and behavioral test is also of importance. Under an FI-300 schedule with food reinforcement, caffeine (6.0 and 12.0 mg/kg) increased responding when measured during the first half-hour after administration (118). Caffeine (24.0 mg/kg) decreased response rate during the third and fourth half-hour.

Adenosine receptor agonists decreased response rate in squirrel monkeys under an FR or FI schedule with food or shock termination as reinforcers (107,108,110,119). Caffeine antagonized the rate-decreasing effects of the adenosine receptor agonist PIA or NECA in squirrel monkeys (108,110). The potency of the agonist in inducing this behavioral effect correlated well with their affinities for the adenosine A_2 but not A_1 receptor (107,108,119).

Caffeine also antagonized the response rate decreasing effects of L-PIA and NECA in rats responding for food reinforcement under a variable ratio (VR)-15 schedule (120). Further, the potency of several xanthines in increasing response rate under an FI corresponded well with their affinities for adenosine receptors (105). Caffeine interacted with the effects of nicotine on response rate under an FI-120 schedule (121). When injected together with an acute injection of nicotine (0.01 to 1.0 mg/kg) that depressed responding, a low dose of caffeine (3.0 mg/kg) increased response rate. Higher dose (30.0 mg/kg) had no effect or reduced response rate in combination with all doses of nicotine.

A number of investigators examined the effects of caffeine on differential reinforcement of low rates (DRL) responding. With such schedules, the animals are required to refrain from responding for a given interval after a reward, and the longer the interval, the more difficult successful learning is. The studies done so far mostly report a decrease in reinforcements due to an increase in the number of responses with too short inter-response times (122–124). Pronounced increases in short inter-response times were observed after systemic injection of amphetamine (125,126). Intermediate doses of caffeine (20.0 and 40.0 mg/kg) increased, whereas an excessive dose (60.0 mg/kg) even decreased response rate in a DRL-18 schedule (127), but no response bursts (responses that occurred within 2.5 seconds of the preceding response) were observed. In contrast, Webb and Levine (124) reported response bursts in mice after systemic caffeine in a DRL-18 task. Response bursts after injection of amphetamine (1.0 or 2.0 mg/kg) but not after injection of caffeine (3.0, 6.0, 12.0 or 24.0, and 48 mg/kg) were observed by Berz and colleagues (123) in rats performing under a DRL-18 schedule. Caffeine as well as amphetamine shifted the peak of the inter-response time distribution to the left (toward shorter inter-response times). In fact, both substances shifted the most frequent response intervals of about 19 seconds in a dose-dependent fashion by a few seconds downward, but only amphetamine produced in addition bursts of the very short response intervals.

Cognitive Performance and Memory

Intellectual functions are particularly difficult to assess. Therefore a wide variety of standardized tests have been employed including arithmetic abilities, writing, problem solving, intelligence tests, etc. In particular, older studies, as reviewed by Estler (4) and Calhoun (40), frequently approached such questions, but the outcomes were not conclusive. Any changes seen were mostly subtle and often inconsistent across similar studies. In a relatively recent study at this laboratory (128), mental maze learning was found to be unaffected by caffeine, although the substance facilitated the regularity and fluency of performance on a letter cancellation task. In the last few years, interest in the effects on intellectual functions not only of caffeine but also other psychoactive substances has decreased. A rather rational argument for this decreased interest can be seen in the fact that changes in any intellectual output can easily be the consequence of indirect effects. In the case of caffeine, the beneficial effects of the substance on endurance, vigilance, and mood could well be the roots of any improvement, and the slight over-excitation of the nervous system, the source of possible reductions in performance.

An important factor in measuring complex cognitive performance can probably be seen in the rather low test-retest reliability of such tasks. Bittner et al. (129) presented the results of a long-term research program on the test-retest reliability of 114 measures of simple and complex performance. The program involved repeated testing of separate groups of 10 to 25 subjects assigned to each of the different tasks over 15 days. It turned out that a surprisingly large proportion of the commonly used tests yielded an unacceptably low test-retest reliability. This holds particularly for complex measures and for difference-related scores such as the Stroop effect, which represented the difference between the response times to conflicting and to nonconflicting stimuli.

This task represents an example of a type of performance that was affected in a different manner in several recent studies. Foreman et al. (130) obtained impairments after 250 mg caffeine. Hasenfratz and Bättig (45) used the same test in a study that differed from that of Foreman in two respects. The task was presented before and after the treatments rather than only after the treatments, and the stimuli were presented with 0- and 1-second delays rather than only with 0-second delays. Caffeine tended to shorten the reaction times to both the conflicting and nonconflicting stimuli for both delay conditions. It also tended to shorten the Stroop effect. However, these effects reached significance only in part, namely for response times to the two stimulus categories when the stimuli were presented with a 1-second delay and for the Stroop effect when the two types of stimulus were presented with no delay. This may be the result of a ceiling effect, as the response times as well as the Stroop difference were generally shorter with 1-second than with 0-second stimulus delay. It may, however, also be a consequence of the lower test-retest reliability of difference scores. In fact, the test-retest reliability coefficients in this study amounted to more than 0.9 for the reaction times for each stimulus category separately, but less than 0.5 for the difference scores of the Stroop effect.

Therefore, the evaluation of effects of caffeine on complex mental functions would call for a large number of both subjects and test repetitions in order to reduce the error term. An early approach toward this goal was chosen by Holck (131), who analyzed the effects of caffeine on solving chess problems. He analyzed performance for 250 problems with caffeine and 250 problems without caffeine and obtained both a remarkable performance stability and an improvement with caffeine, but, understandably, the study was limited to a single subject.

In recent times, more interest has been invested in effects of the substance on various specific memory functions than on complex activities such as reasoning, comprehension, and learning. For this function, the results tend to vary with the type of test used.

In general, the results tend to support the notion proposed by Humphreys and Revelle (132) that arousal, as induced by caffeine, facilitates performance on tasks involving low memory load, whereas it would hinder performance on tasks with high memory load. An example of a low memory load task, involving perhaps no more than simple information transfer, is given by the different types of the Bakan task, for which Bättig and Buzzi (103), Hasenfratz et al. (104), and Frewer and Lader (102) obtained improvements after caffeine. Low memory load is also required for the Sternberg memory task, on which Kerr et al. (92), found improved performance.

Considerably higher memory load is required with the frequently used word recall tests. In these tests, subjects are required to listen to or watch the successive presentation of entire lists of words and then to recall the remembered words. With such tasks, several studies obtained either no effects of caffeine or slight impairments. Loke (133) found no effects with 200 and 400 mg caffeine for easy or difficult words, or for immediate or delayed recall. Foreman et al. (130) also failed to see any effects with 125 or 250 mg caffeine. A slight impairment, particularly for the first words of the lists, and seen by Terry and Phifer (134) with 100 mg caffeine, and Erikson et al. (135), who administered 0, 2, or 4 mg/kg caffeine, also observed a slight impairment, but only in females. Hardly any experimental information is available on possible effects of caffeine on long-term memory, a function that is difficult to assess.

A pointer can be seen in the results of a recent experiment by Lowe (136), who applied the paradigm of state-dependent learning, which is widely used in animal experiments. State-dependent learning implies that a task learned in a particular drug state is remembered better when retention is measured under the same than under another drug (or placebo) state. In one experiment, the subjects had to learn a task after smoking two cigarettes and drinking 0.7 g/kg alcohol and in the other one, after the same dose of alcohol and 300 mg caffeine. In both experiments, retention was tested with either of the two treatments given alone, with the combination of the two, and with no treatment. After learning with alcohol and smoking, retention was almost complete when tested with the same treatment but inferior with the other three. After caffeine and alcohol, retention was superior not only with the same treatment but also with caffeine alone.

Only few studies investigated the effects of caffeine on memory formation in animals. Immediate (2 second) but not delayed (5 minute or 1 hour) injection of caffeine (30.0 mg/kg) after a visual discrimination task improved learning in rats (137). Castellano (138) found improved retention of a Y water maze task after pre- trial as well as posttrial injection of caffeine (1.0 and 2.0 mg/kg) in DBA/2J mice. In an additional experiment (139), he found that pre- and posttrial injection of caffeine (5.0 mg/kg) improved performance in a visual pattern discrimination task in DBA and C57BL mice. In contrast, the performance of BALB mice, who already showed the highest learning ability of all 3 strains tested, was impaired by caffeine.

In the context of learning and memory, it is interesting to note that xanthines, such as theophylline, enhanced long-term potentiation, an electrophysiological model of memory (140). After bath application of xanthines in hippocampal slices of guinea pigs, an increased amplitude of the population spike could be observed up to 30 minutes after tetanic stimulation of mossy fibers with the recording electrode located in the CA3 region.

MOTIVATION AND EMOTION

The question as to how caffeine might shift physiological and behavioral needs upward or downward has received less attention in recent years than the question as to whether coffee might induce a caffeine need. Therefore the closely related question—to what extent caffeine might affect emotions positively or negatively—also merits consideration.

Body Weight Regulation, Food and Water Intake

Given the facts that amphetamine as a stimulant reduces appetite, at least temporarily, and that nicotine as still another stimulant appears to reduce body weight chronically, one could ask whether caffeine, which also possesses stimulant properties, might affect food intake and body weight.

Body weight could be expected to be related to caffeine consumption because caffeine is slightly thermogenic. However, several recent studies reveal a rather inconsistent picture [see review (7)]. In general, increases of oxygen consumption, decreases of the respiratory exchange ratio, and mobilization of free fatty acids were reported in some but not other studies, and hardly in a consistent fashion. Furthermore, Dulloo et al. (141) found that the net gains in caloric expenditure did not exceed 50 to 100 kcal per day. These gains were seen as acute effects of caffeine in subjects who were previously cleared of caffeine by a sufficiently long abstinence washout period. Studies on these functions in nonabstaining subjects to assess the effects of real-life daily consumption are missing so far.

Only a few reports are available on food intake in relation to coffee consumption as a primary factor in body weight regulation. They are all based on questionnaire data and in part suggest that heavy coffee consumption tends to go along with a slightly increased preference for diets with more fats. Using a 24-hour standardized dietary recall, Haffner et al. (142) observed in a sample of more than 2,000 subjects that the percentage of calories consumed as fats increased in men from about 38% for occasional coffee drinkers to 42% in those drinking more than 8 cups per day, and similar increases were seen also for the percentage of saturated fat and dietary cholesterol. No such trends were observed, however, in women. On the other hand, a modest positive relation between coffee consumption and serum cholesterol was observed in both sexes. Mathias et al. (143) also obtained a positive relation between coffee consumption and low density serum lipoproteins but only in the females of the 700-subject sample. However, in contrast to Haffner et al. (142), no relations between coffee and diet were seen. Furthermore, the authors present a review of 14 earlier studies on the coffee/plasma cholesterol relation, which revealed rather conflicting results. In a study of more than 9,000 subjects in Finland, the country with the highest per capita coffee consumption, Tuomilehto et al. (144) reported a minimal increase of plasma cholesterol with increasing coffee consumption but also a parallel increase of dietary fat in both sexes. The most detailed analysis carried out so far was reported by Solvoll et al. (145) on the basis of the data obtained from more than 24,000 subjects. These authors observed increases of total food consumption as well as fat consumption with increasing coffee consumption and also a parallel increase of heavy work, breakfast before 6 A.M., and starting to work early in the morning. Therefore, these reports suggest that relations between coffee consumption and plasma cholesterol are minimal, they tend to go in a positive direction, and are perhaps biased by other life-style variables, particularly as none of the studies suggested any correlations with body weight.

In rats, caffeine (30 and 100 mg/kg) reduced water intake when animals were adapted to a daily 22 hour water deprivation schedule (146). This hypodipsic effect was abolished by injection of benzodiazepines. However, food intake was not significantly affected by caffeine doses smaller than 60 mg/kg (147). Whereas caffeine alone (10 and 20 mg/kg) did not increase feeding, it enhanced feeding induced by glucoprivation (injection of 2DG) in a way similar to amphetamine (148). Injecting the xanthine theophylline also did not alter the total amount of food consumed but disturbed the circadian rhythm of food intake (149). Finally, food deprivation increased caffeine consumption in a two-bottle preference test in rats (150). Caffeine preference was not due to an increased preference for bitter tastes.

A method frequently used to study effects on fluid intake involves the measurement of schedule-induced drinking. High caffeine doses (56 and 100 mg/kg) reduced schedule-induced drinking (FI-60 or FI-90) in rats (115,151,152). A low dose of caffeine (3.125 mg/kg) increased schedule-induced drinking (number of licks) in animals with free access to food in their home cage but not in animals whose weight was reduced to 80% of their free feeding weight (152). However, the number of licks was more than five times higher in animals with reduced access to food than in animals with free access to food in their home cage. A high-licking rate might prevent a further increase in the number of licks per session.

Social Behavior

Social behavior and coffee are closely related in daily life situations. It appears to play an important role not only during the work break and the afternoon chat but especially in the social behavior of politicians and bureaucrats. However, studies related to the underlying reasons and possible benefits are nearly absent so far, and the question remains whether caffeine facilitates social interaction or social interaction increases the need for coffee.

Reports on the effects in humans are somewhat equivocal. Several reports claimed increases in hostility and irritability, while others reported decreases. In psychiatric patients, De Freitas and Schwartz (153) observed decreases of such scores after switching from regular to decaffeinated coffee. Similarly, Podboy and Mallory (154) reported decreases in the number of aggressive outbursts among female mentally retarded patients. On the other hand, Furlong (155) claimed improvements in mood in psychiatric patients after drinking coffee.

The only experimental studies in humans dealt with the effect on aggression. Cherek et al. (156) told subjects pressing buttons for monetary reward that a fictitious person could punish them by money subtraction or noise. Whenever this happened, the subjects could either continue pressing the buttons for money or punish the fictitious person with the same punishments using another button. Caffeine, given in capsules at doses up to 4 mg/kg, decreased such counterattacks and increased monetarily reinforced responses in a dose-dependent fashion, and the same result was also obtained by the same authors in a later study (157) comparing regular and decaffeinated coffee.

A number of studies looked for possible effects of caffeine on social behavior in old and young rats or mice. Caffeine (15, 30 and 60 mg/kg) increased avoidance-irritability behavior (moving away, crouching, squealing, startling) in pairs of mice (64). In rats, it increased (doses of 10, 20 and 40 mg/kg) social investigation of a novel juvenile conspecific (59). In contrast, others found that caffeine (20 and 40 mg/kg) decreased social interaction in pairs of rats (65,158). Further, caffeine (20 mg/kg) suppressed play fighting in juvenile rats, and this effect was age dependent (159,160).

Mood

Mood is certainly a complex area with respect to both the underlying psychological functions and the difficulties of assessment. A further complexity could be seen in the question whether changes in mood are responsible for changes in performance or vice versa, or whether the two can be affected independently. Effects on mood are evaluated by subject self-rating with either scalometric assessment or choices for given adjectives. In recent times, standardized instruments such as the Profile of Mood States (POMS), the Visual Analog Mood Scale (VAMS), The Nestlé Visual Analog Mood Scale (NVAMS), and the Stanford Sleepiness Scale (SSS), have increasingly been preferred. These four scales have recently been employed in two different studies (80,99). In one of the two studies, no effects were obtained for any dose between 32 mg and 256 mg, whereas, in the other one, positive effects were obtained with 64 mg caffeine for three of the four instruments.

In his review, Estler (4) considered the outcome of ten studies on caffeine and mood, the majority of which failed to show significant effects, and suggested that, besides several other factors, the degree of habituation to caffeine might also play an important role. Among the more recent studies, Kuznicki and Turner (161) observed clearer subjective state improvements in high than in low users, as proposed by Estler, but Zahn and Rapoport (162) and Lieberman et al. (80) failed to see any trends in this direction.

On the other hand, negative effects in nonusers, such as increases in tension and nervousness induced by medium doses have occasionally been reported, as for instance recently by Kuznicki and Turner (161). Negative effects by high doses are found regularly in the literature, which from a practical·point of view may be important in protecting individuals against overdoses. Ghoneim et al. (42) assessed mood and plasma caffeine levels ten times across a period of $3^1w4.5_2$ hours after ingestion of a high dose of 6 mg/kg. The mood scales mainly induced items reflecting fatigue, attention, and subjective energy. The scores of the six subjects remained nearly unchanged across the entire period and also failed to antagonize the depression of mood induced by the simultaneous application of diazepam. Loke (133) included in his study mood scales intended to assess negative effects such as tension, nervousness, and restlessness. The dosages of 200 and 400 mg caffeine produced only modest changes of mood in the positive direction, such as decreases in boredom, whereas changes in the negative direction were more prominent, particularly with the higher dose of 400 mg. Furthermore, Griffiths and Woodson (163) observed a slightly greater-than-chance preference for 100 and 200 mg caffeine, chance behavior for 400 mg, and avoidance for 600 mg caffeine in a preference test for caffeine versus placebo capsules.

An aspect that may also play a role is to be seen in the predrug state of the subjects. The more alert a subject feels, the less room remains for a caffeinic improvement. This parameter, however, is difficult to control, as mood can be assessed only in relative terms but not in absolute terms. In addition, the artificial laboratory settings and multiple measurements of different types of performance included in most psychopharmacological studies of caffeine that include mood assessments might per se also affect different aspects of mood. To what extent such results are representative of the effects of habitual daily caffeine intake therefore remains open.

Subjective Recognition of the Caffeine State

A primary prerequisite for a substance to induce dependence would be that it induces specific subjective states. In animals, this is tested widely with the drug state discrimination technique. This or similar techniques, have been used in only a few, more recent studies in humans. The most direct approach would be to ask subjects to guess whether they have received decaffeinated coffee or caffeine-containing coffee. In the many studies that included such a question, the answers were mostly at chance level, as was the case in a recent study at our laboratory by Hasenfratz and Bättig (45). In this experiment, subjects had to perform the Stroop task before and after drinking coffee with 250 mg caffeine or no caffeine. Although they made no difference in scaling coffee strength for the two preparations, they did rate their performance higher after caffeine than after placebo. In a more sophisticated approach, Chait and Johanson (164) applied the drug state discrimination procedure, classically used in animal studies, to 36 volunteers. They were first successfully trained to recognize the state induced by 10 mg amphetamine and by 12.5 and 50 mg benzphetamine. Then, they were tested to see whether they would generalize this discrimination to 100 and 300 mg caffeine. Generalization from amphetamine to benzphetamine as well as to caffeine was generally poor and hardly exceeded chance. A different approach was taken by Griffiths et al. (165). In this experiment the subjects (the seven authors of this study) tried to distinguish between caffeine capsules at descending dosages and placebo capsules. Two capsules were given each day at one-and-one-half-hour intervals. For each dose level the procedure was continued for at least 10 and up to a maximum of 50 days. All subjects easily recognized 178 mg and 100 mg caffeine versus placebo; three subjects were able to detect 56 mg, three others 18 mg, and one subject even 10 mg. Mood changes, however, were obtained only with doses of 100 mg or more. Therefore, it remains open what type of subjective changes allowed the subjects to recognize the lower doses.

This study, in subjects who were informed about the research question and were in addition experienced psychopharmacologists, was recently complemented by Evans and Griffiths (166) with a similar experiment using naive subjects. They were first trained to discriminate 0 versus 300 mg caffeine as "drug A" or as "drug B," respectively, (achieved after 6 to 16 training sessions). The shortest training was needed by the subject with the lowest habitual coffee consumption, and the longest training by the subject with the highest habitual consumption. The subsequent phase of the experiment tested whether the subjects would generalize this discrimination to caffeine doses between 50 and 600 mg. Detecting the presence of caffeine was achieved mostly at the higher dose level of 300 mg or more, whereas the absence of caffeine was detected almost totally for dose levels of 0 and 50 mg, while the guesses remained mostly at chance level for the intermediate doses. The prominent self-reported cues for the detection of caffeine included feeling jittery, nervous, or anxious as opposed to headache, tiredness, or no effect for the detection of placebo.

In drug discrimination studies with animals, the animals are trained to press one of two levers to obtain a reward. Pressing one lever is only correct and rewarded, with, e.g., a food pellet, when they are under the influence of a specific drug; pressing the other lever is correct when they are injected with saline. After this drug-state stimulus control of lever pressing has been established, other drugs are injected, and the number of lever presses of the drug lever and the saline lever are counted and taken as indices, whether the animal feels it is under the influence of the test drug or not. Rats can learn such a discrimination with caffeine doses as low as 10 mg/kg (167).

The development of tolerance of caffeine could be demonstrated by using the drug discrimination paradigm. When caffeine (30mg/kg) was injected twice daily for $3\frac{1}{2}$ days, rats reacted in the test situation as if under the influence of a three to four times lower dose (168). Further, tolerance could be demonstrated using higher training and lower test concentrations of caffeine (169,170).

Rats trained to discriminate between caffeine and saline partially generalized to the methylxanthine derivatives theophylline and theobromine (167,169). A complete generalization was found in one study to aminophylline (171). When theophylline was used as the training drug, rats again only partially generalized to caffeine (170,172).

Rats trained to discriminate between caffeine and saline partially generalized to d-amphetamine (167,169,171) and completely to cocaine and methylphenidate (167,168). Conversely, rats trained to discriminate d-amphetamine from saline generalize only partially from amphetamine to caffeine [e.g., (173)]. However, other experiments failed to find any generalization from caffeine to d-amphetamine or methylphenidate (169). A complete generalization could be found from caffeine to the α_1 adrenergic receptor agonist 2-(2-chloro-5-trifluoromethylphenylimino) imidazolidine (167).

The discriminative stimulus effects of caffeine could be partially blocked by adenosine receptor agonists (2-CA, CHA, L-PIA), the benzodiazepine receptor agonist diazepam, pentobarbital, and the beta adrenergic receptor blocker propranolol (167). A complete block could be obtained with the alpha adrenergic receptor blocking agents prazosin, yohimbine, and phentolamin (167). The dopamine D2 receptor antagonist spiperone and the serotonergic antagonist pizotyline failed to antagonize stimulus control induced by caffeine (171). Further, diazepam blocked the discriminative stimulus properties of a 10 mg/kg training dose of caffeine and its generalization to a dose of 100 mg/kg caffeine (167).

In summary, drug discrimination experiments revealed that rats under the influence of caffeine responded in part as if under the influence of the psychomotor stimulant drugs d-amphetamine or cocaine and, less effectively, other xanthines. However, the results of different authors have not been consistent from study to study. Further, the discriminative stimulus effects of caffeine appear to be dependent on its effect on noradrenergic receptors, particularly those involving the α_1 receptors (167). Adenosine receptor agonists were less effective. Dopaminergic or serotonergic antagonists failed to block the discriminative stimulus effects of caffeine.

The Reward Value of Caffeine

The successful demonstration of caffeine discrimination is not a sufficient argument for assuming a potential for the development of dependence. Many drugs, particularly dopamine agonists and some antidepressants, are easily recognized without producing a desire for self-application. A more direct approach is given by testing whether animals would self-administer pure caffeine or whether humans would drink coffee for its caffeine content.

In order to study this, Griffiths and Woodson (163) gave subjects a choice between differentially coded caffeine and placebo capsules. Before each choice they were familiarized on preceding days with the effects of the caffeine and the placebo capsule, but were never informed which of the two capsules was the "active" one. As a general tendency, caffeine was preferred over placebo at the lower dose levels of 100 and 200 mg and avoided at the high level of 600 mg, whereas 400 mg produced chance behavior. However, on the individual level, only 5 of the 12 subjects developed caffeine preference for at least one dose and only four revealed caffeine avoidance at the 400 or 600 mg dose level.

A more critical argument for dependence could be seen in demonstrations of the amount of work or money that would be spent in order to obtain caffeine. Griffiths et al. (174) had subjects perform ergometer cycling in order to obtain coffee, with or without caffeine, or placebo capsules. With increasing work requirements, the subjects became apparently less interested in performing the required output, as the daily number of servings decreased from about ten initially to two servings when 32 minutes were required. Further, the decrease for placebo capsules was faster than for caffeine capsules or for cups of coffee, irrespective of whether they contained caffeine or not. This may suggest that the taste of coffee, along with the post-absorptional pharmacological effects, constitutes an important element for the desirability of this beverage.

A further criterion of drug reward can be seen in the phenomenon of titration. Titration could be assumed when subjects increase the number of cups, when the caffeine content is decreased and vice versa. Griffiths et al. (175) studied this in a group with extremely high coffee consumption, reporting on average 14 cups per day, residing in the research ward. The daily number of cups remained, however, quite stable regardless of the amount of coffee per cup, the amount of caffeine, and caffeine pre-loads. Even replacing caffeinated with decaffeinated coffee did not appreciably change the daily number of cups. On the other hand, even in these high consumption subjects, high doses exceeding the accustomed level produced avoidance. This low level or even absence of caffeine titration was also recently observed by Benowitz et al. (176) in a smoking abstinence study. As smoking accelerates caffeine metabolism and clearance, coffee abstinence can be expected to raise plasma caffeine levels if the number of cups per day remains unchanged.

In the sample studied by these authors, plasma caffeine increased to levels about 250% higher after 12 or 26 weeks of abstinence. This increase was already present after a few days of smoking abstinence. The number of cups of coffee remained unchanged for up to 12 weeks of smoking abstinence and decreased by no more than about 25% in those subjects who maintained smoking abstinence for 26 weeks.

A further aspect of dependence was the possible occurrence of withdrawal symptoms provoked by sudden caffeine abstinence after chronic use. A number of occasional reports of withdrawal consequences have been published since the early part of this century and have been reviewed by Griffiths and Woodson (177). These reports concern mostly casual observation and were very heterogeneous, reaching from no effect to mental confusion, and transient fatigue and slight headache were among the more frequent observations. A systematic observation was carried out by Griffiths et al. (175) in a small group of excessively heavy consumers with nearly 1,000 mg or more self-reported caffeine intake per day. These subjects were switched under blind conditions to decaffeinated coffee. On the first day of withdrawal, subjective activity and alertness were lowered, but psychomotor performance was not affected. Slight sleepiness and reductions in mood persisted also on the second day and slight headache on the third day of abstinence. Given the modest magnitude of this effect, it would certainly be interesting to investigate the matter further not only by comparing heavy and moderate users but also by attempting to include more objective measurements in addition to the subjective and staff-rated aspects of behavior.

In animals, reward effects of caffeine were seen mostly to very modest extents and depended on particular experimental conditions. Intravenous self-administration of caffeine has been reported in the rat (178) and rhesus monkey (179), but not all the animals self-administered caffeine. In monkeys, self-administration of caffeine (1.0, 2.5, and 5.0 mg/kg per injection) was highly inconsistent. Priming (179) and time-out schedules [for review (180)] were necessary to initiate self-administration in some of the animals. Periods of drug intake alternated with periods of abstinence (179). This variability in caffeine self-administration was also observed by Griffiths and Woodson (180) in individual monkeys on a day-to-day basis. A failure to maintain intravenous self-administration of caffeine in rats (181) and in rhesus monkeys (182) has been reported by other authors. Even after one-month programmed administration, only one out of four rhesus monkeys self-administered caffeine (183). A preference for a caffeine-containing solution could be found only with very low concentrations of caffeine (150) or after prolonged forced exposure to a caffeine solution (184).

Testing whether animals would prefer a place associated with the injection of caffeine by using a place-preference paradigm, Brockwell and colleagues (185) could demonstrate conditioned place preference with caffeine (3.0 mg/kg) in rats, suggesting a rewarding effect of the caffeine injections. When the dose of caffeine was increased (30.0 mg/kg), place preference was replaced by place aversion. This higher dose also led in the same animals to taste aversion. Brockwell and Beninger (186) further demonstrated that the adenosine A_2 antagonist CGS 15943 but not the A_1 antagonist CPX produced a significant place preference.

In contrast, not only was more robust self-administration observed in rats for amphetamine and cocaine [e.g., (179)] and in humans for amphetamine (187), but these behaviors also developed without using time-out schedules and without priming pretreatments. Furthermore, whereas amphetamine and cocaine maintained high levels of self-administration, caffeine tended to maintain lower levels of self-administration [for review, see (180)].

Caffeine may also interact with other drugs. Schulte-Daxboek and Opitz [1981; cited in (180)] observed increased caffeine consumption following chronic nicotine treatment in rats. Further, when rats were pretreated with caffeine (20.0 mg/kg), they acquired cocaine self-administration more rapidly (188). The authors argued that this facilitating effect of caffeine on cocaine self-administration might be due to the ability of caffeine to enhance cocaine's effect on the mesolimbic dopamine system.

Anxiety and Stress

Occasionally high levels of coffee consumption have been related to increased levels of anxiety, particularly among psychiatric patients. An early report by Greden (189) even viewed anxiety and caffeinism as a diagnostic dilemma. Eaton and McLeod (190) examined this hypothesis on the basis of data obtained from the U.S. National Center for Health Statistics: the Health and Nutrition Examination Survey. From the nationwide sample, 3,854 subjects reported high levels of anxiety, stress, strain, and pressure, but they were evenly distributed across the different categories of coffee consumption. Lee et al. (191) compared different data from 43 clinically diagnosed anxiety-disorder patients and 124 control patients. No difference was seen in habitual coffee consumption between the cases and controls, but cases who reported becoming anxious in response to drinking scored higher than the controls on a standardized anxiety symptom checklist. Whereas there appeared to be no evidence that high levels of habitual coffee consumption induced anxiety, the picture was different for acute challenges with caffeine loads in excess of the habitual consumption. Charney et al. (192) presented further evidence that the anxiogenic effect of acute high doses of caffeine was perhaps greater in patients with panic disorders than in controls. After the high dose of 10 mg/kg, the patients' anxiety ratings, nervousness, and fear considerably exceeded those of the controls, although increases of plasma cholesterol and caffeine were comparable for both groups.

The observation that acute high doses of caffeine increased feelings of nervousness, anxiety, and tension was quite common in studies using standardized mood assessments. This relation might even be seen as a protective factor against the overdosing of caffeine through drinking coffee or other caffeine-containing preparations.

Another question was whether external demands and professional stress induced increases in coffee consumption. Conway et al. (193) reported increases of coffee consumption in U.S. Navy company commanders during periods of increased occupational demands of recruit training. Loke (194) similarly reported, on the basis of questionnaires, that college students drank more coffee when they were preparing for examinations.

Studies on the interaction of stress and caffeine have concentrated so far on the cardiovascular effects of such challenges. Such studies, recently reviewed by Bättig (7), mostly required the subjects to perform various mental tasks with or without additional acute loads of caffeine of about 3 mg/kg. Generally the cardiovascular effects of caffeine and stress were simply additive or even less than additive, although possible effects on mental performance were not considered.

Two recent studies carried out at this laboratory were intended to obtain more information on the possible interactions between anxiety, stress, caffeine, and performance. In the first study by Höfer and Bättig (195), 338 healthy, normotensive women were screened for their coffee consumption and personality profile using the FPI personality inventory, which scores the main dimensions of extraversion, masculinity, and neuroticism (or emotional lability) as well as for nine subscales differentially related to the main scales. Coffee consumption was negatively correlated with restraint and depression, both of which correlate with emotional lability. It was further negatively correlated with the Spielberger trait-anxiety index but was positively correlated with sociability and self-confidence, two dimensions correlated with extraversion. Finally, it was also positively correlated with morning type in a separate morning/evening type questionnaire. Although all these significant correlations were modest, they suggest by their internal consistency that caffeine consumption might be avoided more by nervous and anxious subjects, whereas extraverted, self-confident, and sociable subjects tended more toward greater coffee consumption.

The second study, by Hasenfratz and Bättig (196), investigated whether stress susceptibility, stress, and caffeine might interact on both performance and psychophysiological effects. Toward this goal a $2 \times 2 \times 2$ group design was employed comparing high and low stress-susceptible subjects, split for active versus passive coping with painful electric stimuli, and treatment of 0 versus 3.3 mg/kg caffeine added to decaffeinated coffee. The low and high stress-susceptible subjects were selected from the 338 subjects of the previous study using a self-developed 35-item stress-susceptibility scale derived from the 212 items of the FPI personality questionnaire and chosen by face validity and controlled for homogeneity. The recruitment of these subjects was more difficult than expected, because the subjects with high stress-susceptibility scores were highly reluctant to participate in experiments requiring the endurance of electrical pain stimuli. As a result, the low stress-susceptible group consisted of subjects with extremely low FPI scores for nervousness, depression, irritability, restraint, and emotional lability, high scores for masculinity and extraversion, and low Spielberger trait-anxiety scores; the high stress-susceptible group included subjects with scores for all dimensions situated in the opposite direction but within, rather than outside of, the upper range of the normal values. As a consequence, the selection resulted in a low stress-susceptible group versus a "borderline" high stress-susceptible, or even a "control" group.

The analysis of the multiple data showed that each of the experimental factors, caffeine versus placebo, low stress susceptibility versus controls, and active versus passive coping with the electric pain stimuli, produced significant effects, but no interactive effects were obtained for any of the measured parameters.

The low stress-susceptible subjects revealed, in contrast to their counterparts, greater cardiac outputs, greater stroke volumes, and longer left ventricular ejection times, as evaluated by impedance cardiography, and their plethysmographic responses at the finger and earlobe habituated more rapidly. They did not differ, however, from the other group either in subjective pain and discomfort or in electrical pain threshold, but they rated their subjective performance level higher and revealed lower state-anxiety scores.

The active/passive coping paradigm was superimposed on a task of subject-paced rapid information processing, presented before and after intake of test beverages. The subjects allocated to the active coping group were instructed that pain stimuli would be delivered for errors or reaction times that were too long, whereas the passive coping group was instructed that the pain stimuli would be delivered regardless of the level of performance. In fact, the number of pain stimuli was equal for both groups according to a yoked procedure. Active coping resulted in higher response rates and also in more commission errors. Both types of coping increased blood pressure, but with active coping, heart rate and left ventricular ejection times increased considerably more, whereas pulse velocity measured at the earlobe decreased more during active than during passive coping.

Finally, caffeine increased blood pressure and pulse velocity for all experimental periods, lowered the cardiac pre-ejection periods and increased the respiratory amplitudes for the stress phases of the experiment only. The substance increased the EEG peak frequencies in the α and β bands and decreased, in part, the reaction times to the task stimuli. These experimental findings underline the independence of caffeine and stress under conditions of a high stress load and a relatively high caffeine dose after previous coffee abstinence.

In rats, an anxiogenic effect of caffeine (20 and 40 mg/kg) could be found in the social interaction test of anxiety (158,197). Smaller or no effects of caffeine (40 mg/kg) were found using the plus maze or punished drinking as tests for anxiety (197). Other authors even postulated an anxiolytic effect of small doses of caffeine (3.13 and 6.25 mg/kg) as reflected in an increased intake of a 1.5% NaCl solution (198). Data from the three studies further suggest a complex involvement of benzodiazepine binding sites with caffeine's effect on measures of anxiety. File and co-workers (158,197) also provide evidence for an involvement of adrenergic receptors in the anxiogenic action of caffeine.

In humans and rats, high but not low doses of caffeine can influence "stress-hormone" plasma levels [for review, see (199)]. A dose of 500 mg led to an increase in human serum cortisol levels reaching significance 2 hours after ingestion. In rats, systemic injection of 50 mg/kg caffeine increased plasma levels of corticosterone, decreased those for thyrotropin, and left prolactin levels unchanged. In mice, caffeine (3 and 90 mg/kg/day in the drinking water) increased somewhat pathophysiological changes in psychosocially stressed animals (200). Chronic but not acute social stress induced an increase in adenosine receptors similar to the increase observed after chronic caffeine (201).

DISCUSSION: CAFFEINE A "MINOR STIMULANT"

In textbooks, caffeine usually appears in the chapter on stimulants with amphetamine and cocaine. The results available so far from studies on humans and animals raise the question whether caffeine should not be viewed differently. One question might evolve by considering daily-life and pharmacological dose-effect relationships and comparing observations in animals and humans. Animal and human experiments differ primarily in the behavioral functions tested. Locomotor activity and operant performance have been extensively studied in rodents but quite neglected in human studies. Performance and cognitive functions have been mainly investigated in humans and hardly in rodents. In both cases, however, it appears that effects of caffeine are mainly stimulant but only modestly dose dependent and, at least in rodents, subject to rather rapid and near complete tolerance.

This picture varies if one considers the target functions of caffeine. In this respect many questions remain open, and the available data are inconclusive as to whether all effects of caffeine are due directly or indirectly to its effect on a single functional system such as the mesolimbic and mesocortical structures underlying arousal or effects on different functional systems. There are certainly good arguments for seeing the mesocortical projections as a main target of the action of caffeine, as discussed in the chapter by Snel. However, considering the time courses of the different actions and their dose dependence, more differential concepts might also be considered. Effects on sleep, for instance, could be due to direct effects on the suprachiasmatic circadian pacemaker, as in its time course the effect resembles more that of a shift in the internal clock than a transient inhibition of deep sleep. Furthermore, the sleep-disturbing effects of caffeine appear to be better reproducible and dose dependent than many of the effects on different types of performance. A similar problem arises for the decreases in hand steadiness, which appear only with rather high doses and which also tend to last longer than would be expected on the basis of the development of plasma caffeine levels. The latter could therefore represent an effect per se, due to the reduction of inhibitory control of muscle action, for which the cerebellar output is of primary importance. In practical terms, the effects of caffeine on different kinds of psychomotor and cognitive performance merit particular interest. These effects are mainly accelerative, as evidenced by the results obtained with measuring reaction times in humans or timing behavior (DRL) in rats. The frequently assumed specific effects on endurance and vigilance could also be an indirect consequence of a nonspecific accelerating effect of caffeine on cortical processes. This view gains support from experiments that measured vigilance not at a constant frequency of stimulus presentation, but with the procedure of continuously subject-paced presentation of the stimuli. In presenting stimuli at a constant speed, one may easily miss initial improvements that have been successfully detected with a subject-paced presentation. Taken together, however, the profile of caffeinic effects remains so far poorly delineated.

The same holds for the second question of the dose-effect relation and its relevance for the daily intake. The dosages used in laboratory experiments were several times higher than the content range of an average serving, which hardly exceeds 100 mg. In addition, most experiments required the subjects to abstain at least overnight from all caffeine sources, thereby circumventing the limitations given by acute tolerance. Acute tolerance was demonstrated convincingly for the effects on blood pressure, as outlined by Mosqueda-Garcia et al. (this volume). For this function, acute tolerance develops and dissipates rapidly within a few days. On the other hand, possible acute tolerance to the behavioral effects of caffeine has not been studied systematically so far. The same holds to a lesser extent for chronic tolerance consisting of long-lasting changes in sensitivity to caffeine. Although an increasing number of experiments suggests that sensitivity to the effects of caffeine is lower in frequent than in occasional users, it remains open to what extent this may be the result of chronic tolerance and to what extent it reflects individual differences in sensitivity to the substance.

The question as to whether coffee drinking or other sorts of caffeine intake should be seen as a phenomenon of drug dependence has gained increased attention only in the last few years. Holtzman (202) recently proposed this view and argued that caffeine consumption as a relatively stable habit with hardly any documented evidence for negative effects on health might therefore represent a promising model for studying the mechanism and dynamics of the development of drug dependence. James (91) went even further and proposed the development of withdrawal techniques for excessive users. In this context, he discusses the outcome of a few recent studies using behavioral programs to reduce caffeine intake. From these studies it appears that the reduction of caffeine intake by excessive users is relatively easy, that few, if any, withdrawal symptoms and hardly any relapses are to be expected. This limited evidence adds to the studies on withdrawal, self-application, and drug state discrimination discussed in this review, which all provide only modest if any support for the dependence hypothesis. Considering this situation, one might easily come to the conclusion that the factors underlying the popularity of coffee drinking remain widely unknown or speculative.

Generally, it appears, however, that most people adhere to relatively fixed patterns of intake and avoid dosages that would induce nervousness, anxiety, or sleepless nights. This suggests that consumption tends to remain within the individual limits of tolerance and sensitivity, which vary widely from subject to subject.

There remain, therefore, two possible explanations for coffee consumption, both of which need to be further explored and which might also be complementary rather than exclusive. One possibility would be that taste, smell, and the habituated ritual constitute the main factor and the other that caffeine might smooth out the transient dips in performance and arousal during the waking state, as suggested by Dews (5). If so, caffeine could be considered as a candidate for the class of minor stimulants.

REFERENCES

1. Weiss B, Laties VG. Enhancement of human performance by caffeine and the amphetamines. *Pharmacol Rev* 1962;14:1–36.
2. Gilbert RM. Caffeine as a drug of abuse. In: Gibbons RJ, Isreal Y, Kalant H, Popham RE, Schmidt W, Smart RG, eds. *Research advances in alcohol and drug problems*; vol. 3. New York: J. Wiley and Sons, 1976;49–176.
3. Eichler O. *Kaffee und Coffein*, 2nd ed. Berlin: Springer-Verlag, 1976.
4. Estler C-J. Caffeine. In: Hoffmeister F, Stille G, eds. *Psychotropic agents, Part III, Alcohol and psychotomimetics, psychotropic effects of central acting drugs*. Berlin: Springer-Verlag, 1982;369–89.
5. Dews PB. Behavioral effects of caffeine. In: Dews PB, ed. *Caffeine: perspectives from recent research*. Berlin: Springer-Verlag, 1984;86–103.
6. Rall TW. Central nervous system stimulants: The methylxanthines. In: Gilman AG, Goodman LS, Rall TW, Murad F, eds. *Goodman and Gilman's the pharmacological basis of therapeutics*. 7th ed. New York: Macmillan Publishing Co., 1985;589–603.
7. Bättig K. Coffee, cardiovascular and behavioral effects: current research trends. *Rev Environ Health* 1991;9:53–84.
8. Katims JJ, Annau Z, Snyder SH. Interactions in the behavioral effects of methylxanthines and adenosine derivatives. *Journal of Pharmacol Exp Therap* 1983;227:167–73.
9. Snyder SH, Katims JJ, Annau Z, Bruns RF, Daly JW. Adenosine receptors and behavioral actions of methylxanthines. *Proc Nat Acad Sci USA* 1981;78:3260–4.
10. Schultz J. Adenosine 3',5'-monophosphate in guinea pig cerebral cortical slices: effect of benzodiazepines. *J Neurochem* 1974;22:685–90.

11. Smellie FW, Davis CV, Daly JW, Wells JN. Alkylxanthines: inhibition of adenosine-elicited accumulation of cyclic AMP in brain slices and brain phosphodiesterase activity. *Life Sci* 1979;24:2475–82.
12. Berkowitz BA, Tarver JH, Spector S. Release of norepinephrine in the central nervous system by theophylline and caffeine. *Eur J Pharmacol* 1970;10:64–71.
13. Fredholm BB, Fuxe K, Agnati L. Effect of some phosphodiesterase inhibitors on central dopamine mechanisms. *Eur J Pharmacol* 1976;38:31–8.
14. Hadfield MG, Milio C. Caffeine and regional brain monoamine utilization in mice. *Life Sci* 1989;45:2637–44.
15. Polc P, Bonetti EP, Pieri L, et al. Caffeine antagonizes several central effects of diazepam. *Life Sci* 1981;28:2265–75.
16. Boulenger J-P, Patel J, Marangos PJ. Effects of caffeine and theophylline on adenosine and benzodiazepine receptors in human brain. *Neurosci Lett* 1982;30:161–6.
17. Kaplan GB, Greenblatt DJ, Leduc BW, Thompson ML, Shader RI. Relationship of plasma and brain concentrations of caffeine and metabolites to benzodiazepine receptor binding and locomotor activity. *Journal of Pharmacol Exp Therap* 1989;248:1078–83.
18. Nistri A, Berti C. Caffeine-induced potentiation of GABA effects on frog spinal cord: an electrophysiological study. *Brain Res* 1983;258:263–70.
19. Roca DJ, Schiller GD, Farb DH. Chronic caffeine or theophylline exposure reduces γ-aminobutyric acid/benzodiazepine receptor site interactions. *Molec Pharmacol* 1988;30:481–5.
20. Finn IB, Holtzman SG. Tolerance to caffeine-induced stimulation of locomotor activity in rats. *Journal of Pharmacol Exper Therap* 1986;238:542–6.
21. Chou DT, Khan S, Forde J, Hirsh KR. Caffeine tolerance: behavioral, electrophysiological and neurochemical evidence. *Life Sci* 1985;36:2347–58.
22. Thithapandha A, Maling HM, Gillette JR. Effects of caffeine and theophylline on activity of rats in relation to brain xanthine concentrations. *Proc Soc Exp Biol Med* 1971;139:528–36.
23. Christensen HD, Whitsett TL. Measurement of xanthines and their metabolites by means of high pressure liquid chromatography. In: Hawk GL, ed. *Biological/biomedical applications of liquid chromatography.* New York: Marcel Dekker, 1979;507–37.
24. Zielke HR, Zielke CL. Lack of a sustained effect on catecholamines or indoles in mouse brain after long term subcutaneous administration of caffeine and theophylline. *Life Sci* 1986;39:565–72.
25. Aeschbacher HU, Milon H, Wurzner HP. Caffeine concentrations in mice plasma and testicular tissue and the effect of caffeine on the dominant lethal test. *Mut Res* 1978;57:193–200.
26. Storm van Leeuwen W. Quantitative pharmakologische Untersuchungen über die Reflex-funktionen des Rückenmarkes an Warmblütern. I. Mitteilung. Wirkung von Chloroform, Strychnin und Koffein. *Pflügers Arch ges Physiol Menschen Tiere* 1913;154:307–42.
27. Schoen R. Beiträge zur Pharmakologie der Körperstellung und der Labyrinthreflexe. XXI. Mitteilung: Coffein. *Naunyn-Schmiedebergs Arch Pharmakol Exp Pathol* 1926;113:246–56.
28. Sant'Ambrogio G, Frazier DT, Boyarsky LL. Effect of caffeine on spinal reflexes. *Proc Soc Exp Biol Med* 1962;109:273–6.
29. Jacobson BH, Edwards SW. Effects of ingested doses of caffeine on neuromuscular reflex response time in man. *Int J Sports Med* 1990;11:194–7.
30. Jacobson BH, Edgley BM. Effects of caffeine on simple reaction time and movement time. *Aviat Space Environ Med* 1987;58:1153–6.
31. Tarnopolsky MA, Atkinson SA, MacDougall JD, Sale DG, Sutton JR. Physiological responses to caffeine during endurance running in habitual caffeine users. *Med Sci Sports Exerc* 1989;21:418–24.
32. Brooks GA, Fahey TD. *Exercise physiology: human bioenergetics and its applications.* New York: John Wiley & Sons, 1984;234.
33. Delbeke FT, Debackere M. Caffeine: use and abuse in sports. *Int J Sports Med* 1984;5:179–84.
34. Ben-Ezra V, Vaccaro P. The influence of caffeine on the anaerobic threshold of competitively trained cyclists. *Med Sci Sports Exerc* 1982;14:176.

35. Knapik JJ, Jones BH, Toner MM, Daniels WL, Evans WJ. Influence of caffeine on serum substrate changes during running in trained and untrained individuals. In: Knuttgen H, Vogel J, Poortmans J, eds. *Biochemistry of exercise*. Champaign, IL: Human Kinetics, 1983;514–19.
36. Casal DC, Leon AS. Failure of caffeine to affect substrate utilization during prolonged running. *Med Sci Sports Exerc* 1985;17:174–9.
37. Gaesser GA, Rich RG. Influence of caffeine on blood lactate response during incremental exercise. *Int J Sports Med* 1985;6:207–11.
38. Elkins RN, Rapoport JL, Zahn TP, et al. Acute effects of caffeine in normal prepubertal boys. *Am J Psychiatry* 1981;138:178–83.
39. Rapoport JL, Jensvold M, Elkins R, et al. Behavioral and cognitive effects of caffeine in boys and adult males. *J Nerv Ment Dis* 1981;169:726–32.
40. Calhoun WH. Central nervous system stimulants. In: Furchtgott E. ed. *Pharmacological and biophysical agents and behavior*. New York: Academic Press, 1971;181–268.
41. Nash H. Psychological effects and alcohol-antagonizing properties of caffeine. *Quarterly J Stud Alcohol* 1966;27:727–34.
42. Ghoneim MM, Hinrichs JV, Chiang C-K, Loke WH. Pharmacokinetic and pharmacodynamic interactions between caffeine and diazepam. *J Clin Pharmacol* 1986;6:75–80.
43. Loke WH, Hinrichs JV, Ghoneim MM. Caffeine and diazepam: Separate and combined effects on mood, memory, and psychomotor performance. *Psychopharmacology* 1985;87:344–50.
44. Roache JD, Griffiths RR. Interactions of diazepam and caffeine: Behavioral and subjective dose effects in humans. *Pharmacol Biochem Behav* 1987;26:801–12.
45. Hasenfratz M, Bättig K. Action profiles of smoking and caffeine: Stroop effect, EEG and peripheral physiology. *Pharmacol Biochem Behav* 1992;42:155–61.
46. Patacchioli FR, Taglialatela G, Angelucci L, Cerbone A, Sadile AG. Adrenocorticoid receptor binding in the rat hippocampus: strain-dependent co-variations with arousal and habituation to novelty. *Behav Brain Res* 1989;33:287–300.
47. Dews PB. The measurement of the influence of drugs on voluntary activity in mice. *Brit J Pharmacol* 1953;8:46–8.
48. Estler C-J. Effect of α- and β-adrenergic blocking agents and parachlorophenylalanine on morphine- and caffeine-stimulated locomotor activity of mice. *Psychopharmacology* 1973;28:261–8.
49. Estler, C-J. Influence of pimozide on the locomotor hyperactivity produced by caffeine. *J Pharm Pharm* 1979;31:126–7.
50. Heim F, Haas B. Der Einfluss von Megaphen auf Motilität und Sauerstoffverbrauch weisser Mäuse in Ruhe und Erregung. *Arch Exp Pathol Pharmakol* 1955;226:395–402.
51. Heim F, Hack B, Mitznegg P, Ammon HPT, Estler C-J. Coffein-antagonistische Wirkungen des Theobromins und coffeinartige Eigenschaften von Theobromin-Metaboliten. *Arzneimittel Forsch* 1971;21:1039–43.
52. Knoll J. Motimeter, a new sensitive apparatus for the quantitative measurement of hypermotility caused by psychostimulants. *Arch int pharmacodyn* 1961;no. 1-2:141–54.
53. Menge G. Tierexperimentelle Untersuchungen zur zentral stimulierenden Wirkung eines neuen Theophyllin-Derivates. *Arzneimittel Forsch* 1961;11:271–3.
54. Cohen C, Welzl H, Bättig K. Effects of nicotine, caffeine, and their combination on locomotor activity in rats. *Pharmacol Biochem Behav* 1991;40:121–3.
55. Collins C, Richards PT, Starmer GA. Caffeine-phenacetin interaction in the rat: effects on absorption. *J Pharm Pharmac* 1977;29:217–21.
56. Meliska CJ, Loke WH. Caffeine and nicotine: differential effects on ambulation, rearing and wheel-running. *Pharmacol Biochem Behav* 1984;21:871–5.
57. Oettinger R, Martin JR, Rosenberg E, Bättig K. Effects of tunnel maze complexity on caffeinic hyperactivity in the rat. *Pharmacol Biochem Behav* 1985;23:85–90.
58. Kaplan GB, Tai NT, Greenblatt DJ, Shader RI. Separate and combined effects of caffeine and alprazolam on motor activity and benzodiazepine receptor binding in vivo. *Psychopharmacology* 1990;101:539–44.
59. Holloway WR, Jr., Thor DH. Caffeine and social investigation in the adult male rat. *Neurobehav Toxicol Teratol* 1983;5:119–25.
60. Hughes RN, Greig AM. Effects of caffeine, methamphetamine and methylphenidate on reactions to novelty and activity in mice. *Neuropharmacology* 1976;15:673–6.

61. Griebel G, Misslin R, Vogel E. Behavioural effects of selective A$_2$ adenosine receptor antagonists, CGS 21197 and CGS 22706, in mice. *Neuroreport* 1991;2:139–40.
62. Marriott AS. The effects of amphetamine, caffeine and methylphenidate on the locomotor activity of rats in an unfamiliar environment. *Int J Neuropharmacol* 1968;7:487–91.
63. Valzelli L, Bernasconi S. Behavioral and neurochemical effects of caffeine in normal and aggressive rats. *Pharmacol Biochem Behav* 1973;1:251–4.
64. Hilakavi LA, Durcan MJ, Lister RG. Effects of caffeine on social behavior, exploration and locomotor activity: interactions with ethanol. *Life Sci* 1989;44:543–53.
65. File SE, Baldwin HA, Johnston AL, Wilks LJ. Behavioral effects of acute and chronic administration of caffeine in the rat. *Pharmacol Biochem Behav* 1988;30:809–15.
66. Wanner HU, Bättig K. Pharmakologische Wirkungen auf die Laufleistung der Ratte bei verschiedener Leistungsbelohnung und verschiedener Leistungsanforderung. *Psychopharmacology* 1965;7:182–202.
67. Kehrhahn OH. Das Verhalten männlicher Albinomäuse im Laufrad-Versuch. *Arzneimittel Forsch* 1973;23:981–91.
68. Buckholtz NS, Middaugh LD. Effects of caffeine and L-phenylisopropyladenosine on locomotor activity of mice. *Pharmacol Biochem Behav* 1987;28:179–85.
69. Phillis JW, Barraco RA, DeLong RE, Washington DO. Behavioral characteristics of centrally administered adenosine analogs. *Pharmacol Biochem Behav* 1986;24:263–70.
70. Holtzman SG. Complete, reversible, drug-specific tolerance to stimulation of locomotor activity by caffeine. *Life Sci* 1983;33:779–87.
71. Finn IB, Holtzman SG. Pharmacologic specificity of tolerance to caffeine-induced stimulation of locomotor activity. *Psychopharmacology* 1987;93:428–34.
72. Meliska CJ, Landrum RE, Loke WH. Caffeine effects: interaction of drug and wheel-running experience. *Pharmacol Biochem Behav* 1985;23:633–5.
73. Meliska CJ, Landrum RE, Landrum TA. Tolerance and sensitization to chronic and subchronic oral caffeine: Effects on wheel-running in rats. *Pharmacol Biochem Behav* 1990;35:477–9.
74. Boyd EM, Dolman M, Knight LM, Sheppard EP. The chronic oral toxicity of caffeine. *Can J Physiol Pharmacol* 1965;43:995–1007.
75. Haslam DR. Individual differences in pain threshold and level of arousal. *Br J Psychol* 1967;58:139–42.
76. Cass LJ, Frederick WS. The augmentation of analgesic effect of aspirin with phenacetin and caffeine. *Current Therap Res* 1962;12:583–8.
77. Baptisti A, Chermish SM, Gruber CM. Use of non-narcotic analgesic drugs in postpartum patients. *Arch Internat Pharmacodyn* 1966;159:234–9.
78. Lasagna L. Drug interaction in the field of analgesic drugs. *Proc Royal Soc Med* 1965;58(Pt. 2):978–83.
79. Lim RKS, Miller DG, Guzman F, et al. Pain and analgesia evaluated by the intraperitoneal bradykinin-evoked pain method in man. *Clin Pharmacol Ther* 1967;8:521–42.
80. Lieberman HR, Wurtman RJ, Emde GG, Coviella ILG. The effects of caffeine and aspirin on mood and performance. *J Clin Psychopharmacol* 1987;7:315–20.
81. Ward N, Whitney C, Avery D, Dunner D. The analgesic effects of caffeine in headache. *Pain* 1991;44:151–5.
82. Paalzow G, Paalzow L. The effects of caffeine and theophylline on nociceptive stimulation in the rat. *Acta pharmacol toxicol* 1973;32:22–32.
83. Yarbrough GG, McGuffin-Clineschmidt JC. In vivo behavioral assessment of central nervous system purinergic receptors. *Eur J Pharmacol* 1981;76:137–44.
84. Fernstrom JD, Fernstrom MH. Effects of caffeine on monoamine neurotransmitters in the central and peripheral nervous system. In: Dews PB, ed. *Caffeine: perspectives from recent research.* Berlin: Springer-Verlag, 1984;107–18.
85. Goldstein L, Murphree HB, Pfeiffer CC. Quantitative electroencephalography in man as a measure of CNS stimulation. *Annals NY Acad Sci* 1963;107:1045–56.
86. Šulc J, Brožek G, Cmíral J. Neurophysiological effects of small doses of caffeine in man. *Activ Nerv Sup* 1974;16:217–8.
87. Saletu B. The use of pharmaco-EEG in drug profiling. In: Hindmarch I, Stonier P. eds. *Human psychopharmacology: measures and methods.* vol 1. Chichester: John Wiley & Sons, 1987;173–200.

88. Clubley M, Bye CE, Henson TA, Peck AW, Riddington CJ. Effects of caffeine and cyclizine alone and in combination on human performance, subjective effects and EEG activity. *Br J Clin Pharmacol* 1979;7:157–63.
89. Pollack VE, Teasdale T, Stern J, Volavka J. Effects of caffeine on resting EEG and response to sine wave modulated light. *EEG Clin Neurophysiol* 1981;51:470–6.
90. Künkel H. Vielkanal-Eeg-Spektralanalyse der Coffein-Wirkung. *Z Ernährungswiss* 1976; 15:71–9.
91. James JE. *Caffeine and health.* London: Academic Press, 1991.
92. Kerr JS, Sherwood N, Hindmarch I. Separate and combined effects of the social drugs on psychomotor performance. *Psychopharmacology* 1991;104:113–9.
93. Walsh JK, Muehlbach MJ, Humm TM, Dickins QS, Sugerman JL, Schweitzer PK. Effect on caffeine on physiological sleep tendency and ability to sustain wakefulness at night. *Psychopharmacology* 1990;101:271–3.
94. Johnson LC, Freeman CR, Spinweber CL, Gomez SA. Subjective and objective measures of sleepiness: Effect of benzodiazepine and caffeine on their relationship. *Psychophysiology* 1991;28:65–71.
95. Radulovacki M, Miletich RS, Green RD, N^6 (phenylisopropyl) adenosine (L-PIA) increases slow wave sleep (S2) and decreases wakefulness in rats. *Brain Res* 1982;246: 178–80.
96. Radulovacki M, Walovitch R, Yanik G. Caffeine produces REM sleep rebound in rats. *Brain Res* 1980;201:497–500.
97. Virus RM, Ticho S, Pilditch M, Radulovacki M. A comparison of the effects of caffeine, 8-cyclopentyltheophylline, and alloxazine on sleep in rats. *Neuropsychopharmacology* 1990;3:243–9.
98. Yanik G, Glaum S, Radulovacki M. The dose-response effects of caffeine on sleep in rats. *Brain Res* 1987;403:177–80.
99. Lieberman HR, Wurtman RJ, Emde GG, Roberts C, Coviella ILG. The effects of low doses of caffeine on human performance and mood. *Psychopharmacology* 1987;92:308–12.
100. Fagan D, Swift CG, Tiplady B. Effects of caffeine on vigilance and other performance tests in normal subjects. *J Psychopharmacol* 1988;2:19–25.
101. Bakan P, Belton JA, Roth JC. In: Buckner DA, McGrath JJ, eds. *Vigilance: a Symposium.* New York: McGraw-Hill, 1963;22–8.
102. Frewer LJ, Lader M. The effects of caffeine on two computerized tests of attention and vigilance. *Human Psychopharmacol* 1991;6:119–28.
103. Bättig K, Buzzi R. Effect of coffee on the speed of subject-paced information processing. *Neuropsychobiology* 1986;16:126–30.
104. Hasenfratz M, Jaquet F, Aeschbach D, Bättig K. Interactions of smoking and lunch with the effects of caffeine on cardiovascular functions and information processing. *Human Psychopharmacol* 1991;6:277–84.
105. Coffin VL, Spealman RD. Psychomotor-stimulant effects of 3-isobutyl-1-methylxanthine: comparison with caffeine and 7-(2-chloroethyl) theophylline. *Eur J Pharmacol* 1989;170: 35–40.
106. Davis TRA, Kensler CJ, Dews PB. Comparison of behavioral effects of nicotine, d-amphetamine, caffeine and dimethylheptyl tetrahydrocannabinol in squirrel monkeys. *Psychopharmacologia* 1973;32:51–65.
107. Katz JL, Prada JA, Goldberg SR. Effects of adenosine analogs alone and in combination with caffeine in the squirrel monkey. *Pharmacol Biochem Behav* 1988;29:429–32.
108. Spealman RD. Psychomotor stimulant effects of methylxanthines in squirrel monkeys: relation to adenosine antagonism. *Psychopharmacology* 1988;95:19–24.
109. Stinnette MJ, Isaac W. Behavioral effects of d-amphetamine and caffeine in the squirrel monkey. *Eur J Pharmacol* 1975;30:268–71.
110. Glowa JR, Spealman RD. Behavioral effects of caffeine, N^6-(L-phenylisopropyl) adenosine and their combination in the squirrel monkey. *J Pharmacol Exp Therap* 1984;231:665–70.
111. McKim WA. The effect of caffeine, theophylline and amphetamine on operant responding of the mouse. *Psychopharmacology* 1980;68:135–8.
112. Mechner F, Latranyi M. Behavioral effects of caffeine, methamphetamine, and methylphenidate in the rat. *J Exp Anal Behav* 1963;6:331–42.
113. Logan L, Carney JM, Holloway FA, Seale TW. Effects of caffeine, cocaine and their combination on fixed-interval behavior in rats. *Pharmacol Biochem Behav* 1989;33:99–104.

114. Carney JM. Effects of caffeine, theophylline and theobromine on scheduled controlled responding in rats. *Brit J Pharmacol* 1982;75:451–4.
115. McMillan DE. Effects of d-amphetamine and caffeine on schedule-controlled and schedule-induced responding. *J Exp Anal Behav* 1979;32:445–56.
116. Glowa JR. Some effects of *d*-amphetamine, caffeine, nicotine and cocaine on schedule-controlled responding of the mouse. *Neuropharmacology* 1986;25:1127–35.
117. Harris RA, Snell D, Loh HH. Effects of stimulants, anorectics, and related drugs on schedule-controlled behavior. *Psychopharmacology* 1978;56:49–55.
118. Meliska CJ, Brown RE. Effects of caffeine on schedule-controlled responding in the rat. *Pharmacol Biochem Behav* 1982;16:745–50.
119. Spealman RD, Coffin VL. Behavioral effects of adenosine analogs in squirrel monkeys: relation to adenosine A_2 receptors. *Psychopharmacology* 1986;90:419–21.
120. Logan L, Carney JM. Antagonism of the behavioral effects of L-phenylisopropyladenosine (L-PIA) by caffeine and its metabolites. *Pharmacol Biochem Behav* 1984;21:375–9.
121. White JM. Behavioral interactions between nicotine and caffeine. *Pharmacol Biochem Behav* 1988;29:63–6.
122. Ando K. Profile of drug effects on temporally spaced responding in rats. *Pharmacol Biochem Behav* 1975;3:833–41.
123. Berz S, Bättig K, Welzl H. The effects of caffeine and selective adenosine receptor agonists on DRL learning (in preparation).
124. Webb D, Levine TE. Effects of caffeine on DRL performance in the mouse. *Pharmacol Biochem Behav* 1978;9:7–10.
125. Pradhan SN, Dutta SN. Comparative effects of nicotine and amphetamine on timing behavior in rats. *Neuropharmacology* 1970;9:9–16.
126. Sidman M. Technique for assessing the effects of drugs on timing behavior. *Science* 1955; 122:925.
127. Sanger DJ. The effects of caffeine on timing behavior in rodents: comparisons with chlordiazepoxide. *Psychopharmacology* 1980;68:305–9.
128. Bättig K, Buzzi R, Martin JR, Feierabend JM. The effects of caffeine on physiological functions and mental performance. *Experientia* 1984;40:1218–23.
129. Bittner AC, Jr., Carter RC, Kennedy RS, Harbeson MM, Krause M. Performance evaluation tests for environmental research (PETER): Evaluation of 114 measures. *Percep Mot Skills* 1986;63:683–708.
130. Foreman N, Barraclough S, Moore C, Mehta A, Madon M. High doses of caffeine impair performance of a numerical version of the Stroop task in men. *Pharmacol Biochem Behav* 1989;32:399–403.
131. Holck HGO. Effect of caffeine upon chess problem solving. *J Comp Psychol* 1933;301–11.
132. Humphreys MS, Revelle W. Personality, motivation, and performance: a theory of the relationship between individual differences and information processing. *Psychol Rev* 1984; 91:153–84.
133. Loke WH. Effects of caffeine on mood and memory. *Physiol Behav* 1988;44:367–72.
134. Terry WS, Phifer B. Caffeine and memory performance on the AVLT. *J Clinical Psychol* 1986;42:860–3.
135. Erikson GC, Hager LB, Houseworth C, Dungan J, Petros, Beckwith BE. The effects of caffeine on memory for word lists. *Physiol Behav* 1985;35:47–51.
136. Lowe G. State-dependent retrieval effects with social drugs. *Br J Addict* 1988;83:99–103.
137. Paré W. The effect of caffeine and seconal on a visual discrimination task. *J Comp Physiol Psychol* 1961;54:506–9.
138. Castellano C. Effects of caffeine on discrimination learning, consolidation, and learned behavior in mice. *Psychopharmacology* 1976;48:255–60.
139. Castellano C. Effects of pre- and post-trial caffeine administrations on simultaneous visual discrimination in three inbred strains of mice. *Psychopharmacology* 1977;51:255–8.
140. Tanaka Y, Sakurai M, Goto M, Hayashi S. Effect of xanthine derivatives on hippocampal long-term potentiation. *Brain Res* 1990;522:63–8.
141. Dulloo AG, Geissler CA, Horton T, Collins A, Miller DS. Normal caffeine consumption: influence on thermogenesis and daily energy expenditure in lean and post-obese human volunteers. *Am J Clin Nutr* 1989;49:44–50.
142. Haffner SM, Knapp JA, Stern MP, Hazuda HP, Rosenthal M, Franco LJ. Coffee consumption, diet, and lipids. *Am J Epidemiol* 1985;122:1–12.

143. Mathias S, Garland C, Barrett-Connor E, Wingard DL. Coffee, plasma cholesterol, and lipoproteins: a population study in an adult community. *Am J Epidemiol* 1985;121:896–905.
144. Tuomilehto J, Tanskanen A, Pietinen P, et al. Coffee consumption is correlated with serum cholesterol in middle-aged Finnish men and women. *J Epidemiol Commun Health* 1987; 41:237–42.
145. Solvoll K, Selmer R, Løken EB, Foss OP, Trygg K. Coffee, dietary habits, and serum cholesterol among men and women 35–49 years of age. *Am J Epidemiol* 1989;129:1277–88.
146. Cooper SL. Caffeine-induced hypodipsia in water-deprived rats: relationships with benzodiazepine mechanisms. *Pharmacol Biochem Behav* 1982;17:481–7.
147. Cox RH, Jr., Maickel RP. Interactions of caffeine with various amphetamines on rat food consumption and avoidance responding. *Neuropharmacology* 1976;15:767–71.
148. McDermott LJ, Grossman SP. The effects of amphetamine or caffeine on the response to glucoprivation in rats with rostral zona incerta lesions. *Pharmacol Biochem Behav* 1980; 12:949–57.
149. Sakata T, Kodama J, Fukushima M. Feeding patterns of theophyllinized rats and effects of dextrose on their food intake. *Physiol Behav* 1976;17:797–802.
150. Heppner CC, Kemble ED, Cox WM. Effects of food deprivation on caffeine consumption in male and female rats. *Pharmacol Biochem Behav* 1986;24:1555–9.
151. Barone FC, Wayner MJ, Kleinrock S. Effects of caffeine on FT-1 min schedule induced drinking at different body weights. *Pharmacol Biochem Behav* 1979;11:347–50.
152. Wayner MJ, Jolicoeur FB, Rondeau DB, Barone FC. Effects of acute and chronic administration of caffeine on schedule dependent and schedule induced behavior. *Pharmacol Biochem Behav* 1976;5:343–8.
153. De Freitas SB, Schwartz G. Effects of caffeine on chronic psychiatric patients. *Amer J Psychiat* 1979;136:1337–8.
154. Podboy JW, Mallory WA. Caffeine reduction and behavior change in the severely retarded. *Mental Retard* 1977;40.
155. Furlong FW. Possible psychiatric significance of excessive coffee consumption. *Can Psychiat Assoc J* 1975;20:577–83.
156. Cherek DR, Steinberg JL, Brauchi JT. Effects of caffeine on human aggressive behavior. *Psychiat Res* 1983;8:137–45.
157. Cherek DR, Steinberg JL, Brauchi JT. Regular or decaffeinated coffee and subsequent human aggressive behavior. *Psychiat Res* 1984;11:251–8.
158. Baldwin HA, File SE. Caffeine-induced anxiogenesis: The role of adenosine, benzodiazepine and noradrenergic receptors. *Pharmacol Biochem Behav* 1989;32:181–6.
159. Holloway WR, Jr., Thor DH. Caffeine: Effects on the behaviors of juvenile rats. *Neurobehav Toxicol Teratol* 1983;5:127–34.
160. Holloway WR, Jr., Thor DH. Interactive effects of caffeine, 2-chloroadenosine and haloperidol on activity, social investigation and play fighting of juvenile rats. *Pharmacol Biochem Behav* 1985;22:421–6.
161. Kuznicki JT, Turner LS. The effects of caffeine on caffeine users and non-users. *Physiol Behav* 1986;37:397–408.
162. Zahn TP, Rapoport JL. Autonomic nervous system effects of acute doses of caffeine in caffeine users and abstainers. *Int J Psychophysiol* 1987;5:33–41.
163. Griffiths RR, Woodson PP. Reinforcing effects of caffeine in humans. *J Pharmacol Exper Therap* 1988;246:21–9.
164. Chait LD, Johanson CE. Discriminative stimulus effects of caffeine and benzphetamine in amphetamine-trained volunteers. *Psychopharmacology* 1988;96:302–8.
165. Griffiths RR, Evans SM, Heishman SJ, et al. Low-dose caffeine discrimination in humans. *J Pharmacol Exper Therap* 1990;252:970–8.
166. Evans SM, Griffiths RR. Dose-related caffeine discrimination in normal volunteers: individual differences in subjective effects and self-reported cues. *Behav Pharmacol* 1991;2: 345–56.
167. Holtzman SG. Discriminative stimulus properties of caffeine in the rat: noradrenergic mediation. *Journal of Pharmacol Exp Therap* 1986;239:706–14.
168. Holtzman SG. Discriminative stimulus effects of caffeine: tolerance and cross-tolerance with methylphenidate. *Life Sci* 1987;40:381–9.
169. Modrow HE, Holloway FA, Carney JM. Caffeine discrimination in the rat. *Pharmacol Biochem Behav* 1981;14:683–8.

170. Modrow HE, Holloway FA. Drug discrimination and cross generalization between two methylxanthines. *Pharmacol Biochem Behav* 1985;23:425–9.
171. Winter JC. Caffeine-induced stimulus control. *Pharmacol Biochem Behav* 1981;15:157–9.
172. Carney JM, Holloway FA, Modrow HE. Discriminative stimulus properties of methylxanthines and their metabolites in rats. *Life Sci* 1985;36:913–20.
173. Kuhn DM, Appel JB, Greenberg I. An analysis of some discriminative properties of d-amphetamine. *Psychopharmacology* 1974;39:57.
174. Griffiths RR, Bigelow GE, Liebson IA. Reinforcing effects of caffeine in coffee and capsules. *J Exper Anal Behav* 1989;52:127–40.
175. Griffiths RR, Bigelow GE, Liebson IA. Human coffee drinking: Reinforcing and physical dependence producing effects of caffeine. *J Pharmacol Exper Therap* 1986;239:416–25.
176. Benowitz NL, Hall SM, Modin G. Persistent increase in caffeine concentrations in people who stop smoking. *Br Med J* 1989;298:1075–6.
177. Griffiths RR, Woodson PP. Caffeine physical dependence: a review of human and laboratory animal studies. *Psychopharmacology* 1988;94:437–51.
178. Atkinson J, Enslen M. Self-administration of caffeine by the rat. *Arzneimittelforschung/Drug Research* 1976;26:2059–61.
179. Deneau G, Yanagita T, Seevers MH. Self-administration of psychoactive substances by the monkey. *Psychopharmacologia* 1969;16:30–48.
180. Griffiths RR, Woodson PP. Reinforcing properties of caffeine: Studies in humans and laboratory animals. *Pharmacol Biochem Behav* 1988;29:419–27.
181. Collins RJ, Weeks JR, Cooper MM, Good PI, Russell RR. Prediction of abuse liability of drugs using IV self-administration by rats. *Psychopharmacology* 1984;82:6–13.
182. Hoffmeister F, Wuttke W. Self-administration of acetylsalicylic acid and combinations with codeine and caffeine in rhesus monkeys. *Journal of Pharmacol Exp Therap* 1973;186:266–75.
183. Schuster CR, Woods JH, Seevers MH. Self-administration of central stimulants by the monkey. In: Sjöqvist F, Tottie F. eds. *Abuse of central stimulants.* Stockholm: Almqvist & Wiksell, 1969;339–47.
184. Vitiello MV, Woods SC. Caffeine: Preferential consumption in rats. *Pharmacol Biochem Behav* 1975;3:147–9.
185. Brockwell NT, Eikelboom R, Beninger RJ. Caffeine-induced place and taste conditioning: production of dose-dependent preference and aversion. *Pharmacol Biochem Behav* 1991;38:513–7.
186. Brockwell NT, Beninger RJ. Differential effects of A1 and A2 adenosine receptor antagonists on place conditioning and motor activity in rats. *Soc Neurosci Abst* 1990;16:1194.
187. Kramer JC. Amphetamine abuse. Pattern and effects of high dose taken intravenously. *J Am Med Assoc* 1967;201:305–9.
188. Horger BA, Wellman PJ, Morien A, Davies BT, Schenk S. Caffeine exposure sensitizes rats to the reinforcing effects of cocaine. *NeuroReport* 1991;2:53–6.
189. Greden JF. Anxiety or caffeinism: a diagnostic dilemma. *Amer J Psychiatry* 1974;131:1089–92.
190. Eaton WW, McLeod J. Consumption of coffee or tea and symptoms of anxiety. *Amer J Pub Health* 1984;74:66–8.
191. Lee MA, Cameron OG, Greden JF. Anxiety and caffeine consumption in people with anxiety disorders. *Psychiat Res* 1985;15:211–7.
192. Charney DS, Heninger GR, Jatlow PI. Increased anxiogenic effects of caffeine in panic disorders. *Arch Gen Psychiat* 1985;42:233–43.
193. Conway TL, Vickers RR, Jr., Ward HW, Rahe RH. Occupational stress and variation in cigarette, coffee, and alcohol consumption. *J Health Soc Behav* 1981;22:155–65.
194. Loke WH. Caffeine consumption by college undergraduates. *Psychol: A J Human Behav* 1988;25:8–10.
195. Höfer I, Bättig K. Coffee consumption, blood pressure tonus and reactivity to physical challenge in 338 women. (submitted).
196. Hasenfratz M, Bättig K. No psychophysiological interactions between caffeine and stress? *Psychopharmacology* (in press).
197. Baldwin HA, Johnston AL, File SE. Antagonistic effects of caffeine and yohimbine in animal tests of anxiety. *Eur J Pharmacol* 1989;159:211–5.

198. Tang M, Kuribara H, Falk JL. Anxiolytic effect of caffeine and caffeine-clonazepam interaction: evaluation by NaCl solution intake. *Pharmacol Biochem Behav* 1989;32:773–6.
199. Spindel ER, Wurtman RJ. Neuroendocrine effects of caffeine in rat and man. In: Dews PB, ed. *Caffeine*. Berlin: Springer-Verlag, 1984;129–41.
200. Henry JP, Stephens PM. Caffeine as an intensifier of stress-induced hormonal and pathophysiologic changes in mice. *Pharmacol Biochem Behav* 1980;13:719–27.
201. Boulenger J-P, Marangos PJ, Zander KJ, Hanson J. Stress and caffeine: effects on central adenosine receptors. *Clin Neuropharmacol* 1986;9:79–83.
202. Holtzman SG. Caffeine as a model drug of abuse. *Trends Pharmacol Sci* 1990;11:355–6.

Caffeine, Coffee, and Health,
edited by S. Garattini.
Raven Press, Ltd., New York © 1993.

10

Coffee and Caffeine

Sleep and Wakefulness

Jan Snel

*Faculty of Psychology, University of Amsterdam, 1018 WB Amsterdam,
The Netherlands*

Since the sleep-wake rhythm level reflects the circadian arousal rhythm, caffeine should affect sleep and waking. Sleep was measured objectively by recording the EEG and certain physiological variables during sleep, and, subjectively, by subjective reports on sleep quality. In general, caffeine in doses not exceeding 400 mg was given mainly to young adults shortly before going to bed. Caffeine induced restless sleep predominantly in the first half of the sleep. Effects of caffeine on sleepiness were assessed by measuring sleep latency, mood, and task performance. With moderate doses of caffeine, sleep latency increased, mood did not change, and task performance improved on easy tasks but tended to be impaired on complex tasks. Important factors in studies on the effects of caffeine on sleep and waking are the design, the subjects' age, sex, personality, and consumption habits. The general conclusion is that caffeine modulates the level of arousal and that, depending on this interaction, it may have divergent and even contradictory effects on sleep and waking.

SLEEP AND WAKING

The 24-hour endogenous arousal cycle shows a peak in late afternoon and a trough between 3:00 and 4:00 in the morning. Sleep and wakefulness are manifestations of this circadian cycle. During sleep, there are smaller ultradian cycles, the so-called *sleep cycles,* lasting about 90 minutes each, which thus occur six times during a normal sleep period. Some authors assume that this ultradian rhythm still exists during waking and manifests itself as fluctuations of arousal and alertness.

The periodic changes in the EEG during sleep each night in a reliable and characteristic way are called the sleep structure. This sleep structure is used to describe the quality and depth of sleep and runs through stage 1 (alpha rhythm: 8–12 Hz) and stage 4 to the rapid eye movement (REM)-stage. Stages 1 and 2 together are called *light sleep*. Stage 2 or the transition from the period of falling asleep to deep sleep is characterized by the onset of sleep spindles (12–15 cps) and K-complexes. During light sleep the EEG pattern is desynchronized, involving high EEG frequencies with small amplitudes. Stages 3 and 4 together are called *deep sleep* or *slow wave sleep* (SWS), and the EEG shows low frequencies with large amplitudes. In stage 3, the EEG shows large, slow delta waves (0.5–3 cps). In stage 4, more than 50% of the EEG consists of this delta rhythm. Stages 1 to 4 are called non-REM sleep (NREM sleep). When the sleeping person has reached stage 4, there is a quick return through stages 3, 2, and 1 to a state in which rapid eye movements (REM sleep) occur.

Physiological characteristics of REM sleep, compared to NREM sleep, include irregular heart and respiration rate, absent muscle tonus (except for the muscles of the extremities), a higher threshold to awaken the sleeper, and detailed dreams. At the start of the night, more NREM sleep, particularly more SWS, is found, whereas in the second half increasingly more REM sleep and light sleep can be observed. One change from NREM to REM is called a *sleep-cycle*.

Although sleep as a biological rhythm is determined largely by endogenous factors with a free-running length of about 25 hours, there are also exogenous factors, or so-called *Zeitgebers*, that play an important role in the exact timing of the sleep-wake rhythm in 24 hours such as the succession of light and dark, and the pattern of work and leisure time.

In 1972, Müller-Limmroth (1) argued that the antihypnotic or nonspecific fatigue-compensating effects of caffeine were due to the inhibition of inhibitory neurons in the medial reticular formation (RF). This hypothesis is plausible since, in the medial part of the RF, two nuclei are found that have specific characteristics that regulate sleep. These are the serotonergic, sleep-promoting raphe system, found in the medial hindbrain that is surrounded by the diffuse ascending reticular activating system (ARAS) and the noradrenergic locus coeruleus. The activity of the ARAS of the brainstem is gated presumably (2) through the thalamic nucleus reticularis to regulate thalamic inhibition of cortical areas. Thus, the sleep-wake cycle is the result of interrelated activity of several subcortical and cortical structures. It implies that effects of caffeine on the sleep-wake cycle depend both on the level of arousal, determined by more or less constant "trait" factors such as age and personality, and by short-term "state" factors such as time of day, fatigue, or nutritional items, such as caffeine. Aspects of synthesis, release and metabolism of neurotransmitters in the CNS are critical in the sleep-wake process. Experimental evidence on the cellular action of caffeine points to a nonspecific effect that consists of blocking of the adenosine receptors, inhibition of phosphodiesterase, and a modulation of the calcium-flux (3). Hence, it is plausible to assume a significant influence of coffee and caffeine on this cycle; caffeine intake during the day and before going to sleep should affect wakefulness and sleep. Figure 1 shows normal sleep in healthy aged and young.

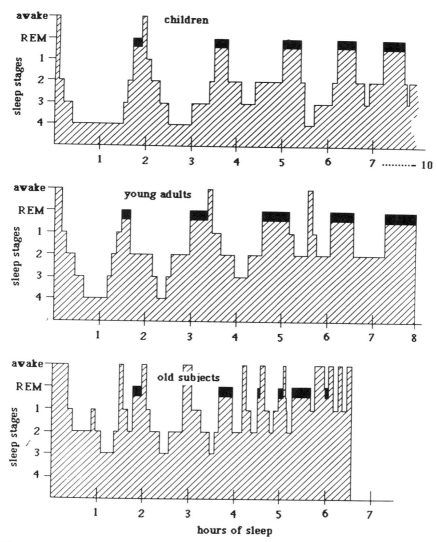

FIG 1. Hypnograms of normal children, age 5 to 13 years, young adults age 19 to 30 years, and subjects over 70 years of age.

Arousal Level

Age

Bättig (4) concluded from his detailed review that the rate of general metabolism is increased by caffeine. However, this effect may depend on the kinetics of neurotransmitters that interact with age and sex. With aging there are reductions in the synthetizing enzymes of dopamine, norepinephrine, and acetylcholine in the brain. Also, with aging, reductions in the catecholamine receptors, a higher metabolite concentration in the liquor and an age-related MAO concentration in brain tissue, blood platelets, and plasma in various areas of the brain have been found (5). It is possible that the altered metabolism of the brain catecholamines in older people causes greater sensitivity to caffeine.

The metabolic removal of caffeine from the blood remains subject to considerable intra- and interindividual differences. In the preterm infant, the half-life ranges from 65 to 105 hours (6,7), falling to about 80 hours in newborn full-term infants (8), and to 14 hours at the age of 3 to 5 months. The adult half-life of about 5 hours is already attained at the age of 5 to 6 months and tends to diminish in the very old (9). Thus, sleep and waking in very young people may be more affected by caffeine than they are in older people. Indeed, effects of caffeine on sleep have been assessed in the very young. The suggestion that transplacentally transported doses of caffeine would have a detectable effect upon neonatal sleep and behavior among full-term infants (10) was tested in forty "full-term healthy" neonates between 24 and 48 hours of age. The dependent measures were sleep-state observation and a commonly used method to assess infant behavior. Each subject was observed for 75 minutes in epochs of 30 seconds by five observers. The mean umbilical cord level of caffeine at birth was 1.224 μg/ml $\pm$ 1.192 (range 0.065 μg/ml to 5.688 μg/ml). The mean caffeine level in saliva taken approximately 40 hours after birth was 0.65 μm/ml $\pm$ 0.628. The correlation between these two levels was 0.87, which confirms the extended half-life in very young infants. The correlations between maternal reported intake and actual levels in the infant were 0.53 ($p < 0.0001$) for saliva and 0.49 ($p < 0.001$) for cord serum levels. The results showed only one significant effect on the sleep data and 2 out of 11 on the behavioral aspects, viz., the number of state changes and startles. The tentative interpretation was that nontoxic caffeine levels in the neonate, received from the placenta and breast milk, preferentially affect the general arousal level and state organization, but do not significantly affect spontaneous state-changes or noninteractive behavior.

This could be further verified in 11 mother-infant pairs. In a double-blind cross-over study (11) after five days of caffeine abstinence, the mothers (daily caffeine intake: 54 to 877 mg) received in two periods of five days, daily 5 × 100 mg/packet or decaffeinated packets. During the caffeine period, the infants, mean age 53 days ± 16, received milk with a caffeine concentration ranging from 1.6 to 6.2 μg/ml or 0.3–1.0 mg/kg/day. During the no-caffeine period, the level was 0.25 μg/ml in the milk. No significant difference in mean heart rate or sleep time was detected between the two observation periods. No significant difference in sleep time was observed by the mothers during these two periods. These results suggest again that moderate coffee drinking by lactating women does not affect the behavior of breast-fed infants aged between 29 and 77 days.

In the elderly, the amplitude of the sleep-wake cycle is diminished and, as a consequence, there is a stronger tendency to fall asleep during the day and to stay awake at night (12). Minors and Waterhouse (13) found, in 321 aged subjects, that they slept more frequently during the day, were less physically and socially active, and had less intra-individual variation in their daily habits (cf. 14). Armstrong-Esther et al. (15) studied the effects of hospitalization on elderly people and found more incontinence, sleep disturbance, cognitive and behavioral changes and more confusion. Internal desynchronization is found in 70 % of the elderly (16) and more time and effort are needed to synchronize desynchronized circadian rhythms or to adapt to a 13-hour shift in the wake-sleep cycle (17). Elderly people as compared to the young have a shorter total sleep time (TST), less alpha activity (8–12 Hz), a greater amount of stage 2, while the time spent in stage 4 (deep sleep) is shorter and with less delta activity (1–3 Hz), and they have more problems staying awake during the daytime (18–20). There are no great sex-related sleep differences in ≥58-year-old people, although men show higher percentages of stage 1 and 2 (light sleep) and women more stage 3 and 4 (deep sleep), a longer REM-latency and fewer REM periods (21). Neurophysiological data support the greater vulnerability of the sleep-wake cycle in the elderly manifested as a slow but steady loss of brain mass, illustrated by a 45% smaller number of cells in the nucleus suprachiasmaticus, the pacemaker of the sleep-wake cycle, in the RF and the frontal cortex (22), and a higher norepinephrine level, especially in situations that demand active involvement (23). These changes are characterized by a delayed return to basal levels (19). The results support the concept of heightened sympathetic tone in the aged inducing only light sleep that is fragmented and has more awakenings. A supposed mechanism behind these age-related differences (19) is the difficulty that elderly people have, like very young children, in suppressing on-going motor and mental activity. This may explain why a third of people older than 60 years have sleep complaints.

Sleep disturbances induced by caffeine in older people might be caused by an increased sensitivity to caffeine. Brezinová (24) found in 50 to 63-year-old moderate caffeine users a tendency to more REM-sleep after a 330 mg caffeine dose, at least in the first part of the night. She also found a markedly reduced TST compared with younger people, as in the literature. These effects lasted longer, the older the subject was. During the wash-out night, older subjects tended to have more numerous and longer persisting sleep complaints than younger subjects. In contrast to this, in seven 23 to 28-year-old medical students, Gresham et al. (25) found no effect of 5 mg/kg caffeine mixed in 400 ml orange juice on the time spent in EEG-recorded stage 1 sleep and REM-sleep. It was not reported whether the subjects had to observe a caffeine abstinence period. Although middle-aged and aged people have greater caffeine-related sleep disturbances than younger people, this does not necessarily mean that sensitivity to caffeine varies with age. Kalow (26) found a correlation of 0.47 ($p < 0.001$) between habitual caffeine consumption and age in 68 subjects (0–9 cups/day; mean 2.46 cups/day). Only two out of seven correlations (range -0.006 to 0.274) between metabolic factors and caffeine consumption approached significance (see also: 27,28). Four subjects between 35 and 42 years old and four 43 to 49 years old (all $\leq$ 3 cups/day) stayed in the sleep lab for 19 nights: three adaptation nights and four discrete experimental blocks of four nights each (29). Within each block, there was a readjustment night, a caffeine night, a wash-out night and a second treatment night. Thirty minutes before bedtime, each subject received 4.6 mg/kg caffeine dissolved in 150 ml warm water or a placebo. There was no convincing EEG evidence of caffeine rebound effects on wash-out nights, although the subjects felt more satisfied with their sleep on wash-out nights than after placebo nights.

Sex

The caffeine clearance rate is slowed down by oral contraceptives and during pregnancy. Nevertheless, attention is rarely paid to differences in effects of caffeine due to sex. In the large epidemiological Tromsø heart study in 125,840 respondents (30), 10% and 8% of the women drinking 8 cups and <8 cups per day, respectively, reported insomnia problems against 5% for both consumption categories in the men. In an epidemiological cross-sectional study (31) in 4,558 Australians (mean age 41.3 ± 13.7 years), it was observed that, with increasing caffeine intake, the perceived difficulty in sleeping and several other complaints increased significantly. The relative risk of experiencing symptoms with a consumption of 240 mg caffeine/day (the population average) compared to caffeine-abstainers was 1.4 for insomnia in males and females. Arnold et al. (32) tested 75 female and 82 male undergraduates after $\geq$10 hours caffeine abstinence between 8:00 A.M. and 12:00 A.M. The women were assessed during the first five days of their menstrual cycle; they were not taking oral contraceptives. The caffeine doses were 0, 2, or 4 mg/kg. World list recall was facilitated in females, but impaired in males at the 2 mg/kg dose. The authors concluded that the effects of caffeine on word list memory in females may vary according to the level of estrogen in the subject's system. Since the estrogen level varies over the menstrual cycle, it may affect consumption habits of caffeine and other substances. In 226 males (aged 16 to 70 years) and 245 women (aged 16 to 69 years) (33) coffee consumption was positively related to the number of cigarettes smoked per day in men but not in women.

Personality

Arousal level might be the common factor (34,35) that underlies personality traits such as extroversion-introversion, impulsivity, and sensation seeking. If so, different effects of caffeine may be expected in high- and low-aroused persons. Under identical conditions, introverts are more highly aroused than extroverts, low impulsives more than high impulsives, and low sensation seekers more than high sensation seekers. Manipulating the level of arousal by caffeine shows rather consistently that moderate doses of caffeine impair performance in introverts, and improve it in extroverts (36,37), and a higher coffee consumption in extroverts (38). High impulsives show a tendency to higher caffeine consumption (39) and after caffeine an improvement of test performance (40–45). In word recall tests, however, caffeine did not interact with the level of impulsivity (32,46). Andrucci et al. (39) indicated a strong and consistent positive correlation between sensation seeking and self-reported caffeine use. Revelle et al. (47) suggested that effects of differences in personality may actually reflect phase differences in arousal. Performance in a complex verbal reasoning test was improved by 200–300 mg caffeine in high impulsives (low aroused) but impaired in low impulsives in the morning, but the reverse was found in the evening. These data can be understood from Revelle's assumption that arousal has an inverted U relation to performance, that caffeine increases arousal, that arousal varies diurnally and that high impulsives lag several hours behind low impulsives in the phase of their circadian rhythm (see the chapter by Bättig and Welzl for details on personality and caffeine).

Time of Day

After lunch a drop in performance and alertness may occur. In order to determine the effects of caffeine given before and after lunch, 32 university students completed two performance tasks with and without a 3 mg/kg dose of caffeine after abstaining from caffeine for 3 hours (48). Caffeine improved the performance of a vigilance task and removed the post-lunch drop in performance found in the noncaffeinated condition. Effects of time of day were studied (49) in 48 healthy female subjects, aged 19 to 32 years, randomly assigned to an afternoon or an evening group. The effects of combinations of temperature (29°C and 18°C) and boring or highly interesting tasks on sleepiness (SSS) were assessed using a visual analogue scale and a drowsiness scale, on visual reaction time, and on an activation/sedation scale (cf. 50). Negative effects of boredom were largely confined to the afternoon group. There was a curvilinear relationship with fatigue increasing around 3:00 P.M., falling by 4:00 P.M.; in the evening this trend was linear. Based on their control for effects of food, the authors' conclusion was that the generally referred to post-lunch dip in attention is better referred to as the afternoon pressure for sleep (APS).

Hill and Hill (51) investigated the relationship between time of day and mood at 8:30 A.M. and at 4:15 P.M. in 25 office workers aged 23 to 53 years. Total mood disturbance was greater in the morning with more tension and depressive feelings. In a similar study (52), six healthy men aged 22 ± 3 yrs were measured at 3:00 A.M., 9:00 A.M., 3:00 P.M., and 9:00 P.M. on the Profile of Mood States (POMS) test and a physical exertion test. Time of day and fatigue together explained 51% of the variance in peak power. One of the conclusions was that feelings of fatigue and subsequent performance are dependent on certain times of day. The findings so far suggest that variations in performance, caffeine treatment effects, and mood are a function of time of day and reflect fluctuations in the circadian arousal rhythm.

Seven hospital physicians, aged 29 to 38 years, were followed during night call duties for one night with a maximum of 3 hours sleep, and the two days thereafter by having them record their feelings of sleepiness and physical fatigue, and sleep patterns (53). The subjects showed almost maximum degrees of tiredness between 3:00 A.M. and 6:00 A.M. during night call and reported elevated sleepiness the following day. Unfortunately, no data were analyzed on the role of caffeine.

The effect of a 1-hour nap was assessed on early morning performance, sleepiness, and sleep latency after 12 healthy men had slept only 4 hours the night before (54). The effect of the nap was most beneficial when taken at 4:30 A.M., at the trough in the circadian arousal rhythm (cf. 55). Rogers et al. (56) studied the effect of a 1-hour nap taken at 2:00 A.M. on performance overnight in six women between 20 and 32 years (mean 25 years). They took no caffeine from 1:00 P.M. on the day of the experiment and at 11:15 P.M. received a placebo or a 300 mg caffeine tablet. Performance on press-button tasks, stimuli sequence memory, letter cancellation, and reaction time tasks was measured at 135 minute intervals from 5:00 P.M. until 8:45 A.M. Caffeine improved performance overnight on almost all tasks, but the nap taken at 2:00 A.M. had only a limited beneficial effect compared with the placebo.

In four healthy male radar surveillance shiftworkers, performance was measured between 8:00 A.M. and 5:00 P.M. and overnight between 5:00 P.M. and 8:00 A.M. (57). During the study, the same diet and decaffeinated coffee were provided. An overnight EEG-sleep recording preceded the day-night schedule, which consisted of a 9-hour workday that started at 8:00 A.M. on days 1 and 2; night-time work lasted 15 hours and started at 5:00 P.M. After a three-day interval, the schedule was repeated. Caffeine or placebo was given at 11:00 P.M. Performance measures were taken during the day and during the night shift with 3-hour intervals. Caffeine showed significant improvements in overnight performance compared to the placebo in 11 out of 14 tasks, most clearly at 2:00 A.M. and 5:00 A.M. The authors point out that the deterioration in performance during night shifts that last longer than 9 hours will coincide with the nadir of impaired performance between 3:00 A.M. and 6:00 A.M. and may be alleviated by the use of mild stimulants such as caffeine. The conclusion is that caffeine is most effective in the early morning, indicating that caffeine effects interact with the level of arousal.

Paradoxical Effects of Caffeine

The general balance in arousal of several concurrently active systems in the nervous system determines the efficacy of caffeine, i.e., the lower the arousal the greater the effect, but ceiling effects may be found during the day. This suggests that caffeine does not necessarily increase arousal but may under certain circumstances lower the system's activation. In everyday life, both outcomes can be observed. Since the assumption is that caffeine always leads to an (over) activated system, deactivating effects of caffeine are called *paradoxical* effects, such as found in hyperkinetic children with doses up to 6 mg/kg/BW (58–62). However, a survey of these effects of caffeine in doses ranging from 3 to 12 mg/kg showed varying effects on vigilance and behavior of hyperactive children (63).

In a situation of overarousal, such as extreme stress situations such as demanding situations at work, people drink coffee to relax. Experimental support for the relaxing effects of caffeine was found in interviews (64) with 180 15 to 82-year-old coffee drinkers (mean 3.8 cups/day). The morning effects, especially its reported calming action (0.31; $p < 0.01$) were involved in the development of a liking for coffee. Although this relaxation effect of caffeine may reflect an interaction with relief of withdrawal symptoms (65), it does illustrate that caffeine intake depends on the subject's arousal state at that moment and thus may modulate feelings of well being.

There is experimental evidence that high doses of caffeine cause sleep in rats (66). Parallel to this, cerebral serotonin and 5-HIAA-levels were increased. Regestein (67) describes six cases of heavy coffee drinkers (5 to 12 cups per day) who felt very groggy in the morning and complained of excessive sleepiness during day time. After discontinuation of caffeine consumption, sleepiness decreased or remitted. Therefore, heavy caffeine consumption apparently may provoke sleepiness. The author suggests three explanations for the pathological sleepiness: nocturnal withdrawal of caffeine, direct sedative action of caffeine as reported for small doses (68), or specific arousal characteristics.

Sensitivity, Habituation, and Tolerance

Those who are sensitive to coffee benefit from its activating effect, but, for the same reason, they avoid it late at night. Healthy students and hospital personnel (aged 22 to 45 years) were divided into two groups based on their experience with the effects of caffeine on their sleep, reported mainly as a delay in falling asleep after drinking coffee in the evening (28). The subjects took a challenge dose of 300 mg at 4:00 P.M. after an abstinence period of 16 hours. Subjects who had a history of coffee-induced wakefulness were light or nondrinkers (0–2 cups/day) and had a caffeine half-life of 7.4 hours (range 4.1 to 12.2). In the symptom-free group, who drank 3 to 6 cups /day, the half-life was 4.2 hours (range 3.2 to 4.9). These differences were reflected in the caffeine plasma levels at midnight.

Eighteen 21 to 35-year old, healthy, light-to-moderate coffee consumers (mean 155 mg; range 3 to 402 mg/day) were allowed to choose, in a discrete choice procedure, between the self-administration of color-coded capsules containing placebo, 100, or 300 mg caffeine (69). When subjects were divided into caffeine-sensitive choosers and nonchoosers, there was a consistent relation between caffeine choice and subjective effects. Nonchoosers reported predominantly aversive effects after caffeine, whereas choosers reported stimulant and mood-improving effects.

Those who are insensitive to caffeine, mostly the habitual drinkers, drink coffee in the morning and throughout the day without its having any influence on their sleep. While light users reported dysphoric symptoms such as nervousness and more awakenings at night, heavy consumers reported stimulant and euphoric effects, but irritability, headache, and restlessness in its absence (70). Whether these differences are due to an initial sensitivity, adaptation to caffeine, or some other factors is not clear. Caffeine delayed sleep onset in both groups, but this delay was more marked in light users than in heavy users. Goldstein et al (71,72) found large inter-individual differences in the disturbance of the soundness of sleep. Heavy coffee consumers tended to sleep better on placebo nights. Light consumers slept worse on caffeine nights. In the treatment of sleep complaints, attention should be paid to these different effects of caffeine related to different patterns of usage (73).

Apparently, for those who are accustomed to drinking large amounts of coffee, the chance of experiencing caffeine-induced sleep disturbances decreases with time. A nice illustration was given by Ogunremi and Mamora (74). They investigated the acute effects of caffeine-rich kolanut and coffee on sleep in ten young Nigerian university students (mean height 1.6 m, 56 kg BW). After one adaptation night, they took two spoonfuls of black coffee (50.22 g or 480 mg caffeine) or two whole nuts of cola acuminata (749 mg caffeine) or cola vera (2,414 mg) before sleep. Sleep-EEG was recorded all night. Since these two varieties of kolanuts are widely consumed and habitually chewed over long periods by all age groups, it suggests that high tolerance to caffeine would have developed. The black coffee resulted in "paradoxical" effects on sleep, while the kolanuts did induce a strongly disturbed sleep. In conclusion: inter-individual differences in the response to caffeine might be determined not only by intrinsic factors, but also by changes in the physiological system related to regular caffeine consumption.

Whether tolerance develops to all of coffee's effects is not clear (75). In 239 homemakers (76), the heavy coffee consumers (≥5 cups/day) reported less caffeine-induced wakefulness during their sleep and less nervousness after coffee in the morning and reported more desirable effects compared to the light users (1 to 2 cups/day). In 18 occasional or nondrinkers (71), caffeine consumption was followed by an irritated stomach and feelings of agitation but no increase in alertness or feelings of well being. The 38 heavy drinkers, on the other hand, reported feelings of anxiety and agitation after a placebo night, but caffeine relieved these unpleasant effects. The heavy drinkers reacted dose dependently to caffeine more positively, with feelings of heightened alertness, attentiveness, and a sense of well-being. Colton et al. (75) found similar results in habitual coffee users (≥1 cup/day). Their conclusion was that habitual coffee users are significantly less sensitive than noncoffee drinkers to the activating effects of caffeine on sleep (cf. 77). However, Hollingworth (78) could not find differences in reported quality and quantity of sleep dependent on habitual caffeine use. Brezinová (24) studied the effects of sleep quality of a dose of 2 to 3 cups of coffee taken just before going to bed. The subjects, in their late fifties, had a daily consumption of 2.7 ± 2 cups of coffee and 3.3 ± 3 cups of tea and were studied on nonconsecutive nights; in between they slept at home. She noted substantial sleep disturbances without tolerance to caffeine, which suggests an absence of long-term tolerance to the action of caffeine at least in this age group (cf. 72). Considering the fact that heavy coffee drinkers, and maybe the elderly, do not develop complete tolerance to the sleep-disturbing effects of caffeine and that depriving these subjects of their habitual daily doses may lead to serious sleep disturbances, it is recommended to exclude them from sleep research.

CAFFEINE AND SLEEP

The studies reviewed (Table 1) generally follow the same procedure of asking subjects to abstain from caffeine-containing beverages some hours before going to sleep. In most studies, 30 minutes before going to bed, caffeine is given in specified doses (Table 2), brewed in coffee, instant coffee, decaffeinated coffee, or sometimes together with a placebo like flavored lactose, fruit juices, etc. The coffee is sometimes mixed to compensate for taste differences. The doses range on average from 1 to 4 cups, minimum 40 to 160 mg, or maximum 100 to 400 mg. It is assumed that the subject will refrain from exertion beyond the normal daily activity pattern. Sometimes

TABLE 1. *Descriptive characteristics of subjects in studies on effects of caffeine on sleep*

Ref	Author	N	Age in years	M/F	Subject descriptors
78	Hollingworth, 1912	16	19–39	10 M	Coffee drinkers and noncoffee drinkers
90	Mullin et al., 1933	8	?	M	Children
95	Marbach et al., 1962	12	?	?	Various?
25	Gresham et al., 1963	7	23–28	?	Normal medical students
70	Goldstein, 1964	230	22–26	M	Medical students: 23% noncoffee, 17%, 1 cup/day; 37%, 2–4 cups/day; 23%, >4 cups/day
72	Goldstein et al., 1965	20	±24	M	m = 2.9 cups/day; range 0–8 cups/day
91	Schwertz, Marbach, 1965	12	?	?	
75	Colton et al., 1968	149	±24	138 M	Second year medical student; noncoffee drinkers: ≤1 cup/day; coffee drinkers: >1 cup/day
92	Stradomsky, 1970	90	15–85 (42)	M	Various hospital patients
98	Forrest et al., 1972	42	46.4	41 M	Medical and surgical patients; BW 67.4 kg
1	Müller-Limmroth, 72	?	?	?	?
85	Karacan et al., 1973	8	21–29	M	4 with and 4 without sleep complaints after coffee
24	Brezinová, 1974	6	50–63 (56)	2 M	Volunteers; m = 2.7 ± 2.0 cups/day; tea m = 3.3 ± 3.0 cups/day; caffeine: 291.3 mg/day
143	Karacan et al., 1974	18	20–30	M	Normal volunteers
124	Saletu et al., 1974	10	19–45 (30.2)	M	Normal volunteers
82	Brezinová et al, 1975	6	50–63	2 M	see (38)
84	Karacan et al., 1975	18	20–30	M	Mentally health young people
142	Ginsberg, Weintraub, 1976	12	?	?	Senile dement; m = 2–3 cups/day
144	Karacan et al., 1976	8	36–59	M	Normal
79	Karacan et al., 1976	18	20–30	M	Normal, healthy; m = 3 cups/day; range 1–4 cups/day; without sleep complaints
145	Browman et al., 1977	365	19–65 (36.1)	232 M	Laborers
29	Karacan et al., 1977	8	35–42	M	Normal: 4 Ss 35–42 years old; 4 43–49 years old
80	Nicholson, Stone, 1980	6	20–31	M	Healthy?
74	Ogunremi, Mamora, 1980	10	17–20 (18)	8 M	Students
86	Hirshkowitz et al., 1982	8	21–29	M	Healthy volunteers
81	Okuma et al., 1982	8	19–25 (21.1)	M	Healthy students, only 1–2 cups/day
89	Hicks et al., 1983	170	22	?	Students
28	Levy, Zylber-Katz, 1983	12	20–45 (30.3)	?	Students, hospital personnel sleep complaints After 0–2 cups/day, with 3–6 cups/day none
83	Gaillard et al., 1985	12	?	?	Healthy, young grown-ups
11	Ryu, 1985	11	22–74 days	?	Breast-fed normal infants
31	Shirlow, Mathers, 1985	3761	20–70	2189 M	Healthy, medicine-free volunteers, full-term healthy
10	Hronsky, Emory, 1987	40	24–48 hours	?	
88	Nicholson et al., 1989	10	20–31	M?	Healthy?
67	Regestein, 1989	6	29–52	4 M	Extremely heavy coffee consumers
106	Johnson et al., 1990	80	20.3 ± 2.74	M	Healthy naval school students
121	Bonnet, Arand, 1991	12	?	M	Young adults
97	Pantelios et al., 1991	140	18–49 (23.2)	?	Students

M, male; F, female; ?, unknown; m, mean; sd, standard deviation.

this is explicitly requested. In quite a few studies, the subjects are asked to perform exertion tasks before going to bed. Most studies are double-blind and except for the dosage, there is acceptable standardization.

The prediction is that, in view of the half-life of caffeine, coffee consumed before going to sleep, at a time of decreasing arousal, will negatively affect sleep, most notably the first part.

Sleep-EEG

Modulation of sleep is a well-established effect of caffeine. Karacan et al. (79) studied the effects of 1, 2, or 4 cups of coffee (31, 64, or 128 mg) on sleep in 18 habitual high coffee users under double-blind conditions in 13 consecutive nights. Abstinence was always from 12:00 P.M. and caffeine was given 30 minutes before lights out. Total sleep time (TST) or sleep length decreased and sleep onset latency (SOL) increased in a dose-related manner. Especially the highest dose produced changes in all measures, i.e., increasing the number of stage shifts and awakenings during sleep, the time in stages 0, 1, and REM of the first cycle and the latency to stage 3. The latency to stages 1 and 2 decreased while that to stages 3 and 4 increased. Their conclusion was that coffee taken shortly before retiring would disturb sleep and notably in the first part of the night (1,80).

Müller-Limmroth (1) studied eight subjects (age, abstinence period, ingestion time before going to bed not given) after a dose of 200 mg caffeine. Sleep was disturbed by caffeine during the first 3 hours, but sleep length did not change. SWS was reduced 18 minutes over the whole night, 17 minutes of which were lost in the first 3 hours of sleep. Muscle tone measured at the bottom of the mouth increased. The results fit in with the general pattern of caffeine-induced sleep disturbance and parallel the average elimination rate of caffeine.

Experimental sleep disturbance was induced in eight healthy low-consumption (≤2 cups/day) students, age 19 to 25 years (mean 21.1 years), who were assigned at random to the various conditions (81). The effects of two other substances on sleep were also assessed. They were asked to abstain from caffeine on the day of the experiment and during the study, not to take naps or to engage in strenuous activities during the day. After two adaptation nights, EEG-sleep was recorded after ingestion of 150 mg 30 minutes before the start of the recordings. A reduction in TST, time awake, SWS, stage 2, and total amount of REM sleep was found as well as an increase in SOL. As for the NREM sleep stages, it appeared that light sleep (stages 1 and 2) increased at the expense of SWS (stages 3 and 4). Again, this occurred especially in the first part of sleep. This effect was stronger when higher doses of caffeine were used. The effects of caffeine on sleep-EEG measures were not always consistent, possibly due to differences in age. In healthy 50- to

TABLE 2. Effects of caffeine on sleep

Ref	Author	Minutes before bedtime	Dose	TST	SOL	WASO	Stage 1	Stage 2	Stage 3	Stage 4	Stage changes	REM latency	REMp
78	Hollingworth	10 days	65–390	–	worse sleep quality with >390 mg caffeine								
90	Mullin et al.	45	130–390			+s							
95	Marbach et al.	15–30	420		intake at 4:00 P.M., 6:00 P.M., and 8:00 P.M.								
25	Gresham et al.	15	350				0						
70	Goldstein	30	150–300		+s	+s			–s	–s			
72	Goldstein et al.	60	300		+s	+s			–s	–s			
91	Schwertz, Marbach	600	800		+	+							
75	Colton et al.	40	150		+s								
92	Stradomsky	60?	200	–t	+	habitual users and abstainers: no differences							
98	Forrest et al.	15?	250	–	+	+							
1	Müller-Limmroth	?	200	0	+	+a	0	0	–a	–a			0
85	Karacan et al.	30	320		+	+						–	+f
24	Brezinová	15	150–440	–	+a	+	+a	+a	–a	–a	+		+a,f
143	Karacan et al.	30	80,160,320	–	+	+	+	+	+		+		
124	Saletu et al.	600	450	no effects on objective and subjective sleep									
82	Brezinová et al.	15	300	–	+	+	+	0	0	0	0		0
84	Karacan et al.	30	80,160,300	–	+	+	+	–	–		+		+
142	Ginsberg	30?	50,140,230	0	0	0	0						+

#	Study		Dose
144	Karacan et al.	30	80,160,320
79	Karacan et al.	30	80,160,320
145	Browman et al.	irrel.	?
29	Karacan et al.	30	320
80	Nicholson, Stone	10	100,200,300
74	Ogunremi	60	480
86	Hirskowitz	30	80,160,320
81	Okuma et al.	30	150
89	Hicks et al.	irrel.	0–≥650
28	Levy, Zylber-Katz	?	260–350
83	Gaillard et al.	15	340
11	Ryu	5 days	1.4–4.2
31	Shirlow, Mathers	irrel.	240 ± 140
10	Hronsky	irrel.	0.65 µg/ml ± 3.16
88	Nicholson	10	100–300
67	Regestein	irrel.	500–1300
106	Johnson	±24 hours	250
121	Bonnet, Arand	?	1200
97	Pantelios	irrel.	correlational

Annotations appearing in the table body:

- 86 Hirskowitz: no effects on spindles
- 28 Levy, Zylber-Katz: sleep complaints in 2 cups/day users; none in 3 cups/day
- 31 Shirlow, Mathers: also no effect on TST as rated by the mothers
- 10 Hronsky: dose-dependent sleep difficulties; stage 1 × maternal caffeine use .28 $p < .05$
- 67 Regestein: paradoxically: subjects reported more sleep
- 106 Johnson: dose given at 5:15 A.M.; no details on sleep
- 121 Bonnet, Arand: sleep efficiency −

TST, total sleep time; SOL, sleep onset latency; WASO, wakefulness after sleep onset; REMp, rapid eye movement period; +, increase; −, decrease; 0, no change; t, trend; ?, unknown or estimate; s, subjective judgment; [a] only or notably present during the first 3 hours of sleep; [b] appears more in the hours 4 to 6 of sleep; [c] appears more in the hours 1, 2, 5, and 6 of sleep; [d] appears less in the hours 3 to 6 of sleep; [e] increase of latencies of later REM periods; [f] total REM time unchanged.

63-year-old subjects after a dose of 300 mg, Brezinová et al. (24) found less time spent in stages 2, 3 + 4, but not in REM time, although TST decreased, and SOL and the time spent in stage 1 increased. In younger subjects, aged between 35 and 49 years, Karacan et al. (29) found a decrease only in stage 2 after 320 mg caffeine. In Brezinová's studies (24) in six normal subjects, baseline sleep was compared with sleep after 300 mg caffeine, taken 15 minutes before lights out. Four nonconsecutive nights followed three adaptation nights (cf. 82). The effect of 4.6 mg/kg caffeine on sleep was evaluated in 12 healthy young adults (83). They were recorded for three nights, after an adaptation night. Caffeine increased wakefulness and markedly reduced stage 4, which returned to normal in the placebo night. It was not reported whether the subjects were caffeine deprived and when exactly they took the caffeine dose. In Karacan's study (84) 18 healthy young males (aged 20 to 30 years) were tested after one adaptation night in 12 consecutive nights divided into two randomized periods of 6 treatment nights. Doses were 31, 64, 128 coffee solids (36 mg/100 mg coffee solids) and 4 mg/kg brewed in 150 ml hot water. Except for the lowest dose, coffee and caffeine decreased TST and the percentage of stage 4 and increased the percentage of stages 0 and 1, REM in the first sleep-cycle, and the number of sleep-awakenings. The number of stage changes increased as well, but only for the high coffee dose. A completely dose-dependent relationship was found for TST. There were no differences between natural coffee and caffeine only. Four of eight healthy male medical students aged 21 to 29 years reported sleep difficulties if they drank coffee shortly before retiring; four reported no effects (85). Twelve consecutive nights were spent in the laboratory, in a counterbalanced order of three baseline nights (BL) and 2 × 4 treatment nights with 128 mg coffee solids/kg (±4 cups) dissolved in 150 ml hot water or without coffee solids as placebo. On BL nights the subjects drank nothing. EEG sleep parameters were supplemented with pre- and post-sleep questionnaires. On nights with caffeine, there were significantly more stage shifts, awakenings, REM periods, a longer latency to the first REM-p, increased time between REM-p, and latency to the first awakening relative to the BL. In addition the subjects felt less comfortable, had more restless sleep, and felt less rested in the morning. There were no significant differences between the BL and decaffeinated (DC) nights, but subjects estimated they slept longer on the DC night than the BL night. The difference in reported sensitivity to caffeine was not related to changes in EEG parameters and questionnaire responses.

An extensive collection of data from 16 studies was summarized (86) to evaluate the effects of a variety of drugs, including caffeine, on sleep spindle activity during stage 2 and NREM sleep (stage 2, 3, and 4) in eight normal subjects. Drinking caffeinated beverages was prohibited after 7:00 P.M., retiring and arising times were as at home. Caffeine 1.1 mg, 2.2 mg or 4.4 mg/kg was mixed with 100 mg of coffee solids in 150 ml hot water and ingested 30 min before sleep. Caffeine gave a marginal decrease ($p < 0.10$) in average spindle length and number (86,87) but only at the low dose, which was ascribed to random causes, such as a statistical artifact. Compared to the placebo, less delta activity was found overall and in the 2-cup and 4-cup equivalent, but not in the low-dose groups.

Modulations of the characteristics of sleep are interrelated so it is difficult to assess the effect of caffeine independently on each of these aspects. An interesting attempt was made (88) on data concerning 50 overnight sleeps with doses of 100 mg (six sleeps), 200 mg (six sleeps) and 300 mg (38 sleeps). The aim of the study was to identify the effect of caffeine on total sleep time (TST) and total REM sleep adjusted for TST. Using a common regression equation, an estimate could be made of the change in REM sleep brought about by caffeine, independent of nocturnal wakefulness or decreased TST. The fraction of total REM sleep spent in 100-minute intervals from sleep onset was significantly less compared to the placebo in the intervals 300 to 400 and 400 to 500 minutes, 25.3 versus 33.7 minutes ($p < 0.001$) and 17.2 versus 25.9 minutes respectively ($p < 0.05$). However, when corrected for TST, there was no difference. Caffeine significantly reduced TST (-9.9%), the length of the second REM-period (36.2%), stage 2 (-13.5%) and stages 3 + 4 or SWS (-19.2%), and increased time awake ($+169\%$) and the time spent in stage 1 ($+21.9\%$).

In summary, sleep quality measured objectively by EEG measures is impaired by moderate doses of caffeine. Sleep after coffee ingestion is characterized by serious restlessness as is borne out by an increased SOL, and light sleep (stages 1 and 2), and diminished sleep depth. These changes are particularly evident in the first part of sleep. This picture is completed by more stage changes, more and longer awakenings, and a lower sleep efficiency, predominantly caused by a lengthened SOL. TST decreases dose dependently. Since generally subjects themselves are aware of wake periods during sleep, changes in TST and SOL correspond well with subjective judgment of sleep quality (79,80,89). The number of stage changes tends to increase, although not always (80,82). The latency to the first REM-p is shortened by caffeine, sometimes dose dependently (84) and, occasionally, the later REM-p are delayed (80). REM pressure increases particularly in the first part of the night, but there are exceptions (24,25,85). Caffeine induces a fragmented REM sleep and sometimes a REM rebound.

Motility, Body Temperature and Heart and Respiratory Rate

Body Motility

Changes in body motility and temperature induced by caffeine during sleep have received little attention (24,90–92). Mullin et al. (90) used doses from two (130 mg) to six (390 mg) grains. The doses were ingested 45 to 60 minutes before retiring on three consecutive nights. Markedly increased motility, albeit not tested statistically, was observed notably in the first half of sleep and was ascribed to the inability of the subject to fall asleep. In a double-blind design (91) 12 subjects (age unknown) came to the laboratory for three consecutive 40-hour stays at intervals of 32 hours. The subjects were unaware of the nature of the study. They were told that the study was being done to assess the effects of vitamins on work aptitude. Treatments were placebo (lactose) and four times 200 mg caffeine daily, based on the subjects' estimated average daily ingestion of four cups. The doses were given at 2:00 A.M., 8:00 A.M., 2:00 P.M., and 8:00 P.M. after a 10-hour abstinence period. A vigilance task, a moderately heavy physical task, and a psychomotor task were each performed four times in a chamber (32°C, 50% relative humidity) to simulate work conditions. Caffeine induced an increase in body temperature and motility but a decrease in heart rate. The effects on sleep were characterized by a greater restlessness due to longer SOL and more awakenings.

Müller-Limmroth (1) found that the tonus of the gross musculature was elevated during REM sleep, but not in the initial stages of sleep. In another study (89) sleep motility was studied double-blind in 90 male subjects (15 to 85 years; mean 42 years) after having ingested 200 mg commercially available coffee or caffeine-free coffee between 8:00 and 8:30 P.M. In addition to longer SOL, there was a tendency to a shorter TST, and more awakenings due to caffeine. Motility was increased similarly from the first hour of sleep (+100%) to the last hour of sleep (+88%). Effects on motility again show that caffeine is related to increased restlessness throughout the night.

The literature offers two interpretations. Müller-Limmroth (1) states that caffeine increases muscle tonus (cf. 93) and, since muscular tension is an expression of emotions, caffeine increases emotional tension. Levenson and Bick (94) ascribe the greater contraction of the striated muscles, including the cardiac muscle, after caffeine intake to a lowered reflex threshold, which is monophasic with lower caffeine doses but biphasic with higher doses: first a lowering, then a heightening. Mullin et al. (90), however, concluded, from the literature and their own experiment with children, that caffeine causes only a monophasic dose-dependent threshold lowering of muscle tone. Taken together it appears that caffeine increases motility throughout sleep.

Body Temperature

Caffeine raises body temperature by 0.3°C throughout the night (91). However, this effect occurs only after intake of 190 mg caffeine (1). Without caffeine, body temperature during sleep is about 1°C lower than during the day. Since worse sleep quality is associated with a smaller temperature decrease, it implies that poor sleep quality goes together with an insufficiently lowered body temperature.

Heart and Respiratory Frequency

Heart rate is lower at night after caffeine use (75,91,95). Colton et al. (75) studied the effects of caffeine on heart rate in 149 second-year students who were divided into nonusers (<1 cup/day) and coffee drinkers (>1 cup/day). From noon they abstained from caffeine and took a 150 mg dose or placebo packets 40 minutes before bedtime. Only nonusers reported sleep disturbances. The mean decrease in heart rate of 3.7 bpm after caffeine in noncoffee drinkers was significantly greater than in coffee drinkers (1.7 bpm). These changes were independent of heart rate before the beverage was consumed. The authors accounted for the unexpected bradycardia as due to either the mild dose, or a difference in tolerance, or the variable interval between the ingestion and the time of observation. Another alternative may be that the effects on heart rate were due to an interaction of tolerance, withdrawal effects, and caffeine.

Marbach et al. (95) studied 12 subjects who had to do physical exercise (1 watt/kg) and a psychosensory activity for 6 hours between 1:45 P.M. and 7:45 P.M. in a temperature of 32°C and 60% relative humidity. The subjects could drink at 3:30, at 4:00, and at 6:00 P.M. during the exercise and after it at 8:00 P.M. The caffeine intake totaled 6 mg/kg, dissolved in water and was given after an abstinence period of 20 hours. Measurements of heart rate and respiratory rate were made each hour between 11:00 P.M. and 7:00 A.M. Relative to placebo (water) condition, no change in respiration rate was found, but there was a significant, progressive decrease of heart rate throughout the night, except for the first hour, which stabilized from 1:00 A.M. until morning. The authors concluded that caffeine has a reducing effect on heart rate during sleep. This seemingly paradoxical effect was attributed to a neutralizing reflex of the vagus (96) by a too-low caffeine dose or by the change from strenuous exercise to a state of rest. Respiratory frequency appears not to be affected by caffeine (95). There has been no report of blood pressure measurements.

Subjective Sleep Quality

It is widely believed that people who complain about their sleep quality should reduce their coffee intake. To test this, Pantelios et al. (97) gave 140 students (18 to 49 years; mean 23.2 years) a questionnaire and diaries to assess the daily consumption of caffeine-containing beverages and their sleep. Caffeine use showed a significant, but low, correlation to TST (-0.22) and lights-out time (0.22) on week nights (Sunday to Thursday). Reported caffeine use during the last 4 hours of the day was not significantly correlated to any of the sleep variables. When age was partialled out, lights-out time and TST remained correlated with caffeine use (0.27 and −0.21, respectively) and SOL with caffeine consumption (0.18) during the 4 hours before bedtime. Higher coffee consumers reported later lights-out times and shorter TST on week nights. The impression was that those who consume more caffeine do not sleep differently from those who consume little or none, which may point to tolerance.

An extensive study was done by Goldstein (72) in 230 medical students who received 150 and 200 mg caffeine in decaffeinated coffee after an 18 hour abstinence period. Prolonged SOL and less sound sleep were found, regardless of whether the experiment was said to deal with hypnotic drugs or was presented as a study on the effects of caffeine. In subjects accustomed to a large intake (≥5 cups/day), coffee caused less wakefulness during the night than in light users.

The hypothesis of a relationship between habitual sleep duration, overall sleep satisfaction, and daily caffeine consumption was tested in 170 undergraduates who responded to a health-habits questionnaire (86). Habitual short sleepers (≤6 hours) used 3.6 times more caffeine than habitual long sleepers (≥8 hours). Heavy caffeine users (≥8 cups/day) had an average of 25% less TST than very moderate or noncaffeine users, and showed lower sleep efficiency (TST/Time In Bed). Sleep satisfaction was significantly related to habitual sleep length but not to daily caffeine intake. There was a tendency for the heavy users to be dissatisfied with their sleep, suggesting that heavy users see their level of insomnia as a sleep problem.

In 42 medical and surgical patients (mean age 46.4 years), 250 mg caffeine or a lactose placebo was administered at 9:30 A.M. after abstinence from coffee, tea, or cola from 6:00 P.M. (98). The effects were evaluated on the patient's report of his sleep and functioning the following day. The poorest night's sleep was reported, as well as the longest sleep latency and the shortest sleep period, after receiving caffeine in comparison to either placebo, 100 mg pentobarbital, or the combination of caffeine and pentobarbital. In addition, the adverse effect on sleep caused more nervousness and sleepiness during the day (see also: 84); but other investigators (85,90) found dose-dependent restlessness only during the night. After caffeine intake, the subjective sleep quality of noncoffee drinkers, indicated on self-rating analogue scales, was 35% poorer than in the no-caffeine and decaffeinated condition, and there was a tendency to be less vigilant in the morning (24,84).

Six healthy 20 to 31-year-old male volunteers had their first experimental night in the laboratory after two adaptation nights (80). After one week of caffeine abstinence, 100, 200, and 300 mg caffeine taken at "lights out" had no effects on sleepiness rated on a 100 mm analogue scale. The EEG measures showed a longer SOL; less stage 3, TST, and SWS, more awakenings, and decreased REM sleep, occurring only later in the night. The next morning they reported a poorer sleep quality but no change in SOL and wakefulness during their sleep. The results, however, were not confirmed in a second study. In Stradomsky's (92) double-blind study, 42 out of 90 patients reported not feeling rested on waking up after caffeine consumption the previous night. The number of complaints in the caffeine condition rose by two-thirds, but decreased by 10% in the placebo condition and by 25% when decaffeinated coffee had been given. In addition, there were more serious problems in falling asleep (12 out of 90), sleep-through (9 out of 90) and getting up (9 out of 90); in the caffeine-free condition no problems were reported.

Satisfaction with one's own sleep seems closely related to the time spent sleeping but not to the amount of coffee used, as was noted in students (99). This relationship between caffeine and sleep satisfaction is found only with high doses of caffeine. With 600 mg of caffeine, TST decreased by 1 hour, and there was a clear tendency to describe sleep as less satisfying. Thus, while there is a dose-dependent relationship with TST, dissatisfaction with one's own sleep starts only with relatively higher doses while with lower doses this association is not always found. In other words, sleeping time may be reduced without this having any direct negative effects on subjective sleep quality. The tentative conclusion is that subjective sleep quality is affected negatively by caffeine, notably with higher doses (>400 mg), and most prominently for SOL, sleep length, and awakenings at night. With light-to-moderate doses (<300 mg) these effects are inconsistent and less prevalent in habitual consumers.

CAFFEINE AND WAKEFULNESS

The level of arousal fluctuates daily from a low level early in the morning (4:00 to 5:00 A.M.) to a peak in the afternoon. Hence, to reliably evaluate the effects of caffeine on wakefulness and alertness, the level of arousal in its circadian fluctuation needs to be determined. Unfortunately, an attempt has not always been made to establish the level of arousal at the time of measurement. Another problem is the concept of wakefulness. One might say that wakefulness is the probability of not falling asleep. An accepted method to assess wakefulness or its reverse, drowsiness, is the multiple sleep latency test (MSLT), designed by Carskadon et al. (100) to measure in a standard setting the likelihood of falling asleep by using EEG recordings as the criterion (Fig. 2). The degree of wakefulness can also be evaluated by asking subjects to indicate their degree of wakefulness or sleepiness on a standardized measure, e.g., the Stanford sleepiness scale (SSS) (101).

A third frequently used method is to determine the change in mood, e.g., with the profile of mood states (POMS) (102); a scale with the factors, vigour, fatigue, tension, depression and anger. Further deductions of the effects of

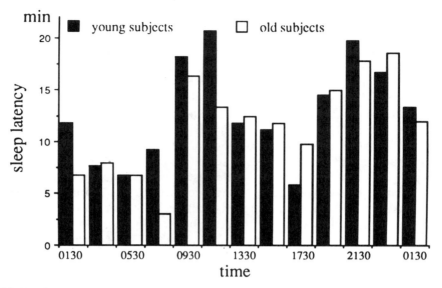

FIG. 2. Mean sleep latency on Multiple Sleep Latency Tests (MSLT) of 8 young subjects and 10 old subjects. (Based on ref. 12.)

caffeine on wakefulness can be made from behavioral manifestations during task performance.

Daytime

Effects of caffeine on daytime sleepiness (MSLT) were investigated (103) in 80 naval personnel using the SSS and visual analogue scale (VAS; 50). They were nonsmokers (age 20.3 ± 2.7 years) with a daily caffeine intake of ≤3 cups. At 9:45 P.M. and 5:15 A.M., they received a substance-filled capsule always with placebo in the evening and either 250 mg caffeine or placebo in the morning. Bedtime was from 10:00 P.M. to 5:00 A.M. Sleep EEG recordings as part of the MLST on each of the two treatment days were made every 2 hours between 7:00 A.M. and 5:00 P.M. In caffeine-treated subjects, MSLT latencies were longer, and throughout the day subjective sleepiness was mitigated somewhat, more so in the first part of the day. A conclusion was that the relationship between these two measures depends upon time of day, probably mediated by the subject's arousal level. Diurnal variations in caffeine's effects on alertness and cognitive function were assessed in ten healthy men (aged 19 to 28; caffeine intake <3 cups/day) (104). Seven days before the study, they were asked to maintain a regular sleep schedule and to refrain from caffeine intake. Following baseline testing (BL), the subjects came to the laboratory at 8:00 A.M. from day 1 to 13 and drank a caffeinated beverage (250 mg) or a caffeine-free beverage at 8:30 A.M. On these days, auditory evoked potentials (AEP) were recorded at 8:00 A.M., 2:30 and 4:30 P.M.; the MSLT was administered at 10:00 A.M., 12:00, 2:00, 4:00, and 6:00 P.M. The subjects were more alert on day 1, and mean MSLT sleepiness as well as naps differed between BL and day 1. This activation was also evident after repeated exposure on day 13, at a lower but still significantly higher level than BL. The lower alertness at mid-afternoon (data at 2:00 and 4:00 P.M. combined), compared to the other times on day 13, suggested the development of tolerance at a susceptible time of day. This was corroborated with the AEP-findings.

Johnson et al. (105) studied the effect of 250 mg caffeine and benzodiazepines on sleepiness (MSLT, VAS, and SSS), cognitive and psychomotor performance, and mood (POMS). Caffeine was effective in reducing sleepiness and performance impairments caused by a benzodiazepine treatment the following day. Mood did not change. In a similar set-up with identical doses (106), higher subjective sleepiness was associated with poorer mood and poorer performance. Caffeine reduced these relationships, most obviously in the early morning.

In 24 male students (normal sleepers, nonsmokers 21 to 36 years old, with a daily caffeine intake of <250 mg) the alerting effect of caffeine was assessed with the MSLT at different times of day (107). Caffeine (250 mg dissolved in 300 ml hot water or 97% caffeine free instant coffee) or decaffeinated instant coffee was given at 9:00 A.M. and 1:00 P.M. The MSLT was administered at 10:00 A.M., 12:00, 2:00, and 4:00 P.M. Analysis of variance revealed that caffeine, compared to placebo, improved alertness and auditory vigilance. Although the sleep-latency in the caffeine group diminished 3 hours posttreatment, the latencies remained above those of the placebo treatment, indicating that caffeine increased wakefulness and that this effect diminished over time.

In another similar experiment, sleep restriction until 2:30 A.M. was introduced (108). Sleep latency was approximately 4 minutes longer with the 300 mg dose than with 0 mg dose. There was no sleep-restriction-dose interaction. This suggests that the basal level of sleepiness does not interact with the alerting effects of caffeine. In other words, caffeine up to 300 mg produces the same amount of increased wakefulness when the basal sleepiness level is normal as when it is significantly increased (cf. 109,110). Twenty female subjects, aged ±42.2 years were given a dose of 0, 150, or 450 mg caffeine in 100 ml grapefruit juice or decaffeinated coffee in the late afternoon (110). They were tested in a continuous speed and monetarily reinforced information-processing task. Fatigue-induced performance decrements were significant across sessions but, interestingly, no interaction was found between arousal state and caffeine. Corresponding results were found by Regina et al. (111), Plath et al. (108), and more recently by Lorist and Snel (112) in well-rested and fatigued subjects, implying that caffeine can possibly improve performance beyond mere compensation for fatigue. Effects of caffeine on vigilance, an index of wakefulness, are in general positive. Twenty nonfatigued, 18 to 47 years old healthy males abstained from caffeine for 12 hours (plasma level 0.3 μg/ml) (113). The doses ran from 0, 32, 64, to 256 mg and were ingested at 8:00 A.M. Subsequently, subjects raised their mood (POMS and VAS), sleepiness (SSS) and anxiety. A battery of performance and mood tests were used, based on previous studies and with proven sensitivity to caffeine. All testing was done between 8:40 and 11:00 A.M. Caffeine significantly increased vigilance and decreased visual reaction time (see also 114).

The effects of a placebo or 250 mg and 500 mg caffeine capsules were assessed (115) in nine healthy habitual coffee drinkers (range 230 to 670 mg; mean 428 ± 146 mg, 18 to 40 years). Before testing they abstained from caffeine for 24 hours. One to 2 hours after intake, several biochemical and physiological parameters and self-rating of alertness all pointed to an increased level of arousal. Ratings of headache and tiredness were decreased by caffeine.

Leathwood and Pollet (50) compared the effects of caffeine (100 mg), tryptophan (500 mg), tyrosine (500 mg), or placebo on mood. Sixty subjects used an 11-item 7-point mood questionnaire to rank the four treatments double-blind, on a sedation/stimulation scale. Caffeine significantly increased the scores for wakefulness, clarity of mind, energy, vigour, and efficiency. Caffeine was found to be the most stimulating compared to the other substances. Dose-dependent effects of caffeine (0, 200, 400, 600 mg) were found by Roache and Griffiths (116) in nine healthy males.

Caffeine in moderate doses (≤300 mg) seems to have a beneficial effect on wakefulness in the daytime, in parallel to the metabolic rate. Caffeine compensates to a large extent for sleep-restriction induced fatigue. Increased alertness may in some cases improve performance beyond the level of placebo but apparently only in easy tasks; in more difficult tasks it may impair performance. It is difficult to draw a firmer conclusion since wakefulness has been measured with different methods and ratings of sleepiness may be unreliable because of the unknown validity of some of the instruments used and the possible bias in the subject's reporting.

Nighttime

Walsh et al. (117) assessed the effect of a single caffeine dose of 4 mg/kg in 300 ml caffeine-free instant coffee (±2–4 cups of coffee) administered at 11:20 P.M. to ten normal-sleeping adults (21 to 37 years; mean 30.3 years). Caffeine reduced objective sleepiness (MSLT) and promoted alertness. This study was continued by Muehlbach et al. (118) in 12 healthy volunteers (age 25.75 years; range 19 to 36 years) pretrained to an 80% error-free criterion on a visual simulated assembly line task. On one night they took 300 ml instant decaffeinated coffee with or without 4 mg/kg caffeine added. The

findings on mood from Walsh's study (117) were replicated, except that subjective sleepiness increased significantly in the course of the night, regardless
of condition. Performance was better in the caffeine condition with a trend
($p = 0.052$) to decrease as the night progressed. However, this decrease was
significantly stronger ($p < 0.04$) for the placebo condition. The conclusion
was that the risk of sleepiness-related performance deficits on night shift may
be reduced with caffeine in spite of significant subjective sleepiness reported
during the early morning hours.

The effect of caffeine on the adjustment to night shifts (N-S) was further
examined in eight healthy nurses (age 28.5 ± 5.3 years), who were regular
coffee consumers (mean 5.1 ± 1.4 cups/day) (119). During the first two nights
of a three-night N-S, 250 mg was given at 4:00 and 11:00 P.M. No effect was
found on performance, on TST, or on time of retiring. Caffeine increased the
oral temperature between 4:00 and 8:00 A.M. by a significant, but negligible,
0.22°C on night 3 (cf. 1,91). Sleep quality was rated significantly lower after
the second night of coffee consumption, but a deteriorating trend was observed only for fatigue and vigor on the POMS. After discontinuation of
caffeine during the third night, fatigue and vigor were significantly worse
than on the placebo night. The conclusion was that the benefits of caffeine
during N-S are clearly outweighed by the negative effects on mood after the
caffeine period as a result of poorer sleep.

Puzzling results were found in 28 nurses (mean age 29.2 ± 6.8 years)
(120). The subjects completed among other tests, a 5-point self-rating scale of
alertness filled out before bedtime and sleep logs on awakening. More caffeine was consumed during the N-S than on free days (2.73 versus 1.83 cups)
and nighttime alertness was lower. The correlation between the change in
caffeine intake and the change in alertness for the N-S, rated just before
bedtime, was −0.42 ($p < 0.05$) and for the early morning shift −0.41 ($p <$
0.05). This may either mean that a high level of caffeine intake is followed
by a low alertness level, or that caffeine is taken because of a low alertness
level during the shift but cannot compensate sufficiently because of too low
consumption. More detailed research is needed to clarify the role of caffeine
during N-S.

Only a few studies are known in which subjects were disturbed during their
sleep to assess effects on wakefulness and alertness. In Bonnet's experiments
(121,122), auditory 1,000 Hz stimuli were presented five to eight times during
sleep to measure awakening thresholds and subsequent sleep latencies. Subjects were six normal 8-hour sleeping males (aged 21 to 23 years) who took
400 mg caffeine or placebo at 11:15 P.M. and were asked to go to sleep at
11:30 P.M.. Initial effects of caffeine were marked during the first half of the
night and tended to last throughout the night. Sleep latencies increased compared to placebo at all points except late at night, indicating that the efficacy
of caffeine wears off with time. Effects of caffeine taken in an awake state
during the night were associated with increased wakefulness and alertness.

Hence caffeine, moderately used, might be a useful antidote to fatigue. Again, it was not clear whether caffeine was the cause of increased alertness or a compensation for fatigue. Also, the apparent negative rebound effects of caffeine on sleep, daytime fatigue and vigor call for a more thorough analysis of its efficacy in situations of sustained wakefulness and sleep deprivation.

DISCUSSION

Some investigators suggest that effects of caffeine on sleep cannot be revealed below a dosage of 200 mg, even when administered shortly before sleep. To allow firmer conclusions more variable and higher doses are recommended. Nevertheless doses <200 mg are useful to assess at which dose exactly sleep complaints develop. A general point of criticism that applies to the literature reviewed concerns the administration of caffeine in a situation of decreasing arousal, viz. just before going to bed. Although such a procedure will almost certainly guarantee effects, it is not an "ecologically" valid method. In order to give a more valid indication of the effect on sleep in the everyday situation, it is suggested that, as is usual practice, caffeine be administered 4 to 5 hours before bed time. Because of the average caffeine half-life of 5 hours in the adult, effects on sleep will then hardly be found. For example, Engleman (123) gave 11 medical students each a total dose of 1,000 mg, divided in doses of 200 mg every 2 hours between 7:00 A.M. and 5:00 P.M. after a maximum night's sleep of 3 hours. The results suggested that regular caffeine intake during the day with the last dose at 5:00 P.M. may not substantially affect nighttime sleep (cf. 124). By varying the time of ingestion and dose instead of administering caffeine just before sleep, with doses not exceeding 400 mg, the nature of the effects on sleep complaints will no doubt also vary. The pattern of the absolute changes can be interpreted in a more qualitative way and should be useful for a better understanding of sleep complaints.

In addition, more attention should be paid to differences in effects on sleep and wakefulness due to age and sex. Although it is well known that the general metabolism and the sleep-wake pattern in the very young and the aged differ from that of the young adult, hardly any attempt has been made to assess their impact. Other comments concern the experimental design, subject parameters, and the interpretation of caffeine effects.

Design Aspects

In a deceptive situation, Kirsch & Weichsel (125) made subjects believe that they were assigned to the caffeine condition, while in a double-blind condition subjects knew they might receive a placebo. In both conditions only decaffeinated coffee was present. The treatments produced different and in some instances opposite effects on pulse rate, systolic blood pressure and mood. The results cast doubt on the validity of double-blind experimental drug designs as commonly used, which may lead to spurious conclusions.

Christensen et al. (126) studied the influence of expectancy on the reporting of caffeine-related symptoms in 62 undergraduates. In the expectancy condition with specific instructions on the effects of caffeine, the subjects received a cellulose-filled gelatin capsule that ostensibly was filled with caffeine; in the nonexpectancy condition this was a placebo. The subjects in the expectancy group reported higher alertness, more caffeine-related symptoms (all $p < 0.05$), and 90% of them remembered the instructions compared with 50% of the nonexpectancy group (127). Similarly, some of the effects found in placebo conditions may reflect expectancies on the effects of caffeine (128,129). In conclusion, the way in which subjects are informed on aspects concerning the influence of caffeine may influence the experimental outcome.

Reliability of Collected Data

Gathering reliable and valid data on caffeine consumption is a prerequisite for interpretation of results. However, associations between self-reporting of caffeine use and laboratory screening are not sufficient to guarantee the correct classification of subjects. James et al. (130) obtained saliva samples of 142 first- and second-year medical students and tested them for caffeine and paraxanthine. They found correlations of 0.31 and 0.42 respectively for caffeine and paraxanthine with questionnaires on consumption data. Even poorer results were found by Little et al. (131) in 28-year-old women (mean 3.4 caffeine containing drinks/day). They were interviewed and kept a daily record for four days (mean 2.6 drinks/day). The difference in daily consumption between the interview and questionnaire data was significant ($p < 0.001$). Blood and urine samples were taken at the end of the recording period. Using the caffeine urine assay as the criterion, 17% of negative screens were associated with caffeine use in the interview.

Subjects' judgments of their own sleep corresponded roughly with the more objective EEG and non-EEG measures (124) and were dose dependent (79,84). Estimates of TST and SOL were accurate and showed higher correlations with EEG parameters of sleep than with any other questionnaire item. Weiss et al. (99), however, found that sleep evaluation by patients themselves did not correspond with sleep as evaluated by nurses; for those who experience poor sleep (71), the correlation between objective and reported sleep quality was even worse. Further, nocturnal sleep quality, objectively measured, is not necessarily correlated with subjective daytime sleepiness even in caffeine studies. Johnson et al. (106) found that nocturnal sleep was associated with objectively measured sleepiness (MSLT) but not with subjective daytime sleepiness. Apparently, the subject's expectation on the efficacy of caffeine influences his perception of wakefulness and alertness and may be a cause of the discrepancies found with more objective wakefulness/sleepiness measures. The discrepancy between objective sleep parameters and reported sleep or wakefulness may be a source of invalid conclusions.

Interindividual Variability

Usually information on caffeine consumption patterns is given retrospectively, but the actual level is not checked or measured in plasma or saliva. There is wide inter-individual variability in the half-life of caffeine. Relevant factors are age (with age-related changed perception of the smell and taste of caffeine: 132,133), body weight (Abernathy et al., 134; Goldstein et al., 72), sex, pregnancy, oral contraceptives (7,135), and liver cirrhosis (alcohol) (124). In order to draw more valid conclusions, caffeine concentration and metabolic rate should be known, especially in long-term situations such as sleep and during chronic performance tasks.

Smoking cigarettes tends to increase the demethylation rate of caffeine (8,124,136), while caffeine in turn might increase nicotine consumption (137,138). Apart from a stimulating effect of caffeine on the CNS, an increase of the caffeine metabolizing liver enzymes has been found in smokers, shortening or diminishing the effects of caffeine on sleep and wakefulness. Hence, habitual intake of caffeine and/or nicotine should be checked carefully before the experiment, and concentrations should be determined in plasma or saliva.

Confounders of Caffeine Effects

Reinforcing properties of caffeine have been found in several studies (139,140). In Griffiths' 1989 study, six of ten healthy heavy coffee drinkers (140) preferred 100 mg caffeine capsules to placebos under conditions of concurrent availability, and this preference was independent of previous abstinence. When progressively increasing amounts of work were required for a cup of coffee, there was an orderly decrease in the number of cups taken, except for the caffeinated coffee or the caffeine capsules. They concluded that caffeine alone has reinforcing effects and that there are individual differences in both caffeine positive reinforcement and caffeine avoidance. A second conclusion was that caffeine dependency and caffeine withdrawal symptoms may substantially potentiate its reinforcing effects. The results indicate that real or expected benefits in mood or subjective well-being experienced by coffee drinkers contribute to or reinforce arousal-related caffeine consumption.

Withdrawal effects may confound the effects of caffeine even when taking into account time of measurement, consumption habit, and sensitivity to caffeine. The caffeine withdrawal syndrome starts on average after 12-(76,141) to 24-hours abstinence with a peak between 20 and 48 hours and may last one week (139,141). Main symptoms are headaches, jitteriness, irritation, fatigue, and lethargy. Withdrawal symptoms may already start after a relatively short-term exposure from 6 to 15 days with doses ≥600 mg/day and may appear in 25 to 100% of heavy consumers, sooner than in low consumers. Since withdrawal effects may interact with the effects of caffeine treatment, no instructions should be given concerning abstinence from caffeine before experiments to assess the effects of caffeine treatment.

Placebo Effect

In eight out of 14 placebo nights, eight subjects, including the authors (90), estimated their average caffeine intake before bedtime as 275 mg. On an average, two of these eight nights were experienced as extremely restless, with the subjects' estimated caffeine intake rising to 390 mg. Similar placebo effects were found (94) on the auditory threshold. These subjective observations indicate a tendency to attribute restlessness in "placebo" nights to caffeine: a reversed placebo effect. A "reversed placebo effect" was also found by Goldstein (70). When the subjects were told that caffeine was used, wakefulness was minimal. Yet identical amounts of caffeine, offered blindly, caused more wakefulness. The absence of placebo effects may be found when subjects do not know that caffeine is involved. Medical students participating in a so-called "class experiment on hypnotics" or "a clinical trial on the effects of a drug on sleep" (70) received a "hypnotic," actually 200 mg caffeine. The treatment resulted in longer time to fall asleep and less sound sleep. The strength of this experiment was that the subjects were unaware of being given caffeine. However, the fact of having received a drug may have been sufficient to induce a placebo effect. Hence, a placebo effect might be absent in subjects who are accustomed to receiving medication.

Twelve demented patients with a history of sleeping problems were studied in a nursing home (142). A placebo, 48, 138, or 228 mg caffeine did not bring about differences on sleep as rated by the nursing staff. Even more surprising was the fact that three patients improved their sleep duration after the 138-mg dose.

Although the results suggest that caffeine may be beneficial to sleep in subjects who are unaware of caffeine treatment and ingest medication as a daily routine, interactions with other drugs on sleep and alertness cannot be ruled out. Nevertheless, in order to determine the effects of caffeine alone, treatment should normally be given unknown and concealed.

CONCLUSION

The central theme is that effects of caffeine on sleep and wakefulness are dependent on the state of arousal. The implication is that in states of low arousal caffeine will induce stimulating effects, whereas in states of high arousal it may have less stimulating effects or even inhibitory effects. In general, the experimental evidence shows that caffeine in doses up to 300 mg given shortly before sleep on the descending slope of the circadian arousal rhythm will affect sleep negatively. Caffeine given during the daytime, after a normal night's rest, will affect wakefulness positively. Important factors to take into account are age, sex, and personality. Most studies have been done on young adults around 25 to 30 years of age. Hence, when drawing conclusions on the influence of age on effects of caffeine, this particular age group forms the reference norm. In the very young, the circadian arousal rhythm is still in the process of stabilization, and the caffeine's metabolic half-life is longer than in the young adult. Hence, sleep and wakefulness in the very young are more affected. In elderly people, the sleep-wake cycle is stable, but is characterized by low amplitudes. Disturbances of the rhythm tend to last longer, due possibly to impaired ability to return to baseline. In the elderly, caffeine increases alertness during the daytime, and lowers the tendency to fall asleep, but sleep is more impaired than in younger adults.

There is hardly any evidence of the role of sex in the different effects of caffeine on sleep and wakefulness. Since the hormonal balance of men and women differs notably in young adults—and most studies have been done in this age group—interpretations of the effects of caffeine are probably more valid for men. Personality traits too may be a serious confounder in the effects of caffeine, if not controlled for. People who are predisposed to increased behavioral activity are supposed to have a low level of arousal. In this state of arousal, caffeine appears to have beneficial effects on wakefulness, sleep, and performance. In people predisposed to high levels of arousal, the reverse seems to be true. However, the reliability of these personality-related effects of caffeine is affected by time of day and suggests that differences attributed to personality may in fact depend on phase differences in arousal. Daily caffeine consumption is almost always reported retrospectively and is generally not screened in the laboratory. This is surprising since chronic users react less strongly in a nonabstaining state than non- or light users, and withdrawal effects are more intense in heavy users after an abstinence period.

Methodological considerations indicate that caffeine administered double-blind compared to deceptive administration may reveal divergent results. Also, expectancy on the efficacy of caffeine may lead to different effects on aspects of alertness and sleep. Taking these findings together, any conclusion on the effects of caffeine on sleep and wakefulness can only be tentative. At low levels of arousal, caffeine, in moderate doses, appears to have activating effects as expressed in heightened alertness and a decreased tendency to fall asleep. At high levels of arousal, caffeine in moderate doses may induce over-arousal, leading to prolonged wakefulness and impaired sleep.

ACKNOWLEDGMENTS

I would like to thank Dr. Gerrit HD van der Stegen, Dr. Martin Elton, and Dr. Bertie Maritz for their critical comments on an earlier version of this manuscript.

REFERENCES

1. Müller-Limmroth W. Der Einfluss von coffeinhaltigem und coffeinfreiem Kaffee auf den Schalf des Menschen. *Z Ernährungswiss* 1972;Suppl.14:46–53.
2. Yingling CD, Skinner JE. Gating of thalamic input to cerebral cortex by nucleus reticularis thalami. In: Desmedt JE, ed. *Attention, voluntary contraction and event-related cerebral potentials*, vol 1. Basel: Karger, 1977;70–96.
3. Rall TW. Drugs used in the treatment of asthma. In: Goodman Gilman A, Rall, TW, Nies AS, Taylor P. *The pharmacological basis of therapeutics.*, 8th ed. New York: Pergamon Press, 1990;618–37.
4. Bättig K. The physiological effects of coffee consumption. In: Clifford MN, Willson KC, eds. *Caffeine, botany, biochemistry and production of beans and beverages*. Croom Helm: London, Sydney, 1985;394–439.
5. Goldman J, Coté L. Aging of the brain: Dementia of the Alzheimer's type. In: Kandel ER, Schwartz JH eds. *Principles of neural science* 3rd ed. Amsterdam: Elsevier, 1992;974–83.
6. Elias PS. Current biological problems with coffee and caffeine. *Café cacao thé* 1986;(2): 121–38.
7. Pozniak PC. the carcinogenicity of caffeine and coffee. A review. *J The Amer Dietetic Ass* 1985;85:1127–33.
8. Barone JJ, Grice HC. Report of the 5th International Caffeine Workshop, Cancun 1984. *Food Chem Toxicol* 1985;23:389–407.
9. Schnegg M, Lauterburg BH. Quantitative liver function in the elderly assessed by galactose elimination capacity, amniopyrine demethylation and caffeine clearence. *J Hepatol* 1986; 3(2):164–71.
10. Hronsky SL, Emory EK. Neurobehavioral effects of caffeine on the neonate. *Infant Beh Dev* 1987;10(1):61–80.
11. Ryu JE. Effect of maternal caffeine consumpton on heart rate and sleep time of breast-feed infants. *Dev Pharmacol Ther* 1985;8:355–63.
12. Richardson GS, Carskadon MA, Orav EJ, Dement WC. Circadian variation of sleep tendency in elderly and young adult subjects. *Sleep* 1982;5(2):S82–94.
13. Minors DS, Waterhouse JM. Ageing and life style—implications for circadian rhythms. In: Morgan E, ed. *Chronobiology of Medicine—Basic Research and Applications*. Eur Soc Chronobiol. Frankfurt am Main: Lang, 1990.
14. Fanelli MT. Stevenhagen KJ. Characterizing consumption pattern by food frequency methods: core foods and variety of foods in diets of older Americans. *J Am Diet Assoc* 1985; 85(12):1570–6.
15. Armstrong-Esther CA, Bonner AB, Browne KD, Hawkins L. Cognitive impairment in the elderly and its relationship to their circadian rhythms. In: Morgen E, ed. *Chronobiology and medicine—basic research and applications*. Eur Soc Chronobiol. Frankfurt am Main: Lang, 1990.
16. Wever RA. *The circadian system of man. Results of experiments under temporal isolation*. New York: Springer Verlag, 1979.

17. Brown FM, Graeber RC. *Rhythmic aspects of behavior*. Hillsdale, New Jersey: Lawrence Erlbaum Ass, 1982.
18. Prinz PN. Sleep changes with aging. In: Eisdorfer C, Fann WE, eds. *Psychopharmacology of Aging*, New York: Spectrum Publications, Inc. 1980;1–12.
19. Prinz PN, Dustman RE, Emmerson R. Electrophysiology and aging. In: Birren JE, Schaie KW, eds. *Handbook of the psychology of aging*, 3rd ed. New York: Academic Press, 1990;135–47.
20. Miles LE, Dement WC. Sleep and aging. *Sleep* 1980;3(2):119–220.
21. Rediehs MH, Reis JS, Creason NS. Sleep in old age: focus on gender differences. *Sleep* 1990;13(5):410–24.
22. Swaab DF. *Aging of the brain and Alzheimer's disease*. Amsterdam: Elsevier, 1986.
23. Prinz PN, Vitiello MV, Smallwood RG, Schoene RB, Halter JB. Plasma norepinephrine in normal young and aged men: relationship with sleep. *J Geront* 1984;39(5):561–7.
24. Brezinová V. Effect of caffeine on sleep: EEG study in late middle age people. *Br J Clin Pharm* 1974;1:203–8.
25. Gresham SC, Webb WB, Williams RL. Alcohol and caffeine: effect on inferred visual dreaming. *Science* 1963;140:1226–7.
26. Kalow W. Variability of caffeine metabolism in humans. *Arzneim-Forsch/Drug Research* 1985;35:319–24.
27. Grant DM, Tang BK, Kolow W. Variability in caffeine metabolism. *Clin Pharmacol Ther* 1983;33:591–601.
28. Levy MD, Zylber-Katz E. Caffeine metabolism and coffee-attributed sleep disturbances. *Clin Pharmacol Ther* 1983;33:770–5.
29. Karacan I, Thornby JL, Salis P, et al. The effect of natural coffee, decaffeinated coffee and caffeine in normal middle-aged men. *Sleep Res* 1977;6:73.
30. Jacobson BK, Hansen V. Caffeine and health. *Br Med J Clin Res* 1988;296(6617):291.
31. Shirlow MJ, Mathers CD. A study of caffeine consumption and symptoms: indigestion, palpitations, tremor, headache and insomnia. *Int J Epidem* 1985;14:239–48.
32. Arnold ME, Petros TV, Beckwith BE, Coons G, Norman N. The effects of caffeine, impulsivity, and sex on memory for word lists. *Physiol Behav* 1987;41(1):25–30.
33. Carmody TP, Brischetto CS, Matarazzo JD, O'Donnell RP, Conner WE. Co-concurrent use of cigarettes, alcohol, and coffee in healthy, community-living men and women. *Health Psychol* 1985;4(4):323–35.
34. Eysenck HJ. *The biological basis of personality*. Springfield: Thomas, 1967.
35. Eysenck MW. *Attention and arousal*. Berlin: Springer Verlag, 1982.
36. Gilliland K. The interactive effect of introversion-extraversion with caffeine induced arousal on verbal performance. *J Res Personality* 1980;14:482–92.
37. Gupta U. Personality, caffeine and human cognitive performance. *Pharmacopsychoecologia* 1988;1(2):79–84.
38. Perez Sanchez J. Variables de personalidad y consumo de cafe. *Revista de Psicologia General y Aplicada*. 1986;41(1):127–34.
39. Andrucci GL, Archer RP, Pancoast DL. The relationship of MMPI and sensation seeking scales to adolescent drug use. *J Personality Assessment* 1989;53(2):253–66.
40. Anderson KJ, Revelle W, Lynch MJ. Caffeine, impulsivity and memory scanning: a comparison of two explanations for the Yerkes-Dodson Effect. *Motivation & Emotion* 1989; 13(1):1–20.
41. Bowyer PA, Humphreys MS, Revelle W. Arousal and recognition memory; the effects of impulsivity, caffeine and time on task. *Personality & Individual Differences* 1983;4(1): 41–9.
42. Terry WS, Phifer B. Caffeine and memory performance on the AVLT. *J Clin Psychol* 1986;42(6):860–3.
43. Gupta U, Gupta BS. Caffeine differentially affects kinesthetic after effect in high and low impulsives. *Psychopharmacology* 1990;102(1):102–5.
44. Anderson KJ, Revelle W. Impulsivity, caffeine and proof reading: a test of the Easterbrook hypothesis. *J Exp Psychol: Human Perc Perf* 1982;8(4):614–24.
45. Anderson KJ, Revelle W. The interactive effects of caffeine, impulsivity and task demands on a visual search task. *Personality and individual differences* 1983;4(2):127–34.
46. Erikson GC, Hager LB, Houseworth C, Dungan J, Petros T, Beckwith BE. The effects of caffeine on memory for word lists. *Physiol Behav* 1985;35(1):47–51.

47. Revelle W, Humphreys MS, Simon L, Gilliland K. The interactive effects of personality, time of day and caffeine: a test of the arousal model *J Exp Psychol Gen* 1980;109(1):1–31.
48. Smith AP, Rusted JM, Eaton-Williams P, Savory M, Leathwood P. Effects of caffeine given before and after lunch on sustained attention. *Neuropsychobiol* 1990;23(3):160–3.
49. Mavlee V. Sleepiness, time of day, boredom and room temperture. In: Horne J, ed. *Sleep '90 Proceedings of the Xth European Congress on Sleep Research*, Strassbourg 1990. Bochum: Pontenagel Press, 1990;55–8.
50. Leathwood PD, Pollet P. Diet-induced mood changes in normal populations. *J Psychia Res* 1983;17(2):147–54.
51. Hill CM, Hill JC. Influence of time of day on response to the profile of mood states. *Perceptual Motor Skills* 1991;72:434.
52. Hill DW, Smith JC. Effect of time of day on the relationship between mood state, anaerobic power, and capacity. *Perceptual Motor Skills* 1991;72:83–7.
53. Arnetz BB, Akerstedt T, Anderzen I. Sleepiness in physicians on night call duty. *Work & Stress* 1990;4(1):71–3.
54. Gillberg M. The effects of two alternative timings of a one-hour nap on early morning performance. *Biol Psychol* 1984;19(1):45–54.
55. Tilley AJ, Warren P. Retrieval from semantic memory during a night without sleep. *Quarterly J Exp Psychol* 1984;36A(2):281–9.
56. Rogers AS, Spencer MB, Stone BM, Nicholson AN. The influence of a 1 h nap on performance overnight. *Ergonomics* 1989;32(10):1193–205.
57. Borland RG, Rogers AS, Nicholson AN, Pascoe PA, Spencer MB. Performance overnight in shiftworkers operating a day-night schedule. *Av Sp Envir Med* 1986;57(3):241–9.
58. Reichard CC, Elder ST. The effects of caffeine on reaction time in hyperkinetic and normal children. *Am J Psychiatry* 1977;134(2):144–8.
59. Harvey DH, Marsh RW. The effects of de-caffeinated coffee versus whole coffee on hyperactive children. *Developmental Med & Child Neurol* 1978;20(1):81–6.
60. Firestone P, Poitras-Wright H, Douglas V. The effects of caffeine on hyperactive children. *J Learning Disabilities* 1978;11(3):133–41.
61. Conners CK. The acute effects of caffeine on evoked response, vigilance, and activity level in hyperkinetic children. *J Abn Child Psychol* 1979;7(2):145–51.
62. Zahn TP, Rapoport JL. Acute autonomic nervous system effects of caffeine in prepubertal boys. *Psychopharmacol* 1987;91:40–1.
63. Elkins RN, Rapoport JL, Zahn TP, et al. Acute effects of caffeine in normal prepubertal boys. *Am J Psychiatry* 1981;138(2):178–83.
64. Cines BM, Rozin P. Some aspects of the liking for hot coffee and coffee flavor. *Appetite* 1982;31(1):23–34.
65. Pilette WL. Caffeine: psychiatric grounds for concern. *J Psychiatric Nursing and Mental Health Services* 1983;21:19–24.
66. Jaffe JH. Drug addiction and drug abuse. In: Goodman LS, Gilman A, eds. *The pharmacological basis of therapeutics,* 3rd ed. New York: MacMillan, 1975.
67. Regestein QR. Pathological sleepiness induced by caffeine. *The Am J Med* 1989;87:586–8.
68. Snyder SH. Adenosine as mediator of the behavioral effects of xanthines. In: Dews PB, ed. *Caffeine, perspectives from recent research*. Berlin: Springer, 1984;129–41.
69. Stern KN, Chait LD, Johanson CE. Reinforcing and subjective effects of caffeine in normal human volunteers. *Psychopharmacol (Berlin)* 1989;98(1):81–8.
70. Goldstein A. Wakefulness caused by caffeine. *Naunyn-Schmiedebergs Arch Exp Path u Pharmak* 1964;248:269–78.
71. Goldstein A, Kaizer S, Whitby O. Psychotropic effects of caffeine in man IV. Quantitative and qualitative differences associated with habituation to coffee. *Clin Pharmacol Ther* 1969a;10:489–97.
72. Goldstein A, Warren R, Kaizer S. Psychotropic effects of caffeine in man I. Individual differences in sensitivity to caffeine-induced wakefulness. *J Pharmacol Exp Ther* 1965; 149:156–9.
73. Sawyer DA, Julia HL, Turin AC. Caffeine and human behavior: arousal, anxiety and performance effects. *J Behav Med* 1982;5(4):415–39.
74. Ogunremi OO, Mamora AO. Cola Acuminata (Kolanut) and coffee: acute effects on sleep of Nigerians. *Psychopathologie Africaine* 1980;XVI(1):69–75.

75. Colton T, Gosselin RE, Smith RP. The tolerance of coffeedrinkers to caffeine. *Clin Pharmacol Ther* 1968;9:31–9.
76. Goldstein A, Kaizer S. Psychotropic effects of caffeine in man. III. A questionnaire survey of coffee drinking and its effects in a group of housewives. *Clin Pharmacol Ther* 1969b; 10:477–88.
77. Winsor AL, Strongin EI. A study of the development of tolerance for caffeinated beverages. *J Exp Psychol* 1933;16:725–34.
78. Hollingworth AL. The influence of caffeine on mental and motor efficiency. *Arch Psychol* 1912;20:1–166.
79. Karacan I, Thornby JL, Anch AM, Booth GH, Williams RL, Salis PJ. Dose-related sleep disturbances induced by coffee and caffeine. *Cl Pharmacol Therap* 1976b;20:682–9.
80. Nicholson AN, Stone BM. Heterocyclic amphetamine derivatives and caffeine on sleep in man. *Br J Clin Pharmac* 1980;9:195–203.
81. Okuma T, Matsuoka H, Matsue Y, Toyomura K. Model insomnia by methylphenidate and caffeine and use in the evaluation of temazepam. *Psychopharmacology* 1982;76:201–8.
82. Brezinová V, Oswald I, Loudon J. Two types of insomnia: too much waking or not enough sleep. *Br J Psychiatr* 1975;126:439–45.
83. Gaillard J-M, Sovilla J-Y, Blois R. The effects of clonazepam, caffeine and the combination of the two drugs on human sleep. In: Koella WP, Ruther E, Schulz H, eds. *Sleep '84 Proceedings of the VIIth European Congress on Sleep Research,* Münich 1984. Stuttgart, New York: Fischer Verlag, 1985;314–5.
84. Karacan I, Thornby JI, Booth GH, et al. Dose response effects of coffee on objective (EEG) and subjective measures of sleep. In: Levin P, Koella WP, eds. *Sleep '74 Proceedings of the IIIrd European Congress on Sleep Research. Rome 1974;* Basal: Karger, 1975; 504–9.
85. Karacan I, Booth GH, Thornby JI, Williams RL. The effect of caffeinated and decaffeinated coffee on nocturnal sleep in young adult males. *Sleep Res* 1973;2:64.
86. Hirshkowitz M, Thornby JI, Karacan I. Sleep spindles: pharmacological effects in humans. *Sleep* 1982;5:85–94.
87. Hirshkowitz M, Karacan I, Thornby JI, Salis PJ, Williams RL. Sleep spindles: results from dose-response studies. *Sleep Res* 1980;9:286.
88. Nicholson AN, Belyavin AJ, Pascoe PA. Modulation of rapid eye movement sleep in humans by drugs that modify monoaminergic and purinergic transmission. *Neuropsychopharmacol* 1989;2(2):131–43.
89. Hicks RA, Hicks GJ, Reyes JR, Cheers Y. Daily caffeine use and the sleep of college students. *Bull Psyconom Soc* 1983;21:24–5.
90. Mullin FJ, Kleitman N, Cooperman NR. Studies on the physiology of sleep X. The effects of alcohol and caffeine on motility and body temperature during sleep. *Am J Physiol* 1933; 106:478–87.
91. Schwertz MT, Marbach G. Effets physiologiques de la caféine et du meprobamate au cours du sommeil chez l'homme. *Arch Sci Physiol* 1965;119:425–79.
92. Stradomsky N. Untersuchungen über Schlafbewegungen nach coffeinhaltigem und coffeinfreiem Bohnenkaffee. *Med Klin* 1970;65:1372–6.
93. White BC, Lincoln CA, Pearce NW, Reeb R, Vaida C. Anxiety and muscle tension as a consequence of caffeine withdrawal. *Science* 1980;209(4464):1547–8.
94. Levenson HS, Bick EC. Psychopharmacology of caffeine. In: Jarvik ME, ed. *Psychopharmacology in the practice of medicine.* New York: Appleton-Century-Crofts, 1977;451–67.
95. Marbach GH, Schaff G, Schwertz MT. Effects de l'alcool et de la caféine sur la fréquence cardiaque et la fréquence respiratoire au cours du sommeil. *Comp Rend Soc Biol* 1962; 156:1522–5.
96. Bolton S, Null G. Caffeine, Psychological effects, Use and Abuse. *Orthomolecular Psychiatr* 1981;10:202–11.
97. Pantelios G, Lack L, James J. Caffeine consumption and sleep. *Sleep Res* 1989;18:65.
98. Forrest WH, Weldon Bellville J, Brown BW. The interaction of caffeine with pentobarbital as a night time hypnotic. *Anesthesiology* 1972;36:37–41.
99. Weiss BL, McPartland RJ, Kupfer DJ. Once more: the inaccuracy of non EEG estimations of sleep. *Am J Psychiat* 1973;130:1282–5.
100. Carskadon MA, Dement WC, Mitler MM, Roth T, Westbrook PR, Keenan S. Guidelines

for the Multiple Sleep Latency Test (MSLT). A standard measure of sleepiness. *Sleep* 1988;9:518–24.

101. Hoddes E, Zarcone V, Smythe H, Phillips R, Dement WC. Quantification of sleepiness: a new approach. *Psychophysiol* 1973;10:431–6.

102. McNair DM, Lorr M, Droppleman LF. *Profile of Mood States* San Diego: Educational and Testing Service, 1981.

103. Johnson LC, Freeman CR, Spinweber CL, Gomez SA. Subjective and objective measures of sleepiness: effect of benzodiazepine and caffeine on their relationship. *Psychophysiol* 1991;28(1):65–71.

104. Lipschutz L, Berman S, Spielman AJ. Acute and chronic caffeine administration: alertness, cognition, and diurnal variation. *Sleep Res* 1990;19:74.

105. Johnson LC, Spinweber CL, Gomez SA. Benzodiazepine and caffeine: effect on daytime sleepiness, performance, and mood. *US Naval Health Research Center Report* 1988 Rept. no. 88–51:1–27.

106. Johnson LC, Spinweber CL, Gomez SA, Steven A. Benzodiazepine and caffeine: effect on daytime sleepiness, performance, and mood. *Psychopharmacol* 1990;101(2):160–7.

107. Zwyghuizen-Doorenbos A, Roehrs TA, Lipschutz L, Timms V. Effects of caffeine on alertness *Psychopharmacol* 1990;100(1):36–9.

108. Plath D, Roehrs TA, Zwyghuizen-Doorenbos A, Sicklesteel J, Wittig RM, Roth T. The alerting effects of caffeine after sleep restriction. *Sleep Res* 1989;18:124.

109. Lumley M, Roehrs T, Asker D, Zorick F, Roth T. Ethanol and caffeine effects on daytime sleepiness/alertness *Sleep* 1987;10(4):306–12.

110. Bättig K, Buzzi R. Effect of coffee on the speed of subject-paced information processing. *Neuropsychobiol* 1986;16(2–3):126–30.

111. Regina EG, Smith GM, Kepier CG, McKelvey RK. Effects of caffeine on alertness in simulated automobile driving. *J Appl Psychol* 1974;59(4):483–9.

112. Lorist MM, Snel J. *Specific effects of caffeine on information processing*. Progress Report PEC-ICO, University of Amsterdam 1991;1–28.

113. Lieberman HR, Wurtman RJ, Emde GG, Roberts C, Coviella ILG. The effects of low doses of caffeine on human performance and mood. *Psychopharmacol* 1987;92(3):308–12.

114. Pons L, Trenque T, Bielecki M, Mopulin M, Potier JC. Attentional effects of caffeine in man: comparison with drugs acting upon performance. *Psychiatry Res* 1988;23(3):329–33.

115. Bruce M, Scott N, Lader M, Marks V. The psychopharmacological and electrophysiological effects of single doses of caffeine in healthy human subjects. *Br J Clin Pharmacol* 1986; 22(1):81–8.

116. Roache JD, Griffiths RR. Interactions of diazepam and caffeine: behavioral and subjective dose effects in humans. *Pharmacol Biochem Behav* 1987;26(4):801–12.

117. Walsh JK, Muehlbach MJ, Humm TM, Stokes Dickins Q, Sugerman JL, Schweitzer PK. Effect of caffeine on physiological sleep tendency and ability to sustain wakefulness at night. *Psychopharmacol* 1990;101(2):271–3.

118. Muehlbach MJ, Schweitzer PK, Stuckey ML, Walsh JK. The effect of caffeine on continuous performance at night. *Sleep Res* 1991;20:464.

119. Koopmans R, Van Boxtel CJ. The influence of caffeine on the adjustment to night shift. *Chronopharmacology*. PhD Thesis, University of Amsterdam, 1990;171–82.

120. Kräuchi K, Nussbaum P, Wirz-Justice A. Consumption of sweets and caffeine in the night shift: relation to fatigue. In: Horne J, ed. *Sleep '90 Proceedings of the Xth European Congress on Sleep Research,* Straasbourg 1990. Bochum: Pontenagel Press, 1990;62–4.

121. Bonnet MH, Arand DL. Chronic caffeine effects on sleep, metabolism, and daytime alertness *Sleep Res* 1991;20:211.

122. Bonnet MH, Arand DL. The effect of caffeine use on mood and personality *Sleep Res* 1991;20:172.

123. Engleman H, Ronald P, Shapiro CM. The effect of caffeine and sleep deprivation on daytime performance. Paper presented at the Xth European Congress on Sleep Research, Strasbourg, France, 1990.

124. Saletu B, Allen M, Itil TM. The effects of Coca Cola, caffeine, antidepressants and C chlorpromazine on objective and subjective sleep parameters. *Pharmakopsychiatry* 1974; 254:307–21.

125. Kirsch I, Weixel LJ. Double-blind versus deceptive administration of a placebo. *Behavioral Neuroscience* 1988;102(2):319–23.

126. Christensen L, White B, Krietsch K, Steele G. Expectancy effects in caffeine research. *Int J Addictions* 1990;25(1):27–31.
127. Christensen L, Miller J, Johnson D. Efficacy of caffeine versus expectancy in altering caffeine-related symptoms. *J Gen Psychol* 1991;118(1):5–12.
128. Murray JR. Psychophysiological aspects of coffee consumption. *Psychol Rep* 1988;62(2):575–87.
129. Bradley JR, Petree A. Caffeine consumption, expectancies of caffeine-enhanced performance and caffeinism symptoms among university students. *J Drug Education* 1990;20(4):319–28.
130. James JE, Bruce MS, Lader MH, Scott NR. Self-report reliability and symptomatology of habitual caffeine consumption. *Br J Clin Pharmacol* 1989;27(4):507–14.
131. Little RE, Uhl CN, Labbe RF, Abkowitz JL, Phillips LR. Agreement between laboratory test and self-reports of alcohol, tobacco, caffeine, marijuana and other drug use in postpartum women. *Soc Sci Med* 1986;22(1):91–8.
132. Murphy C, Gilmore M. Quality-specific effects of aging on the human taste system. *Perception and Psychophysics* 1989;45(2):121–8.
133. Gilmore M, Murphy C. Aging is associated with increased Weber ratios for caffeine, but not for sucrose. *Perception and Psychophysics* 1989;46(6):555–9.
134. Abernethy DR, Todd EL, Schwartz JB. Caffeine disposition in obesity. *Br J Clin Pharm* 1985;20:61–6.
135. Curatolo PW, Robertson D. The health consequences of caffeine—a review. *Ann Intern Med* 1983;98(part 1):641–53.
136. Parsons WD, Neims AM. Effects of smoking on caffeine clearance. *Cl Pharm Therap* 1978;24:40–5.
137. Downing RW, Rickels K. Coffee consumption, cigarette smoking and reporting of drowsiness in anxious patients treated with benzodiazepines or placebo. *Acta Psychiat Scan* 1981;64:398–408.
138. Welin L, Svärdsudd K, Tibblin G, Wilhelmsen L. Coffee, traditional riskfactors, coronary heart disease, and mortality. In: MacMahon B, Sugimura, eds. *Coffee and Health* Banbury report 17, Cold Spring Harbor Laboratory, 1984;219–29.
139. Griffiths RR, Woodson PP. Reinforcing effects of caffeine in humans. *J Pharmacol Exp Ther* 1988;246(1):21–9.
140. Griffiths RR, Bigelow GE, Liebson IA. Reinforcing effects of caffeine in coffee and capsules. *J Exp An Behav* 1989;52(2):127–40.
141. Van Dusseldorp M. Headache caused by caffeine withdrawal among moderate coffee drinkers switched from ordinary to decaffeinated coffe: a 12-week double blind trial. *Br Med J* 1990;300:1558–9.
142. Ginsberg R, Weintraub M. Caffeine in the "sundown syndrome"—report of negative results. *J Geront* 1976;31:419–20.
143. Karacan I, Thornby JL, Booth GH, et al. Dose-response effects of natural and decaffeinated coffee and caffeine on the sleep of normal young adult males. *Sleep Res* 1974;3:56.
144. Karacan I, Thornby JL, Anch AM, et al. Dose-response effects of coffee on the sleep of normal middle-aged men. *Sleep Res* 1976a;5:71.
145. Browman CP, Gordon GC, Tepas DI, Walsh JK. Reported sleep and drug habits of workers: a preliminary report. *Sleep Res* 1977;6:111.

Caffeine, Coffee, and Health,
edited by S. Garattini.
Raven Press, Ltd., New York © 1993.

11

Effects of Caffeine on Human Information Processing

A Cognitive-Energetic Approach

Odin van der Stelt and Jan Snel

*Faculty of Psychology, University of Amsterdam, 1018 WB Amsterdam,
The Netherlands*

Two hypotheses have been proposed about the way caffeine affects human performance, one of which emphasizes *nonspecific energetic* and the other *specific cognitive* effects of caffeine. Consistent with traditional, unidimensional energetic views, these hypotheses have been developed and evaluated in relative isolation. In this chapter both hypotheses are found to be partly supported by experimental evidence. In accordance with the cognitive-energetic model formulated by Sanders (1), it is argued that the hypotheses should be conceived as largely complementary rather than competitive. The effects of caffeine on performance appear to be a function of both the energetic state of the subject and the cognitive task demands. Implications for future research are given, and an experimental example along these lines is presented. The conclusion is reached that caffeine may have selective rather than general actions on information processing.

INTRODUCTION

Two hypotheses can be distinguished concerning the manner in which caffeine alters human performance. The first is associated with Barmack (1940) (2) suggesting that caffeine acts on "some central process or processes concerned with alertness" that function to "allay the development of a bored attitude to a task." Barmack observed that caffeine enhanced the rate of adding during a 2-hour period, but initial adding performance was not affected. It was further suggested on the basis of subjective ratings that the supposed "anti-fatigue" or "anti-hypnotic" properties of caffeine could also be involved, but the former hypothesis was preferred. Barmack's hypothesis refers both to physiological effects of caffeine, taking the form of an increase in central nervous system activation [i.e., reticular activating system (3)], and to concomitant subjective effects, namely that the drug is supposed to reduce feelings of boredom and/or fatigue. This implies that the actions of caffeine on performance are *indirect* as well as *nonspecific* since they emerge only when the subject's state is unfavorable for optimal efficiency, irrespective of the nature of the task demands.

The second hypothesis is associated with Nash (1962) (4) and suggests that caffeine acts directly on "specific neural capacities" that are inherently involved in task performance. Nash examined the effects of caffeine in a large number of short-term tasks and found some performances improved, while other tasks were not affected. According to Nash, the drug effects were demonstrated under conditions of alertness, since the task duration was short and subjective ratings were hardly affected. Nash's hypothesis implies that the effects of caffeine on performance are both *direct* and *specific* because they are observed when the subject's state is suitable or optimal for current activity depending on the type of task used. Thus, although both Barmack's and Nash's hypotheses consist of two assumptions, not necessarily linked, Barmack stresses *nonspecific energetic* functions, while Nash assumes that *specific cognitive* functions are affected by caffeine [see (1)].

This section considers Barmack's assumption that caffeine affects performance indirectly. Thus, the question is addressed as to whether the enhancing effects of caffeine on performance are confined, entirely or primarily, to conditions unfavorable for the maintenance of the alert state. Subsequently, Nash's assumption that caffeine affects performance selectively is examined.

BARMACK'S ASSUMPTION

Barmack's assumption seems to be supported by a number of studies on caffeine involving continuous performance over a period of 30 minutes or more (5–15). The vigilance task has been mainly used. In a vigilance task, subjects are required to detect infrequent and unpredictable target stimuli among repetitive background stimuli. In general, these tasks demand sustained attention, perceptual discrimination, and decision making, but they require little motor action. Performance in vigilance tasks has been shown to be sensitive to a wide range of environmental conditions such as noise, sleep loss, incentives, rest pauses, drugs, etc. and task modifications such as changing the event rate, sensory modality (visual or auditory), or target discrimination type (successive or simultaneous discrimination, sensory or cognitive) (16–20). Vigilance performance is characterized by a drop in detection rate (or speed) as a function of time on task. The decrease in the number of correct detections ("hits") is generally accompanied by a decrease in false detections ("false alarms"). Application of the theory of signal detection has demonstrated that two functionally distinct mechanisms are responsible for the decline in detection rate and false-alarm rate, namely, sensitivity decrement and criterion shifts. Accordingly, performance may fall because the observer's ability to discriminate the signals, or perceptual sensitivity, decreases over time. On the other hand, sensitivity may remain stable, and a more conservative criterion the observer uses in reporting detections, that is, an increase in the response criterion, may account for the drop in vigilance.

The mechanisms controlling the vigilance decrement differ as a function of the event rate and other task parameters. It seems that in visual and auditory low event-rate tasks the vigilance decrement is associated with an increase in the response criterion over time, signifying that the subject is becoming more cautious in making positive responses. In contrast, in high event-rate vigilance tasks, with stimuli every 2 or 3 seconds, when the demand of a high stimulus processing rate is combined with either a memory load, provoked by rapid successive discriminations involving memory, or a perceptual load from degraded stimuli, it seems that perceptual sensitivity declines over time (19,20).

The vigilance decrement implies perceptual and/or cognitive impairment and has been attributed to inhibition, reduced arousal, fluctuations in target expectancy, neural habituation, fatigue, and related constructs (16,17), but no single one of these constructs appears sufficient to explain the major findings on vigilance in the literature. Multiple theoretical explanations may be required to account for different aspects of performance on different kinds of vigilance tasks (19,20).

It has been reasonably well established that caffeine can improve performance in a variety of sustained tasks (5–15). For instance, beneficial effects of caffeine have been found in tasks of auditory vigilance (8,10,12–15) and visual vigilance (6,7,11,13). Caffeine has also been shown to improve long-term performance in simple arithmetic tasks (2,6) and to increase the regularity and stability of performance in a 30-minute letter cancellation task (21). In addition, caffeine can improve performance in prolonged tasks related to the operation of vehicles such as flying an airplane (5,6) or driving an automobile (6,7,9). Typically, the enhancing effects of caffeine in such sustained tasks are less likely to be observed in subjects who have just started the task than in those who have already been working for a time (2,5,6,8,9,14,21). When the duration of visual vigilance performance is short (22), however, or when stimulus duration is long and stimulus rate low, "allowing subjects to take short rest periods during testing, thereby alleviating boredom" (23), no significant caffeine effects have been found.

This pattern of results seems consistent with Barmack's assumption that the action of caffeine on performance is indirect and related to the subject's state of alertness or fatigue. Additional support for this view may be provided by studies showing that, even in relatively brief tasks, effects of caffeine on performance can be modulated by variables supposed to be associated with the subject's state such as personality (24–26), time of day (25), age (22,27,28), or drugs [e.g., alcohol (29,30) and diazepam (31–33)].

Reservations

Despite experimental evidence that appears to fit Barmack's assumption, there are difficulties concerning manipulation and measurement of the state of the subject. One marked problem is that few studies have examined the effects of caffeine on performance in fatigued or bored subjects in comparison to fresh, alert subjects (34). Far more systematic studies must be undertaken that vary the state of the subject through random assignment before Barmack's assumption that the effects of caffeine are state-dependent can be well accepted. Another problem is the complex relationship between performance and subjective measures of effects of state changes. While a caffeine-induced improvement of performance has been demonstrated in parallel with beneficial effects on self-reported alertness, boredom, and/or fatigue (2,5,10,12–14,33), an enhancement of performance without these subjective effects has also been demonstrated (4,11,13,28), as well as a lack of drug effect on performance with these subjective effects (10,28,33,35–37). Thus a beneficial effect of caffeine on self-reported alertness or fatigue may be neither a necessary nor a sufficient condition for a beneficial influence on performance.

Furthermore, Barmack's assertion that caffeine affects central activation, or that caffeine affects "arousal" (24–26,38), is problematic. Relatively few studies on caffeine have measured the stage of activation independently of performance using autonomic or electrocortical measures [e.g., (10,11,21, 22,37)]. Although in some studies that have used psychophysiological measures, the direction of physiological changes induced by caffeine seemed consistent with increased activation, virtually no systematic relationship has been observed between these physiological changes and changes in performance efficiency. It should be noted that the physiological measures used are generally derived over relatively long time periods, and they appear to index the "background" state or changes in activity of physiological systems that are not, or only indirectly, related to the specific neural functions that are engaged by discrete task events (39). Such tonic physiological measures presumably reflect comparatively slow fluctuations in the general state of alertness of the subject, representing physiological changes that are not directly related to the information-processing task. In contrast, phasic or stimulus-induced responses, such as the electrodermal response, the heart rate response, the pupillary response, or the event-related brain potential (ERP), are derived over very short time periods and, through the use of time-locked averaging methods, these measures are assumed to represent physiological changes that are related in time to the cognitive function under study (16,39–41). Phasic physiological measures attained this way reflect aspects of physiological reactions to discrete or distinct events and are possibly more specifically related to the information-processing demands of the task. Unfortunately, these phasic measures have been largely ignored in studies of effects of caffeine on task performance.

Conclusions

Barmack's assumption that the effects of caffeine on performance are indirect, or mediated by an increase in central activation, appears to be supported by subjective and performance data on sustained performance. These studies show that caffeine can improve several types of prolonged performances (2,5–15,21), usually as a function of time on task (2,5,6,8,9,14,21), which can be accompanied by beneficial effects on self-reported alertness, interest, and/or fatigue (2,5,10,12–14). In addition to caffeine's effects on long-term performance as a function of time on task, converging evidence for Barmack's assumption may be provided by studies showing interactions between caffeine and other central state-related variables on performance (24–33). Still, the evidence for this widespread assumption has been inferred rather than demonstrated, because relatively few studies on the effects of caffeine on performance have varied the state of activation systematically or have measured activation independently of performance by means of psychophysiological measures.

Concerning subjective measures, there are indications (4–6,10,11,13, 28,35–37) that the influence of caffeine on performance efficiency has a weak association with the influence upon self-reported mood state, which suggests that the actions on performance and subjective state are, more or less, independent. These findings argue against Barmack's assumption that caffeine improves performance merely by retarding the development of unfavorable attitudes, such as boredom or fatigue, toward the task. Instead, these subjective data seem to support Nash's view that caffeine can enhance performance under conditions of alertness, implying that it can have effects beyond a mere restoration of performance degraded as a result of a suboptimal state.

Corresponding results have been presented by Bättig and Buzzi (11), who found that caffeine improved vigilance performance independently of the decline over time, and a number of investigators have reported beneficial effects of caffeine on short-term performance. In sum, while the enhancing effects of caffeine on performance appear to be most pronounced when the subject's state is unsuitable for current activity, as a consequence of, say, prolonged work, personality, age, circadian rhythms, or drugs, caffeine may also improve performance directly, raising it above placebo or normal levels.

Comment

The results from studies on the effects of caffeine on sustained performance are still rather disappointing. Although the enhancing effects of caffeine on prolonged performance appear superficially independent of the exact nature of the activity, this issue can hardly be addressed since the specific information-processing requirements of the tasks used are by no means completely known, and task parameters that could be involved in long-term performance (16,17,19,20) have rarely been manipulated. Yet, the type of work does appear to play a role in the effects of caffeine on sustained performance because not all prolonged tasks are sensitive to these effects (e.g., 23).

It can only roughly be stated that an important condition for obtaining enhancing effects of caffeine on long-term performance is probably that the task has to be repetitive and monotonous and has to demand continuous attention. As already expressed by Barmack, current evidence has certainly substantiated that the performance in such monotonous tasks is likely to be associated with a decline in efficiency (16,17,42) and development of boredom (42) over time, as well as with changes in both autonomic and electrocortical measures indicative of a reduction in physiological activation with time (16,19). On the whole, however, the studies on prolonged performance provide no information about the specific way in which caffeine improves efficiency, and the aspects of the task that may or may not be involved.

In addition, studies on the effects of caffeine on vigilance have not used signal detection methods of analysis, and only a few report both the number of hits and false alarms. Nevertheless, some studies on vigilance did have a high event-rate and load on memory (e.g., 8,10–13,15), which suggests that changes in perceptual sensitivity as a function of caffeine could well have been invoked (see also 43). Indeed, results in some of these studies suggest an enhancement in detection rate with caffeine and no change in false-alarm rate (12,13,15). Hence, these findings may indicate that caffeine can genuinely enhance detection efficiency, or the efficiency with which stimulus information is extracted, accumulated, and utilized, and it appears unlikely that some kind of strategic change (speed at the expense of accuracy) underlies the effects of caffeine in such vigilance tasks.

NASH'S ASSUMPTION

Nash's hypothesis is often considered less well supported than Barmack's (3). The effects of caffeine on short-duration tasks designed to assess specific cognitive functions have been criticized as inconsistent, subtle, and difficult to interpret (34). Briefly, several factors might have contributed to the obscurity of caffeine's effects on cognitive performance. First, due to the large individual differences in the effects of caffeine on performance (44), and their limited size (6,34), a within-subjects rather than between-subjects design might sometimes have been more appropriate. Second, the nontheoretical nature of the tasks used in studies of caffeine, the lack of replications, and the lack of manipulation of task variables produced results that are difficult to interpret (see 45). The additive factors method (AFM) provides a useful conceptual framework for studying effects of drugs on human information processing (1,45,46). Third, due to the complexity and diversity of the pharmacological actions of caffeine, it appears likely that the effects on performance are mixed patterns of facilitation and interference. For instance, detrimental caffeine effects have been observed on hand steadiness (4,6,31,37) and eye-hand coordination (47) that might reduce or obscure possible favorable effects in tasks involving fine-motor coordination (writing, drawing, etc.) or visually guided manual responses such as pointing (see 48). Fourth, caffeine's effects might be difficult to detect because of a ceiling, either because the measurement scale cannot go higher, or because the subject is alert and motivated in such a way that performance is already at its maximum, leaving little room for drug-induced enhancement. As a consequence, caffeine's effects are easier to detect when performance is degraded by fatigue, boredom, lowered alertness, etc. (6).

Finally, the actions of caffeine on performance can be sensitive to a variety of variables that may affect performance but that are not usually related to the cognitive function the task is supposed to evaluate. These include several state-related variables as outlined earlier (24–33), task variables such as intensity (29), stimulus rate (49), or practice (50), and variables associated with the pharmacokinetics of caffeine, such as dosage (10,27,48), pattern of consumption (22,23) or time after treatment (10,28,30). The latter interaction indicates why it is implausible that the predominant or typical effect of caffeine on task performance is exerted uniformly over the course of its action.

This variety of influences on caffeine's effects on performance has given variable, but not completely contradictory, results. Consonant with Nash's hypothesis, enhancing effects of caffeine have been found on short-term tasks, which appeared to be dependent on the nature of the task.

Nash (4) evaluated the effects of caffeine in several test batteries. Beneficial effects were found on a number of tasks with a duration ranging from 1 to 12 minutes, such as adding, immediate recall, writing expansiveness, and associative productivity containing free-association and word fluency. Caffeine also increased the total number of words written in response to incomplete sentences that had to be finished as rapidly as possible, using a single word or phrase. The author claimed that the drug effects were obtained in conditions of alertness, because the tasks were brief, and subjective measures were hardly affected by caffeine. Nash did not find effects of caffeine in other tasks, which involved for example abstract reasoning, language usage, deduction, time estimation, or detection of arithmetical errors. On the basis of these findings, Nash concluded that "speeded" tests are more sensitive to effects of caffeine than "power" tests.

A similar conclusion was reached in a comprehensive review by Weiss and Laties (6) suggesting that "a very wide range of behavior (with the notable exception of intellectual tasks) can be enhanced by caffeine." Likewise, Lienert and Huber (51) showed that coffee enhanced the "dynamic" factors of intelligence, while the "cognitive" factors were either not, or negatively, affected by the drug. Similarly, caffeine has been found to antagonize the decrement in performance due to ethanol (30) and diazepam (31–33) as a function of the type of task used. For instance, caffeine counteracted the performance decrement produced by diazepam in a digit and symbol cancellation task, but not in an immediate recall task (31–33). Moreover, within the symbol cancellation task, caffeine antagonized the diazepam-induced impairment only when one target, but not when two or four targets, had to be maintained in memory (31). Again, it was concluded that caffeine facilitated the speed, but not the memory, component of the task (31,32). In sum, this pattern of results suggests that the influence of caffeine on performance depends on the specific task demands, which argues against Barmack's nonspecific view.

Reservations and Implications

The interpretation of the previous results is a problem because most tasks used to evaluate the effects of caffeine have a weak theoretical background and questionable validity (see 45). For example, Nash's assertion that caffeine might act upon specific neural capacities as "adding capacity" is not evident. The contemporary view presumes that tasks and cognitive functions are performed by complex aggregates of smaller, functionally distinct processing units (1,45,46,52), which might be differentially affected by a drug. Likewise, enhancing effects of caffeine found on, say, a memory task do not necessarily imply that caffeine did affect memory function.

At first, such an implication is rather nonspecific. Several types of memory can be distinguished (e.g., echoic, iconic, short-term, long-term, etc.) and several subprocesses (e.g., storage or retrieval) possibly differently sensitive to effects of the drug. Second, such a statement can be unwarranted since it is possible that, instead of memory, caffeine enhanced other mental processes (e.g., attentional, perceptual, or motor processes) that to some degree subserve performance in the memory task. In fact, Nash (4) pointed out that the caffeine-related improvement of immediate recall was brought about by changes in the subjects' capacity to "take full advantage of the rapid influx of auditory information, to organize this information so that it might best be assimilated and formed into a stable memory trace." The suggestion is that immediate recall was enhanced by caffeine as a result of beneficial influences on perceptual and/or attentional processes. This implies that caffeine did not have a specific or direct effect on immediate recall and that the effect could also be demonstrated when this aspect of memory function was not involved in the task. In short, the meaning of significant effects of caffeine on most tasks reported in the literature is ambiguous, because it is not evident what a task is supposed to measure and which mental functions are affected by the drug. One way that might solve these problems is to evaluate drug effects within a theoretical framework based on the additive factors method (AFM) (1,46). The AFM assumes that task performance is mediated by a sequence of mental operations or processing "stages" that must be carried out in order to produce an appropriate response when a stimulus is presented. Drug effects on performance (i.e., on the latency of the response) are examined as a function of one or more task variables that are supposed to be related to these specific stages of information processing. According to the AFM, when the effects of a drug and effects of a particular task variable on performance are additive, then the assumption is that the drug did not affect the processing stage associated with this task variable. When they interact, it is taken to indicate that the drug affected the processing stage manipulated by the task variable.

Referring to the memory example above, the suggestion that caffeine affects memory processes would have received stronger support if the memory load of the task had been manipulated and caffeine had shown significantly larger effects under the high- than low-load condition.

The alternative, that caffeine affects perceptual processing, could also have been examined by manipulation of experimental variables assumed to affect this type of processing such as stimulus intensity, stimulus similarity, or stimulus quality. Evaluating the effects of drugs as a function of task variables or components rather than integral tasks may allow stronger and more specific statements about the kinds of cognitive functions that are sensitive to effects of a drug and the way in which a drug alters performance.

Conclusions

Nash's hypothesis that caffeine selectively affects cognitive functions may be supported indirectly by studies showing that tasks requiring "speed" are more sensitive to caffeine than tasks requiring "power." Indeed, the general picture is that caffeine can improve performance on tasks that may be characterized as relatively passive, automatic, "data-driven," or "bottom-up" in nature such as tapping (10,14,28,53), simple auditory reaction time (10,12, 30,53), visual choice reaction time (13,28,33,54), simple arithmetic (2,4,6, 51,53), cancellation (6,21,31–33), and vigilance (6–8,10–15), while tasks that are more active, subject-regulated, "schema-driven" or "top-down" in nature, involving, for example, analogical reasoning (3,4), numerical reasoning (3,30,51), reading comprehension (3,6), strenuous arithmetic (55,56), or short-term memory (10,31–33,36,48,57), seem to be hardly affected by the drug.

It may, therefore, be deduced that more elementary peripheral (perceptual and/or motor) processing operations are more sensitive to the effects of caffeine than central processing operations (i.e., decision making, memory, or translatory operations). Again, the evidence for this deduction is indirect, because most results come from studies that have examined the effects of caffeine on individual tasks with little consideration of the specific processing components involved in performing the task. In addition, the evidence is not entirely compelling because the enhancing effects of caffeine reported in the above studies have not always been demonstrated on similar tasks in other studies (e.g., 31,32,37). On the other hand, the suggestion that caffeine enhances the motor side of information processing is strengthened by observations in a simple reaction task (58) and choice reaction task (28,54) in which caffeine reduced motor or movement time, implying that the drug reduced the duration of processing beyond the central stage of response selection.

ENERGETICS AND COGNITION

The views of Barmack and Nash have been developed and evaluated in relative isolation. They can be characterized by differences in the way caffeine affects performance, and the kinds of mental functions involved. Thus, while Barmack (2) used one long-term task and emphasized that caffeine affects nonspecific vigilance or arousal functions, Nash (4) used several short-term tasks and stressed that caffeine may affect specific cognitive functions. Both investigators share a lack of manipulation of task parameters.

In this section, the sharp break between the two hypotheses and associated experimental situations is questioned, and a more integrative approach is proposed. As a first step, the development of the concept of arousal—from a general system of arousal to specific systems—is outlined. The traditional application of this concept in research on the effects of environmental conditions on performance is debated, and an alternate approach is described, in terms of the cognitive-energetic model of Sanders (1). The implications of the latter approach for the views of Barmack and Nash and for future research on caffeine are given, and an experimental example along these lines is presented. Finally, to consider the possibility that caffeine affects performance indirectly and selectively, some effects of caffeine are modeled on those seen transiently during the orienting response (OR). The OR can be conceived at least partly as an involuntary attention response to salient events in the environment (59,60), or phasic arousal reaction, which may be specifically related to information-processing activities (1,61).

Arousal

The concept of *energy mobilization, activation,* or *arousal* gained popularity in experimental psychology during the late 1950s. This concept refers to the view of the living organism as an energy system (62). The arousal concept describes a hypothetical state that was believed to vary on a continuum from a low level in coma or deep sleep to a high level in extreme effort or intense excitement. This general state could be observed in behavior, expressed by self-reporting, and measured using autonomic or electrocortical indices of physiological activity. Arousal was conceived as a diffuse, nonspecific, and widespread brain process associated with the "intensity," but not with the "direction," of behavior (62–64). The application of the arousal concept to the interpretation of the effects of environmental conditions (e.g., prolonged work, noise, drugs, etc.) on performance usually involved the Yerkes-Dodson law (65). This law states that the quality of performance is a curvilinear (inverted U) function of arousal; that is, as arousal increases, performance first improves and then deteriorates. The additional assumption incorporated into this law is that the decrement of task performance with increasing arousal is more likely in relatively complex or difficult tasks than in simple ones (59).

This application of the arousal concept adequately described the effects of a wide range of environmental conditions on performance, provided a framework for these kinds of observations, and offered a plausible physiological basis for environmental influences on performance in terms of changes in brainstem activation (17,18).

In contrast to the modeling of the human organism as an energy system, another metaphor that has guided much of the research in experimental psychology since the 1950s and that is still the most generally accepted manner of viewing mental activity in contemporary cognitive psychology, is the conceptualization of the organism as an information-processing system. The information-processing approach consists of studying the flow of information through the system, monitoring the sequence of processing, and transformations between input and output (e.g., 66). In its various forms, the information-processing metaphor has guided research on quite complex behavior and has allowed the generation of extensive theories concerning the nature of such phenomena as perception, memory, attention, problem solving, language, and decision making.

A problem for the biological psychologist is, however, that the computer metaphor cannot easily account for the variability and flexibility intrinsic to human behavior, since it is assumed that, in principle, the operation characteristics of information-processing systems are invariant (39). This makes it difficult to incorporate changes in information processing and performance as a function of environmental or internal states. In short, energetic or intensive aspects of information processing have not been well integrated into the mainstream of cognitive psychology (39,67,68).

The conceptualizations of the human organism based predominantly on either "energy" or "computation" notions have had considerable impact on research interests and theoretical emphasis. The two frameworks and associated research areas have been developed in relative isolation, and attempts to build theoretical bridges are scarce in the psychological literature (67,68). Indeed, such a state of affairs is in line with the classical sharp distinction between *nonspecific* energetic and *specific* cognitive functions as determinants of behavior, a distinction that has frequently been used in the history of experimental psychology in terms of "drive versus habit" (69), "energizing versus guiding" (63) or "capacity versus structure" (59) (see 67). There is, however, increasing evidence that the strong emphasis on either activation or structure is arbitrary (see also 70). One line of evidence concerns the concept of arousal. On the basis of psychophysiological research (71–73) and behavioral research (1,18,67,74) a nonspecific and unidimensional arousal or activation concept seems no longer tenable, and a multiplicity of functionally distinct activation states seems to be progressively gaining acceptance.

From General to Specific Arousal

Lacey (71) has criticized the unidimensionality of arousal on the basis of dissociations and rather low quantitative relations between simultaneous cortical, autonomic, and behavioral measures of arousal. In addition, dissociations could be demonstrated within the same autonomic measure, namely heart rate, as a function of the task demands. Lacey proposed different forms of arousal and suggested that the pattern of physiological responses is context specific. Likewise, on the basis of a range of neuropsychological and psychophysiological data, Pribram and McGuinness (72) assume three neurally distinct, but interacting attentional systems—arousal, activation, and effort—that operate upon the information-processing system. *Arousal* is defined in terms of phasic physiological responses to input, *activation* as tonic physiological readiness to respond, and *effort* as the coordinating activity between arousal and activation. Instead of a nonspecific, diffuse arousal system, this view implies several qualitatively different activation states that subserve specific information-processing functions.

Behavioral research on the effects of environmental conditions raised some additional problems for a simple unidimensional arousal concept. One problem is that the direction of the effects of combinations of environmental variables on performance may vary (17,18). For example, an incentive and noise both effectively counteract the effects of sleep deprivation, but, whereas an incentive also reduces the impairment of time on task, noise appears to increase it (18). Another problem concerns the findings that different environmental conditions seem to produce qualitatively different patterns of cognitive change. For example, whereas noise appears to induce a tendency to increase speed at the expense of accuracy, and a decrease in the use of working memory, an incentive generally brings about an overall increase in these indices of performance (18). Similarly, the effects of amphetamines in choice reaction tasks appear to be affected by variables associated with motor activity, but not by variables related to aspects of perceptual processing, while barbiturates appear sensitive to perceptual, but not to motor processing-related variables (1).

Clearly, these data are difficult to reconcile with the idea that all environmental conditions affect one single, general arousal system. Moreover, such findings suggest that the impact of an environmental variable on performance is dependent on the nature of the task demands, i.e., task performance seems to be a function of both the current pattern of activation and the cognitive task demands. Consistent with physiological findings, these behavioral data suggest a strong interdependence between energetic and cognitive aspects of information processing. The implication for a theory of human performance is that both dimensions should no longer be examined separately, but should be related and considered together. Indeed, this has led to models of human performance that assume several, interacting arousal or energetic systems associated with specific information-processing functions (e.g. 1,38,45,73).

One model that aims to relate energetic and cognitive aspects of human information processing was formulated by Sanders (1). This model emerged from the study of the effects of environmental stressors on choice reaction-time tasks that were interpreted along the lines of the AFM. In line with Pribram and McGuinness (72), Sanders' model assumes three energetic mechanisms: two basal mechanisms—one related to input processing (arousal), one to output processing (activation)—and a higher mechanism (effort) that controls the basal mechanisms and is also related to the central stage of response choice. According to the model, the duration of processing in a stage is determined by the subject's energetic state and by computational demands. The principal assumption of the model is that environmental stressors such as barbiturates, amphetamines, and sleep loss have specific rather than general effects on processing stages in choice reaction tasks, and Sanders presents evidence consistent with this assumption. The conclusion is reached that barbiturates act on arousal, amphetamines on activation, while sleep loss may act on both mechanisms.

The major advantages of Sanders' cognitive-energetic model seem to be that it can be used to generate precise and testable predictions and that it provides an alternative method and theoretical framework for considering effects of environmental conditions on performance.

Implications for Research on Caffeine

A cognitive-energetic view on caffeine, performance, and information processing implies that the hypotheses of Barmack and Nash are one-sided and can be conceived as largely complementary rather than competitive. That is, the impact of caffeine on task performance may be a function of both the energetic state of the subject and the information-processing demands of the task. Future research, therefore, should concern the relations between the effects on performance of caffeine, state-related variables (e.g., time of day, noise, drugs, incentive or reinforcement, sleep deprivation, anxiety, etc.), and processing stage-related variables (e.g., stimulus quality, memory set size, time uncertainty, etc.). Psychophysiological measures can be used to complement performance and subjective measures as an index of the subject's energetic state. Of particular utility in this framework is the event-related brain potential (ERP). This tool from the emerging field of cognitive psychophysiology (75) may be useful to evaluate both energetic and cognitive aspects of human information processing (73).

ERPs are small, transient voltage fluctuations elicited in conjunction with sensory, cognitive, or motor events. These phasic brain potentials can be detected by time-locked averaging methods in the scalp-recorded electroencephalogram (EEG). They may be described in terms of a series of positive and negative peaks or components that occur at characteristic times (e.g., N100 is a negative peak occurring approximately 100 ms after stimulus onset). In addition to polarity and latency, ERP components can be characterized by their scalp topography and sensitivity to experimental manipulations. Early ERP components, occurring within 100 ms or so after stimulus onset, have been termed *exogenous* (76), because they seem to be determined mainly by physical stimulus parameters and show little variation as a function of cognitive task demands. Exogenous components are inevitably elicited by appropriate stimulation, and some of the components that occur within approximately 50 ms poststimulus have been identified with neural activity in distinctive structures of the sensory pathways.

Certain longer-latency, *endogenous* ERP components are less sensitive to the physical attributes of the eliciting stimulus. Some endogenous components are elicited even in the absence of an external stimulus as long as the absence itself has meaning or delivers information to the subject (e.g., the omission of an anticipated stimulus). Endogenous components seem to be sensitive to variations in the psychological context of the evoking stimulus and to reflect active cognitive processing of stimulus information on the part of the subject. For example, the P300 component is a large positive peak with maximum amplitude at the parietal electrode sites, which is generally elicited only by unexpected stimuli that are relevant to the subject's task (i.e., requiring a motor response or cognitive decision) (77). Since ERPs are patterns of neural activity at the physiological level and seem to be related to specific perceptual, cognitive, and motor acts at the psychological level, these measures may be especially valuable in psychopharmacological research (e.g., 78).

AN EXPERIMENTAL EXAMPLE

A recent study by Lorist, van der Stelt, and Snel (in preparation) examined the effects of 250 mg caffeine on ERP in a combined visual-attention–memory-search task paradigm (see 79,80). At the beginning of this task, a set of letters displayed on a screen had to be memorized. This set of two or four letters is called the *memory set*. These letters are labeled *targets;* letters not included in the memory set are referred to as *nontargets*. During testing, subjects had to attend to two letters when presented on one diagonal of the screen designated as *relevant* (the relevant stimuli) and to ignore the stimuli presented on the other diagonal (the *irrelevant* stimuli). They were instructed to press a button whenever a target was presented on the relevant diagonal (i.e., a relevant target); nontargets presented on the relevant diagonal (i.e., relevant nontargets) required attention but no motor response. The stimuli were flashed one at a time, in random order, and with equal probabilities; they were presented for 400 ms, and interstimulus intervals varied randomly between 2,050 ms and 2,450 ms. The memory set letters did not change throughout a block of trials. The variables in the study included attention (relevant or irrelevant), memory load (two or four letters), stimulus category (target or nontarget), and drug (placebo or caffeine), which were varied in a within-subjects design. Reaction time (RT) was significantly longer under the high- than low-memory load condition (679 ms versus 557 ms). In the high-memory load condition the number of misses and false alarms also increased. The RT under the caffeine condition was significantly shorter than under the placebo condition (593 ms versus 643 ms), but the number of errors did not differ as a function of drug. The interaction between memory load and drug on RT did not reach significance, which according to the AFM suggests that the hypothetically central stage of memory search was not affected by caffeine. The ERP elicited by correctly detected targets contained a large P300 component that occurred between 300 and 700 ms post-stimulus. This broad positive deflection was most pronounced over the centro-posterior scalp, and less distinct under the high- than low-memory load condition.

In spite of the fact that the P300 component is usually absent when stimuli are not relevant for the subject's task and are ignored (81,82), in the present study a distinct, rather sharp P300 peak was elicited by irrelevant stimuli. Unlike the P300 to relevant target and relevant nontarget stimuli, this late positive peak was also prominent at the frontal midline electrode site. This P300 peak to irrelevant stimuli, probably due to the relatively long interstimulus interval (83) and the passive nature of the ignore condition (84), suggests that the subjects' attention was involuntarily drawn by the irrelevant, obtrusive inputs and that, to some extent, this irrelevant information had been processed (see 82,84). The interesting finding was that, while subjects under the placebo condition seemed to find it difficult to ignore the irrelevant inputs as indicated by the large P300 peaks, subjects under the caffeine condition found it even more difficult. Caffeine had large effects on the amplitude of the P300 peaks elicited by irrelevant stimuli, irrespective of memory load or stimulus category. Caffeine showed only minor effects on the P300 peaks in response to relevant stimuli.

These ERP findings suggest that caffeine increased the availability of energy resources that are more or less automatically allocated to appropriate environmental inputs. In other words, caffeine could have enhanced cortical orienting or *involuntary attention* (59,60,73). In particular this finding shows the utility of ERP measures for assessing ongoing cognitive operations without demanding an overt response by the subject. Consistent with the proposed functional role of the orienting response in human information processing (1,61), the data may indicate that the caffeine-induced reduction in RT was related to enhancing effects on sensory and perceptual processing. In addition, given that P300 latency appears to depend on the duration of stimulus evaluation processes relatively independent of the time required for response selection and execution (77,82), the lack of drug effect in the present study on the P300 peaks elicited by the relevant target stimuli suggests that response (post-evaluation) processes were also affected by caffeine. These findings, in combination with the behavioral data, imply effects of caffeine on the input and output side of information processing but negligible effects on central processing (i.e., memory search and target detection). These conclusions require substantiation in future research.

Caffeine, Attention, and the Orienting Response

Studies of caffeine using tonic measures of autonomic or electrocortical activity (see 22,37,44,53–56,85,86) and behavioral results from studies reviewed earlier indicate that caffeine can increase general alertness or tonic arousal and can modulate slow fluctuations in arousal resulting from imposed or natural changes in state (e.g., prolonged work, drugs, age, or circadian rhythms). Additionally, studies using phasic physiological measures (6,85–87) suggest that caffeine can modulate momentary or short-term physiological responses to input, which may be closely related to changes in attention and may be particularly important in interpreting the effects on both sustained and short-term performance (see 16,17,41,59). The results of our ERP study indicated that caffeine facilitated orienting toward task-irrelevant stimuli. The orienting response (OR) might serve as a bridge between Barmack's energetic view and Nash's cognitive view since it has been considered as a phasic arousal reaction besides having functional significance for perceptual and cognitive processes (e.g., 59,61,72,73). According to Kahneman (59), the OR should be viewed as a loosely organized set of physiological responses, elicited by novel or significant stimuli, that consists of an inhibition of ongoing motor activity, intense processing of the alerting stimulus, and various preparations for future stimuli and responses.

Although the effects of the OR are exogenously induced and are typically short lived, there is some evidence of similarities, between these effects and the effects of caffeine. First, in experimental subjects, caffeine appears to heighten the sensitivity to color (88) and luminance (89,90). An increase in sensory sensitivity is also believed to occur during the OR (91,92). Second, a moderate OR is accompanied by an "agreeable rise in excitement and interest" (92). Subjective reactions of this nature can also accompany caffeine ingestion (93). Third, increases in the size and stability of the OR in schizophrenics have been produced by Soviet investigators through the use of caffeine (92). Fourth, the pattern of facilitation and interference of caffeine's effects on performance seems coherent with the distinction between the orienting reaction (OR) and the defense reaction (DR) (91). The OR has been associated with an increased intake of information (e.g., 94) and enhanced performance in various tasks (95–97), while the DR (which is partly mediated by the same neural systems as the OR) has been characterized by "an attempt to shut off further input" (72) and is related to impaired performance (97).

Fifth, physiological data indicate that caffeine stimulates the reticular formation (44) as well as central noradrenergic and serotonergic systems (98) and suppresses medial thalamic activity (44), brain structures that are presumed to play a role in behavioral orienting (see 92,99,100). Note that these neurotransmitter systems, especially the raphe-serotonergic system, may well be involved in tonic behavioral state changes too, such as the sleep-wake cycle (100). Finally, in experimental subjects, caffeine enhanced the electrodermal response to nonsignal stimuli (85,86), retarded electrodermal habituation (86), and, in a double-foreperiod reaction-time task, caffeine increased the amplitude of the early component of the contingent negative variation (CNV) (87). These psychophysiological reactions have been associated with the OR (101). Additionally, in our ERP study, caffeine showed substantial effects on the amplitude of the P300 peak elicited by irrelevant, but not by relevant, stimuli. In particular, the different effects of caffeine in this study as a function of attention or relevance are interesting because they suggest that caffeine affects the OR to *nonsignal,* but not to *signal,* stimuli.

Siddle (102) suggests that nonsignal and signal OR may possess different functional properties in terms of stimulus selection and information processing. The responses elicited by nonsignal stimuli may "serve to maximize the gathering of information from all aspects of the perceptual field," while those elicited by signal stimuli may "serve to maximize the gathering of particular information by focusing attention on one particular aspect of the field." That is, nonsignal OR may be associated with *involuntary attention,* which is presumed to be governed by enduring dispositions (59), while signal OR may be associated with *voluntary attention,* which appears to be deter-

mined by the momentary task instructions (59,60,61,73). Luria and Homskaya (103) present neuropsychological evidence consistent with this position, indicating that the two kinds of OR have different kinds of cerebral
organization. A neurophysiological animal model for attention constructed
by Skinner and Yingling (94) provides further support for this view. This
model distinguishes two systems that jointly regulate the transmission of
information through the sensory relay nuclei of the thalamus to the cortex.
One system, mediated by the mesencephalic reticular formation (MRF), has
a widespread, diffuse organization and is associated with generalized, tonic
control over transmission of sensory input. This system is reflexively activated by salient inherent features of the stimulus (i.e., nonsignal stimuli),
resulting in a nonspecific facilitatory effect on neural transmission of information to the cortex. A second system, the mediothalamic-frontocortical system
(MTFCS), has a modality-specific organization and exerts selective, phasic,
inhibitory control over neural processing. This system is responsive to derived (conditioned) features of the stimulus (i.e., signal stimuli), suppressing
the transmission of activity to the cortex evoked by irrelevant information.
In short, the MRF regulates the amount of reflexive orienting (involuntary
attention), while the MTFCS seems to control the degree of sensory filtering
(selective attention). Thus, the distinction between involuntary and voluntary attention seems to be well supported (see also 73).

The implication is that caffeine may affect involuntary attention, while
voluntary attention seems less responsive. Indeed, as indicated before, relatively passive or data-driven task situations, associated with receptive attention to environmental events [e.g., vigilance tasks, conditioning paradigms
(6), and orienting or habituation paradigms (85,86)], seem to be more sensitive
to the effects of caffeine than internally driven task situations that require
active subject-regulated attention and complex conceptual operations.

In accordance with more traditional (91,92) and contemporary views (1,61,
73,99), Skinner and Yingling assume that the principal function of the OR is
sensory and perceptual facilitation. As expressed by Sokolov (91), the OR
increases the sensitivity or discriminatory power of sensory "analyzers,"
meaning a comprehensive system that includes the receptors, peripheral
pathways, specific cortical areas, and the efferent system that provides feedback to the analyzers. This function may be viewed not only with reference
to facilitation of analysis of the eliciting stimulus, but also in terms of facilitation of perception of future stimuli (59,101). Given some resemblance between the effects of the OR and those of caffeine, this may imply that caffeine
enhances the brain's responsivity to sensory input and facilitates perceptual
efficiency, which was tentatively proposed on the basis of our ERP findings.
However, central as well as motor effects of the OR have been implied (see
59,104), and it has been argued that effects of the OR pervade a number
of systems, so that "they are likely to transcend individual stages in the

information-processing sequence'' (101), which could, in principle, also apply to effects of caffeine.

Conclusions and Discussion

The effects of caffeine on task performance need to be specified. Since caffeine is a widely used psychotropic agent, it may be relevant not only on the basis of theoretical considerations, but also from an applied point of view to establish the environmental conditions (state-related variables), and the kinds of cognitive operations (processing stage-related variables) that are sensitive to the effects of caffeine. In addition, caffeine's effects may vary as a function of other aspects of the environment (monotony, isolation, etc.) or task (stimulus rate, sensory modality, practice, feedback, etc.), and thus the influence of these aspects needs investigation. It may be advantageous to be able to predict the types of work and variety of states that are likely to be affected by caffeine, especially any that might be adversely affected.

Concerning detrimental effects of caffeine on task performance, a number of studies have demonstrated caffeine-induced deficiencies. Adverse effects of caffeine have been observed on short-term memory (33,49,105). Caffeine-induced performance deficiency has been observed on digits backwards, but an enhancement on digits forwards (4); also, coffee impaired some cognitive factors of intelligence but facilitated the speed factors (51); a caffeine-induced impairment was observed in a novel perceptual-restructuring task, but an improvement when the task was practiced (50); finally, caffeine impaired performance in a visual search task with a memory load of six letters but showed an improvement with a memory load of two letters (106).

At first, this pattern of results appears to suggest that beneficial, but also adverse, effects of caffeine on performance are, in part, determined by the required type of cognitive operations (peripheral versus central) or mode of information processing (involuntary versus voluntary attention, automatic versus controlled processing) (see 73,79) rather than the task itself. Second, these results seem consistent with the Yerkes-Dodson law (65) since detrimental effects of caffeine are more likely in complex or difficult tasks than in easy task situations. The Yerkes-Dodson law can also incorporate the findings that a caffeine-induced deficiency in tasks of moderate or high complexity often occurs as a function of variables supposed to be associated with the level of arousal, such as dose (24,48), personality (24–26), or time of day (25). One problem is that the Yerkes-Dodson law is a descriptive formulation that, without specifications, has minimal explanatory or predictive value. Reformulations of the inverted-U hypothesis, although producing discordant views, have attempted to relate changes in arousal and performance to changes in attention. These reformulations point out that detrimental effects of high arousal on performance may be related to either an excessive narrowing or broadening of attention (107). A narrowing of attention (i.e., an increase in selectivity) as a function of arousal, Easterbrook's hypothesis (108), implies that a performance decrement may involve reduced intake and deficient use of task-relevant information. In contrast, a performance decrement associated with a broadening of attention (i.e., reduced selectivity) may involve a more uneven and less precise allocation of attention (59); increased distractability and more off-task processing such as facilitation of the processing of task-irrelevant information, facilitation of irrelevant or competing responses, or enhanced attention to bodily reactions or thoughts rather than to the task (74,107).

There is some evidence that may be congruous with a broadening of attention as a function of caffeine. For instance, the ERP data from our study indicate that caffeine enhanced the processing of irrelevant input, but, despite this, the substance did not adversely affect the performance measures. However, the interpretation proposed to account for these results was based on the assumption that caffeine facilitated the processing of both irrelevant and relevant stimuli. Although caffeine primarily had effects on the ERP elicited by irrelevant stimuli, it was presumed that the effects on the ERP to relevant stimuli were largely obscured by superimposed effects reflecting the increased processing requirements associated with the *attend* condition as compared to the *ignore* condition. This assumption is consistent with the observation that the P3 peak to relevant stimuli was more pronounced and prolonged than the P3 peak to irrelevant stimuli, as well as with the general observation that responses elicited by signal stimuli are larger than those elicited by nonsignal stimuli (59,91,101). Moreover, caffeine did show minor effects on the P3 peak to relevant stimuli.

A study by Broverman and Casagrande (50) provides more support that a caffeine-induced performance decrement may be provoked by a reduced ability to select input, or to inhibit irrelevant input. In this study, caffeine had unfavorable effects on a novel perceptual-restructuring task in which the subjects' ability was required to "inhibit automatized perceptual responses to obvious stimulus attributes in favour of responses to less obvious visual cues." Given that caffeine enhances activity in the reticular formation (44), this result is consistent with the framework of Skinner and Yingling (94) in which effects of the phylogenetically older brainstem orienting mechanism (MRF) are capable of overruling the effects of the higher selective attention mechanism (MTFCS). In addition, caffeine-induced performance deficiency as a result of increased response generalization may also be involved. Caffeine has been shown to reduce performance in a difficult numerical Stroop task (48) that demanded the inhibition of competing motor responses. This is in agreement with Weiss and Laties (6), who implied that caffeine can provoke a tendency to produce quick or strong but false reactions that need to be suppressed.

Thus, the pattern of findings appears to indicate that caffeine-induced facilitation, or weakened inhibition, of the processing of both irrelevant input and output may be involved in the drug's adverse effects on performance efficiency although it must be stressed that relatively few studies on the effects on performance have found detrimental effects of moderate doses. In this chapter the findings reviewed concerning the effects of caffeine suggest that the principal action on performance is indirect and specific. Caffeine may have specific effects on energetic or attentional mechanisms that control human information processing. There seem to be three major, interrelated functions of attention (109): (a) orienting to sensory events, (b) detecting signals for focal (conscious) processing, and (c) maintaining a vigilant or alert state. The suggestion is that caffeine may affect orienting to produce sensory and perceptual facilitation and possibly acts on alerting to enhance the generation of motor actions, whereas detection, which is related to central and memory processes, may not be affected. In terms of Sanders' model (1), the basal mechanisms of arousal and activation may be more sensitive to the effects of caffeine than the higher effort mechanism.

Assuming that caffeine has both sensory and motor effects, enhancement of performance can be expected when the task or task condition requires relatively simple decisions and reactions. Since it may be difficult in task situations that require rapid and continuous decisions of a fairly simple nature to sustain the attention necessary for efficient performance over long periods of time (16,20), the enhancing effects of caffeine in such situations are likely to be observed as a function of time on task. Caffeine enhances the capacity of smoothly coupling input to output, which may be generally beneficial for ordinary routine behavior. As a consequence, a performance decrement is plausible when the task situation involves complex decisions, or a high degree of central processing, which (in order to avoid fast but inadequately considered reactions) requires that the direct link between input and output be "uncoupled" (1). According to Pribram and McGuinness (72), the process controlled by effort that allows the uncoupling to take place is habituation, which might be retarded by caffeine (86).

Finally, two illustrations are presented how the energetic effects of caffeine may modulate higher brain functions. Luria (60) found that caffeine in a patient with occipital lesions reduced the symptoms of simultanagnosia. This form of visual agnosia consists of an impairment in appreciating more than one aspect of a stimulus configuration at a time. On the basis of this finding, and some other clinical observations, Luria suggests that caffeine may have a direct beneficial influence on visual perception. This finding may also indicate that caffeine acts on visual spatial attention (i.e., orienting) to enhance perceptual function. According to Skinner and Yingling's model, one way by which caffeine facilitates visual information processing is to increase the amount of input from the peripheral visual system to the striate cortex by stimulation of the MRF (i.e., an increase in generalized control) and/or inhibition of the MTFCS (i.e., a reduction in selective control). Another way might be by caffeine acting on cholinergic or noradrenergic systems innervating neurons in visual areas to enhance the "signal-to-noise" ratio of the selective responses of these cells to visual inputs (100,110). Measurements of caffeine's physiological and psychological effects could produce a more comprehensive picture, relating the influences of this substance on the mediating brain mechanisms to their consequences on human information processing.

ACKNOWLEDGMENTS

The helpful comments of Drs. Martin Elton, Leon Kenemans, and Bertie Maritz are gratefully acknowledged.

REFERENCES

1. Sanders AF. Towards a model of stress and human performance. *Acta Psychol* 1983;53: 61–97.
2. Barmack JE. The time of administration and some effects of 2 grs of alkaloid caffeine. *J Exp Psychol* 1940;27:690–8.
3. Bachrach H. Note on the psychological effects of caffeine. *Psychol Rep* 1966;18:86.
4. Nash H. *Alcohol and caffeine*. Springfield: Thomas, 1962.
5. Payne RB, Hauty GT. The effects of experimentally induced attitudes upon task proficiency. *J Exp Psychol* 1954;47:267–73.
6. Weiss B, Laties VG. Enhancement of human performance by caffeine and the amphetamines. *Pharmacol Rev* 1962;14:1–36.
7. Baker WJ, Theologus GC. Effects of caffeine on visual monitoring. *J Appl Psychol* 1972; 56:422–7.
8. Keister ME, McLaughlin RJ. Vigilance performance related to extraversion-introversion and caffeine. *J Exp Res Person* 1972;6:5–11.
9. Regina EG, Smith GM, Keiper CG, McKelvey RK. Effects of caffeine on alertness in simulated automobile driving. *J Appl Psychol* 1974;59:483–9.
10. Clubley M, Bye CE, Henson TA, Peck AW, Riddington CJ. Effects of caffeine and cyclizine alone and in combination on human performance, subjective effects and EEG activity. *Br J Clin Pharmacol* 1979;7:157–63.
11. Bättig K, Buzzi R. Effect of coffee on the speed of subject-paced information processing. *Neuropsychobiology* 1986;16:126–30.
12. Lieberman HR, Wurtman RJ, Emde GG, Coviella ILG. The effects of caffeine and aspirin on mood and performance. *J Clin Psychopharmacol* 1987;7:315–20.
13. Lieberman HR, Wurtman RJ, Emde GG, Roberts C, Coviella ILG. The effects of low doses of caffeine on human performance and mood. *Psychopharmacology* 1987;92:308–12.
14. Fagan D, Swift CG, Tiplady B. Effects of caffeine on vigilance and other performance tests in normal subjects. *J Psychopharmacol* 1988;2:19–25 (abstract).
15. Zwyghuizen-Doorenbos A, Roehrs TA, Lipschutz L, Timms V, Roth T. Effects of caffeine on alertness. *Psychopharmacology* 1990;100:36–9.
16. Mackworth JF. *Vigilance and habituation*. Middlesex: Penguin;1969.
17. Broadbent DE. *Decision and stress*. London: Academic Press;1971.
18. Hockey R. Varieties of attentional state: the effects of environment. In: Parasuraman R, Davies DR, eds. *Varieties of attention*. Orlando: Academic Press, 1984;449–83.
19. Parasuraman R. Sustained attention in detection and discrimination. In: Parasuraman R, Davies DR, eds. *Varieties of attention*. Orlando: Academic Press, 1984;243–71.
20. Parasuraman R. Sustained attention: a multifactorial approach. In: Posner MI, Marin OSM, eds. *Attention and performance XI*. Hillsdale, NJ: Erlbaum; 1985;493–511.
21. Bättig K, Buzzi R, Martin JR, Feierabend JM. The effects of caffeine on physiological functions and mental performance. *Experientia* 1984;40:1218–23.

22. Rapoport JL, Jensvold M, Elkins R, et al. Behavioral and cognitive effects of caffeine in boys and adult males. *J Nerv Ment Dis* 1981;169:726–32.
23. Loke WH, Meliska CJ. Effects of caffeine use and ingestion on a protracted visual vigilance task. *Psychopharmacology* (Berlin) 1984;84:54–7.
24. Gilliland K. The interactive effect of introversion-extraversion with caffeine induced arousal on verbal performance. *J Res Person* 1980;14:482–92.
25. Revelle W, Humphreys MS, Simon L, Gilliland K. The interactive effect of personality, time of day, and caffeine: a test of the arousal model. *J Exp Psychol: Gen* 1980;109:1–31.
26. Anderson KJ, Revelle W. Impulsivity, caffeine, and proofreading: a test of the Easterbrook hypothesis. *J Exp Psychol: Hum Percept Perf* 1982;8:614–24.
27. Cattell RB. The effects of alcohol and caffeine on intelligent and associative performance. *Br J Med Psychol* 1930;10:20–33.
28. Swift CG, Tiplady B. The effects of age on the response to caffeine. *Psychopharmacology* (Berlin) 1988;94:29–31.
29. Carpenter JA. The effects of caffeine and alcohol on simple visual reaction time. *J Comp Physiol Psychol* 1959;52:491–6.
30. Franks HM, Hagedorn H, Hensley VR, Hensley WJ, Starmer GA. The effect of caffeine on human performance, alone and in combination with ethanol. *Psychopharmacologia* (Berlin) 1975;45:177–81.
31. Loke WH, Hinrichs JV, Ghoneim MM. Caffeine and diazepam: separate and combined effects on mood, memory, and psychomotor performance. *Psychopharmacology* (Berlin) 1985;87:344–50.
32. Ghoneim MM, Hinrichs JV, Chiang C-K, Loke WH. Pharmacokinetic and pharmacodynamic interactions between caffeine and diazepam. *J Clin Psychopharmacol* 1986;6:75–80.
33. Roache JD, Griffiths RR. Interactions of diazepam and caffeine: behavioral and subjective dose effects in humans. *Pharmacol Biochem Behav* 1987;26:801–12.
34. Dews PB. Behavioral effects of caffeine. In: Dews PB, ed. *Caffeine perspectives from recent research*. New York: Springer-Verlag, 1984;86–103.
35. Goldstein A, Kaizer S, Warren R. Psychotropic effects of caffeine in man. II. Alertness, psychomotor coordination, and mood. *J Pharmacol Exp Ther* 1965;150:146–51.
36. Loke WH. Effects of caffeine on mood and memory. *Physiol Beh* 1988;44:367–72.
37. Bruce M, Scott N, Lader M, Marks V. The psychopharmacological and electrophysiological effects of single doses of caffeine in healthy human subjects. *Br J Clin Pharmacol* 1986; 22:81–7.
38. Humphreys MS, Revelle W. Personality, motivation, and performance: a theory of the relationship between individual differences and information processing. *Psychol Rev* 1984; 91:153–84.
39. Hockey GRJ, Coles MGH, Gaillard AWK. Energetical issues in research on human information processing. In: Hockey GRJ, Gaillard AWK, Coles MGH, eds. *Energetics and human information processing*. Dordrecht: Martinus Nijhoff, 1986;3–21.
40. Tecce JJ. Attention and evoked potentials in man. In: Mostofsky DI, ed. *Attention: contemporary theory and analysis*. New York: Appleton-Century-Crofts, 1970;331–65.
41. Beatty J. Task-evoked pupillary response, processing load, and the structure of processing resources. *Psychol Bull* 1982;91:276–92.
42. O'Hanlon JF. Boredom: practical consequences and a theory. *Acta Psychol* 1981;49: 53–82.
43. Bowyer PA, Humphreys MS, Revelle W. Arousal and recognition memory: the effects of impulsivity, caffeine and time on task. *Person Individ Diff* 1983;4:41–9.
44. Bättig K. The physiological effects of coffee consumption. In: Clifford MN, Willson CK, eds. *Coffee: botany, biochemistry and production of beans and beverage*. London: Croom Helm, 1985;394–439.
45. Gaillard AWK. The evaluation of drug effects in laboratory tasks. In: Hindmarch I, Aufdembrinke B, Ott H, eds. *Psychopharmacology and reaction time*. Chichester: Wiley, 1988; 15–24.
46. Sternberg S. On the discovery of processing stages: some extension of Donders' method. *Acta Psychol* 1969;30:276–315.
47. Putz-Anderson V, Setzer JV, Croxton JS. Effects of alcohol, caffeine and methylchloride on man. *Psychol Rep* 1981;48:715–25.

48. Foreman N, Barraclough S, Moore C, Mehta A, Madon M. High doses of caffeine impair performance of a numerical version of the stroop task in men. *Pharmacol Biochem Behav* 1989;32:399–403.
49. Erickson GC, Hager LB, Houseworth C, Dungan J, Petros T, Beckworth BE. The effects of caffeine on memory for word lists. *Physiol Behav* 1985;35:47–51.
50. Broverman DM, Casagrande E. Effect of caffeine on performances of a perceptual-restructuring task at different stages of practice. *Psychopharmacology* (Berlin) 1982;78:252–5.
51. Lienert GA, Huber HP. Differential effects of coffee on speed and power test. *J Psychol* 1966;63:269–74.
52. Posner MI, Peterson SE, Fox PT, Raichle ME. Localization of cognitive operations in the human brain. *Science* 1988;240:1627–31.
53. Gilliland AR, Nelson D. The effects of coffee on certain mental and physiological functions. *J Gen Psychol* 1939;21:339–48.
54. Smith DL, Tong JE, Leigh G. Combined effects of tobacco and caffeine on the components of choice reaction time, heart rate, and hand steadiness. *Percept Mot Skills* 1977;45:635–9.
55. Lane JD, Williams RB. Caffeine affects cardiovascular responses to stress. *Psychophysiology* 1985;22:648–55.
56. France C, Ditto B. Caffeine effects on several indices of cardiovascular activity at rest and during stress. *J Beh Med* 1988;11:473–81.
57. Mitchell VE, Ross S, Hurst PM. Drugs and placebos: effects of caffeine on cognitive performance. *Psychol Rep* 1974;35:875–83.
58. Jacobson BH, Edgley BM. Effects of caffeine in simple reaction time and movement time. *Aviat Space Environ Med* 1987;58:1153–6.
59. Kahneman D. *Attention and effort.* Englewood Cliffs, NJ: Prentice-Hall, 1973.
60. Luria AR. *The working brain.* Harmondsworth: Penguin, 1973.
61. Öhman A. The orienting response, attention, and learning: an information-processing perspective. In: Kimmel HD, van Olst EH, Orlebeke JF, eds. *The orienting reflex in humans.* Hillsdale: Erlbaum, 1979;443–71.
62. Duffy E. *Activation and behavior.* New York: Wiley, 1962.
63. Hebb DO. Drives and the C.N.S. (conceptual nervous system). *Psychol Rev* 1955;62:243–54.
64. Malmo RB. Activation: a neuropsychological dimension. *Psychol Rev* 1959;66:367–86.
65. Yerkes RM, Dodson JD. The relation of strength of stimulus to rapidity of habit formation. *J Comp Neurol Psychol* 1908;18:459–82.
66. Neisser U. *Cognitive psychology.* New York: Appleton-Century-Crofts, 1967.
67. Gopher D, Sanders AF. S-Oh-R: Oh stages! Oh resources! In: Prinz W, Sanders, AF, eds. *Cognition and motor processes.* Berlin: Springer-Verlag 1984;231–53.
68. Gopher D. In defence of resources: on structures, energies, pools and the allocation of attention. In: Hockey GRJ, Gaillard AWK, Coles MGH, eds. *Energetics and human information processing.* Dordrecht: Martinus Nijhoff, 1986;353–71.
69. Hull CL. *Principles of behavior.* New York: Appleton-Century-Crofts, 1943.
70. Wickens CD. Processing resources in attention. In: Parasuraman R, Davies DR, eds. *Varieties of attention.* Orlando: Academic Press, 1984;63–102.
71. Lacey JI. Somatic response patterning and stress: some revisions of activation theory. In: Appley MH, Trumbull R, eds. *Psychological stress.* New York: Appleton-Century-Crofts, 1967;14–37.
72. Pribram KH, McGuinness D. Arousal, activation, and effort in the control of attention. *Psychol Rev* 1975;82:116–49.
73. Kok A. Internal and external control: a two-factor model of amplitude change of event-related potentials. *Acta Psychol* 1990;74:203–36.
74. Eysenck MW. *Attention and arousal.* Berlin: Springer-Verlag, 1982.
75. Donchin E. *Cognitive psychophysiology.* Hillsdale, NJ: Erlbaum, 1982.
76. Donchin E, Ritter W, McCallum WC. Cognitive psychophysiology: the endogenous components of the ERP. In: Callaway E, Tueting P, Koslow SH, eds. *Event-related brain potentials in man.* New York: Academic Press, 1978;349–441.
77. Donchin E, Coles MGH. Is the P300 component a manifestation of context updating? *Behav Brain Sci* 1988;11:357–74.
78. Callaway E. The pharmacology of human information processing. *Psychophysiology* 1983;20:359–70.

79. Shiffrin W, Schneider W. Controlled and automatic human information processing: II. Perceptual learning, automatic attending, and a general theory. *Psychol Rev* 1977;84: 127–90.
80. Okita T, Wijers AA, Mulder G, Mulder LJM. Memory search and visual spatial attention: an event-related brain potential analysis. *Acta Psychol* 1985;60:263–92.
81. Duncan-Johnson CG, Donchin E. On quantifying surprise: the variation in event-related potentials with subjective probability. *Psychophysiology* 1977;14:456–67.
82. Pritchard WS. Psychophysiology of P300. *Psychol Bull* 1981;89:506–40.
83. Jong HLooren de, Kok A, Rooy JCGMvan. Early and late selection in young and old subjects: an ERP study. *Psychophysiology* 1988;25:657–71.
84. Johnson R Jr. A triarchic model of P300 amplitude. *Psychophysiology* 1986;23:367–84.
85. Zahn TP, Rapoport JL. Autonomic nervous system effects of acute doses of caffeine in caffeine users and abstainers. *Int J Psychophysiol* 1987;5:33–41.
86. Davidson RA, Smith BD. Arousal and habituation: differential effects of caffeine, sensation seeking and task difficulty. *Person Indiv Diff* 1989;10:111–9.
87. Münte T-F, Heinze H-J, Künkel H, Scholz M. Personality traits influence the effects of diazepam and caffeine on CNV magnitude. *Neuropsychobiology* 1984;12:60–7.
88. Kravkov SV. The influence of caffeine on the color sensitivity. *Acta Ophthal* 1939;17: 89–92.
89. Diamond AL, Cole RE. Visual threshold as a function of test area and caffeine administration. *Psychon Sci* 1970;20:109–11.
90. Diamond AL, Smith EM. The effects of caffeine on terminal dark adaption. In: Moskowitz HR et al., eds. *Sensation and measurement*. Dordrecht-Holland: D. Reidel Publishing Company, 1974;339–49.
91. Sokolov EN. *Perception and the conditioned reflex*. Oxford: Pergamon, 1963.
92. Lynn R. *Attention, arousal and the orientation reaction*. Oxford: Pergamon, 1966.
93. Griffiths RR, Evans SM, Heishman SJ, et al. Low-dose caffeine discrimination in humans. *J Pharmacol Exp Ther* 1990;252:970–8.
94. Skinner JE, Yingling CD. Central gating mechanisms that regulate event-related potentials and behavior. In: Desmedt JE, ed. *Attention, voluntary contraction and event related cerebral potentials*. Basel: Karger, 1977;30–69.
95. Maltzman I, Raskin DC. Effects of individual differences in the orienting reflex on conditioning and complex processes. *J Exp Res Person* 1965;1:1–16.
96. Maltzman I, Mandell MP. The orienting reflex as a predictor of learning and performance. *J Exp Res Person* 1968;3:99–106.
97. Carroll D. Physiological response to relevant and irrelevant stimuli in a simple reaction time situation. *Ergonomics* 1973;16:587–94.
98. Fernstrom JD, Fernstrom MH. Effects of caffeine on monoamine neurotransmitters in the central and peripheral nervous system. In: Dews PB, ed. *Caffeine perspectives from recent research*. New York: Springer-Verlag, 1984;107–18.
99. Tucker DM, Williamson PA. Asymmetric neural control systems in human self-regulation. *Psychol Rev* 1984;91:185–215.
100. Foote SL, Morrison JH. Extrathalamic modulation of cortical function. *Ann Rev Neurosc* 1987;10:67–95.
101. Rohrbaugh JW. The orienting reflex: performance and central nervous system manifestations. In: Parasuraman R, Davies DR, eds. *Varieties of attention*. Orlando: Academic Press, 1984;323–73.
102. Siddle D. The orienting response and stimulus significance: some comments. *Biol Psychol* 1979;8:303–9.
103. Luria AR, Homskaya ED. Frontal lobes and the regulation of arousal processes. In: Mostofsky DI, ed. *Attention: contemporary theory and analysis*. New York: Appleton-Century-Crofts, 1970;303–30.
104. Bernstein AS. The orienting response and stimulus significance: further comments. *Biol Psychol* 1981;12:171–85.
105. Terry WS, Phifer B. Caffeine and memory performance on the AVLT. *J Clin Psychol* 1986;42:860–3.
106. Anderson KJ, Revelle W. The interactive effects of caffeine, impulsivity, and task demands on a visual search task. *Person Indiv Diff* 1983;4:127–34.

107. Jennings JR. Bodily changes during attending. In: Coles MGH, Donchin E, Porges SW, eds. *Psychophysiology, systems, processes and applications*. Amsterdam: Elsevier, 1986; 268–89.
108. Easterbrook JA. The effect of emotion on cue utilization and the organization of behavior. *Psychol Rev* 1959;66:183–201.
109. Posner MI, Peterson SE. The attention system of the human brain. *Ann Rev Neurosc* 1990; 13:25–42.
110. Beatty J. Computation, control, and energetics: a biological perspective. In: Hockey GRJ, Gaillard AWK, Coles MGH, eds. *Energetics and human information processing*. Dordrecht: Martinus Nijhoff, 1986;43–52.

Caffeine, Coffee, and Health,
edited by S. Garattini.
Raven Press, Ltd., New York © 1993.

12

Reproductive Effects of Caffeine

Experimental Studies in Animals

Delphine Purves and Frank M. Sullivan

Division of Pharmacology and Toxicology, United Medical and Dental Schools of Guy's and St. Thomas's Hospitals, Guy's Hospital Campus, University of London, London SE1 9RT, United Kingdom

This chapter reviews the animal studies carried out to investigate the effects of caffeine on male and female fertility, pregnancy, lactation, and postnatal development. It also includes a risk assessment of caffeine use for humans.

Overall the effect of caffeine on male fertility is limited, except at high doses or with prolonged treatment. Marked testicular atrophy has been conclusively demonstrated only at doses of caffeine above 250 mg/kg/day, and it is possible that the testicular pathology is a side-effect of reduced body weight. Caffeine levels that had no effect on body weight (up to 122 mg/kg/day) had little effect on testicular weight and atrophy, while higher doses (258 mg/kg/day), which severely reduced body weight, also resulted in adverse effects on the testes. Doses of 80 mg/kg/day in the rat and 122 mg/kg/day in the mouse have no effect on male fertility.

In general, the effects of caffeine or high intakes of coffee on female fertility in rodents appears to be quite limited, although in some studies, time to pregnancy and birth weight have been affected. Effects on birth weight, pup weight, and perinatal mortality have also been demonstrated especially in the later generations of multigenerational studies. Nevertheless, it is apparent that most parameters of female fertility (i.e., number of conceptions, resorptions, implantations and births, sex ratio, and litter size), are largely unaffected by exposure up to 60 mg/kg/day of caffeine (in drinking water) in rats, and 74 mg/kg/day in mice.

Numerous studies carried out since 1960 have shown that very high doses of caffeine (around 200 mg/kg) could produce teratogenic effects in mice and rats. However, caffeine below a dose of 80 mg/kg/day, fails to produce any clear teratogenic effects in rats, and most workers have reported teratogenic effects only with doses of 100 mg/kg/day or more.

It is incorrect, however, to state that caffeine is a teratogen at doses of 100 mg/kg/day or above since the effects of caffeine are very much related to the mode of administration. In all the above studies, caffeine was given as a single bolus dose either by gavage or by injection. Equal or higher quantities of caffeine administered by gavage either as divided doses over a day in drinking water or in the diet, fail to produce any dose-related abnormalities. Only very high doses of caffeine (330 mg/kg/day) in the diet of rats resulted in any malformations. In the same study, 180 mg/kg/day caffeine resulted in no teratogenic effects.

Teratogens may be classified as "peak blood level" type or "area under the curve" types. Caffeine may be considered a teratogen of the "peak blood level" type, and a level of 60 µg/ml or more in plasma is required for teratogenicity. Lower doses of caffeine however, although not teratogenic, can adversely affect the fetus and, in particular, may result in growth retardation and delayed skeletal ossification.

In both rats and mice, exposure to caffeine during pregnancy and lactation may result in increased mammary development and therefore increased milk production without affecting the composition of milk. The resulting increase in pup weaning weight, however, is not a consistent finding in many of the other studies cited.

Behavioral teratology studies have been carried out in mice, rats and primates. It is evident that although prenatal exposure to greater than 20 mg/kg/day of caffeine can cause behavioral and developmental alterations in animals, the effects are subtle and somewhat inconsistent, so that no definite conclusions on the "behavioral teratological effect" of caffeine can be drawn at present.

A detailed risk assessment of the teratogenic risk of caffeine for humans has been carried out based on the animal data. Because of the classification of caffeine as a "peak plasma level" teratogen, the classical methods of safety margin assessment based on "dose" are inappropriate. Given the plasma level of caffeine needed to produce teratogenic effects, it would seem impossible to produce them in humans at sublethal doses; this conjecture is borne out by the epidemiological evidence.

INTRODUCTION

Caffeine is one of the most widely and routinely consumed pharmacologically active substances. It is assumed to be harmless to humans. While the use of other agents with similar "high social profiles," such as alcohol or tobacco, is generally limited or refrained from during pregnancy, use of coffee, cola drinks, and tea, etc. remains relatively unrestrained. In the last two decades, the question has arisen as to whether such confidence in caffeine is merited. Animal data have been vital in determining the answer to this question, and a review of the most important effects of caffeine on animal reproduction is presented below. An assessment of the relevance of these animal data to humans has also been undertaken.

FERTILITY

Many investigations have been published on the effect of caffeine on reproduction, but few have separated the effects on male and female fertility. A brief summary of the available data on these aspects of reproduction are presented below.

Male Fertility

The majority of investigations into the effects of caffeine on male fertility have been carried out in the rat; the results have been conflicting (1–4). Two main investigations have produced quite different results, and these will be reviewed in detail; the results of smaller studies will also be mentioned.

In a study that set out to determine whether caffeine or other methylxanthines, alone or in combination with sodium nitrite, might nitrosate and produce carcinogenic nitrosamines in vivo (2), significant findings on the effect of caffeine on male fertility were discovered incidentally. Three separate experiments were set up—the first two using Osborne-Mendel rats and the third Holtzman rats, which were dosed with caffeine, sodium nitrite, theobromine, and theophylline. This review will detail only the results from the caffeine groups.

In the first experiment, five-week-old Osborne-Mendel rats (20 per group) were given a diet supplemented with 0.5% caffeine (controls received normal diet) for 64 weeks. The study was then terminated. The average dose was calculated to be approximately 258 mg/kg/day (5). Caffeine had no significant effect on survival, but food consumption, weight gain, and terminal mean body weight were significantly reduced. Relative organ weights of kidney, liver, and spleen were not significantly different from controls, but testicular weight in animals treated with caffeine was significantly reduced to 64% that of controls. The most marked observation was the symmetrical, bilateral testicular atrophy seen in all caffeine-treated animals. The testes were approximately one-third the size of the controls', and showed aspermatogenesis. In addition, there was some associated atrophy of accessory organs (epididymis, seminal vesicle, and prostate gland).

In the second experiment, five- to six-week-old Osborne-Mendel males (20 per group) were treated with 0.5% dietary caffeine and killed at 14 and 75 weeks. Relative testicular weight, similarly, was reduced to 58% of control values in animals treated with caffeine, and testicular atrophy was observed in most (4 of 5) caffeine-treated animals at 14 weeks, and all at 75 weeks. This is an important observation since it demonstrates that testicular atrophy occurred in young treated animals and not just in aged animals where such findings are quite common. Aspermatogenesis was seen in only 1 of 5 (20%) and 5 of 8 (62%) caffeine-treated animals, and oligospermatogenesis was present in 3 of 5 (60%) and 3 of 8 (38%), at 14 and 75 weeks, respectively. All testes (6 of 6) from controls were normal. There was no effect on survival in any groups, but terminal body weight was significantly reduced. In this second experiment, cytogenetic analysis of spermatogonial cells was carried out, and a significant and severe decrease in the mitotic index was discovered in the caffeine-treated group (0.01% for caffeine and 0.26% for normal controls). There was no effect on cytogenetic damage, however, as measured by chromosomal breaks.

Finally, when 41 four-week-old Holtzman rats were fed with 0.5% caffeine until termination at 19 weeks, food consumption, weight gain, terminal body weight, and relative testicular weight (to 51% that of controls) were significantly reduced in caffeine-treated animals. In addition, these also had bilateral testicular atrophy and most (10 of 11) displayed aspermatogenesis. Mortality was greater, but not significant, for caffeine-treated animals. Serum analysis showed there was a nonsignificant increase in testosterone and a significant increase in cholesterol with caffeine treatment.

In this study, three separate experiments with two different strains of rat showed that 0.5% caffeine in the diet (on average, 258 mg/kg/day) resulted in testicular atrophy and aspermatogenesis. It was also demonstrated, although not reviewed here, that 0.5% theobromine was nearly as toxic as caffeine but theophylline had a much less toxic effect (2). It is worth noting, however, that body weight was significantly reduced compared with controls in all experiments, and this in itself can affect the testes.

There is some evidence that caffeine in high doses can cause testicular atrophy in rats, but not all investigations have demonstrated detrimental effects of caffeine on male fertility (3,4,6–8). The most important study to conclude that caffeine had no effect on male fertility was carried out for the Food and Drug Administration in the United States (3). Seventy-five male Osborne-Mendel rats, ten to eleven weeks old, were dosed daily by gavage, with either 40 to 80 mg/kg body weight of aqueous caffeine, each divided into two separate doses. Controls received only vehicle. The treatment was continued over 22 days during which the male rats were mated with untreated females, commencing at the end of the second day of treatment. The *only* effect was a significant reduction in body weight of the caffeine-treated males by day 7, but this remained significant only from days 14 to 22 in animals treated with 80 mg/kg/day of caffeine. There was no significant difference in testicular weight, pregnancy rate, litter size, number of litters, birth weight, or survival of pups at birth. The conclusion drawn from these results was that caffeine at the levels described had little potential to produce adverse effects on male reproduction. Similar findings were discovered in a study of Wistar rats in which both males and females were treated with caffeine (9). The details of this investigation are described here (see the section on Female

Fertility). Briefly, 10 mg/kg/day of caffeine administered in the diet of both sexes throughout *five* successive pregnancies resulted in *only* reduced birth weights for the first four pregnancies, and reduced birth weight and increased neonatal mortality in the fifth pregnancy.

In a multigeneration investigation with CD-1 mice, (see the section on Female Fertility), doses of caffeine of up to 37 mg/kg/day were administered continuously in drinking water to both sexes for four generations without affecting fertility (10).

Negative results have also been obtained with HA/ICR mice (11). In each group, 15 male mice were given either 0.02, 0.06, 0.2, or 0.6 mg/ml of caffeine in their drinking water (equivalent to doses of 3.6, 13.4, 49, and 122 mg/kg/day) for eight weeks prior to mating. Treatment was then terminated, and six from each group were then mated with untreated females for another eight weeks. Terminal body weight was unaffected. There was no significant effect on the number of implantations per female, although there was a significant decrease in the number of pregnancies in the two top doses. The authors suggest that this is indicative of high levels of caffeine affecting male mating behavior rather than male fertility. There was no significant effect on embryonic mortality.

When the effect of exposure to 30 mg/kg/day of caffeine during pregnancy on the fetal gonad was examined in a more recent study (4) (for details see section on Female Fertility), there was only a marginal slowing of the morphogenic organization of the seminiferous cords, although the number of Leydig cells was significantly reduced compared with untreated controls. Other in vitro studies have shown that caffeine (5–6 mM) significantly increases motility of bovine (6), hamster (7), and murine (8) sperm and, in consequence, the fertilization of ova (8).

Summary of Effects on Male Fertility

It appears that, overall, the effect of caffeine on male fertility is limited, except at high levels (2) or with prolonged treatment (9). Marked testicular atrophy only has been conclusively demonstrated at doses above 250 mg/kg/day (2). It is possible that the testicular pathology is a side effect of reduced body weight. Caffeine levels that had no effect on body weight (up to 122 mg/kg/day) had little effect on testicular weight and atrophy (3,11), while higher doses (258 mg/kg/day) that severely reduced body weight (2) also resulted in adverse effects on the testes. It seems, however, that doses of 80 mg/kg/day in the rat (3) and 122 mg/kg/day in the mouse (11) have no effect on male fertility.

Female Fertility

The first and perhaps one of the most comprehensive studies on female fertility was carried out by Palm and his colleagues in 1978 (12). Groups of

25 young, virgin, Sprague-Dawley female rats (F_0) were given either 12.5, 25, or 50% brewed coffee in their drinking water (equivalent to approximately 9, 19, or 38 mg/kg/day caffeine) for five weeks prior to mating (with untreated males) and throughout gestation. Some dams were sacrificed on day 19 of gestation, and the remainder littered and nursed their offspring. Coffee treatment was continued in the latter group until day 37 postpartum. The female offspring (F_1 generation) were given no further treatment but were mated at 100 days of age with F_1 males. These rats littered and nursed their offspring (F_2 generation) for 28 days.

There was no significant effect on most parameters of reproduction in the original dams (F_0), including mean days to pregnancy, the mean number of resorptions, fetuses per litter, fetal weight, or sex ratio. There was also no dose-related difference in fetal size, although fetal length and width were significantly increased with the 12.5 and 50% coffee-treated groups. In dams that had littered, there was no effect on litter size, number of live pups, birth weight, or pup weight (at day 38).

There was no difference in pregnancy rates between the F_1 and F_0 matings, but the mean days to pregnancy were significantly increased in the two top dose groups. There was no difference, however, in litter size, birth weight, pup weight (at day 28), or in survival rates in the F_2 generation compared with the F_1.

In addition to these coffee-treated groups, 25 females were dosed with 30 mg/kg/day of caffeine either by gavage or in drinking water from day 0 of pregnancy to birth. No treatment was given prior to mating or after birth. As before, some dams were sacrificed on day 19 of gestation and others littered and nursed their offspring (F_1 generation). F_1 rats were mated at 100 days postpartum.

There was a significant increase in mean days to pregnancy with F_1 matings for both modes of treatment. In addition, the group dosed via drinking water showed a significant decrease in the survival rates in the F_1 generation, although body weight was unaffected. There were no other significant differences noted in either the F_1 or F_2 offspring, but relative fetal organ weights of the F_1 generation, though variable, tended to be smaller in treated animals.

It would seem from this initial study that caffeine at doses up to 38 mg/kg/day has only limited effects on female fertility, and these results are supported by other investigations (4,13,14). In another study with rats, groups of 30 pregnant Sprague-Dawley rats were fed 0.25, 0.5, or 1.0 g of caffeine per kg of diet (equivalent to 16, 35, or 62 mg/kg/day) throughout gestation and lactation (13). They were mated again to produce a second litter, and the treatment was continued. There was no effect on litter size or pup weight, and no abnormalities were detected. With the top dose of caffeine, however, there was a significant reduction in birth weight in the first litter only. Cross-fostering of pups between treated and untreated dams showed that dosing only during pregnancy or only during lactation had no significant effect on litter size, birth weight, or development.

An investigation in mice also failed to detect any effect of caffeine on female fertility (14). Twenty-seven female C3H/HeMei mice were given 0.05% caffeine in their drinking water (equivalent to approximately 74 mg/kg/day) from weaning (20 days of age) until termination. Eleven were sacrificed for examination but the rest were mated on day 63 postpartum. The dams littered, then nursed six of their offspring (three males and three females) until weaning, when the trial was terminated. There was little effect on maternal weight gain except on day 63, and no significant effect on rate of pregnancy, length of gestation, or litter size was observed. There was no significant difference for time taken to vaginal opening, the pattern of estrous cycles, or virgin ovarian weight in the offspring of controls (which received tap water ad libitum) and treated animals. Development of mammary glands in virgin mice was also unaffected, with a similar degree of formation of end-buds and their DNA content between controls and treated animals.

Another group examined the effect of caffeine intake during pregnancy on sexual differentiation of fetal gonads in rats (4). Pregnant Wistar rats were dosed daily by gavage with 30 mg/kg body weight of caffeine from days 1 to 20 of gestation and sacrificed on days 13, 14, 15, and 20 of gestation. Fetal gonads were examined by light and electron microscopy. It was discovered that fetal ovarian differentiation and germ cell proliferation were unaffected by the caffeine exposure in pregnancy. More marked effects on female fertility have been demonstrated however in a more recent paper by the same group (15). Virgin Wistar rats were dosed daily by gavage with either 30 or 60 mg/kg of caffeine during pregnancy only. The total dose was fractionated into three 8-hourly aliquots. Some dams were sacrificed on day 20 of gestation but the rest littered and nursed their offspring (F_{1a} generation). Treatment was ceased either the day before sacrifice, or the day before birth. The dams were mated again eight weeks after delivery of the first litter but were not treated again with caffeine. A second litter was produced (F_{1b} generation). Untreated females from the first litter were also mated to produce a second generation (F_2).

In the F_{1a} litters, there was a significant reduction in birth weight and pup weight (at 13 weeks of age) in both treated groups. In the top dose group, mortality at birth was significantly increased and litter size significantly decreased. There was no effect on length of gestation or sex ratio. In the F_{1b} litters, a significant reduction in birth weight was observed only in the group previously treated with caffeine. Interestingly, birth weight was significantly increased in treated animals, with a significant increase in the length of gestation (1 day) in the F_2 generation rats, that had not been treated with caffeine. No other effects were observed.

These results suggest that higher levels (60 mg/kg/day) of caffeine may have more marked and persistent effects on female fertility than lower doses, affecting both birth weight and survival of offspring. Such effects on birth weight and survival have also been seen in investigations of fertility where both male and females have been treated with caffeine (9,10,16,17).

One study used Sprague-Dawley weanling rats, which were given 25, 50, or 100% brewed or instant coffee (equivalent to doses of 20, 40, or 80 mg/kg/day of caffeine) as their sole source of fluid from shortly after weaning for approximately 30 weeks, when the trial ended (16). Treatment began 91 days prior to the first mating. Ten days after weaning the first litter, the females were mated again with the same male, and were sacrificed on days 13 or 21 of gestation. There were no effects on body weight or food consumption in the adults (F_0), although fluid consumption was significantly reduced with 100% coffee, while with 25% and 50% coffee, it was significantly increased. In the first litter, there was no effect on the number of conceptions, the number of live pups at birth, neonatal mortality (by day 4), or number of pups weaned. There was a dose-related decrease in pup weight (by day 4), but the difference was only significant for 100% coffee. With the second mating, there was no significant difference in the conception rate, number of implantations per dam, number of live or dead fetuses, nor fetal weight. Similar results were found in a study by the same group in which decaffeinated coffee instead of tap water was used as a control (17).

A more extensive study used Wistar rats (9). Twelve-week-old rats were divided into breeding pairs, four of which consumed an average of 10 mg/kg/day of caffeine in their diet. Animals were mated for five successive pregnancies and deliveries, with deliveries approximately 25 days apart. No significant difference in litter size or sex ratio was seen in any of the pregnancies, but there was a significant reduction in weight of weanlings in all treated groups (on average 20% less than controls). Pup weight was on average 32% less than that of controls by the fourth pregnancy. There was no effect on neonatal mortality in the first four pregnancies, but birth weight was significantly reduced and mortality increased by the fifth pregnancy, so that by day 6 of age, mortality had reached 44% compared to 3.1% in controls. Crown–rump length was significantly reduced only at birth in offspring of the fifth pregnancy. No malformations were observed.

Two investigations in mice have produced similar findings (10,18). The first was one of the earliest studies to administer caffeine to mice in the drinking water (18). NMRI-inbred mice were given caffeine in their drinking water from 14 days prior to mating until days 14 to 18 of gestation, when they were sacrificed. The average daily intake of caffeine was 50 mg/kg body weight. There was no effect on implantations, resorptions, or litter size, but fetal weight was significantly reduced. Of 745 caffeine-treated fetuses, seven were malformed (there were no malformations in the 561 controls), leading the authors to conclude that caffeine is a weak teratogen. The second was a comprehensive multigeneration study in mice, in which no significant effects on fertility by caffeine were noted (10). Charles River CD-1 mice received 4–5, 12–18, or 25–37 mg/kg/day of caffeine in their drinking water. Both sexes were treated from four weeks prior to the initial mating and continuously throughout the trial. Twenty females and ten males were mated to produce the F_1 generation. The offspring (F_1) were paired and bred for two successive pregnancies. The first was raised and the second sacrificed at birth. These mating procedures were repeated with the F_2 and F_3 generations. All matings were out-crosses except for the F_1; brother-sister matings were also carried out.

There was no significant effect on body weight or water consumption, although it did appear to increase with later generations. Generally, there were no consistent dose-related effects. Number of conceptions, number of births, litter size, number of pups weaned, sex ratio, and age of sexual maturity in females were not significantly affected by the treatment. There was also no significant difference in pup weight at weaning, although it was reduced in the F_2 and F_3 generations. No difference in the incidence of abnormalities was noted.

Summary of the Effects on Female Fertility

In general, the effects of caffeine on female fertility in rodents appears to be quite limited, affecting mainly time to pregnancy and birth weight (12–14). More marked effects on birth weight, pup weight, and perinatal mortality have been demonstrated (9,10,15–17), and these tended to be magnified in later generations (9,10). It is nevertheless apparent that most parameters of female fertility (i.e., number of conceptions, resorptions, implantations and births, sex ratio, and litter size), are largely unaffected by exposure to caffeine up to 60 mg/kg/day (in drinking water) in rats (13,15), and 74 mg/kg/day in mice (14).

REPRODUCTION AND TERATOLOGY

In most of the investigations described above, caffeine treatment was begun either before mating or given only to preceding generations and, as such, affected fertility. In all the following studies, caffeine was given after conception so they are considered investigations of embryo-fetal toxicity, teratology, and developmental toxicology of caffeine. Numerous investigations on these effects have been carried out in animals over the last three decades, but this review has concentrated on the larger, well-conducted studies that perhaps provide the most reliable results; smaller trials are mentioned more briefly.

History

One of the earliest studies (and, perhaps, the most important, in terms of alerting people to the possible detrimental effects of caffeine on reproduction) was carried out by Nishimura and Nakai in 1960 (19). One hundred SMA mice were injected once i.p. with 250 mg/kg of caffeine. Each group was dosed on a different day, between days 7 and 15 of pregnancy. There was some increase in the resorption rate with all caffeine-treated groups, and there was a peak incidence of malformations (18 to 43%) in treatments late in pregnancy (i.e., on days 10 to 14 of pregnancy). The malformations consisted mainly of digital defects, hematomas, or cleft palate. This investigation was one of the first to demonstrate that caffeine could be teratogenic if given in high enough doses.

In a second study, Nishimura injected ICR-JCL mice i.p. or s.c. with 200 mg/kg of caffeine, either in one dose or in two divided doses (with 2 or 4 hour intervals between injections) on day 12 of pregnancy. Fetal weight was significantly reduced, and the percentage of abnormal fetuses increased (20). A single, daily injection of caffeine resulted in malformations in 18% to 21% of fetuses, compared with only 6% if the dose was fractionated. Cleft palate was the major abnormality observed, and only two fetuses had digital defects. Several studies that followed confirmed these results in mice (20–25).

Table 1 summarizes some important studies of caffeine on reproduction in mice. Generally, high doses of caffeine (≥ 100 mg/kg/day) result in malformations, mainly cleft palate and digital abnormalities, while lower levels of caffeine, although less effective, are reported to have reproductive and teratogenic effects. Not all investigations, however, have demonstrated these effects (26–28).

More Recent Investigations

Following the results from the mouse, which indicated the potential teratogenic nature of caffeine, more extensive and comprehensive investigations were set up to produce reliable and conclusive data for risk assessment in humans. Most of these studies were carried out in the rat.

One of the largest investigations was commissioned by the Food and Drug Administration in the United States (29). It was set up in an attempt to resolve the question of caffeine's teratogenicity and to assess its danger to humans from consumption of cola beverages—at that time, the regulation of caffeine levels in cola drinks was in question.

Osborne-Mendel rats were orally intubated from days 0 to 19 of gestation with 0, 6, 12, 40, 80, or 125 mg/kg of caffeine, and each group contained 49 and 59 pregnant dams. Animals were sacrificed on day 20 of gestation. Maternal toxicity was apparent at 125 mg/kg of caffeine, since six dams died during

TABLE 1. A summary of the effects of caffeine on reproduction in the mouse

Study (ref no.)	Strain	Route of administration	Dose (mg/kg/day)	Days of gestation treated	Reproductive effects			Teratogenic effects	
					Rate of resorption	Fetal weight	Others[a]	Cleft palate	Other malformations
Group D'Etude, 1969 (26)	Swiss	Gavage	75	5–?	No effect	No effect	No effect	Present (NS)	Present (NS)
Bertrand et al., 1970 (27)	Balb/c	Gavage	50	5–18	Increased	ND	ND	No effect	No effect
	Swiss	Gavage	75	5–18	ND	ND	ND	No effect	No effect
	Balb/c	Gavage	75	5–18	Increased	ND	ND	No effect	No effect
Bertrand et al., 1965 (31)	Balb/c	Gavage	50	6–18	ND	ND	ND	No effect	Present (NS)
Elmazar et al., 1981 (23)	Albino CD-1	Gavage	200	14	No effect	ND	ND	Present (NS)	Present (NS)
	Albino CD-1	Gavaga	300	14	Increased	ND	ND	Present (NS)	Present (NS)
Elmazar et al., 1982 (24)	Albino CD-1	Gavage	50	6–16	No effect	ND	No effect	Present (NS)	Present (NS)
	Albino CD-1	Gavage	150	6–16	Increased	Reduced	No effect	Present (NS)	Present (SIG)
	Albino CD-1	Drinking water	140–178	5–18	No effect	No effect	No effect	No effect	Present (NS)
	Albino CD-1	Drinking water	207–242	5–18	No effect	Reduced	Skeletal variation	No effect	Present (NS)
Murphy and Benjamin, 1981 (28)	White	Diet (coffee)	4.8	0–birth	No effect	No effect	No effect	No effect	No effect
	White	Diet (coffee)	9.6	0–birth	No effect	Reduced	Shorter fetuses	No effect	No effect
	White	Diet (coffee)	14.4	0–birth	Increased	Reduced	Shorter fetuses	No effect	No effect
	White	Diet (coffee)	19.2	0–birth	Increased	Reduced	Shorter fetuses	No effect	No effect
	White	Diet (coffee)	24.0	0–birth	Increased	Reduced	Shorter fetuses	No effect	No effect
Nishimura and Nakai, 1960 (19)	SMA	Intraperitoneal	250	7,15[b]	Increased	ND	ND	Present (NA)	Present (NA)
Fujii et al., 1969 (20)	ICR-JCL	Intraperitoneal	200	12	Increased	Reduced	ND	Present (SIG)	Present (SIG)
	ICR-JCL	Subcutaneous	200	12	Increased	Reduced	ND	Present (SIG)	Present (SIG)
Scott, 1983 (25)	Albino CD-1	Intraperitoneal	80	11–12	No effect	No effect	ND	Present (NA)	Present (NA)
	Albino CD-1	Intraperitoneal	100–150	11–12	No effect	No effect	ND	Present (NA)	Present (NA)
	Albino CD-1	Intraperitoneal	175–250	11–12	Increased	No effect	ND	Present (NA)	Present (NA)

[a] Skeletal variations, litter size etc.; [b] animal dosed on one day between day 7 to 15.
ND, not determined; NA, no statistical analysis; NS, nonsignificant; SIG, significant ($p < 0.05$).

TABLE 2. *A summary of the effects of*

Study (ref no.)	Strain	Route of administration	Dose (mg/kg/day)	Days of gestation treated	Rate of resorption
Collins et al., 1981 (29)	Osborne-Mendel	Gavage	6	0–19	No effect
			12	0–19	No effect
			40	0–19	No effect
			80	0–19	Increased
			125	0–19	Increased
Ikeda et al., 1982 (30)	Osborne-Mendel	Gavage	80	0–14	No effect
		Drinking water	80	11–15	No effect
Smith et al., 1987 (34)	Wistar	Gavage	10	6–20	No effect
			100	6–20	Increased
Palm et al., 1978 (12)	Sprague-Dawley	Gavage	30	0–19	No effect
		Drinking water	30	0–19	No effect
Collins et al., 1983 (40)	Osborne-Mendel	Drinking water	10	0–19	No effect
			27.4	0–19	Increased
			50.7	0–19	No effect
			86.6	0–19	No effect
			115.8	0–19	No effect
			160–204.5	0–19	Increased
Fujii and Nishimura, (41)	Sprague-Dawley	Diet	180	0–22	Increased
			330	0–22	Increased
Ritter et al., 1982 (38)	Wistar	Intraperitoneal	75	12	Increased
			150	12	Increased

[a] Litter size, fetal length etc.
ND, not determined; NA, no statistical analysis; NS, non significant; SIG, significant ($p < 0.05$).

the treatment period. Maternal food consumption and, consequently, weight gain was lower in all experimental groups throughout gestation.

There was a significant decrease in the numbers of live fetuses per litter in the two top dose groups, with a correlated increase in the resorption rate, and fetal weight and crown–rump length were significantly reduced. An increase in malformations was also detected, but ectrodactyly, the main abnormality observed, was seen *only* in the two top dose groups (present in 11% and 28.5% of fetuses exposed to 80 mg/kg and 125 mg/kg doses, respectively). Edematous fetuses were found with 40, 80, and 125 mg/kg doses, but the number was increased significantly only in the group treated with 125 mg/kg. Hemorrhages were detected in fetuses from all groups but were only significantly increased with levels of 80 and 125 mg/kg of caffeine. Skeletal ossification variations occurred in all groups and was dose related. A statistically significant increase in sternebral ossification retardation was seen even in the lowest dose level of 6 mg/kg. The authors concluded that there was a clear no-effect threshold for frank terata at 40 mg/kg/day of caffeine.

Numerous studies have demonstrated similar results in rats (27,30–34); these have been comprehensively detailed in previous reviews of the subject *caffeine on reproduction in the rat*

Reproductive effects			Teratogenic effects	
Fetal weight	Skeletal variations	Others[a]	Ectrodactyly	Other malformations
No effect	Increased	No effect	No effect	No effect
No effect	Increased	No effect	No effect	No effect
No effect	Increased	No effect	No effect	No effect
Reduced	Increased	Short fetuses	Present (SIG)	No effect
Reduced	Increased	Short fetuses	Present (SIG)	No effect
ND	ND	ND	Present (NA)	ND
ND	ND	ND	No effect	No effect
No effect	No effect	No effect	No effect	No effect
Reduced	Increased	Short fetuses	Present (SIG)	Present (SIG)
No effect	Increased	No effect	No effect	No effect
No effect	Increased	No effect	No effect	No effect
No effect	No effect	No effect	No effect	No effect
No effect	No effect	No effect	No effect	No effect
No effect	Increased	No effect	No effect	No effect
Reduced	Increased	Short fetuses	No effect	No effect
Reduced	Increased	Short fetuses	No effect	Present (NS)
Reduced	Increased	Short fetuses	No effect	No effect
Reduced	Increased	ND	No effect	Present (NS)
Reduced	Increased	ND	No effect	Present (SIG)
No effect	ND	ND	No effect	Present (SIG)
No effect	ND	ND	No effect	Present (SIG)

(5,35–37), and some are summarized in Table 2. Generally, teratogenic effects have been detected only with high, single gavage (27,29,31–34) or i.p. (38) doses (≥80–100 mg/kg/day) of caffeine, and other methods of caffeine administration have had either no teratogenic effects (32,34,39,40), or resulted only in frank terata at comparatively high levels (330 mg/kg/day) of caffeine (41).

A Possible Mechanism for the Teratogenicity of Caffeine

The fact that high, single doses of caffeine are necessary before a teratogenic effect can be detected may be explained by examining blood levels of caffeine. In the study for the FDA, only single, oral gavage doses of 80 mg/kg or more were shown to produce frank terata, while doses up to 205 mg/kg/day in drinking water were not teratogenic (29). Another study, also commissioned by the FDA, examined the pharmacokinetics involved (30). Osborne-Mendel rats were given 80 mg/kg/day of caffeine, either in drinking water from days 9 to 15 of gestation or by gavage from days 0 to 14. Radioactive caffeine was supplied in drinking water on days 12 to 15, and by gavage on day 12 of pregnancy. With the former, radioactivity was monitored every 6 hours for the three days, and with the latter, radioactivity was measured at various time intervals between 1 and 24 hours after 9:00 A.M. Blood levels of caffeine in μg/ml were calculated from these measurements. Animals were sacrificed on day 15 of pregnancy. The mean peak blood levels in animals treated with caffeine in their drinking water were 5.74 ± 2.30 μg/ml and 4.23 ± 2.71 μg/ml at 12 and 24 hours, respectively, while with gavage doses, the peak of 63.09 ± 4.73 μg/ml was reached in 1 hour. No abnormalities were observed in fetuses treated with caffeine in drinking water but ectrodactyly was found in 11 fetuses out of five litters from dams treated by gavage (unfortunately, no concomitant controls were carried out so statistical analysis was impossible).

Similar results were produced by a study in which CD-1 mice were given 150 mg/kg/day of caffeine either in drinking water or by gavage in a sustained-release pellet from days 6 to 14 of pregnancy (24). The blood levels from the treatment with drinking water peaked at 5.3 ± 1.29 μg/ml and 5.4 ± 0.59 μg/ml at 3 and 15 hours, respectively, while the peak with the sustained-release pellet was 16.4 ± 0.91 μg/ml at 2 hours. Malformations were significantly increased only in animals that had been dosed by gavage.

An interesting finding was seen in a different trial by the same group (34). Female Wistar rats were dosed by gavage from days 6 to 20 of pregnancy with 100 mg/kg/day of caffeine, either in one bolus dose or as four 3-hourly fractions of 25 mg/kg. Ectrodactyly was significantly increased only in the group that had received a single daily dose of 100 mg/kg of caffeine, with 25 of 170 fetuses affected. A single bolus dose of 100 mg/kg of caffeine produced a high incidence of malformed fetuses, while the same dose divided into four doses given at 3-hourly intervals was not teratogenic. Peak blood levels for the single daily gavage was 80 μg/ml (range of 60 to 110 μg/ml) at 2 to 5 hours, and 30 μg/ml (range of 25 to 35 μg/ml) at 5 hours after the first dose for the fractionated dosing regime [unpublished data quoted by Smith (34)]. An earlier study already mentioned (20), also demonstrated that a single daily injection of 200 mg/kg of caffeine in ICR-JCL mice resulted in malformations in 18% to 21% of fetuses, compared with only 6% if the dose was divided into two 2-hourly or four hourly doses. So it is apparent that high peak blood levels of caffeine correlate with its teratogenic activity.

It has been previously shown that chemicals that exert teratogenic effects can be divided into two classes: those that are teratogenic only when some critical threshold level in the blood or tissue is exceeded ("peak blood level" teratogens), and those whose action depends on the "area under the curve" when the blood level is plotted against time. This was elegantly demonstrated by Nau and his colleagues in Berlin (42–45). In an investigation of the mode of action of the antiepileptic drug valproic acid, they dosed mice with either single injections or continuous infusions of sodium valproate via implanted mini-osmotic pumps. These pumps permitted the production of sustained steady-state blood levels of valproate in the mice. By comparing the peak blood levels and the areas under the curves obtained from these two methods of administration, they showed clearly that the dose and area under the curve were correlated with fetal weight reduction and retardation, while the peak level attained was correlated with the neural tube defects. A certain blood level had to be attained before the teratogenic effects of the valproate were seen, making a single, high dose most effective; in short, the effects of valproate depended on the kinetics. They also reported that cyclophosphamide, although less well studied, was a teratogen of the other type; the teratogenic effects depended on the area under the curve, and repeated low doses were in this case more effective teratogenically than single high doses.

Caffeine may be considered a teratogen of the "peak blood level" type since only single high doses produce teratogenicity. The blood level data show that a level of 60 μg/ml or more of caffeine is required (24,30,34,45).

Delayed Skeletal Ossification

Although caffeine is teratogenic only at relatively high doses, lower nonteratogenic doses administered by most methods may have other adverse reproductive effects (on rates of resorptions, fetal weight and length, number of viable fetuses per litter, litter size) (29,34,39,40,46–48). One effect, consistently demonstrated by most investigations, is a delay in skeletal ossification (12,17,24,29,40,41) (see Table 1).

A detailed investigation of skeletal effects was carried out in a second teratology study commissioned by the FDA in the United States (49). Caffeine was administered in drinking water to pregnant Osborne-Mendel rats. Three dose ranges were used: 24.7 to 29.0 mg/kg/day (low), 42.7 to 48.8 mg/kg/day (medium), and 70.6 to 75.1 mg/kg/day (high), and animals from each group were killed either on day 20 of gestation (fetuses), on postnatal day 0 (neonates), or on postnatal day 6 (pups). Approximately half the fetuses were stained with Alizarin Red S, a dye that stains osteoid (the material that comprises bone). In the medium- and high-dose treatments with caffeine, there was a significant reduction in viable fetuses and an increase in fetal sternebral variations and other skeletal defects, such as missing centra and reduced ossification of the dorsal arch. No reduction in fetal weight was found. In neonates killed on day 0 postpartum, a significantly increased incidence of delayed sternebral ossification was seen in all caffeine-treated animals, but only pups in the high-dose group showed a significant increase in incompletely ossified sternebrea by day 6. No other skeletal effects were seen. No frank terata was found in this study. The results suggest that caffeine delayed the process of ossification rather than impaired bone development in fetuses, since the effect had disappeared by day 6 postpartum in the low- and medium-dose groups.

Results from another study supported this finding (46). Caffeine administered by gavage in a dose of 100 mg/kg to pregnant Sprague-Dawley rats—either from days 7 to 19, days 7 to 16, days 16 to 19, or only on day 19—had no significant effect on the number of resorptions or litter size; but aphalangia (complete ablation of the distal segment of a digit) was found in six fetuses (1.6%) from four litters of the group treated from days 7 to 19. A difference in alizarin-staining for assessing the ossification in the fetuses was revealed; short-term treatment (days 16 to 19) decreased the staining as much or more than long-term treatment (days 7 to 19). In those rats in which long-term treatment was discontinued by day 16 (treated on days 7 to 16), the effect on staining of the fetuses was not as great as in those treated until day 19 and, in some instances, was not significantly different from controls. This suggested that the fetus was more susceptible to caffeine's effect on ossification late in pregnancy. The author concluded that caffeine slows the rate of ossification rather than causing a permanent abatement, arguing that such short-term treatment was unlikely to cause lasting impairment to bone development.

More recent studies have examined the effect of protein-enriched diets on the development of bones in rats treated with dietary caffeine (50–53). In Sprague-Dawley rats fed a 20% protein diet supplemented with caffeine in doses of either 5, 10, or 20 mg/kg body weight from day 8 to day 22 of gestation when they were sacrificed, there was no significant effect on maternal or fetal body weight (50). Fetal mandibular weight was significantly increased, however, in animals exposed to 5 mg/kg body weight of caffeine, while with the two top doses it was significantly decreased.

These results were confirmed in another similar study (51). Sprague-Dawley rats were again fed a 20% protein diet supplemented with 20 mg/kg body weight of caffeine from day 9 of gestation until killed on day 15 postpartum. There was no effect on maternal or pup weight gain, but both the mandibles and femurs were significantly smaller and lighter in caffeine-treated pups. Cranial bones were unaffected. Interestingly, supplementing the caffeine diets with zinc (0.6 g/kg of diet) counteracted the effect of caffeine on bone development (51).

In another study, a high protein diet also modified the effect of caffeine on ossification (53). Sprague-Dawley rats were fed either a 20% or 40% protein diet supplemented to provide 20 mg/kg of caffeine, from day 7 of gestation until killed at parturition with no effect on birth weight or litter size. Mandibular weight was significantly reduced in the animals exposed to caffeine in a 20% protein diet, but those treated with a 40% caffeine-supplemented protein diet were unaffected. Thus, the effect of caffeine on the development of fetal mandibles was shown to be modified by different levels of maternal dietary protein.

The effect of maternal dietary caffeine on fetal bones has also been shown to be persistent (52). Holtzman rats were fed 10 mg/kg of caffeine in a diet supplemented with 20% protein from day 9 of gestation to day 22 postpartum. Male weanlings were fed only the 20% protein diet with no added caffeine and were killed on day 56 postpartum. There was no effect on body weight in the pups, but mandibular and femur weights were significantly reduced, and the femurs were also significantly shorter in the offspring of caffeine-treated animals. This study demonstrated therefore, not only impaired growth and development of fetal bone resulting from maternal intake of caffeine during gestation and lactation, but it also showed that these effects persisted in the adolescent offspring (52). Maternal intake of caffeine results in a delay in ossification in animals, a reversible effect that can be favorably modified by protein or zinc dietary supplements (50–53). The fact that, in most cases, it is not accompanied by a dose-related decrease in fetal weight indicates that the phenomenon is not merely a reflection of overall fetal retardation (46,49–53).

Summary of Reproductive and Teratogenic Effects of Caffeine

Below a dose of 80 mg/kg/day, caffeine fails to produce any clear teratogenic effects in rats (29), and the evidence supporting this conclusion has been detailed in other comprehensive reviews of caffeine's teratogenic capabilities (5,35–37), summarized in Table 2. Only the study by Collins and his co-workers (29) has shown caffeine to be teratogenic in rats at 80 mg/kg/day; most workers have reported teratogenic effects only with doses of 100 mg/kg/day or more of caffeine (27,31–34).

It would be incorrect, however, to state that caffeine is a teratogen at doses of 100 mg/kg/day or above, since the effects of caffeine are very much related to the mode of administration. In all the studies mentioned above, caffeine was given as a single bolus dose either by gavage or by injection (27,29, 31–34). Equal or higher quantities of caffeine administered either as divided doses over a day (34,39), in drinking water (40), or in the diet (32) fail to produce any dose-related abnormalities. Only very high doses of caffeine (330 mg/kg/day) in the diet of rats resulted in any malformations (41). In this same study, 180 mg/kg/day caffeine resulted in no teratogenic effects. Caffeine may be considered a teratogen of the "peak blood level" type, and a level of 60 μg/ml or more in plasma is required for teratogenicity (24,30,34). Lower doses of caffeine, although not teratogenic, can adversely affect the fetus, resulting particularly in growth retardation (48,54,55) and delayed skeletal ossification (12,17,46,49–53).

LACTATION

Few studies have investigated the effect of caffeine on lactational performance, but three papers recently addressed this aspect of reproduction (56–58). Hart and Grimble (1990) (56) looked at the effect of methylxanthines at concentrations occurring in tea. Pregnant Wistar rats were given 50 mg/

kg/day caffeine in their drinking water (controls received tap water) from day 0 of pregnancy to day 14 postpartum. Litter sizes were adjusted to eight pups per dam during lactation. Similar experiments were also carried out with theobromine and theophylline, but only the results for caffeine are reviewed here. Caffeine treatment had no significant effect on body weight or food or water consumption in dams during pregnancy. Food and fluid consumption were significantly greater in caffeine-treated dams during lactation, however, but there was no significant difference in body weight. Milk volume was significantly increased in caffeine-treated dams, but the composition of the milk was unaffected; protein, lactose, triacylglycerol production and fatty acid content were unaltered. Litter weights were significantly greater by day 13 of lactation for animals exposed to caffeine.

A recent extensive study in mice reached similar conclusions (58). Primiparous, 10-week-old ND/4 mice were mated and given 500 mg/L caffeine in their drinking water from days 1 to 18 of pregnancy. The caffeine was then removed (no data on maternal body weight or fluid consumption was presented so no dose level in g/kg/day could be determined). Some dams were sacrificed at day 18 of pregnancy to examine the mammary glands. The survivors gave birth and nursed the offspring until day 15 of lactation when the trial was terminated, and the mammary glands examined. Two other separate trials were similarly set up: in one, eight pups/dam were cross-fostered at birth to dams that had received the same caffeine treatment or control treatment during pregnancy; in the other, pups were removed from the dams for 4 hours and the milk harvested on days 5, 10, and 15 of lactation for analysis. Results of the first experiment showed that, although birth weight was unaffected, litter weight was significantly greater at the end of lactation in caffeine-treated dams (litter size was relatively constant between dams), indicating an enhanced lactational performance. Mammary wet weight and mammary DNA were significantly increased on day 18 of pregnancy and day 15 of lactation in dams exposed to caffeine, indicating that the increased lactational performance may have been due to increased mammary development. Mammary RNA was also increased but, since the RNA/DNA ratio was unaffected, the authors concluded that there was no increase in secretory activity per cell. The same effects, including an increase in litter weight, were seen in the cross-fostering experiment but only when the foster mother (rather than the natural mother) had received the caffeine. This indicated that the effects were due to differences in the lactation period and not to differences in offspring at birth. The composition of the milk was unaffected by caffeine, with neither fat nor protein content significantly altered on days, 5, 10, or 15 of lactation; based on this finding, the authors suggested that caffeine affected only the volume of milk production.

In conclusion, a recent research in both rats and mice has shown that exposure to caffeine (at the described levels) during pregnancy and lactation may result in increased mammary development and, consequently, increased milk production, without affecting the composition of the milk (56–58). The resulting increase in pup weaning weight on the other hand is not a consistent finding in many of the other studies cited earlier in this review.

POSTNATAL DEVELOPMENT

In addition to reproductive and teratogenic effects, caffeine has been shown to affect postnatal behavior and development in the offspring of treated animals. The term *behavioral teratology* has been coined to describe these postnatal effects. Various parameters of development were measured and the major ones are briefly summarized below.

Pre-weaning parameters include the day of eye opening, eruption of incisors, surface-righting reflex, air-righting reflex, auditory startle, and development of open-field activity. The first two are self explanatory; the surface-righting test measures the time taken for a pup to right itself (all four feet on the surface) from a prone position; the air-righting test measures the ability of a pup held by its limbs in a supine position (upside-down) and released twelve inches above a surface to land on all four limbs; and the test for auditory startle measures the day on which a sudden noise will regularly elicit a startle reaction. Open-field activity is usually measured by determining the pattern of locomotion, rearing, defecation and/or urination that occurs within a set time on a flat surface of specified size.

Post-weaning tests tend to be more complex in design, measuring higher nervous system activity, and include passive and active avoidance tests, position discrimination, and maze learning. It is impossible to describe the details of all these tests, but essentially they measure the ability of an animal to learn and retain knowledge of simple or complex tasks. Many other tests, not mentioned here, are used to measure motor activity and behavior, but those cited above tend to be the more commonly used parameters.

The first and perhaps most comprehensive examination of the effect of caffeine on postnatal development in rats was carried out by Sobotka and his colleagues (59). There have been many other investigations since then, but since most of them are similarly in design, it is appropriate to detail the original study and mention only the results of others. In this first investigation (59), three groups of pregnant Sprague-Dawley rats were given 0.0125, 0.025, or 0.5% caffeine (approximate doses: 23, 49 or 92 mg/kg/day) in their drinking water from day 7 of gestation to the day of weaning (day 22). Controls received normal tap water. Dams gave birth and nursed their offspring until weaning. There were no significant effects on maternal weight gain, food or water consumption (except increases in dams during lactation), or litter size. There were slight reductions in pre-weaning body weight for pups of low and high dose caffeine-treated dams, but the mid-dose group was unaffected. Post-weaning body weights were not significantly different. The only pre-weaning parameter affected by caffeine was eye opening, but this was not dose related. On day 13 of weaning, eye opening was significantly delayed in female offspring in the high-dose group and males in the mid-dose group. Open field activity and the surface righting reflex were unaffected by all dose levels.

Only male pups were examined for post-weaning behavior. Passive avoidance and motor activity were unaffected by caffeine. Open-field behavior, on the other hand, was significantly increased in all doses, with an increase in the number of rearings inversely related to dose. There was also enhanced performance in position discrimination tasks, but this was not dose related. This was the first demonstration of an effect of caffeine on postnatal development and showed that, while there was little effect in the neonate, some behavioral changes in post-weaning adolescents had occurred (59). Numerous investigations (summarized in Table 3) have demonstrated similar results in the rat, although there is some variation between studies (60–72). For example, three investigations demonstrated a delay in eye opening (59,64,67), while three others failed to show this response (61,65,73), even when strains and treatments were very similar [compare Sobotka et al. (59) and Gullberg et al. (65)]. Such conflicting data is also seen for most other parameters of postnatal behavior in the rat (Table 3).

TABLE 3. *A summary of the effects of*

Study (ref. no.)	Strain	Route and dose range	Eye opening	Incisor eruption
Sobotka et al., 1979 (59)	Sprague-Dawley	Drinking water 23–92 mg/kg/day	Delayed	ND
Peruzzi et al., 1985 (64)	Sprague-Dawley	Drinking water 27–188 mg/kg/day	Delayed	No effect
Gullberg et al., 1986 (65)	Sprague-Dawley	Drinking water 23–135 mg/kg/day	No effect	ND
Butcher et al., 1984 (61)	Sprague-Dawley	Drinking water 25–90 mg/kg/day	No effect	Delayed
Hughes and De'Ath, 1983 (73)	Wistar	Intraperitoneal 20 mg/kg/day	No effect	ND
West et al., 1986 (67)	Charles River Albino	Gavage 5–75 mg/kg/day	Delayed	Delayed
Swenson et al., 1990 (72)	Sprague-Dawley	Subcutaneous 60 mg/kg/day	ND	ND
Nakamoto et al., 1991 (71)	Sprague-Dawley	Diet 20 mg/kg/day	ND	ND
Grimm and Fieder, 1988 (63)	Wistar	Drinking water 25–75 mg/kg/day	ND	ND
Hughes and Beveridge, 1986 (66)	Wistar	Intraperitoneal 10–40 mg/kg/day	ND	ND
Hughes and Beveridge, 1990 (70)	Wistar	Drinking water 28–36 mg/kg/day	ND	ND
Glavin and Krueger, 1985 (62)	Wistar	Drinking water 12.5–35 mg/kg/day	ND	ND

ND, not determined.

There have been few investigations in other species. One study, in which two strains of mice were dosed with up to 100 mg/kg/day caffeine in drinking water from the day before mating until parturition, found a significant increase in open-field activity in female C57BR offspring (9 to 15 months of age) but not in males, nor was it observed in Balb/C mice (60). Caffeine did not affect spontaneous alternation in either strain, and the results from the passive avoidance tasks were variable, although some significant difference was noted for both strains.

In the only investigation to date in primates, caffeine was administered to 40 cynomogus monkeys at two dose levels; the low group received 10 to 15 mg/kg/day, and the high group received 25 to 35 mg/kg/day in their drinking water (75). The animals were treated for at least eight weeks prior to mating. The reproductive history of all these monkeys was unknown since they had been captured in the wild. Nineteen controls produced 19 live infants; 21 low-dose monkeys produced 14 live infants, 2 miscarriages, and 5 stillbirths; in the high-dose group, 20 monkeys produced live infants, 5 miscarriages, and 6 stillbirths. The investigators could find no cause for death in the stillbirths other than that the lungs were not inflated. No gross malformations were detected. Birthweight of female infants was decreased with increasing caffeine but was significant only when the results of the treated groups were

caffeine on postnatal development in the rat

Surface righting	Air righting	Auditory startle	Open-field activity (OFA)	Post weaning OFA	Complex tasks
No effect	ND	ND	No effect	Increased	No effect
Delayed	Delayed	ND	ND	Increased	ND
ND	Delayed	Delayed	No effect	ND	ND
No effect	ND	Delayed	Increased	Increased	No effect
No effect	ND	ND	ND	No effect	ND
ND	No effect	Delayed	No effect	No effect	Increased
ND	ND	ND	ND	ND	No effect
ND	ND	ND	ND	Increased	ND
ND	ND	ND	No effect	Increased	Increased
ND	ND	ND	ND	Increased	ND
ND	ND	ND	ND	Increased	ND
ND	ND	ND	ND	No effect	ND

added together. This was a poorly conducted study, and the protocol had to be extensively altered due to large numbers of unexpected stillbirths and miscarriages. The offspring nevertheless showed impaired performance with a spatial delayed-to-sample task (69). It is therefore evident that, although prenatal exposure to greater than 20 mg/kg/day of caffeine can cause behavioral and developmental alterations in animals, the effects are subtle and somewhat inconsistent, so that no definite conclusions on the "behavioural teratological effect" of caffeine can be drawn at present.

SUMMARY OF THE ANIMAL DATA

This chapter examines the effect of caffeine on animal reproduction. Different strains and species differ somewhat in their sensitivity to caffeine, but in general the effects on reproduction are comparable. The importance of the mode of administration should be emphasized, and it is clear that caffeine is a weak teratogen when given in a single bolus dose of 80 mg/kg or more to rats and 50 mg/kg to mice. When administered in multiple low doses in drinking water or in diet (below 300 mg/kg/day), caffeine has no teratogenic effects. Even levels of 204.5 mg/kg/day of caffeine in drinking water have been shown to exert no teratogenic effects. Nevertheless, nonteratogenic levels of caffeine may still affect other aspects of reproduction, with consequent adverse effects on the fetus. Other effects, including those on fertility and postnatal development, are less well established, and results are too inconsistent at present for definite conclusions to be drawn.

CONSIDERATION OF ANIMAL DATA FOR RISK ASSESSMENT IN HUMANS

In attempting to assess the teratogenic hazard for humans, consideration must be given to the critical blood or plasma level necessary for teratogenesis and not just to the total daily dose to which they are exposed. The use of conventional safety margins for dealing with "peak level" teratogens is inappropriate. Most normal caffeine consumers have peak plasma caffeine levels of approximately 2 to 5 µg/ml, and heavy coffee drinkers (six or more cups a day) would rarely reach 10 µg/ml. Clear pharmacological effects of caffeine are seen only at levels well above this and, except in cases of poisoning, such levels are not normally seen. The dose of 80 mg/kg used in animal studies is around one-third to one-fifth the LD50 and, as discussed above, deaths are common in animals at the higher dose levels. The teratogenic plasma threshold for caffeine was calculated to be 60 µg/ml from the animal data (24,30,34) (see section above on blood levels). It is inconceivable that humans could approach a blood level of 60 µg/ml except in a deliberate overdose attempt and, considering the available animal data, it seems extremely unlikely that caffeine presents any teratogenic hazard to humans. This surmise is borne out by epidemiological studies (74).

A safety margin for caffeine cannot be set using traditional factors. From the available animal teratology data, the probable blood level of caffeine required to produce teratogenic effects is in excess of 60 μg/ml. Although this level can be reached only with single, large bolus doses and cannot be reached by consumption of solutions of caffeine over a period of several hours, one can extrapolate from this figure to arrive at a theoretical dose that is teratogenic for humans through consumption of caffeinated beverages.

Administration of 80 mg/kg/day of caffeine to pregnant rats in drinking water resulted in a mean peak plasma caffeine level of 5.7 μg/ml (30). The peak required to elicit a teratogenic effect is 63.09 $\pm$ 4.73 μg/ml, which was produced by the equivalent dose administered as a single bolus dose (30). The plasma level of caffeine produced through administration in drinking water, then, is below its teratogenic threshold by a factor of approximately 10. In theory, then, 80 $\times$ 10 = 800 mg/kg/day of caffeine administered in drinking water might produce a peak plasma concentration of caffeine of approximately 60 μg/ml. Using these hypothetical data, 800 mg/kg/day caffeine is equivalent to a human (weighing 60 kg) consuming 48,000 mg (800 $\times$ 6) of caffeine a day, or 480 cups of coffee, 1,200 cups of tea or, 1,370 cans of cola. It is perhaps more to the point that 5 to 10 g of caffeine is the suggested lethal dose for humans.

REFERENCES

1. Bachmann G, Haldi J, Wynn W, Ensor C. Reproductivity and growth of albino rats on a prolonged daily intake of caffeine. *J Nutr* 1946;32:239.
2. Friedman L, Weinberger MA, Farber MT, et al. Testicular atrophy and impaired spermatogenesis in rats fed high levels of the methylxanthines caffeine, theobromine, or theophylline. *J Environ Pathol Toxicol* 1979;2:687.
3. Whitby KE, Collins TFX, Welsh JJ, et al. Reproduction study of caffeine administration to male Osborne-Mendel rats. *Fd Chem Toxic* 1986;24:277.
4. Pollard I, Williamson S, Magre S. Influence of caffeine administered during pregnancy on the early differentiation of fetal rat ovaries and testes. *J Dev Physiol* 1990;13:59.
5. Dews PB. *Caffeine.* New York: Springer-Verlag; 1984.
6. Garbers DL, First NL, Sullivan JJ, Lardy HA. Stimulation and maintenance of ejaculated bovine spermatozoan respiration and motility by caffeine. *Biol Reprod* 1971;5:336.
7. Morton B, Chang TSK. The effect of fluid from the cauda epididymis, serum components and caffeine upon the survival of diluted epididymal hamster spermatozoa. *J Repro Fert* 1973;35:255.
8. Pomeroy KO, Dodds JF, Seidel GE, Jr. Caffeine promotes in vitro fertilization of mouse ova within 15 minutes. *J Exp Zool* 1988;248:207.
9. Dunlop M, Court JM. Effects of maternal caffeine ingestion on neonate growth in rats. *Biol Neonate* 1981;39:178.
10. Thayer PS, Kensler CJ. Exposure of four generations of mice to caffeine in drinking water. *Toxicol Appl Pharmacol* 1973;25:169.
11. Thayer PS, Kensler CJ. Genetic tests in mice of caffeine alone and in combination with mutagens. *Toxicol Appl Pharmacol* 1973;25:157.
12. Palm PE, Arnold EP, Rachwall PC, Leyczek JC, Teague KW, Kensler CJ. Evaluation of

the teratogenic potential of fresh-brewed coffee and caffeine in the rat. *Toxicol Appl Pharmacol* 1978;44:1.

13. Aeschbacher HU, Milon H, Poot A, Wurzner HP. Effect of caffeine on rat offspring from treated dams. *Toxicol Letts* 1980;7:71.

14. Nagasawa H, Sakurai N. Effects of chronic ingestion of caffeine on mammary growth and reproduction in mice. *Life Sciences* 1986;39:351.

15. Pollard I, Jabbour H, Mehrabani PA. Effects of caffeine administration during pregnancy on fetal development and subsequent functions in the adult rat: prolonged effects on a second generation. *J Toxicol Environ Health* 1987;22:1.

16. Nolen GA. The effect of brewed and instant coffee on reproduction and teratogenesis in the rat. *Toxicol Appl Pharmacol* 1981;58:171.

17. Nolen GA. A reproduction/teratology study of brewed and instant decaffeinated coffees. *J Toxicol Environ Health* 1982;10:769.

18. Knoche C, Konig J. Prenatal toxicity of diphenylpyraline-8-chlorotheophylinate, with reference to experiments with thalidomide and caffeine. *Anzneimittel-forsch* 1964;14:415.

19. Nishimura H, Nakai K. Congenital malformations in offspring of mice treated with caffeine. *Proc Soc Exp Biol Med* 1960;104:140.

20. Fujii T, Sasaki N, Nishimura H. Teratogenicity of caffeine in mice related to its mode of administration. *Jap J Pharmac* 1969;19:134.

21. Snigorska B, Bartel H. Studies in the teratogenic influence of caffeine in the fetuses of white mice. *Folia Morphologica (Warsz)* 1970;29:353.

22. Bartel H, Gnacikowska M. Histological studies on the influence of caffeine on embryonic development of the limbs in mice. *Folia Morphologica (Warsz)* 1972;31:178.

23. Elmazar MMA, McElhatton PR, Sullivan FM. Acute studies to investigate the mechanism of action of caffeine as a teratogen in mice. *Human Toxicol* 1981;1:53.

24. Elmazar MMA, McElhatton PR, Sullivan FM. Studies on the teratogenic effects of different oral preparations of caffeine in mice. *Toxicol* 1982;23:57.

25. Scott WJ. Caffeine-induced limb malformations: Description of malformations and quantitation of placental transfer. *Teratology* 1983;28:427.

26. Group d'Etude des Risques Teratogenes. Experimental teratogenesis: study of caffeine with mice. *Therapie* 1969;24:575.

27. Bertrand M, Girod J, Rigaud MF. Ectrodactylie provoquee par la cafeine chez les Rongeurs. Role des facteurs specifiques et genetiques. *C R Soc Biol* 1970;164:1488.

28. Murphy SJ, Benjamin CP. The effects of coffee on mouse development. *Microbiols Letters* 1981;17:91.

29. Collins TFX, Welsh JJ, Black TN, Collins EV. A study of the teratogenic potential of caffeine given by oral intubation to rats. *Regulatory Toxicology and Pharmacology* 1981;1: 355.

30. Ikeda GJ, Sapienza PP, McGinnis ML, Bragg LE, Walsh JJ, Collins TFX. Blood levels of caffeine and results of fetal examination after oral administration of caffeine to pregnant rats. *J Appl Toxicol* 1982;2:307.

31. Bertrand M, Schwam E, Frandon A, Vagne A, Alary J. On the systematic and specific teratogenic effect of caffeine in rodents. *C R Soc Biol* 1965;159:2199.

32. Leuschner F, Schwerdtfeger W. Uber den Einfluss von Coffein und anderen Methylxanthinen auf die Fortpflanzung von Wistar Ratten. In: Heim F, Ammon HPT, eds. *Coffein und andere Methylxanthine*. Stuttgart: F.K. Schattauer Verlag; 1969:209.

33. Leuschner F, Czok G. Reversibility of prenatal injuries induced by caffeine in rats. *ASIC (Paris) Cinquieme Colloque International sur la Chimie des Cafes, Lisbonne* 1973;388.

34. Smith SE, McElhatton PR, Sullivan FM. Effects of administering caffeine to pregnant rats either as a single daily dose or as divided doses four times a day. *Fd Chem Toxic* 1987;25: 125.

35. Collins TFX. Review of reproduction and teratology studies of caffeine. *FDA By lines* 1979; September:352.

36. Collins TFX, Welsh JJ, Black TN, Ruggles DI. Teratogenic potential of caffeine in rats. In: *Alternative dietary practices and nutritional abuses in pregnancy. Proceedings of a workshop*. National Academy Press, 1981:97–107.

37. Federation of American Societies for Experimental Biology (FASEB). *Evaluation of the health aspects of caffeine as a food ingredient*. Springfield, VA: NTIS, 1978.

38. Ritter EJ, Scott WJ, Wilson JG, Mathinos PR, Randall JL. Potentiative interactions between caffeine and various teratogenic agents. *Teratology* 1982;25:95.
39. Gilbert EF, Pistey WR. Effect on the offspring of repeated caffeine administration to pregnant rats. *J Repro Fert* 1973;34:495.
40. Collins TFX, Welsh JJ, Black TN, Ruggles DI. A study of the teratogenic potential of caffeine ingested in drinking water. *Fd Chem Toxic* 1983;21:763.
41. Fujii T, Nishimura H. Adverse effects of prolonged administration of caffeine on rat fetus. *Toxicol Appl Pharmacol* 1972;22:449.
42. Nau H. Teratogenic valproic acid concentrations: infusion by implanted minipumps versus conventional injection regimen in the mouse. *Toxicol Appl Pharmacol* 1985;80:243.
43. Nau H, Scott WJ. Teratogenicity of valproic acid and related substances in the mouse: drug accumulation and pHi in the embryo during organogenesis and structure-activity considerations. *Arch Toxicol* 1987;suppl. 11:128.
44. Nau H, Scott, WJ. *Pharmacokinetics in teratogenesis. Vol 1. Interspecies comparison and maternal embryonic-fetal drug transfer.* Boca Raton, Florida: CRC Press, Inc., 1987.
45. Sullivan FM, Smith SE, McElhatton PR. Interpretation of animal experiments as illustrated by studies on caffeine. In: Nau H, Scott WJ, Eds. *Pharmacokinetics in Teratogenesis.* Volume 1; Boca Raton, Florida: CRC Press, Inc., 1987:123–7.
46. Muther TF. Caffeine and reduction of fetal ossification in the rat: fact or artifact. *Teratology* 1988;37:239.
47. Tanaka H, Nakazawa K, Arima M. Maternal caffeine and fetal development in rats. *Teratology* 1982;26:20A.
48. Loosli R, Loustalot P, Schalch WR, Sievers K, Stenger EG. Joint study in teratogenicity research. *Proceedings of the European Society for the study of drug toxicity* 1964;4:214.
49. Collins TFX, Welsh JJ, Black TN, Whitby KE, O'Donnell MW. Potential reversibility of skeletal effects in rats exposed in utero to caffeine. *Fd Chem Toxic* 1987;25:647.
50. Nakamoto T, Grant S, Yazdani M. The effects of maternal caffeine intake during pregnancy on mineral contents of fetal rat bone. *Res Exp Med* 1989;189:275.
51. Sasahara H, Yamano H, Kakamoto T. Effects of maternal caffeine with zinc intake during gestation and lactation on bone development in newborn rats. *Archs Oral Biol* 1990;35:425.
52. Schneider PE, Miller HI, Nakamoto T. Effects of caffeine intake during gestation and lactation on bones of young growing rats. *Res Exp Med* 1990;190:131.
53. Driscoll PG, Joseph F, Nakamoto T. Prenatal effects of maternal caffeine intake and dietary high protein on mandibular development in fetal rats. *Br J Nutr* 1990;63:285.
54. Nakamoto T, Shaye R. Protein-energy malnutrition in rats during pregnancy modifies the effects of caffeine on fetal bones. *J Nutr* 1986;116:633.
55. Tanaka H, Nakazawa K, Arima M, Iwasaki S. Caffeine and its dimethylxanthines and fetal cerebral development in rat. *Brain Dev* 1984;6:355.
56. Hart AD, Grimble RF. Effect of methylxanthines on lactational performance of rats. *Ann Nutr Metab* 1990;34:297.
57. Hart AD, Grimble RF. The effect of methylxanthines on milk volume and composition, and growth of rat pups. *Br J Nutr* 1990;64:339.
58. Sheffield LG. Caffeine administered during pregnancy augments subsequent lactation in mice. *J Anim Sci* 1991;69:1128.
59. Sobotka TJ, Spaid SL, Brodie RE. Neurobehavioral teratology of caffeine exposure in rats. *Neurotoxicology* 1979;1:403.
60. Sinton CM, Valatx JL, Jouvet M. Gestational caffeine modifies offspring behaviour in mice. *Pyschopharmacology* 1981;75:69.
61. Butcher RE, Vorhees CV, Wootten V. Behavioral and physical development of rats chronically exposed to caffeinated fluids. *Fundam Appl Toxicol* 1984;4:1.
62. Glavin GB, Krueger H. Effects of prenatal caffeine administration of offspring mortality, open-field behaviour and adult gastric ulcer susceptibility. *Neurobehav Toxicol Teratol* 1985;7:29.
63. Grimm VE, Frieder B. Prenatal caffeine causes long lasting behavioral and neurochemical changes. *Int J Neurosci* 1988;41:15.
64. Peruzzi G, Lombardelli G, Abbracchio MP, Coen E, Cattabeni F. Perinatal caffeine treatment: behavioral and biochemical effects in rats before weaning. *Neurobehav Toxicol Teratol* 1985;7:453.

65. Gullberg EI, Ferrell F, Christensen HD. Effects of postnatal caffeine exposure through dam's milk upon weanling rats. *Pharm Biochem Behavior* 1986;24:1695.
66. Hughes RN, Beveridge IJ. Behavioral effects of prenatal exposure to caffeine in rats. *Life Sci* 1986;38:861.
67. West GL, Sobotka TJ, Brodie RE, Beier JM, O'Donnell MW. Postnatal neurobehavioral development in rats exposed in utero to caffeine. *Neurobehav Toxicol Teratol* 1986;8:29.
68. Hughes RN, Beveridge IJ. Effects of prenatal exposure to chronic caffeine on locomotor and emotional behavior. *Psychobiology* 1987;15:179.
69. Gilbert SG, Rice DC. Effect of *in utero* caffeine exposure on spatial and non-spatial matching to sample performance in infant monkeys. *Society of Toxicology Meeting, Miami Beach* 1990;12-16th February:1212.
70. Hughes RN, Beveridge IJ. Sex and age dependent effects of prenatal exposure to caffeine on open field behaviour, emergence latency and adrenal weights in rats. *Life Sciences* 1990; 47:2075.
71. Nakamoto T, Roy G, Gottschalk SB, Yazdani M, Rossowska M. Lasting effects of early chronic caffeine feeding on rats' behaviour and brain in later life. *Physiol Behav* 1991;49: 721.
72. Swenson RR, Beckwith BE, Lamberty KJ, Krebs SJ, Tinius TP. Prenatal exposure to AVP or caffeine but not oxytocin alters learning in female rats. *Peptides* 1990;11:927.
73. Hughes RN, De'Ath CP. Effect of prenatal caffeine on behaviour of young rats. *Psychol Psychiat* 1983;11:504.
74. Leviton A. Caffeine consumption and the risk of reproductive hazards. *J Repro Med* 1988; 33:175.
75. Gilbert SG, Rice DC, Reuhl KR, Stavric B. Adverse pregnancy outcome in the monkey (*Macaca fascicularis*) after chronic caffeine exposure. *Pharmacol Exp Therap* 1988;245: 1048.

Caffeine, Coffee, and Health,
edited by S. Garattini.
Raven Press, Ltd., New York © 1993.

13

Coffee, Caffeine, and Reproductive Hazards in Humans

Alan Leviton

*Department of Neurology, Children's Hospital/Harvard Medical School,
Boston, Massachusetts 02115*

Observational studies of women have evaluated the association between consumption of caffeine-containing beverages and the risk of delayed conception, spontaneous abortion, prematurity, low birthweight, and congenital malformations. The design and analytic deficiencies of many of these studies limit the inferences that can be based on their findings. The larger and higher quality studies tend to show no relationship between caffeine (or coffee) consumption and pregnancy adversities.

INTRODUCTION

The relationship between coffee consumption and reproductive hazards has been reviewed frequently in the past decade (1–14). In part, the plethora of reviews reflects the abundant number of papers added to the field each year. Thus, I could justify another review by saying it was the most up to date when it was written in late 1991. I wanted, however, to justify it in another way, especially for people who had no epidemiologic training. I wanted this review to help them appreciate the minefield that is the topic of coffee consumption and reproductive epidemiology.

Unlike other reviews of this field, the framework of this review is a catalogue of the limitations that characterize many of the studies. Built on this framework are specific examples from the literature. This review is not exhaustive, however. Rather, it is intended to be a primer that will enable the reader to identify, in future reports, the limitations tabulated here.

The major limitations of the studies that have evaluated coffee and caffeine consumption as risk factors for reproductive hazards are listed in Table 1. Some of the studies that have each limitation are identified in Tables 2 to 6. The exposure information was collected and presented in so many ways that I believed that Tables 2 to 6 should have more exposure information than would be conveyed by the five exposure limitations listed in Table 1.

SAMPLE SELECTION

One philosophy in epidemiology is that the ideal observational study approximates a randomized clinical trial (15). For example, those exposed (i.e., who drink coffee) should be as similar as possible to those who are not exposed (i.e., who drink no coffee). Although a theoretical goal, this is rarely, if ever, achieved. A body of literature attests to the differences between coffee consumers and abstainers (16–20).

Another desirable characteristic of epidemiological studies is that subjects be representative of their groups. In a cohort study, the women recruited should be representative of all those who (a) intend to become pregnant (if assessing delayed conception or infertility), or (b) have become pregnant.

Investigators do not always achieve their goals, in part because those evaluating the relationships between coffee/caffeine consumption and reproductive adversities tend to use samples of convenience. This process is sometimes started when a sample recruited for other purposes is found (post hoc) to have an adversity associated with coffee/caffeine consumption (21). A report of such an unexpected finding appears to prompt investigators to review data they had collected for other purposes to see whether the coffee/caffeine relation with the reproductive adversity is seen in their own sample.

Samples of convenience are also used for a combination of other reasons. It appears that few epidemiologists who study reproductive hazards start out with coffee/caffeine consumption as their primary focus. Indeed, one gets the impression that coffee and caffeine are incidental interests. Nevertheless, many investigators ask their subjects about coffee and caffeine consumption, apparently to divert attention from other risk factors (e.g., cigarette smoking and alcohol consumption) or for completeness.

Unfortunately, such a sample of convenience may pose problems of inference (15). For example, half of the sample recruited by Barr and her colleagues (22) was in the top quintile of alcohol consumption. Similarly, Fried and O'Connell (23) emphasized consumption of cannabis, alcohol, and tobacco in selecting their sample.

In another study, members of the Church of Latter Day Saints (Mormons) were selected because of their presumed homogeneity and low probability of life-style characteristics that might adversely influence fetal well-being (24). Not only are Mormons a heterogeneous group, but those Mormons who deviate from church teachings in one area are more likely than their peers to deviate from the church's teachings in other areas (25).

If proved fertility conveys information about the risk of a woman's conceiving in the future, then any study of delayed conception or reduced fertility, ideally, should be limited to women who have conceived or, preferably, given birth to full-term healthy children. The published studies evaluating caffeine/coffee consumption and subfecundity have utilized opportunistic

TABLE 1. *Some of the most striking limitations of the studies listed in Tables 2–6.*

Sample selection

The basic axion is that participants in a study should be representative of all in their category (women desiring to conceive, etc). This axiom can be violated in the following ways:

S-1 Selecting a convenience sample
S-2 Selecting as cases only the most extreme examples of the disorder
S-3 Selecting controls who are not suitable
    Women who differed from cases in their risk of the outcome
    Women who might not acknowledge pregnancy characteristics, events, and
       exposures as readily as cases.
S-4 Selecting only the most cooperative

Exposure

1. Crude (rarely/frequently)
2. Basis of dichotomization not justified
3. Ignoring consumption changes during pregnancy. The assumption that consumption at one time (i.e., before pregnancy) is the same months later (i.e., throughout pregnancy) is not supported by the literature.
4. Assuming that every cup of coffee has the same caffeine content.
5. Considering caffeine from a few sources only (e.g., coffee and tea but not cola, medications, etc).

Inference

The basic goal is to avoid having confounders distort our perception of the relationship between exposure and outcome. The following practices appear to have prevented investigators from achieving this goal.

A. Not controlling for potentially important confounders
    I-1. No multivariate analysis at all
    I-2. Control of one confounder at a time
    I-3. Ignoring potentially important confounders (e.g., alcohol consumption, previous pregnancy history, nausea)
B. Controlling inadequately for obvious confounders (e.g., viewing tobacco smoking as a dichotomous variable rather than as a continuous variable)
    I-4. Dichotomizing variables that should be continuous, the data, by the most important confounder candidates
    I-5. Not stratifying (or failing to convince the reader that the data were indeed examined in different strata)
C. Inferential errors related to post-hoc analyses
    I-6. Subsample analyses
    I-7. Viewing hypothesis generation as hypothesis testing

samples, and no effort appears to have been made to evaluate the beverage/fertility relationship separately in nulliparous women and those who had conceived previously (see I-5 in Table 1).

In a case-referent (case-control) study, the cases and the referent group (usually identified as *controls*) should be representative of those with and without the outcome. The representativeness of case groups is called into question when details about case selection are not provided. Caan and Goldhaber (26) selected their 34 low-birthweight and 97 growth-retarded newborns from a population of 9,000 babies. If intrauterine growth retardation is defined as birthweight less than the tenth percentile for gestational age, then approximately 900 babies should have been eligible. Including only 97 without accounting for the other 803 raises doubts about case selection procedures.

The controls should also be representative of all those without the outcome of interest. Some investigators did not even describe control selection procedures (27).

Reasonable people may argue about the best control for any outcome studied. In their effort to evaluate whether consumption of caffeine-containing beverages increased the risk of delivering a malformed baby, Rosenberg and her colleagues (28) selected as controls for each group of malformations mothers of children with other malformations. The investigators argued persuasively against the generalized teratogenic effects of caffeine. Their claim that mothers of malformed babies may selectively recall pregnancy experiences differently from mothers of babies without malformations has since been documented (29).

The case-referent design is essential when investigators are first studying a rare phenomenon (e.g., any specific group of malformations). The more extensive cohort design can be used for relatively common phenomena and has the distinct advantage of ascertaining exposure on an ongoing basis (and before selective recall can set in).

The effects of caffeine/coffee consumption on birthweight can be studied using the case-referent design or the cohort design. Only ten of sixteen studies of fetal growth evaluated birthweight as a continuous variable (Table 2). For a case-referent study, however, a dichotomous outcome is needed. Where should the line be drawn between converting a continuous variable into a low-frequency adverse outcome and the larger group of those without the adversity? In seven studies, low birthweight was defined as less than 2.5 kg (26,32–37), small-for-gestational-age (not defined by Furuhashi and his colleagues), or intrauterine growth retardation (i.e., less than the tenth percentile in birthweight for gestational age) (26,37). These dichotomous entities may be heterogeneous themselves (38).

Power is the word epidemiologists use to denote a study's ability to avoid the (β or type II) error of inferring no difference between two groups when, in truth, a difference does exist. *Power* is defined as one minus the β error (i.e., power = $1 - \beta$). Thus, the greater the power, the smaller the β error. In addition, the larger the sample size, the more powerful the study. For example, Berkowitz and her colleagues (39) reported that their study had a power of 0.9 to conclude that coffee and tea consumption were not associated with a tripling of the risk of preterm delivery, but only a power of 0.8 to conclude that coffee and tea consumption were not associated with a two-and one-half fold increased risk of prematurity. Sample sizes of 48 (31) and 52 (40) must be expected to have virtually no power.

EXPOSURE

Ascertaining exposure to coffee and caffeine correctly is essential if investigators are to claim a relationship with a reproductive hazard. One of the major building blocks of an argument that the exposure causes the outcome is a dose-response relationship. To claim that coffee/caffeine consumption causes a reproductive adversity requires that women who consume the most be at highest risk. As will become apparent, measuring exposure is one of the more formidable problems facing epidemiologists who want to study the correlates and effects of coffee and caffeine consumption.

Serving Size

Not everybody drinks from the same size cup (41). Some people drink their coffee from what might be called a teacup (180 ml to the brim), others from an eight-ounce cup, and others from a mug (usually varying in size from 300 to 480 ml). Some people fill their cup only three-quarters full to allow the addition of milk or cream, whereas others will do so to avoid spilling it when moved from where it is poured to where it is consumed. Others may not drink all they have poured.

A serving of caffeine-containing soda can vary from 180 to 360 ml. These are only the beginnings of the exposure-ascertainment obstacle course. A tall glass filled with ice cubes may provide less than half the cola that would be available from the same glass without any ice cubes.

Caffeine Content

The wide variability in coffee roasting, grinding, and brewing methods reflects both regional and personal preferences (42,43). Epidemiologists are limited in their ability to assess caffeine content. Recall by questionnaire may overestimate consumption by some and underestimate consumption by others when compared to information obtained with diaries (44). In a recent report, current caffeine consumption was assessed at one time and retrospectively at least three years later for the same time (45). Breast cancer cases tended to underreport their daily past caffeine consumption by about 75 mg, whereas controls underreported theirs by about 40 mg. Pregnant controls were more likely than women who miscarried to report lower caffeine consumption when reinterviewed six months after the first interview (46).

Plasma content of methylxanthine metabolites do not necessarily correlate with reported caffeine consumption as assessed by a questionnaire (47). Although such discrepancies may reflect varying time intervals between consumption and phlebotomy, they call into question the validity of reported caffeine consumption. Then too, similar methylxanthine blood levels, despite reported differences in consumption, might reflect differences in metabolic degradation rates.

Problems with consumption during pregnancy are a special set of problems. First, nausea during the first and second trimesters appears to be associated with a decrease in coffee and caffeine consumption (48). Second, the pathways associated with methylxanthine degradation are markedly slowed near the end of pregnancy (49–51). Presumably to avoid the dysphoria associated with elevated plasma levels of methylxanthine metabolites, women appear to reduce their consumption of coffee and caffeine during pregnancy (19,30,52,53). In addition, some women reduce their caffeine consumption in anticipation of becoming pregnant or upon confirmation that they are pregnant (30,48). Because of these phenomena, as well as problems of reliability and validity, the ideal study would measure coffee/caffeine consumption before and repeatedly throughout pregnancy. Unfortunately, this is not possible for case-referent studies in which the relatively rare outcome is usually first apparent after birth. Even more unfortunate is the lack of repeated measures of consumption for outcomes that can be studied prospectively (e.g., birthweight, a delayed conception, etc).

Some case-referent studies have asked women after delivery about their usual consumption (24,54), rather than about consumption at a specific time just before or during pregnancy. Other investigators have not made clear what period the consumption measure refers to (27,28,33,35,55,56).

ANALYSIS

Epidemiologists apply the term *confounder* to variables that distort our perception of the relationship between an exposure and an outcome (57). Invariably, these variables are associated with the exposure and with the outcome (even among those not exposed).

An example of a confounder is maternal age. Coffee consumption appears to increase with age between adolescence and menopause (58). The risk of a number of reproductive hazards also appears to increase with the number of years beyond age 25 or 30 (59). Thus, unless the investigators take into account maternal age, they might find a relationship between coffee consumption and a reproductive hazard, not because coffee increases the risk of that hazard, but merely because of an association between maternal age and both the exposure and the hazard.

Coffee drinkers differ in a number of ways from those who do not drink coffee, and those who consume the most coffee differ from those who consume less (16–20,60–62). Compared to people who drink no coffee or drink only small amounts, those who consume large amounts of coffee tend to consume more tobacco and alcohol. Socially undesirable behaviors tend to be underreported (63). Perhaps that is why some people tend not to fully acknowledge their alcohol and tobacco consumption. Whether this is particularly true for pregnant women has yet to be determined. Consider the possibility that some people who underreport their tobacco and alcohol consumption fully acknowledge their coffee consumption. In such a situation, the coffee consumption variable conveys information about the amount of alcohol and tobacco consumed. As a consequence, when the socially unacceptable behavior is underreported but coffee consumption is not, the coffee consumption variable conveys information not only about coffee consumption but also about the socially unacceptable behavior. Morrison (64) proposed that this type of confounding accounts for some of the reported association between coffee consumption and one malignancy.

A recent publication calls attention to the Morrison hypothesis, but not by name (65). Among women who did not smoke, caffeine consumption was not associated with any birthweight reduction. Among smokers, however, those who consumed 400 mg of caffeine per day gave birth to babies 6.5% lighter than did women who consumed no caffeine. The most obvious interpretation is that caffeine exacerbates a tobacco effect. For epidemiologists trained to accept the admonition that they might be wrong (15), an alternative interpretation is that the caffeine consumption variable provides improved information about the true (but inadequately acknowledged) consumption of tobacco and alcohol.

Another example of confounding is most pertinent to the study of fetal wastage, or perhaps what is more appropriately termed *spontaneous abortion*. In this instance, nausea is the confounder. Nausea is associated with a reduction in caffeine consumption (48). However, nausea is *less* common in the pregnancies that culminate in spontaneous abortion than in pregnancies resulting in an apparently healthy baby (48,66,67). Zena Stein and Mervyn Susser (68) offer the view that hormones produced by the recently implanted placenta contribute to nausea. Thus, the larger and better functioning the placenta, the higher the levels of these hormones (especially chorionic gonadotropin) and the greater the likelihood a viable implantation will continue to term. Thus, a woman whose placenta is not producing the anticipated levels of hormones is unlikely to have nausea, and she is unlikely to reduce her caffeine consumption. In addition, she is more likely to miscarry than women who are nauseated. As a consequence, failure to reduce caffeine consumption may be a marker of a suboptimal implantation rather than a cause of any fetal adversity.

Investigators who do not control/adjust for potentially important confounders have no basis for claiming any relationship between an exposure and an outcome. Some investigators have controlled for one confounder at a time (30,53). Others have not made any adjustment whatsoever (24,33,35,40,44). A number of competent investigators have sometimes not controlled for all the variables, or, if they have, have not reported such efforts at adjustment.

For example, Rosenberg and her colleagues did not describe adjusting for alcohol in their study of malformations. Srisuphan and Bracken (69) selected as confounders only those with a p value of 0.1 or less. The potential problems of this criterion are described elsewhere (70).

Some investigators have chosen to throw away valuable information. Smoking is associated with birthweight reduction in a dose-response manner (71). Thus, it would seem prudent to classify smokers by their amount of smoking. Some investigators, however, have dichotomized smoking as a yes/no variable (33,36,54,72). Caan and Goldhaber (26) did not do any better when they dichotomized smoking at the 10-cigarettes-per-day level. The work of Brooke and his colleagues (19) illustrates how the careful attention to smoking eliminates the apparent association between coffee consumption and birthweight.

CONCLUSIONS

With this understanding of the basic problems that plague the literature about coffee/caffeine consumption and reproductive hazards, it is now appropriate to move on to specific hazards.

Low Birthweight

Fully 15 reports have been published on the relationship between coffee/caffeine consumption and birthweight (Table 2). The larger (32,34) and better-conducted (19) studies tend to show no relationship, although this is not always the case (32). Thus, the likelihood is that coffee and caffeine consumption do not reduce birthweight.

Prematurity

Premature onset of labor and premature rupture of membranes account for most deliveries before the 37th week of gestation (Table 3) (73). Vaginal bleeding (including placenta previa and abruptio placentae) and maternal illness (most often preeclampsia) are the disorders that tend to prompt physicians to evacuate the uterus before term. These four physiological disturbances indicate the heterogeneity of what is termed *prematurity*.

None of the ten studies that evaluated the relationship between maternal coffee/caffeine consumption and prematurity considered gestational age as a continuum. Even the three largest studies, each with cohorts of more than 10,000 women, dichotomized gestational age, defining prematurity as less than 37 weeks (32–34). As with birthweight, the larger and higher quality

TABLE 2. Studies of the association between coffee/caffeine consumption and the risk of reduced birthweight

First author	Birthweight		Daily coffee/caffeine consumption		Other limitations	
	Sample size	Birthweight outcome	When assessed	Group considered exposed	Sample	Inference
Mau (54)	5,200	<2.5 kg	First trimester	"Frequent consumers"		I-2
Linn (34)	12,205	<2.5 kg	After (for first trimester)	4+ cups		
Kuzma (77)	5,093	Continuum	During (63%) After (37%)	Mg caffeine		
Barr (22)	462	Continuum	All trimesters	Mg caffeine	S-1	
Furuhashi (35)	9,921	Small for GA	During preg (NOS)	5+ cups		
Watkinson (30)	286	Continuum	After (for all trimesters)	Mg caffeine		I-2
Beaulac-Baillargon (78)	913	Continuum	After	300+ mg		I-3, I-4, I-3
Fried (23)	667	Continuum	All trimesters	300+ mg		I-3
Martin (36)	3,654	Continuum <2.5 kg	First, second trimester	300+ mg	S-1	
Tierson (79)	400	Continuum	All trimesters	Mg caffeine	S-1	
Munoz (31)	48	Continuum	Third trimester	Any coffee	S-1	I-1
Brooke (19)	1,513	Continuum	All trimesters	Cups of coffee, mg caffeine		
Caan (26)	131 cases 136 controls	IUGR, <2.5 kg	After (for first trimester)	300+ mg	S-1, S-3	I-4
Fenster (37)	1,230	IUGR, <2.5 kg	After (for first trimester)	300+ mg		I-4, I-5
Olsen (32)	11,858	Continuum <2.5 kg	Third trimester	8+ cups	S-1	

GA, gestational age; NOS, not otherwise specified; IUGR, intrauterine growth rate.

TABLE 3. Studies of the association between coffee/caffeine consumption during pregnancy and the risk of giving birth prematurely

| First author | Sample size[a] | Outcome | Daily coffee/caffeine consumption | | Other limitations | |
			When assessed	Group considered exposed	Sample	Inference
Mau (54)	5,200	GA <260 days	First trimester	"Frequent consumers"		I-2
van den Berg (33)	15,000	GA <37 weeks	During pregnancy (NOS)	7+ cups		I-2, I-4
Hogue (72)						
Weathersbee (24)	449	Premature birth	After	600+ mg	S-4	I-4
Berkowitz (39)	(175:313)[b]	GA <37 weeks	After	4+ cups		
Linn (34)	12,205	GA <37 weeks	After (for first trimester)	4+ cups		
Tebbutt (40)	52	Preterm labor	First trimester	400 mg		I-3
Furuhashi (35)	9,921	Preterm labor	During pregnancy (NOS)	5+ cups		I-1
Martin (36)	3,654	GA <37 weeks	First trimester	300+ mg	S-1	
Fenster (37)	1,230	GA <37 weeks	After (for first trimester)	300+ mg		I-4, I-5
Olsen (32)	11,858	GA <37 weeks	Third trimester	8+ cups	S-1	

[a] All are cohort samples except for Berkowitz et al.
[b] Cases:controls.
GA, gestational age; NOS, not otherwise specified.

TABLE 4. *Studies of the association between coffee/caffeine consumption and the risk of delayed conception/infertility*

First author	Sample size	Outcome	Daily coffee/caffeine consumption How assessed	Daily coffee/caffeine consumption Group considered exposed	Other limitation Sample	Other limitation Inference
Wilcox (21)	104	Delayed conception	Prospective	100 + mg	S-1, S-4	I-3, I-6, I-7
Christianson (75)	6,303	Delayed conception	Prospective	7 + cups	S-1	I-4
Joesoef (62)	2,817	Delayed conception	Prospective	233 g[a]	S-1	
Joesoef (62)	(1818:1765)[b]	Primary infertility	Retrospective	3 + cups	S-1	
Williams (74)	3,010	Delayed conception	Prospective	4 + cups	S-1	
Olsen (76)	11,886	Delayed conception	Retrospective	8 + cups		

[a] Reported as 7 grams per month.
[b] Cases:controls.

cohort studies (32,34) found no contribution of coffee and caffeine consumption to the occurrence of prematurity.

Delayed Conception/Infertility

Following the hypothesis generated by Wilcox and his colleagues (21) that as little as 100 mg of caffeine per day impairs fertility, other investigators looked back at data they collected for other purposes (Table 4). Some decided that the association they saw between delayed conception and consumption of four cups of coffee per day (74) and seven cups per day (75) warranted only a letter to the editor. More complete reports of three samples, however, have shown no evidence of dose-response relationships between coffee/caffeine consumption and the risk of delayed conception (62,76) or persistent infertility (62). It seems reasonable to conclude that coffee and caffeine consumption by women does not impair fertility.

Congenital Malformations

Laboratory animals given high doses of caffeine do show an increased risk of facial clefts and limb anomalies (see the chapter by Purves and Sullivan). Epidemiological studies, however, have not shown any relationship between maternal coffee/caffeine consumption and facial clefts (28,55) and skeletal anomalies (55) in the offspring (Table 5).

By and large, the congenital malformation studies have tended to be of higher quality than the studies of other reproductive adversities. When malformations of all organs are the outcome of interest, no relationship is seen with maternal coffee and caffeine consumption (32,34,35).

TABLE 5. Studies of the association between coffee/caffeine consumption during pregnancy and the risk of congenital malformations in the fetus

| First author | Sample size | | Malformations | Daily coffee/caffeine consumption | | Other limitations | | |
	Cases	Controls		When assessed	Group considered exposed	Sample	Inference
Borlee (27)	190	162	Any	After	8+ cups	S-3?	I-3
Linn (34)	12,205[a]		Any	After (for first trimester)	4+ cups		
Rosenberg (28)	300	712	Inguinal hernia	After	400+ mg		I-3
	101	712	Neural tube	After	400+ mg		I-3
	277	712	Cardiac	After	400+ mg		I-3
	120	712	Cleft palate	After	400+ mg		I-3
	299	712	Cleft lip	After	400+ mg		I-3
Kurpa (55)	112	706	CNS	After	4+ cups		
	241	706	Orofacial	After	4+ cups		
	210	706	Skeletal	After	4+ cups		
	143	706	Cardiovascular	After	4+ cups		
Furuhashi (35)	9,921[a]		Any	During pregnancy (NOS)	5+ cups	S-1	I-3
Olsen (32)	11,858[a]		Any	Third trimester	8+ cups		

[a] Cohort.
CNS, Central nervous system; NOS, not otherwise specified.

TABLE 6. *Studies of the association between coffee/caffeine consumption and the risk of spontaneous abortion*

First author	Sample size	Daily coffee/caffeine consumption		Other limitations	
		When assessed	Group considered exposed	Sample	Inference
Weathersbee (24) Warburton (80)	449	After	600 + mg	S-4	I-4
Furuhashi (35)	9,921	During pregnancy (NOS)	5 + cups		I-1
Watkinson (30)	284	After (all 3 trimesters)	300 + mg		I-2
Srisuphan (69)	3,135	First, second trimester	151 + mg	S-1	I-3
Hansteen (56)	361 cases 249 controls	First, second trimester	4 + cups		
Fenster (48)	607 cases 1,284 controls	After	300 + mg		I-4, I-5

NOS, not otherwise specified.

Spontaneous Abortion

The Stein-Susser (68) hypothesis that nausea is a confounder has not been considered by any group investigating the relationship between coffee consumption and early fetal wastage. I believe that the seven studies tabulated in Table 6 should not be viewed as adequate tests of whether coffee or caffeine consumption contributes to the risk of spontaneous abortion. Until investigators consider the Stein-Susser hypothesis, no study can be viewed as having adequately evaluated the relationship between coffee/caffeine consumption and the risk of miscarriage.

REFERENCES

1. Morris MB, Weinstein L. Caffeine and the fetus: is trouble brewing? *Am J Obstet Gynecol* 1981;140:607–10.
2. Dews P. Caffeine. *Annu Rev Nutr* 1982;2:323–41.
3. James JE, Stirling KP. Caffeine: a survey of some of the known and suspected deleterious effects of habitual use. *Br J Addiction* 1983;78:251–8.
4. Briggs GG, Freeman RK, Yaffe SJ. *Drugs in pregnancy and lactation,* 2nd edition. Baltimore: Williams & Wilkins; 1983.
5. Ernster VL. Epidemiologic studies of caffeine and human health. In: Spiller GA, ed. *Progress in clinical and biological research;* vol. 159. *The methylxanthine beverages and foods: chemistry, consumption and health effects.* New York: Alan R. Liss; 1984:377–400.
6. Leviton A. Epidemiologic studies of birth defects. In: Dews PB, ed. *Caffeine: perspective from recent research.* Berlin: Springer-Verlag, 1984:188–200.
7. Brown NA, Scialli AR. Update on caffeine. *Reprod Toxicol* 1987;6:13–8.

8. Heller J. What do we know about the risks of caffeine consumption in pregnancy? *Br J Addict* 1987;82:885–9.
9. Nolen GA. The developmental toxicology of caffeine. In: Kalter H, ed. *Issues and reviews in teratology;* vol. 4. New York: Plenum Publishing; 1988:305–50.
10. Leviton A. Caffeine consumption and the risk of reproductive hazards. *J Reprod Med* 1988; 33:175–8.
11. Nash J, Persaud TVN. Reproductive and teratological risks of caffeine. *Anat Anz Jena* 1988;167:265–70.
12. Al-Hachim G. Teratogenicity of caffeine; a review. *Eur J Obstet Gynecol Reprod Biol* 1989; 237–47.
13. Narod SA, De Sanjose S, Victora C. Coffee during pregnancy: a reproductive hazard? *Am J Obstet Gynecol* 1991;164:1109–14.
14. McKim EM. Caffeine and its effects on pregnancy and the neonate. *J Nurse-Midwifery* 1991;36:226–31.
15. Feinstein A. Scientific standards in epidemiologic studies of the menace of daily life. *Science* 1988;242:1257–63.
16. Jacobsen BK, Thelle DS. The Tromso Heart Study: is coffee drinking an indicator of a life style with high risk for ischemic heart disease? *Acta Med Scand* 1987;222:215–21.
17. Leviton A, Pagano M, Allred E, el Lozy M. Correlates of coffee and caffeine consumption. In: *Douzieme colloque scientificue international sur le cafe;* Proceedings of the 12th International Colloquium on Coffee, Montreux, June 29–July 3, 1987. Paris: Association Scientifique Internationale du Cafe (ASIC), 1988:93–9.
18. Schreiber GB, Maffeo CE, Robins M, Masters MN, Bond AP, Morganstein D. Measurement of coffee and caffeine intake: implications for epidemiologic research. *Prev Med* 1988; 17:280–94.
19. Brooke OG, Anderson HR, Bland JM, Peacock JL, Stewart CM. Effects on birth weight of smoking, alcohol, caffeine, socioeconomic factors, and psychosocial stress. *BMJ* 1989;298: 795–801.
20. Puccio EM, McPhillips JB, Barrett-Connor E, Ganiats TG. Clustering of atherogenic behaviors in coffee drinkers. *Am J Public Health* 1990;80:1310–3.
21. Wilcox A, Weinberg CR, Baird DD. Caffeinated beverages and decreased fertility. *Lancet* 1988;2:1453–5.
22. Barr HM, Streissguth AP, Martin DC, Herman CS. Infant size at 8 months of age: relationship to maternal use of alcohol, nicotine and caffeine during pregnancy. *Pediatrics* 1984;74: 336–41.
23. Fried PA, O'Connell CM. A comparison of the effects of prenatal exposure to tobacco, alcohol, cannabis and caffeine on birth size and subsequent growth. *Neurotoxicol Teratol* 1987;9:79–85.
24. Weathersbee PS, Olsen LK, Lodge JR. Caffeine and pregnancy: a retrospective survey. *Postgrad Med* 1977;62:64–9.
25. Gardner JW, Lyon JL. Cancer in Utah Mormon women by church activity level. *Am J Epidemiol* 1982;116:258–65.
26. Caan BJ, Goldhaber MK. Caffeinated beverages and low birthweight: A case-control study. *Am J Public Health* 1989;79:1299–1300.
27. Borlee I, Lechat MF, Bouckaert A, Misson C. Le cafe facteur de risque pendant la grossesse? *Louvain Medical* 1978;97:284–97.
28. Rosenberg L, Mitchell AA, Shapiro S, Slone D. Selected birth defects in relation to caffeine-containing beverages. *JAMA* 1982;247:1429–32.
29. Werler MM, Pober BR, Nelson K, Holmes LB. Reporting accuracy among mothers of malformed and nonmalformed infants. *Am J Epidemiol* 1989;129:415–21.
30. Watkinson B, Fried PA. Maternal caffeine use before, during and after pregnancy and effects upon offspring. *Neurobehav Toxicol Teratol* 1985;7:9–17.
31. Munoz LM, Lonnerdal B, Keen CL, Dewey KG. Coffee consumption as a factor in iron deficiency anemia among pregnant women and their infants in Costa Rica. *Am J Clin Nutr* 1988;48:645–51.
32. Olsen J, Overvad K, Frische. Coffee consumption, birthweight, and reproductive failures. *Epidemiology* 1991;2:370–4.
33. van den Berg BJ. Epidemiologic observations of prematurity: effects of tobacco, coffee and

alcohol. In: Reed DM, Stanley FJ, eds. *The epidemiology of prematurity*. Munich: Urban and Schwarzenberg, 1977;157–76.

34. Linn S, Schoenbaum SC, Monson RR, Rosner B, Stubblefield PG, Ryan KJ. No association between coffee consumption and adverse outcomes of pregnancy. *N Engl J Med* 1982;306: 141–5.

35. Furuhashi N, Sato S, Suzuki M, Hiruta M, Tanaka M, Takahashi T. Effects of caffeine ingestion during pregnancy. *Gynecol Obstet Invest* 1985;19:187–91.

36. Martin T, Bracken MB. The association between low birthweight and caffeine consumption during pregnancy. *Am J Epidemiol* 1987;126:813–21.

37. Fenster L, Eskenazi B, Windham GC, Swan SH. Caffeine consumption during pregnancy and fetal growth. *Am J Public Health* 1991;81:458–61.

38. Villar J, Belizan JM. The timing factor in the pathophysiology of the intrauterine growth retardation syndrome. *Obstet Gynecol Surv* 1982;8:499–506.

39. Berkowitz GS, Holford TR, Berkowitz RL. Effects of cigarette smoking, alcohol, coffee and tea consumption on preterm delivery. *Early Hum Dev* 1982;7:239–50.

40. Tebbutt IH, Teare AJ, Meek JH, Mallett KA, Hawkins DF. Caffeine, theophylline and theobromine in pregnancy. *Biol Res Pregnancy Perinatol* 1984;5:174–6.

41. Schreiber GB, Robins M, Maffeo CE, Masters MN, Bond AP. Confounders contributing to the reported associations of coffee or caffeine with disease. *Prev Med* 1988;17:295–309.

42. Lelo A, Miners JO, Robson R, Birkett DJ. Assessment of caffeine exposure: caffeine content of beverages, caffeine intake, and plasma concentrations of methylxanthines. *Clin Pharmacol Ther* 1986;39:54–9.

43. Galasko CT, Furman KI, Alberts E. The caffeine contents of non-alcoholic beverages. *Food Chem Toxicol* 1989;27:49–51.

44. Rapoport JL, Berg CJ, Ismond DR, Zahn TP, Neims A. Behavioral effects of caffeine challenge. *Arch Gen Psychiatry* 1984;41:1073–9.

45. Friedenreich CM, Howe GR, Miller AB. An investigation of recall bias in the reporting of past food intake among breast cancer cases and controls. *Ann Epidemiol* 1991;1:439–53.

46. Fenster L, Swan SH, Windham GC, Neutra RR. Assessment of reporting consistency in a case-control study of spontaneous abortions. *Am J Epidemiol* 1991;133:477–88.

47. Kennedy JS, von Moltke LL, Harmatz JS, Engelhardt N, Greenblatt DJ. Validity of self-reports of caffeine use. *J Clin Pharmacol* 1991;31:677–80.

48. Fenster L, Eskenazi B, Windham GC, Swan SH. Caffeine consumption during pregnancy and spontaneous abortion. *Epidemiology* 1991;2:168–74.

49. Aldridge A, Bailey J, Neims AH. The disposition of caffeine during and after pregnancy. *Seminars in Perinatol* 1981;5:310–4.

50. Knutti R, Rothweiler H, Schlatter C. The effect of pregnancy on the pharmacokinetics of caffeine. *Arch Toxicol* (Suppl) 1982;5:187–92.

51. Brazier JL, Ritter J, Berland M, Khenfer D, Faucon G. Pharmacokinetics of caffeine during and after pregnancy. *Dev Pharmacol Ther* 1983;6:315–22.

52. Hook EB. Changes in tobacco smoking and ingestion of alcohol and caffeinated beverages during early pregnancy: are these consequences, in part of feto-protective mechanisms diminishing maternal exposure to embryotoxins: In: Kelly S, Hook EB, Janerich DT, Portar H, eds. *Birth defects: risks and consequences*. New York: Academic Press; 1976:173–83.

53. Hook EB. Dietary cravings and aversions during pregnancy. *Am J Clin Nutr* 1978;31: 1355–62.

54. Mau G, Netter P. Are coffee and alcohol consumption risk factors in pregnancy? *Geburtshilfe Frauenheilkd* 1974;34:1018–22.

55. Kurppa K, Holmberg PC, Kuosma E, Saxen L. Coffee consumption during pregnancy and selected congenital malformations: a nationwide case-control study. *AJPH* 1983;73:1397–9.

56. Hansteen I-L. Occupational and lifestyle factors and chromosomal aberrations of spontaneous abortions. *Mutation and the Environment*, Part B; 1990;467–75.

57. Last JM. *A Dictionary of epidemiology*. New York: Oxford University Press; 1983:21.

58. Barone JJ, Roberts H. Human consumption of caffeine. In: Dews PB, ed. *Caffeine. Perspectives from recent research*. Berlin: Springer-Verlag; 1984:59–73.

59. Kline J, Stein Z, Susser M. *Conception to birth. Epidemiology of prenatal development*. New York: Oxford University Press; 1989:259–94.

60. Istvan J, Matarazzo JD. Tobacco, alcohol, and caffeine use: a review of their interrelationships. *Psychol Bull* 1984;95:301–26.

61. Carmody TP, Brischetto CS, Matarazzo JD, et al. Co-occurrent use of cigarettes, alcohol, and coffee in healthy, community-living men and women. *Health Psychol* 1985;4:323–5.
62. Joesoef MR, Beral V, Rolfs RT, Aral SO, Cramer DW. Are caffeinated beverages risk factors for delayed conception? *Lancet* 1990;335:136–7.
63. Paganini-Hill A, Ross RK. Reliability of recall of drug usage and other health-related information. *Am J Epidemiol* 1982;116:114–22.
64. Morrison AS. Control of cigarette smoking in evaluating the association of coffee drinking and bladder cancer. In: MacMahon B, Sugimura T, eds. *Banbury Report 17: Coffee and health*. Cold Spring Harbor Laboratory; 1984:127–34.
65. Peacock JL, Bland JM, Anderson HR. Effects on birthweight of alcohol and caffeine consumption in smoking women. *J Epidemiol Comm Hlth* 1991;45:159–63.
66. Weigel MM, Weigel RM. Nausea and vomiting of early pregnancy and pregnancy outcome. An epidemiological study. *Br J Obstet Gynaecol* 1989;96:1304–11.
67. Weigel RM, Weigel MM. Nausea and vomiting of early pregnancy and pregnancy outcome. A meta-analytical review. *Br J Obstet Gynaecol* 1989;96:1312–8.
68. Stein Z, Susser M. Miscarriage, caffeine and the epiphenomena of pregnancy: Specifying the analytic model. *Epidemiology* 1991;2:163–7.
69. Srisuphan W, Bracken MB. Caffeine consumption during pregnancy and association with late spontaneous abortion. *Am J Obstet Gynecol* 1986;155:14–20.
70. Dales LG, Ury HK. An improper use of statistical significance testing in studying covariables. *Int J Epidemiol* 1978;7:373–5.
71. Hebel JR, Fox NL, Sexton M. Dose-response of birth weight to various measures of maternal smoking during pregnancy. *J Clin Epidemiol* 1988;41:483–9.
72. Hogue C. Coffee and pregnancy. *Lancet* 1981;1:554.
73. Tucker JM, Goldenberg RL, Davis RO, Copper RL, Winkler CL, Hauth JC. Etiologies of preterm birth in an indigent population: is prevention a logical expectation? *Obstet Gynecol* 1991;77:343–7.
74. Williams MA, Monson RR, Goldman MB, Mittendorf R. Coffee and delayed conception. *Lancet* 1990;335:1603.
75. Christianson RE, Oechsli FW, van den Berg BJ. Caffeinated beverages and decreased fertility. *Lancet* 1989;1:378.
76. Olsen J. Cigarette smoking, tea and coffee drinking, and subfecundity. *Am J Epidemiol* 1991;133:734–9.
77. Kuzma JW, Kissinger D. Patterns of alcohol and cigarette use in pregnancy. *Neurobehav Toxicol Teratol* 1981;3:211–21.
78. Beaulac-Baillargeon L, Desrosiers C. Caffeine-cigarette interaction on fetal growth. *Am J Obstet Gynecol* 1987;157:1236–40.
79. Tierson FD, Hook EB. The effect of some embryotoxins in the maternal diet on pregnancy outcome. *Am J Phys Anthropol* 1987;72:262–3.
80. Warburton D, Stein Z, Kline J, Strombino B. Environmental influences on rates of chromosome anomalies in spontaneous abortions. *Am J Hum Genet* 1980;32:92A.

Caffeine, Coffee, and Health,
edited by S. Garattini.
Raven Press, Ltd., New York © 1993.

14

Experimental Studies on Carcinogenicity and Mutagenicity of Caffeine

Ulrich Mohr, Makito Emura, and Margrit Riebe-Imre

Institute of Experimental Pathology, Hannover Medical School, DW-3000 Hannover 61, Germany

Possible mutagenic and/or carcinogenic effects of coffee or caffeine are discussed in this chapter, which is concerned solely with experimental data obtained from animal or in vitro studies.

No carcinogenic effects of coffee alone could be detected. In combination experiments, coffee exhibited rather an inhibitory effect on the carcinogenicity of known mutagens in rodents. After administration of caffeine, the incidence or multiplicity of certain organ tumors were unaffected in a number of studies, but enhanced tumor rates have also been described. Many groups reported caffeine effects in combination with known carcinogens, ranging from clear enhancement to clear inhibition of the occurrence of certain organ tumors. It should be taken into consideration, however, that the results of these in vivo carcinogenicity studies are mostly qualitatively and quantitatively inadequate for evaluation purposes.

Experiments aimed at detecting mutagenic effects of coffee or caffeine similarly revealed contradicting results. Coffee and caffeine, investigated for in vivo as well as in vitro mutagenicity, could not be definitely categorized as a mutagen or nonmutagen. Simultaneous administration of coffee with known mutagens resulted in inhibition of the mutagens' genotoxic effect, whereas the combination of caffeine and mutagens in a number of different assay systems led to either an increase or a decrease of the induced mutation rates.

In conclusion, it can be stated that concern about the carcinogenicity of coffee or caffeine today plays a subordinate role. With respect to the occasionally observed cytogenic effects of caffeine, the main emphasis is placed on the need for further investigation of the mechanisms of caffeine action.

INTRODUCTION

Possible adverse effects of coffee or caffeine on human health have been discussed from behavioral, physiological, pharmacological, and reproductive viewpoints, based on both epidemiological and experimental data. In this chapter, discussion will be focused on the carcinogenic and mutagenic effects of caffeine. Since these effects in humans are also to be dealt with in other chapters, this contribution concerns itself solely with experimental data obtained in microbes, plants, insects, rodents, and mammalian (including human) cell cultures. In addition, knowledge accumulated up to the early 1980s tells us that caffeine, as long as its intake is limited to a moderate degree, has no carcinogenic and mutagenic potential in rodents or in humans (1,2). Since then, many additional experimental studies have been published. These studies will be the primary concern of this chapter, therefore, to see whether they again allow us to draw a similar conclusion.

CARCINOGENICITY

Effects of Coffee Alone (Table 1)

In a study on the carcinogenicity of coffee, pregnant Swiss mice received 1% instant coffee in their diet throughout gestation and lactation. The offspring then received a diet containing 0, 1, 2.5, or 5% instant coffee for two years. Coffee dose-dependently impaired the growth of the animals, but in the higher doses a better survival rate was observed compared with the controls. There was no clear enhancement of tumor formation. Only lymphosarcomas showed a certain decrease in incidence (3).

F_1-generation Sprague-Dawley rats (55 males and 55 females per group) were given freshly brewed regular coffee at concentrations of 25, 50, and 100% in drinking water ad libitum. These F1 rats derived from P generation females that were provided with 50% coffee in drinking water for about five weeks prior to copulation and throughout gestation and lactation. There was essentially no effect from the coffee on the tumor incidence, although there appeared to be some equivocal evidence of a relationship between coffee consumption and the number of primary tumor-bearing animals (4).

TABLE 1. *Carcinogenicity tests with coffee alone*

Animal system	Coffee application	Response	Reference
Mouse	Pregnant mothers 1%, offspring up to 5% instant coffee in drinking water	Tumor formation in general unaffected; only lymphosarcomas slightly decreased	(3)
Rat	P-generation females 50%, F_1-generation 25, 50, and 100% regular coffee in drinking water	Tumor incidence unaffected	(4)

TABLE 2. *Carcinogenicity tests with coffee in combination with carcinogens*

Animal system	Carcinogen combined with coffee	Response	Reference
Inhibitory effects of coffee only			
Rat	I.p. injection of azaserine and high-fat diet	Pancreatic tumors decreased	(5)
Hamster	S.c. Injection of N-nitrosobis(2-oxypropyl)amine and high-fat diet	Adenocarcinoma incidence slightly decreased	(5)
Rat	I.v. injection of 7,12-dimethylbenz[a]anthracene	Mammary tumor incidence unaffected; mammary carcinoma multiplicity decreased	(6)
Rat (females)	7,12-dimethylbenz[a]anthracene by gavage	Mammary tumor formation unaffected	(6)

Effects of Coffee in Combination with Carcinogens (Table 2)

Effects of coffee on the carcinogenicity of known chemical carcinogens were investigated in three different species. Woutersen et al. (5) treated 40 male Wistar rats 19 days after birth with single i.p. injection of the pancreatic carcinogen, azaserine, at 30 mg/kg body weight. The animals then received a diet with low or high fat content or high fat plus coffee given as a drinking fluid increasing from 25% to 100% over four weeks. The animals were autopsied 15 months after the end of the carcinogen treatment. Body weights in the group receiving high fat combined with coffee were significantly lower than in the group fed the high-fat diet alone. Occurrence of pancreatic tumors was significantly reduced in the coffee group as compared to the high-fat control group. This should, however, be discussed considering the strongly reduced body weights of the coffee-treated group.

The influence of coffee on the carcinogenicity of N-nitrosobis(2-oxypropyl)amine was examined using a similar experimental regimen (5). Six-week-old male Syrian golden hamsters received two weekly s.c. injections of the carcinogen (20 mg/kg) and were then fed a low-fat or high-fat diet, or a high-fat diet plus coffee as the drinking fluid. The experiment was terminated 12 months after the second carcinogen injection. The group given high fat plus coffee did not show different body weights as compared to the high-fat control group. The number of adenocarcinomas was slightly, but not significantly, lower in the high fat plus coffee group than in the group with high fat alone.

In a study reported by Welsch et al. (6), female Sprague-Dawley rats, 53 to 55 days old, received a single i.v. injection of 7,12-dimethylbenz[a]anthracene (DMBA) at 20 mg/kg. The animals were given moderate or full strength or decaffeinated coffee as drinking fluid from 29 days before to three days after DMBA application. Other female rats, 54 to 55 days old, were treated with a single DMBA dose of 5 mg by gavage, followed three days later by treatment with coffee in the drinking fluid. In the rats treated with DMBA by gavage, coffee did not show any influence on the mammary tumor formation. In the group that received the DMBA intravenously, moderate as well as high doses of coffee significantly reduced the mammary carcinoma multiplicity, whereas the mammary tumor incidence was not affected. No effect was observed in the rat group given decaffeinated coffee. Only after addition of caffeine to the decaffeinated coffee was tumor multiplicity reduced. These results were confirmed in a similar study in which rats were fed a defined diet containing 5% corn oil with coffee given as the drinking fluid (7).

Effects of Caffeine Alone (Table 3)

Only a few studies have been performed to test the carcinogenicity of caffeine alone. In the study by Takayama and Kuwabara (8), eight-week-old Wistar rats were maintained on a basal diet and given tapwater alone (control) or with caffeine (experimental). One group of 50 males and 50 females served as control. A second group of 50 males and 50 females received 0.1% caffeine in tapwater (total consumption: 14.5 g for males and 13.9 g for females) for 78 weeks. A third group of 50 males and 50 females were given 0.2% caffeine in the same way (total consumption: 26.6 g for males and 21.7 g for females). All surviving rats were killed at 104 weeks. When benign and malignant tumors were evaluated together, the numbers of tumor-bearing animals were 24 of 46 for males and 41 of 50 for females in the control, 31 of 48 for males and 44 of 48 for females in the 0.1% caffeine group, and 18 of 44 for males and 37 of 50 for females in the 0.2% caffeine group. There was no significant difference in the tumor sites between the control and treated groups. When only the malignant tumors were evaluated, however, there was a dose-dependent increase in the incidence of adenocarcinomas in the mammary gland (1

TABLE 3. *Carcinogenicity tests with caffeine alone*

Animal system	Caffeine application	Response	Reference
Mouse (females only)	0.05% in drinking water	Mammary gland tumors and hyperplasia increased	(10,11)
Mouse	250 and 500 mg/L in drinking water	Tumor incidence unaffected, tumor multiplicity increased	(12)
Rat	0.1–0.2% in drinking water	Mammary gland adenocarcinomas increased	(8)
Rat	0.2% in drinking water	Pituitary adenomas and hyperplasia increased	(9)
Rat	Up to 2,000 mg/L in drinking water	No carcinogenic effect	(13)

of 96 for males and females in the control, 3 of 96 for males and females in the 0.1% caffeine group, 8 of 94 for males and females in the 0.2% caffeine group).

In a study with Wistar rats (9), a group of 40 four-week-old females was given 0.2% caffeine in drinking water for 12 months (mean total dose of caffeine; 13.5 g per rat). Another group of 40 females was given tapwater only as the control (survival rate at the end of the study, 30 of 40). Pituitary adenomas occurred with a significantly enhanced incidence in the caffeine-treated group (22 of 40 compared to 8 of 30 in the control). Pituitary hyperplasia was also observed in 5 of 40 rats given caffeine and in 1 of 30 control rats.

In C3H/He mice, the incidence of mammary gland tumors was enhanced by caffeine significantly above the spontaneous level (10). Eighteen virgin mice received 0.05% caffeine in drinking water from the age of 20 days until the end of the experiment (25 months of age). Thirty-six virgin mice were given tapwater only as the control. In contrast, for definition, the breeder mice were those that gave birth once and retired from breeding after the first lactation. Tumor development was monitored by palpation every seven days. Mammary tumorigenesis was significantly higher in the caffeine-treated groups of both virgin and breeder mice than in controls, when simultaneously considering the incidence and the age of tumor onset. With a similar experimental regimen, mammary hyperplastic alveolar nodules of virgin mice of SHN, SLN, GR/A, and C3H/He developed significantly earlier in the caffeine-treated group (0.05% caffeine in drinking water) than in the control (tapwater) group (11).

Groups of 37 to 43 female C3H mice were treated at eight weeks of age with 0 (control), 250, or 500 mg/L caffeine in drinking water for 43 weeks. The incidence of animals bearing mammary carcinomas and mean time to tumor appearance were not significantly affected by caffeine; however, the tumor multiplicity (number of tumors per animal) increased significantly in the groups given 500 mg/L caffeine (12).

In the study by Mohr et al. (13), groups of 50 male and 50 female 28-day-old Sprague-Dawley rats were given 200, 430, 930, or 2,000 mg/L of caffeine in drinking water for 104 weeks. Mean daily intake was 12, 26, 49, and 102 mg/kg for males and 15, 37, 80, and 170 mg/kg for females. Two control groups of 50 males and 50 females received drinking water only. The incidence of tumors in various organs of treated rats did not exceed that of the control group. No unusual tumors or tumor sites were seen in animals receiving caffeine.

As the IARC Working Group objectively judges (14), only two of the above-mentioned studies, both of which used rats, can be regarded as full-scale carcinogenesis studies on caffeine to be incorporated for the strict evaluation of the results. Although some chronic studies, already referred to, have also been conducted in mice, they are not as comprehensive as current standards require. It is generally acknowledged that the response to xenobiotics differs greatly from species to species and caffeine alone appears to possess no complete carcinogenicity.

Effects of Caffeine in Combination with Carcinogens (Table 4)

Caffeine administration in combination with known carcinogens or other compounds has shown various effects: stimulation, inhibition, or no effects on the induced carcinogenesis. Ten-week-old Sprague-Dawley rats were fed benzo(a)pyrene (BaP) in the diet (average dose 6 or 39 mg/kg per year) or

TABLE 4. *Carcinogenicity tests with caffeine in combination with carcinogens*

Animal system	Carcinogen combined with caffeine	Response	Reference
Enhancing effects of caffeine			
Mouse	S.c. injection of urethane, topical administration of anthranil	Skin papilloma incidence increased	(17)
Mouse	4-nitroquinoline-N-oxide	Skin papilloma incidence increased	(18)
Mouse	Intragastric intubation of 7,12-dimethylbenz[a]anthracene	Mammary gland tumor incidence unaffected, multiplicity increased	(12)
Rat	Benzo[a]pyrene in the diet or by gavage	Forestomach papillomas increased	(15)
Rat	4HAQO	Pancreatic nodules increased	(16)
Rat	Intragastric intubation of 7,12-dimethylbenz[a]anthracene	Mammary gland carcinomas increased	(19)
Rat	Intragastric intubation of 7,12-dimethylbenz[a]anthracene	Carcinoma multiplicity increased	(6)
Rat	7,12-dimethylbenz[a]anthracene and dietary fat	Mammary gland carcinoma multiplicity increased	(20)
Inhibitory effects of caffeine			
Mouse (virgin females)	17β-estradiol or progesterone	Mean tumor latency increased	(29)
Mouse	S.c. injection of urethane	Lung tumor incidence reduced	(30)
Rat	I.p. injection of diethylnitrosamine	Liver tumor incidence decreased	(26)
Rat	Dietary 2-acetylaminofluorene	Tumor incidence unaffected	(27)
Rat (females only)	S.c. implantation of diethylstilbestrol	Mammary tumor incidence and multiplicity decreased, latency lengthened	(28)
Rat	Intragastric intubation of 7,12-dimethyl-benz[a]anthracene	Mammary carcinoma multiplicity decreased	(6)

given BaP by gavage in an aqueous solution of 1.5% caffeine (average dose, 6, 18, or 39 mg/kg per year) for life (15). Rats given BaP in caffeine developed significantly more papillomas of the forestomach than those given BaP in the diet.

Partially pancreatectomized male Wistar rats were treated at six weeks of age with various subcutaneous doses of caffeine in combination with 7 mg/kg of i.v.-injected 4-hydroxyaminoquinoline-1-oxide (4HAQO) (16). When groups of 9 to 18 rats received multiple s.c. injections of 0, 30, 60, or 120 mg/kg caffeine before single i.v. injection of 4HAQO, the number of macroscopic pancreatic nodules in the group with 30 mg/kg caffeine was significantly higher than in the control group after 52 weeks, when the rats were killed.

Caffeine given 6 hours before urethane also yielded increased incidence of skin papillomas (17). Groups of 30 six- to eight-week-old female ICR mice were given a single s.c. injection of 25 mg/mL urethane in saline. Two weeks later, topical application of anthranil was started with a twice-weekly regimen. At various times between 24 hours before and 6 hours after the urethane injection, caffeine was injected s.c. at a single dose of 100 μg/g. In the animals killed at 45 weeks after the start of anthranil, only the caffeine administered 6 hours before urethane significantly enhanced the incidence of skin papillomas. Induction of skin papillomas by 4-nitroquinoline-1-oxide (4NQO) was also stimulated by 0.8 mg caffeine painted topically (18).

In the case of mammary gland carcinomas induced by 7,12-dimethylbenz(a)anthracene (DMBA), however, administration of caffeine after the carcinogen enhanced the tumorigenicity. Three groups of 30 female Sprague-Dawley rats received a single intragastric intubation of 5 mg DMBA in 1 mL of sesame oil at 53 days of age. Three days later, continuous administration of caffeine followed at a dose of 0, 250, or 500 mg/L in drinking water. The experiment ended 21 weeks after DMBA treatment, and increased incidences of mammary carcinomas were observed (19). Groups of 40 to 41 female Sprague-Dawley rats received single intragastric administration of 5 mg DMBA at 53 to 55 days of age. Three days later, treatment with caffeine (100 to 860 mg/L in drinking water) started and continued until 12 or 18 weeks after DMBA. In the group with caffeine given after DMBA for 12 weeks, a significant increase in the multiplicity of carcinomas was observed (6). Groups of 54 to 55 female BD2F1 mice received weekly intragastric intubation of 1 mg DMBA at eight weeks of age for six weeks. One week after the last intubation, the animals received 0, 250, or 500 mg/L caffeine in drinking water for 20 weeks, at which point the experiment was terminated. The mammary carcinoma multiplicity was significantly enhanced in the group with 500 mg/L caffeine. There were no effects on the incidence of tumor-bearing animals and tumor latency (12). Four groups of 20 female Sprague-Dawley rats (50 days old) received a single gastric intubation of 20 mg DMBA. In addition, they were treated variously with caffeine (10 mg/kg) in their drinking water and fat in their diet. In a group of animals that received both caffeine and fat, the mammary tumor multiplicity was considerably more enhanced than the control and other treatment groups; the tumor latency was also significantly reduced in this group (20).

Besides such earlier works as published by Rothwell (21), Mirvish et al. (22), Theiss and Shimkin (23), Zajdela and Latarjet (24), and Nomura (25), a number of studies have been published since the early 1980s that show inhibitory effects on various carcinogenic or other specific agents.

Groups of BD VI and Wistar rats (25 and 30 males, respectively) received 0 or 600 mg/L caffeine in the drinking water. Three days later, i.p. injections with 80 mg/kg N-diethylnitrosamine (DEN) were begun and continued weekly for ten weeks. Caffeine was given for another two weeks and all animals were killed 24 weeks after the beginning of the DEN treatment. Although high morality (40%) was observed, there was a significant decrease in the incidence of liver tumors in the caffeine group (26).

Groups of 15 or 20 male ACI rats (six weeks of age) were given 0.02% 2-acetylaminofluorene (2AAF) in the diet and 0 or 0.2% caffeine in drinking water (total caffeine intake 3.26 g per rat) for 18 weeks. Thereafter they were maintained on a basal diet and with no caffeine for 15 weeks. The multiplicity of liver tumors (number of tumors per animal) was significantly reduced in the caffeine group, although the tumor incidence (number of tumor-bearing animals) was not affected by caffeine. However, caffeine caused a significant reduction in the intake of the 2AAF diet (27).

Four-month-old female ACI rats (24 to 30 animals per group) received s.c. implantation of 5 mg diethylstilbestrol (DES) one week after the start of caffeine treatment at doses of 0, 1 mg/mL (approx. 60 mg/kg/day) and 2 mg/mL (120 mg/kg/day) in the drinking water for 10.5 months (end of experiment). The latency of mammary tumors was significantly lengthened and their incidence as well as their multiplicity was decreased with the increasing doses of caffeine. The difference from the control was significant at the highest caffeine dose (28). In a study with the same experimental regimen as previously mentioned (6), a diet containing 5% or 20% (w/w) corn oil was used instead of standard chow. Caffeine intake (430 to 500 mg/L) before and during the DMBA treatment significantly decreased the multiplicity of mammary carcinomas (7).

Two strains of virgin female GR mice (110 GR/A and 92 GRS/SN mice) were treated continuously for 24 weeks with 17-estradiol (0.5 mg/L in the drinking water) and progesterone (30 mg implanted s.c. together with 10 mg cholesterol) starting at eight to ten weeks of age. One week after the start of hormone treatment, one half of the hormone-treated mice were given caffeine (500 mg/L) in drinking water for 23 weeks (end of experiment). Caffeine significantly reduced the mammary tumor multiplicity and significantly increased the mean tumor latency (29).

Female ICR/Jcl mice (25 days old) received a single s.c. injection of urethane (0.1 mg/g). They were then immediately given multiple injections of a total of 70 μg/g (0.35 mol) caffeine at 6-hour intervals up to 36 hours after urethane treatment. The experiment was terminated five months after urethane. The lung tumor incidence was significantly reduced in the caffeine group (30). In most of the studies in which tumor incidence was reduced by caffeine, body weight was also considerably decreased, although the causal relationship was not clear.

Several other studies have demonstrated practically no effects of caffeine on the incidence of tumors (tumor-bearing animals) induced by known carcinogens such as N-nitroso-N-butyl(4-hydroxy-butyl)amine (NBHBA) (31–33) and urethane (17). In these studies caffeine was given simultaneously with or after the carcinogen. When caffeine was given before the carcinogen initiation, the tumor incidence was enhanced (16,17). In a few studies, caffeine did not affect the incidence of rats bearing mammary tumors induced by DMBA applied simultaneously with and/or after caffeine, although the tumor multiplicity increased due to caffeine (6,7,12,19).

When the results of the studies of caffeine combined with known carcinogens/mutagens are evaluated on the basis of the number of tumor-bearing animals, the effects of caffeine are overwhelmingly negative (two studies with inhibition and ten studies with no effects) other than enhancing (three studies). Based on the tumor multiplicity in specific organs such as pancreas, mammary gland, and liver, the caffeine effects are indefinable (four inhibitory and five enhancing studies).

Theophylline (a total dose of 63 μg/g) injected i.p. into 25-day-old ICR/Jcl mice many times within 36 hours after a single s.c. injection of urethane (0.1 mg/g) did not affect lung tumor incidence when examined five months after urethane (30). With the same experimental regimen in the same publication, a total of 63 μg/g theobromine significantly reduced the incidence of mice bearing lung tumors induced by urethane. Skin tumors induced by ultraviolet light (total dose, 107 ergs/mm^2) on the ears of 10-to 12-week-old Swiss mice, were significantly inhibited by the application of 40 μL of 0.2% theophylline in acetone/chloroform (24).

MUTAGENICITY

Effects of Coffee Alone (Table 5)

Mutagenic (genetic) and related effects of coffee have been thoroughly reviewed in the IARC Monograph Vol. 51 (14). Only the main points are summarized here. Freshly brewed coffee, instant coffee, and decaffeinated coffee induced prophage lambda in lysogenic *Escherichia coli* K12, and brewed coffee was shown to induce reverse mutations in *E. coli* (34). Altogether, 15 papers describe the mutagenicity of brewed coffee in the *Salmonella* mutation assay. Of these, ten studies revealed positive results and five

TABLE 5. *Mutagenicity tests with coffee alone*

Assay system	Genetic endpoint	Published results	
		Mutagenic	Nonmutagenic
E. coli	Prophage induction	+	
	Reverse mutations	+	
S. typhimurium	Reverse mutations	+	+
Drosophila	Somatic mutations	+	
	Mitotic recombinations		+
	Sex chromosome losses		+
	Sex-linked recessive lethal mutations		+
	Dominant lethal mutations		+
Rodent cells in vitro	Sister chromatid exchanges	+	
Human blood lymphocytes	Sister chromatid exchanges	+	
	Chromosomal aberrations	+	
Mice in vivo	Sister chromatid exchanges		+
	Micronuclei		+
Hamsters in vivo	Sister chromatid exchanges		+
	Micronuclei		+
Human erythrocytes/ reticulocytes in vivo	Micronuclei	+	

negative results when no exogenous metabolic activation was used. In the presence of a mammalian activation system, however, mainly negative results were obtained. Nine out of 14 studies showed mutagenicity of instant coffee in *Salmonella* only without metabolic activation. Even in the case of decaffeinated coffee, six out of seven studies reported mutagenic responses without metabolic activation and three described a possible slight mutagenic effect of decaffeinated coffee after enzymatic activation.

Graf and Würgler (35) investigated mutagenic effects of brewed and instant coffee in *Drosophila*. Both types of coffee appeared to induce somatic mutations and mitotic recombinations, but failed to induce sex chromosome losses, sex-linked recessive lethal or dominant lethal mutations.

Mutagenic effects of coffee were also described in mammalian cell systems in vitro. Tucker et al. (36) observed sister chromatid exchanges in Chinese hamster ovary cells after treatment with brewed, instant, and decaffeinated coffee, and in human peripheral lymphocytes only after treatment with brewed coffee. Aeschbacher et al. (37) reported chromosomal aberrations in human lymphocytes induced by all three coffee types, both with and without metabolic activation. No sister chromatid exchanges or micronuclei were induced by instant coffee in hamsters or mice in vivo (38,39). Smith et al. (40) found an induction of micronuclei in human erythrocytes/reticulocytes in vivo.

TABLE 6. *Mutagenicity tests with coffee in combination with mutagens*

Assay system	Genetic endpoint	Mutagen combined with caffeine	Response
Inhibitory effects of caffeine only			
S. typhimurium	SOS induction	UV light	Suppression
		2-(2-furyl)-3(5-nitro-2-furyl)acrylamide	Suppression
		4-nitroquinoline-N-oxide	Suppression
		N-methyl-N'-nitro-N-nitrosoguanidine	Suppression
	Reverse mutations	Methylurea	Decrease
Mouse in vivo	Micronuclei	Mitomycin C	Decrease
		Cyclophosphamide	Decrease
		Procarbazine	Decrease
		Adriamycin	Unaffected

Effects of Coffee in Combination with Mutagens (Table 6)

In the *Salmonella* mutation assay, brewed, instant, and decaffeinated coffee suppressed SOS DNA repair induction by ultraviolet (UV) light, 2-(2-furyl)-3-(5-nitro-2-furyl)acrylamide, 4-nitroquinoline-N-oxide, and N-methyl-N'-nitro-N-nitrosoguanidine (41). All three coffee types inhibited mutagenesis resulting from the nitrosation of methylurea in *Salmonella typhimurium* TA 1535 (42).

In the mouse in vivo micronucleus test, mutagenicity of mitomycin C, cyclophosphamide, and procarbazine (but not adriamycin) was significantly reduced by the administration of instant coffee 2 hours before clastogen treatment. Similar results were observed with brewed and decaffeinated coffee on the micronucleus induction by mitomycin C and with brewed coffee on the procarbazine effect (43). However, instant coffee did not influence the formation of micronuclei induced by N-nitrosodimethylamine (39).

Effects of Caffeine Alone (Table 7)

The large number of publications dealing with genetic and related effects of caffeine, either alone or in combination with other compounds, have been reviewed in the IARC Monograph Vol. 51 (14). In short, of 11 studies carried out with *E. coli* (without exogenous microsomal activation), six demonstrated mutagenicity (various types) of caffeine. By contrast, in more than 30 studies using various tester strains of *S. typhimurium*, tested mostly with and without exogenous activation systems, caffeine was consistently nonmutagenic. With other microbes such as *Bacillus subtilis, Ophiostoma, Xanthomonas, Plectonema, Physarum, Dictostelium, Schizosaccharomyces*, and *Saccharomyces*, most of the results were positive (without exogenous activation).

TABLE 7. Mutagenicity tests with caffeine alone

Assay system	Genetic endpoint	Published results	
		Mutagenic	Nonmutagenic
E. coli	Point mutations	+	+
S. typhimurium (Ames-Test)	Reverse mutations		+
Different microbial assays (without metabolic activation)	Point mutations	+	
Plant systems	Point mutations	+	
	Chromosomal aberrations	+	
	Mitotic crossing-over	+	
	Mitotic recombination	+	
Drosophila	Sex-linked lethal mutations		+
	Aneuploidy	+	+
Rodent cells in vitro	DNA strand breaks	+	+
	Unscheduled DNA synthesis		+
	HPRT locus mutations		+
	Sister chromatid exchanges	+	+
	Micronuclei	+	
	Chromosomal aberrations	+	
	Morphologic transformation		+
Human blood lymphocytes	Unscheduled DNA synthesis		+
	HPRT locus mutations		+
Different human cells in vitro	Sister chromatic exchanges	+	
	Chromosomal aberrations	+	
Rodents in vivo (bone marrow or blood cells)	Sister chromatid exchanges	+	+
	Micronuclei	(+)	+
	Chromosomal aberrations	(+)	+
	Dominant lethal mutations		+
			+

In plants such as *glycine, allium, hordeum* (barley), *vicia, coreopsis, ustilago,* or *nicotiana,* caffeine induced point mutation, chromosomal mitoses, chromosomal (chromatid) breaks, mitotic crossing-over, or mitotic recombination. In only three out of six studies with *vicia,* caffeine did not induce chromosomal aberrations (interchanges). Of 11 studies using *Drosophila* for sex-linked lethal mutation, seven showed negative results and another two equivocal results. Of 13 studies again using *Drosophila* for the aneuploidy test, eight were positive and five were negative. Chromosomal aberrations were inducible with caffeine in this species when the cells were in G2 or early mitosis.

Various mammalian cell systems have also been employed. In CHO cells, DNA strand breaks were induced by caffeine, while in V79 and Syrian hamster embryo cells this was not the case. In the latter, unscheduled DNA synthesis was also negative. In both CHO and V79 cells, mutation at various gene loci (including HPRT) was not induced by caffeine. Sister chromatid exchange (SCE) was not inducible in Chinese hamster Don, C1-1, or V79 cells, whereas it was induced in mouse blastocysts. Micronuclei were induced by caffeine in a rat kidney cell line (NRK) and in cultured mouse pre-implantation embryo cells. Chromosomal aberrations were also induced by caffeine in various cell lines derived from Chinese hamsters (in all six reports). Morphological in vitro transformation was not observed in the Syrian hamster embryo cell systems after treatment with caffeine.

Neither unscheduled DNA synthesis nor HPRT locus mutation was induced by caffeine in human blood cells. Of six studies with normal human lymphocytes, one reported negative data for the induction of SCE and two reported equivocal data. In one study with human fibroblasts, caffeine induced SCE. In one of three studies using lymphatic cells from xeroderma pigmentosum patients, equivocal data for SCE were obtained, and the other two studies showed weak enhancement of SCE due to caffeine treatment. In contrast, chromosomal aberrations were caused by caffeine in eight of nine studies with various human cells, including lymphocytes, HeLa cells, and embryonic cells. When usual levels of caffeine contained in coffee were tested, however, no significant increase of chromosomal aberrations was observed (37). In one study with HeLa cells, the data were negative. In lymphocytes from patients with heritable chromosome fragility, caffeine enhanced expression of fragile sites on chromosomes (44).

The in vivo SCE test, mostly in bone marrow cells, gave positive results in four out of seven studies. The results of one test were equivocal. In contrast, the in vivo micronucleus test showed negative effects of caffeine in 8 out of 11 studies. Chromosomal aberrations in in vivo tissues were inducible in only 2 out of 11 studies, including one study with equivocal responses. The dominant lethal test with mice was negative in all of 16 studies; in another study the results were equivocal.

Summarizing the results of the whole battery of tests, the mutagenicity of caffeine alone is difficult to determine, but considering the results of only the mammalian in vivo experiments, the mutagenicity of caffeine is present though quite weak. Various tests with human cells, however, indicate that caffeine might have certain adverse cytogenetic effects, although the tested concentrations were mostly at levels equivalent to or far exceeding the theoretical lethal dose for humans. Theophylline and theobromine have both shown similar results, although the results of the latter in human cells were rather equivocal.

Effects of Caffeine on the Mutagenicity of Other Compounds (Table 8)

In V79 cells, caffeine at nontoxic dose levels after polycyclic aromatic hydrocarbon (PAH) treatment failed to show any effects on the frequency of SCE and ouabain resistance induced by various epoxide derivatives of benzo(a)pyrene (BaP) (45), although cell survival was synergistically reduced. In another study with V79 cells that were pretreated with high doses (over 60 μM) of methylnitrosourea (MNU) and posttreated with 1 mM caf-

TABLE 8. *Mutagenicity tests with caffeine in combination with mutagens*

Assay system	Genetic endpoint	Mutagen combined with caffeine	Response
Enhancing effects of caffeine			
Rodent cells in vitro	Sister chromatid exchange	Benzo[a]pyrene	Unaffected
	Ouabain resistance	Benzo[a]pyrene	Unaffected
	Thioguanine resistance	Methylnitrosourea	Increased
Human lymphocytes in vitro	Chromosomal aberrations	Mitomycin C	Increased
		X-irradiation	Increased
		Gibberellic acid	Increased
		Ellipticine	Increased
	Sister chromatid exchange	Mitomycin C	Increased
	Micronuclei	Gamma-irradiation	Increased/decreased
Plants:			
Barley		Propane sultone	Increase
Allium root tips	Chromosomal aberrations	Acetaldehyde	Increase
Drosophila	Dominant lethal mutations	Ethylmethanesulphonate	Increase
		Methylmethanesulphonate	Increase
Inhibitory effects of caffeine			
S. typhimurium	Point mutations	9-aminoacridine/ethionine	Decreased
		UV light	Unaffected or decreased
		Mitomycin C	Decreased
		Aromatic amines	Decreased
E. coli	Spontaneous mutation of different loci	None	Increased/decreased
	Point mutations	9-aminoacridine	Decreased
Rodent cells in vitro	Thioguanine resistance	4-nitroquinoline-N-oxide	Decreased
	Tumor promotion	Benzo[a]pyrene with a tumor promoter	Decreased

feine, significant enhancement was observed in the mutation (thioguanine resistance) frequency (46).

Posttreatment of human lymphocytes with caffeine considerably enhanced the induction of chromatid and isochromatid breaks and chromatid exchanges by mitomycin C(1 μg/mL) (47). In gamma-irradiated human lymphocytes that were stimulated by phytohaemagglutinin (PHA) after irradiation, posttreatment with 1 mM caffeine significantly decreased the frequency of micronuclei, while caffeine significantly enhanced the micronuclei frequency when PHA stimulation preceded the irradiation (48). In x-irradiated human lymphocytes, immediate posttreatment with 5×10^{-4} M caffeine considerably enhanced the frequency of chromosomal aberrations (49). Caffeine posttreatment (10^{-3} M) at the G2 phase of the cell cycle significantly potentiated the activity of gibberellic acid (3 to 10 mM) to induce chromosomal aberrations in human lymphocytes (50). Posttreatment of human lymphocytes with caffeine (1 mM) yielded about twofold enhancement in the induction of chromosomal aberrations and abnormal metaphases by 3 μg/mL ellipticine (antitumor alkaloid) (51). Subsequent treatment with cytosine arabinoside (5 × 10^{-6} M) potentiated this caffeine effect another twofold. Mutagenesis was observed in caffeine potentiation of propane sultone in *Hordeum* (52). Caffeine (2.5 mM) strongly potentiated the frequency of chromatid-type aberrations in *allium* root-tip cells when given immediately after the treatment with 0.1% acetaldehyde (53).

Pretreatment with 0.5% caffeine significantly increased the frequency of dominant lethality in *Drosophila* induced by 0.1 mM ethylmethane sulphonate or methylmethane sulphonate (54). A considerable number of studies, using various test systems, have also been carried out on the inhibitory effects of caffeine on diverse mutagenic agents. In an excision-proficient strain of *Salmonella* treated with 9-aminoacridine (9AA) (0 to 150 μg/plate), the yield of mutants was almost completely abolished by the simultaneous presence of both caffeine (500 μg/mL) and ethionine (160 μg/plate) although caffeine or ethionine alone did not show such an effect (55). Using an excision-deficient strain of *Salmonella*, caffeine (1 mg/mL) was shown to significantly inhibit the formation of UV-induced base-pair substitution mutants, whereas the frameshift mutation was only marginally affected (56). The reversion from his − to his + induced by mitomycin C (up to 10 μg/plate) was also significantly inhibited by simultaneous caffeine (0 to 2 mg/mL) treatment in excision-proficient strains of *Salmonella* (57,58). In another study using *Salmonella*, caffeine (up to 0.37 mM) in the mixture of mouse liver microsomal activation system and 2-amino-3,4-dimethylimidazo(4,5-f)quinoline, 3-amino-1-methyl-5H-pyrido(4,3-b)indole, or 2-amino-3,8-dimethylimidazo(4,5-f)-quinoxaline prior to bacterial exposure, significantly inhibited the occurrence of revertants following exposure to one of these aromatic amines (59). The results of this study were interpreted by the authors to indicate a certain inhibitory action of caffeine on promutagen activation by microsomal enzymes.

Caffeine (0.5 or 1 mg/mL) was antimutagenic for spontaneous mutations in *E. coli* to revert from 6-azauracil sensitivity to resistance and from inability to utilize melibiose to melibiose utilization. It enhanced spontaneous reversions from lactose nonutilization to utilization and fucose sensitivity to resistance, and it had no effect on the spontaneous mutation from deoxygalactose sensitivity to resistance (60).

Caffeine, at levels up to 3 mg/mL during treatment with 0.1 mM 9AA of wild type *E. coli*, caused a decrease in the yield of frameshift reversions of at least three orders of magnitude (61).

In V79 cells, the induction of mutants resistant to 6-thioguanine by 4NQO was strongly reduced by the presence of caffeine (1 mM), which inhibited metabolic activation of 4NQO (62) similar to the previous observation by Alldrick and Rowland (59) in *Salmonella* exposed to aromatic amines.

There are a few studies showing that caffeine inhibits mammalian cell transformation induced by diverse chemical carcinogens (63), but reports to the contrary are also available (64). In Syrian hamster embryo cells, the activity of a tumor promoter (12-0-tetradecanoyl-phorbol-13-acetate, 0.08 M) to stimulate the morphological transformation initiated by BaP (0.2 μM) was almost completely inhibited by 200 μg/mL caffeine or 50 μg/mL theophylline (65). On the whole, the results of the studies with various test systems on the enhancing or suppressing effects of caffeine on diverse mutagens/carcinogens do not permit any clear prediction. Caffeine appears to enhance the effects of (other) mutagens/carcinogens, especially when taking into account mammalian cells including human cells and particularly in the case of human lymphocytes, although experimental conditions such as the time point of juvenilization by PHA seem to considerably influence the results. However, mutation at HPRT locus or unscheduled DNA synthesis has not been reported in any human cells in vitro. The results of the above mutagenicity studies may indicate that the main mechanisms of caffeine action involve its interaction with the repair of the damage caused either spontaneously or by mutagens/carcinogens in DNA and related structures. It is also possible that caffeine interacts with the enzymatic activation efficacy of promutagens/procarcinogens and other compounds. In connection with this and another chemotherapeutic viewpoint for tumors, it seems important to note also the potentiation of cell killing effects of caffeine in other compounds in certain mammalian and tumor cell systems (66–71).

CONCLUSION

After close study of several recently published review articles (72–78), it is interesting to observe that concern about the carcinogenicity of caffeine now plays a subordinate role. The main emphasis is placed on the need for further investigation of the mechanisms of caffeine action (75–77).

Compared to the number of in vivo investigations of the effects of caffeine in combination with known carcinogens, there are only a few studies on the carcinogenicity of coffee or caffeine alone. In addition, the results of these studies are mostly inadequate, both qualitatively and quantitatively, for evaluation (14). Caffeine as an adenosine agonist may influence the metabolic activity of various organs, particularly hormone-dependent organs. Caffeine can cause hyperfunction in some of them, which may in turn cause an acceleration of the aging processes and of spontaneous tumorigenesis. Indeed, in Syrian hamsters given caffeine in drinking water for a total experimental period of 90 days, a significant number of treated animals developed a follicular stimulation of the thyroid glands (Kamino et al. manuscript in preparation). This is conceivably a phenomenon unique to Syrian hamsters, however, in view of the negative results with Sprague-Dawley rats (9). In other studies cited where the tumor incidence in hormone-dependent organs is enhanced, the first tumor appearance is also usually accelerated (8,11,12). The data from the studies on the effects of combined coffee or caffeine and known carcinogens have shown inhibitory or no effects on the incidence of tumor-bearing animals much more frequently than enhancing effects. Taking the results of all mutagenicity studies with various test systems together, coffee or caffeine, whether alone or combined with mutagens, have each shown equivocal effects. As far as the results of studies in mammalian, and in particular human cell systems are concerned, coffee or caffeine appears to some extent to possess cytogenic effects. However, such chromosomal changes may also be interpreted as physiological reactions of cells developing drug resistance after exposure to high doses of coffee or caffeine (79), although this remains to be proved. Quite a few studies have also shown inhibitory effects of caffeine on the tumorigenesis induced by known carcinogens. In this connection, mention should be made of recent attempts that explore possible caffeine potentiation of the cell killing effect of certain tumor therapeutics.

ACKNOWLEDGMENT

The authors are grateful to Ms. Gillian Teicke for her editorial help.

REFERENCES

1. Grice AC. The carcinogenic potential of caffeine. In: Dews PB, ed. *Caffeine*. Berlin Heidelberg: Springer-Verlag, 1984;201–20.
2. Haynes RH, Collins JDB. The mutagenic potential of caffeine. In: Dews PB, ed. *Caffeine*. Berlin Heidelberg: Springer-Verlag, 1984;221–38.
3. Stalder R, Luginbühl H, Bexter A, Würzner H-P. Preliminary findings of a carcinogen bioassay of coffee in mice. In: MacMahon B, Sugimura T, eds. *Coffee and health (Banbury Report 17)*, Cold Spring Harbor, New York, CSH Press, 1984;79–88.
4. Palm PE, Arnold EP, Nick MS, Valentine JR, Doerfler TE. Two-year toxicity/carcinogenicity study of fresh-brewed coffee in rats initially exposed in utero. *Toxicol Appl Pharmacol* 1984;74:364–82.
5. Woutersen RA, van Garderen-Hoetmer A, Bax J, Scherer E. Modulation of dietary fat-promoted pancreatic carcinogenesis in rats and hamsters by chronic coffee ingestion. *Carcinogenesis* 1989;10:311–6.
6. Welsch CW, DeHoog JV, O'Connor DH. Influence of caffeine and/or coffee consumption on the initiation and promotion phases of 7,12-dimethylbenz(a)anthracene-induced rat mammary gland tumorigenesis. *Cancer Res* 1988;48:2068–73.
7. Welsch CW, DeHoog JV. Influence of caffeine consumption on 7,12-dimethylbenz[a]anthracene-induced mammary gland tumorigenesis in female rats fed a chemically defined diet containing standard and high levels of unsaturated fat. *Cancer Res* 1988;48:2074–7.
8. Takayama S, Kuwabara N. Long-term study on the effect of caffeine in Wistar rats. *Gann* 1982;73:365–71.
9. Yamagami T, Handa H, Takeuchi J, Munemitsu H, Aoki M, Kato Y. Rat pituitary adenoma and hyperplasia induced by caffeine administration. *Surg Neurol* 1983;20:323–31.
10. Nagasawa H, Konishi R. Stimulation by caffeine of spontaneous mammary tumorigenesis in mice. *Eur J Cancer Clin Oncol* 1988;24:803–5.

11. Nagasawa H, Konishi R. Precancerous mammary hyperplastic alveolar nodules in four strains of virgin mice with different mammary tumor potentials: influence of chronic caffeine ingestion. *Eur J Cancer Clin Oncol* 1987;23:1019–23.
12. Welsch CW, DeHoog JV, O'Connor DH. Influence of caffeine consumption on carcinomatous and normal mammary gland development in mice. *Cancer Res* 1988;48:2078–82.
13. Mohr U, Althoff J, Ketkar MB, Conradt P, Morgareidge K. The influence of caffeine on tumour incidence in Sprague-Dawley rats. *Food Chem Toxicol* 1984;22:377–82.
14. IARC Working Group. *IARC monographs on the evaluation of carcinogenic risks to humans. Coffee, tea, mate, methylxanthines and methylglyoxal; vol 51.* Lyon: International Agency for Research on Cancer, 1991.
15. Brune H, Deutsch-Wenzel RP, Habs M, Ivankovic S, Schmahl D. Investigation of the tumorigenic response to benzo(a)pyrene in aqueous caffeine solution applied orally to Sprague-Dawley rats. *J Cancer Res Clin Oncol* 1981;102:153–7.
16. Denda A, Yokose Y, Emi Y, et al. Effects of caffeine on pancreatic tumorigenesis by 4-hydroxyaminoquinoline 1-oxide in partially pancreatectomized rats. *Carcinogenesis* 1983; 4:17–22.
17. Armuth V, Berenblum I. The effect of caffeine on two-stage skin carcinogenesis and on complete systemic carcinogenesis. *Carcinogenesis* 1981;2:977–9.
18. Hoshino H, Tanooka H. Caffeine enhances skin tumor induction in mice. *Toxicol Lett* 1979; 4:83–5.
19. Welsch CW, Scieszka KM, Senn ER, DeHoog JV. Caffeine (1,3,7-trimethylxanthine), a temperate promoter of DMBA-induced rat mammary gland carcinogenesis. *Int J Cancer* 1983;32:479–84.
20. Minton JP, Abou-Issa H, Foecking MK, Sriram MG. Caffeine and unsaturated fat diet significantly promotes DMBA-induced breast cancer in rats. *Cancer* 1983;51:1249–53.
21. Rothwell K. Dose-related inhibition of chemical carcinogenesis in mouse skin by caffeine. *Nature* 1974;252:69–70.
22. Mirvish SS, Cardesa A, Wallcave L, Shubik P. Induction of mouse lung adenomas by amines or ureas plus nitrite and by N-nitroso compounds: effects of ascorbate, gallic acid, thiocyanate, and caffeine. *J Nat Cancer Inst* 1975;55:633–6.
23. Theiss JC, Shimkin MB. Inhibiting effect of caffeine on spontaneous and urethan-induced lung tumors in strain A mice. *Cancer Res* 1978;38:1757–61.
24. Zajdela F, Latarjet R. Inhibition of skin carcinogenesis in vivo by caffeine and other agents. *Nat Cancer Inst Monogr* 1978;50:133–40.
25. Nomura T. Timing of chemically induced neoplasia in mice revealed by the antineoplastic action of caffeine. *Cancer Res* 1980;40:1332–40.
26. Balansky RM, Blagoeva PM, Mirtchea Z. The influence of selenium and caffeine on chemical carcinogenesis in rats, mutagenesis in bacteria, and unscheduled DNA synthesis in human lymphocytes. *Biol Trace Element Res* 1983;5:331–43.
27. Hosaka S, Nagayama H, Hirono I. Suppressive effect of caffeine on the development of hepatic tumors induced by 2-acetylaminofluorene in ACI rats. *Gann* 1984;75:1058–61.
28. Petrek JA, Sandberg WA, Cole MN, Silberman MS, Collins DC. The inhibitory effect of caffeine on hormone-induced rat breast cancer. *Cancer* 1985;56:1977–81.
29. VanderPloeg LC, Welsch CW. Inhibition by caffeine of ovarian hormone-induced mammary gland tumorigenesis in female GR mice. *Cancer Lett* 1991;56:245–50.
30. Nomura T. Comparative inhibiting effects of methylxanthines on urethan-induced tumors, malformations, and presumed somatic mutations in mice. *Cancer Res* 1983;4:1342–46.
31. Nakanishi K, Fukushima S, Shibata M, Shirai T, Ogiso T, Ito N. Effect of phenacetin and caffeine on the urinary bladder of rats with N-butyl-N-(4-hydroxybutyl)-nitrosamine. *Gann* 1978;69:395–400.
32. Nakanishi K, Hirose M, Ogiso T, Hasegawa R, Arai M, Ito N. Effects of sodium saccharin and caffeine on the urinary bladder of rats treated with N-butyl-N-(4-hydroxybutyl)-nitrosamine. *Gann* 1980;71:490–500.
33. Kunze E, Rath G, Graewe T. Effect of phenacetin and caffeine on N-butyl-N-(4-hydroxybutyl)nitrosamine-initiated urothelial carcinogenesis in rats. *Urol Int* 1987;42:108–14.
34. Kosugi A, Nagao M, Suwa Y, Wakabayashi K, Sugimura T. Roasting coffee beans produces compounds that induce prophage lambda in E. coli and are mutagenic in E. coli and S. typhimurium. *Mutat Res* 1983;116:179–84.

35. Graf U, Würgler FE. Investigation of coffee in Drosophila genotoxicity tests. *Food Chem Toxicol* 1986;24:835–42.
36. Tucker JD, Taylor RT, Christensen ML, Strout CL, Hanna ML. Cytogenetic response to coffee in Chinese hamster ovary AUXB1 cells and human peripheral lymphocytes. *Mutagenesis* 1989;4:343–8.
37. Aeschbacher HU, Ruch E, Meier H, Wurzner HP, Munoz-Box R. Instant and brewed coffees in the in vitro human lymphocyte mutagenicity test. *Food Chem Toxicol* 1985;23:747–52.
38. Aeschbacher HU, Meier H, Ruch E, Würzner HP. Investigation of coffee in sister chromatid exchange and micronucleus tests in vivo. *Food Chem Toxicol* 1984;22:803–7.
39. Shimizu M, Yano E. Mutagenicity of instant coffee and its interaction with dimethylnitrosamine in the micronucleus test. *Mutat Res* 1987;189:307–11.
40. Smith DF, MacGregor JT, Hiatt RA, et al. Micronucleated erythrocytes as an index of cytogenetic damage in humans: demographic and dietary factors associated with micronucleated erythrocytes in splenectomized subjects. *Cancer Res* 1990;50:5049–54.
41. Obana H, Nakamura S-I, Tanaka R-I. Suppressive effects of coffee on the SOS responses induced by UV and chemical mutagens. *Mutat Res* 1986;175:47–50.
42. Stich HF, Rosin MP, Bryson L. Inhibition of mutagenicity of a model nitrosation reaction by naturally occurring phenolics, coffee and tea. *Mutat Res* 1982;95:119–28.
43. Abraham SK. Inhibition of in vivo genotoxicity by coffee. *Food Chem Toxicol* 1989;27:787–92.
44. Smeets D, Verhagen A, Hustinx T. Familial and individual variation in chromosome fragility. *Mutat Res* 1989;212:223–9.
45. Bowden GT, Hsu IC, Harris CC. The effect of caffeine on cytotoxicity, mutagenesis, and sister-chromatid exchanges in Chinese hamster cells treated with dihydrodiol epoxide derivatives of benzo(a)pyrene. *Mutat Res* 1979;63:361–70.
46. Onfelt A, Jenssen D. Enhanced mutagenic response of MNU by post-treatment with methylmercury, caffeine or thymidine in V79 Chinese hamster cells. *Mutat Res* 1982;106:297–303.
47. Okoyama S, Kitao Y. Inhibition of chromosome repair by caffeine or isonicotinic acid hydrazide on chromosome damage induced by mitomycin C in human lymphocytes. *Mutat Res* 1981;81:75–80.
48. Boyes BG, Koval JJ. Clastogenic interactions of radiation and caffeine in human peripheral blood cultures. *Mutat Res* 1983;108:239–49.
49. Karsdon J, van Rijn J, Berger H, Natarajan AT. Increased frequency of spontaneous and X-ray-induced chromosomal aberrations in lymphocytes from neonates and the influence of caffeine—an in vitro study. *Mutat Res* 1989;26:13–9.
50. Arutyunyan RM, Zalinyan GG. Cytogenetic effect of natural modifiers of mutagenesis in a human lymphocyte culture. Effect of caffeine during induction of chromosomal aberrations by gibberellic acid. *Cytol Genet* 1987;21:28–33.
51. Sakamoto-Hojo ET, Takahashi CS. Clastogenic action of ellipticine over the cell cycle of human lymphocytes and influence of posttreatments with caffeine and ara-C at G2. *Mutat Res* 1991;248:195–202.
52. Singh C, Kaul BL. Caffeine potentiation of propane sultone mutagenesis in barley. *Mutat Res* 1985;144:239–42.
53. Cortes F, Mateos S, Ortiz T, Pinero J. Effects of caffeine and inhibitors of DNA synthesis on chromatid-type aberrations induced by acetaldehyde in root-tip cells. *Mutat Res* 1987;180:183–8.
54. El-Zawahri MM, Al-Ghaith LK. Potentiating effects of caffeine on mutagenicity and teragenicity of alkylating agents. *Environ Mol Mutagen* 1989;14(Suppl 15):55.
55. MacPhee DG, Nagel BA, Podger DM. Mutagenesis and antimutagenesis in Salmonella: influence of ethionine and caffeine on yields of mutations induced by 2-aminopurine and 9-aminoacridine. *Mutat Res* 1983;111:283–93.
56. MacPhee DG, Leyden MF. Effects of caffeine on ultraviolet-induced base-pair substitution and frameshift mutagenesis in Salmonella. *Mutat Res* 1985;143:1–3.
57. Kim J, Levin RE. Influence of caffeine on mitomycin C induced mutagenesis. *Microbios* 1986;46:15–20.
58. Kim J, Levin RE. Mechanism of caffeine repression of mitomycin C induced reversion in Salmonella typhimurium strain T A 94. *Microbios* 1988;53:216–7.

59. Alldrick AJ, Rowland IR. Caffeine inhibits hepatic-microsomal activation of some dietary genotoxins. *Mutagenesis* 1988;3:423–7.
60. Clarke CH, Shankel DM. Antimutagenic specificity against spontaneous and nitrofurazone-induced mutations in *Escherichia coli* K12ND160. *Mutagenesis* 1989;4:31–4.
61. Pons FW, Muller P. Strong antimutagenic effect of caffeine on 9-aminoacridine-induced frameshift mutagenesis in *Escherichia coli* K12. *Mutagenesis* 1990;5:363–6.
62. Tsuda H, Yoshida D, Mizusaki S. Caffeine inhibition of the metabolic activation of a carcinogen, 4-nitroquinoline-1-oxide, in cultured Chinese hamster cells. *Carcinogenesis* 1984;5:331–4.
63. Kakunaga T. Caffeine inhibits cell transformation by 4-nitroquinoline-1-oxide. *Nature* 1975;258:248–50.
64. Donovan PJ, DiPaolo JA. Caffeine enhancement of chemical carcinogen-induced transformation of cultured Syrian hamster cells. *Cancer Res* 1974;34:2720–7.
65. Rivedal E, Sanner T. Caffeine and other phosphodiesterase inhibitors are potent inhibitors of the promotional effect of TPA on morphological transformation of hamster embryo cells. *Cancer Lett* 1985;28:9–17.
66. Byfield JE, Murnane J, Ward JW, Calabro-Jones P, Lynch M, Kulhanian F. Mice, men, mustards and methylated xanthines: the potential role of caffeine and related drugs in the sensitization of human tumours to alkylating agents. *Br J Cancer* 1981;43:669–83.
67. Sivak A, Rudenko L, Teague LG. Variations among species and cell types in the effects of caffeine on mutagen-induced cytotoxicity and postreplication repair of DNA. *Environ Mutagen* 1982;4:143–62.
68. Iliakis G, Nusse M. Effects of caffeine on X-irradiated synchronous, asynchronous and plateau phase mouse ascites cells: the importance of progression through the cell cycle for caffeine enhancement of killing. *Int J Radiat Biol* 1983;43:649–63.
69. Sawecka J, Golos B, Malec J. Modification by caffeine of acute cytotoxic response of cultured L5178Y cells to hydroxyurea treatment. *Neoplasma* 1987;34:369–77.
70. Mourelatos D, Dozi-Vassiliades J, Kotsis A, Gourtsas C. Enhancement of cytogenetic damage and of antineoplastic effect by caffeine in Ehrlich ascites tumor cells treated with cyclophosphamide in vivo. *Cancer Res* 1988;48:1129–31.
71. Tomita K, Tsuchiya H. Caffeine enhancement of the effect of anticancer agents on human sarcoma cells. *Jpn J Cancer Res* 1989;80:83–8.
72. Grice HC. Genotoxicity and carcinogenicity assessments of caffeine and theobromine. *Food Chem Toxicol* 1987;25:795–6.
73. Rosenkranz HS, Ennever FK. Evaluation of the genotoxicity of theobromine and caffeine. *Food Chem Toxicol* 1987;25:247–51.
74. Rosenkranz HS, Ennever FK. Genotoxicity and carcinogenicity assessments of caffeine and theobromine. Reply to comments. *Food Chem Toxicol* 1987;25:795–6.
75. Pozniak PC. The carcinogenicity of caffeine and coffee: A review. *J Am Diet Assoc* 1985;85:1127–33.
76. Somani SM, Gupta P. Caffeine: a new look at an age-old drug. *Int J Clin Pharmacol Ther Toxicol* 1988;26:521–33.
77. Wolfrom D, Welsch CW. Caffeine and the development of normal, benign and carcinomatous human breast tissues: a relationship? *J Med* 1990;21:225–50.
78. Abbott PJ. Caffeine: a toxicological overview. *Med J Australia* 1986;145:518–21.
79. Hahn P, Kapp LN, Morgan WF, Painter RB. Chromosomal changes without DNA overproduction in hydroxyurea-treated mammalian cells: implications for gene amplification. *Cancer Res* 1986;46:4607–12.

Caffeine, Coffee, and Health,
edited by S. Garattini.
Raven Press, Ltd., New York © 1993.

15

Coffee and Cancer Epidemiology

Carlo La Vecchia

*Department of Epidemiology, Mario Negri Institute for Pharmacological
Research, 20157 Milan, Italy*

Epidemiological studies of coffee consumption and cancer risk are reviewed. Data are limited but largely reassuring for several cancer sites, including oral cavity, esophagus, stomach, liver, breast, ovary, kidney, and lymphoreticular neoplasms. Greater attention has been centered on three cancer sites, i.e., pancreas, colorectum, and urinary bladder. The possible association between coffee consumption and pancreatic cancer gained widespread attention following a report published in 1981. Only one out of 19 studies published since then however, has shown a significant positive association. Thus, there is now substantial evidence that coffee is not related to pancreatic carcinogenesis. No consistent association with colorectal cancer was observed in four cohort studies. Among the 12 case-control studies reviewed, nine showed a lower relative risk (RR) of colorectal cancer among coffee users, two found no association, and one showed a RR above unity. Published evidence on the coffee-colorectal cancer issue is therefore consistent with a potential protection. A plausible biological explanation has been given in terms of reduction of bile acids and neutral sterol secretion in the colon. Over 30 case-control studies have been published on the coffee-bladder cancer issue over the last two decades. Compared with nonconsumers of coffee, the RR in most studies tends to be elevated in drinkers, but such an increase is generally neither dose nor duration related. This makes it possible to confidently exclude a strong association between coffee and bladder cancer, while at the same time indicating that coffee drinking is a risk indicator. Whether this indicator is nonspecific—and due to some bias or confounding that is not totally identified—or includes some aspect of causality is still open to debate.

INTRODUCTION

Over the last three decades, the relationship between coffee and cancer risk has been extensively investigated. There are several digestive, bladder, and other urinary-tract, breast, genital, and lymphoid neoplasms among various cancer sites considered. The data were extensively reviewed in 1990 by a Working Group of the International Agency for Research of Cancer (IARC) (IARC Monograph No. 51) (1). This chapter will therefore only summarize the issues on which conclusions were reached by the IARC working group, while giving greater attention to the topics that were considered still open to debate.

SUMMARY OF EPIDEMIOLOGICAL DATA ON COFFEE FROM THE IARC MONOGRAPH NO. 51

The IARC Monograph 51 (1) reviewed data on descriptive and analytical epidemiology on all cancer sites combined: bladder and urinary tract, breast, large bowel, pancreas, ovary, stomach, upper digestive tract, and a few other sites including liver, lung, and lymphoid neoplasms.

Descriptive Epidemiology

Descriptive studies of temporal trends and geographical patterns (ecological studies) showed no consistent relationship between various measures of coffee consumption or disappearance and cancer rates. It is not surprising, in view of the large number of tests performed, that some significant differences were observed, but only the strength and consistency of the correlations for pancreatic cancer reported by several studies were difficult to attribute to the change alone. Still, there are some features of the descriptive epidemiology of pancreatic cancer (such as the difficulties and uncertainties of diagnosis and certification of the disease, with the consequent higher rates in developed areas of the world and the substantial upward trends in recent decades) that may well be the only explanation for the correlations. No consistent association was found between coffee consumption and bladder cancer rates in ecological and descriptive epidemiology studies.

All Cancer Sites

At least three cohort studies and one case-control study examined the relationship between coffee consumption and incidence or mortality from a broad spectrum of diseases.

The first study (2,3) was based on information collected on a cohort of 23,912 Seventh-day Adventists in 1960, followed up until 1980. Besides bladder cancer, there was a positive association between coffee consumption and fatal colon cancer (relative risk, RR = 1.7 for ≥2 cups per day). The risk estimate for pancreatic cancer was below unity. The apparent association with colorectal cancer persisted after allowance for indicator foods (eggs and meat), as well as weight (3), but it is difficult to state whether it reflects other correlates of adherence to the rules of the Seventh-day Adventists' life-style.

The study by Jacobsen et al. (4) was based on a cohort of 13,314 Norwegian men and 2,891 women, who provided information on coffee consumption from 1967 to 1969 and were followed up to 1978. No significant positive association was found between coffee consumption and disease. The risk estimates were below unity (RR = 0.6) for both colon and rectal cancer and of borderline significance for colon cancer. Other inverse associations were observed for kidney and nonmelanomatous skin cancers.

The study by Nomura et al. (5), based on a cohort of 7,355 Japanese men in Hawaii, found elevated risks of cancers of the lung and the urinary bladder and a reduced risk for rectal cancer (RR = 0.5) but not for colon cancer. However, after allowance for smoking and age, using multiple logistic regression, none of the trends in risk was significant. The RRs for pancreatic cancer were above unity, but the absolute number of cases (n = 21) was too small to permit statistical inference.

The number of cases was substantially greater in an Italian hospital-based case-control study (6). That study found no association between coffee consumption and cancers of the esophagus, stomach, pancreas, and liver, but significant inverse trends were observed for colon and rectum, with RRs for highest versus lowest level of intake of 0.6 and 0.7, respectively.

Cancer of the Bladder and Other Urinary Sites

The evidence accumulated over the last two decades from over 30 case-control studies on coffee and urinary tract cancers conducted in broadly heterogeneous populations was considered remarkably consistent: the relative risks for bladder cancer tends to be higher in coffee drinkers than in nondrinkers, but the risk is neither dose nor duration related (1).

An important confounding factor is cigarette smoking, which is related to both coffee consumption and bladder cancer risk. The difference between crude and adjusted odds ratios varies, however, from one study to another, and misclassification of smoking status is unlikely to totally explain the positive results for all the studies. Other possible residual confounding must therefore be considered, such as diet or occupational exposure, although the similar associations found in males and females suggest that occupational exposures cannot account totally for the positive results.

The IARC working group examined 26 studies, 22 of which were used to make evaluations. Sixteen of them showed a moderately higher risk of bladder cancer in coffee drinkers compared to nondrinkers; in seven of these the association was significant, and in three there was evidence of a dose-risk relationship. No relationship was observed in the other six studies. Lifelong nonsmokers were also considered separately to obtain information on the impact of the potential distorting effect of tobacco. The relationship with coffee was still observed, although (in part because of the lower numbers) it was less clear.

Although the data are limited, a similar pattern of risk was apparent for transitional cell cancers of the renal pelvis and ureter, whose etiology and pathogenesis are in several aspects similar to those of bladder cancer. Published data on adenocarcinoma of the kidney are scarce as well, but what exists does not indicate any consistent association with coffee.

Data on decaffeinated coffee from six case-control studies were reviewed, but its effect was not clearly distinguishable from coffee containing caffeine.

Cancer of the Breast

Seven case-control studies were considered, and there was no evidence in any of them of an association with coffee—all the relative risk estimates being close to unity. Adequate allowance was made, in most studies, for major recognized risk factors for breast cancer and any potential confounding factors, so the existence of any meaningful association is unlikely.

Large Bowel Cancer

Although the cohort studies were not considered particularly informative, 11 of the 12 case-control studies considered showed an inverse association between coffee consumption and colorectal cancer risk; in five studies it was significant. The data were not considered conclusive, but nonetheless compatible with a protective effect of coffee.

Cohort studies were not informative in regard to large bowel cancer, although some data were provided by six prospective studies. None of them found significant associations, and the apparently high risks were reduced by allowance for smoking.

Cancer of the Pancreas

Twenty-one case-control studies that provided data on the coffee-pancreatic cancer relationship were considered. A large study published in the early 1980s showed a strong positive association with coffee consumption, and another found a significant relationship with decaffeinated coffee. Of the subsequent 19 studies, 10 found moderate positive associations, which tended, however, to be weaker after allowance for smoking. No association was observed in the remaining studies. The working group recognized the existence of a modest association between elevated coffee consumption and pancreatic cancer, but remarked that this could be noncausal and might reflect bias or confounding. While data on decaffeinated coffee were more scarce, they were considered negative.

Cancer of the Ovary

Seven case-control studies of ovarian cancer included data on coffee. Risks were significantly elevated in two of them, and a slightly increased risk was found in the remaining five. Interpretation of the findings, however, was not clear.

Cancer of the Stomach

Data on coffee and gastric cancer risk from five case-control studies were reviewed. There was no evidence of association in any of them. Evidence from published studies based on different populations indicates, then, that coffee, while it certainly has an impact on gastric secretion, is unlikely to have any major impact on gastric carcinogenesis.

Cancers of the Upper Digestive Tract

Six studies providing data on cancers of the oral cavity, pharynx, and esophagus were considered. There was no evidence of an association with coffee consumption per se in any of them, except for a possible association with very high temperature.

Other Cancer Sites

One case-control study of cancer of the liver, two cohort, and one case-control study of lung cancer, and a cohort study on Hodgkin's disease, non-Hodgkin's lymphomas, lymphatic and myeloid leukemia, and malignant melanoma all furnished data on coffee consumption. No association was observed with any of these cancer sites. Some association with cancer of the vulva was found in a case-control study and with cancer of the cervix in a cohort study.

The IARC Monograph 51 (1) thus provided substantially reassuring evidence on the relationship between coffee consumption and a number of important cancer sites. There was still scope for debate for cancers of the large bowel, pancreas, bladder, and other urinary tract sites, which will therefore be reviewed in greater detail.

CANCER OF THE COLON AND RECTUM

The relation between coffee and colorectal cancer has been extensively studied. Summary results from the main studies are given in Table 1. Among four cohort studies, one involving over 23,000 Seventh-day Adventists (2,3) found a significant direct trend in risk, with an RR of 1.5 for the highest consumption level; a study of 7,355 Japanese men in Hawaii (5) showed no consistent association. A third study on a cohort of Norwegians (over 13,000 men and about 3,000 women) (4) reported nonsignificantly reduced RR of 0.6 both for colon and rectal cancer. Finally, the cohort study of a retirement community in California (7) showed no consistent association between the amount of coffee drunk and colorectal cancer risk.

Nine case-control studies of colorectal cancer from the United States (8–10), Japan (11), France (12), Belgium (13), Italy (7,14), Singapore (15), and Spain (16) showed RRs for coffee consumption consistently below unity, with risk estimates of 0.6 to 0.8 for the upper consumption levels. No association was observed in studies from Japan (17) and Yugoslavia (18), while a direct association was found in a study from Utah (19). Among the studies included in Table 1, three reported RR above unity, four found no consistent association, and nine reported RR below unity. The trends in risk were significant in two studies showing direct and in three showing inverse associations.

Only one study was added to the review published in the IARC monograph; it was a relatively small investigation of a selected population [members of the Church of Latter Day Saints (Mormons)] (19) with low coffee consumption, that reported inconsistent results between males and females. The fact that the results of this study were inconsistent with most published evidence is not surprising, considering the peculiar correlates that may influence coffee consumption in this particular population.

Besides the studies included in Table 1, at least three other epidemiological investigations of colorectal cancer mentioned coffee: one of them showed a direct association for colon, but not for rectum cancer (20); one showed no relation (21), and one showed a protective effect of high levels of coffee consumption (22).

Published evidence on the coffee-colorectal cancer issue is therefore not completely consistent, although studies suggesting some protection by coffee, particularly among case-control investigations, are more numerous than those showing no or positive associations. The absence of a consistent pattern of risk among cohort studies is more difficult to interpret, and probably (at least in part) attributable to the small absolute numbers of cases. A biological interpretation of the potential protection of coffee against large intestine cancer has been given as a reduction of bile acid and neutral sterol secretion in the colon by substances in coffee, since bile acids are potent promoters of colon carcinogenesis in animals (14,23,24).

TABLE 1. *Coffee and colorectal cancer: main results from selected studies*

Study, country	Site	Sex	Type of study	Number of cases	Relative risk for level of coffee consumption		
					1 (Low)	2 (Intermediate)	3 (High)
Higginson, 1966, United States (8)	Colorectum	M + F	Case-control	340	1[a]	0.5	0.6
Haenszel et al., 1973, United States (9)	Colorectum	M + F	Case-control	179	1[a]	0.7	
Watanabe et al., 1984, Japan (11)	Colon	M + F	Case-control	138	1[a]	0.8	
	Rectum	M + F		65	1[a]	0.7	
Tajima and Tominaga, 1985, Japan (17)	Colon	M + F	Case-control	65	1[a]	1.2	1.1
	Rectum	M + F		51	1[a]	1.3	1.0
Phillips and Snowdon, 1985, United States (3)	Colorectum	M + F	Cohort	100	1[a]	1.5	1.5[b]
Nomura et al., 1986, Hawaii, Japanese (5)	Colon	M	Cohort	108	1[a]	1.4	1.1
	Rectum	M		60	1[a]	0.9	0.7
Macquart-Moulin et al., 1986, France (12)	Colorectum	M + F	Case-control	399	1[a]	0.6	0.6
Jacobsen et al., 1986, Norway (4)	Colon	M + F	Cohort	100	1[a]		0.6
	Rectum	M + F		63	1[a]		0.6
Wu et al., 1987, United States (7)	Colorectum	M	Cohort	58	1[a]	1.3	1.5
		F		68	1[a]	1.5	1.2
Tuyns et al., 1988, Belgium (13)	Colon	M + F	Case-control	453	1[a]	0.9	0.6[b]
	Rectum	M + F		365	1[a]	0.9	0.7
La Vecchia et al., 1989, Italy (6)	Colon	M + F	Case-control	455	1[a]	0.9	0.6[b]
	Rectum	M + F	Case-control	295	1[a]	0.9	0.7[b]
Lee et al., 1989, Singapore (15)	Colorectum	M + F	Case-control	203	1[a]	0.7	0.7
Jarebinski et al., 1989, Yugoslavia (18)	Rectum	M + F	Case-control	98	1[a]	1.0	0.8
Rosenberg et al., 1989, United States (10)	Colon	M + F	Case-control	717	1[a]	1.0	0.7[b]
	Rectum	M + F		538	1[a]	1.1	1.2
Benito et al., 1990, Spain (16)	Colorectum	M + F	Case-control	286	1[a]	0.6	0.8
Slattery et al., 1990, United States (19)	Colon	M	Case-control	112	1[a]	1.7	2.2[b]
		F		119	1[a]	1.3	0.9

[a] Reference category.
[b] Statistically significant ($p < 0.05$).

CANCER OF THE PANCREAS

The possible association between coffee consumption and the risk of pancreatic cancer has gained widespread attention since 1981, when MacMahon et al. (25) reported a significantly higher risk with increasing daily consumption of coffee. This finding, however, has not been confirmed by most subsequent studies (26). Only one study (40) out of the 19 (26–44) published since then has shown a significant positive association (see Table 2 for an overview of published investigations).

When the results of various studies published before 1987 were pooled to obtain an overall risk estimate for coffee consumption (36), there seemed to be evidence of a moderate effect. Even when the data from MacMahon et al. (25), who first proposed the association, were excluded from the pooled analysis, the RR was 1.2 (95% confidence interval: C.I. = 1.0–1.5) for moderate drinkers and 1.4 (95% C.I. = 1.1–1.8) for heavy drinkers compared to nondrinkers.

It is possible, however, that this small association is not causal, but explainable through residual confounding with cigarette smoking [the single recognized risk factor for pancreatic cancer (45)], or other sources of bias, since only crude allowance was possible on published data (36). Subsequent studies were, if anything, even more reassuring, several of them reporting RR below unity in the highest consumption categories. This is also true for the three studies published after the IARC monograph (42–44), so the evidence is probably more reassuring now than at the time of that overview. A strong association between coffee and pancreatic cancer can therefore now be excluded, but, although the majority of the studies are largely or completely reassuring, it is still not possible to totally exclude some small association.

CANCER OF THE BLADDER AND OTHER URINARY TRACT SITES

Since the early 1970s, the possible association between coffee consumption and bladder cancer risk has been a topic of widespread interest for cancer epidemiologists. In 1971, Cole (46) reported an RR of 1.2 in men and of 2.6 in women who drank coffee compared to nondrinkers, in a population-based case-control study from the Boston area. Since then, more than two dozen case-control studies have been published on the topic (47–78). Their main results are summarized in Table 3 (users versus nonusers) and Table 4 (dose-risk relationships and the significance of the linear trend in risk). Whenever possible, combined relative risks are derived from data presented in strata of sex, age, race, and other possible covariates.

Compared with nonconsumers of coffee, the relative risk in most studies

TABLE 2. *Coffee and pancreatic cancer: main results from selected studies[a]*

Study, country	Number of cases	Relative risk estimates for level of coffee consumption			
		1 (No)	2 (Low)	3 (Intermediate)	4 (High)
MacMahon et al., 1981, United States (25)	369	1[b]	1.8	2.7[c]	
Jick and Dinan, 1981, United States (26)	83	1[b]	0.7	0.5	
Nomura et al., 1981, Hawaii, (27)	28	1[b]	2.8	1.8	2.9
Goldstein, 1982, United States (28)	91	1[b]	1.8	1.6	
Severson et al., 1982, United States (29)	22	1[b]		1.0	
Wynder et al., 1983, United States (30)	275	1[b]	1.0	1.0	1.0
Kinlen and McPherson, 1984, Britain (31)	216	1[b]		0.9	
Gold et al., 1985, United States (32)	201	1[b]	1.2	1.7	1.4
Mack et al., 1986, United States (33)	490	1[b]	—	1.4	1.6
Hsieh et al., 1986, United States (34)	176	1[b]	1.4	1.4	2.3
Norell et al., 1986, Sweden (35)	99	1[b]	1.6	1.0	
La Vecchia et al., 1987, 1989, Italy (6,36)	214	1[b]	—	1.1	1.0
Raymond et al., 1987, Switzerland (37)	88	1[b]	0.9	1.3	
Falk et al., 1988, United States (38)	363	1[b]	0.7	0.6	1.0
Olsen et al., 1989, United States (39)	212	1[b]	0.9	0.7	0.6
Clavel et al., 1989, France (40)	161	1[b]	2.2	3.5	5.0[c]
Cuzick and Babiker, 1989, Britain (41)	216	1[b]	0.9	0.6	1.4
Farrow and Davis, 1990, United States (42)	148	1[b]	0.7	2.0	1.1
Jain et al., 1991, Canada (43)	249	1[b]	0.9	0.9	0.9
Ghadirian et al., 1991, Canada (44)	179	1[b]	0.4	0.8	0.5

[a] All, except Nomura et al., 1981, Snowdon and Phillips, 1984, and Jacobsen et al., 1986, were case-control studies.
[b] Reference category.
[c] Statistically significant ($p < 0.05$).

TABLE 3. Summary of results of case-control studies of bladder cancer and coffee consumption, users versus nonusers

Study, country	Subjects (Cases, Controls)		Sex	Relative risk[a] (95% C.I.)	Significance	Comments
Dunham et al., 1968; (47) Fraumeni et al., 1971, United States (48)	493	527	Both	1.5	Not significant, RR significant in black females	Adjusted for age and cigarette smoking
Cole, 1971, United States (46)	345	351	M	1.2 (0.8–1.9)		Adjusted for age and smoking (nonsmokers <½ pack/≥½, pack per day)
	100	100	F	2.6 (1.3–5.1)		Similar relation among nonsmokers, nonoccupationally exposed to carcinogens
Bross and Tidings, 1973, United States (49)	360	1,178	M	1.5	Not given	Adjusted for smoking, levels unspecified
	120	1,482	F	0.8		
Morgan and Jain, 1974, Canada (50)	158	158	M	0.7	Not significant	Unadjusted, mailed questionnaire
	74	74	F	1.3		
Simon et al., 1975, United States (51)	135	290	F	2.1 (1.1–4.3)		RR = 1.9 (not significant) after adjustment for smoking in 2 categories
Miller, 1977, Canada (52)	400	400	M	1.4/0.8	Not significant after adjustment for smoking	Regular/instant coffee, adjusted for smoking
	118	118	F	0.8/1.7		
Wynder and Goldsmith, 1977, United States (53)	574	574	M	1.5	Not significant	Adjusted for smoking (4 levels)
	158	158	F	1.3		
Miller et al., 1978, Canada (54)	183	366	M	1.3	RR significant for females	
	72	144	F	1.6		
Mettlin and Graham, 1979, United States (55)	569	1,025	M	1.5 (0.9–2.5)		Adjusted for smoking (two levels) from published data
Howe et al., 1980, Canada (56)	480	480	M	1.4 (0.9–2.0)		Unadjusted estimates from matched analysis
	152	152	F	1.0 (0.5–2.4)		

Study	No. cases	No. controls	Sex	Relative risk (95% CI)	Findings	Comments
Cartwright et al., 1981, U.K. (57)	631	789	M	1.1 (0.9–1.4)		Adjusted for age, type of case (incident/prevalent) and smoking
	210	271	F	0.8 (0.6–2.1)		No heterogeneity according to type of coffee (instant/ground)
Morrison et al., 1982, England, Japan (58)	1,417	1,839	Both	1.0 (0.8–1.2)		Adjusted for age, sex, study area and smoking
Najem et al., 1982, United States (59)	75	142	Both	1.8 (0.1–10.0)		Unadjusted estimates, low power
Sullivan, 1982, United States (60)	82	169	Both	Not given	Significant association for ground coffee in white males, decaffeinated and ground for white females	No relation with duration. Unadjusted for covariates
Hartge et al., 1983, United States (61)	2,982	5,782	Both	1.4 (1.1–1.8)		Adjusted for sex, age, race, geographic area, and tobacco history
Marrett et al., 1983, United States (62)	412	493	M	1.3 (1.1–1.6)		Adjusted for age and smoking
			F	1.1 (0.8–1.4)		
Mommsen et al., 1983, Denmark (63,64)	165	165	M	No association		Details not given for males; only one female case and five controls, nondrinkers. ≥2 versus <2 cups/day
	47	94	F	2.6 (0.4–8.8)		
Rebelakos et al., 1985, Greece (65)	300	300	Both	1.7 (1.2–2.3)		Adjusted for age, sex, and smoking
Ohno et al., 1985, Japan (66)	293	589	Both	0.9 (0.7–1.2)		Adjusted for sex
Gonzales et al., 1985, Spain (67)	58	116	Both	0.6	Not significant	"Habitual consumers". Unadjusted
Jensen et al., 1986, Denmark (68)	371	771	Both	~1.4	Not significant	Including papillomas. Adjusted for age, sex, smoking (never/current + lifetime pack years), tea and soft drinks

TABLE 3. *Continued*

Study, country	Subjects (Cases, Controls)		Sex	Relative risk[a] (95% C.I.)	Significance	Comments
Claude et al., 1986, Germany (69)	340	340	M	1.8	Significant trend in males	Adjusted for smoking (never/ever + lifetime pack years)
	91	91	F	1.1		
Piper et al., 1986, United States (70)	173	173	F	1.6 (0.8–3.2)		Age 20–49 only, unadjusted
				0.7 (0.4–1.5)		Adjusted for smoking
Bravo et al., 1986, Spain (71)	406	406	M	1.9 (1.4–2.6)		Matched for age and area of residence; unadjusted
	53	53	F	2.3 (1.1–5.1)		
Kabat et al., 1986, United States (72)	76	238	M	1.1 (0.8–1.5)		Nonsmokers only from the American Health Foundation dataset
	76	254	F			
Iscovich et al., 1987, Argentina (73)	117	117	Both	2.4 (1.4–4.4)		Adjusted for sex; Adjusted for smoking
Slattery et al., 1988, United States (74)	419	889	Both	~1.2	Not significant	Adjusted for age, sex, diabetes, bladder infections, smoking
Ciccone and Vineis, 1988, Italy (75)	567	798	M	1.0	Not significant	Adjusted for smoking (never/ex/current)
			F	0.9		
Risch et al., 1988, Canada (76)	826	792	M	0.9 (0.6–1.3)		Adjusted for smoking (cumulated pack years) and history of diabetes
			F	1.9 (1.0–3.4)		
La Vecchia et al., 1989, Italy (77)	163	188	Both	1.8	Not significant	Adjusted for age, sex, area of residence, social class, smoking
Clavel and Cordier, 1991, France (78)	690	690	Both	1.5	Not significant	Adjusted for age, sex, hospital, place of residence and smoking

[a] Reference category: coffee nonusers.

tends to be elevated in drinkers, but this increase is generally not dose or duration related.

This risk pattern was clear in the largest case-control study on bladder cancer published by Hartge et al. (61) based on 2,982 cases and 5,782 general-population controls interviewed in a collaborative, population-based study in ten geographical areas of the United States. The ever versus never coffee drinking RRs, after simultaneous allowance for sex, age, race, geographical area, and tobacco consumption, were 1.6 (95% C.I = 1.2–2.2) for males, 1.2 (95% C.I. = 0.8–1.7 for females), and 1.4 (95% C.I. = 1.1–1.8) for both sexes combined. When various consumption levels were considered, the RR was significantly above unity (RR = 1.5, 95% C.I. = 1.1–1.9) for males who drank over 64 cups of coffee per week, but no steady dose-risk relationship was evident in either sex. Likewise, there was no association with duration of coffee drinking. No interaction was observed with geographical area, race, occupation, artificial sweetener use, or history of urinary tract infections. The authors noted that adjustment for smoking reduced the ever versus never RR from 1.8 to 1.4, and that residual confounding by tobacco (or other corre-lates of coffee drinking) would only partly explain the persistent relationship between bladder cancer and coffee, which was still present when only sub-jects who claimed to be lifelong nonsmokers were considered.

Other studies published before 1990 are summarized in the IARC mono-graph 51 (1). Information on coffee and bladder cancer from another case-control and one cohort study has been published since then. The cohort study (79) was based on 34,198 Seventh-day Adventists in California who had provided information on life-style and dietary habits in 1976. Since the end of 1982, 52 histologically confirmed bladder cancers were registered. Compared with nondrinkers of coffee, the smoking-adjusted RRs were 1.0 for less than one cup per day, 0.4 for one cup, and 2.0 for two or more cups of coffee per day. The trend in risk was not significant, but the pattern was similar in smokers and nonsmokers.

In a case-control study from France, Clavel and Cordier (78) collected data on 690 cases of histologically confirmed bladder cancer and 690 age-, sex-, and hospital-matched controls. About 70% of the cases were not infiltrating. Compared with noncoffee drinkers, the RRs, adjusted for age, sex, hospital, and place of residence, were 1.5 for one to four cups per day, 2.0 for five to seven cups, and 3.8 for over seven cups of coffee per day. The trend in risk was significant. After allowance for smoking, these risk estimates declined to 1.2, 1.5, and 2.9, and the trend in risk was no longer significant. Among males, the trends in risk for coffee drinking were significant both in nonsmok-ers and in smokers.

The results of the recent studies on bladder cancer are, therefore, consis-tent with previous data from different parts of the world on the coffee-bladder cancer relationship. This makes it possible to confidently exclude a strong association between coffee and bladder cancer, while at the same time sug-

TABLE 4. Summary of cae-control studies of bladder cancer and coffee consumption: dose-risk relationship

Study, country	Sex	Relative risk for level of coffee consumption							Significance (trend) p
		1 (Lowest)	2	3	4	5	6	7 (Highest)	
Cole, 1971, United States (46)	M	1[a]	1.3	1.2	1.3	—	—	—	Not given
	F	1[a]	1.6	3.8	2.2	—	—	—	Not given
Fraumeni et al., 1971, United States (48)	M, White	1[a]	1.4	2.0	1.7	—	—	—	Not given
	M, Black	1[a]	2.1	2.9	2.1	—	—	—	
	F, White	1[a]	0.7	0.4	0.3	—	—	—	
	F, Black	1[a]	10.0	4.6	2.2	—	—	—	
Bross and Tidings, 1973, United States (49)	M	1[a]	1.3	1.5	1.6	—	—	—	Not given
	F	1[a]	0.9	1.0	0.8	—	—	—	
Morgan and Jain, 1974, Canada (50)	Both	1[a]	0.6	0.9	0.8	1.1	—	—	N.s.
Simon et al., 1975, United States (51)	F	1[a]	2.2	1.9	2.3	—	—	—	0.28
Wynder and Goldsmith, 1977, United States (53)	M	1[a]	1.4	1.9	2.0	—	—	—	N.s.
	F	1[a]	1.0	1.9	1.3	—	—	—	N.s.
Mettlin and Graham, 1979, United States (55)	Both	1[a]	1.2	1.1	1.8	1.3	—	—	N.s.
Howe et al., 1980, Canada (56)	M	1[a]	1.6	1.3	1.5	—	—	—	N.s.
	F	1[a]	0.7	1.7	1.3	—	—	—	N.s.
Morrison et al., 1982, United States (58)	M	1[a]	0.8	0.7	0.9	0.8	0.8	1.5	N.s.
	F	1[a]	0.8	0.6	1.7	0.9	0.7	1.0	N.s.
United Kingdom	M	1[a]	1.1	0.9	0.9	0.8	—	—	N.s.
	F	1[a]	1.4	0.4	1.2	1.0	—	—	N.s.
Japan	M	1[a]	1.0	1.2	1.3	1.9	—	—	N.s.
	F	1[a]	0.7	—	0.7	—	—	—	N.s.

Study	Category								Significance
Hartge et al., 1983, United States (61)	M	1[a]	0.9	1.0	1.1	1.0	1.2	1.5	N.s.
	F	1[a]	0.9	0.8	0.9	0.7	0.9	0.8	N.s.
Marrett et al., 1983, United States (62)	M	1[a]	1.6	2.0	2.0	—	—	—	Significant
	F	1[a]	1.3	1.2	1.0	—	—	—	N.s.
Rebelakos et al., 1985, Greece (65)	Both	1[a]	1.2	1.7	2.7	0.7	—	—	0.02
Ohno et al., 1985, Japan (66)	M	1[a]	0.7	0.6	1.1	1.8	—	—	N.s.
	F	1[a]	0.7	0.8	0.6	—	—	—	N.s.
Jensen et al., 1986, Denmark (68)	Both	1[a]	1.4	1.2	1.4	1.8	—	—	0.12
Claude et al., 1986, Germany (69)	M	1[a]	1.4	1.4	2.3	—	—	—	<0.05
	F	1[a]	1.3	1.9	2.2	—	—	—	N.s.
Piper et al., 1986, United States (70)	F	1[a]	0.9	1.9	2.1	—	—	—	N.s.
Bravo et al., 1986, Spain (71)	M	1[a]	2.0	2.7	—	—	—	—	<0.01
Kabat et al., 1986, United States (72)	M	1[a]	0.9	1.4	1.4	0.5	—	—	N.s.
	F	1[a]	1.5	0.8	0.7	2.4	—	—	N.s.
Iscovich et al., 1987, Argentina (73)	Both	1[a]	1.1	4.4	12.0	—	—	—	<0.01
Slattery et al., 1988, United States (74)	Both	1[a]	1.2	1.1	1.6	—	—	—	N.s.
Ciccone and Vineis, 1988, Italy (75)	M	1[a]	0.8	1.0	1.2	0.8	—	—	N.s.
	F	1[a]	1.4	1.0	0.7	0.8	—	—	N.s.
Risch et al., 1988, Canada (76)	M	1[a]	1.1	1.2	0.9	—	—	—	N.s.
	F	1[a]	1.0	1.9	1.1	—	—	—	N.s.
La Vecchia et al., 1989, Italy (77)	Both	1[a]	2.0	1.6	—	—	—	—	0.10
Clavel and Cordier, 1991, France (78)	Both	1[a]	1.2	1.4	2.4	—	—	—	N.s.

[a] Reference, category.
N.s., not significant.

393

gesting that coffee drinking represents an indicator of risk. Whether this indicator is nonspecific or includes some aspects of causality is still open to debate.

In biological terms, caffeine and the large number of substances other than caffeine contained in coffee have a wide spectrum of direct as well as indirect metabolic activities. It is conceivable that even small amounts of coffee may bring about changes in the levels of carcinogens or anticarcinogens in the bladder epithelium, since most substances or metabolites are secreted through the urinary tract and are consequently in direct contact with the bladder mucosa. On the other hand, (although it is less likely) coffee drinking may have some influence on the diagnostic pattern of bladder cancer, systematically interfering with the likelihood of interview. These and other possible sources of error or bias may at first sight appear to be mere speculations. Considerable amount of epidemiological research, however, has systematically, and with remarkable consistency, shown an association between coffee and bladder cancer. Even apparently less plausible hypotheses should therefore be considered and, if possible, tested in future research.

With reference to other urinary tract neoplasms, data were recently published (80) from a case-control study of 410 cases of renal cell adenocarcinoma and 605 neighborhood controls in the Boston metropolitan area. The relative risks for coffee were 1.4 for moderate versus low intake and 1.2 for high versus low intake. None of these estimates was statistically significant.

OTHER CANCER SITES

Data on coffee consumption and breast cancer risk from a cohort study of 14,593 Norwegian women has been published over the last two years, with a total of 152 incident cases (81). The risk estimates for heavy coffee consumption were below unity for lean women and above unity for overweight women. This interaction, although statistically significant, is difficult to interpret in the absence of replication by other studies and plausible biological interpretations.

CONCLUSIONS

This updated overview of coffee and cancer epidemiology provides further reassuring information on the absence of any meaningful association of coffee with most common cancers, including digestive tract, breast, and genital tract neoplasms. In relation to the three main issues still open when the IARC monograph on coffee (1) (pancreas, colorectum, and bladder) was published, the data for pancreatic cancer are now more reassuring: two (42,43) out of three recently published studies, found RR close to unity for the highest consumption category, and one (44) not significantly below unity.

One additional study was available on colorectal cancer (20). It was based, however, on a peculiar population of Mormons with a low and probably selected pattern of coffee consumption and was therefore difficult to interpret. The data are nonetheless consistent with the suggestion that coffee has a protective effect on colon (or colorectal) cancer.

One cohort study (79) and one case-control study (78) were recently added to the over two-dozen studies already published on the coffee-bladder cancer relationship. In both studies, the risk-estimate was above unity in heavy coffee drinkers, but the association was not significant after allowance for smoking, and there was some inconsistency in the dose-risk relationship.

Taken as a whole, the analytical studies are indeed consistent with an association between coffee consumption and a possibly increased risk of bladder cancer. However, the notable absence of replication of findings in the two sexes in several studies, the general lack of dose-response relationships, and the same findings reported for different types of coffee (irrespective of their dose or caffeine content) cast doubt on whether the association is causal. It is possible that some unidentified correlate of coffee consumption influences the risk of bladder cancer.

REFERENCES

1. World Health Organization. *IARC monogr eval carcinog risk hum.* Lyon: IARC, 1991;51.
2. Snowdon DA, Phillips RL. Coffee consumption and risk of fatal cancers. *Am J Public Health* 1984;74:820–3.
3. Phillips RL, Snowdon DA. Dietary relationships with fatal colorectal cancer among Seventh-day Adventists. *J Natl Cancer Inst* 1985;74:307–17.
4. Jacobsen BK, Bjelke E, Kvale G, Heuch I. Coffee drinking, mortality and cancer incidence: results from a Norwegian prospective study. *J Natl Cancer Inst* 1986;76:823–31.
5. Nomura A, Heilbrun LK, Stemmermann GN. Prospective study of coffee consumption and the risk of cancer. *J Natl Cancer Inst* 1986;76:587–90.
6. La Vecchia C, Ferraroni M, Negri E, et al. Coffee consumption and digestive tract cancers. *Cancer Res* 1989;49:1049–51.
7. Wu AH, Paganini-Hill A, Ross RK, Henderson BE. Alcohol, physical activity and other risk factors for colorectal cancer: a prospective study. *Br J Cancer* 1987;55:687–94.
8. Higginson J. Etiological factors in gastrointestinal cancer in man. *J Natl Cancer Inst* 1966; 37:527–45.
9. Haenszel W, Berg JW, Segi M, Kurihara M, Locke FB. Large-bowel cancer in Hawaiian Japanese. *J Natl Cancer Inst* 1973;51:1765–79.
10. Rosenberg L, Werler MM, Palmer JR, et al. The risks of cancers of the colon and rectum in relation to coffee consumption. *Am J Epidemiol* 1989;130:895–903.
11. Watanabe Y, Tada M, Kawamoto K, et al. A case-control study of cancer of the rectum and the colon (Jpn). *Nippon Shokakibyo Gakkai Zasshi* 1984;81:185–93.
12. Macquart-Moulin G, Riboli E, Cornee J, Charnay B, Berthezène P, Day N. Case-control study on colorectal cancer and diet in Marseilles. *Int J Cancer* 1986;38:183–91.
13. Tuyns AJ, Kaaks R, Haelterman M. Colorectal cancer and the consumption of foods: a case-control study in Belgium. *Nutr Cancer* 1988;11:189–204.
14. La Vecchia C. Epidemiological evidence on coffee and digestive tract cancers: a review. *Dig Dis* 1990;8:281–6.
15. Lee HP, Gourley L, Duffy SW, Day NE, Esteve J, Lee J. Colorectal cancer and diet in an Asian population—a case-control study among Singapore Chinese. *Int J Cancer* 1989;43: 1007–16.

16. Benito E, Obrador A, Stiggelbout A, et al. A population-based case-control study of colo-rectal cancer in Majorca. I. Dietary factors. *Int J Cancer* 1990;45:69–76.
17. Tajima K, Tominaga S. Dietary habits and gastro-intestinal cancers: a comparative case-control study of stomach and large intestinal cancers in Nagoya, Japan. *Jpn J Cancer Res* 1986;76:705–16.
18. Jarebinski M, Adanja B, Vlajinac H. Case-control study of relationship of some biosocial correlates to rectal cancer patients in Belgrade, Yugoslavia. *Neoplasma* 1989;36:369–74.
19. Slattery ML, West DW, Robinson LM, et al. Tobacco, alcohol, coffee, and caffeine as risk factors for colon cancer in a low-risk population. *Epidemiology* 1990;1:141–5.
20. Graham S, Dayal H, Swanson M, Mittelman A, Wilkinson G. Diet in the epidemiology of cancer in colum and rectum. *J Natl Cancer Inst* 1978;61:709–14.
21. Dales LG, Friedman GD, Ury HK, Grossman S, Williams SR. A case-control study of relationships of diet and other traits to colorectal cancer in American blacks. *Am J Epidemiol* 1979;109:132–44.
22. Abu-Zeid HA, Choi NW, Hsu PH. Factors associated with risk of cancer of the colon and rectum. *Am J Epidemiol* 1981;114:442.
23. Bjelke E. Colon cancer and blood-cholesterol [Letter]. *Lancet* 1974;i:1116–7.
24. Jacobsen BK, Thelle DS. Coffee, cholesterol, and colon cancer: is there a link? *Br Med J* 1987;294:4–5.
25. MacMahon B, Yen S, Trichopoulos D, Warren K, Nardi G. Coffee and cancer of the pancreas. *N Engl J Med* 1981;384:630–3.
26. Jick H, Dinan BJ. Coffee and pancreatic cancer [Letter]. *Lancet* 1981;ii:92.
27. Nomura A, Stemmermann GN, Heilbrun LK. Coffee and pancreatic cancer [Letter]. *Lancet* 1981;ii:415.
28. Goldstein HR. No association found between coffee and cancer of the pancreas [Letter]. *N Engl J Med* 1982;306:997.
29. Severson RK, Davis S, Polissar L. Smoking, coffee and cancer of the pancreas [Letter]. *Br Med J* 1982;285:214.
30. Wynder EL, Hall NEL, Polansky M. Epidemiology of coffee and pancreatic cancer. *Cancer Res* 1983;43:3900–6.
31. Kinlen LJ, McPherson K. Pancreas cancer and coffee and tea consumption: a case-control study. *Br J Cancer* 1984;49:93–6.
32. Gold EB, Gordis L, Diener MD, et al. Diet and other risk factors for cancer of the pancreas. *Cancer* 1985;55:460–7.
33. Mack TM, Yu MC, Hanisch R, Henderson BE. Pancreas cancer and smoking, beverage consumption, and past medical history. *J Natl Cancer Inst* 1986;76:49–60.
34. Hsieh C-C, MacMahon B, Yen S, Trichopoulos D, Warren K, Nardi G. Coffee and pan-creatic cancer (Chapter 2) [Letter]. *N Engl J Med* 1986;315:587–9.
35. Norell SE, Ahlbom A, Erwald R, et al. Diet and pancreatic cancer: a case-control study. *Am J Epidemiol* 1986;124:894–902.
36. La Vecchia C, Liati P, Decarli A, Negri E, Franceschi S. Coffee consumption and risk of pancreatic cancer. *Int J Cancer* 1987;40:309–13.
37. Raymond L, Infante F, Tuyns AJ, Voirol M, Lowenfels AB. Diet and cancer of the pan-creas. *Gastroenterol Clin Biol* 1987;11:488–92.
38. Falk R, Pickle LW, Fontham ET, Correa P, Fraumeni JF Jr. Life-style risk factors for pancreatic cancer in Louisiana: a case-control study. *Am J Epidemiol* 1988;128:324–36.
39. Olsen GW, Mandel JS, Gibson RW, Wattenberg LW, Schuman LM. A case-control study of pancreatic cancer and cigarettes, alcohol, coffee and diet. *Am J Public Health* 1989;79:1016–9.
40. Clavel F, Benhamou E, Auquier A, Tarayre M, Flamant R. Coffee, alcohol, smoking and cancer of the pancreas: a case-control study. *Int J Cancer* 1989;43:17–21.
41. Cuzick J, Babiker AG. Pancreatic cancer, alcohol, diabetes mellitus and gall-bladder dis-ease. *Int J Cancer* 1989;43:415–21.
42. Farrow DC, Davis S. Risk of pancreatic cancer in relation to medical history and the use of tobacco, alcohol and coffee. *Int J Cancer* 1990;45:816–20.
43. Jain M, Howe GR, St. Louis P, Miller AB. Coffee and alcohol as determinants of risk of pancreas cancer: a case-control study from Toronto. *Int J Cancer* 1991;47:384–9.
44. Gharidian P, Simard A, Baillargeon J. Tobacco, alcohol, and coffee and cancer of the

pancreas. A population-based, case-control study in Quebec, Canada. *Cancer* 1991;67: 2664–70.
45. Boyle P, Hsieh CC, Maisonneuve P, et al. Epidemiology of pancreas cancer (1988). *Int J Pancreatol* 1989;5:327–46.
46. Cole P. Coffee-drinking and cancer of the lower urinary tract. *Lancet* 1971;i:1335–7.
47. Dunham LJ, Rabson AS, Stewart HL, Frank AS, Young JL. Rates, interview, and pathology study of cancer of the urinary bladder in New Orleans, Louisiana. *J Natl Cancer Inst* 1968;41:683–709.
48. Fraument JF Jr, Scotto J, Dunham LJ. Coffee-drinking and bladder cancer. *Lancet* 1971; 11:1204.
49. Bross IDJ, Tidings J. Another look at coffee drinking and cancer of the urinary bladder. *Prev Med* 1973;2:445–50.
50. Morgan RW, Jain MG. Bladder cancer: Smoking, beverages and artificial sweeteners. *Can Med Assoc J* 1974;111:1067–70.
51. Simon D, Yen S, Cole PH. Coffee drinking and cancer of the lower urinary tract. *J Natl Cancer Inst* 1975;54:587–91.
52. Miller AB. The etiology of bladder cancer from the epidemiological viewpoint. *Cancer Res* 1977;37:2939–42.
53. Wynder EL, Goldsmith R. The epidemiology of bladder cancer. A second look. *Cancer* 1977;40:1246–68.
54. Miller CT, Neutel CI, Nair RC, Marrett LD, Last JM, Collins WE. Relative importance of risk factors in bladder carcinogenesis. *J Chron Dis* 1978;31:51–6.
55. Mettlin C, Graham S. Dietary risk factors in human bladder cancer. *Am J Epidemiol* 1979; 110:255–63.
56. Howe GR, Burch JD, Miller AB, et al. Tobacco use, occupation, coffee, various nutrients and bladder cancer. *J Natl Cancer Inst* 1980;64:701–13.
57. Cartwright RA, Adib R, Glashan R, Gray BK. The epidemiology of bladder cancer in West Yorkshire. A preliminary report on nonoccupational aetiologies. *Carcinogenesis* 1981;2: 343–47.
58. Morrison AS, Buring JE, Verhoek WG, et al. Coffee drinking and cancer of the lower urinary tract. *J Natl Cancer Inst* 1982;68:91–4.
59. Najem GR, Louria DB, Seebode JJ, et al. Life time occupation, smoking, caffeine, saccharine, hair dyes and bladder carcinogensis. *Int J Epidemiol* 1982;11:212–7.
60. Sullivan JW. Epidemiologic survey of bladder cancer in greater New Orleans. *J Urol* 1982; 128:281–3.
61. Hartge P, Hoover R, West DW, Lyon JL. Coffee drinking and risk of bladder cancer. *J Natl Cancer Inst* 1983;70:1021–6.
62. Marrett LD, Walter SD, Meigs JW. Coffee drinking and bladder cancer in Connecticut. *Am J Epidemiol* 1983;117:113–27.
63. Mommsen S, Aagaard J, Sell A. An epidemiological study of bladder cancer in a predominantly rural district. *Scand J Urol Nephrol* 1983;17:307–12.
64. Mommsen S, Aagaard J, Sell A. A case-control study of female bladder cancer. *Eur J Cancer Clin Oncol* 1983;19:725–9.
65. Rebelakos A, Trichopoulos D, Tzonou A, Zavitsanos X, Velonakis E, Trichopoulos A. Tobacco smoking, coffee drinking, and occupation as risk factors for bladder cancer in Greece. *J Natl Cancer Inst* 1985;75:455–61.
66. Ohno Y, Aoki K, Obata K, Morrison AS. Case-control study of urinary bladder cancer in metropolitan Nagoya. *NCI Monogr* 1985;69:229–34.
67. Gonzales CA, Lopez-Abente G, Errezola M, et al. Occupation, tobacco use, coffee and bladder cancer in the county of Mataro (Spain). *Cancer* 1985;55:2031–4.
68. Jensen OM, Wahrendorf J, Knudsen JB, Sorensen BL. The Copenhagen case-control study of bladder cancer. II. Effect of coffee and other beverages. *Int J Cancer* 1986;37:651–7.
69. Claude J, Kunze E, Frentzel-Beyme R, Paczkowski K, Schneider J, Schubert H. Life-style and occupational risk factors in cancer of the lower urinary tract. *Am J Epidemiol* 1986; 124:578–89.
70. Piper JM, Matanoski GM, Tonascia J. Bladder cancer in young women. *Am J Epidemiol* 1986;123:1033–42.
71. Bravo P, del Rey J, Sanchez J, Conde M. Café y analgésicos como factores de riesgo del cancer de verjiga. *Arch Esp Urol* 1986;39:337–41.

72. Kabat GC, Dieck GS, Wynder EL. Bladder cancer in nonsmokers. *Cancer* 1986;57:362–7.
73. Iscovich J, Castelletto R, Estève J, et al. Tobacco smoking, occupational exposure and bladder cancer in Argentina. *Int J Cancer* 1987;40:734–40.
74. Slattery ML, West DW, Robinson LM. Fluid intake and bladder cancer in Utah. *Int J Cancer* 1988;42:17–22.
75. Ciccone G, Vineis P. Coffee drinking and bladder cancer. *Cancer Lett* 1988;41:45–52.
76. Risch HA, Burch JD, Miller AB, Hill GB, Steele R, Howe GR. Dietary factors and the incidence of cancer of the urinary bladder. *Am J Epidemiol* 1988;127:1179–91.
77. La Vecchia C, Negri E, Decarli A, D'Avanzo B, Liberati C, Franceschi S. Dietary factors in the risk of bladder cancer. *Nutr Cancer* 1989;12:93–101.
78. Clavel J, Cordier S. Coffee consumption and bladder cancer risk. *Int J Cancer* 1991;47:207–12.
79. Mills PK, Beeson WL, Phillips RL, Fraser GE. Bladder cancer in a low risk population. Results from the Adventist health study. *Am J Epidemiol* 1991;133:230–9.
80. Maclure M, Willet WC. A case-control study of diet and risk of renal adenocarcinoma. *Epidemiology* 1990;1:430–40.
81. Vatten LJ, Solvoll K, Løken EB. Coffee consumption and the risk of breast cancer. A prospective study of 14,593 Norwegian women. *Br J Cancer* 1990;62:267–70.

Caffeine, Coffee, and Health,
edited by S. Garattini.
Raven Press, Ltd., New York © 1993.

Overview

Silvio Garattini

Mario Negri Institute for Pharmacological Research, 20157 Milan, Italy

It is remarkable to consider how many chemicals we are ingesting when we drink a cup of coffee. Several hundred have already been identified, and no doubt others await disclosure. Probably few other dietary components have been studied in this respect so thoroughly as coffee. However, the variability of coffee's constituents is endless because they depend on the soil where the coffee is grown, on the variety of plant, on the degree of roasting of the beans, and on the way the coffee is brewed. Putting these variables together helps explain certain differences in the composition of coffee consumed in different countries. However, coffee is no exception because any vegetable we eat is made up of a number of chemical species. The special interest in coffee is probably because it is perceived as much as a psychostimulant than as a routine item in a meal.

It is probably because coffee is often drunk to increase alertness that attention has focused on what is considered its pharmacologically active principle, i.e., caffeine. This trimethylxanthine is also present in different amounts depending on many variables. For instance, contrary to general belief, a cup of Italian espresso coffee may contain relatively little caffeine (about 30 to 80 mg compared to about 100 to 150 mg in a standard American cup of coffee) when it is prepared with blends rich in Arabica beans (this variety contains 50% less caffeine than the Robusta coffee), is roasted more than in other countries (caffeine sublimates and is therefore lost with heating), and remains in contact with water for only a very short time (the amount of caffeine extracted from coffee is proportional to the length of contact with hot water). Therefore caffeine intake differs widely across different populations; in fact, ten cups of coffee in Italy may deliver less caffeine than five cups in the United States.

The consumption of caffeine is difficult to assess because it is found not only in coffee but also in tea (about 50% less than coffee at equal volume) and in several soft drinks. In addition, caffeine is a constituent of several commonly used analgesics (about 150 mg per dose depending on the product).

Knowledge of caffeine is extensive and was originally derived from its medical use; it is believed that caffeine shortens psychomotor reaction time and total sleep time and increases vigilance, sleep latency, and waking time. Learning and memory are increased and sustained attention is enhanced. Beneficial effects on performance have been observed although the degree depends on the type of task involved and the type of personality. However some of these effects are controversial.

Despite the large number of published studies, results are contradictory probably because changes are frequently very subtle and difficult to detect. This may be related to the fact that a certain degree of tolerance arises with time and reflects a certain self-selection, too, because people who are sensitive to caffeine tend not to consume beverages containing it. More data are needed about the psychostimulant effects of coffee than on caffeine alone.

In interpreting the results with caffeine, for comparison across animal species including humans, it is important to recall that the dose is a measure "exogenous" to the body. In the body the dose becomes a concentration (per ml of fluid or per g of tissue). Because of differences in the kinetics of caffeine, the same dose may result in quite different concentrations in various animal species depending on the rate of absorption, distribution, metabolism, and excretion. In the same species the same dose may yield different concentrations depending on the individual, his/her age, sex, concomitant use of other drugs, life-style, and exposure to different environments. In pregnancy, for instance, there is a considerable increase in the half-life of caffeine and therefore an increase in exposure.

On changing the dose, the plasma area under the curve changes in the same direction but not always proportionally. For instance in rats, raising the dose from 1 mg/kg to 100 mg/kg the body exposure to caffeine increases by almost 400 times, indicating a dose-dependent kinetics. In experimental work it is easier to administer caffeine by injection or by gavage, but these routes of administration are not representative of its use in beverages where the daily intake is split into several "doses" over time. Therefore data on caffeine pharmacology and toxicology can seldom be employed to assess the effects of coffee.

Another far-reaching difference lies in the metabolism of caffeine; the primary metabolites of caffeine, the dimethylxanthines (theophylline, theobromine, and paraxanthine) have stimulant effects that differ in potency. These metabolites are formed to different extents in various animal species. In humans, paraxanthine is the principal metabolite (in blood) after orally administered caffeine, whereas theophylline is the major metabolite in monkeys. The pharmacology of paraxanthine in animals and in humans still remains largely unexplored.

The questions discussed for the central effects of caffeine apply equally to its cardiovascular activity, where the effects are subtle and require relatively high doses. Acutely, there is an increase in blood pressure that is not accompanied by bradycardia probably because the increase in sympathetic traffic responsible for the hypertensive effect is accompanied by an inhibition of the baroreflex induced by caffeine. However there is a rapid rise in tolerance to the cardiovascular effects.

Once again, the abundance of caffeine studies contrasts with the paucity of studies using actual coffee. Thus, even if we have plenty of data on caffeine, much remains to be learned about the other constituents of coffee. We need to know more about their quantities, their pharmacology, and their toxicology.

Despite the number of publications available, we still do not know the mechanism of action of caffeine itself particularly its psychostimulant and cardiovascular effects. Previous suggestions that caffeine inhibits phosphodiesterase activity with a consequent increase in second messenger cyclic-adenosine monophosphate (AMP) are losing ground because this effect requires toxic doses of caffeine. The inhibition of phosphodiesterase may explain the convulsant action of caffeine at high doses and possibly also the impairment of DNA repair mechanism exerted by high concentrations in vitro. More interesting is the suggestion that caffeine interferes with the benzodiazepine receptors that regulate GABA activity. An antagonistic effect on these receptors could account for its stimulant effect due to the general inhibitory action of GABA (γ-ammino butyric acid). However despite evidence of an antagonism between caffeine and benzodiazepines in vitro and in vivo, the concentrations of caffeine reached after coffee consumption leave doubts about the significance of this effect in real life. It is more likely that caffeine has an antagonistic effect on adenosine receptors, which could be attained at concentrations closer to those reached in vivo. Studies in progress are complicated by the multiplicity of adenosine receptors and by their roles in different tissues.

Recent findings provide solid evidence of an increase in sympathetic tone induced by caffeine through increased release of noradrenaline. This also occurs with moderate consumption of coffee and may explain the rise in blood pressure and, if it occurs in brain, too, also the stimulant activity of caffeine. However, as already mentioned, tolerance to this effect arises very rapidly. In parallel to the experimental studies, an array of epidemiological studies has been made, both retrospective and prospective, to investigate possible health problems induced by coffee and caffeine. These studies have an intrinsic limitation deriving from the frequent close positive correlation between smoking and/or alcohol consumption and coffee. It is difficult to isolate the effect related to coffee from those due to smoking and alcohol. It is also difficult to define coffee consumption precisely because of the differences in the origin of coffee beans, their degree of roasting, and the various ways of preparing coffee even in the same population. The reference category is another obstacle because "nondrinkers" of coffee may also differ in their other dietary habits or life-styles, and even in their diseases.

It has therefore been proposed—and it is worth exploring, in analogy with epidemiological studies on alcohol—that the reference group should comprise people who only occasionally drink coffee, or who take only small amounts.

Despite these limitations, the numerous studies available strongly suggest that the risks associated with coffee consumption are very low. All epidemiological studies considering myocardial infarction are negative in terms of moderate consumption of coffee (fewer than five cups a day) while there are contrasting results at higher doses. It should, however, be stressed that confounding factors—mostly smoking and sedentary habits—are difficult to isolate, and therefore more studies are needed to analyze the rate of myocardial infarction in groups of "nonsmokers-coffee drinkers."

The results of a study of 10,000 hypertensive patients at risk of cardiovascular disease were also negative even for high coffee consumption. In fact there were no changes in mortality, cerebrovascular events, or cardiovascular diseases in relation to the consumption of caffeine after correction for smoking. The elevation of blood cholesterol detected mostly in Scandinavian countries is probably related to the method of preparing coffee (only boiled coffee) and is not seen when other methods are used. The caffeine content of their coffee is lower than elsewhere, due to the exclusive use of Arabica beans. The recent detection in coffee of a principle inducing hypercholesterolemia awaits confirmation although the concentrations are unlikely to be high enough to raise blood cholesterol under normal conditions of use. Furthermore, there is no risk of hypertension for moderate or high consumers of coffee.

Considerable attention has been paid to the effect of coffee consumption on reproduction and pregnancy in experimental and clinical studies. In animal studies, caffeine is teratogenic at doses that are almost impossible to reach in humans, the peak level being more important than the total exposure over time. However a delay in bone formation, which is made up very rapidly after birth, has been observed at lower doses. Whether women who drink a large number of cups of coffee tend to have lower-weight babies is still unclear. However this finding is confounded by smoking and alcohol and by the fact that coffee consumption rises with age and aging itself is a source of problems of pregnancy. Relatively few studies have investigated the relation between coffee consumption and spontaneous abortions and such studies could be useful.

Finally the relation between caffeine and cancer has been studied in great detail starting from experimental studies indicating a mutagenic effect of caffeine at high concentrations. Caffeine studies in animals, aimed at establishing its role as a cancer promoter, have produced contradictory results because depending on the dose, the sequence of administration, and the experimental model employed, caffeine may apparently raise or lower cancer incidence. High doses, which are unlikely to be reached in humans, have always been used.

Epidemiological studies, recently summarized in an ad hoc International Agency for Research on Cancer (IARC) monograph, have not detected any particular effect of coffee on the incidence of most cancers. There are still some doubts about an increase of risk of bladder cancer in coffee drinkers, although this is not dose related and lacks any plausible biological explanation, and, in fact, there are good reasons to believe that smoking may be a confounding factor. It is worth mentioning that most studies show some protection from coffee against colorectal cancer. Changes in the excretion of biliary sterols has been proposed as an explanation for this observation, but substantiation by adequate studies is required.

Taken together, the information available to date is reassuring about the safety of coffee—particularly when drunk in moderation. Most of the accusations against coffee have not been confirmed by investigations carried out with proper scientific methodology. However it is almost certain that other types of concern will eventually be raised. It is therefore easy to predict that there will be no end to the studies on the effects of coffee, caffeine, and—it is hoped—the other constituents of coffee. This is certainly justified by the widespread habit of coffee drinking and by the need to be sure that this habit does not constitute a public health problem.

Industry and research groups should therefore be ready to push ahead with their efforts to gain better knowledge of the composition, consumption, and biological effects of coffee, particularly as regards those subgroups of the population who might eventually be at risk.

Subject Index